David K. Eiteman
University of California, Los Angeles
Arthur I. Stonehill
Oregon State University
Michael H. Moffett
Thunderbird—The American Graduate School of International Management

Multinational Business Finance

7th Edition

With a contribution by
Cheol S. Eun
Georgia Institute of Technology

Addison-Wesley Publishing Company
Reading, Massachusetts • Menlo Park, California • New York
Don Mills, Ontario • Wokingham, England • Amsterdam • Bonn
Sydney • Singapore • Tokyo • Madrid • San Juan • Milan • Paris

World Student Series

Cover Designer: John Kane
Senior Manufacturing Coordinator: Judith W. Sullivan
Senior Marketing Manager: Dave Theisen
Marketing Manager: Craig Bleyer
Permissions Editor: Mary Dyer
Production Services: York Production Services
Illustrator: American Composition and Graphics
Compositor: York Production Services
Cover image © John Lund/Tony Stone Worldwide

FASB Statement No. 52, *Foreign Currency Translation,* is copyrighted by the Financial Accounting Standards Board, 401 Merritt 7, P.O. Box 5116, Norwalk, CT 06856-5116, U.S.A. Portions are reprinted with permission. Copies of the complete document are available from the FASB.

Reprinted with corrections, December 1994.

ISBN 0-201-84553-9

1 2 3 4 5 6 7 8 9 10-DOC-99 98 97 96 95

Preface

As the field of international finance has evolved, so has the content of *Multinational Business Finance*. As in previous editions, we perceive the multinational firm to be a unique institution that acts as a catalyst and facilitator of international trade and as an important producer and distributor in host countries where its affiliates are located. The success of a multinational firm continues to be dependent on its ability to recognize and benefit from imperfections in national markets for products, factors of production, and financial assets.

Also carried over from earlier editions is the theme that volatile exchange rates may increase risk, but they also create great opportunities for both investors and firms to profit, given a proper understanding of exchange-risk management.

The seventh edition continues to recognize the increasing importance of global integration of money and capital markets, a trend that is creating expanded opportunities for both investors and organizations that need to raise capital. Although global integration of financial markets removes some market imperfections, which impede the flow of capital internationally, excellent opportunities continue to exist for investors to increase their returns while lowering their risks through international portfolio diversification and for firms to lower their cost of capital by sourcing it internationally.

New to the Seventh Edition

The seventh edition of *Multinational Business Finance* has been revised to reflect changes in the field of international finance occurring since the end of 1992. In particular:

- **Interest Rate Risk Management.** A completely new chapter (Chapter 14) has been added detailing the theory of interest rate risk, its measures, financial instruments used in its management (caps, floors, collars, swaps, swaptions, etc.), and industry practices in this growing area of international financial management. A new case study of interest rate risk management at British Columbia Hydro is also included.

- **New Case Studies.** Six new case studies have been added to the seventh edition to show real-world applications and issues on current multinational financial topics. Subjects include a case study of the tribulations of the Finnish markka; a transaction exposure case analysis of the infamous problems of Lufthansa's purchase of 20 Boeing 737 aircraft; a case analysis of how a U.S.-based petrochemical producer dealt with the problems of the September 1992 European Monetary System crisis, and others.

- **Sourcing Equity for the Multinational Firm.** New sections (Chapter 12) detail the significance of expanding international equity listings and share issues by multinational firms. Examples include the listing of Daimler-Benz on the New York

Stock Exchange, Euroequity issues related to privatization of national firms in both western and eastern Europe, Latin America and the Far East, directed share issues by Hafslund Nycomed (Norway), and an equity infusion into Bang and Olufsen (Denmark) by Philips NV (the Netherlands) as part of a strategic alliance.

- **Chapter Openers:** *Global Views*. Each chapter begins with an example of current business practices, trends, or events which directly apply to the theory and analysis of the chapter. These *Global Views* serve to demonstrate to students, often in the context of an article from the popular business press, the way many of the subtle issues of multinational finance are found in practice. Example: a *Global View* shows how Disney (US) earned hundreds of millions of dollars from Euro Disney in 1993 through royalties, although Euro Disney suffered a loss of over $900 million!

- **Expanded Coverage of Currency Options with Spreadsheet Software.** Chapter 6, describing the valuation principles of foreign currency options has been completely rewritten and expanded to cover the basics of option pricing and how premiums change with market conditions. A particularly powerful addition is an option-pricing spreadsheet template written by Jim Bodurtha of the University of Michigan that allows the student to "price their own" currency options for analysis.

- **Advanced Topics in Currency Risk Management.** A completely new advanced topics chapter (Chapter 23) has been added to allow the instructor or student who wishes to study further the principles of currency hedging, including optimal hedging, beta calculations, delta hedging, and second generation option products.

- **Strategy and Direct Foreign Investment.** This chapter (Chapter 17) has been completely revised to include more on network and internationalization theories (the Uppsala University, Sweden, contribution) and Michael Porter's competitive advantage of nations.

- **Multinational Taxation.** The chapter (Chapter 21) on taxation has been thoroughly revised, simplified, and moved in front of working capital management for more effective coverage.

- **Suggested Outlines for Traditional and New Short Courses.** The instructor's manual includes suggested chapter combinations for different short-course construction, including selected cases, chapter problems, and potential projects.

Audience

The seventh edition of *Multinational Business Finance* is appropriate for the same audiences as the first six editions. Earlier editions have been widely used in international financial management courses in university degree programs, university-run executive programs, and company management development programs.

Readers will find *Multinational Business Finance* most meaningful if they have the background knowledge or experience equivalent to a basic finance course. A previous course in international economics is desirable, but the text is designed to cover sufficient economic material so that a separate background is not essential.

Supplements

An instructor's manual will be provided to teachers who adopt this book for classroom use. The manual includes a disk, which contains a variety of spreadsheets that would be useful in solving end-of-chapter problems. A video collection of 12 MacNeil-Lehrer reports is also available to adopters.

Acknowledgments

The authors are very grateful to the numerous persons who have provided critical comments and suggestions to improve both the current and earlier editions of this book. The seventh edition has benefitted immensely from comments we received on the sixth edition, both from formal reviews and from colleagues' replies to a questionnaire.

Special thanks goes to Charles F. Kane of Stratus Computer/Boston College, Chuck Kwok of the University of South Carolina, Jay Choi of Temple University, Ham Dethero of St. Mary's College, Torben Juul Andersen of Unibank (Denmark), Russell Taussig of the University of Hawaii at Manoa, Peter Yeung of Bank of America – Asia Ltd. (Hong Kong), and Karen Wallace of ARCO Chemical, who provided many insightful inputs into the manuscript of the seventh edition. Cheol Eun deserves a special thanks for allowing us to continue using his contributions carried over from earlier editions.

Adopters Surveyed

We take this opportunity to thank the following persons for their responses to surveys of adopters of previous editions:

Otto Adleberger
Essen University, Germany

Raj Aggarwal
John Carroll University

Stephen Archer
Willamette University

Hossein G. Askari
George Washington University

James Baker
Kent State University

Morten Balling
Aarhus School of Business, Denmark

Arindam Bandopadhyaya
University of Massachusetts at Boston

Ari Beenhakker
University of South Florida

Carl Beidleman
Lehigh University

Nancy Bord
University of Hartford

Tom Brewer
Georgetown University

Kevin Cheng
New York University

Jay Choi
Temple University

J. Markham Collins
University of Tulsa

Kerry Cooper
Texas A&M University

Roy Crum
University of Florida

Farmarz Damanpour
James Madison University

David Distad
University of California, Berkeley

Mark Eaker
University of Virginia

Rodney Eldridge
George Washington University

Vihang Errunza
McGill University

William R. Folks, Jr.
University of South Carolina

Anne Fremault
Boston University

Fariborg Ghadar
George Washington University

Martin Glaum
Justus-Lievig-Universitat Giessen,
Germany

Deborah Gregory
University of Georgia

Robert Grosse
University of Miami at Coral Gables

Christine Hekman
Claremont Graduate School

James Hodder
University of Wisconsin, Madison

Laurent Jacque
Tufts University

Veikko Jaaskelainen
Helsinki School of Economics and
Business Administration, Finland

Fred Kaen
University of New Hampshire

Robert Kemp
University of Virginia

W. Carl Kester
Harvard Business School

Seung Kim
St. Louis University

Paul Korsvold
Norwegian School of Management

Chris Korth
University of South Carolina

Chuck Kwok
University of South Carolina

Sarah Lane
Boston University

Martin Laurence
William Paterson College

Wilbur Lewellen
Purdue University

Arvind Mahajan
Texas A&M University

Charles Maxwell
Murray State University

Charles McCord
Auburn University

Jeanette Medewitz
University of Nebraska at Omaha

Robert Mefford
University of San Francisco

Eloy Mestre
American University

Gregory Noronha
Old Dominion University

John Olienyk
Colorado State University

Lars Oxelheim
Lund University, Sweden

Yoon S. Park
George Washington University

Louis Poinacheck
New York University

Yash Puri
University of Massachusetts at Lowell

R. Ravichandran
University of Colorado at Boulder

Scheherazade Rehman
George Washington University

Lee Remmers
INSEAD, France

Jeff Rosenslog
Emory University

David Rubenstein
University of Houston

Alan Rugman
University of Toronto

Mehdi Salehizadeh
San Diego State University

Roland Schmidt
Erasmus University, The Netherlands

Hamid Shomali
Golden Gate University

Luc Soenen
California Polytechnic State University

Marjorie Stanley
Texas Christian University

Jahangir Sultan
Bentley College

Kishore Tandon
CUNY – Bernard Baruch College

Russell Taussig
University of Hawaii at Manoa

Lee Tavis
University of Notre Dame

Michael Williams
University of Texas at Austin

Brent Wilson
Brigham Young University

Richard Wright
McGill University

Alexander Zampieron
Bentley College

Emilio Zarruk
Florida Atlantic University

The final product is also the end result of the many valuable reviews and suggestions received on earlier editions, all of which have guided us as our thoughts evolved over the years. Particularly helpful have been comments from:

Academia (present or former affiliation)

Robert T. Aubey
University of Wisconsin, Madison

David Babbel
University of Pennsylvania

Finbarr Bradley
University of Dublin, Ireland

Michael Brooke
University of Manchester, England

Robert Carlson
Wake Forest University

Robert Chia
National University of Singapore

Frederick D.S. Choi
New York University

Mark Ciechon
University of California, Los Angeles

Alan N. Cook
Baylor University

Robert Cornu
Cranfield School of Management, UK

Steven Dawson
University of Hawaii at Manoa

Gunter Dufey
University of Michigan

Cheol S. Eun
Georgia Institute of Technology

Lewis Freitas
University of Hawaii at Manoa

Ian Giddy
New York University

Manolete Gonzales
Oregon State University

Alfred Hofflander
University of California, Los Angeles

Ronald A. Johnson
Northeastern University

Gordon Klein
University of California, Los Angeles

Steve Kobrin
University of Pennsylvania

Eric Y. Lee
Fairleigh Dickinson University

Donald Lessard
Massachusetts Institute of Technology

Rita Maldanado-Baer
New York University

Edmund Outslay
Michigan State University

R.J. Rummel
University of Hawaii at Manoa

Lemma Senbet
University of Maryland

Alan Shapiro
University of Southern California

Hany Shawky
State University of New York, Albany

Norman Toy
Columbia University

Harald Vestergaard
Copenhagen Business School

Joseph D. Vu
University of Illinois, Chicago

Industry (present or former affiliation)

Paul Adaire
Philadelphia Stock Exchange

Barbara Block
Tektronix, Inc.

Holly Bowman
Bankers Trust

Payson Cha
HKR International, Hong Kong

John A. Deuchler
Private Export Funding Corporation

Kåre Dullum
Gudme Raaschou Investment Bank,
Denmark

Steven Ford
Hewlett-Packard

David Heenan
Theo Davies, Hawaii

Sharyn H. Hess
Foreign Credit Insurance Association

Aage Jacobsen
Gudme Raaschou Investment Bank,
Denmark

Ira G. Kawaller
Chicago Mercantile Exchange

Kenneth Knox
Tektronix, Inc.

Arthur J. Obesler
Eximbank

I. Barry Thompson
Continental Bank

Gerald T. West
Overseas Private Investment Corporation

Willem Winter
First Interstate Bank of Oregon

Inevitably woven into the fabric of this book are ideas received from faculty and students at institutions where we have taught. These include our home universities of University of California, Los Angeles, Oregon State University, and Thunderbird – AGSIM. Our visiting stints have been at the Hong Kong University of Science and Technology, Hong Kong; University of California, Berkeley; University of Michigan, Ann Arbor;

Cranfield School of Management, U.K.; University of Hawaii at Manoa; Northern European Management Institute, Norway; Copenhagen Business School, Denmark; Aarhus School of Business, Denmark; Helsinki School of Economics and Business Administration, Finland; Institute for the Development of Executives, Argentina; National University of Singapore; International Center for Public Enterprise, Yugoslavia; Beijing Institute of Chemical Engineering Management, People's Republic of China; and Dalian University of Science & Technology, People's Republic of China. Further ideas came from consulting assignments in Argentina, Belgium, Canada, Denmark, Hong Kong, Indonesia, Japan, Malaysia, Mexico, the Netherlands, Norway, People's Republic of China, Taiwan, the United Kingdom, and Venezuela.

We would also like to thank all those with Addison-Wesley who have worked so diligently on this seventh edition: Julia Berrisford, Marjorie Williams, Patsy DuMoulin, and Ericka Perry. Dolores Wolfe and her associates at York Production Services also receive our thanks.

Finally, we would like to rededicate this book to our parents, the late Wilford Eiteman, Sylvia Eiteman, the late Harold Stonehill, Norma Stonehill, and Bennie Ruth and Hoy Moffett, who gave us the motivation to become academicians and authors. We thank our wives, Keng-Fong, Kari, and Megan, for their patience through the years spent preparing this edition. Karen Schnatterly deserves special thanks for her excellent research assistance.

Frazier Park, California	D.K.E.
Corvallis, Oregon	A.I.S.
Glendale, Arizona	M.H.M.

About the Authors

David K. Eiteman David K. Eiteman is Professor Emeritus of Finance at the John E. Anderson Graduate School of Management at UCLA, and from 1992 to 1994 he was visiting professor of management accounting at the Hong Kong University of Science & Technology (Hong Kong). He has also held teaching or research appointments at the National University of Singapore, Dalian University (China), the Helsinki School of Economics and Business Administration (Finland), University of Hawaii at Manoa, University of Bradford (UK), Cranfield School of Management (UK), and IDEA (Argentina). He is currently president of the society for Economics and Management in China, and he is a former president of the Western Finance Association.

Professor Eiteman received a B.B.A. (Business Administration) from the University of Michigan, Ann Arbor (1952), M.A. (Economics) from the University of California, Berkeley (1956), and a Ph.D. (Finance) from Northwestern University (1959).

He has authored or co-authored four books and twenty-nine other publications. His articles have appeared in *The Journal of Finance, Financial Analysts Journal, Journal of International Business Studies, California Management Review, Columbia Journal of World Business, Management International, Business Horizons, MSU Business Topics, Public Utilities Fortnightly*, and others.

Arthur I. Stonehill Arthur I. Stonehill is currently a Professor of Finance and International Business, Emeritus, at Oregon State University. He currently holds a split appointment at the University of Hawaii at Manoa and Copenhagen Business School (Denmark). He has been a member of the faculty at Oregon State University since 1966. He has also held teaching or research appointments at the University of California, Berkeley, Cranfield School of Management (UK), and the North European Management Institute (Norway). He is past President of the Academy of International Business, and was a western area director of the Financial Management Association.

Professor Stonehill received a B.A. (History) from Yale University (1953), an M.B.A. from Harvard Business School (1957), and a Ph.D. from the University of California, Berkeley (1965). In 1989 he was awarded an honorary doctorate from the Aarhus School of Business (Denmark), and in 1992 awarded an honorary doctorate from the Copenhagen Business School (Denmark).

He has authored or co-authored seven books and twenty-three other publications. His articles have appeared in *Financial Management, Journal of International Business Studies, California Management Review, Journal of Financial and Quantitative Analysis, Journal of International Financial Management and Accounting, The Investment Analyst* (UK), *Nationaløkonomisk Tidskrift* (Denmark), *Sosialøkonomen* (Norway), *Journal of Financial Education*, and others.

Michael H. Moffett   Michael H. Moffett is Associate Professor of Finance at Thunderbird – The American Graduate School of International Management. He formerly was Associate Professor of Finance and International Business at Oregon State University. He has also held teaching or research appointments at the University of Michigan, Ann Arbor, the Brookings Institution, the University of Hawaii at Manoa, the Aarhus School of Business (Denmark), the Helsinki School of Economics and Business Administration (Finland), the University of Ljubljana (Yugoslavia), and the University of Colorado, Boulder.

Professor Moffett received a B.A. (Economics) from the University of Texas at Austin (1977), a M.S. (Resource Economics) from Colorado State University (1979), a M.A. (Economics) from the University of Colorado, Boulder (1983), and a Ph.D. (Economics) from the University of Colorado, Boulder (1985).

He has authored, co-authored, or contributed to five books and eight other publications. His articles have appeared in the *Journal of Financial and Quantitative Analysis*, *Journal of International Money and Finance*, *Journal of International Financial Management and Accounting*, *Journal of Contemporary Policy Issues*, *Brookings Discussion Papers in International Economics*, and others. He is also co-author of *International Business* with Michael Czinkota and Ilkka Ronkainen of Georgetown University.

Brief Contents

Part 1 **The International Financial Environment**   1

    Chapter 1 Introduction to Multinational Business Finance   1
    Chapter 2 The International Monetary System   25
    Chapter 3 Balances and Imbalances of Payments   59

Part 2 **Foreign Exchange Markets**   80

    Chapter 4 The Foreign Exchange Market   80
    Chapter 5 International Parity Conditions   108
    Chapter 6 Foreign Currency Options   146

Part 3 **Managing Foreign Exchange Exposure**   181

    Chapter 7 Transaction Exposure: Measurement and Management   181
    Chapter 8 Operating Exposure   219
    Chapter 9 Accounting Exposure   251

Part 4 **Financing from a Global Perspective**   281

    Chapter 10 Internationalizing the Cost of Capital   281
    Chapter 11 Designing the Financial Structure   304
    Chapter 12 Sourcing Equity Internationally   321
    Chapter 13 Sourcing Debt Internationally   344
    Chapter 14 Interest Rate Risk Management   369

Part 5 **Trade Financing**   411

    Chapter 15 International Banking   411
    Chapter 16 Import and Export Financing   438

Part 6 **Foreign Investment Decisions**   467

    Chapter 17 Corporate Strategy and Foreign Investment   467
    Chapter 18 Political Risk Management   500
    Chapter 19 Multinational Capital Budgeting   525
    Chapter 20 International Portfolio Investments   547

Part 7   **Controlling International Operations**   **570**

Chapter 21 Principles of Multinational Taxation   570
Chapter 22 Working Capital Management   598
Chapter 23 Advanced Topics in Currency Risk Management   641

Glossary   **674**

Author Index   **687**

Subject Index   **689**

Index of Named Cases and Problems   **696**

Contents

Part 1   The International Financial Environment   **1**

Chapter 1 Introduction to Multinational Business Finance   **1**
   Global View American Multinational Profits Feel the Squeeze   1
   International Business   2
   Multinational Financial Activities   5
   Organization of This Book   6
   What Is the Goal of Management?   10
   Market Imperfections: A Rationale for the Continued Prosperity of the
      Multinational Firm   13
   Global View "Come Back Multinationals"   14
   Summary   17
   Questions   18
   Bibliography   20
   Appendix The Theory of Comparative Advantage   22

Chapter 2 The International Monetary System   **25**
   Global View Can Central Banks Turn the Tide?   25
   Currency Values and Terminology   26
   A Brief History of the International Monetary System   28
   Contemporary Currency Arrangements   37
   The European Monetary System (EMS)   41
   Eurocurrencies   46
   Summary   48
   Decision Case The Finnish Markka   48
   Questions   54
   Bibliography   55
   Appendix The Creation of Eurodollars   56

Chapter 3 Balances and Imbalances of Payments   **59**
   Global View U.S.—Japan: Counting What Counts   59
   Measuring the Balance of Payments   60
   Imbalances in the Balance of Payments   67
   Major Country Trends in Trade and Capital Flows   71

Summary   74
Decision Case Ecuadorian Debt for Development   74
Questions   78
Bibliography   79

Part 2   Foreign Exchange Markets   **80**

Chapter 4 The Foreign Exchange Market   **80**
Global View The Global Greenback   80
Geographic Extent of the Foreign Exchange Market   81
Functions of the Foreign Exchange Market   82
Market Participants   83
Size of the Market   86
Transactions in the Interbank Market   91
Foreign Exchange Rates and Quotations   92
Global View Roots of the $ Sign   93
Summary   100
Questions   101
Bibliography   103
Appendix Foreign Currency Futures   105

Chapter 5 International Parity Conditions   **108**
Global View Forecasting: In Trends We Trust   108
Parity Conditions   109
Prices and Exchange Rates   110
Interest Rates and Exchange Rates   117
Forward Rate as an Unbiased Predictor of the Future Spot Rate   124
Prices, Interest Rates, and Exchange Rates in Equilibrium   127
Exchange Rate Forecasting   129
Summary   134
Questions   135
Bibliography   138
Appendix An Algebraic Primer to International Parity Conditions   142
The Law of One Price   142
Purchasing Power Parity   142
Covered Interest Arbitrage (CIA) and Interest Rate Parity (IRP)   143
Fisher Effect   144
International Fisher Effect   145

Chapter 6 Foreign Currency Options   **146**
Global View French Bank Stages Mock Options Market on Super Bowl
    to Teach Businesses How to Hedge Their Risks   146

Vocabulary   147
Foreign Currency Options Markets   148
Foreign Currency Speculation   151
Option Pricing and Valuation   158
Summary   170
Questions   171
Bibliography   174
Appendix A Currency Option Pricing Theory   176
Appendix B Cumulative Normal Probability Tables   179

Part 3   Managing Foreign Exchange Exposure   181

Chapter 7 Transaction Exposure: Measurement and Management   181

Global View Sony's Hedging Is More Profitable Than Its Sales   181
Types of Foreign Exchange Exposure   182
Measurement of Transaction Exposure   186
Contractual Hedges   188
Foreign Exchange Contractual Hedging in Practice   199
Summary   203
Decision Case Lufthansa   204
Questions   210
Bibliography   216

Chapter 8 Operating Exposure   219

Global View Daring to Hedge the Unhedgeable   219
Transaction Exposure to Operating Exposure   220
Operating Exposure Defined   221
Measuring the Impact of Operating Exposure   222
Illustration of Operating Exposure   223
Managing Operating Exposure at the Strategic Level
    Through Diversification   230
Global View Sourcing from Thailand   231
Managing Operating Exposure by Changing Operating Policies   233
Managing Operating Exposure by Changing Financing Policies   237
Operating Exposure Management in Practice   241
Summary   243
Illustrative Case An Example of Operating Exposure Management:
    Statoil of Norway   244
Questions   245
Bibliography   249

Chapter 9 Accounting Exposure   **251**
    Global View Rethinking Functional Currencies   251
    Current Rate Method   252
    Monetary/Nonmonetary Method   253
    Temporal Method   254
    Technical Aspects of Translation   254
    Current Rate and Monetary/Nonmonetary Translation Example   257
    Comparison of Accounting Exposure with Operating Exposure   261
    Consolidation of Accounts   262
    Managing Accounting Exposure   265
    Summary   268
    Decision Case Computer International, Inc.   269
    Questions   276
    Bibliography   279

Part 4   Financing from a Global Perspective   **281**

Chapter 10 Internationalizing the Cost of Capital   **281**
    Global View Foreign Firms Tap U.S. Capital Markets   281
    Improving Market Liquidity   282
    Overcoming Market Segmentation   284
    Novo Industri A/S (Novo)   288
    Are Capital Markets Segmented Today?   294
    Summary   295
    Questions   297
    Bibliography   299
    Appendix Weighted Average Cost of Capital   301

Chapter 11 Designing the Financial Structure   **304**
    Global View Capital and Ownership Structure   304
    Theory of Optimal Financial Structure   305
    Financial Structure of Foreign Affiliates   309
    Choosing Among Sources of Funds to Finance Foreign Affiliates   315
    Summary   317
    Questions   318
    Bibliography   319

Chapter 12 Sourcing Equity Internationally   **321**
    Global View Privatization and ADRs   321
    Why CrossList on Foreign Stock Exchanges?   322

Barriers to Crosslisting   325
Where to Crosslist   326
Sourcing New Equity Shares in International Markets   331
Global View "A New Kind of Arbitrage"   335
Summary   339
Questions   339
Bibliography   341

Chapter 13 Sourcing Debt Internationally   **344**

Global View Foreign Companies Borrow in Cheap U.S. Markets   344
Debt Management and Funding Goals   345
International Debt Markets: Instrument Choices   350
International Bank Loans   351
The Euronote Market   353
The International Bond Market   357
Summary   363
Questions   364
Bibliography   367

Chapter 14 Interest Rate Risk Management   **369**

Global View Interest Rate Risk Management at Apple   369
Growing Need for Interest Rate Risk Management   370
Defining Interest Rate Risk   370
Management of Interest Rate Risk   373
Outright Instruments and Techniques   377
Option-Based Instruments and Techniques   387
Counterparty Risk   397
Summary   399
Decision Case British Columbia Hydro   400
Questions   406
Bibliography   409

Part 5   Trade Financing   **411**

Chapter 15 International Banking   **411**

Global View Foreign Banks Return to Mexico   411
International Financial Centers   412
International Strategies of Banks   416
Types of Banking Offices   419
Comparing Bank Services   425
Risks in International Lending to Developing Countries   427

Analysis of Country Risk   430
Strategies for Managing Country Risk   433
Summary   434
Questions   435
Bibliography   436

Chapter 16 Import and Export Financing   438
Global View The Ukraine's Eximbank's Problems   438
Benefits of the System   440
Letter of Credit   442
Draft   448
Bill of Lading   452
Additional Documents   453
Summary: Documentation in a Typical Trade Transaction   454
Government Programs to Help Finance Exports   456
Countertrade   458
Summary   463
Questions   464
Bibliography   465

Part 6   Foreign Investment Decisions   467

Chapter 17 Corporate Strategy and Foreign Investment   467
Global View Giants in China Build-Up   467
Whether to Invest Abroad   469
Does the Firm Have a Sustainable Competitive Advantage in the Home Market?   470
Product and Factor Market Imperfections   473
Internalization   477
Where to Invest Abroad   479
The Internationalization Process   479
Multinational Firms in a Network Perspective   480
Global View When Two Giants Meet   481
How to Invest Abroad: Modes of Foreign Involvement   481
Summary   487
Decision Case Silica Glass, Inc.   489
Questions   495
Bibliography   497

Chapter 18 Political Risk Management   500
Global View Foreign Investment in China   500
Macro Risks   502
Micro Risk: Goal Conflict   503

Micro Risk: Corruption   508
Host Government Regulations That Hinder Operations of Multinational Firms   509
Assessing Political Risk   513
Global View The U.S.'s Country-Risk Problem   513
Negotiating the Environment Prior to Investment   515
Operating Strategies After the Investment Decision   516
Crisis Planning   519
Summary   521
Questions   521
Bibliography   523

Chapter 19 Multinational Capital Budgeting   525

Global View Of Mice, Men and Money   525
Foreign Complexities   526
Project Versus Parent Valuation   527
Kim Electronics (Kimtron)   532
Summary   541
Questions   542
Bibliography   545

Chapter 20 International Portfolio Investments   547

Global View Currency Risk and Overseas Investment   547
Global Risk Diversification: A Case for International Investment   548
Risk and Return in the World Stock Markets   551
Choice of an Optimal International Portfolio   553
Effect of Fluctuating Exchange Rates   557
Performance of International Mutual Funds   560
Do Multinationals Provide International Diversification?   562
A Word of Caution   564
Summary   565
Questions   566
Bibliography   567

Part 7   Controlling International Operations   570

Chapter 21 Principles of Multinational Taxation   570

Global View California's Unitary Tax and Barclays   570
Tax Morality   571
Tax Neutrality   572
National Tax Environments   573
Tax Dimensions of Multinational Operations   578
U.S. Taxation of Foreign-Source Income   582

Foreign Tax Credits   584
Foreign Sales Corporation (FSC)   589
Possessions Corporation   592
Global View Puerto Rico's Shaky Tax Credit   593
Summary   594
Questions   595
Bibliography   596

Chapter 22 Working Capital Management   598
Global View SmithKline Beecham and Global Netting   598
Constraints on Positioning Funds   599
Unbundling International Fund Transfers   599
International Dividend Remittances   600
Royalties, Fees, and Home Office Overhead   601
Transfer Pricing   604
Managerial Incentives and Evaluation   607
Blocked Funds   610
Managing International Cash Balances   615
Managing Receivables   621
Inventory Management   626
Summary   628
Decision Case Tektronix B   628
Questions   636
Bibliography   639

Chapter 23 Advanced Topics in Currency Risk Management 641
Global View Lost in a Maze of Hedges   641
The Currency Hedge Ratio   642
Financial Engineering and Risk Management   648
Second-Generation Currency Risk Management Products   652
Global View Hedging with the Mexican Cobertura   653
Exotic Options   658
Summary   662
Decision Case ZAPA Chemical and BuBa   663
Questions   670
Bibliography   672

Glossary   674
Author Index   687
Subject Index   689
Index of Named Cases and Problems   696

Chapter 1
Introduction to Multinational Business Finance

Global View
American Multinational Profits Feel the Squeeze

Everyone knows that U.S. corporations have become increasingly global in their operations—a development that has increased the sensitivity of their bottom lines to currency shifts and foreign economic trends. But the fastest growth of American direct investment abroad hasn't necessarily been in areas one might suspect.

"To a surprising degree," says economist Rosanne M. Cahn of First Boston Corp., "U.S. corporations seem to prefer to form direct-investment ties in the more stable, developed countries and to avoid heavy investment in their fast-growing developing world." Cahn draws this conclusion from Commerce Dept. reports on foreign profits of U.S. companies from 1982 to 1991, the last year for which detailed numbers are available. The data indicate that such profits—which reflect acquisitions as well as expanded subsidiary operations—rose at a compound annual rate of 10.8% in that nine-year period. That's almost twice as fast as domestic profits of the same U.S. multinationals.

Foreign profits earned in Europe were particularly strong, rising at a 16.6% annual rate in dollars (and a 14.5% pace in European currency terms). But foreign profits earned outside of Europe, Canada, and Japan grew at only half the rate of total overseas profits. Such data, says Cahn, suggest that "as recently as a year or so ago, U.S. companies were still not expanding direct investment outside of industrialized countries with any conviction." Apparently, their primary strategy to take advantage of low labor costs in the developing world is still focused on importing cheap goods made by local companies.

The upshot is that developed countries now account for more than two-thirds of the foreign profits of U.S. companies. And Europe, whose share has risen from 43%

of all foreign profits in 1982 to just over 60% in 1991, is by far the area of deepest concentration. Scanning various industries, one finds that U.S. multinationals in oil, drugs, soaps, computers, electronic components, motor vehicles, tobacco, advertising, and data processing each derived at least a third of their total sales from foreign markets in 1991.

All this implies that the multinationals could take a sizeable hit this year. Whereas their foreign operations normally contribute perhaps 30% of their total profits, the foreign share jumped to over 70% in 1991, as the U.S. recession and huge write-offs ravaged domestic earnings. In 1993, however, the deepening recession in much of Europe combined with weakening European currencies against the dollar suggest that overseas profits will be unusually slim.

Source: "Where America's Bottom Line May Be Squeezed Overseas." Reprinted from 9/20/93 issue of *Business Week,* by special permission, © 1993 by McGraw-Hill, Inc.

Business, everyone's business, is international. The world economy of the 1990s is internationalized, globalized, and multinationally integrated, regardless of whether individuals in specific countries or specific firms recognize or acknowledge it. As firms expand their sales, their input sourcing, their structures, and their very profits across borders, the problems of financial management become more important and more complex. This book is intended to provide the reader possessing a solid understanding of business and finance with a sophisticated understanding of the many issues, areas of analysis and activity, and ultimately decision making related to the financial management activities of the multinational firm.

International Business

For several centuries international economists have used the classical economic theory of *comparative advantage* to explain trade movements between nations. Springing from the writings of Adam Smith and David Ricardo in the eighteenth and nineteenth centuries, the theory in simple terms states that everyone gains if each nation specializes in the production of those goods it produces relatively most efficiently and imports those goods that other countries produce relatively most efficiently (see this chapter's appendix for a detailed explanation). The theory has supported free-trade agreements, such as the recently concluded North American Free Trade Agreement (NAFTA).

The doctrine of comparative advantage made an initial assumption that although the products of economic activity could move internationally, the factors of production were relatively fixed in a geographic sense. Land, labor, and capital were assumed to be internationally immobile. Although the early economists did not go beyond these initial three factors, by implication such other factors as managerial skills, worker education, and research and development abilities were assumed to be largely attributes of particular nations.

The still growing post–World War II wave of direct foreign investment and the growth of multinational business enterprises is perhaps the major economic phenomenon of the last half of the twentieth century. This development, which holds such potential for the economic betterment of the world's population, runs counter to the postulates of Smith and Ricardo in that it is based on international mobility of the most important factors of production in the twentieth century.

- Capital raised in London by a Belgium-based corporation may finance the acquisition of machinery by a subsidiary located in Australia.

- A management team from French Renault may take over a U.S.-built automotive complex in the Argentine.

- Clothing for dolls, sewn in Korea on Japanese-manufactured sewing machines according to U.S. specifications, may be shipped to northern Mexico for assembly with other components into dolls being manufactured by a U.S. firm for sale in New York and London during the Christmas season.

- A Hong Kong bank originally developed with British management and capital buys control of a major upstate New York banking chain, which in turn finances the construction in Korea of ships intended for the Greek merchant marine.

Of Mice, Men, and Money   Paris—It looks like being a winter of discontent for Euro Disney. On November 10th the company, which runs a big amusement park outside Paris modelled on American ones owned by its parent firm, Walt Disney, said that it had lost a whopping FFr5.3 billion ($960m) in the year to the end of September. Unless it can solve its problems soon, Euro Disney could end up on the scrap-heap.

What then? So far Walt Disney, which owns 49% of Euro Disney, has been steadfastly supportive of its troubled European offspring. Even when Euro Disney loses money, its parent can still cream off management fees and royalties.

Source: "Of Mice, Men and Money," 11/13/93, p. 79. ©1993 The Economist Newspaper Ltd. Reprinted with permission.

Virtually every large firm in the world today has become multinational to some extent. Every dimension of international business and competitiveness, except culture (see Euro Disney above), appears to be mobile.

Classification of International Business Activities

Cross-border business transactions are divided into three categories:

- **International.** The traditional international activity of business is importing and exporting. Goods are produced in the domestic market and then exported to foreign buyers. Financial management problems of this basic international trade activity focus on the payments process between the foreign buyer (seller) and the domestic seller (buyer).

- **Multinational.** As international business expands, the firm needs to be closer to the consumer, closer to cheaper sources of inputs, or closer to other producers of the same product to gain from their activities. It needs to produce abroad as well as sell abroad. As the domestic firm expands operations across borders, incorporating activities in other countries, it is classified as a *multinational*.

- **Transnational.** As the multinational firm expands its branches, affiliates, subsidiaries, and network of suppliers, customers, distributors, marketers, and all others that fall under the firm's umbrella of activities, the once traditional "home country" becomes less and less well defined. Firms like Unilever, Philips, Ford, Sony, Schlumberger, Royal Dutch Shell, and Asea Brown Boveri have become intricate networks with home offices defined differently for products, processes, capitalization, and even taxation.

Exhibits 1.1 and 1.2 provide a small sample of six multinational firms and how their total sales and assets were distributed worldwide in 1992. A close examination of individual firms often reveals some expected and unexpected business distributions. For example, ARCO, a U.S.-based petrochemical conglomerate, has the majority of its sales and assets in the United States, with a significant presence in Europe. Benetton, the Italian textile manufacturer and retailer, is still heavily entrenched in Europe, its "home," with over 80% of its sales in European markets and nearly that proportion of its assets.

Exhibit 1.1   Multinational Diversification of Sales for Six Multinationals in 1992

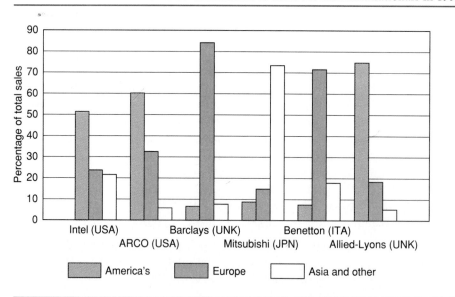

Exhibit 1.2   Multinational Diversification of Assets for Six Multinationals in 1992

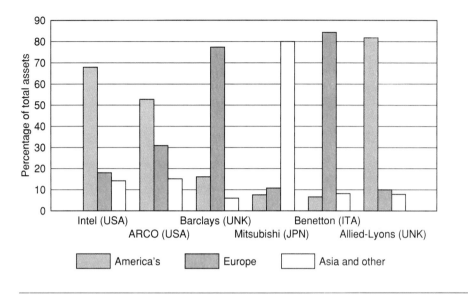

Source: Derived by authors from Worldscope database for end of year 1992 values. Home country sales and assets are combined with other countries in its "home" area. "Asia and other" includes Japan, Australia, and other Pacific Rim and Africa markets.

Yet other firms are not so predictable. Allied-Lyons, a British-based food conglomerate, recorded over 75% of its sales in the Americas (nearly all in the United States and Canada) in 1992, with over 80% of its assets also located in the Americas, a somewhat surprising result for a British firm. Intel of the United States recorded only roughly 50% of its sales in the Americas where 70% of its assets were located.

Although this simple illustration is not a statistically significant result, it does demonstrate the geographical diversity of multinational firms. The complexities that are introduced by worldwide operations pose a problem for multinational business finance, which may in the end prove as much art as science.

Multinational Financial Activities

Financial management, even in a domestic environment, is one of those curious combinations of mathematical precision (principal and interest payments, initial public offerings, current asset management, etc.) and the prime source of all random behavior: human behavior. When the financial management activities must stretch across geographic, cultural, political, and jurisdictional boundaries, the attention needed to organization and goals is critical.

Traditional Areas of Financial Management

Finance focuses on cash flows. The management activities related to the "financial plumbing" of the firm are normally organized into four major areas:

- **Capital structure.** Determination of what proportions of debt and equity are necessary for the firm's maximum financial health and long-term competitiveness.

- **Capital budgeting.** Analysis of investment opportunities and lines of business activity that are considered by the firm.

- **Long-term financing.** Selection, issuance, and management of long-term sources of equity and debt capital by the firm.

- **Working capital management.** Management of the levels and composition of the current assets of the firm (cash, receivables, inventories) and their proper funding.

Many other financial management issues and topics are frequently forced into the "miscellaneous" category at the end of textbooks, including international finance. That approach obviously assumes international issues do not fundamentally change anything that has come before it. We disagree.

Multinational Finance and Management Activities

We argue that the definitions of such basic financial concepts as rate of return and risk may not be universally accepted. Instead, these definitions may be culturally determined norms, varying by country. Later in this introductory chapter we explain how the emergence of the multinational firm as a major actor on the international stage challenges traditional concepts of international economics. Market imperfections create the environment in which such firms thrive.

Organization of This Book

Exhibit 1.3 provides a "map" to the topics covered in this book. Our primary focus is *managerial:* the individual decision maker working within a multinational business with specific areas of financial responsibility.

Part 1 describes the international financial environment. Chapter 1 raises the question whether finance theory is culturally determined or universal. Chapter 2 presents an overview of the international monetary system. Chapter 3 provides an overview of the balance of payments and its relationship to currency regimes.

Part 2 is a comprehensive analysis of foreign exchange rates and instruments. Chapter 4 describes contemporary currency trading and quotation, in addition to the principal currency instrument, the *forward contract.* Chapter 5 is key to the understanding of international finance: the theoretical principles that link exchange rates, interest rates, and inflation rates, termed *international parity conditions.* Chapter 6 is expressly

Exhibit 1.3 *Organization of Multinational Business Finance, Seventh Edition*

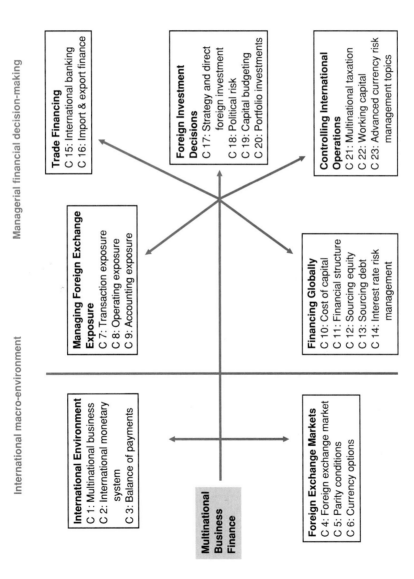

International macro-environment

Managerial financial decision-making

International Environment
C 1: Multinational business
C 2: International monetary system
C 3: Balance of payments

Managing Foreign Exchange Exposure
C 7: Transaction exposure
C 8: Operating exposure
C 9: Accounting exposure

Trade Financing
C 15: International banking
C 16: Import & export finance

Foreign Investment Decisions
C 17: Strategy and direct foreign investment
C 18: Political risk
C 19: Capital budgeting
C 20: Portfolio investments

Controlling International Operations
C 21: Multinational taxation
C 22: Working capital
C 23: Advanced currency risk management topics

Financing Globally
C 10: Cost of capital
C 11: Financial structure
C 12: Sourcing equity
C 13: Sourcing debt
C 14: Interest rate risk management

Foreign Exchange Markets
C 4: Foreign exchange market
C 5: Parity conditions
C 6: Currency options

Multinational Business Finance

devoted to the detailed understanding and use of foreign currency options, one of the most rapidly growing areas of international finance.

Operating Exposure Management at Pirelli   One of the most complex and geographically diverse manufacturing companies in the world, Milan-based Pirelli, has managed to keep its foreign exchange exposure under tight control.

   With subsidiaries in 12 countries in Europe and six in the US and Asia, Pirelli has avoided the need for intense trading activity. Supplying a market with products made in one country and sold in another gives Pirelli its transaction risk, but its response to this exposure is to keep a tight control on distribution. It has set up a central buying company that purchases the necessary materials and then resells them to its subsidiaries.

Source: "Operating Exposure Management at Pirelli," *Corporate Finance*, 10/93, p. 21. Reprinted with permission.

Although Parts 1 and 2 are fundamental to the understanding of the field of international finance, it is Parts 3 through 7 that are the true purpose of this book. Whereas Parts 1 and 2 define the macro environment of multinational business and finance, micro financial management is the focus of the remainder of the book.

   Part 3 details the three primary currency *exposures* of the multinational firm, the first and most visible significant departure in managerial concern from traditional financial management. Chapter 7 introduces the three exposures, and then proceeds to analyze in detail *transaction exposure management*. Chapter 8 extends the concepts of firm exposure to exchange rates from the very short run to the long term and the total competitive environment in its analysis of *operating exposure*. Chapter 9 concludes the section with a continuing source of debate, *accounting exposure management*.

Despite Slump in Sales, Honda Raises Its Prices   Honda Motor Company told U.S. dealers last week that it plans to raise base prices of its Honda and Acura brand cars for the second time in three months, largely to counter profit pressures aggravated by the yen's record strength against the dollar.

Source: "Despite Slump in Sales, Honda Raises Its Prices," 4/12/93. Reprinted by permission of *The Wall Street Journal*, © 1993 Dow Jones & Co., Inc. All Rights Reserved Worldwide.

   Part 4, the financing of the firm from a global perspective, is an area of subtle but significant theoretical departures from the traditional theory of corporate finance. Chapters 10 and 11 analyze how a firm can internationalize its cost and availability of capital while maintaining an optimal financial structure. These chapters also stress that a multinational's access to low-cost capital can contribute significantly to its competitiveness. Chapters 12 and 13 analyze in pragmatic terms the menus and methods available to firms utilizing international equity and debt markets, respectively. Chapter 14, the concluding chapter of this "financing" part, describes the newest area of international interest (pardon the pun), the management of interest rate risk.

> **First Hong Kong Corporate Euro**   Cheung Kong Holdings, the flagship of property tycoon Li Ka-Shing's business interests, has launched the first Eurobond issue by a Hong Kong company. The $500 million bond, issued via the company's Cayman Islands-based financial subsidiary, is one of the biggest from a private corporate this year.
>   The bond, launched at 83 basis points over the five-year Treasury, has a coupon of 5.5% and matures on September 30, 1998, a year after the UK Government's 99-year lease on the colony expires. The fact that Goldman Sachs had little difficulty in selling its $350 million allocation demonstrates investors' confidence in Hong Kong's future.
>
> Source: "First Hong Kong Corporate Euro," *Corporate Finance*, 10/93, p. 4. Reprinted with permission.

Part 5, simply entitled trade financing, describes two of the perennial mainstays of international business: international banking in Chapter 15 and import/export financing in Chapter 16. Although neither of these subjects is "glossy" in context, they are as important and fundamental to international business activity as any portfolio diversification or financial option.

Part 6 focuses on the investment decisions inherent in international business. Chapter 17 describes the strategic, behavioral, and economic motivations that lead a firm to move from domestic to international to multinational activity. Chapter 18 describes political risk measurement and management. Chapter 19 provides a capital budgeting analysis of the intricate process of evaluating potential foreign investments. This too is an area that departs significantly from the traditional theory of domestic corporate finance. Chapter 20 concludes Part 6's discussion of investment decisions by focusing on why investors diversify their portfolios internationally and whether or not the shares of multinational firms are part of this process.

> **It Wasn't Only Gorbachev That Fell Overnight**   There are times when markets react so strongly to political events that economic factors are completely swamped and have little or no influence. Yesterday was such a day, following news that Mr. Mikhail Gorbachev had been replaced as president of the Soviet Union.
>
> Source: "It Wasn't Only Gorbachev That Fell Overnight," *Financial Times*, 8/20/91, p. 32. Financial Times Copyright.

Part 7, controlling international operations, includes the analysis of taxation, and working capital management. Chapter 21 provides an overview of the primary tax systems used worldwide, as well as a detailed description of the computation of taxes for foreign-source income for U.S.-resident firms. Chapter 22 analyzes many of the methods and tradeoffs in the management of working capital within a multinational firm, an area which in practice may dominate most of the everyday financial management activity of the multinational. Chapter 23 concludes the part with a detailed description of advanced topics in currency risk management evolving in the 1990s.

Two final notes deserve repeating prior to concluding our overview of multinational business finance:

1. *Finance,* whether domestic or international, focuses on cash flows;

2. *Management* focuses on the decision makers and their use of information, intellect, and insight in the solution of financial and strategic problems.

Exhibit 1.4 provides one opinion of some of these guiding principles of corporate financial management, those of Peter Drucker. Although we personally may not agree with all of Mr. Drucker's ideas (as we wind our way through the book some of these differences should become apparent), they provide some preliminary clues to the human element in the financial management problem. Our discussion now turns to the goals—that should guide the financial manager of a multinational firm.

Exhibit 1.4   Peter Drucker on International Corporate Treasury Management

1. **Exchange rates are inherently unstable and will remain so.** Fixed exchange rates are not from Genesis. It must be accepted that governments mess with exchange rates.

2. **Predicting currency rates is a foolish game.** Talk and emotions often move exchange rates in unpredictable directions. Imponderables such as these make it dangerous to engage in rate-dependent financial maneuvers. In other words, you had better hedge.

3. **Not to hedge is to speculate.** Exchange rates are a cost of production that financial executives must manage. A MNC with 60 percent foreign sales had better sell forward this year's expected earnings.

4. **MNCs must take advantage of global markets.** Most MNCs still finance largely in one country. This is an increasingly dubious luxury. Managers should protect earnings by financing capital in the same currency.

5. **MNCs finances must be managed centrally and for the entire group.** The CFO needs to be divorced from any single operation and must manage on a worldwide basis. Earnings, cash, and investment streams must be company-wide, not national.

6. **Finance managers cannot blame corporate losses on market volatility.** The company's business is not finance but making widgets. In the next violent currency fluctuation—and it will occur during the business life of everyone working today—many managers will find that corporate profits are down, say, 40 percent owing to foreign exchange (FX). This will not be accepted and the company will say, "You are paid to protect us from that."

7. **You must give your up-and-coming staff true international experience.** The best training ground is not in business school but in the treasury function. Most important, do not wait until managers are at very high levels before you move them around. When they are still quite mobile, expose them to the realities of multinational business.

Source: *Keynote Address,* Peter Drucker, Chief Financial Officers Conference, sponsored by Business International, San Francisco, 1990. Reprinted with permission.

What Is the Goal of Management?

The introductory course in finance is usually taught within this framework: maximizing shareholder's wealth is *the goal of management.* This perspective is dominant not only in the Anglo-American-based courses but also to some extent in basic finance courses taught in the rest of the world.[1] One has only to observe that the same textbooks, or translated versions, are used worldwide. Even when local authors write basic finance textbooks for their own national markets, they often adopt the same subjective model used in the Anglo-American markets.

Although the idea of maximizing shareholder wealth is probably realistic, both in theory and practice, in the Anglo-American markets, it is not realistic elsewhere. This is because some basic differences in corporate and investor philosophies exist between the Anglo-American markets and those in the rest of the world. Therefore, one must realize that the *universal truths* taught in basic finance courses are actually *culturally determined norms*. If management's goal is unclear, it is obviously not possible to determine what information or criteria, and ultimately what decisions, should be made in financial management.

The Shareholder Wealth Maximization Model

The Anglo-American markets are characterized by a philosophy that maintains a firm's objective should be to *maximize shareholder wealth* (SWM model). More specifically, the firm should strive to maximize the return to shareholders, measured by the sum of capital gains and dividends, for a given level of risk. Alternatively, the firm should minimize the risk to shareholders for a given rate of return.

The SWM model assumes as a universal truth that the stock market is efficient. The share price is always correct because it captures all of the expectations of return and risk as seen by investors. It quickly incorporates new information in the share price. Share prices are the best allocators of capital in the macro economy.

The SWM model also treats the definition of risk as a universal truth. Risk is defined as the added risk the firm's shares brings to a diversified portfolio. The total operational risk of the firm can be eliminated through portfolio diversification by the investors. Therefore, this *unsystematic risk,* the risk of the individual security, should not be a prime concern for management unless it increases the prospect of bankruptcy. *Systematic risk,* the risk of the market in general, cannot be eliminated. This is the risk that the share price will be a function of the stock market.

The field of *agency theory* is a study of how shareholders can motivate management to accept the prescriptions of the SWM model. For example, liberal use of stock options should encourage management to think like shareholders of the firm. Whether these inducements succeed or not is open to debate. However, if management deviates too much from this objective—of working to maximize the returns to the shareholders—the board of directors should replace them. In cases where the board is too weak or ingrown to accomplish this, the discipline of the equity markets could do it through a takeover. This discipline is made possible by the *one-share-one-vote rule* that exists in most Anglo-American markets.

---

[1]Anglo-American is defined to mean the United States, United Kingdom, Canada, Australia, and New Zealand.

The Corporate Wealth Maximization Model

In contrast to the SWM model, the continental European and Japanese equity markets are characterized by a philosophy that a corporation's objective should be to *maximize corporate wealth.*[2] This means a firm should treat shareholders on a par with other corporate interest groups, such as management, labor, the local community, suppliers, creditors, and even the government. The goal is to earn as much as possible in the long run, but to retain enough to increase the corporate wealth for the benefit of all interest groups.

The definition of corporate wealth is much broader than just financial wealth, such as cash, marketable securities, and unused credit lines. It includes the firm's technical, market, and human resources. "Consequently, it goes beyond the wealth measured by conventional financial reports to include the firm's market position as well as the knowledge and skill of its employees in technology, manufacturing processes, marketing and distribution, and administration of the enterprise."[3]

The corporate wealth maximization (CWM) model does not assume equity markets are either efficient or inefficient. It does not really matter because the firm's financial goals are not exclusively shareholder oriented. In any case, the model assumes the long-term "loyal" shareholders should influence corporate strategy, not the transient portfolio investor.

The CWM model assumes *total risk,* that is, operating and financial risk, does count. It is a specific corporate objective to generate growing earnings and dividends over the long run with as much certainty as possible, given the firm's mission statement and goals. Risk is measured more by product market variability than by short-term variation in earnings and share price.

One might wonder why shareholders do not enforce their own objectives when management does *not* act as their agent. The answer is that the non-Anglo-American markets are not characterized by the corporate "one-share-one-vote" rule. On the contrary, dual classes of voting shares, restrictions on how many shares can be voted, and restrictions on foreign ownership of shares are the norm. Furthermore, many other anti-takeover defenses exist that make it difficult to replace management except by internal pressure from the board of directors.

Universal Truth or Culturally Determined Norm?

In summary, with respect to the financial goal of the firm, what is a "universal truth" and what is a "culturally determined norm"?

1. Universal truth: Firms are composed of competing and cooperating stakeholder groups. Which stakeholder group dominates is a culturally determined norm, with

---

[2]This description of the corporate wealth maximization model is adapted from Gordon Donaldson and Jay Lorsch, *Decision Making at the Top: The Shaping of Strategic Direction,* New York: Basic Books, 1983.

[3]Ibid., pp. 162–163.

a distinct difference between the Anglo-American markets and the rest of the world.

2. Universal truth: Most firms try to maximize their value. How that value is measured and from whose perspective is a culturally determined norm.

3. Universal truth: Most firms are risk averse. How that risk is measured and from whose perspective is a culturally determined norm.

Market Imperfections: A Rationale for the Continued Prosperity of the Multinational Firm

As we noted in the beginning, the ability of the multinational firm to serve as a conduit for the movement of all goods, services, and factors of production has driven international business. But, like water flowing from a higher level to a lower level, the differentials—the imperfections—motivate and perpetuate activity.

Risk and Rate of Return

Multinational firms strive to take advantage of imperfections in national markets for products, factors of production, and financial assets. Imperfections in the market for products translate into market opportunities for multinational firms. Large international firms are better able to exploit such competitive factors as economies of scale, managerial and technological expertise, product differentiation, and financial strength than are their local competitors. In fact, multinational firms thrive best in markets characterized by international oligopolistic competition, where these factors are particularly critical. In addition, once multinational firms have established a physical presence abroad, they are in a better position than purely domestic firms to identify and implement market opportunities through their own internal information network.

In some cases the common stock of multinational firms may serve as a vehicle for investors who wish to hold internationally diversified portfolios but are prevented from achieving diversification because of perceived and real imperfections in the market for financial assets. For example, international portfolio investors can be frustrated by foreign exchange controls, withholding taxes on dividends, capital market controls, lack of full disclosure, and lack of knowledge about foreign securities markets. The multinational firms' common stock may be perceived as a convenient proxy for international diversification without the headaches involved in dealing with foreign securities markets.

Multinational Firms and Host Countries: The Potential for Goal Conflict

From an economic perspective, host countries welcome multinational firms because they are viewed as agents of technology transfer and host country economic development. From a business perspective, multinational firms are eager for opportunities to

Global View
"Come Back Multinationals"

The flow of foreign direct investment by multinational companies was five times greater, at $50 billion, in 1986 than it was 15 years earlier. In the early 1970s any prediction of such growth would have provoked fresh demands for a United Nations "code of conduct" to control the behavior of what were then widely labeled as exploitative giants. No longer. The UN still wants such a code, but its most recent report on the activities of what it calls "transnational corporations" stresses the good that such companies do. Third-world governments are coming to appreciate the employment, skills, exports and import-substitutes that they deliver.

The developing world's resentment of the direct investment of multinationals once stemmed from these companies' very rationale for setting up factories abroad. One of their reasons was to gain better access to foreign markets: this was construed as a threat to crowd-out local firms. Their second reason was the quest for lower manufacturing costs: this was exploitation. The fact that a search for fickle comparative advantage led such companies to invest abroad was taken to imply a lack of commitment to the society and employment of the host country. The UN report debunks many of these bogeyman assumptions.

- One old bogey was size—the idea that multinationals are always big, powerful and liable to abuse their power. Although giant corporations certainly account for a large share of the world economy, smaller companies are nowadays just as likely as big ones to invest abroad.

- Multinationals increase employment in their host countries. The UN's conservative estimate of direct employment by multinationals is 65m, or 3% of the world's labor force. Add indirect employment, such as jobs created by suppliers and by the general lift to an economy that multinationals can provide—and such companies may generate 6% of world employment.

- Foreign investors increase a host country's output and exports. This is especially important for developing, or newly industrializing, countries which need fast growth and foreign exchange to service bank debt. Foreign-owned companies accounted for 55% of Singapore's employment in manufacturing industry in 1982, 63% of its manufacturing output and 90% of its exports of manufactured goods. They produced 70% of Zimbabwe's industrial output. In 1983 nearly 30% of Argentina's manufacturing output and exports came from multinationals. It is often easier for a multinational to export than for an indigenous firm to do so. It has better distribution and marketing networks overseas, and can sometimes circumvent protectionism in other countries more effectively.

Such truths are hitting home; but there is still some third-world resistance to multinationals in the service industries. This is a pity, because the UN report shows that services are taking an increasing share of multinationals' foreign direct invest-ment—particularly, but not only, within the rich countries.

Slowly the message is registering: the best multinational code for the third world may well be the one that you can dial, and that gets you through.

Source: Adapted from *The Economist*, 11/26/88, p. 73. © 1988 The Economist Newspaper Ltd. Reprinted with permission.

invest in geographic locations where they can earn a rate of return high enough to com-pensate them for the perceived level of risk. National and international market imperfec-tions provide these opportunities.

Although a strong economic and business rationale exists for the success of multina-tional firms, they must live with host country economic, political, social, and religious goals and the potential for conflict with such goals. Thus maximizing the value of the multinational firms for the benefit of their shareholders may conflict with concepts of national sovereignty, which nearly always override the rights of individual firms, multi-national or domestic. Therefore, in choosing operational financial goals and making pol-icy decisions to implement these goals, financial executives of multinational firms must recognize the institutional, cultural, and political differences among host countries, which in turn lead to different national perceptions of the proper goals of a business entity.

Multinational Firms and Fluctuating Exchange Rates

An understanding of foreign exchange risk is essential for managers and investors in today's environment of volatile foreign exchange rates. The present international mone-tary system is characterized by a mix of floating and managed exchange rate policies pursued by each nation in its own best interest. As we describe in Chapter 2, some cur-rencies are tied to the U.S. dollar, some to the European Union (EU) currencies, some to the Japanese yen, some to the U.K. pound, and some are floating freely without a refer-ence currency. This rather complex system has led to violent shifts in the relative value of various currencies, with a consequent gain or loss in relative purchasing power.

Currency Values and Trade Politics   The dollar plunged nearly 4% against the yen, amid speculation that the Clinton administration will try using a strong yen to prod a Japanese market opening. But last night the U.S. issued a statement that its policy hasn't changed and that it doesn't endorse manipulating exchange rates.

The White House is preparing a two-pronged trade attack, deciding to renew the tough Super 301 trade provision and planning trade-sanction proceedings over cellular telephones. Most of corporate America, however, doesn't want a trade war with Japan that threatens to flare out of control.

Source: "Currency Values and Trade Politics," 2/15/94. Reprinted by permission of *The Wall Street Journal*, © 1994 Dow Jones & Co., Inc. All rights reserved worldwide.

When a currency increases in relative value, as was the case for the U.S. dollar between 1981 and 1985, exports from the United States decline because their prices become too high when converted to the currency of the foreign importer. Likewise, imports into the United States increase because they cost less in U.S. dollar terms when converting from a foreign currency. The loss of exports hurts gross national product and employment in the United States, but low-cost imports benefit consumers and help keep a lid on inflation. Thus any firm that exports or imports, or even a domestic firm that competes against imports, is directly affected by changes in the value of the U.S. dollar. All firms must understand foreign exchange risk in order to anticipate increased competition from imports or to realize increased opportunities for exports.

Multinational firms have the advantage of being geographically diversified. They need to understand foreign exchange risk in order to shift production to countries with relatively undervalued currencies and to promote sales in countries with over-valued currencies. They also typically have access to international sources of funds. The relative cost of these funds, after considering exchange rate effects, is likely to change, thereby giving multinational firms an opportunity to lower their cost of capital.

Multinational Firms and Capital Market Integration

Daimler-Benz Lists on the New York Stock Exchange   New York—Foreign companies are falling in love with American finance. The latest illustration of the widespread appeal of U.S. capital markets is Daimler-Benz AG's decision to list its shares on the New York Stock exchange, beginning today. To qualify for listing, the diversified German auto maker had to undertake a costly, excruciating revision of its accounting practices that 2 1/2 weeks ago caused a $592 million first-half loss, the company's first since World War II.

Source: "Daimler-Benz Lists on the New York Stock Exchange," 10/5/93, p. A1. Reprinted by permission of *The Wall Street Journal*, © 1993 Dow Jones & Co., Inc. All rights reserved worldwide.

During the past decade an explosive growth has occurred in the use of international capital markets to lower a firm's cost of capital. This growth has been fueled in part by a trend toward liberalizing securities markets in the most important world capital markets, which has motivated a large net increase in international portfolio investment. The United States was the first to liberalize, after the Securities and Exchange Commission pressured the investment community to adopt negotiated rather than fixed commissions when executing securities trades. Subsequently the European Union countries have adopted rules that should eventually lead to an integrated money and capital market, although their capital markets are not yet liberalized to the extent of those in the United States. The "Big Bang" of October 1986 was the U.K. version of capital market liberalization. Even the Japanese capital market has been slowly liberalized. Foreign firms have been admitted to the Tokyo Stock Exchange. Restrictions on the use of yen as an international currency have been eased and foreign firms may raise capital in Japan.

Although global integration is well started, many restrictions on the free flow of capital still exist. Furthermore, performances of stock and bond markets vary widely among countries and over time. Therefore opportunities still exist for both firms and portfolio investors to benefit from diversifying internationally.

Summary

The field of multinational business finance is something of a blend, a borscht, a stew, a chowder, which blends elements of corporate finance with international economics. However, it is not merely an extension of these fields using international examples. On the contrary it challenges some of the basic concepts of these fields.

- Definitions of *rate of return* and *risk* are not universally accepted. Indeed, meaning is based on culturally determined norms, varying by country. In the Anglo-American markets, the shareholder wealth maximization (SWM) model is probably the culturally determined norm. In the non-Anglo-American markets, the corporate wealth maximization (CWM) model may be the culturally determined norm. There are distinct differences between these models with respect to the treatment of rate of return and risk.

- One reason such differences exist is the one-share-one-vote rule. In the SWM model, it provides the means to discipline management in case it does not act in the shareholders' interests. In the CWM model, the one-share-one-vote rule is not the norm. Moreover, many takeover defenses exist, making it more difficult to discipline management except by internal pressure.

- Multinational firms are usually welcome in host countries to the extent they transfer technology, market access, and investment capital. However, many potential areas of goal conflict exist.

- Market imperfections are the rationale for the continued prosperity of multinational firms. It permits them to make competitive profits and to reduce risk though diversification.

- Although unexpected changes in exchange rates, interest rates, and commodity prices can be a threat, if properly understood, they can lead to profitable opportunities. Multinational firms are prepositioned to recognize these opportunities and to take advantage of them.

- Although capital markets are becoming more integrated, opportunities still exist for both firms and portfolio investors to benefit from diversifying internationally.

Questions

1. Comparative Advantage and Twentieth Century Transnationalism

The classical theory of comparative advantage has long been the pillar of modern international economic theory. But comparative advantage was based on the assumption that the factors of production such as labor and capital were immobile, or "trapped" in their home country. Following this principle, how would you answer the following questions:

    a.   Is this assumption realistic in the world we live in today in which firms move workers and obtain capital across many borders?

    b.   Even if this assumption was no longer relevant, are the principles of comparative advantage and the benefits of international trade still true?

2. Evolving Forms of International Business Organization

Using the three basic forms of international business organization described in this chapter (international, multinational, transnational), determine which category each of the following firms or activities belongs to:

    a.   Disney (US), with wholly owned theme parks in the United States, a licensed theme park in Japan, and a minority ownership in a theme park in France.

    b.   A garlic grower in Gilroy, California.

    c.   A croissant stand in the Toronto, Canada, airport.

    d.   Princess Cruise Lines, operating passenger cruises out of Miami and several cities on the Pacific coast.

    e.   A barber in Aarhus, Denmark.

3. Peter Drucker's "Principles"

All seven of the points made by Peter Drucker listed in Exhibit 1.4 will be covered in this book (as well as many more). However, from what you know now, from what logic tells you, with which of the points do you agree, and with which do you disagree?

4. Come Back Multinationals: Crowding Out and Exploitation

As discussed in the Global View "Come Back Multinationals," foreign direct investment continues to grow in a world that has not always been so receptive to growth.

    a.   Why have many multinationals in many countries traditionally been accused of crowding out and exploitation?

    b.   Cite arguments and evidence that multinational firms may not be the villains today they were once believed to be.

5. The Goal of Management

Before you can "manage," you must be clear on what goals you are pursuing, for yourself and for your firm. The two major philosophies described in the chapter, shareholder wealth maximization and corporate wealth maximization, could potentially lead management of a firm to make very different decisions.

    a. A leveraged buyout is a financial maneuver in which a group of investors gain control of a firm and then liquidate its assets (i.e., break it up) in order to pay off the purchase price. How would this be perceived in a country that believed in corporate wealth maximization? In shareholder wealth maximization?

    b. In an interlocking directorate, the members of the governing board of one firm also sit on the governing board of a second firm. How is this practice likely to be perceived between the two philosophies?

6. European Union's Fifth Directive

The Company Law Directorate of the European Commission of the European Union has proposed the so-called Fifth Directive. If passed, this directive would require one-share-one-vote for common stock but permit up to 50% of equity capital to consist of nonvoting preferred stock. The Fifth Directive has been through many iterations because of intense opposition from member countries that permit dual classes of common stock.

    a. Discuss the pros and cons of passing the Fifth Directive into law for all of the member countries of the European Union.

    b. Suggest alternative laws that might accomplish the same purposes but be more acceptable to the majority of member countries.

7. Universal versus Culturally Determined Norms

Explain whether the following financial tasks are actually guided by universal principles or culturally determined principles:

    a. Calculation of the discount rate to be used in a capital budgeting analysis.

    b. Determination of the optimal mix of debt and equity for a firm's financial structure.

    c. Establishing the policy of what proportion of net profits are to be distributed to shareholders and what proportion retained by the firm for future growth needs (dividend policy).

8. One-Share-One-Vote Versus Dual Classes of Stock

The U.S. Securities and Exchange Commission has recently reaffirmed the desirability of U.S. firms pursuing a "one-share-one-vote" policy. On the other hand, many European companies have two types of share capital, A and B shares, with differential voting rights. Why do you believe the Europeans allow this differential in voting rights?

9. Japanese Financial Goals

It is widely believed the goal of most large Japanese companies is to "maximize corporate wealth" in the long run. The survival of the firm is paramount rather than maximizing shareholders' wealth. What are the characteristics of the Japanese society and business system that make corporate wealth maximization a more desirable goal than shareholder wealth maximization?

Bibliography

Ahn, Mark J., and William D. Falloon, *Strategic Risk Management: How the Global Corporations Manage Financial Risk for Competitive Advantage,* Chicago: Probus, 1991.

Aliber, Robert Z., *Handbook of International Financial Management,* Homewood, Ill.: Dow Jones-Irwin, 1989.

Aliber, Robert Z., *The International Money Game,* 5th ed., New York: Basic Books, 1987.

Aoi, Joichi, "To Whom Does the Company Belong?: A New Management Mission for the Information Age," *Journal of Applied Corporate Finance,* Winter 1994, pp. 25–31.

Brewer, Thomas L., "Government Policies, Market Imperfections, and Foreign Direct Investment," *Journal of International Business Studies,* First Quarter 1993, pp. 101–120.

Buckley, Peter J., and Mark Casson, eds., *Multinational Enterprises in the World Economy: Essays in the Honour of John Dunning,* Aldershot, Hants, England: Edward Elgar, 1992.

Buckley, Peter J., and Jeremy Clegg, *Multinational Enterprises in Less Developed Countries,* New York: St. Martin's Press, 1991.

Choi, Frederick D. S., "International Data Sources for Empirical Research in Financial Management," *Financial Management,* Summer 1988, pp. 80–98.

Donaldson, Gordon, "The Corporate Restructuring of the 1980s—and its Import for the 1990s," *Journal of Applied Corporate Finance,* Winter 1994, pp. 55–69.

Dufey, Gunter, and Ian Giddy, *50 Cases in International Finance,* 2nd ed., Reading, Mass.: Addison-Wesley, 1992.

Elfstrom, Gerard, *Moral Issues and Multinational Corporations,* New York: St. Martin's Press, 1991.

Giddy, Ian H., *Global Financial Markets,* Lexington, MA: D.C. Heath, 1994.

Grabbe, J. Orlin, International Financial Markets, 2nd ed., New York: Elsevier, 1991.

Holland, John, *International Financial Management,* 2nd ed., New York and Oxford, U.K.: Basil Blackwell, 1992.

Investing, Licensing and Trading Conditions Abroad, New York: Business International, a reference service that is continually updated.

Lessard, Donald R., "Corporate Finance in the 1990's: Implications of a Changing Competitive and Financial Context," Chapter 1 in *Handbook of International Accounting,* Frederick D. S. Choi, ed., New York: Wiley, 1991.

Lessard, Donald R., "Global Competition and Corporate Finance in the 1990's," *Journal of Applied Corporate Finance*, Winter 1991, pp. 59–72.

Lessard, Donald R., *International Financial Management, Theory and Application,* 2nd ed., New York: Wiley, 1987.

Levi, Maurice, *International Finance: Financial Management and the International Economy,* 2nd ed., New York: McGraw-Hill, 1990.

Levich, Richard M., "Recent International Financial Innovations: Implications for Financial Management," *Journal of International Financial Management and Accounting,* vol.1, no. 1, Spring 1989, pp. 1–14.

Madura, Jeff, *International Financial Management,* 3rd ed., St. Paul, Minn.: West, 1992.

Miller, Merton H., "Is American Corporate Governance Fatally Flawed?", *Journal of Applied Corporate Finance,* Winter 1994, pp. 32–39.

Phylaktis, Kaate, and Mahmeed Pradhan, eds., *International Finance and the Less Developed Countries,* Basingstoke, England: Macmillan, in association with the Department of Banking and Finance, City University Business School, 1990.

Prahalad, C.K., "Corporate Governance or Corporate Value Added?: Rethinking the Primacy of

Shareholder Value," *Journal of Applied Corporate Finance*, Winter 1994, pp. 40–50.

Shapiro, Alan C., *Multinational Financial Management*, 4th ed., Boston: Allyn & Bacon, 1992.

Solnik, Bruno, *International Investments*, 2nd ed., Reading, Mass.: Addison-Wesley, 1991.

Stopford, John, *Directory of Multinationals*, 4th ed., Basingstoke, Hampshire, U.K.: Macmillan Publishers Ltd., 1993.

Chapter 1 Appendix
The Theory of Comparative Advantage

The theory of comparative advantage and its corollary, the theory of factor proportions, provide a basis for explaining and justifying international trade in a model world assumed to enjoy free trade, perfect competition, no uncertainty, costless information, and no government interference. The theory contains the following features:

- Exporters in country A sell goods or services to unrelated importers in country B (any other country).

- Firms in country A specialize in making products that can be relatively efficiently produced, given country A's endowment of factors of production, that is, land, labor, capital, and technology. Firms in country B do likewise, given the factors of production found in country B. In this way the total combined output of A and B is maximized.

- Since the factors of production cannot be freely moved from country A to country B, the benefits of specialization are realized through international trade.

- How the benefits of the extra production are shared depends on the terms of trade. Each share is determined by supply and demand in perfectly competitive markets in the two countries. Neither country A nor B is worse off than before trade, and typically both are better off, albeit perhaps unequally.

For an example of the benefits of free trade based on comparative advantage, assume country A is relatively efficient at producing food and country B is relatively efficient at producing cloth. Assume each unit of production (land, labor, capital, and technology) in country A can produce either 6 tons of food or 12 yards of cloth, whereas each unit of production in country B can produce either 2 tons of food or 10 yards of cloth. In other words, a production unit in A has an absolute advantage over a production unit in B in both food and cloth. Nevertheless, country A has a larger relative advantage over country B in producing food (6 to 2) than cloth (12 to 10). As long as these ratios are unequal, comparative advantage exists.

	Units of production	Total production (millions of tons or yards)	Total consumption (millions of tons or yards)
Country A			
Food	700,000 × 6 =	4.2	4.2
Cloth	300,000 × 12 =	3.6	3.6
Country B			
Food	700,000 × 2 =	1.4	1.4
Cloth	300,000 × 10 =	3.0	3.0

Assume both countries have one million units of production and the production and consumption situations before trade are as follows:

Now assume that trade is allowed, with the barter ratio between food and cloth being 4 yards of cloth equal 1 ton of food. The barter ratio must end up between the ratios in each of the countries, since without trade nobody in country A would pay more than 2 yards of cloth for 1 ton of food, while in country B nobody would pay more than 5 yards of cloth for 1 ton of food. Assume that country A transfers all units of production from producing cloth to producing food and country B transfers all units of production

	Units of production	Total production (millions of tons or yards)	Trade (millions of tons or yards)	Total consumption (millions of tons or yards)
Country A				
Food	1,000,000 × 6 =	6.0	−1.6	4.4
Cloth	—	—	+6.4	6.4
Country B				
Food	—	—	+1.6	1.6
Cloth	1,000,000 × 2 =	10.0	−6.4	3.6

from producing food to producing cloth. The resulting output is then bartered so both countries consume more food or cloth than they consumed before trade was allowed. The new production and consumption situations after trade could be as follows:

Both countries have benefited from specializing and trading. Country A consumes 200,000 tons more of food and 2.8 million yards more of cloth. Country B consumes 200,000 tons more of food and 600,000 yards more of cloth. Total combined production of both food and cloth has increased through the specialization process, and it only remains for the exchange ratio to determine how the larger output is distributed between the countries.

Although international trade might have approached the comparative advantage model during the nineteenth century, it certainly does not today, for the following reasons:

- Countries do not appear to specialize only in those products that could be most efficiently produced by that country's particular factors of production. Instead, governments interfere with comparative advantage for a variety of economic and political reasons, such as full employment, economic development, national self-sufficiency in defense-related industries, and protection of an agricultural sector's way of life. Government interference takes the form of tariffs, quotas, and other nontariff restrictions.

- At least two of the factors of production, capital and technology, flow directly between countries rather than only indirectly through traded goods and services. This direct flow occurs between related affiliates of multinational firms, as well as between unrelated firms via loans, licenses, and management contracts.

- Although the terms of trade are ultimately determined by supply and demand, the process by which this trade occurs is different from that visualized in traditional trade theory. The terms of trade are determined partly by administered pricing in oligopolistic markets.

■ Comparative advantage shifts over time as less developed countries become more developed and realize their latent opportunities. For example, comparative advantage in producing cotton textiles shifted from the United Kingdom to the United States, to Japan, to Hong Kong, to Taiwan, and to Thailand.

■ The classical model of comparative advantage did not really address certain other issues such as the effect of uncertainty and information costs, the role of differentiated products in imperfectly competitive markets, and economies of scale.

Nevertheless, although the world is a long way from the classical trade model, the principle of comparative advantage is still valid. The closer the world gets to true international specialization, the more world production and consumption can be increased, provided the problem of equitable distribution of the benefits can be solved to the satisfaction of consumers, producers, and political leaders. Complete specialization, however, remains an unrealistic limiting case, just as perfect competition is a limiting case in microeconomic theory.

Chapter 2
The International Monetary System

Global View
Can Central Banks Turn the Tide?

It is pointless for governments and central banks to intervene in the foreign-exchange markets. Such interventions are now a mere drop in a $1 trillion-a-day ocean. The turmoil in Europe's exchange-rate mechanism (ERM) over the past year has demonstrated the futility of trying to take on the power of the markets in the age of footloose finance.

Or so it is commonly thought. But a new study by Kathryn Dominguez and Jeffrey Frankel for the Institute for International Economics, a Washington think-tank, challenges that conventional wisdom. "Does Foreign Exchange Intervention Work?", their study asks. "Yes it does," they answer. Their conclusion is based on an analysis of (hitherto secret) daily intervention data from America's Federal Reserve and Germany's Bundesbank. They crunched all the numbers through a computer and did indeed find a positive relationship between central-bank intervention and subsequent exchange-rate movements.

Only a small part of the impact of intervention stems directly from the actual selling or buying of currency by the central banks. More important, the study argues, is the effect on traders' expectations: the central banks are sending a signal which the markets in most cases tend to heed. But the strength of the signal can vary a lot, depending on how the intervening is done. For maximum effect on the market, the study advises:

- Surprise. The first intervention has the largest impact. If it comes out of the blue, so much the better.

- Publicity. Interventions work best when they are trumpeted, rather than . . . kept entirely secret.
- Co-ordination. Banks acting together can achieve more than a single central bank acting alone.

Unfortunately, all this is of little help to the battered ERM. Even the best-managed interventions will have little effect if they fly in the face of powerful economic fundamentals. Besides, in a quasi-fixed exchange rate system such as the one that the Europeans have tried to operate, intervention loses the element of surprise. Elsewhere, too, the impact would quickly fade if intervention were tried too often. Intervention may be a more useful tool than is commonly believed, but it is one to be used sparingly.

Source: "Gang up, and strike from the blue," 9/18/93, p. 84. © 1993 The Economist Newspaper Ltd. Reprinted with permission.

The increased volatility of exchange rates since 1973 is one of the main economic trends of the past 22 years. Under the current system of partly floating and partly fixed exchange rates, the earnings of multinational firms, banks, and individual investors have been subjected to significant real and paper fluctuations as a result of changes in relative exchange rates. Policies to forecast and react to exchange rate fluctuations are still evolving as understanding of the functioning of the international monetary system grows, as accounting and tax rules for foreign exchange gains and losses become clarified, and as the economic effect of exchange rate changes on future cash flows and market values becomes recognized.

Although volatile exchange rates may increase risk, they also create profit opportunities for both firms and investors, given a proper understanding of exchange risk management. However, in order to manage foreign exchange risk, management must first understand how the international monetary system has evolved over time and how it functions today. The *international monetary system* can be defined as the structure within which foreign exchange rates are determined, international trade and capital flows are accommodated, and balance of payments adjustments made. It also includes all of the instruments, institutions, and agreements that link together the world's currency and money markets. These topics are analyzed in the remainder of this chapter. The case of the Finnish markka, described at the end of this chapter, demonstrates the complexities of a country managing its currency value in the 1990s.

Currency Values and Terminology

A *foreign currency exchange rate* is the price of one country's currency in units of another currency or commodity (typically gold or silver). If the government of a country, for example Taiwan, regulates the rate at which the New Taiwan dollar (NT$) is exchanged for other currencies, the system or *regime* is classified as a *fixed* or *managed exchange rate regime*. The rate at which the currency is fixed, or pegged, is frequently referred to as its *par value*. If, however, the government of the country does not interfere in the exchange or valuation of its currency in any way, it is classified as *floating* or *flexible*.

Changing Currency Values

A definition of terms used in reporting changes in exchange rates is also appropriate prior to a brief history of the international monetary system (if for no other reason than that newspaper accounts often use terminology such as the word *devaluation* incorrectly).

- The term *devaluation* in a narrow and semantically correct sense refers only to a drop in foreign exchange value of a currency that is pegged to gold or to another currency. The opposite of devaluation is *revaluation*.

- The terms *weakening, deterioration,* or *depreciation* refer to a drop in the foreign exchange value of a floating currency. The opposite of weakening is *strengthening* or *appreciating,* which refers to a gain in the exchange value of a floating currency.

- A currency is considered *soft* if it is expected to be devalued or to depreciate relative to major currencies, or if its exchange value is being artificially sustained by its government. A currency is considered *hard* if it is expected to revalue or appreciate relative to major trading currencies.[1]

Fixed Versus Flexible Exchange Rates

Although the following historical section focuses on the exchange rate in isolation, a nation's choice as to which currency regime it follows reflects national priorities about all facets of the macroeconomy, such as inflation, unemployment, interest rate levels, trade balances, and economic growth. The choice between fixed and flexible rates may then change as priorities change.

At the risk of overgeneralizing, the following points aid in the understanding of the history of the global monetary system of the twentieth century—a continuing battle between fixed rates and flexible rates, internal versus external political and economic national priorities. As we analyze these major points, it is obvious the costs associated with what a country desires—for example, a fixed exchange rate—may be too dear when actually put into practice.

- Countries prefer fixed exchange rates. Fixed rates provide stability in international prices for the conduct of trade. Stable prices aid in the growth of international trade.

---

[1]For example, firms in eastern Europe or Latin America often export products and request payment in *hard currencies*. The U.S. dollar, the Japanese yen, the German mark, the Swiss franc, British pound, and a number of other major industrial country currencies that have histories of maintaining their values over time, and are generally acceptable for payments around the world, are considered *hard*.

- Fixed exchange rates are inherently anti-inflationary, requiring the country to follow restrictive monetary and fiscal policies. This restrictiveness, however, can often be a burden to a country wishing to pursue policies that alleviate continuing internal economic problems such as high unemployment or slow economic growth.

- Fixed exchange rate regimes require central banks to maintain large quantities of international reserves (other hard currencies and gold) to be used in the occasional defense of their fixed rate. As the international currency markets have grown rapidly in size and volume, this has become a significant burden to many nations.

- Fixed rates, once in place, may be maintained at rates that are inconsistent with economic fundamentals. As the structure of a nation's economy changes, as its trade relationships and balances evolve, the exchange rate itself should change. Whereas flexible exchange rates allow this to happen gradually and efficiently, fixed rates must be changed administratively—usually too late and at too large of a onetime cost to the nation's economic health.

A Brief History of the International Monetary System

Currencies have been defined historically in terms of gold and other items of value, and the international monetary system has been subject to a variety of international agreements. A brief history of these systems provides useful perspective against which to understand today's system and to evaluate weaknesses and proposed changes in the present system.

The Gold Standard, 1876–1913

Currencies have not always been pegged to other currencies, or to baskets of goods, or even allowed to float freely. Since the days of the Pharaohs (about 3000 B.C.) gold was used as a medium of exchange and a store of value. The Greeks and Romans used gold coins and passed on this tradition through the mercantile era to the nineteenth century. The great increase in trade during the free-trade period of the late nineteenth century led to a need for a more formalized system for settling international trade transactions. One country after another set a *par value* for its currency in terms of gold and then tried to maintain this value. This was the fundamental principle of the *classical gold standard*. The gold standard as an international monetary system gained acceptance in western Europe in the 1870s, with the United States a relative latecomer to the system, not officially adopting the standard until 1879. Although successful for its time, like all systems, it had rules.

The rules of the game under the gold standard were clear and simple. Each country set the rate at which its currency (paper or coin) could be converted to a weight of gold. The United States, for example, declared the dollar to be convertible to gold at a rate of $20.67/ounce of gold, the par value of the dollar. This rate remained in effect until the beginning of World War I. The British pound was pegged at £4.2474/ounce of gold. As long as both currencies were freely convertible into gold, the dollar/pound exchange rate was as follows:

$$\frac{\$20.67/\text{ounce of gold}}{\pounds4.2474/\text{ounce of gold}} = \$4.86656/\pounds$$

Because the government of each country on the gold standard agreed to buy or sell gold on demand with anyone at its own fixed parity rate, the value of each individual currency in terms of gold, and therefore the fixed parities between currencies, was set. Under this system it was very important for a country to maintain adequate reserves of gold to back its currency's value. The system also had the effect of implicitly limiting the rate at which any individual country could expand its money supply. The growth in money was limited to the rate at which additional gold could be acquired by official authorities.

The gold standard worked adequately until the outbreak of World War I interrupted trade flows and the free movement of gold. This caused the main trading nations to suspend the operation of the gold standard.

The Interwar Years and World War II, 1914–1944

During World War I and the early 1920s, currencies were allowed to fluctuate over fairly wide ranges in terms of gold and each other. Theoretically, supply and demand for a country's exports and imports caused moderate changes in an exchange rate about a central value. This was the same function that gold performed under the previous gold standard. Unfortunately, flexible exchange rates did not work as smoothly; exchange rates were increasingly unstable. International speculators, attempting to make a profit on the depreciation of weaker currencies, added to the instability of the markets with their actions. As a result, currency values fell further than warranted by the real economic factors. The reverse happened with strong currencies. The net result was that the volume of world trade did not grow in the 1920s in proportion to world gross national product, and declined even further with the advent of the Great Depression in the 1930s.

Several attempts were made to return to the gold standard during the interwar years. The United States returned to gold in 1919, the United Kingdom in 1925, and France in 1928. The revaluation of the British pound in April 1925 to $4.86656/£ (its prewar parity) resulted in increased unemployment and economic stagnation in the U.K., all in order to restore confidence in the exchange rate system. The problem of finding new and reasonably stable parity values for gold was never solved before the collapse of the Austrian banking system in 1931 caused most trading nations to abandon the gold standard once again.

The United States returned to a modified gold standard in 1934 when the U.S. dollar was devalued to $35.00/ounce of gold from the previous $20.67/ounce in effect prior to World War I. Although the United States returned to the standard, gold was traded only with foreign central banks, not private citizens. From 1934 to the end of World War II, exchange rates were theoretically determined by each currency's value in terms of gold. During World War II and its immediate aftermath many of the world's major currencies lost their *convertibility*, their ability to be readily accepted and exchanged. The dollar was the only major trading currency that continued to be convertible.

The Bretton Woods Agreement and the Gold Exchange Standard, 1944–1973

In 1944, as World War II drew toward a close, a so-called gold exchange standard was adopted by the Allied Powers at Bretton Woods, New Hampshire. The agreement established a dollar-based international monetary system and provided for two new institutions: the International Monetary Fund (IMF), for aiding countries with balance of payments and exchange rate problems, and the International Bank for Reconstruction and Development (World Bank), for post-war reconstruction and general economic development.

Under the provisions of the Bretton Woods Agreement, all countries fixed the value of their currencies in terms of gold but were not required to exchange their currencies for gold. Only the dollar remained convertible into gold (at $35 per ounce). Therefore each country decided what it wished its exchange rate to be vis-à-vis the dollar, and then calculated the gold par value of its currencies to create the desired dollar exchange rate. Participating countries agreed to try to maintain the value of their currencies within 1% of par value by buying or selling foreign exchange or gold as needed. Devaluation was not to be used as a competitive trade policy, but if a currency became too weak to defend, a devaluation of up to 10% was allowed without formal approval by the IMF. Larger devaluations required IMF approval.

The International Monetary Fund. The International Monetary Fund, or IMF, was obviously the key institution in this international monetary system, and it has remained so to the present. The IMF was originally established to render temporary assistance to member countries trying to defend their currencies against cyclical, seasonal, or random occurrences. It also assists countries having structural trade problems if they take adequate steps to correct their problems. However, if persistent deficits occur, the IMF cannot save a country from eventual devaluation. The Soviet Union, one of the Allied Powers that participated in the Bretton Woods meeting, chose not to join the International Monetary Fund or the World Bank. Some of the successors to the Soviet Union are currently seeking membership in both organizations.

To carry out its task, the IMF was originally funded by each member subscribing to a quota based on expected post–World War II trade patterns.[2] Quotas were paid 25% in gold (a country's "gold tranche") and 75% in their local currency. The quotas have been expanded and the distribution revised many times since 1944 to accommodate growth in overall world trade, new membership, and changes in the relative importance of member countries.

Any member nation can borrow funds from the IMF. Under the guidelines presently in effect, each of the 177 member countries can borrow annually up to 150% of its quota,

---

[2]Current international financial statistics covering the IMF and member countries appear in the current month's issue of IMF, *International Financial Statistics,* Washington, D.C.

or up to 450% during a three-year period. Cumulative access, net of scheduled repayments, can be up to 600% of a member's quota.

Relative size of quotas is important as a determinant of voting power. The industrialized countries have always maintained voting control because they supply most of the quotas. At present the United States holds 17.82% of voting control. Other large voting rights are held by Germany (5.55%), Japan (5.55%), France (4.99%), and the United Kingdom (4.99%).[3]

In addition to its quota resources, the IMF has access under certain circumstances to funds that it borrows in the world's capital markets. Under the General Arrangements to Borrow (GAB) and associated agreements, the IMF can use the borrowed funds not only to help GAB members over temporary exchange problems but also to assist nonmembers, such as countries with heavy external debt burdens.

Special Drawing Rights (SDRs). The Special Drawing Right, or SDR, is a standard currency basket created by the International Monetary Fund in 1970 as a type of foreign exchange reserve. It is, in effect, an alternate basket to the other major currency basket used today, the European Currency Unit (discussed later in this chapter).

Originally the weighted average of 16 currencies, the SDR was redesigned in 1981 to approximate the weighted value of the five IMF members having the largest exports of goods and services. These countries and their current weighting are the United States (40%), Germany (21%), Japan (17%), the United Kingdom (11%), and France (11%).[4] The amount of each component currency of the SDR will remain in effect until December 31, 1995, at which time the SDR will again be revised to reflect changes in the relative importance of each country in international trade and finance.

The basic purpose of the SDR is to be a reserve currency that members may use in transactions among themselves and with the IMF. The interest rate on the SDR, a weighted average of the yields on short-term obligations of the five currencies, is used to pay or charge interest to IMF members whose holdings of SDRs exceed or are below their required reserve allocation.

Fixed Exchange Rates, 1945–1973

The currency arrangement negotiated at Bretton Woods and monitored by the IMF worked fairly well during the post–World War II period of reconstruction and rapid growth in world trade. However, widely diverging national monetary and fiscal policies, differential rates of inflation, and various unexpected external shocks eventually resulted in the system's demise. A key element of this system failure was the core currency of the system: the dollar. The U.S. dollar was the main reserve currency held by central banks and was the key to the web of exchange rate values. Unfortunately the

---

[3]International Monetary Fund, *Annual Report,* Washington, D.C.: International Monetary Fund, 1993, pp. 166–167.

[4]International Monetary Fund, *Annual Report,* Washington, D.C.: International Monetary Fund, 1993, p. 95. The specific units of the individual currencies constituting the value of the SDR are as follows: US$—0.572 units; DM—0.453 units; ¥—31.8 units; FF—0.800 units; £—0.0812 units.

United States ran persistent and growing deficits on its balance of payments. This resulted in a heavy capital outflow of dollars (often referred to as the "dumping of dollars on world markets") to finance these deficits and to meet the growing demand for dollars from investors and businesses. Eventually the heavy overhang of dollars held abroad resulted in a lack of confidence in the ability of the United States to meet its commitment to convert dollars to gold.

The Crisis of 1971. On August 15, 1971, President Richard Nixon was forced to suspend official purchases or sales of gold by the U.S. Treasury after the United States suffered outflows of roughly one-third of its official gold reserves in the first seven months of the year. Furthermore, in what was termed "Phase I" of a series of policy changes, the United States temporarily imposed a 10% surcharge on all imports, and all domestic U.S. prices were frozen at existing rates.

Because the price of gold at $35 per ounce was theoretically left unchanged, there was no immediate impact on the amount of international monetary reserves. Nevertheless, the United States served notice to the world that the dollar could no longer be used as the basis for the gold exchange standard (and the nation would no longer abide by the "rules of the game"). In the meantime, exchange rates of most of the leading trading countries were allowed to float in relation to the dollar and thus indirectly in relation to gold.[5] By the end of 1971 most of the major trading currencies had appreciated vis-à-vis the dollar. This was—in effect—a devaluation of the dollar.

Smithsonian Agreement of December 1971. Multilateral bargaining sessions among the world's leading trading nations reached a compromise agreement at the Washington, D.C., meeting of December 17–18, 1971, later known as the *Smithsonian Agreement*. The United States agreed to devalue the dollar to $38 per ounce of gold (an 8.57% devaluation). In return, the other countries present agreed to revalue their own currencies upward in relation to the dollar by specified amounts. Actual revaluations ranged from 7.4% by Canada to 16.9% by Japan. Furthermore, the trading band around par value was expanded from the existing 1% band to plus or minus 2.25%.

March 1973 Decision to Float. The Smithsonian Agreement was less than a year old before market pressures once again forced changes. The British pound was allowed to float in June 1972 and the Swiss franc in January 1973. In early 1973 the U.S. dollar came under attack once again, thereby forcing a second devaluation on February 12, 1973, this time by 10% to $42.22 per ounce. By late February 1973 a fixed-rate system appeared no longer feasible given the extreme surges of speculative flows of currencies. The major foreign exchange markets were actually closed for several weeks in March 1973, and when they reopened, most currencies were allowed to float to levels determined by market forces. Par values were left unchanged. The dollar had floated downward an average of 10% by June 1973.

---

[5]*The Economist* magazine's cover for the week of August 21, 1971, depicted a large inflated U.S. dollar floating in water with the caption "Come on, the water's fine!"

An Eclectic Currency Arrangement, 1973–Present

Since March 1973, exchange rates have become much more volatile and less predictable than they were during the "fixed" exchange rate period, when changes occurred infrequently. The foreign exchange markets have become increasingly dominated by the so-called *triad currencies* consisting of the U.S. dollar, German mark (Deutschemark), and Japanese yen. The dollar and yen float independently. The Deutschemark is the central currency of continental Europe.

Jamaica Agreement of January 1976. At Jamaica an agreement was reached that provides the rules of the game for today's system. Highlights of the Jamaica Agreement are as follows:

- Floating rates were declared acceptable, although member countries are permitted to interfere to even out unwarranted fluctuations caused by sheer speculation. In other words, member countries are no longer expected to maintain a band around par value.

- Gold was demonetized as a reserve asset. The IMF agreed to return 25 million ounces to its members and to sell another 25 million ounces at the going market price (around $2 billion). The proceeds of the sale were to be placed in a trust fund to help the poorer nations. Members could also sell their own gold reserves at market price rather than at the previous par value price.

The U.S. Dollar on a Roller Coaster Ride. Exhibit 2.1 shows how the U.S. dollar has fared relative to the currencies of some major industrial trading partners. The Morgan Guaranty Index depicted in Exhibit 2.1 is the *nominal effective* exchange rate of the U.S. dollar compared with the weighted average basket of the currencies of 15 other industrial countries. The index is weighted by the size of the U.S. bilateral trade in manufactured goods with 15 other industrial countries during the year 1980. The weighted average exchange rates for the years 1980 to 1982 are fixed at an index value of 100. In general the dollar has been volatile and has weakened somewhat over the long run.

The Growing Strength of the Deutschemark and Yen. Exhibit 2.2 shows how the Deutschemark and yen have fared compared to the dollar during the same period as in Exhibit 2.1. Their volatility and long-run strengthening is the mirror image of the dollar's volatility and long-run weakening.

Summary of Currency Events, 1973–Present

Exhibit 2.3 summarizes the key events and external shocks that have impacted currency values since 1973. The most important shocks were, in chronological order, the oil crisis of late 1973, loss of confidence in the U.S. dollar in 1977 and 1978, the second oil crisis in 1979, formation of the European Monetary System in 1979, diversification of foreign exchange reserves by central banks starting in 1979, the strength of the U.S. dollar during the period 1981 to 1985, followed by a rapid decline in the value of the U.S. dollar

Exhibit 2.1   The U.S. Dollar Under Floating Exchange Rates, 1971–1993

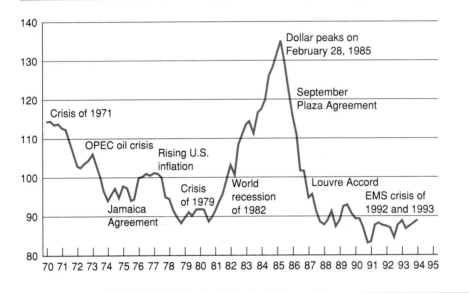

Source: 15-country nominal exchange rate index of the U.S. dollar, Morgan Guaranty, *World Financial Markets,* various issues. 1980–1982 = 100.

from February 1985 until early 1988. Since 1988, world currency values have continued to fluctuate erratically. In addition to the aforementioned Jamaica Agreement (1976), two other agreements during this period deserve special attention.

Plaza Agreement and Louvre Accords.   In September 1985, the finance ministers and central bank governors of the so-called Group of Six industrial countries (U.S.A., France, Germany, United Kingdom, Japan, and Canada) met at the Plaza Hotel in New York City and reached what was later referred to as the Plaza Agreement. They announced it would be desirable for most major currencies to appreciate vis-à-vis the U.S. dollar and pledged to intervene in exchange markets to accomplish this objective. Since the dollar had already started to weaken in value during the spring and summer of 1985, this announcement further accelerated the dollar's decline.

The dollar declined rapidly throughout the rest of 1985, all of 1986, and on into early 1987. In fact, it showed signs of overshooting its purported "natural level" given the changed economic conditions. Therefore in February 1987 the major industrial countries again met and reached a new agreement known as the Louvre Accords. They agreed that exchange rates had been realigned sufficiently and pledged to support stability of exchange rates around their current levels. Although the dollar declined further during 1987, it rallied in early 1988, thereby ending for the moment its dramatic rise and fall during the period from 1980 to 1987.

Exhibit 2.2 The Relative Values of the Dollar, Mark, and Yen, 1970–1993

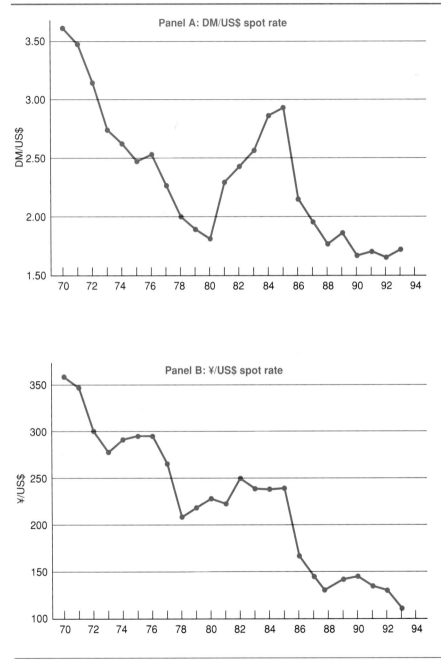

Source: Derived by the authors from the *Federal Reserve Bulletin,* Board of Governors of the Federal Reserve System, Washington D.C., monthly.

Exhibit 2.3 World Currency Events, 1970–1994

Date	Event	Impact
August 1971	Nixon closes the U.S. Gold Window	Suspends purchases or sales of gold by U.S. Treasury; temporary imposition of 10% import surcharge
December 1971	Smithsonian Agreement	Group of Ten reaches compromise whereby the US$ is devalued to $38/oz. of gold; most other major currencies are appreciated versus US$
June 1972	British pound floats	Bank of England allows pound to float
January 1973	Swiss franc floats	Swiss central bank allows franc to float
February 1973	U.S. dollar devalued	Devaluation pressure increases on US$ forcing further devaluation to $42.22/oz. of gold
Feb–March 1973	Currency markets in crisis	Fixed exchange rates no longer considered defensible; speculative pressures force closure of international foreign exchange markets for nearly two weeks; markets reopen on floating rates for major industrial currencies
June 1973	U.S. dollar depreciation	Floating rates continue to drive the now freely floating US$ down by about 10% by June
Fall 1973–1974	OPEC oil embargo	Organization of Petroleum Exporting Countries (OPEC) impose oil embargo eventually quadrupling the world price of oil; because world oil prices are stated in US$, value of US$ recovers some former strength
January 1976	Jamaica Agreement	IMF meeting in Jamaica results in the "legalization" of the floating exchange rate system already in effect; gold is demonetized as a reserve asset; IMF quotas are increased
1977–1978	U.S. inflation rate rises	Carter administration reduces unemployment at the expense of inflation increases; rising U.S. inflation causes continued depreciation of the US$
March 1979	EMS created	European Monetary System (EMS) is created, establishing a cooperative exchange rate system for participating members of the EEC
Summer 1979	OPEC raises prices	OPEC nations raise price of oil once again
Fall 1979	Iranian assets frozen	Carter responds to Iranian hostage crisis by freezing all Iranian assets held in U.S. financial institutions
Spring 1980	U.S. dollar begins rise	Worldwide inflation and early signs of recession coupled with real interest differential advantages for dollar-denominated assets contribute to increased demand for dollars
August 1982	Latin American debt crisis	Mexico informs U.S. Treasury that it will be unable to make debt service payments, Brazil and Argentina follow in months; the "debt crisis" begins
February 1985	U.S. dollar peaks	The U.S. dollar peaks against most major industrial currencies, hitting record highs against the Deutschemark and other European currencies
September 1985	Plaza Agreement	The Group of Ten members meet at the Plaza Hotel in New York to sign an international cooperative agreement to control the volatility of world currency markets and to establish currency target zones
February 1987	Louvre Accord	The Group of Six members state they will "intensify" economic policy coordination to promote global growth

Exhibit 2.3 *continued*

		and reduce external imbalances; members agree that current exchange rates are "consistent with underlying economic fundamentals"
September 1992	EMS Crisis	High German interest rates induce massive capital flows into Germany eventually causing the withdrawal of the Italian lira and British pound from the Exchange Rate Mechanism (ERM)
July 31, 1993	EMS Realignment	EMS adjusts allowable deviation band to ±15% for all member currencies (except Dutch guilder); U.S. dollar continues to weaken against other major industrial currencies such as the yen and Deutschemark; Japanese yen reaches ¥100.25/$ in August 1993

Contemporary Currency Arrangements

So many different currency arrangements exist today that to describe the current international monetary system in any one way, for example as a floating-rate system, is misleading. Although it is true the three most widely traded currencies on global markets (the U.S. dollar, the Japanese yen, the German mark) float against one another, it is important that the multinational enterprise understand the currency regime specifically in place in all markets in which it operates.

Classification of Currency Arrangements

The International Monetary Fund (IMF) classifies today's currency arrangements into seven categories (see Exhibit 2.4). These categories can be briefly described as follows:

1. **Pegged to another currency.** About 50 countries peg their currency to some other currency. For example, the U.S. dollar is the base for 24 other currencies, ranging from Angola's *chintzy* to the *rial* used by the Republic of Yemen. The French franc is the base for 14 currencies, all issued by former French colonies in Africa. Six of the new countries created at the breakup of the Soviet Union peg their currencies to the Russian ruble; another six countries peg their currencies to an important neighbor.

2. **Pegged to a basket.** Some 34 countries peg their currencies to a composite "basket" of currencies, where the basket consists of a portfolio of currencies of major trading partners. The base value of such a basket is more stable than any single currency. Five of these countries peg their currencies to Special Drawing Rights (SDRs). The remaining 29 peg their currencies to their own tailor-made basket, designed to mirror the country's unique trading and investing patterns.

3. **Flexible against a single currency.** Four countries in the Persian Gulf area maintain their currencies within a limited range of flexibility vis-à-vis the U.S. dollar.

Exhibit 2.4   International Monetary Fund Currency Arrangements

| | | *Currency Pegged To* | | | |
U.S. dollar	French franc	Russian ruble	Other currency	IMF's SDR	Other composite
Angola	Benin	Armenia	Bhutan	Libya	Algeria
Antigua	Burkina Faso	Azerbaijan	(Indian	Myanmar	Austria
& Barbuda	Cameroon	Belarus	Rupee)	Rwanda	Bangladesh
Argentina	C. African	Georgia	Estonia	Seychelles	Botswana
Bahamas, The	Republic	Kazakhstan	(Deutschmark)		Burundi
Barbados	Chad	Moldova	Kiribati		Cape Verde
Belize	Comoros	Turkmenistan	(Australian		Cyprus
Djibouti	Congo		dollar)		Fiji
Dominica	Cote d'Ivoire		Lesotho		Hungary
Grenada	Equatorial		(South African		Iceland
Iraq	Guinea		rand)		Jordan
Liberia	Gabon		Namibia		Kenya
Marshall Islands	Mali		(South African		Kuwait
Oman	Niger		rand)		Malawi
Panama	Senegal		Swaziland		Malta
St. Kitts &	Togo		(South African		Mauritania
Nevis			rand)		Mauritius
St. Lucia					Morocco
St. Vincent &					Nepal
The Grenadines					Papua New
Suriname					Guinea
Syrian Arab Rep.					Solomon
Yemen,					Islands
Republic of					Tanzania
					Thailand
					Tonga
					Vanuatu
					Western
					Samoa
					Zimbabwe

4. **Joint float.** The 12 members of the European Union[6] maintain their currencies within a flexible range against other members of their group. This structure, referred to as the European Monetary System (EMS), pegs each member's currency to all the other members' currencies, with a joint float against non-EMS currencies. The EMS is discussed in detail later.

5. **Adjusted according to indicators.** Three countries (Chile, Colombia, and Madagascar) adjust their currencies more or less automatically against changes in a

---

[6]The European Community was officially renamed on January 1, 1994, as the European Union.

Exhibit 2.4 *continued*

Single currency	*Cooperative arrangements*	*Adjusted to a set of indicators*	*Other managed floating*	*Independently floating*	
Bahrain	Belgium	Chile	Cambodia	Afghanistan	Latvia
Qatar	Denmark	Colombia	China,	Albania	Lebanon
Saudi Arabia	France	Madagascar	P.R.	Australia	Lithuania
United Arab	Germany		Croatia	Bolivia	Mongolia
Emirates	Ireland		Ecuador	Brazil	Mozambique
	Luxembourg		Egypt	Bulgaria	New Zealand
	Netherlands		Greece	Canada	Nigeria
	Portugal		Guinea	Costa Rica	Norway
	Spain		Guinea-	Dominican	Paraguay
			Bissau	Republic	Peru
			Indonesia	El Salvador	Phillipines
			Israel	Ethiopia	Romania
			Korea	Finland	Russia
			Lao P.D.	Gambia, The	Sierra Leone
			Rep	Ghana	South Africa
			Malaysia	Guatemala	Sudan
			Maldives	Guyana	Sweden
			Mexico	Haiti	Switzerland
			Nicaragua	Honduras	Trinidad &
			Pakistan	India	Tobago
			Poland	Iran, I.R. of	Uganda
			Sao Tome/	Italy	Ukraine
			Principe	Jamaica	United
			Singapore	Japan	Kingdom
			Slovenia	Kyrgyz. Rep.	United States
			Somalia		Zaire
			Sri Lanka		Zambia
			Tunisia		
			Turkey		
			Uruguay		
			Venezuela		
			Vietnam		

Source: "International Monetary Fund Currency Arrangements," *International Financial Statistics,* International Monetary Fund, September 1993, p.6. Reprinted with permission.

particular indicator. One indicator is the real effective exchange rate, which reflects inflation-adjusted changes in a country's currency vis-à-vis the currencies of its major trading partners.

6. **Managed float.** Some 23 countries maintain what is officially called a "managed float." Each central bank sets the nation's exchange rate against a predetermined

goal, but allows the rate to vary. Central bank support of the rate is *not* automatic. Support is based on each bank's view of an appropriate rate in the context of the country's balance of payments position, foreign exchange reserves, and rates quoted outside of the official market. Intervention is sometimes taken to smooth out daily fluctuations and create an orderly pattern of exchange rate changes. Another intervention goal is to "lean against the wind" by delaying, but not resisting, a fundamental exchange rate change. However, some intervention is in fact an unofficial peg, which is sometimes called a "dirty float."

7. **Independently floating.** In the largest single category listed in Exhibit 2.4 are 44 countries that allow full flexibility through an independent float. These countries' currencies include the most important currencies of the world other than those in the European Monetary System. Their central banks allow exchange rates to be determined by market forces alone, although some central banks may intervene in the market from time to time, usually in an attempt to counter speculative pressures on their currency. However they intervene only as one of many anonymous participants in the free market; they do not "peg" the currency by heavy or continued intervention. The increasing number of countries that allow their currencies to float freely is also indicated by Exhibit 2.5, which summarizes the number of countries in each of the previously described categories.

Exhibit 2.5   Evolving Global Exchange Rate Arrangements (1987–1993)

Classification Status	1987	1988	1989	1990	1991	1992	1993
Currency pegged to:							
U.S. dollar	38	36	32	25	24	24	20
French franc	14	14	14	14	14	14	14
Russian ruble	0	0	0	0	0	6	7
Other currency	5	5	5	5	4	6	6
SDR	8	8	7	6	6	5	4
Other composite	27	31	35	35	33	29	27
Flexibility limited vis-à-vis a single currency	4	4	4	4	4	4	4
Cooperative arrangements	8	8	9	10	10	9	9
Adjusted according to a set of indicators	5	5	5	3	5	3	3
Managed floating	23	22	21	23	27	23	28
Independently floating	<u>18</u>	<u>17</u>	<u>20</u>	<u>25</u>	<u>29</u>	<u>44</u>	<u>49</u>
Total	151	151	152	154	156	167	171

Source: *International Financial Statistics*, International Monetary Fund, Washington D.C., September 1993, p. 6.

[1]For members with dual or multiple exchange markets, the arrangement shown is that in the major market.

[2]Excludes the following seven countries which as of end-June 1993 have not yet formally notified the IMF of their exchange rate arrangements: Czech Republic, Federated States of Micronesia, former Yugoslav Rupublic of Macedonia, San Marino, Slovak Republic, Tajikistan, and Uzbekistan.

[3]All classifications are for end of year except 1993, which is the end of the second quarter.

Attributes of the "Ideal" Currency Arrangement

The global economy is today much more complex than the one in which the gold standard was used prior to World War I. International investment, the cross-border movement of capital, now must be considered in addition to simple merchandise trade flows that dominated international commerce at the turn of the century. If there were such a thing as the "ideal" currency arrangement today, it would possess three attributes:

- *Fixed Exchange Rate.* The value of the currency would be fixed in relationship to other major currencies so traders and investors could be relatively certain of the foreign exchange value of each currency for some extended period into the future.

- *Freedom of Capital Flows.* Complete freedom of monetary flows would be allowed, so traders and investors could move funds from one country or currency to another in response to perceived economic opportunities or risks.

- *Independent Monetary Policy.* Domestic monetary policy would be set by each individual country (normally its central bank) so as to pursue desired national economic policies. These domestic economic goals include limiting inflation, combating recessions, and fostering full employment.

Unfortunately, all three of these attributes cannot be achieved at the same time. For example, countries whose currencies are pegged to each other, as in the European Monetary System, are in effect agreeing to both a common inflation rate and a common interest rate policy. If inflation rates are different but the peg (i.e., fixed exchange rate) is maintained, a low-inflation country's goods will become cheaper in the other countries. This will lead to unemployment in the high-inflation countries. If one country's interest rates are higher than the others and the peg is maintained, investors will move funds (capital flows) from the low-rate country to the high-rate country, creating ever more difficulty in maintaining the peg. The European Monetary System crises of 1992 and 1993 were prime examples of this process.

The European Monetary System (EMS)

The 12 members of the European Union are also members of the European Monetary System (EMS). This group has tried to form an island of fixed exchange rates among themselves in a sea of major floating currencies. Members of the EMS rely heavily on trade with each other, so the day-to-day benefits of fixed exchange rates between them are perceived to be great. The EMS has undergone a number of major changes since its inception in 1979, however, including major crises and reorganizations in 1992 and 1993.

European Currency Unit (ECU)

The *European Currency Unit,* or *ECU,* is a basket or index currency based on a weighted average of the currencies of the 12 members of the European Union. Each member currency is defined in terms of units per ECU. The weights are based on each member's share of intra-European Union trade and the relative size of its GNP. The ECU's value varies over time as the members' currencies float jointly with respect to the

U.S. dollar and other nonmember currencies. Exhibit 2.6 demonstrates how the value of the ECU is determined in terms of the U.S. dollar.[7]

Each of the 12 EMS currencies is assigned a currency component, column (1) in Exhibit 2.6. These currency components are then used as value-scale factors, as they are multiplied by the current spot rate of the EMS currency versus the U.S. dollar (units/US$) listed in column (2). The resulting U.S. dollar value of the component currencies in column (3) are summed to determine the U.S. dollar value of the ECU. Finally, the relative "weights" of the individual currencies in the ECU are determined in

Exhibit 2.6   European Currency Unit Components and Calculation of Relative Weighting

Currency	(1) Currency Component in ECU	(2) Current Spot Rate (units/US$)[1]	(3) US$ Value of Component (US$)	(4) Currency Equivalent (units/ECU)	(5) Currency Weight in ECU (percent)
German mark	0.6242	1.6590	0.376251	1.9141	32.61
Dutch guilder	0.2198	1.8645	0.117887	2.1512	10.22
Belgian franc	3.431	35.65	0.096241	41.1310	8.34
Irish punt[2]	0.008552	1.4060	0.012024	0.8206	1.04
Italian lira	151.8	1594.00	0.095232	1839.07	8.25
Danish krone	0.1976	6.8325	0.028921	7.8830	2.51
French franc	1.332	5.8200	0.228866	6.7148	19.84
British pound	0.08784	1.5070	0.132375	0.7656	11.47
Greek drachma	1.440	233.20	0.006175	269.054	0.54
Spanish peseta	6.885	133.55	0.051554	154.083	4.47
Portuguese escudo	1.393	169.45	0.008221	195.502	0.71
ECU			1.153746		100.00

Source: "The ECU and Its Role in the Process Towards Monetary Union," *European Economy,* Commission of the European Communities, Directorate General for Economic and Financial Affairs, September 1991, no. 48, pp. 121–148. Belgian franc weighting includes that of Luxembourg franc. Exchange rates are closing bid rates for September 1, 1993, and are taken from the *Financial Times* of London, page 28. Financial Times copyright.

[1]British pound and Irish punt spot rates stated as US$/unit.

[2]The Irish currency unit is the "punt" or "pound"; both names are accepted by official authorities. We use *punt* throughout this book for clarity of separation from the British pound.

Column (1): stated currency component as fixed by the EMS
Column (2): daily spot rate as reported to the European Commission
Column (3): column (1) ÷ column (2)
Column (4): column (2) × US$ value of ECU
Column (5): column (3) as a percentage of U.S. dollar value of ECU

---

[7]The official value of the ECU as stated by the European Commission changes daily. Each individual currency is quoted by its home country central bank at 2:15 P.M. daily (Brussels time) versus the U.S. dollar. These quotes are collected by the National Bank of Belgium, which in turn passes the quotes to the European Commission. These rates are then used by the Commission to calculate the official ECU rate of the day, first in US$/ECU, then in each of the currencies of the member states. For additional details of the history of the ECU, see "The ECU and Its Role in the Process Towards Monetary Union," *European Economy,* September 1991, no. 48, pp. 121–145.

column (5) by determining the percentage of the total ECU value in U.S. dollars which the individual currency's component constitutes.[8]

The Exchange Rate Mechanism (ERM)

The *Exchange Rate Mechanism (ERM)* is the process by which the member countries maintain the managed exchange rates. The ERM presently consists of nine countries that actively manage their currencies in order to maintain the EMS parities.[9] The ERM has three features: (1) the stipulation there is a bilateral responsibility for the maintenance of exchange rates; (2) the availability of additional support mechanisms that provide the means and resources for maintaining the parities; (3) a last resort or safety valve of agreed upon realignments when currencies irretrievably diverge from parity.

Bilateral Exchange Rates. The central rates of the EMS are the specified bilateral exchange rates among all member currencies; this actually constitutes a grid of bilateral exchange rates among all members. Each currency is then allowed to range ±15% around these central rates. If the currencies approach these bilateral bounds, "indicators of divergence" are encountered that mandate bilateral actions for the maintenance of the central rates.

The core of the European Monetary System is the pegging of each member's currency to the currency of every other member. This is accomplished by having a central rate for each currency defined in terms of the European Currency Unit (ECU), which becomes the common denominator. For example, the central rate for the German mark on August 1, 1993, was DM 1.94964/ECU, and the central rate for the Spanish peseta was Pta 154.250/ECU. These two central rates are then used to calculate the parity rate—the pegged exchange rate—between the German mark and the Spanish peseta:

$$\frac{Pta154.250/ECU}{DM1.94964/ECU} = Pta79.1172/DM.$$

This is the shaded value shown in Exhibit 2.7 as the parity rate between the mark and the peseta.

Under the Exchange Rate Mechanism agreement of the EMS, the central banks of both countries must intervene to keep actual exchange rates within an appropriate range of this central rate. The EMS grid of August 1993 is illustrated in Exhibit 2.7. Originally,

---

[8]Although the values in column (5) of Exhibit 2.6 are commonly referred to as the "weights" of the individual currencies in the ECU, it should be noted that these values change on a daily basis as the spot rates of the individual currencies change. The true fixed component of the ECU index is actually the initial currency component values listed in column (1). These are the only values in the calculation that do not change from day to day.

[9]Prior to the September 1992 crisis in the EMS, membership in the ERM had reached a peak of 10 active members, with only Greece and Portugal not participants at that time. The large interest differentials between member state currencies in the summer and early fall of 1992 resulted in speculative attacks and capital outflows from a number of members, the result of which was the withdrawal of the British pound and the Italian lira from the ERM in September 1992. As of January 1994, the British pound, Italian lira, and Greek drachma were not committed to ERM parities.

Exhibit 2.7   The European Monetary System Central Exchange Rates and Parity Grid
(August 1, 1993)

Country/ currency[1]	German mark (DM/fc)	Dutch guilder (fl/fc)	Belgian franc (BF/fc)	Irish punt (IR£/fc)	Danish krone (DKr/fc)	French franc (FF/fc)	Spanish peseta (Pta/fc)	Portuguese escudo (Esc/fc)
German mark		1.1267	20.6255	0.4148	3.8144	3.3539	79.1172	98.9177
Dutch guilder	0.8875		18.3056	0.3681	3.3854	2.9766	70.2183	87.7918
Belgian franc[2]	0.0485	0.0546		0.0201	0.1849	0.1626	3.8359	4.7959
Irish punt	2.4110	2.7166	49.7290		9.1968	8.0863	190.76	238.50
Danish krone	0.2622	0.2954	5.4072	0.1087		0.8793	20.7415	25.9324
French franc	0.2982	0.3360	6.1498	0.1237	1.1373		23.5898	29.4937
Spanish peseta	0.0126	0.0142	0.2607	0.0052	0.0482	0.0424		1.2503
Portuguese escudo	0.0101	0.0114	0.2085	0.0042	0.0386	0.0339	0.7998	
Central Rate (units/ECU)[3]	1.94964	2.19672	40.2123	0.808628	7.43679	6.53883	154.250	192.854

Source: Derived from Central Rates as published daily in the *Financial Times* of London.

[1]As of August 1, 1993, the date of the realignment of both EMS central rates and wider ranges of divergence, the United Kingdom, Italy, and Greece were not participating members of the Exchange Rate Mechanism and are thus not part of the parity grid. They are, however, official members of the European Monetary System and may reenter the ERM at any time they desire.

[2]Belgian franc and the Luxembourg franc are listed as one.

[3]Grid parity rates are found by dividing one central rate by another. For example, the grid rate for the German mark versus Dutch guilder cross (DM/fl) is found by dividing the DM central rate, 1.94964, by the fl central rate, 2.19672, resulting in DM0.8875/fl.

this range was ±2.25%; on August 1, 1993, however, the range for all EMS countries, except the Netherlands, was increased to ±15.00%.[10]

Support Mechanisms. Members intervene in the foreign exchange markets through a system of mutual credit facilities. Each member can borrow almost unlimited amounts of foreign currency from other members for periods that can be extended up to three months. A second line of defense includes loans that can be extended to nine months, but the total amount available is limited to a pool of credit, originally about 14 billion ECUs, and the size of the member's quota in the pool. Additional funds are available for maturities of from two to five years from a second pool, originally about 11 billion ECUs, but to use these funds, the borrowing member must correct domestic economic policies that are causing its currency to deviate.

[10]The actual points at which member state central banks must intervene in the foreign exchange markets is determined by a rather complex formula combining the allowable range (±15%), a threshold of divergence indicator (75% of the allowable range), and the weight of the individual currency in the ECU on that date (as shown in column (5) of Exhibit 2.6). The weights of the individual currencies in the ECU actually change (slightly) daily, thereby creating a moving target for intervention. The actual percentage range over which an individual currency could move is therefore significantly less than the stated current 15%. For example, using exchange rates and ECU weights for September 1, 1993, the range over which the German mark could move assuming a 33.61% weight is actually ± 7.5814%: .75 × 15.0% × (1 − .3261) = ± 7.5814%.

Realignment. The original ERM terms provided for realignment of parities, but only after mutual agreement among the member countries. However, events in the currency markets during 1992 and 1993 swept away this orderly procedure for re-alignment.

During the summer of 1993, currency speculators tested the resolve of the ERM by attacking the Nordic currencies (Finland, Sweden, and Norway). These were voluntarily attached to the ERM as part of the strategies the Nordic countries employed while applying for membership in the European Union. The speculators won at great profit to themselves but heavy cost to the defending central banks.

Flush with success, the speculators turned on the French franc, the British pound, and Italian lira in rapid succession. Once again, the speculators were so successful that on August 1, 1993, the range of float within the ERM had to be expanded to ±15.00%, except for the Netherlands.

Monetary officials worldwide have learned a painful lesson from this turmoil in the EMS. As discussed in the introductory Global View in this chapter, no amount of official intervention in currency markets or manipulation of interest rates can overcome a determined attack by speculative forces if the economic fundamentals are inappropriate for fixed exchange rates. Chapter 5 explains what is meant by the term *appropriate*.

The Future of the EMS and Maastricht

In December 1991, the 12 members of the European Union met at Maastricht, the Netherlands, and concluded a treaty.

Timetable. The Maastricht Treaty specified a timetable and a plan to replace all the individual currencies with a single currency, called for the moment a European Currency Unit (ECU). Other steps were adopted that would lead to a full European Monetary Union (EMU) by the end of 1996, or at the latest, the end of 1998.

Convergence Criteria. In order to prepare for the EMU, the Maastricht Treaty calls for the integration and coordination of the member countries' monetary and fiscal policies. Few financial market differences should exist by the time the EMU starts. The EMU would be implemented by a process called *convergence*. Before becoming a full member of the EMU, each member should meet the following convergence criteria:

1. Nominal inflation should be no more than 1.5% above the average for the three members of the European Union with the lowest inflation rates during the previous year.

2. Long-term interest rates should be no more than 2% above the average for the three members with the lowest interest rates.

3. The fiscal deficit should be no more than 3% of gross domestic product.

4. Government debt should be no more than 60% of gross domestic product.

The convergence criteria are so tough that few, if any, of the members currently can satisfy them.

Strong Central Bank. A strong central bank, called the European Central Bank (ECB), would be established. It has since been decided that Frankfurt, Germany, would be the host city. It would be modeled after the U.S. Federal Reserve System. An independent central bank would dominate the 12 continuing country central banks. The individual country central banks would regulate banks resident within their borders, but all financial market intervention and the issuance of ECUs would be the sole responsibility of the ECB. The single most important mandate of the ECB should be to promote price stability within the European Union.

The first major hurdle for the EMU was simply the acceptance of the treaty. Denmark had been successful in gaining the right to conduct a popular vote of its citizens to determine whether the degree of integration described by Maastricht was indeed desirable. In June 1992, the Danes voted "nej" (no). The Irish and French immediately scheduled popular votes in their own countries in view of the possibility that the treaty was not desired. The Irish vote in July 1992 resulted in a relatively strong show of support; the French vote in September 1992 was an extremely narrow yes vote. The French result was immediately dubbed "le petit oui."

Although the Maastricht Treaty has now been successfully approved by all of the member states of the European Union, the recent crises in the EMS indicate the Union may be moving further away—rather than closer—to an integrated financial market. The widening of the divergence bands on August 1, 1993, is a clear indication of the problems that continue to plague the goal of a single currency for the European Union.

Eurocurrencies

Eurocurrencies are sometimes viewed as another kind of money, although in reality they are domestic currencies of one country on deposit in a second country. Their value is identical to that of the same currency "at home." For example, a Eurodollar is a U.S. dollar-denominated interest-bearing deposit in a bank outside the United States. The bank may be a foreign bank, the overseas branch of a U.S. bank, or a special "offshore" entity called an International Banking Facility (IBF), which is described in Chapter 15.

Eurocurrency Characteristics

Eurodollar time deposit maturities range from call money and overnight funds to longer periods. Certificates of deposit are usually for three months or more and in million-dollar increments. Note that a Eurodollar deposit is not a demand deposit; it is not created on the bank's books by writing loans against required fractional reserves, and it cannot be transferred by a check drawn on the bank having the deposit. Eurodollar deposits are transferred by wire against an underlying balance held in a bank located within the United States. A domestic analogy would be the transfer of deposits held in savings and loan associations, which is done by having the association write a check on a commercial bank. The appendix to this chapter illustrates how a Eurodollar is created, loaned to a customer via the interbank market, and eventually repaid.

Any convertible currency can exist in "Euro-" form. Thus the Eurocurrency market includes Euromarks (Deutschemarks deposited in banks outside Germany), Eurosterling (British pounds deposited outside the United Kingdom), and Euroyen (Japanese yen deposited outside Japan), as well as Eurodollars.

Eurocurrency markets serve two valuable purposes: (1) Eurocurrency deposits are an efficient and convenient money market device for holding excess corporate liquidity; (2) the Eurocurrency market is a major source of short-term bank loans to finance corporate working capital needs, including the financing of imports and exports.

Banks in which Eurocurrencies are deposited are sometimes called "Eurobanks." A Eurobank is "a financial intermediary that simultaneously bids for time deposits and makes loans in a currency other than that of the country in which it is located."[11] Eurobanks are major world banks that conduct a Eurocurrency business in addition to all other banking functions. Thus the Eurocurrency operation that qualifies a bank for the name "Eurobank" is in fact a department of a large commercial bank, and the name springs from performance of this function.

History of the Eurodollar Market

The modern Eurodollar market was born shortly after World War II, when eastern European holders of dollars, including the various state trading banks of the Soviet Union, were afraid to deposit their dollar holdings in the United States because these deposits might be attached by U.S. residents with claims against communist governments. Therefore eastern European holders deposited their dollars in western Europe, particularly with two Soviet banks: the Moscow Narodny Bank in London and the Banque Commerciale pour l'Europe du Nord in Paris. These two banks redeposited the funds in other banks, especially in London. Additional dollar deposits were received from various central banks in western Europe, which elected to hold part of their dollar reserves in this form to obtain a higher yield. Commercial banks also placed their dollar balances in the market for the same reason as well as because specific maturities could be negotiated in the Eurodollar market. Additional dollars came to the market from European insurance companies with a large volume of U.S. business. They found it financially advantageous to keep their dollar reserves in the higher yielding Eurodollar market. International refugee funds were another source of deposits.

Although the basic causes of the growth of the Eurodollar market are economic efficiencies, a number of unique institutional events during the 1950s and 1960s helped its growth. In 1957, British monetary authorities responded to a weakening of the pound by imposing tight controls on U.K. bank lending in pounds to nonresidents of the United Kingdom. Encouraged by the Bank of England, U.K. banks turned to dollar lending as the only alternative that would allow them to maintain their leading position in world finance. Although New York was "home base" for the dollar and had a large domestic money and capital market, international trading in the dollar centered in London because of that city's expertise in international monetary matters and its proximity in time and distance to major customers.

Additional support for a European-based dollar market came from the balance of payments difficulties of the United States during the 1960s, which temporarily segmented the U.S. domestic capital market from that of the rest of the world. Ultimately,

---

[11]Gunter Dufey and Ian H. Giddy, *The International Money Market,* Englewood Cliffs, N.J.: Prentice Hall, 1978, p. 10.

however, the Eurocurrency market continues to thrive because it is a large international money market relatively free from governmental regulation and interference.

Summary

- The international monetary system has evolved from the gold standard at the beginning of the century to the floating rate system that is used today.

- The Jamaica Agreement of January 1976 provided the rules for today's floating rate system. This agreement "legalized" the float of the U.S. dollar, which had actually begun in March 1973.

- The global experience under a system of floating exchange rates (for the major industrial countries) has been largely an unstable one. The series of events we have recounted for the 1973 to 1993 period constitute a series of shocks to a system that somehow survived such battering.

- The European Monetary System was formed in March 1979. The EMS has combined the elements of rules and cooperation in a new version of currency exchange that to date has been relatively successful.

- The world monetary system has shown a movement toward regional currency blocs, forming what is commonly referred to as a "triad" (United States, Japan, Germany) dominance of currencies.

- Eurocurrencies are domestic currencies of one country on deposit in a second country. Their value is identical to that of the same currency "at home."

Decision Case
The Finnish Markka[12]

The Finnish markka—like its home country—was the subject of massive economic changes in the early 1990s. With the disintegration of the Soviet Union and the Eastern Bloc economies, it was increasingly apparent to Finland that future economic survival lay in a closer relationship with western Europe. One of the major linkages between any country and its business partners is its currency. The Finnish markka was therefore the subject of a government-instituted policy of linking its value to the currencies of western Europe in 1991. The rough road traveled by the markka during this period, being first fixed to the ECU, then devalued versus the ECU, and finally floated against the ECU, is a study in the dynamics of the workings of the international financial markets. Exhibit

---

[12]Michael H. Moffett, University of Michigan, March 1993/January 1994. Reprinted with permission. The author would like to thank Veikko Jaaskelainen of the Helsinki School of Economics and Business Administration and Ian Giddy of New York University for helpful comments.

Exhibit 2.8   The Finnish Markka: The FIM/ECU and FIM/US$ Exchange Rate

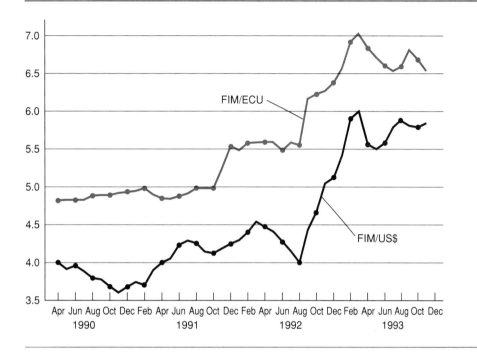

2.8 provides a brief illustration of the markka's decline against the European Currency Unit (ECU) and the U.S. dollar.

Pegging the Markka to the ECU

On June 7, 1991, the Finnish Parliament approved the unilateral linkage of the markka to the European Currency Unit (ECU). Prior to this time the markka was managed against an index of major world currencies. The currencies included in the previous index constituted a cross section of major Finnish trading partners, including the U.S. dollar and the Japanese yen. With the breakup of the East Bloc and the newfound growth of the countries of the European Community (EC), Finland believed its economic future lay with increasing integration with the EC. Although not formalized at this time, if Finland were to consider eventual membership in the EC, and be considered for membership by the EC, it would need to stabilize its currency with respect to the ECU. The new exchange range and exact fluctuation range of ± 3% was set against a midpoint defined in FIM/ECU.

The pegging or fixing of the markka to the ECU was not without its controversy, however. As referred to in Exhibit 2.9, the controversy was focused more on the "no devaluation policy" than on the shifting focus of exchange rate policy to the ECU. Many in and out of government argued that the Finnish export sector needed a boost, and a devaluation of the markka would provide that stimulus by making Finnish products

Exhibit 2.9   Finnish Markka Linked to ECU

Finland's new centre-right Government and the Bank of Finland decided in June to link the markka to the European Currency Unit (ECU) without devaluation. The decision was taken unilaterally by Finland. Sweden and Norway had earlier taken similar action. Immediately after the Government and the Bank of Finland had announced their intention to align themselves more and more closely with European monetary policy, domestic interest rates began falling. At the same time, the Government banished the possibility of devaluation from the country's economic policy—at least momentarily.

For Finland, the change in the currency system means that the markka's exchange rate will be more stable in relation to Western European currencies. The exclusion of the American dollar and the Japanese yen from the Finnish currency basket increases the exchange-rate risks with which Finnish companies must contend, because the markka will no longer follow the development of those currencies' exchange rates.

The strongest criticism of the ECU decision, especially the no-devaluation part of it, came from Finnish export industries and MTK, the organisation representing farmers and forest owners. The Chairman of Confederation of Finnish Industries, Casimir Ehrnrooth, later resigned in protest at the decision. Finland's decision was welcomed in international circles. Both the Commission of the European Communities and individual EC countries expressed their satisfaction. One immediate effect of the ECU linkage was to reverse the outward flow of currency that had been a problem for Finland in recent months.

Source: *Blue Wings,* Finnair Inflight Magazine, August/September 1991, p. 30. Reprinted with permission.

relatively cheaper for Western buyers. The Finnish export sector had yet to recover from the devastating loss of exports to the East Bloc. The trade deficit and balance of payments of Finland continued to worsen.

The Finnish government's stand, however, was that the reason for fixing the markka's value to the ECU was to demonstrate *stability,* and devaluing the markka at the same time would not be consistent with that goal. The government declared itself committed to the fixed value of the FIM/ECU, and stood ready to defend its currency with whatever measures might be required. Markets—particularly international currency markets—however, often have their own ideas.

The November Speculative Attack

The events of November 1991 serve as a classic example of the pressures that may accumulate versus a managed currency's value. Throughout October and early November there were increasing concerns that Finland's continuing balance of payments deficit signaled the need for devaluation of the markka (see Exhibit 2.10).

As more and more currency speculators came to the conclusion the markka would have to be devalued, they contributed to the devaluation pressures by speculating on its fall. By borrowing as much short-term markka as possible, the currency

Exhibit 2.10   Finmark Under Attack

Stockholm—Finland's central bank caved in to a massive wave of currency speculation and allowed the markka to float in global foreign-exchange markets, presaging an imminent devaluation of as much as 20%, analysts said. The decision to uncouple the markka from its fixed intervention range against the European currency unit came after the close of trading Thursday in Helsinki.

In volatile international trading, the markka immediately plunged nearly 10%. London traders said the markka stabilized at about 5.5270% ECU, compared with about 5.0100% ECU at the close of trading in Helsinki. The weakest markka value allowed under the central bank's previous exchange-rate policy was 5.0220% ECU.

Source: Stephen D. Moore, "Finland Let's Markka Float: Devaluation Due," 11/15–16/91. Reprinted by permission of *The Wall Street Journal Europe*, © 1991 Dow Jones & Co., Inc. All rights reserved worldwide.

Exhibit 2.11   Devaluation of Markka

On November 14, 1991, the Bank of Finland decided to temporarily float the markka because of mounting pressure against the currency in the foreign exchange market. On the following day, November 15, the Government decided on the basis of a proposal by the Parliamentary Supervisory Board of the Bank of Finland to raise the limits of the markka's fluctuation range against the ECU by 14 percent, implying a 12.3 percent fall in the external value of the markka. The new midpoint is 5.55841 (FIM/ECU), and the markka may now fluctuate against the ECU in a range of 5.39166 to 5.72516.

Source: *The Bank of Finland Bulletin*, December 1991, vol. 65, no. 12, p. 11.

speculator could convert them into some other major currency. Once the expected devaluation occurred, the speculator could then use the foreign currency balances to convert back to markka, repay the short-term markka debt, and profit as a result of the devaluation.

The markka was finally officially devalued November 14, 1991. The official announcement by the Bank of Finland is shown in Exhibit 2.11. The Bank of Finland believed the 12.3% devaluation was large enough to take the markka to a value that could be maintained within the new range set.

The Crisis of September 1992: The Markka Floats

Although surviving a major speculative attack on its value in April 1992, the situation once again reached a crisis in September 1992. The markka was not simply devalued against the ECU this time, it was set free to float (see Exhibit 2.12). And float—or

Exhibit 2.12   Finland Lets Markka Float

Stockholm—The Bank of Finland allowed the markka to float freely against all currencies, abandoning its attempts to maintain a fixed exchange rate policy and paving the way for the second devaluation of the markka in less than 10 months. Sveriges Riksbank, the central bank in neighboring Sweden, responded to the spillover from the Finnish crisis by raising its marginal interest rate to 24% from 16%, the biggest single interest rate increase in the Riksbank's 324-year history.

   In Brussels, a spokesman for the European Community Commission said it regretted Finland's decision to abandon the link with the EC's semi-fixed currency grid and allow the markka to float. He noted that any candidate country to join the EC's planned economic and monetary union must respect the membership rules for the European Monetary Union agreed to in the Maastricht Treaty.

Source: Robert Flint, "Finland Let's Markka Float, Leading to Record Increase in Swedish Interest Rate," 9/9/92. Reprinted by permission of *The Wall Street Journal,* © 1992 Dow Jones & Co., Inc. All rights reserved worldwide.

sink—it did. By March 1993 the markka had depreciated from about FIM6.2/ECU in September to over FIM7.1/ECU.[13]

   If it is any consolation to the Finns, the currency crisis to which the markka fell victim in early September swept across the European Community in the second and third weeks of September. When it was all over, the British pound sterling and the Italian lira had both withdrawn from active participation in the European Monetary System and allowed their currencies to float. Continuing attacks on the Spanish peseta, Portuguese escudo, and Irish punt forced their devaluation within the EMS. By November, the Swedish krona and Norwegian krone had both been devalued versus the ECU as well.

   Although misery may love company, the falling values of other "satellite currencies" to the central currencies of Europe, the ECU and the German mark, was little comfort. As described in Exhibit 2.13, the Finnish government relied heavily on the international financial markets for the sale of much of its government debt, and that market was now in question. If the government of Finland states its intention to borrow a foreign currency such as the U.S. dollar, and at the same time is experiencing rapid currency depreciation, foreign investors question the ability of the borrower to actually repay the debt.

   Access to international financial markets is critical for countries of all sizes, but most importantly for those that are relatively small. Economic growth requires capital, and without access to international sources, government and industry may be forced to

---

[13]Against the U.S. dollar it was even worse. The markka fell from FIM 4.0/USD in August 1992 to more than FIM 6.0/USD in March 1993.

Exhibit 2.13   Finland's Reception in the International Financial Market

The Republic of Finland was in New York last Friday, presenting its economic policies and prospects to the local investment community. Friday's meeting had been planned some time before the European currency crisis had started to build momentum, and it provided a useful lesson for US investors on what recent events will mean for those nations whose currencies were whipped senseless by the hurricane of speculation that swept through Europe last week.

Matti Vanhala, a member of the board of the Bank of Finland, assured his audience that the decision to float the Finnish markka was taken before, not after, the Bank had spent a high proportion of the national foreign currency reserves in supporting the currency. Central bank governor Sirkka Hamalainen was due to present a speech to the investors, but was unable to attend. In her prepared notes, she said that the markka would be "fixed against EC currencies again, but only when it is realistic to do so. Our ambitions concerning integration in Europe, including membership in the EC, have not changed." However, her speech added that it was "impossible to say how long it will take before a credible basis exists for fixing the exchange rate."

One of the big tasks facing the Republic, along with other European nations caught in the currency crossfire, is the rebuilding of foreign exchange reserves, which the central bank governor admitted to having been "insufficient" when the currency storm first started to brew up. Partly as a result of this, estimated borrowings by the central government for the current year are estimated to rise to 30% of GDP, or around FIM150bn, and nearly 40% of GDP next year. 41% of Finnish government debt has been raised in the domestic markets, the rest in foreign ones.

Most European market professionals' view that there was no point in talking about what the currency crisis might have cost Finland, or any other issuer in terms of yield [price of debt]. Investors at the moment aren't buying at any price. "It is like the old Russian joke. The taxis in Moscow were very cheap, but you just couldn't get any."

Source: "Finland: Biding Time," *International Financing Review* (IFR), Issue 947, 9/9/1992, p. 7. Reprinted with permission.

settle for slower growth and lower prospects. Only time will tell the degree to which the markka will eventually be "markked down."

Case Questions

1. What did Finland really believe it would gain by pegging the value of the Finnish markka to the ECU?

2. What conditions motivate international investors and speculators to aid the exchange rate goals of central banks? To hinder the goals?

3. How is this repeated cycle of devaluation and depreciation likely to alter Finland's access to the international capital markets?

Questions

1. Fixed Versus Flexible Exchange Rates

Why is it that some of the largest industrial powers such as Japan, the United States, and Germany allow their individual currencies to float in value against the others while other countries like Finland continue to attempt to maintain fixed exchange rates?

2. The Gold Standard

What were the rules of the game under the gold standard? Why, if the gold standard was so successful in maintaining fixed exchange rates, did the major industrial countries leave it?

3. The Bretton Woods Agreement

How did the Bretton Woods system differ from the gold standard? Why design the new system around the U.S. dollar rather than gold or silver?

4. The 1967 Devaluation of the Pound

Although most of the attention focused historically on the Bretton Woods system is on the crises of 1971, the devaluation of the British pound in 1967 was considered by many an omen of things to come. Use your library to research the problems arising in and out of Great Britain leading to the 1967 devaluation.

5. Eclectic Currency Arrangements

The variety of currency arrangements listed in Exhibit 2.4 clearly depicts a world that is in little agreement regarding the form of currency arrangements which is "best" for the individual country. What characteritics of countries (e.g., size, openness, historical affiliations, etc.) do you think have a hand in determining a specific country's choice?

6. Global Currency Arrangement Trends

What forces do you believe are driving the world currency arrangements as described in Exhibit 2.4 and 2.5? Will these continue throughout the remainder of the twentieth century?

7. European Monetary System and ECU (CO2A.WK1)

The calculation methodology of the European Currency Unit (ECU) was described in Exhibit 2.6. Using currency quotations from a recent newspaper or other periodical, calculate the value of the ECU. How has its value changed since the date of Exhibit 2.6?

8. The EMS and Maastricht

What must happen in the European Union for Maastricht to successfully construct a "single currency for Europe"?

9. Central Banks and Currency Values

How do the principles of central bank intervention in currency markets described in the chapter-opening Global View relate to the actions taken by the Central Bank of Finland (Suomen Pankki) in 1991 and 1992 described in the end-of-chapter Decision Case?

Bibliography

Agmon, Tamir, Robert G. Hawkins, and Richard M. Levich, eds., *The Future of the International Monetary System,* Lexington, Mass.: Lexington Books, 1984.

Arshanapalli, Bala, and John Doukas, "Integration of Euro-Money Markets," *Journal of Multinational Financial Management,* vol. 2, no. 3/4, 1993, pp. 107–126.

Claassen, Emil-Maria, *International and European Monetary Systems,* New York: Praeger, 1990.

Coffey, Peter, *The European Monetary System— Past, Present and Future,* 2nd ed., Dordrecht, the Netherlands; Lancaster, U.K.: Kluwer Academic Publishers, 1987.

Cooper, Richard N., *The International Monetary System: Essays in World Economics,* Cambridge, Mass.: MIT Press, 1987.

Dornbusch, Rudiger, "Exchange Rate Economics: 1986," *The Economic Journal,* March 1987, pp. 1–18.

Errunza, Vihang, Kedreth Hogan, and Mao-Wei Hung, "The Impact of the EMS on Exchange Rate Predictability," *Journal of Multinational Financial Management,* vol. 2, no. 3/4, 1993, pp. 73–94.

Friedman, Irving, *Reshaping the Global Money System,* Lexington, Mass.: Lexington Books, 1987.

Genberg, Hans, "The European Monetary System," in *The Handbook of International Financial Management,* Robert Z. Aliber, ed., Homewood, Ill.: Dow Jones-Irwin, 1987, pp. 732–758.

Jorion, Philippe, "Properties of the ECU as a Currency Basket," *Journal of Multinational Financial Management,* vol. 1, no. 2, 1991, pp. 1–24.

Koromzay, Val, John Llewellyn, and Stephen Potter, "The Rise and Fall of the Dollar: Some Explanations, Consequences and Lessons," *The Economic Journal,* March 1987, pp. 23–43.

McKibben, Warwick J., and Jeffrey D. Sachs, "Comparing the Global Performance of Alternative Exchange Agreements," *Journal of International Money and Finance,* vol. 7, no. 4, December 1988, pp. 387–410.

Schinasi, Garry J., "European Integration, Exchange Rate Management, and Monetary Reform: A Review of the Major Issues," *International Finance Discussion Papers,* Board of Governors of the Federal Reserve System, no. 364, October 1989.

Shafer, Jeffrey R., and Bonnie E. Loopesko, "Floating Exchange Rates After Ten Years," *Brookings Papers on Economic Activity,* Washington, D.C.: Brookings Institution, 1983.

Taylor, Dean, "Official Intervention in the Foreign Exchange Market, or Bet Against the Central Bank," *Journal of Political Economy,* April 1982, pp. 356–368.

Chapter 2 Appendix
The Creation of Eurodollars

Eurodollar creation can be explained with a simple example. Assume a French Firm (FF) has $10 million in a soon-maturing certificate of deposit (CD) in a New York Bank (NYB) on which it is earning 8%. The $10,000,000 shows on the books of the two entities as follows (000 omitted):

New York Bank (NYB)		French Firm (FF)	
	$CD_{FF@8.00\%}$ 10,000	$CD_{NYB@8.00\%}$ 10,000	

The French Firm wants to continue holding U.S. dollars but would like a higher rate of interest. A London Bank (LB) offers to pay 8.25% on dollar-denominated deposits with a three-month maturity. When the New York Bank CD matures, the French Firm instructs its New York Bank to transfer funds to the London bank, where the sum is placed in a three-month Eurodollar deposit account paying 8.25%. Because the London Bank maintains a correspondent account with the New York Bank, the actual "transfer" is effected by the New York Bank debiting the account of the French Firm and crediting the demand deposit (DD) correspondent account of the London Bank. The books now look like this:

New York Bank (NYB)	
	~~$CD_{FF@8.00\%}$~~ ~~10,000~~
	DD_{LB} 10,000

London Bank (LB)		French Firm (FF)	
DD_{NYB} 10,000	$CD_{FF@8.25\%}$ 10,000	$CD_{LB@8.25\%}$ 10,000	

Transfer of the dollar deposit from the New York Bank to the London Bank creates a Eurodollar deposit: A bank outside of the United States (the London Bank) now has a deposit liability denominated in dollars rather than in British pounds. Behind this dollar liability lies a dollar asset in the form of a demand deposit held by the London Bank with the New York Bank. Hence total deposits in the United States have not diminished, but a New York Bank's liability to a foreign firm has become a liability to a foreign bank. In three months the London Bank must return $10,000,000 (plus interest) to the French Firm, which it will do by giving the French Firm a demand deposit on a New York Bank, or transferring a New York deposit to any party specified by the French Firm.

At this point, the London Bank is temporarily holding a dollar demand deposit in New York, on which it is earning nothing, while simultaneously owing dollars to the French Firm on which it has promised to pay 8.25%. If the London Bank is not to lose on the transaction, it must loan its dollar asset (the New York demand deposit) to an entity at a rate higher than the 8.25% it is paying. Suppose the London Bank loans $10,000,000 to an Italian Bank (IB) at 8.50%. The books would then look like this:

New York Bank (NYB)

	~~CD$_{FF@8.00\%}$~~	~~10,000~~
	~~DD$_{LB}$~~	~~10,000~~
	DD$_{IB}$	10,000

London Bank (LB)				French Firm (FF)	
~~DD$_{NYB}$~~	~~10,000~~			CD$_{LB@8.25\%}$ 10,000	
Loan$_{IB@8.50\%}$	10,000	CD$_{FF@8.25\%}$	10,000		

Italian Bank (IB)

DD$_{NYB}$	10,000	Loan$_{LB@8.50\%}$	10,000

The New York Bank's deposit liability is now shifted to the Italian Bank, and the London Bank owns a dollar asset in the form of a dollar loan to the Italian Bank on which it is earning one-quarter of a percent more than it is paying the French Firm for the funds. The Italian Bank is paying 8.50% for the dollars and (for the moment) is earning nothing.

This chain of lending and relending at slightly higher interest rates can continue for some time. To end the sequence, assume the Italian Bank loans dollars to an Italian Manufacturer (IM) at 8.75%. The dollars in New York are transferred to the account of the Italian Manufacturer, and the books look like this:

New York Bank (NYB)

	~~CD$_{FF@8.00\%}$~~	~~10,000~~
	~~DD$_{LB}$~~	~~10,000~~
	~~DD$_{IB}$~~	~~10,000~~
	DD$_{IM}$	10,000

London Bank (LB)				French Firm (FF)	
~~DD$_{NYB}$~~	~~10,000~~			CD$_{LB@8.25\%}$ 10,000	
Loan$_{IB@8.50\%}$	10,000	CD$_{FF@8.25\%}$	10,000		

Italian Bank (IB)				Italian Manufacturer (IM)	
~~DD$_{NYB}$~~	~~10,000~~	Loan$_{LB@8.50\%}$ 10,000		DD$_{NY}$ 10,000	Loan$_{IB@8.75\%}$ 10,000
Loan$_{IM@8.75\%}$	10,000				

The Italian Manufacturer (IM) borrowed the funds for a business purpose, perhaps to pay for the purchase of new machine tools from the United States. If so, the Italian Manufacturer transfers the money to the machine tool manufacturer and the deposit in New York becomes a bank liability to that domestic firm. The residual value of the Eurodollar deposit is that any U.S. person or firm will accept it as payment for goods or services.

Each bank in the chain between the New York Bank and the Italian Manufacturer has a dollar asset as well as a dollar liability and is earning a profit on the spread between the interest rates. The underlying dollar deposit remains in the New York Bank (or in some other U.S. bank) but ownership of it shifts from one depositor to another and eventually back to an American entity.

To repay the loan in six months, the Italian Manufacturer must either buy or accumulate (perhaps from exports to the United States) dollars and transfer them to the Italian Bank, which will transfer the dollars to the London Bank, which will transfer the dollars back to the French Firm in the form of a deposit in New York.

The sequence of events just described could have evolved in other directions. Any holder of Eurodollar balances could have invested them in the New York money market, in shares of common stock traded in the United States, in the U.S. real estate market, or directly in a U.S. subsidiary. In all these cases, as in the original, a demand deposit in a U.S. bank is behind each Eurodollar transaction. Foreign banks accepting time deposit in Eurodollars do not "create" funds or expand the dollar money supply in the fashion described in textbooks on domestic money and banking. This is because they do not create new demand deposits in return for loans, as do domestic banks, but simply transfer deposits held in New York at a markup in interest rates.

One might ask why the French Firm did not deposit its dollars directly in the Italian Bank to earn a higher rate, or why the Italian Manufacturer did not borrow directly from the London Bank at the lower rate being charged there. Part of the answer lies in the imperfections of international capital markets and part in participants' different perceptions of risk. The French Firm may not have known of the Italian bank nor had any easy way to find out that a bank in Italy was paying a higher rate for Eurodollar deposits. In addition the French Firm may simply have had more confidence in British banks—a confidence born of geographical proximity and a long history of association, or it may have wanted to be a good bank client so the London Bank would provide other services in the future.

The Italian Bank may or may not have aggressively pursued the dollar deposit of the French Firm. The Italian Manufacturer might be unknown in London and so unable to borrow there without first going through a long process of establishing a credit rating. If the Italian Manufacturer were unknown in London, it might have to pay the London Bank a rate higher than the rate paid to the Italian Bank.

Chapter 3
Balances and Imbalances of Payments

Global View
U.S.—Japan: Counting What Counts

Tokyo—Daily headlines notwithstanding, the trade problem between the U.S. and Japan is not the American trade deficit. The flows of economic activity measured by official trade statistics represent a tiny and steadily decreasing share of the economic linkages between the two countries. These data, remember, do not count the revenues from services or from licenses or from intellectual property or from goods manufactured by U.S. firms in third countries but sold in Japan or from goods both manufactured and sold by U.S. firms in Japan. All they count is that relatively small universe of things physically produced in the U.S., crated, loaded into ships or planes, passed through customs, and then uncrated and sold in Japan.

When a U.S. software house sells its leading-edge program in Tokyo, the trade data capture little, if any, of the value added. When a U.S. chip manufacturer sells its products in Osaka, the sales may count toward the 20% of the market earmarked for U.S. firms, but—if the chips were, as likely, fabricated in Malaysia—they do not show up in the trade data. When a U.S. sportswear manufacturer retails in Hokkaido garments sewn in Indonesia or Taiwan, the sales do not matter to those who count bilateral trade flows. When Japanese consumers see a U.S. movie or use their U.S.-originated credit cards, trade watchers essentially ignore their activities.

In the mid-1980s, if you included in the trade figures all the sales in Japan of "American" (as consumers perceive them) goods and services, the numbers would show that the Japanese bought—per capita—four times as much "American" stuff as Americans bought "Japanese" stuff. Since then, the ratio has only grown larger.

Source: Kenichi Ohmae, "U.S.—Japan: Counting What Counts," 3/22/94. Reprinted by permission of *The Wall Street Journal*, © 1994 Dow Jones & Co., Inc. All rights reserved worldwide.

The balance of payments (BOP) is an accounting system that measures all economic transactions between residents of one country and residents of all other countries. Economic transactions include exports and imports of goods and services, capital inflows and outflows, gifts and other transfer payments, and changes in a country's international reserves.

A country's own balance of payments is important to business managers, investors, consumers, and government officials because it influences, and is influenced by, other key macroeconomic variables such as gross national product, employment, price levels, exchange rates, and interest rates. Monetary and fiscal policy must take the balance of payments into account at the national level.

At the corporate level, business policy decisions must include consideration of the firm's balance of payments impact on host and home country alike. A foreign country's balance of payments may be important for international managers and investors for any of the following reasons:

- The balance of payments helps forecast a country's market potential, especially in the short run. A country experiencing a serious balance of payments deficit is not likely to import as much as it would if it were running a surplus.

- The balance of payments is an important indicator of pressure on a country's foreign exchange rate, and thus on the potential for a firm trading with or investing in that country to experience foreign exchange gains or losses.

- Continuing deficits in a country's balance of payments may signal future controls over payment of dividends and interest, license fees, royalty fees, or other cash disbursements to foreign firms or investors.

In this chapter we first describe how the balance of payments is measured, including a number of summary measures or aggregates often used to describe particular components of the overall balance of payments. The second major section details trade and current account imbalances, as well as capital account imbalances, and looks at the policy implications. We conclude with a comparison of the balance of payments of the United States, Germany, and Japan in recent years.

Measuring the Balance of Payments

Balance of payments accounts are a systematized procedure for measuring, summarizing, and stating the effect of all financial and economic transactions between residents of one country and residents of the remainder of the world during a particular time period. If expenditures abroad by residents of one nation exceed what the residents of that nation can earn or otherwise receive from abroad, that nation is generally deemed to have a "deficit" in its balance of payments. However, if a nation receives from abroad more than it spends, that nation incurs a "surplus." Balance of payments accounts show the size of any deficit or surplus by several different measures, and also indicate the manner in which a deficit was financed or the proceeds of a surplus invested.

Debits and Credits

In dealing with the rest of the world, a country earns foreign exchange on some transactions and expends foreign exchange on others. Transactions that earn foreign exchange are recorded in the balance of payments statistics as a "credit" and are marked by a plus (+) sign. As a general matter, credits are obtained by selling to nonresidents either real or financial assets or services. For example, the export of U.S.-made jet aircraft by Boeing and McDonnell Douglas earns foreign exchange and is therefore a credit. The sale to a foreign resident of a service, such as an airline trip on a U.S. carrier, also earns foreign exchange and is a credit. When that foreigner purchases a ticket on a U.S. air carrier, that purchase is the sale of a U.S. service to a nonresident — regardless of whether the trip itself is from a U.S. city to a foreign city, from New York to San Francisco, or from London to Cairo.

Borrowing abroad brings in foreign exchange and is therefore recorded as a credit. This type of transaction may be viewed as though it were the export of U.S. securities (shares of stock, bonds, promissory notes, etc.) to foreigners; thus it generates foreign exchange in a manner analogous to the export of such tangible merchandise as machines. An increase in accounts payable due to foreigners by U.S. residents has the same balance of payments effect as more formal borrowing in the world's capital markets.

Transactions that expend foreign exchange are recorded as "debits" and are marked with a minus (−) sign. The foremost example is the import of goods from foreign countries. When U.S. residents buy automobiles from Japan or wine from France, foreign exchange is expended and the import is recorded as a debit. Similarly, when U.S. residents purchase foreign services, such as insurance taken out with a London carrier, or ship merchandise in a vessel owned by a Greek shipping company, foreign exchange is used. Lending to foreigners also uses foreign exchange and is recorded as a debit; foreign lending may be considered as equivalent to the importing of foreign securities.

Businesspeople usually need access to the balance of payments of foreign countries rather than their home country. A useful source for such data is the annual presentation of the International Monetary Fund (IMF). This source is valuable for comparing various countries because a common format is used for each nation and because all monetary amounts are restated in one currency, the U.S. dollar. IMF data for the United States for the period 1985 to 1992 appears in Exhibit 3.1.

Analytical Arrangement

In any balance of payments presentation, all transactions between residents and nonresidents are conceptually divided into two analytical categories, the sum of which is zero. Thus in one sense the balance of payments is always in balance. You can visualize the statement as having an imaginary horizontal line drawn across the list of accounts such that all transactions "above the line" are financed by all transactions "below the line." This imaginary line may be drawn higher or lower, depending on the analytical need of the person evaluating the accounts.

The IMF format in Exhibit 3.1 facilitates a variety of analytical perspectives, with a user able to regard as "above the line" any cumulative partial balance from Group A

Exhibit 3.1   U.S. Balance of Payments Statistics, Aggregated Presentation: Transactions Data, 1985–1992 (billions of U.S. dollars)

		1985	1986	1987	1988	1989	1990	1991	1992
1. A.	Current Account, excl. Group E	−121.79	−147.54	−163.45	−126.67	−101.19	−90.46	−8.48	−66.30
2.	Merchandise: exports f.o.b.	215.91	223.35	250.21	320.23	361.70	388.71	416.94	440.14
3.	Merchandise: imports f.o.b.	−338.09	−368.41	−409.77	−447.19	−477.38	−497.55	−490.75	−536.28
4.	Trade balance	−122.18	−145.06	−159.56	−126.96	−115.68	−108.84	−73.81	−96.14
	Services: credit	66.38	78.23	88.42	98.72	113.89	132.02	145.66	159.40
	Services: debit	−70.84	−77.70	−87.50	−94.37	−97.70	−112.35	−113.08	−117.08
	Income: credit	97.73	97.04	106.61	131.38	153.88	160.15	145.86	130.95
	Reinvested earnings	*14.34*	*8.44*	*15.85*	*10.90*	*14.77*	*19.48*	*13.18*	*15.29*
	Other investment income	*76.75*	*80.56*	*80.72*	*108.54*	*125.93*	*124.08*	*114.07*	*95.30*
	Other	*6.64*	*8.04*	*10.04*	*11.94*	*13.18*	*16.59*	*18.61*	*20.36*
	Income: debit	−69.90	−75.90	−88.37	−110.56	−129.98	−128.50	−119.61	−110.55
	Reinvested earnings	*.39*	*.75*	*.78*	*−.67*	*8.52*	*16.28*	*19.92*	*12.59*
	Other investment income	*−68.27*	*−74.41*	*−86.41*	*−106.34*	*−134.87*	*−140.54*	*−134.20*	*−116.97*
	Other	*−2.02*	*−2.24*	*−2.74*	*−3.55*	*−3.63*	*−4.24*	*−5.33*	*−6.17*
5.	Total goods, services, and income	−98.81	−123.39	−140.41	−101.79	−75.59	−57.52	−14.98	−33.42
	Private unrequited transfers	−9.56	−10.12	−10.55	−11.87	−12.32	−12.39	−14.05	−14.48
	Total, excl. official unrequited transfers	−108.37	−135.51	−150.96	−113.66	−87.91	−69.91	−29.03	−47.90
	Official unrequited transfers	−13.42	−14.03	−12.49	−13.01	−13.28	−20.55	20.55	−18.40
	Grants (excluding military)	*−11.28*	*−11.87*	*−10.28*	*−10.50*	*−10.77*	*−21.86*	*−18.51*	*−15.96*
	Other	*−2.14*	*−2.16*	*−2.21*	*−2.51*	*−2.51*	*1.31*	*39.06*	*−2.44*
B.	Direct Investment and Other L.T. Capital, excl. Groups E through G	79.02	85.03	61.49	93.77	85.57	2.00	16.00	−17.61
	Direct investment	6.61	18.52	31.04	41.82	38.87	12.45	−5.16	−32.42
	In United States	*20.01*	*35.63*	*58.22*	*57.27*	*67.87*	*45.14*	*23.97*	*2.37*
	Abroad	*−13.40*	*−17.11*	*−27.18*	*−15.45*	*−29.00*	*−32.69*	*−29.13*	*−34.79*
	Portfolio investment	64.41	71.59	31.06	40.30	43.50	−33.00	8.60	14.19
	Other long-term capital Resident official sector	−1.00	−.42	−1.23	1.07	2.42	3.70	5.86	−.28

down through Group F. Most of the partial balances from Group A down have a name and particular analytical use.

Trade Balance. The *trade balance* is the net balance on merchandise trade. Lines 2 and 3 under Group A of Exhibit 3.1 show exports and imports of merchandise such as wheat, machinery, automobiles, bananas, aircraft, and oil. In each year the United States ran a deficit on its trade balance, as shown on line 4. In 1992, the United States exported $440.14 billion of merchandise and imported $536.28 billion for a "trade deficit" (line 4) of $96.14 billion. (The minus sign for a balance indicates a deficit.)

Exhibit 3.1 *continued*

		1985	1986	1987	1988	1989	1990	1991	1992
	Disbursements on loans extended	−5.90	−7.14	−4.85	−5.91	−3.93	−6.65	−10.82	−5.21
	Repayments on loans extended	4.30	5.65	7.19	9.92	6.29	10.36	16.23	5.07
	Other	.60	1.07	−3.57	−2.94	.06	−.01	.45	−.14
	Deposit money banks	9.00	−4.66	.62	10.58	.78	18.85	6.70	.90
	Other sectors	−	−	−	−	−	−	−	−
6.	**Total, Groups A plus B**	**−42.77**	**−62.51**	**−101.96**	**−32.90**	**−15.62**	**−88.46**	**7.52**	**−83.91**
	C. Other Short-Term Capital, excl. Groups E through G	23.76	13.28	49.20	−3.33	30.12	11.19	−14.22	54.19
	Resident official sector	−1.44	−.52	−1.96	−.15	1.80	3.77	−.71	6.24
	Deposit money banks	24.30	26.76	45.88	5.49	10.91	−1.05	−13.08	40.32
	Other sectors	.90	−12.96	5.28	−8.67	17.41	8.47	−.43	7.63
	D. Net Errors and Omissions	24.81	15.45	−4.11	−.04	2.43	47.46	−15.08	−12.34
7.	**Total, Groups A through D**	**5.80**	**−33.78**	**−56.86**	**−36.27**	**16.93**	**−29.81**	**−21.78**	**−42.06**
	E. Exceptional Financing	−	−	−	−	−	−	−	−
	Total, Groups A through E	**5.80**	**−33.78**	**−56.86**	**−36.27**	**16.93**	**−29.81**	**−21.78**	**−42.06**
8. F.	Liabilities Constituting Foreign Authorities' Reserves	−1.96	33.46	47.72	40.19	8.34	32.04	16.02	38.14
9.	**Total, Groups A through F**	**3.84**	**−.32**	**−9.14**	**3.92**	**25.27**	**2.23**	**−5.76**	**−3.92**
10. G.	Reserves	−3.84	.32	9.14	−3.92	−25.27	−2.23	5.76	3.92
	Monetary gold	.01	.01	−	−	.01	−	−	−
	SDRs	−.90	−.25	−.51	.13	−.53	−.20	−.18	2.32
	Reserve position in the Fund	.91	1.50	2.07	1.02	.47	.66	−.37	−2.66
	Foreign exchange assets	−3.86	−.94	7.58	−5.07	−25.22	−2.70	6.31	4.27
	Other claims	−	−	−	−	−	−	−	−
	Use of Fund credit and loans	−	−	−	−	−	−	−	−
	Memorandum items								
	Total change in reserves	−8.21	−5.11	2.58	−1.79	−26.81	−8.68	5.61	6.38
	of which: revaluations	−4.37	−5.43	−6.56	2.13	−1.55	−6.45	−.15	2.46

Source: "The United States Balance of Payments Statistics, Aggregated Presentation," *International Monetary Fund Balance of Payments Statistics,* International Monetary Fund, 1993, Vol. 42, Part 1, p. 742. Reprinted with permission.

Balance on Current Account. Although the merchandise trade balance is an often quoted summary measure, especially by politicians, it is not necessarily the most important. Countries like the United States and Japan have relatively large service sectors, such as airline transportation, tourism, construction, and banking. These services constitute a significant proportion of the overall balance of payments. In 1992, for example, the United States ran a surplus in its balance on service trade, selling services (a credit) to foreigners of $159.40 billion while purchasing services (a debit) of $117.08 billion. The U.S. net surplus on services (not shown on any line) was $42.32 billion ($159.40 billion − $117.08 billion).

The *current account* expands the trade balance concept to include earnings and expenditures on account of services, just mentioned, and for investment income. When the net effect of these items is added to the merchandise trade balance, the resultant balance on "goods, services, and income" measures the net effect of both physical trade and what is sometimes called "invisible" trade in services, plus income payments.

The investment income component of the current account is the flow of earnings from different forms of capital or portfolio investments made in prior periods. For example, the income a U.S. corporation currently earns on a manufacturing facility constructed in Canada in previous years falls into the current account. The initial investment of capital, however, was a "capital outflow" recorded in the capital accounts back in the year when originally made. Just as corporate investment expenditures in any one year lead, hopefully, to investment income in subsequent years, so capital outflows in a nation's BOP accounts lead, hopefully, to current account inflows in subsequent years.

As shown on line 5 under Group A (Total: goods, services, and income), the balance on trade and invisibles deteriorated from 1985 through 1987. This was due to the exceptional strength of the dollar during those years of the Reagan presidency. Since 1987 the annual deficit on trade and invisibles has been dropping. Analysis of the balance down through "goods, services, and income" presumes the outcome is determined "autonomously" by the actions of independent and private parties on the basis of price, availability, and quality. In other words, the balance is not managed or manipulated by government policies.

The remaining items in Group A, private and official unrequited transfers, measure unilateral transfers not matched by a quid-pro-quo transaction. Unrequited transfers include sums sent home by migrant workers, parental payments to students studying abroad, Fulbright grants, private gifts, pension payments to retirees living abroad, and governmental gifts or grants.

The net sum of all merchandise, service, income, and unrequited transfers is the balance on "current account," shown at the top of Group A on line 1. The balance on current account is the measure most frequently used in economic policy analysis because it comes closest to measuring the effect of current international payments on a nation's economy. Newspaper publicity on balance of payments usually focuses on either the balance on trade or the balance on current account. Line 1 of Exhibit 3.1 shows the U.S. deficit on current account reached a peak of $163.45 billion (line 1) in 1987 and has diminished steadily until it increased again in 1992.

Basic Balance. Group B in the IMF presentation provides data on long-term capital flows, including direct foreign investments, portfolio investments, and other long-term capital movements. Long-term capital flows are presumed to be "autonomous" because of fundamental desires to invest for the long run. During the years 1985 through 1990 the United States ran a surplus (credit balance) on direct investment, meaning that on balance foreigners invested more in the United States than did U.S. residents in foreign countries. The balance was reversed in 1992.

The *basic balance* is the net result of activities in Groups A and B together. This balance is useful in evaluating long-term trends in the balance of payments because it does not include volatile, easily reversible, short-term capital flows. The United States had a deficit on its basic balance account throughout the period 1985 to 1992, except 1991, as shown on line 6. In 1992 the deficit was $83.91 billion.

Overall Balance, or Official Settlements Balance. Group C measures short-term capital movements, such as transactions in money market instruments and bank deposits, and changes in outstanding corporate account receivable and account payable balances. In one sense these are "autonomous," in that they are made by private parties. From another perspective, however, they are often induced by the monetary policies of various countries. For this reason short-term capital movements are sometimes regarded as volatile and readily reversible rather than as fundamental and stable in nature.

Group D measures errors and omissions, transactions that are known to have occurred but for which no specific measure was made. The account arises because balance of payments statistics are gathered on a single-entry basis, rather than on a double-entry basis as in corporate accounting, from statistics collected when goods move through customhouses or funds flow through the banking system. Many transactions are not recorded but are known to have occurred because other components of the statistical series reveal an imbalance. For example, one large unrecorded account for the United States is illegal narcotics imports; drug dealers just don't report such transactions! Because most errors and omissions are in current account or capital items, the errors and omissions balance is placed before striking the balance labeled "Total, Groups A through D."

The *overall balance,* also called the *official settlements balance,* is the net result of activities in Groups A through D (line 7). It is one of the most frequently used measures because it represents the sum of all autonomous transactions that must be financed by the use of official reserves or of other nonreserve official transactions that are often viewed as being a substitute for reserve transactions. It is a comprehensive balance often used to judge a country's overall competitive position in terms of all private transactions with the rest of the world. Deficits or surpluses in the overall balance are frequently used to judge pressure for exchange rate changes. The overall balance of the United States has been negative during the years 1985 to 1992, except 1985 and 1989, ending 1992 with a negative $42.06 billion.

Other Adjustments. Groups E and F in Exhibit 3.1 constitute transactions that have governmental attributes but are not counted in official reserves. *Exceptional financing* is financing mobilized by a country's monetary authorities that falls outside of the definitions of official reserves. Examples would be postponing the repayment of government foreign currency debt or drawing on private banking loans to finance transactions that would otherwise have depleted the country's reserve assets. This account appears mostly with countries having foreign exchange reserve difficulties, and seldom appears for reserve currency countries such as the United States.

Liabilities constituting foreign authorities' reserves refers to changes in private bank liabilities that are held as foreign exchange reserve by central banks of other countries. Note that the entry for 1992 is a credit of $38.14 billion (line 8), meaning that on a net basis foreign central banks increased their deposits in U.S. private banks by this amount. This credit almost offset the official settlements deficit of $42.06 billion.

Changes in Reserves. The net result of activities in Groups A through F (line 9 in Exhibit 3.1) must be financed by changes in *official monetary reserves*. The sum of changes in reserves on line 10 is identical to line 9 except the sign is reversed. In other words, the balance on line 9 was financed by the various accounts in Group G. These consist of changes in the holdings of monetary gold, special drawing rights (SDRs), the U.S. reserve position with the IMF, and U.S. holdings of foreign exchange assets. The sum of these, $3.92 billion, represents the 1992 increase in foreign exchange reserves held by the United States. The major component was an increase of $4.27 billion in U.S. holding of foreign exchange assets, that is, the currencies of other countries.

Balance of Payments: An Interpretive Summary

Exhibit 3.2 provides a brief conceptual overview of the interrelationships just discussed, based on data for the year 1992. The merchandise trade balance for 1992 was a deficit of $96.14 billion, meaning the United States imported that much more than it exported. This is the account balance that is the most well recognized and publicized of the various BOP summary statistics. It is often used by politicians and labor leaders to rationalize limits on free trade, and of course can be used by businesses to explain how their operations benefit a country. The merchandise trade balance, when supplemented with the balance on international services, income, and official and private unrequited transfers,

Exhibit 3.2   The U.S. Balance of Payments: Commonly Used Summary Measures (billions of U.S. dollars)

Group	Category Component	Balance in 1992	Cumulative Total	Popular Name
A	Merchandise Trade, net	−96.14		"Trade Balance"
	Other current items	29.84		
	Current Account	−66.30		
			−66.30	"Current Account Balance" (Sum of Group A)
B	Direct Investment, net	−32.42		
	Portfolio Investment, net	14.19		
	Other long-term items	0.62		
	Long-Term Capital	−17.61		
			−83.91	"Basic Balance" (Sum of A + B)
C	Short-Term Capital	+54.19		
D	Errors and Omissions	−12.34		
			−42.06	"Overall Balance" (Sum of A + B + C + D)

Source: *Balance of Payments Statistics*, International Monetary Fund, December 1993, p. 742.

results in the current account balance. The current account balance for 1992 was a deficit of $66.30 billion.

To the current account deficit must be added a net deficit in long-term investments of $17.61 billion, leading to a basic balance deficit of $83.91 billion. With the additions of an inflow of $54.19 billion in short-term capital and a negative $12.34 billion in errors and omissions, the overall balance was a deficit of $42.06 billion for 1992.

Imbalances in the Balance of Payments

The significance of a deficit or surplus in the balance of payments (BOP) has changed since the advent of floating exchange rates. Traditionally, BOP measures were used as evidence of pressure on a country's foreign exchange rate. This pressure led to governmental transactions that were compensatory in nature, forced on the government by its need to settle the deficit or face a devaluation.

Exchange Rate Impacts

The relationship between the balance of payments and exchange rates can be illustrated by use of a simplified equation that summarizes balance of payments data:

$$\underset{(X - M)}{\underset{\text{Balance}}{\text{Current Account}}} \quad + \quad \underset{(CI - CO)}{\underset{\text{Balance}}{\text{Capital Account}}} \quad + \quad \underset{FXB}{\underset{\text{Balance}}{\text{Reserve}}} \quad = \quad \underset{BOP}{\underset{\text{Payments}}{\text{Balance of}}}$$

where
- X = exports of goods and services
- M = imports of goods and services
- CI = capital inflows
- CO = capital outflows
- FXB = the foreign exchange reserve balance of the country

The effect of an imbalance in the balance of payments of a country works somewhat differently depending on whether that country has fixed exchange rates, floating exchange rates, or a managed exchange rate system.

Fixed Exchange Rate Countries. Under a fixed exchange rate system the government bears the responsibility to assure a BOP near zero. If the sum of the current and capital accounts does not approximate zero, the government is expected to intervene in the foreign exchange market by buying or selling official foreign exchange reserves. If the sum of the first two accounts is greater than zero, a surplus demand for the domestic currency exists in the world. To preserve the fixed exchange rate, the government must then intervene in the foreign exchange market and sell domestic currency for foreign currencies or gold so as to bring the BOP back near zero.

If the sum of the current and capital accounts is negative, an excess supply of the domestic currency exists in world markets. Then the government must intervene by buying the domestic currency with its reserves of foreign currencies and gold. It is obviously important for a government to maintain significant foreign exchange reserve balances to allow it to intervene effectively. If the country runs out of foreign exchange reserves, it will be unable to buy back its domestic currency and will be forced to devalue.

Floating Exchange Rate Countries. Under a floating exchange rate system, the government of a country has no responsibility to peg the foreign exchange rate. The fact that the current and capital account balances do not sum to zero will automatically (in theory) alter the exchange rate in the direction necessary to obtain a BOP near zero. For example, a country running a sizable current account deficit [$(X - M) < 0$], with a capital account balance of zero ($CI - CO = 0$) will have a net BOP deficit. An excess supply of the domestic currency will appear on world markets, and like all goods in excess supply, the market will rid itself of the imbalance by lowering the price. Thus the domestic currency will fall in value, and the BOP will move back toward zero. As we see in Chapter 5, exchange rate markets do not always follow this theory.

Managed Floats. Although still relying on market conditions for day-to-day exchange rate determination, countries operating with managed floats often find it necessary to take actions to maintain their desired exchange rate values. They therefore seek to alter the market's valuation of a specific exchange rate by influencing the motivations of market activity, rather than through direct intervention in the foreign exchange markets.

The primary action taken by such governments is to change relative interest rates, thus influencing the economic fundamentals of exchange rate determination. In the context of our equation, a change in domestic interest rates is an attempt to alter the term ($CI - CO$), especially the short-term component of these capital flows, in order to restore an imbalance caused by the deficit in the current account. As we discuss in detail in Chapter 5, the power of interest rate changes on international capital and exchange rate movements can be substantial. A country with a managed float that wishes to "defend its currency" may choose to raise domestic interest rates to attract additional capital from abroad. This will alter market forces and create additional market demand for the domestic currency. In this process, the government "signals" exchange market participants that it intends to take measures to preserve the currency's value within certain ranges. The process also raises the cost of local borrowing for businesses, however, and so the policy is seldom without domestic critics.

Economic Development Impacts

Apart from implications for pressure on foreign exchange rates, the balance of payments has also been used for economic development analysis. In that context a deficit or surplus in the current account is not inherently "good" or "bad" for a country. From a national income viewpoint, a deficit on current account might have a negative effect on GNP and employment if underemployment exists, whereas a surplus could have a positive effect. However, if full employment exists, a current account deficit which can be financed abroad would allow the import of investment goods that would not have been possible otherwise.

From a program viewpoint, economic development usually requires a net import of goods and services (deficit in the current account) financed by foreign savings. Less developed countries find it nearly impossible to generate sufficient domestic savings or technical and managerial know-how to reach the "takeoff" point without external aid.

Finally, from a liquidity viewpoint, a deficit could mean a country is building up a net long-term creditor position vis-à-vis the rest of the world through direct foreign investments and long-term loans while simultaneously building up its short-term liabilities to the rest of the world.

Note that a country's trade or current account must be viewed against the rest of the world, not just on a bilateral basis vis-à-vis one other country. If country A exports only to country B, which exports the same dollar value to country C, which exports the same dollar value to country A, each country is in balance overall but seriously out of balance with a single other country.

Exhibit 3.3 shows the multilateral balances among the European Community, the United States, and the Pacific Rim countries in 1992. Notice that Europe runs a trade deficit with both Asia and the United States, the United States runs a surplus with Europe but a deficit with Asia, and Asia runs a surplus with both Europe and the United States.

Exhibit 3.3   World Trade Profile

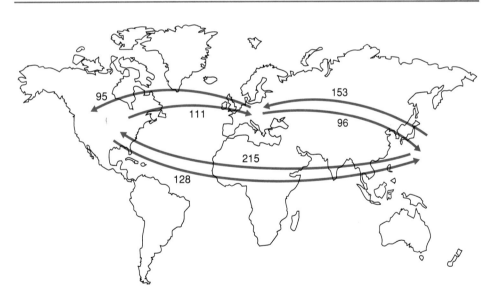

Imports and exports among the European Community, the United States, and the Pacific Rim nations in 1992 (billions of dollars)

Source: "European Economic Review," *International Herald Tribune,* 12/9/93, p. 15. Reprinted with permission. Data from U.S. Department of Commerce and the German Ministry of Economics.

Issues in International Capital Flows

International economic and financial problems in the 1990s are not confined to the current account. The capital account and its subject financial flows are of equal concern to business firms and governments.

Capital flows across countries are typically classified in terms of maturity, short term and long term, and whether the investment represents some degree of control over the target investment. Short-term capital flows respond primarily to interest rate differentials and expectations of interest rate changes across countries. As we detail in Chapter 4, speculators and arbitragers are able to move massive quantities of capital around the world in moments in search of the highest returns. This allows small interest differentials to be exploited by the astute investor.

Short-Term Capital Flows. Short-term debt instruments, such as the U.S. Treasury bill (maturities of 13, 26, and 52 weeks), have at different times in the past decade offered relatively high rates of return and low levels of risk for investors worldwide. Their relatively high yields during the early 1980s, combined with the "safe haven" argument that the United States constituted one of the most stable political and economic environments, induced significant capital flows from abroad (particularly from Japan). This portfolio investment from abroad was the subject of much of the debate over foreign financing of the U.S. government budget deficit during the Reagan administration.

Long-Term Capital Flows. Long-term capital flows play a significant role in the balance of payments structure of many nations. Whereas short-term capital tends to follow interest rates, long-term capital is typically attracted to economic and business environments expected to provide significant long-run stability and economic growth.

The classification of international capital flows is also premised on the degree of control over a target investment by a foreign investor. In the United States, the acquisition of 10% or more of the equity of a U.S. enterprise is considered sufficient for a foreign investor to exercise some influence on the management and operations of the firm. Such investment is then categorized as *direct foreign investment* (DFI), and the firm itself is reclassified as the U.S. affiliate of a foreign company. The definitional requirement for DFI varies across countries, with West Germany requiring 25%, and both the United Kingdom and France specifying 20% as the point of DFI. If ownership is less than the DFI threshold level, or the investment is a debt instrument, it is summarily classified as portfolio investment.

DFI is often further subdivided into the nature of the investment itself: (1) "greenfield" projects in which the capital is used for the construction of new production, sales, or commercial facilities; and (2) "acquisition" investments that are essentially the purchase of preexisting enterprises or operations. Greenfield investments are looked upon by most governments as a strong potential contributor to economic welfare, and are normally encouraged and courted. Acquisitions, however, are increasingly a source of emotional and political concern as foreign business firms buy the assets and maybe technology of domestic enterprises. Such acquisitions often become the topic of emotional "sovereignty" as residents of the countries receiving these capital inflows worry over the potential loss of home control. A recent example is the failure of the Swedish shareholders of Volvo to approve a merger with French Renault for fear the French would dominate what would otherwise remain a major Swedish corporation.

Capital Flight. A final issue is that of capital flight. Although no single accepted definition of capital flight exists, Ingo Walter's discussion has been one of the more useful.

> International flows of direct and portfolio investments under ordinary circumstances are rarely associated with the capital flight phenomenon. Rather, it is when capital transfers by residents conflict with political objectives that the term "flight" comes into general usage.[1]

Although not limited to heavily indebted countries, the rapid and sometimes illegal transfer of convertible currencies out of a country poses significant economic and political problems. Many heavily indebted countries have suffered significant capital flight, which has compounded their problems of debt service.

Four primary mechanisms exist by which capital may be moved from one country to another. Transfers via the usual international payments mechanisms, regular bank transfers, are obviously the easiest, lowest cost, and legal. Transfer of physical currency by bearer (the proverbial smuggling of cash out in the false bottom of a suitcase) is more costly and for transfers out of many countries, illegal. The illegality may be proscribed for balance of payments reasons or to make difficult the movement of money from the drug trade or other illegal activities. The third form of movement is the transfer of cash into collectibles or precious metals, which are then in turn transferred across borders. The fourth form of transfer, and the one most typically associated with capital flight, is that of the false invoicing of international trade transactions. Capital is successfully moved through the underinvoicing of exports or the overinvoicing of imports, where the difference between the invoiced amount and the actually agreed upon payment is deposited in banking institutions in a country of choice. Some of the dollar loans originally extended to Latin American countries are suspected of having been redeposited in the same lending banks but under the ownership of new identities.

Major Country Trends in Trade and Capital Flows

Exhibits 3.4, 3.5, and 3.6 provide graphical representations of the current account balances and overall balances of the United States, Japan, and West Germany for the past decade. A number of trends are evident.

Exhibit 3.4 shows balances on current account and overall balance for the United

---

[1]Ingo Walter, "The Mechanisms of Capital Flight," in *Capital Flight and Third World Debt*, edited by Donald R. Lessard and John Williamson, Washington, D.C.: Institute for International Economics, 1987, p.104.

Exhibit 3.4   U.S. Balance of Payments (billions of U.S. dollars)

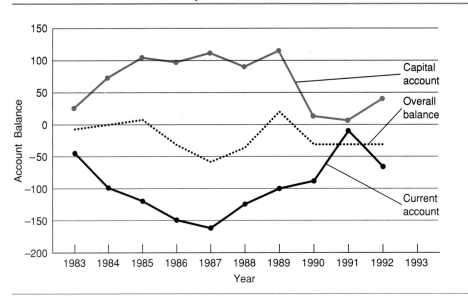

Source: Adapted from *Balance of Payments Statistics,* International Monetary Fund, Washington, D.C., 1993.

Exhibit 3.5   Japanese Balance of Payments (billions of U.S. dollars)

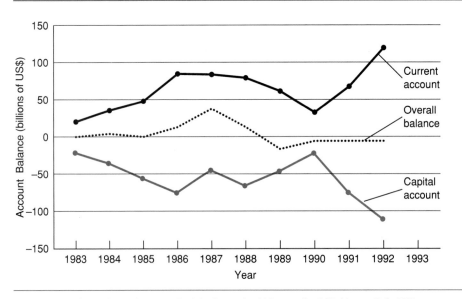

Source: Adapted from *Balance of Payments Statistics,* International Monetary Fund, Washington, D.C., 1993.

Exhibit 3.6 German Balance of Payments (billions of U.S. dollars)

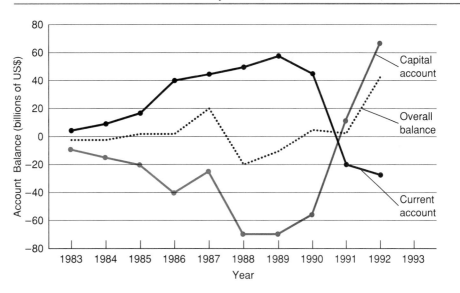

Source: Adapted from *Balance of Payments Statistics,* International Monetary Fund, Washington, D.C., 1993.

States. The magnitude of the current account deficit of the United States, beginning in 1984, is striking. This deficit was over $100 billion each year from 1985 to 1989, although dropping steadily after 1987. The current account deficit was offset, by and large, by massive inflows of capital. The improvement in the overall balance of payments for the United States in 1988 and 1989 coincides with the fall of U.S. interest rates and the dollar over this period. The deficit of 1990 is attributable to the failure of capital flows to offset the continued current account deficit.

For Japan and West Germany over the same period, a largely reciprocal relationship is evident. Growth in the U.S. current account deficit coincided with the rapid increase in Japan's current account surplus through 1987. Since 1987 the magnitude of the surplus has diminished. Also since 1987 the Japanese trade surplus has dropped in size. During these years the yen more than doubled in value versus the U.S. dollar, meaning that Japan's BOP surplus measured in U.S. dollars increased more rapidly than the same surplus measured in yen.

The current account surplus of Germany grew steadily through 1989 before starting to diminish. As with Japan, Germany has been a net investor in other countries and so has run a deficit in its capital account. After the unification of Germany, much of German investment has shifted from abroad to internal use. The strength of the Deutschemark has made German goods less competitive internationally, resulting in a shrinking current account surplus.

Summary

- Although termed a balance of payments, the BOP is actually an income statement that summarizes receipts and disbursements on all economic transactions between residents of one country and residents of all other countries.

- The balance of payments consists of three major components: (1) the current account balance; (2) the capital account balance; and (3) the overall balance. The current account balance, which includes imports and exports of merchandise and service trade, has traditionally been the focus of attention. However, the 1980s saw a massive growth in the level of capital flows internationally, resulting in increased interest in the capital account balance and its subcomponents.

- The capital account balance combines both short-term capital flows and long-term capital investment. Short-term flows often follow the highest and yet safest real returns on short-term debt instruments, for example, the U.S. Treasury bill in the mid-1980s. Long-term capital flows are normally attracted to countries thought to offer more stable and profitable business environments for longer periods of time.

- The chapter concluded with a brief overview of the major balance of payment accounts of the United States, Japan, and Germany. The United States experienced a continuing surplus in its capital account while suffering a record deficit in the current account during the 1980s. Both Japan and Germany, however, exhibited opposite positions with large surpluses in the current account and deficits in their capital account balances.

Decision Case
Ecuadorian Debt for Development[2]

Jack is nervous. Jack Van de Water is the Director for International Education Programs at Oregon State University, and therefore responsible for managing the financing of all study-abroad programs. It is May 1991 and one of the causes of Jack's nervousness is the need to decide whether or not the university is to take part in the "Debt for Development" program (hereafter DFD) in financing its study programs in the country of Ecuador. The DFD program is designed to aid not-for-profit entities like universities in increasing their spending capabilities abroad while contributing to the reduction of large foreign debt levels suffered by many developing countries.

---

[2]Michael H. Moffett, Oregon State University, May 1991. Reprinted with permission.

Ecuador and Debt

Ecuador is another in the long line of Latin American countries attempting to deal with large levels of foreign debt. This debt is made up of loans taken out by the government of Ecuador and other semigovernment institutions in Ecuador (like utilities, railroads, etc.) during the late 1970s and early 1980s when the prospects for economic development in that part of the world were quite strong. Ecuador, like Brazil and Mexico, went to the international capital markets to obtain funds, to speed up its rate of industrialization. The debt was primarily in the form of U.S. dollars, a currency with wide international purchasing power at the time. The capital was intended to improve the internal infrastructure and manufacturing industries of Ecuador to allow it to generate increased earnings—particularly in export markets where it could be paid in U.S. dollars—so the debt could be serviced and eventually repaid. Things, however, did not quite work out that smoothly.

The internal and external sectors of the Ecuadorian economy did not grow sufficiently to generate the large amounts of foreign currency earnings needed for debt service during the 1980s. By 1987, a large amount of Ecuadorian debt was classified as in arrears, and by 1988 a substantial secondary market had developed for the sale of dollar debt owed by Ecuador to commercial banks throughout the world. Ecuador, like other heavily indebted countries, was faced with few alternatives to service dollar-denominated debt: (1) export (or run a net export surplus); or (2) borrow additional dollars. The second alternative was not considered overly attractive by either the borrower or the lenders. The export market was relatively stable, but not growing sufficiently to service the existing levels of debt. A new alternative arose: Miss the debt-service payments!

The term *debt,* as normally used in reference to developing countries, consists of long-term borrowings by government or semigovernment entities from the international capital markets. The lenders are governments, international aid and development organizations like the International Monetary Fund (IMF), and large commercial banks worldwide. Although the first two organizations do not operate on the basis of profit, the commercial banking sector does operate in an increasingly competitive mode. As the debt crises of the early 1980s came and stayed, many of the commercial banks tried to either reschedule their loans to foreign borrowers (thus effectively redefining the loan as not being in arrears on servicing its obligations) or to rid themselves of their foreign debt completely. It is this dumping of debt, in which the commercial banks are willing to sell their loans to unrelated third parties, which feeds the growing secondary market for third world debt. Since the loans are often not currently being serviced by the borrowing country, and the prospects for payment in full are often poor, the banks are willing to sell the loans at a considerable discount from the face value of the loan.

The Debt for Development Program

The DFD program is described in its own literature as follows: "The Debt for Development Coalition, Inc., represents not-for-profit organizations committed to finding ways to turn the international debts of countries into economic development opportunities."

If a portion of the external debt of developing nations can be converted—by donation or purchase—into local currencies, not-for-profit organizations can use the funds for development projects needed to help spur economic growth in Latin America, Africa, Asia, and the Pacific.

Coalition members are U.S. colleges and universities, cooperatives, private volunteer organizations, and research institutes engaged in economic development programs overseas. The coalition also maintains close cooperation with various U.S. environmental organizations.

The coalition works closely with private organizations in debtor nations to identify programs important to each country's economic priorities such as education, public health, nutrition, agriculture, small business enterprises, research, housing, credit, and natural resource management programs.

The DFD program arose from the growing activity in what is called debt for equity swaps. Many of the indebted countries wished to alter the nature of their obligations from debt to participating equity, where the holder would see returns tied to the profits (or losses) of the enterprises associated with the capital. The idea was to encourage long-term equity involvement in the country, rather than the debt repayment at any cost posture of most debt holders.

The Debt for Development swap is something akin to a debt for equity swap. The dollar debt is swapped for sucre-denominated debt in this case, however, rather than into the equity ownership of a sucre-denominated enterprise. Most debt holders have traditionally opposed debt redenomination schemes due to the weakness and inconvertibility of many of the developing country currencies. A country heavily indebted in dollars might reissue all debt in its own currency, essentially printing money to repay the debt. This is commonly thought to be too dangerous for all parties, resulting in depreciated values in repayment and inducing the country to undertake inflationary policies not in its own best interest. The DFD program, however, altered this process substantially by limiting the actual sucre to be swapped and by requiring a debt swap with a repayment schedule matching that of the initial debt obligation. The first and foremost concern on the part of an indebted country like Ecuador is that the debt and debt service is in a foreign currency, in this case U.S. dollars. This swap program would allow Ecuador to exchange sucre debt for dollar debt.

Ecuadorian Debt for Development

The DFD program would work in the following way. Commercial banks holding Ecuadorian debt would sell their loans to the DFD program participant. The debt would be sold at a discount, with the banks receiving partial repayment in dollars and writing the remainder of the loans off as bad debt obligations. The U.S. government, as well as the governments of several other large industrial countries having banks with third world debt, have provided tax relief to aid commercial banks to write off these loans through "advantaged loan loss reserves."

Ecuadorian debt has been quoted at between $0.16 and $0.20 per dollar of face value debt throughout late 1990 and early 1991. The third party—Oregon State University—would purchase dollar-denominated debt. The debt would then be swapped, with the Ecuadorian government crediting Oregon State with $0.50 for every dollar in debt face value. The Ecuadorian government would then exchange this discounted dollar value for the domestic currency, sucre, at the official government exchange rate, sucre 970/$.

Several other countries follow a slightly different procedure whereby the country would swap the debt at 100 percent face value, but then exchange the dollar debt to domestic currency at a significantly altered (overvalued) exchange rate. The indebted country thus gains one way or the other in the actual exchange of dollar debt for domestic currency. Ecuador thus succeeds in reducing its dollar-denominated debt obligations to foreign banks, and essentially assures the proceeds of the conversion will be spent in the domestic economy (sucre do not buy anything anywhere else)!

There is, however, a final twist to this specific program. Ecuador, although anxious to retire or replace existing dollar-denominated debt with domestic currency, does not wish to add to inflationary pressures by pumping up its money supply. The government of Ecuador therefore will swap the debt as described, but for sucre-denominated bonds, not cash. These bonds would then be serviced by sucre-denominated cash flows (coupons) to be paid quarterly until maturity on October 31, 1996. The payment schedule and maturity matches the schedules of the original debt.

This last feature poses a problem for Jack (he is to the point of facial "ticks" now; twitching). Given the limited resources a university possesses in conducting study-abroad programs, he needs all the sucre value possible for use in the current period. Jack inquires as to the liquidity of these government bonds, and is told the market is "thin," but the bonds will likely be able to be sold at discounts ranging from 10 to 30% depending on financial and inflationary conditions.

Jack's Dilemma

Jack was now running short of time. He had to decide whether to commit his resources and his study-abroad program financing, approximately $50,000 for the 1991–1992 academic year, to the DFD program or not. Jack then summarized the major points he needed to weigh in the pro and con columns of the dog-eared Big Chief tablet on his desk.

Case Questions

1. What are the probable sucre proceeds of the debt swap program for Jack's $50,000? Given that there are a range of values over which many of the variables could change, create a best case, moderate case, and worst case scenario for Jack.

2. What are the obvious and not so obvious risks in participating in this debt swap program for Oregon State University? Which of the explicit variables appears to be most important to the actual sucre proceeds?

3. If Jack proceeded with the DFD swap program, what should be his immediate concerns when gaining possession of the sucre-denominated Ecuadorian government bonds? How will Jack's expectations of inflation alter his bond or cash management for the coming year?

Questions

1. BOP Summary Measures
Using the balance of payments data for the United States in Exhibit 3.1, construct a summary table like that of Exhibit 3.2 for the United States in 1992. How have the fundamental balances changed?

2. Balance on Current Account
The current account of a country frequently receives much attention because it is largely composed of merchandise trade. What "balance" (surplus or deficit) do most countries wish to see reflected in their own current account balance? Is a surplus better or worse than a deficit in merchandise trade?

3. Balance on Capital Account
Given what most countries wish to experience in their current account (question 2), what should these same countries expect to experience in their individual capital accounts? For the long-term productivity growth of a country, what do you think would be the best "balance" in long-term capital flows?

4. Capital Flight
Explain why capital flight is such a serious problem for countries in managing their balance of payments during periods of crisis.

5. Foreign Direct Investment (FDI) and Portfolio Investment
The topic of FDI is one filled with emotion in many countries. Why do so many countries, whether it be France, Canada, the United States, or Japan, frequently restrict the ability of foreign residents to purchase assets such as land or natural resources in their countries?

6. Management's Use of the Balance of Payments
Many students find discussion of BOP quite "boring," yet issues related to a country's BOP frequently cover the front page of daily and weekly business periodicals. Why is a concept as macro in scope important for decision making by business management?

7. U.S. Balance of Payments: Changing Trends (C03A.WK1)
Using Exhibit 3.1 (or the C03A.WK1 template) answer the following questions regarding the trends in U.S. balance of payments subaccounts in the late 1980s and early 1990s:

   a. What was the *basic balance* for the United States in 1990–1992?
   b. Which of the merchandise trade components, exports or imports, appears to be more volatile between 1985 and 1992?
   c. What was the *balance of payments* for the United States in 1991 and 1992, and which measure is most appropriate?
   d. What is the most striking change in recent years among the U.S. balance of payments subaccount balances?

8. Japanese and German Balance of Payments (C03A.WK1, C03B.WK1, C03C.WK1)
Use Exhibits 3.4, 3.5, and 3.6 (or C03A.WK1, C03B.WK1, and C03C.WK1) to answer the following question: How have the changes in the U.S. balance of payments compared with those of Japan and Germany in the early years of the 1990s?

Bibliography

Bergsten, Fred C., and Shafique Islam, *The United States as a Debtor Country,* Washington, D.C.: Institute of International Economics, 1990.

Brown, Brendan, *The Flight of International Capital: A Contemporary History,* New York and London: Croom Helm, 1987.

Carvounis, Chris C., *The United States Trade Deficit of the 1980s,* Westport, Conn.: Quorum Books, 1987.

de Vries, Margaret Garritsen, *Balance of Payments Adjustment, 1945–1986: The IMF Experience,* Washington, D.C.: IMF, 1987.

Eichengreen, Barry, and Peter H. Lindert, *The International Debt Crisis in Historical Perspective,* Cambridge, MA: MIT Press, 1990.

Ganitsky, Joseph, and Gerardo Lema, "Foreign Investment Through Debt-Equity Swaps," *Sloan Management Review,* vol. 29, no. 2, Winter 1988, pp. 21–29.

Graham, Edward, and Paul Krugman, *Foreign Direct Investment in the United States,* Washington, D.C.: Institute for International Economics, 1989.

Hufbauer, Gary Clyde, Diane T. Berliner, and Kimberly Ann Elliott, *Trade Protection in the United States: 31 Case Studies,* Washington, D.C.: Institute for International Economics, 1986.

Hutchinson, Michael, and Charles Piggott, "Budget Deficits, Exchange Rates and the Current Account: Theory and U.S. Evidence," *Economic Review,* Federal Reserve Bank of San Francisco, Fall 1984, pp. 5–25.

International Trade: The U.S. Trade Deficit: Causes and Policy Options for Solutions, Washington, D.C.: U.S. General Accounting Office, 1987.

Millman, Gregory J., "Financing the Uncreditworthy: New Financial Structures for LDCs," *Journal of Applied Corporate Finance,* vol. 3, no. 4, Winter 1991, pp. 83–89.

Ohmae, Kenichi, "Lies, Damned Lies, and Statistics: Why the Trade Deficit Doesn't Matter in a Borderless World," *Journal of Applied Corporate Finance,* vol. 3, no. 4, Winter 1991, pp. 98–106.

Tavis, Lee A., ed., *Rekindling Development: Multinational Firms and World Debt,* Notre Dame, Ind.: Notre Dame Press, 1988.

Williamson, John, *Voluntary Approaches to Debt Relief,* Washington, D.C.: Institute for International Economics, 1988.

Williamson, John, and Donald Lessard, eds., *Capital Flight and Third World Debt,* Washington, D.C.: Institute for International Economics, 1987.

Chapter 4
The Foreign Exchange Market

Global View
The Global Greenback

The U.S. dollar, although weakening on a consistent basis over the past decade versus other major currencies like the Japanese yen, is alive and well as the currency of choice in many countries today. A few examples:

- **Cuba.** In the spring of 1994 the Cuban Communist Party legalized the use of the U.S. dollar for transactions in Cuba. Whether the exchange rate between the dollar and Cuban peso is set by the market or the government (the official rate is Pesos1/$, the free market rate is Pesos60/$) is as yet undecided.

- **Argentina.** In an effort to stabilize the economy and the currency of the country, Argentina has pegged the Argentine peso to the U.S. dollar at a rate of Ps0.99/$ since 1991. Residents of Argentina can also hold bank accounts denominated in U.S. dollars as well, assuring that Argentine interest rates are equivalent to U.S. dollar-denominated interest rates on world markets.

- **Panama.** The official currency of Panama, although a separate and sovereign power, has been the U.S. dollar for many years.

- **China.** Despite recent reforms in which the foreign exchange certificate, the currency reserved for the use of foreign visitors alone was removed, the Chinese yuan is still not freely convertible into foreign currencies. The business of Guangdong, the Chinese province neighboring Hong Kong, continues to thrive thanks to the use of the U.S. dollar.

- **Vietnam.** Nightclubs and other businesses frequented by tourists and the new local capitalists require payments for services, including cover charges, in U.S. dollars.

- **Mexico.** Like Hong Kong, Taiwan, and a number of other major U.S.-trading partners, Mexico ties its currency value to the U.S. dollar. What makes Mexico's new program particularly unique is that it has set a crawling-devaluation schedule which allows the new peso to fall .04 centavos per day versus the U.S. dollar.

- **Brazil.** The hyperinflationary environment of Brazil has long made currencies like the U.S. dollar and German mark the only real currencies which hold their value from day to day. It is not unusual to see advertisements stating prices in U.S. dollars rather than the Brazilian cruzeiro real.

Source: This global view draws on a number of sources including: "Hail to the Castrodollar," *The Economist,* July 24, 1993, p. 46; "China's Currency: E pluribus unum," *The Economist,* December 4, 1993, pp. 83–84; "Solid Mexican Peso Scares Some Investors," by Craig Torres, *Wall Street Journal,* Tuesday November 2, 1993, pp. C1, C20; "The Global Greenback," Owen Ullmann, Pete Engardio, Peter Galuszka, and Bill Hinchberger, *Business Week,* August 9, 1993, pp. 40–44.

The foreign exchange market provides the physical and institutional structure through which the money of one country is exchanged for that of another country, the rate of exchange between currencies is determined, and foreign exchange transactions are physically completed. *Foreign exchange* means the money of a foreign country, that is, foreign currency bank balances, banknotes, checks and drafts. A *foreign exchange transaction* is an agreement between a buyer and seller that a fixed amount of one currency be delivered at a specified rate for some other currency.

This chapter describes the operation of the foreign exchange market. Chapter 5 explains the parity conditions that help determine foreign exchange rates, and Chapter 6 describes the market and pricing of foreign currency options. Together, these three chapters explain the foreign exchange market in its broadest interpretation.

This chapter describes the following features of the foreign exchange market:

- The geographical extent of the foreign exchange market.
- The three main functions performed by the market.
- The market's participants.
- The immense transaction volume that takes place daily in the foreign exchange market.
- Types of transactions, including spot, forward, and swap transactions.
- Methods of stating exchange rates, quotations, and changes in exchange rates.

Geographic Extent of the Foreign Exchange Market

Geographically the foreign exchange market spans the globe, with prices moving and currencies traded somewhere every hour of every business day. Major world trading starts each morning in Sydney and Tokyo, moves west to Hong Kong and Singapore, passes on to Bahrain, shifts to the main European markets of Frankfurt, Zurich, and London, jumps the Atlantic to New York, goes west to Chicago, and ends up in San Francisco and Los Angeles. The market is deepest, or most liquid, early in the European afternoon, when markets of both Europe and the U.S. East Coast are open. This period is regarded as the best time to ensure the smooth execution of a very large order.

At the end of the day in California, when traders in Tokyo and Hong Kong are just getting up for the next day, the market is thinnest. During these hours, when the U.S. West Coast is awake and Europe sleeps, aggressive speculators or central banks sometimes try to move prices by trading large blocks, and thus influence European attitudes about particular currencies the following morning. Many large international banks operate foreign exchange trading rooms in each major geographic trading center in order to serve important commercial accounts on a 24-hour-a-day basis. The world of foreign exchange dealing is shown on the map on the front flyleaf of this book.

In some countries, a portion of foreign exchange trading is conducted on an official trading floor by open bidding. Closing prices are published as the official price, or "fixing," for the day, and certain commercial and investment transactions are based on this official price. Business firms in countries with exchange controls often must surrender foreign exchange earned from exports to the central bank at the daily fixing price.

Banks engaged in foreign exchange trading are connected by highly sophisticated telecommunications networks. Professional dealers and brokers obtain exchange rate quotes on desktop computer screens, and communicate with each other by telephone, computer, fax, and telex. The foreign exchange departments of many nonbank business firms also use computer networks to keep in touch with the market and to seek out the best quotations. Reuters, Telerate, and Bloomberg are the leading suppliers of foreign exchange rate information and trading systems. A recent development has been the introduction of automated "matching" systems into computerized quotation systems. Many dealers think computer-executed transactions will replace other, more conventional, trading systems in the near future.

Functions of the Foreign Exchange Market

The foreign exchange market is the mechanism by which one transfers purchasing power between countries, obtains or provides credit for international trade transactions, and minimizes exposure to the risks of exchange rate changes.

Transfer of Purchasing Power

Transfer of purchasing power is necessary because international trade and capital transactions normally involve parties living in countries with different national currencies. Each party usually wants to deal in its own currency, but the trade or capital transaction can be invoiced only in one single currency. If a Japanese exporter sells Toyota automobiles to a Brazilian importer, the exporter could invoice the Brazilian importer in Japanese yen, Brazilian cruzeiros, or any convenient third-country currency such as U.S. dollars. The currency would be agreed upon beforehand.

Whichever currency is used, one or more of the parties must transfer purchasing power to or from its own national currency. If the transaction is in yen, the Brazilian importer must buy yen with cruzeiros. If the transaction is in cruzeiros, the Japanese exporter must sell the cruzeiros received for yen. If U.S. dollars are used, the Brazilian importer must exchange cruzeiros for dollars, and the Japanese exporter must then exchange dollars for yen. The foreign exchange market provides the mechanism for carrying out these purchasing power transfers.

Provision of Credit

Because the movement of goods between countries takes time, inventory in transit must be financed. In the case of the Toyota sale, somebody must finance the automobiles while they are being shipped to Brazil and also while they are "floored" with Toyota dealers in Brazil before final sale to a customer. The elapsed time might be anywhere from a few weeks to six months, depending on how the cars are shipped.

The Japanese exporter may agree to provide this credit by carrying the accounts receivable of the Brazilian importer, with or without interest. Alternatively, the Brazilian importer may pay cash on shipment from Japan and finance the automobiles with its local bank. The foreign exchange market provides a third source of credit. Specialized instruments, such as bankers' acceptances and letters of credit, are available to finance international trade. (These documents are explained in Chapter 16.)

Minimizing Foreign Exchange Risk

Neither the Brazilian importer nor the Japanese exporter may wish to carry the risk of exchange rate fluctuations. Each may prefer to earn a normal business profit on the automobile transaction without exposure to an unexpected change in anticipated profit because exchange rates suddenly change. The foreign exchange market provides "hedging" facilities for transferring foreign exchange risk to someone else. (These facilities are explained in Chapter 7.)

Market Participants

The foreign exchange market consists of two tiers: the interbank or wholesale market, and the client or retail market. Individual transactions in the interbank market are usually for large sums that are multiples of a million U.S. dollars or the equivalent value in other currencies. By contrast, contracts between a bank and its clients are usually for specific amounts, sometimes down to the last penny.

Five broad categories of participants operate within these two tiers: bank and nonbank foreign exchange dealers, individuals and firms conducting commercial or investment transactions, speculators and arbitragers, central banks and treasuries, and foreign exchange brokers.

Bank and Nonbank Foreign Exchange Dealers

Banks, and a few nonbank foreign exchange dealers, operate in both the interbank and client markets. They profit from buying foreign exchange at a "bid" price and reselling it at a slightly higher "offer" (also called "ask") price. Competition among dealers world-wide narrows the spread between bid and offer and so contributes to making the foreign exchange market "efficient" in the same sense as in securities markets.

Dealers in the foreign exchange departments of large international banks often function as "market makers." They stand willing at all times to buy and sell those currencies in which they specialize. They do this by maintaining an "inventory" position in those currencies. They trade with other banks in their own monetary centers and in other centers around the world in order to maintain inventories within the trading limits set by bank policy. Trading limits are important because foreign exchange departments of many banks operate as profit centers, and individual dealers are compensated on a profit incentive basis.[1] Unauthorized violation of trading limits by dealers under profit pressure increases risk and at times has caused embarrassing losses for major banks.

Small- to medium-sized banks are likely to participate but not be market makers in the interbank market. Instead of maintaining significant inventory positions, they buy from and sell to larger banks to offset retail transactions with their own customers. Of course, even market-making banks do not make markets in every currency. They trade for their own account in those currencies of most interest to their customers and become participants when filling customer needs in less important currencies.

Individuals and Firms Conducting Commercial and Investment Transactions

Importers and exporters, international portfolio investors, multinational firms, tourists, and others use the foreign exchange market to facilitate execution of commercial or investment transactions. Their use of the foreign exchange market is necessary but nevertheless incidental to their underlying commercial or investment purpose. Some of these participants use the market to "hedge" foreign exchange risk.

Speculators and Arbitragers

Speculators and arbitragers seek to profit from trading in the market itself. They operate in their own interest, without a need or obligation to serve clients or to ensure a continuous market. Whereas dealers seek profit from the spread between bid and offer in addition to what they might gain from changes in exchange rates, speculators seek all of their profit from exchange rate changes. Arbitragers try to profit from simultaneous exchange rate differences in different markets.

A large proportion of speculation and arbitrage is conducted on behalf of major banks by traders employed by those banks. Thus banks act both as exchange dealers and as speculators and arbitragers. (Banks seldom admit to speculating; instead they see themselves as "taking an aggressive position"!)

---

[1]Currency trading is quite profitable for commercial and investment banks. In the early 1990s, many of the major currency-trading banks in the United States derived 10 to 12% on average of their annual net income from currency trading. But currency trading is also very profitable for the individual. The head of currency trading for Salomon Brothers Inc. in 1993 is purported to have received a total compensation package of $28 million; Salomon's CEO received only $7 million (Michael Siconolfi, "Salomon's Fattest Pay Didn't Go to CEO," *Wall Street Journal,* March 29, 1994, p. C1).

Central Banks and Treasuries

Central banks and treasuries use the market to acquire or spend their country's foreign exchange reserves as well as to influence the price at which their own currency is traded. They may act to support the value of their own currency because of policies adopted at the national level or because of commitments entered into through membership in such joint float agreements as the European Monetary System (EMS). Consequently their motive is not to earn a profit as such, but rather to influence the foreign exchange value of their currency in a manner that will be beneficial to the interests of their citizens. In many instances they do their job best when they willingly take a loss on their foreign exchange transactions.

Foreign Exchange Brokers

Foreign exchange brokers are agents who facilitate trading between dealers without themselves becoming principals in the transaction. For this service they charge a small commission. They maintain instant access to hundreds of dealers worldwide via open telephone lines. At times a broker may maintain a dozen or more such lines to a single client bank, with separate lines for different currencies and for spot and forward markets.

The relationship between banks acting as dealers and brokers is shown in Exhibit 4.1. The customer approaches its own bank, Citibank in New York. Citibank, in turn, can trade directly with Bankers Trust or Manufacturers Hanover in New York, or directly with Barclays or National Westminster in London. Alternatively, Citibank can seek quotes or place orders through a New York broker, who in turn might place the order

Exhibit 4.1 Trading Combinations, New York and London

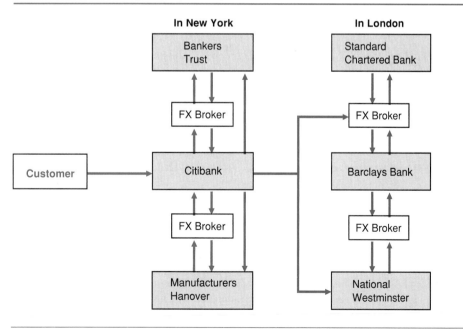

with Bankers Trust or Manufacturers Hanover. Lastly Citibank might contact a broker in London (or any other foreign center) who in turn would place the order with various London banks.

It is a broker's business to know at any moment exactly which dealers want to buy or sell any currency. This knowledge enables the broker to find quickly an opposite party for a client without revealing the identity of either party until after a transaction has been agreed upon. Dealers use brokers for speed and because they want to remain anonymous, since the identity of participants may influence short-term quotes.

Size of the Market

The Bank for International Settlements (BIS), in conjunction with central banks all over the world, conducts a survey of currency trading activity every three years. The most recent survey, conducted in April 1992, estimated global net turnover in the world foreign exchange markets as US$880 billion *per business day.*[2] "Turnover" means the total U.S. dollar value of all spot, outright forward, swap, futures, and options contracts *concluded* (not settled) during the month of April 1992.

The rapid growth in world currency trading is illustrated in Exhibit 4.2. The same BIS survey conducted in 1989 estimated trading at $640 billion per day, and in 1986 at about $200 billion per day. This constitutes an increase of more than 400% between 1986 and 1992! Also depicted in Exhibit 4.2 are the relative shares of the three major currency trading cities: London, New York, and Tokyo. Although Tokyo and New York gained on London's lead in total turnover between 1986 and 1989, the period between 1989 and 1992 resulted in a return to the traditional ranking of London first, New York second, and Tokyo third. The three in total, however, continue to dominate world trading (constituting over 55% in 1992).

Exhibit 4.3 summarizes the April 1992 survey results by currency and instrument. Net global turnover is dominated by trading in U.S. dollars and Deutschemarks, followed by Japanese yen, the U.K. pound sterling, and the Swiss franc in that order. Overall, spot trading (trades settled within two business days) is most important at 47.3% of the total, followed closely by swaps (a sale for one future date with the simultaneous purchase of an equivalent amount for a later date) at 39.0%. Outright forwards (sales for a future date unmatched with a simultaneous purchase) are of significantly less importance. In the United States, Japan, Australia, and Canada, swap trading is larger than spot trading, but in Germany (and to a lesser degree, the United Kingdom) spot trading substantially exceeds swap trading.

Every foreign exchange transaction involves two currencies and so cannot logically be broken down by single currencies alone. The relative importance of major currency pairs is shown in Exhibit 4.4.

---

[2]*Central Bank Survey of Foreign Exchange Market Activity in April 1992,* Bank for International Settlements, Monetary and Economics Department, Basle, Switzerland, March 1993. The BIS survey was compiled from information provided by central banks and monetary authorities in 26 countries. It was adjusted to eliminate double counting and to add estimated activity not covered by the survey.

Exhibit 4.2   Net Daily Trading (Turnover) on World Currency Markets

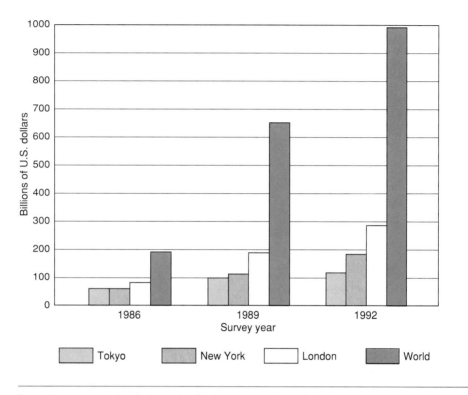

Source: Data drawn from *Bank for International Settlements Annual Report,* Basle, Switzerland, June 1990 and March 1993 issues.

   The U.S. dollar is by far the most important currency in the world's currency markets, constituting 69.0% of total trading in the seven most important currency pairs. Including pairs not reported in Exhibit 4.4, the BIS estimates that the U.S. dollar is on one side of over 80% of reported global turnover.[3] The BIS notes that the U.S. dollar is involved in 93% of deals involving the Australian dollar and in 87% of deals involving the Japanese yen. It is less prominent in deals involving European currencies, constituting 70% of British pound, 64% of Deutschemark, and 60% of French franc deals. The Deutschemark is currently the second most widely traded currency after the U.S. dollar, and is used in cross trades in Europe without having to pass through the U.S. dollar. The mark and dollar together account for 95% of all trading against the Japanese yen, British pound, Swiss franc, Australian dollar, Canadian dollar, and French franc.[4]

   Foreign exchange market transactions by location, rather than currency, show which financial centers are the most important. Exhibit 4.5 shows this data for the 11 countries

---

[3]*Central Bank Survey,* p. 8

[4]Ibid.

Exhibit 4.3 Daily Average Global Foreign Exchange Market Activity in April 1992[a]

BILLIONS OF U.S. DOLLARS	Total	Specified currency against all other currencies										
		U.S. dollar	Deutsche-mark	Japanese yen	Pound sterling	Swiss franc	Australian dollar	Canadian dollar	French franc	ECU	Other EMS	Others
Spot	393.7	283.8	209.3	79.2	56.5	37.8	6.3	8.1	14.9	11.7	36.8	43.2
Outright forward	58.5	44.2	21.3	15.5	9.1	5.1	1.5	2.0	2.3	1.6	5.7	8.7
Swaps	324.3	309.0	72.6	83.3	41.6	23.5	11.4	15.9	13.9	10.8	30.7	35.7
Subtotal	778.1	638.5	303.4	178.1	107.4	66.5	19.2	25.9	31.1	24.1	73.2	88.7
Futures	9.5	9.2	4.0	2.9	1.1	0.7	0.2	0.3	–	–	0.2	0.4
Options	37.7	29.1	19.1	13.2	4.4	2.4	1.0	1.0	0.6	–	0.6	3.7
Total reported	832.0	682.4	329.6	194.4	113.0	69.8	20.4	27.3	31.9	24.4	74.2	96.8
Estimated gaps in reporting	48.0											
Estimated global turnover	880.0											

PERCENT-AGES	Total	U.S. dollar	Deutsche-mark	Japanese yen	Pound sterling	Swiss franc	Australian dollar	Canadian dollar	French franc	ECU	Other EMS	Others
Spot	47.3	41.6	63.5	40.7	50.0	54.1	30.9	29.7	46.7	47.9	49.6	44.6
Outright forward	7.0	6.5	6.5	8.0	8.0	7.2	7.3	7.3	7.2	6.6	7.7	9.0
Swaps	39.0	45.3	22.0	42.9	36.8	33.7	55.9	58.2	43.6	44.3	41.4	36.9
Subtotal	93.5	93.6	92.0	91.6	95.0	95.3	94.1	94.9	97.5	98.8	98.7	91.6
Futures	1.1	1.3	1.2	1.5	1.0	1.0	1.0	1.1	–	–	0.3	0.4
Options	4.5	4.3	5.8	6.8	3.9	3.4	4.9	3.7	1.9	–	0.8	3.8
Total reported	100.0	100.0	100.0	100.0	100.0	100.0	100.0	100.0	100.0	100.0	100.0	100.0

[a]Because two currencies are involved in each transaction, the horizontal sum of transactions in individual currencies for each line adds to twice the total reported turnover in the "total" column.

Source: Adapted from "Reported exchange market turnover net of local and cross-border inter-dealer double-counting in April 1992, by market segment, counterparty and currency. Total reported transactions in all currencies," *Central Bank Survey of Foreign Exchange Market Activity in April 1992*. Basle, Switzerland: Bank for International Settlements, Monetary and Economics Department, March 1993, Table I (p. 6) and Annex Table 1-A. Note that totals do not add in the original BIS data. Percentages calculated by present authors.

Exhibit 4.4   Percentage of Daily Average Global Foreign Exchange Market Activity
by Major Currency Pairs, April 1992

Currency Pair	Spot	Outright forward	Swaps	Subtotal	Futures	Options	Total
$/DM	29.6	21.7	19.4	24.7	41.5	34.3	25.4
$/¥	15.7	20.4	25.0	19.9	29.9	27.9	20.2
$/£	8.5	9.4	11.5	9.8	11.1	4.1	9.5
$/Sfr	5.9	6.1	6.8	6.3	7.2	3.3	6.1
$/C$	2.0	2.9	4.9	3.3	2.9	2.7	3.2
$/A$	1.5	2.1	3.4	2.3	2.0	2.2	2.3
$/FFr	1.3	2.3	3.8	2.4	0.1	1.3	2.3
Sum	64.5	64.9	74.8	68.7	94.7	75.8	69.0
DM/£	4.9	3.1	0.7	3.0	0.1	5.8	3.1
DM/¥	3.9	3.5	0.3	2.3	0.1	6.0	2.5
DM/Sfr	2.9	1.6	0.2	1.7	0.1	2.4	1.7
Other intra-EMS currencies shown excluding DM/£	7.0	4.0	1.0	4.3	0.2	1.4	4.1
All other	16.8	23.0	23.1	20.0	4.9	8.5	19.6
All currency pairs	100.0	100.0	100.0	100.0	100.0	100.0	100.0

Source: Adapted from "Total Net Reported Foreign Exchange Turnover by Currency Pairs in April 1992: Percent of Daily Average Turnover," *Central Bank Survey of Foreign Exchange Market Activity in April 1992,* Basle, Switzerland: Bank for International Settlements, Monetary and Economics Department, March 1993, Table IIb, p. 10. Totals may not add because of rounding.

Exhibit 4.5   Net Daily Foreign Exchange Turnover, April 1992

Rank	Country	Net turnover (billions of US$)	Share (% of total)
1.	United Kingdom	300.2	26.6
2.	United States	192.3	17.0
3.	Japan	126.1	11.1
4.	Singapore	75.9	6.7
5.	Switzerland	68.1	6.0
6.	Hong Kong	60.9	5.4
7.	Germany	56.5	5.0
8.	France	35.5	3.1
9.	Australia	29.8	2.6
10.	Denmark	27.6	2.4
11.	Canada	22.5	2.0
	Fifteen other countries	134.9	12.0
	Total	$1,130.3	100.0%

Source: Extracted from "Foreign Exchange Market Transactions in April 1989 and April 1992, Total," *Central Bank Survey of Foreign Exchange Market Activity in April 1992,* Basle, Switzerland: Bank for International Settlements, Monetary and Economics Department, March 1993, Annex Table 4-B. "Net" turnover means net of local interdealer double counting.

in the world with 2% or more of world volume. The United Kingdom remains the world's major foreign exchange market with almost 27% of world volume, followed by the United States at 17% and Japan at 11%. Foreign exchange trading in Japan, Singapore, and Hong Kong each exceeds that of any European country except the United Kingdom and (except for Hong Kong) Switzerland. This reflects the rise in economic importance of Asia.

Transactions in the Interbank Market

Transactions in the foreign exchange market can be executed on a "spot," "forward," or "swap" basis. A broader definition of the foreign exchange market would include foreign currency options, which are the subject of Chapter 6. A *spot* transaction requires almost immediate delivery of foreign exchange. A *forward* transaction requires delivery of foreign exchange at some future date, either on an "outright" basis or through a "futures" contract. A *swap* transaction is the simultaneous purchase and sale of a foreign currency.

Spot Transactions

A spot transaction in the interbank market is the purchase of foreign exchange with delivery and payment between banks to take place, normally, on the second following business day. The Canadian dollar settles on the first following business day. The date of settlement is referred to as the "value date." On the value date, most dollar transactions in the world are settled through the computerized Clearing House Interbank Payments Systems (CHIPS) in New York, which provides for calculation of net balances owed by any one bank to another and for payment by 6 P.M. that same day in Federal Reserve Bank of New York funds. Spot transactions are the most important single type of transaction, constituting 47.3% of all transactions in the BIS survey (Exhibit 4.3).

A typical spot transaction in the interbank market might involve a U.S. bank contracting on a Monday for the transfer of £10,000,000 to the account of a London bank. If the spot exchange rate was $1.6984/£, the U.S. bank would transfer £10,000,000 to the London bank on Wednesday, and the London bank would transfer $16,984,000 to the U.S. bank at the same time. A spot transaction between a bank and its commercial customer would not necessarily involve a wait of two days for settlement.

Outright Forward Transactions

An outright forward transaction (usually just called "forward") requires delivery at a future value date of a specified amount of one currency for a specified amount of another currency. The exchange rate is established at the time of the agreement, but payment and delivery are not required until maturity. Forward exchange rates are normally quoted for value dates of one, two, three, six, and twelve months. Actual contracts can be arranged for other numbers of months or, on occasion, for periods of more than one year. Payment is on the second business day after the even-month anniversary of the trade. Thus a two-month forward transaction entered into on March 18 will be for a value date of May 20, or the next business day if May 20 falls on a weekend or holiday.

Note that as a matter of terminology one can speak of "buying forward" or "selling forward" to describe the same transaction. A contract to deliver dollars for guilders in six months is both "buying guilders forward for dollars" and "selling dollars forward for guilders."

Although outright forward contracts are quite important for multinational firms, they represent a relatively small proportion of the global volume of trading. According to the BIS survey (Exhibit 4.3), outright forward contracts accounted for only 7% of foreign exchange transactions.

Swap Transactions

A swap transaction in the interbank market is the simultaneous purchase and sale of a given amount of foreign exchange for two different value dates. Both purchase and sale are with the same counterparty. A common type of swap is a "spot against forward." The dealer buys a currency in the spot market and simultaneously sells the same amount back to the same bank in the forward market. Since this is executed as a single transaction with one counterparty, the dealer incurs no unexpected foreign exchange risk.

A more sophisticated transaction is called a "forward-forward" swap. A dealer sells £20,000,000 forward for dollars for delivery in, say, two months at $1.6870/£ and simultaneously buys £20,000,000 forward for delivery in three months at $1.6820/£. The difference between the buying price and the selling price is equivalent to the interest rate differential between the two currencies. Thus a swap can be viewed as a technique for borrowing another currency on a fully collateralized basis. Swap transactions are very important in the interbank market. They represented 39% of foreign exchange transactions in the BIS survey. Swap quotations are discussed in the next section.

Foreign Exchange Rates and Quotations

A foreign exchange *rate* is the price of one currency expressed in terms of another currency. A foreign exchange *quotation* (or *quote*) is a statement of willingness to buy or sell at an announced rate.

Interbank Quotations

The most common way of stating foreign exchange quotations is in terms of the number of units of foreign currency needed to buy one unit of home currency. For example, if the home currency is the U.S. dollar ($) and the foreign currency is the German mark (DM), the exchange rate between dollars and marks might be stated:

DM1.5625/$, read as "1.5625 marks per dollar."

This method, called *European terms,* expresses the rate as the foreign currency price of one dollar (the home currency). This is also called an *indirect quote*. Almost all interbank quotations around the world are stated in European terms.

The alternative method, called *American terms,* is to give the home currency price of one unit of the foreign currency. For example, continuing with our example of the

U.S. dollar as the home currency and the German mark as the foreign currency, the exchange rate between dollars and marks in American terms might be:

$$\textbf{\$0.6400/DM}, \text{ read as "0.6400 dollars per mark."}$$

This is also called a *direct quote*. American terms are normally used in the interbank market for quotations of the British pound, Australian dollar, New Zealand dollar, the Irish punt, and the ECU.[5] American terms are used in quoting rates for most foreign currency options and futures, as well as in retail markets that deal with tourists and personal remittances. Note that in all cases the reciprocal of a direct quote (American terms) is an indirect quote (European terms).

Global View
Roots of the "$" Sign

Eighteen world currencies are called "dollars": U.S. dollar, Australian dollar, Bahamian dollar, Barbados dollar, Belize dollar, Bermudian dollar, Brunei dollar, Canadian dollar, East Caribbean dollar, Guyana dollar, Hong Kong dollar, Jamaican dollar, Liberian dollar, New Taiwan dollar, New Zealand dollar, Singapore dollar, Solomon Islands dollar, and Zimbabwe dollar.

All use the "$" sign to designate their currency, as do many Latin American countries for which the symbol means "peso." The symbol itself seems to have evolved in different places from the Mexican sign "Ps" for pesos or piastres or pieces of eight. The symbol "$" was written after numerals by Spanish Americans and before numerals by English colonists before the sign was officially adopted for the United States dollar in 1785. Another version of the history is that the "$" sign evolved from a broken "8" representing the old Spanish pieces of eight or 8 reales. The two vertical bars came from the Pillars of Hercules and appeared on pieces of eight minted in Mexico City as early as 1732.

The word "dollar" itself comes from an ancient monetary unit, the *Joachimsthaler* or "thaler," minted in the Kingdom of Bohemia as early as 1516. There is no evidence for the view of some that "$" is the superimposed initials of "U" and "S" with the U's bottom loop deleted.

---

[5]The British pound is quoted as the foreign currency price of one pound for historical reasons. For centuries the British pound consisted of 20 shillings, each of which had 12 pence. Multiplication and division with this nondecimal currency was difficult, so the custom evolved for foreign exchange prices in London, then the undisputed financial capital of the world, to be stated in foreign currency units per pound. This practice remained even after sterling changed to decimals in 1971.

Foreign exchange traders often use nicknames for major currencies. "Sterling" means the British pound. "Paris" is used for the French franc, "Kiwi" for the New Zealand dollar, "Aussie" for the Australian dollar, "Swissie" for Swiss francs, and "Sing dollar" for the Singapore dollar.

Bid and Offer Quotations

Interbank quotations are given as a *bid* and *offer* (also referred to as *ask*). A bid is the price (i.e., exchange rate) in one currency at which a dealer will buy another currency. An offer is the price (i.e., exchange rate) at which a dealer will sell the other currency. Dealers bid (buy) at one price and offer (sell) at a slightly higher price, making their profit from the spread between the buying and selling prices.

Bid and offer quotations in the foreign exchange markets are superficially complicated by the fact that the bid for one currency is also the offer for the opposite currency. A trader seeking to buy dollars with marks is simultaneously offering to sell marks for dollars. Assume a bank makes the quotations shown in the top half of Exhibit 4.6 under the heading "European terms (DM/$)." The spot quotations on the first line indicate that the bank's foreign exchange trader will "buy dollars" (i.e., "sell marks") at the bid price of DM1.5625 per dollar. The trader will "sell dollars" (i.e., "buy marks") at the offer price of DM1.5635 per dollar.

The heading "outright quotations" means the full price to all of its decimal points is given. Traders, however, tend to abbreviate when talking on the phone or putting quotations on a video screen. The first term, the bid, of a spot quotation may be given in full: that is, "1.5625." However, the second term, the offer, will probably be expressed only as the digits that differ from the bid. Hence the bid and offer for spot marks would be printed "1.5625-35" on a video screen. On the telephone the trader may say "1.5625 (pause) 35," "1.5625 to 35," or simply "25 to 35," assuming the leading digits are known. The part of the quote omitted because it seldom changes is called the "big figure"; the last two digits used by themselves are called the "small figure."

Exhibit 4.6   Spot and Forward Quotations for the German Mark (DM)

	Quotations as given in interbank market		Reciprocals calculated for convenience of retail customers	
	EUROPEAN TERMS (DM/$)		AMERICAN TERMS ($/DM)	
	Bid	Offer	Bid	Offer
OUTRIGHT QUOTATIONS				
Spot	1.5625	1.5635	0.6396	0.6400
One month forward	1.5567	1.5579	0.6419	0.6424
Three months forward	1.5450	1.5466	0.6466	0.6472
Six months forward	1.5283	1.5301	0.6536	0.6543
POINTS QUOTATIONS				
One month forward	58−56			
Three months forward	175−169			
Six months forward	342−334			

When quotations in European terms are converted to American terms, bid and offer reverse: The reciprocal of the bid becomes the offer, and the reciprocal of the offer becomes the bid. In Exhibit 4.6, the reciprocal of the bid of DM1.5625/$ becomes the offer of $0.6400/DM; the reciprocal of the offer of DM1.5635/$ becomes the bid of $0.6396/DM. For a bank to make a profit, the bid must be smaller than the offer; that is, the bank (like any successful merchant) must sell its "merchandise" (foreign exchange) for more than it buys it. In the European terms quoted, the trader wants to buy one dollar for DM1.5625 and then resell it at DM1.5635, making a profit of DM0.0010 per dollar. Using reciprocals, the trader will buy one mark for $0.6396 and then resell it for $0.6400, also making a profit.

In actuality currency markets are rarely so docile that traders can expect to profit by consistently buying at their bid and selling at their offer. If a trader quotes 1.5625-35 and buys dollars at 1.5625, the dealer's next quote may be 1.5630-40 if the market is going up or 1.5610-20 if it is going down. A trader's profitability depends more on ability to time purchases and sales in each instance. Additionally, since each dealer is a market maker (that is, stands ready to buy or sell at any time for a price), a counterparty may "hit the bid" or force the dealer to buy when the dealer's preference is to sell, or the offer may be "lifted" when the dealer would prefer to buy.

Expressing Forward Quotations on a Points Basis

The spot and forward quotations given in the top half of Exhibit 4.6 are "outright": DM1.5625/$ for the spot bid and DM1.5450/$ for the six-month forward bid. Among themselves foreign exchange traders usually quote forward rates in terms of points, also referred to as "swap rates." The bottom part of Exhibit 4.6 shows forward quotations as they would be given on a points basis. A quotation in points is not a foreign exchange rate as such. Rather it is the difference between the forward rate and the spot rate. Consequently the spot rate itself cannot be given on a points basis.[6]

In the mark/dollar interbank quotations in Exhibit 4.6, the forward dollar is at a discount relative to the spot dollar. Hence points must be subtracted from the spot quotation to obtain the lower forward quotation. The six-month forward outright mark/dollar quotation is derived as follows:

	Bid	Offer
Outright spot:	1.5625	1.5635
less points	−175	−169
Outright forward:	1.5450	1.5466

---

[6]A point is the last digit of a quotation, with convention dictating the number of digits in each quotation. German marks and most other currency prices for the U.S. dollar are expressed to four decimal points. Hence a point is equal to 0.0001 of most currencies. Some currencies, such as the Japanese yen and Italian lira, are traditionally quoted only to two decimal points. The point is used in foreign exchange quotations without the decimal point or the leading zeros. A point quotation refers to the number of points away from the outright spot rate, with the first number referring to points away from the spot bid and the second number to points away from the spot offer. A slash (/) or a dash (-) is often used to separate the bid and offer point quotations on video screens or in print. A pause or the word *to* is used in voice communication.

Traders follow an operational rule that indicates whether the forward quote is at a premium or a discount. When the bid *in points* is larger than the offer *in points,* as in the mark example here, the trader knows the points should be subtracted and the forward quotation is at a discount. If the bid in points is smaller than the offer in points, the trader knows the points should be added and the forward quotation is at a premium.

A forward bid and offer quotation expressed in points is often called a *swap rate.* As we indicated earlier, many forward exchange transactions in the interbank market involve the simultaneous purchase for one date and sale (reversing the transaction) for another date. This "swap" is a way to borrow one currency for a limited time while giving up the use of another currency for the same time; that is, it is a short-term borrowing of one currency combined with a short-term loan of an equivalent amount of another currency. The two parties could, if they wanted, charge each other interest at the going rate for each of the currencies. However it is easier for the party with the higher interest currency to simply pay the *net* interest differential to the other. The swap rate expresses this net interest differential on a points basis rather than as an interest rate. A points quotation and an interest rate differential are equivalent, as we explain in Chapter 5.

Forward Quotations in Percentage Terms

Forward quotations are sometimes expressed in terms of the percent-per-annum deviation from the spot rate. This method of quotation facilitates comparing premiums or discounts in the forward market with interest rate differentials.

With Indirect Quotes. When the foreign currency is quoted on an indirect basis, the formula for the percent-per-annum premium or discount is:

$$\text{Forward premium or discount} = \frac{\text{Spot} - \text{Forward}}{\text{Forward}} \times \frac{360}{n} \times 100,$$

where n = the number of days in the contract (n may also be the number of months, in which case the numerator is 12).

Assume the following quotations where the dollar is the home currency:

	Indirect quote	Direct quote
Spot rate	¥105.65/$	$0.009465215/¥
3-month forward	¥105.04/$	$0.009520183/¥

When n equals the number of days, the annualized three-month forward premium/discount on the yen ($f^\yen$) from a dollar perspective is then calculated as follows:

$$f^\yen = \frac{(S - F_n)}{F_n} \times \frac{360}{n} \times 100.$$

Substituting indirect spot and forward rates, as well as the number of days forward (90),

$$f^Y = \frac{105.65 - 105.04}{105.04} \times \frac{360}{90} \times 100 \approx +2.32\%.$$

The value is positive, signifying the forward yen is selling at a premium relative to the dollar.

With Direct Quotes. When using direct quotes, the formula becomes:

$$\text{Forward premium or discount} = \frac{\text{Forward} - \text{Spot}}{\text{Spot}} \times \frac{360}{n} \times 100.$$

The annualized three-month forward premium on the yen (f^Y) using direct quotes is calculated as follows:

$$f^Y = \frac{(F_n - S)}{S} \times \frac{360}{n} \times 100$$

Substituting the direct spot and forward rates, as well as the number of days forward (90),

$$f^Y = \frac{0.009520183 - 0.009465215}{0.009465215} \times \frac{360}{90} \times 100 \approx +2.32\%.$$

The premium value is positive, again signifying the forward yen is selling at a premium relative to the dollar.

Reading Newspaper Quotations

Foreign exchange rates are quoted in all major world newspapers. The manner of quotation in the *Wall Street Journal* and the *Financial Times,* the world's two major English-language business newspapers, is shown in Exhibit 4.7 for the U.K. pound sterling. Although these quotes are for the same day, they are not identical because of time zone differences.

Exhibit 4.7 U.S. Dollar/British Pound Foreign Exchange Newspaper Quotations

- *Wall Street Journal:* "EXCHANGE RATES"

	U.S.$ equiv.		Currency per U.S.$	
	Fri.	*Thur.*	*Fri.*	*Thur.*
Britain (Pound)	1.4845	1.4800	.6736	.6757
30-day forward	1.4812	1.4767	.6751	.6772
90-day forward	1.4764	1.4718	.6773	.6794
180-day forward	1.4702	1.4653	.6802	.6825

- *Financial Times:* "POUND SPOT - FORWARD AGAINST THE POUND"

Nov 5	*Day's Spread*	*Close (bid-offer)*	*One Month*	*% p.a.*	*Three Months*	*% p.a.*
US	1.4740-1.4875	1.4860-1.4870	0.33-0.32 cmp	2.62	0.82-9.80 pm	2.18

Sources: "Exchange Rates," 11/8/93, p. C14. Reprinted by permission of *The Wall Street Journal,* © 1993 Dow Jones & Co., Inc. All rights reserved worldwide.

"Exchange Rate Quotations," *Financial Times,* 11/8/93. Financial Times copyright.

The *Wall Street Journal* gives American terms quotes under the heading "U.S.$ equiv." and European terms quotes under the heading "Currency per U.S.$." Quotes are for the last two trading days, and are given on an outright basis for spot, one-, three-, and six-month forwards. The heading of the table states that quotes are "selling rates," that is, offer rates. Bid rates are not given. Quotes are for trading among banks in amounts of $1 million or more, as quoted at 3 P.M. Eastern Time by Bankers Trust Company, Telerate, and other sources. The *Journal* states that retail transactions provide fewer units of foreign currency per dollar.

The *Financial Times* presents the latest day's spread and closing bid and offer quotes in its first two columns. One-month and three-month forward quotes are expressed in terms of points rather than on an outright basis, and forward quotes are also expressed in terms of the percent-per-annum deviation from the spot rate. For the U.S. dollar only (but not for other currencies), the 6-month and 12-month forward quotes are given in a footnote.[7]

Cross Rates

Many currency pairs are only inactively traded, so their exchange rate is determined through their relationship to a widely traded third currency. For example, an Australian importer needs Danish currency to pay for purchases in Copenhagen. The Australian dollar (symbol A$) is not quoted against the Danish krone (symbol DKr). However, both currencies are quoted against the U.S. dollar. Assume the following quotes:

Australian dollar	A$1.3806/US$
Danish kroner	DKr6.4680/US$

The Australian importer can buy one U.S. dollar for A$1.3806, and with that dollar buy DKr6.4680. The cross-rate calculation would be

$$\frac{\text{Australian dollar/U.S. dollar}}{\text{Danish kroner/U.S. dollar}} = \frac{\text{A\$1.3806/US\$}}{\text{DKr6.4680/US\$}} = \text{A\$0.2135/DKr.}$$

---

[7]The outright one-month forward bid and ask quotes can be determined from the *Financial Times*'s quotations as follows:

	Bid	Offer
Spot rate (given)	1.4860	1.4870
One month (in points)	−.0033	−.0032
Forward rate	1.4827	1.4838

Because the U.S. dollar is selling forward at a premium ("cpm" is "cents premium"), the forward points are subtracted from the U.S. dollar per pound spot rate to calculate the one-month forward bid and offer outright rates. The resulting one-month forward rate indicates a "stronger" forward U.S. dollar relative to the British pound (requiring fewer dollars per pound). The percent-per-annum (% p.a.) premium on the dollar-per-pound forward rate is calculated from the annualized *average* of the forward points over the initial spot rates:

$$\text{Premium} = \frac{\left[\dfrac{0.0033 + .0032}{2}\right]}{\left[\dfrac{1.4860 + 1.4870}{2}\right]} \times \frac{360 \text{ days}}{30 \text{ days}} \times 100 = +2.62\%.$$

The cross rate could also be calculated as the reciprocal:

$$\frac{\text{Danish kroner/U.S. dollar}}{\text{Australian dollars/U.S. dollar}} = \frac{\text{DKr6.4680/US\$}}{\text{A\$1.3806/US\$}} = \text{DKr4.6849/A\$}.$$

Cross rates are also used by businesses to validate the internal consistency of their separate foreign exchange forecasts. A mark/dollar exchange rate forecast for next year by a firm's German staff may be divided by a franc/dollar forecast by the French staff to see whether the cross rate is reasonable. Such cross checking is important for maintaining consistency across foreign affiliates when drawing up corporatewide performance budgets or setting interaffiliate transfer prices.

Intermarket Arbitrage

Cross rates can be used to check on opportunities for intermarket arbitrage. Suppose the following exchange rates are available:

Dutch guilders (symbol *fl*) per U.S. dollar	*fl*1.9025/US\$
Canadian dollars per U.S. dollar	C\$1.2646/US\$
Dutch guilders per Canadian dollar	*fl*1.5214/C\$

The cross rate between Dutch guilders and Canadian dollars is:

$$\frac{\text{Dutch guilders/U.S. dollar}}{\text{Canadian dollars/U.S. dollar}} = \frac{fl1.9025/\text{US\$}}{\text{C\$}1.2646/\text{US\$}} = fl1.5044/\text{C\$}.$$

However, the cross rate is not the same as the actual quotation of *fl*1.5214/C\$. An opportunity for profit from arbitrage between these three markets (triangular arbitrage) exists. Exhibit 4.8 shows the steps.

A Dutch trader with *fl*1,000,000 can sell that sum in the spot market for US\$525,624. Simultaneously that trader can sell the U.S. dollars for C\$664,704 and exchange the Canadian dollars for *fl*1,011,281, making a risk-free profit of *fl*11,281, before transaction costs, on one "turn." Such intermarket arbitrage should continue until exchange rate equilibrium is reestablished, that is, until the calculated cross rate equals the actual quotation, less a margin for transaction costs.

Measuring a Change in Spot Exchange Rates

Assume the German mark, recently quoted at DM1.5625/\$, suddenly strengthens to DM1.2800/\$. What is the percentage increase in the dollar value of the mark, and thus in the value of mark-denominated accounts receivable or payable from a dollar perspective? The quotation form (direct or indirect) is important when calculating this change.

With Indirect Quotes. The following formula expresses the change in the spot value of the mark from a U.S. dollar perspective:

$$\text{Percentage change} = \frac{\text{beginning rate} - \text{ending rate}}{\text{ending rate}} \times 100$$

$$= \frac{\text{DM1.5625/\$} - \text{DM1.2800/\$}}{\text{DM1.2800/\$}} \times 100 = +22.07\%.$$

Exhibit 4.8   Intermarket Triangular Arbitrage

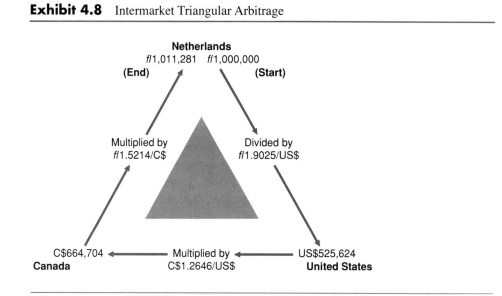

With Direct Quotes. If direct exchange rates are used, the formula changes. Using the same exchange rates, but in this case their reciprocals ($0.6400/DM instead of DM1.5625/$ and $0.78125/DM instead of DM1.2800/$), the formula for the percentage change is as follows:

$$\text{Percentage change} = \frac{\text{ending rate} - \text{beginning rate}}{\text{beginning rate}} \times 100$$

$$= \frac{\$0.78125/\text{DM} - \$0.6400/\text{DM}}{\$0.6400/\text{DM}} \times 100 = +22.07\%.$$

Summary

- Geographically the foreign exchange market spans the globe, with prices moving and currencies traded somewhere every hour of every business day.
- The three functions of the foreign exchange market are to transfer purchasing power, provide credit, and minimize foreign exchange risk.
- The foreign exchange market is composed of two tiers: the interbank market and the client market. Participants within these tiers include bank and nonbank foreign

exchange dealers, individuals and firms conducting commercial and investment transactions, speculators and arbitragers, central banks and treasuries, and foreign exchange brokers.

■   Transactions within the foreign exchange market are executed either on a spot basis, requiring settlement two days after the transaction, or on a forward or swap basis, which requires settlement at some designated future date.

■   A foreign exchange rate is the price of one currency expressed in terms of another currency. A foreign exchange quotation is a statement of willingness to buy or sell currency at an announced rate.

■   European terms, or indirect quotes, are quotations in terms of number of units of a foreign currency needed to buy one unit of the home currency. American terms, or direct quotes, are the number of units of the home currency needed to buy one unit of a foreign currency.

■   Forward quotations may be stated on an outright basis, on a points basis, or as an annual percentage deviation from the spot rate.

■   A cross rate is an exchange rate between two currencies, calculated from their common relationship with a third currency. When cross rates differ from the direct rates between two currencies, intermarket arbitrage is possible.

Questions

1. Luxembourg Franc

The spot Luxembourg franc is quoted against the U.S. dollar in "European terms" in the *Financial Times* as follows:

Bid: LF36.4210   Offer: LF36.5800

   a.   What is the closing mid-point quotation?
   b.   What are the outright bid and ask rates on a direct basis (i.e., "American terms")?

2. Spot and Forward Market Sizes

According to the survey data reported in Exhibit 4.2, which currency market has the largest percentage of its activity in *outright forwards* (besides the "others" category)? Which currencies seem to be the subject of a lot of currency *swaps* activity?

3. Cross Rates and Percentage Change

   a.   What is the percentage change in the value of the Deutschemark if the spot rate moves from ¥77.37/DM to ¥64.97/DM over six months?
   b.   What is the percentage change annualized?

c. What is the percentage change in the value of the Japanese yen over this six-month period, in percent per annum?

4. Computer Trading Screen: Spot Currency Quotations

The quotation screen in a foreign exchange trader's office shows the following spot rates for the U.S. dollar:

Reuters   *Friday, 25 February 1994*

RIC	Latest Spots Bid/Ask	Contributor	Loc	Srce	Deal	Time	High	Low
DEM = ↓	1.7085/95	CITIBANK	NYC	CINY	CITN*D	20:00	1.7206	1.7027
JPY = ↓	104.65/4.75	LTCB	NYC	JYAA	LTNY*J	20:01	105.30	104.30
GBP = ↑	1.4885/95	ROYAL BK CAN	TOR	RBCT	RBCM*G	19:58	1.4935	1.4788
CHF = ↓	1.4265/72	BK MONTREAL	TOR	BMMA	BMMA*C	20:00	1.4375	1.4222
CAD = ↑	1.3509/14	CITIBANK	NYC	CINY	CITN*R	19:59	1.3525	1.3411
AUD = ↓	0.7185/90	NAB	NYC	NABN	NABN*T	20:01	0.7246	0.7188
NZD = ↓	0.5768/75	NAB	NYC	NABN	NABN*W	19:42	0.5785	0.5768
FRF = ↓	5.7985/15	SOC GENERALE	NYC	SGNY	SOGN*F	19:51	5.8470	5.7885

a. If the latest quote on the DEM is lower than previous quotes, is the DEM appreciating or depreciating versus the U.S. dollar?

b. What is the percentage range of movement of the high and low of the Japanese yen?

c. Which of the currency quotations are direct on the dollar and which indirect?

5. Forward Rates on the Australian Dollar

Using the following forward rates on the U.S. dollar/Australian dollar cross, and the present spot rate of US$0.7152/A$, answer the following questions.

Maturity	US$/A$	Maturity	US$/A$
1 month	.7144	6 months	.7107
3 months	.7128	12 months	.7152

a. Is the Australian dollar selling forward at a *premium* or a *discount?*

b. What is the 90-day forward premium on the Australian dollar?

c. What is the 180-day forward premium on the Australian dollar?

d. What would the 270-day forward rate be if the 270-day Eurocurrency deposit rates for U.S. dollars and Australian dollars are 3.5000% and 4.2500% per annum?

6. Eurocurrency Interest Rates and Forward Rates (CO4A.WK1)

Use the following spot rates and Eurocurrency deposit rates pulled from the computer quotation screen in your office to answer the following questions.

Eurocurrency deposit rates (percent per annum)

Maturity	U.S. dollar	Canadian dollar	French franc	Japanese yen	Swiss franc
1 month	3.1875	3.5625	6.4063	2.2500	4.1875
3 months	3.3750	3.6875	6.2813	2.1875	4.0000
6 months	3.5625	3.6875	6.0313	2.1250	3.8750
12 months	3.8125	3.9375	5.6563	2.0938	3.6250
Spot rate	—	C$1.3290/$	FF5.8855/$	¥108.20/$	SF1.4470/$

a. Calculate the 90-day forward rate for the C$/$.
b. Calculate the 180-day forward rate for the C$/$.
c. Calculate the 360-day FF/C$ forward rate.
d. Calculate the 180-day SF/FF forward rate.
e. Calculate the 90-day ¥/SF forward rate.

7. Currency Cross Rates

Using the *bid* spot currency quotes shown in number 4, answer the following questions:

a. What is the current spot rate for JPY/DEM?
b. What is the current spot rate for JPY/CHF?
c. What is the current spot rate for AUD/NZD?

Bibliography

Agénor, Pierre-Richard, *Parallel Currency Markets in Developing Countries: Theory, Evidence, and Policy Implications,* Essays in International Finance, no. 188, Princeton: International Financial Section, Department of Economics, 1992.

Braas, Alberic, and Charles N. Bralver, "An Analysis of Trading Profits: How Most Trading Rooms Really Make Money," *Journal of Applied Corporate Finance,* Winter 1990, pp. 85–90.

Byler, Ezra U., and James C. Baker, "S.W.I.F.T.: A Fast Method to Facilitate International Financial Transactions," *Journal of World Trade Law,* September-October 1983, pp. 458–465.

Coninx, Raymond G.F., *Foreign Exchange Dealer's Handbook,* 2nd ed., Homewood, IL: Dow Jones-Irwin, 1986.

Glassman, Debra, "Exchange Rate Risk and Transactions Costs: Evidence from Bid-Ask Spreads," *Journal of International Money and Finance,* vol. 6, no. 4, December 1987, pp. 479–491.

Goodhart, Charles A.E., and Thomas Hesse, "Central Bank Forex Intervention Assessed in Continuous Time," *Journal of International Securities Markets,* August 1993, pp. 368–389.

Gregory, Ian, and Philip Moore, "Foreign Exchange Dealing," *Corporate Finance,* October 1986, pp. 33–46.

Gupta, Sanjeev, "A Note on the Efficiency of Black Markets in Foreign Currencies," *Journal of Finance,* June 1981, pp. 705–710.

Jacque, Laurent L., "Management of Foreign Exchange Risk: A Review Article," *Journal of International Business Studies,* Spring/Summer 1981, pp. 81–101.

Kubarych, Roger M., *Foreign Exchange Markets in the United States,* rev. ed., New York: Federal Reserve Bank of New York, 1983.

Murphy, John J., *Intermarket Technical Analysis: Trading Strategies for the Global Stock, Bond, Commodity, and Currency Markets*, New York: Wiley, 1991.

Remmers, H. L., FORAD: *International Financial Management Simulation* (Players' Manual, Release 2.4), Fontainebleau, France: INSEAD, 1990.

Sweeney, Richard J., "Beating the Foreign Exchange Market," *Journal of Finance*, March 1986, pp. 163–182.

Sweeney, Richard J., and Edward J.Q. Lee, "Trading Strategies in Forward Exchange Markets," *Advances in Financial Planning and Forecasting*, vol. 4, 1990, pp. 55–80.

Chapter 4 Appendix
Foreign Currency Futures

A foreign currency futures contract is an exchange-traded agreement calling for future delivery of a standard amount of foreign exchange at a fixed time, place, and price. It is similar to futures contracts that exist for commodities (hogs, cattle, lumber, etc.), for interest-bearing deposits, and for gold. As shown in Exhibit 4.3, futures account for 1.1% of global foreign exchange activity.

In the United States the most important market for foreign currency futures is the International Monetary Market (IMM) of Chicago, a division of the Chicago Mercantile Exchange. Contracts traded on the IMM are interchangeable with those traded on the Singapore International Monetary Exchange (SIMEX). Most major money centers have established foreign currency futures markets during the past decade.

Contract Specifications

Contract specifications are defined by the exchange on which they are traded. Using the IMM as an example, the major features that must be standardized are the following:

A specific-sized contract. A German mark contract is for DM125,000. Consequently trading can be done only in multiples of DM125,000.

A standard method of stating exchange rates. "American terms" are used; that is, quotations are the dollar cost of foreign currency units.

A standard maturity date. Contracts mature on the third Wednesday of January, March, April, June, July, September, October, or December. However, not all of these maturities are available for all currencies at any given time. "Spot month" contracts are also traded. These are not spot contracts as that term is used in the interbank foreign exchange market, but are rather short-term futures contracts that mature on the next following third Wednesday, that is, on the next following standard maturity date.

A specified last trading day. Contracts may be traded through the second business day prior to the Wednesday on which they mature. Therefore, unless holidays interfere, the last trading day is the Monday preceding the maturity date.

Collateral. The purchaser must deposit a sum as an initial margin or collateral. This is similar to requiring a performance bond and can be met by a letter of credit from a bank, Treasury bills, or cash. In addition, a maintenance margin is required. The value of the contract is marked to market daily, and all changes in value are paid in cash daily. The amount to be paid is called the variation margin.

Settlement. Only about 5% of all futures contracts are settled by the physical delivery of foreign exchange between buyer and seller. Most often, buyers and sellers offset their original position prior to delivery date by taking an opposite position. That is, if one had bought a futures contract, that position would be closed out by selling a futures contract for the same delivery date. The complete buy/sell or sell/buy is called a "round turn."

Commissions. Customers pay a commission to their broker to execute a round turn and only a single price is quoted. This practice differs from that of the interbank market, where dealers quote a bid and an offer and do not charge a commission.

Clearinghouse a counterparty. All contracts are agreements between the client and the exchange clearinghouse, rather than between the two clients involved. Consequently clients need not worry that a specific counterparty in the market will fail to honor an agreement.

IMM futures contracts are available in nine currencies, as well as in gold, 90-day U.S. Treasury bills, and Eurodollar time deposits.

Reading Newspaper Quotations

Futures trading on the IMM in German marks is reported in the world's newspapers as in Exhibit 4.9. The first line under the headings indicates that German marks were traded in contracts of DM125,000 each at the dollar-per-mark prices shown in the table.

The next three lines deal with contracts that expire in September and December of 1993 and March of 1994. These are the only maturities for mark contracts being traded.

September contracts, meaning contracts that expire on the third Wednesday in September, opened trading on Tuesday at $0.5967/DM. The highest trading price during the day was $0.5986/DM and the lowest trading price was $0.5937/DM. "Settle" refers to settlement price, the daily closing price that is used by the IMM Exchange Clearing House to determine margin calls and invoice prices for deliveries. Thus the last trade for September contracts during the day was $0.5956/DM. "Change" is the difference between today's and the prior day's settlement price. "Lifetime high and low" refers to the highest and lowest prices at which a contract has traded since its introduction. The September contract has traded as high as $0.6720 and as low as $0.5702.

The "open interest" for September contracts is 129,734 contracts. Open interest is the sum of all long (buying futures) and short (selling futures) contracts outstanding. Multiplying 129,734 by the current spot price (not shown in the table) of $0.6700 per mark suggests the market value of outstanding September contracts was approximately

Exhibit 4.9   Foreign Currency Futures Quotations

	Open	High	Low	Settle	Change	Lifetime High	Lifetime Low	Open Interest
W. GERMAN MARK (CME)—125,000 marks; $ per mark								
Sep	.5967	.5986	.5937	.5956	−.0020	.6720	.5702	129,734
Dec	.5930	.5936	.5888	.5907	−.0020	.6650	.5657	12,669
Mr94	.5872	.5872	.5857	.5871	−.0019	.6200	.5646	266
Est vol 44,056; vol Mon 32,551; open int 142,669, −3,444.								

Source: *Wall Street Journal,* Wednesday, September 1, 1993.

$129,734 \times DM125,000 \times 0.6700 = \$10,865,222,500$. The open interest can be used by clients to judge ability to execute a large order. If the order were, say, 5% of the open interest, execution might be possible without a significant change in price. But if the order were, say, 25% of the open interest, execution at prices near current prices might be difficult.

The first number on the last line reports that trading volume for Tuesday was 44,056 contracts, as compared with Monday's 32,551 contracts. The open interest on Tuesday was 142,669 contracts, some 3,444 less than open interest for Monday. Tuesday's open interest can be determined by adding the three volumes shown in the open interest column: $129,734 + 12,669 + 266 = 142,669$.

Foreign Currency Futures Versus Forward Contracts

Foreign currency futures contracts differ from forward contracts in a number of important ways. Exhibit 4.10 provides a comparison of the major features and characteristics of the two instruments. As a general matter, businesses have not found futures a particularly useful device for hedging risks. In part this is because of the constraint of fixed contract sizes and maturities, and in part it is because of the requirement for a margin deposit that must be marked to market every single day, which means either the possibility of an uncertain cash outflow every day or the maintenance of an extra cash deposit with the dealer.

Exhibit 4.10   Comparison of Foreign Currency Futures and Forward Contracts

Characteristic	Foreign currency futures	Forward contracts
Size of Contract	standardized contracts per currency	any size desired
Maturity	fixed maturities, the longest being typically less than one year	any maturity up to one year, sometimes longer
Location	trading occurs on the floor of an organized exchange	trading occurs between individuals and banks with other banks by telecommunications linkages
Pricing	open outcry process in the "pit" by floor traders	prices are arrived at by bid and offer quotes
Collateral	initial margin that is marked to market value on a daily basis	no explicit collateral, but standing bank "relations" necessary
Settlement	rarely delivered upon; settlement normally takes place through the purchase of an offsetting position	the contract is normally delivered upon, although the taking of offsetting positions possible
Commissions	single commission covers both purchase and later sale (round trip)	commissions gained through the bid-offer spreads provided to retail customers
Trading Hours	traditionally traded during exchange hours; several exchanges are now moving to automated 24-hour-a-day trading	negotiated by phone 24 hours a day through bank global networks
Counterparties	unknown to each other due to the auction market structure	parties are in direct contact in setting forward specifications
Liquidity	liquid but relatively small in total sales volume and value	liquid and relatively large in sales volume compared to that of futures contracts

Chapter 5
International Parity Conditions

Global View
Forecasting: In Trends We Trust

In a lecture to bankers and academics in London last month, Bank of England governor Robin Leigh-Pemberton admitted what the market already knew. He told his illustrious audience that there was little if anything that one central bank acting alone can do to influence the foreign exchange markets. Besides providing a short-term breathing space for interest rates the governor said candidly that for any intervention to be at all effective it would have to be "very large indeed." Reaction to his speech was that it was one of the most significant statements to come out of Threadneedle Street for some time.

For the practitioners it was open recognition of what really moves markets: the weight of money and emotion, not the arrogance of politicians or the divine will of central bankers. It is for this reason that talk of target zones and exchange rate bands is a pure chimera, way beyond the resources or will of finance ministers. Even the mighty and aloof Bundesbank will admit in private conversation with its fellow European central bankers the truth of this position.

Certainly the growing band of those who make a living out of second-guessing the market, the foreign exchange forecasters, have always known that the emperor had no clothes. Said leading chartist Brian Marbour, "At the Plaza meeting in September 1985 central bankers and the G5 states (UK, France, Japan, US, West Germany) were very arrogant about their ability to hold sway over the market and in particular the dollar. I sent my clients a telex before the meeting to close all long positions in the dollar. We did not need a Plaza statement; the dollar was going down anyway. What difference will $10 billion of intervention do in a $300 billion-a-day market?"

For Marbour, whose clients are charged some $25,000 a year, the fundamentalist approach ignores the simple laws of supply and demand; for the chartist the figure on the Reuter or Telerate screen represents at any given moment the whole sum of human knowledge. Technical analysis, he says, assesses the psychology of the market in a way that the economists do not. There is, he says with a conviction bordering on the dogmatic, no such thing as value in the market; it is only a perception of value. Likewise it is not the news itself but how the market reacts to the news. Marbour likes to quote George Bernard Shaw: "Foreign exchange movements are like Saturday afternoons, which although occurring at regular intervals, always catch Baker Street station by surprise."

Nobody will be quoted referring to the foreign exchange market as a game of poker but they nearly all talk in terms of busted flushes and buying into an inside straight. But it was Winston Churchill who put his finger on the casino-like mentality and bravado of the foreign exchange markets when, still in the heady days of Bretton Woods, he said: *There is no sphere of human thought in which it is easier to show superficial cleverness and the appearance of superior wisdom than discussing questions of currency and exchange.*

Source: Adapted from "Forecasting: In Trends We Trust," *The Banker*, June 1987, pp. 83–84.

Are changes in exchange rates predictable? How are exchange rates related to interest rates? How does inflation affect exchange rates? What, at least theoretically, is the "proper" exchange rate? These are only a few of the fundamental issues that managers of multinational firms, international investors, importers and exporters, and government officials must deal with every day.

Our approach to answering these questions and more is first to describe the economic fundamentals of international finance, known as *parity conditions*. We then discuss the forecasting needs of multinational firms and investors. We conclude with a discussion of the various approaches to forecasting in practice, including the balance of payments approach, the asset market approach, and technical analysis.

Parity Conditions

Since the present international monetary system is characterized by a mix of freely floating, managed floating, and fixed exchange rates, no single general theory is available to forecast exchange rates under all conditions. Nevertheless, there are certain basic economic relationships, called parity conditions, which help to explain exchange rate movements.

Under a freely floating exchange rate system, future spot exchange rates are theoretically determined by the interplay of differing national rates of inflation, interest rates, and the forward premium or discount on each currency. The following sections explain the theoretical linkages between prices, exchange rates, interest rates, and forward rates. These relationships form the heart of international financial theory.

Prices and Exchange Rates

If the identical product or service can be sold in two different markets, and no restrictions exist on the sale or transportation costs of moving the product between markets, the product's price should be the same in both markets. This is called the *law of one price*. A primary principle of competitive markets is that prices will equalize across markets if frictions or costs of moving the products or services between markets do not exist. If the two markets are two different countries, the product's price may be stated in different currency terms, but the price of the product should still be the same. Comparison of prices would only require a conversion from one currency to the other. For example,

$$P^\$ \times S = P^¥$$

where the price of the product in U.S. dollars ($P^\$$), multiplied by the spot exchange rate (S, yen per U.S. dollar), equals the price of the product in Japanese yen ($P^¥$). Conversely, if the prices of the two products were stated in local currencies, and markets were efficient at competing away a higher price in one market relative to the other, the exchange rate could be deduced from the relative local product prices:

$$S = \frac{P^¥}{P^\$}.$$

Purchasing Power Parity and the Law of One Price

If the law of one price were true for all goods and services, the *purchasing power parity* (PPP) exchange rate could be found from any individual set of prices. By comparing the prices of identical products denominated in different currencies, one could determine the "real" or PPP exchange rate that should exist if markets were efficient.

The "hamburger standard," as it has been christened by *The Economist* (Exhibit 5.1), is a prime example of this law of one price. Assuming the Big Mac is indeed identical in all countries listed, it serves as one form of comparison of whether currencies are currently trading at market rates that are close to the exchange rate implied by Big Macs in local currencies. For example, a Big Mac in Sweden costs SKr25.50; the same Big Mac in the United States is $2.28. This implies a purchasing power parity exchange rate of:

$$\frac{SKr25.50}{\$2.28} = SKr11.18/\$.$$

However, on the date of the survey, the actual exchange rate was SKr7.43/$. Therefore the Swedish kronor is overvalued by:

$$\frac{\$11.18}{\$7.43} = 1.50, \text{ or } 50\%.$$

A less extreme form of this principle would be that in relatively efficient markets the price of a basket of goods would be the same in each market. This simply requires the replacement of the individual product's price with that of a price index. The PPP

Exhibit 5.1   The Law of One Price: The Big Mac Hamburger Standard

Country	(1) Big Mac Price in local currency	(2) Actual exchange rate 4/5/94	(3) Big Mac Prices in dollars	(4) Implied PPP of the dollar	(5) Local currency under(−)/over(+) valuation
United States	$2.30	—	2.30	—	—
Argentina	Peso 3.60	1.00	3.60	1.57	+57
Australia	A$ 2.45	1.42	1.72	1.07	−25
Austria	Sch 34.00	12.0	2.84	14.8	+23
Belgium	BFr 109	35.2	3.10	47.39	+35
Brazil	Cr 1,500	949	1.58	652	−31
Britain	£ 1.81	1.46	2.65	1.27	+15
Canada	C$ 2.86	1.39	2.06	1.24	−10
Chile	Peso 948	414	2.28	412	−1
China	Yuan 9.00	8.70	1.03	3.91	−55
Czech Rep	CKr 50	29.7	1.71	21.7	−27
Denmark	DKr 25.75	6.69	3.85	11.2	+67
France	FFr 18.50	5.83	3.17	8.04	+38
Germany	DM 4.60	1.71	2.69	2.00	+17
Greece	Dr 620	251	2.47	270	+8
Holland	Fl 5.45	1.91	2.85	2.37	+24
Hong Kong	HK$ 9.20	7.73	1.19	4.00	−48
Hungary	Forint 169	103	1.66	73.48	−29
Italy	Lire 4,550	1,641	2.77	1,978	+21
Japan	¥ 391	104	3.77	170	+64
Malaysia	M$ 3.77	2.69	1.40	1.64	−39
Mexico	Peso 8.10	3.36	2.41	3.52	+5
Poland	Zloty 31,000	22,433	1.40	13,478	−40
Portugal	Esc 440	174	2.53	191	+10
Russia	Rouble 2,900	1,775	1.66	1,261	−29
Singapore	$ 2.98	1.57	1.90	1.30	−17
S. Korea	Won 2,300	810	2.84	1,000	+24
Spain	Ptas 345	138	2.50	150	+9
Sweden	SKr 25.50	7.97	3.20	11.1	+39
Switzerland	SwFr 5.70	1.44	3.96	2.48	+72
Taiwan	NT$ 62	26.4	2.35	26.96	+2
Thailand	Baht 48	25.3	1.90	20.87	−17

Source: Adapted from "Big MacCurrencies," *The Economist,* April 9, 1994, p. 88. Original quotations courtesy of McDonald's. United States Big Mac price is the average of New York, Chicago, San Francisco, and Atlanta. British exchange rate and implied PPP rates quoted in U.S. dollar per pound.

Column (1): Prices in local currency; may vary by location.
Column (2): Actual exchange rate on April 5, 1994 (London quotes).
Column (3): column (1) ÷ column (2)
Column (4): column (1) ÷ $2.3028 (price of Big Mac in United States).
Column (5): column (4) ÷ column (2)

exchange rate between the two countries would then be stated:

$$S = \frac{PI^{¥}}{PI^{\$}}$$

where $PI^{¥}$ and $PI^{\$}$ are price indices expressed in local currency for Japan and the United States, respectively. For example, if the identical basket of goods cost ¥1000 in Japan and $10 in the United States, the PPP exchange rate would be:

$$\frac{¥1000}{\$10} = ¥100/\$.$$

This is the *absolute version of the theory of purchasing power parity. Absolute PPP states that the spot exchange rate is determined by the relative prices of similar baskets of goods.*

Relative Purchasing Power Parity

If the assumptions of the absolute version of PPP theory are relaxed a bit more, we observe what is termed *relative purchasing power parity*. This more general idea is that PPP is not particularly helpful in determining what the spot rate is today, but that the relative change in prices between two countries over a period of time determines the change in the exchange rate over that period. More specifically, *if the spot exchange rate between two countries starts in equilibrium, any change in the differential rate of inflation between them tends to be offset over the long run by an equal but opposite change in the spot exchange rate.*

Exhibit 5.2 shows a general case of relative PPP. The vertical axis shows the per-

Exhibit 5.2   Purchasing Power Parity

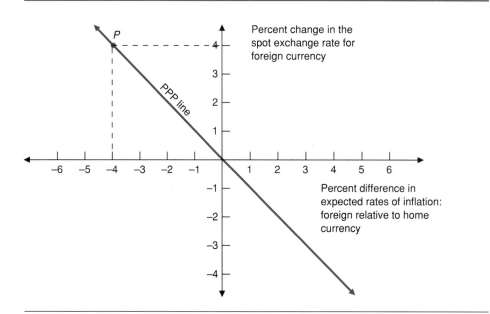

centage appreciation or depreciation of the foreign currency relative to the home currency, and the horizontal axis shows the percentage higher or lower rate of inflation in the foreign country relative to the home country. The diagonal parity line shows the equilibrium position between a change in the exchange rate and relative inflation rates. For instance, point P represents an equilibrium point where inflation in the foreign country, say Japan, is 4% lower than in the home country, say the United States. Therefore, relative PPP would predict the yen would appreciate by 4% per annum with respect to the U.S. dollar.

The main justification for purchasing power parity is that if a country experiences inflation rates higher than those of its main trading partners, and its exchange rate does not change, its exports of goods and services will become less competitive with comparable products produced elsewhere. Imports from abroad will also become more price competitive with higher priced domestic products.

Empirical Tests of Purchasing Power Parity

Extensive testing of both the absolute and relative versions of purchasing power parity and the law of one price has been done.[1] The tests have, for the most part, not proved PPP is accurate in predicting future exchange rates. Goods and services do not in reality move at zero cost between countries, and in fact many goods are not "tradeable," for example haircuts. Many goods and services are not the same quality across countries, reflecting the differences in tastes and resources of the countries of their manufacture and consumption.

Two general conclusions can be made from these tests: (1) PPP holds up well over the very long run but poorly for shorter time periods; (2) the theory holds better for countries with relatively high rates of inflation and underdeveloped capital markets.[2] On the other hand, several problems do exist with these tests.

---

[1]See, for example, Lawrence H. Officer, "The Purchasing-Power-Parity Theory of Exchange Rates: A Review Article," *International Monetary Fund Staff Papers,* March 1976, pp. 1–60. Also see Richard J. Rogalski and Joseph D. Vinso, "Price Level Variations as Predictors of Flexible Exchange Rates," *Journal of International Business Studies,* Spring/Summer 1977, pp. 71–81; Stephen P. Magee, "Contracting and Spurious Deviations from Purchasing Power Parity," in Jacob A. Frenkel and Harry G. Johnson, eds., *The Economics of Exchange Rates,* Reading, Mass.: Addison-Wesley, 1978, pp. 67–74; Lawrence Officer, Edward I. Altman, and Ingo Walter, eds., *Purchasing Power Parity and Exchange Rates: Theory, Evidence, and Relevance,* Contemporary Studies in Economic and Financial Analysis, vol. 35, London: JAI Press, 1982. Barry K. Goodwin, Thomas Grennes, and Michael K. Wohlgenant, "Testing the Law of One Price When Trade Takes Time," *Journal of International Money and Finance,* March 1990, pp. 21–40.

[2]For studies on the validity of PPP in the long run see Jacob Frenkel, "Purchasing Power Parity: Doctrinal Perspective and Evidence from the 1920s," *Journal of International Economics,* May 1978, pp. 169–191; and Michael R. Darby, "Movements in Purchasing Power Parity: The Short and Long Runs," in Michael R. Darby and James R. Lothian, eds., *The International Transmission of Inflation,* 1983. Two of the best studies questioning the validity of PPP in the long run are that of Mark Rush and Steven Husted, "Purchasing Power Parity in the Long Run," *Canadian Journal of Economics,* February 1985, pp. 137–145; and Meher Manzur, "An International Comparison of Prices and Exchanges Rates: A New Test of Purchasing Power Parity," *Journal of International Money and Finance,* March 1990, pp. 75–91.

Problem 1. Most of the tests use an index of prices such as the wholesale price index. This index may be misleading, since only goods that are traded directly affect supply and demand for foreign currencies. Nevertheless, even such nontraded goods as housing and medical costs indirectly affect the price of traded goods through their influence on the overall cost of living and thus on wage demands.

Problem 2. Tests of PPP should be based on comparing a similar market basket of goods in each country. If purchasing power parity is working, and governments do not interfere, the effective prices for a similar basket of goods should be the same in every country once exchange rates and prices have adjusted to worldwide PPP. However, because of differences in taste, level of developments, and income, it is difficult to find identical market baskets among countries. Any consumption-based index is necessarily going to compare "apples and oranges."

Problem 3. Tests of PPP require a knowledge of what the market is forecasting for differential inflation rates, but the data that are available are either realized historical inflation rates or existing differential interest rates used as a proxy for expected inflation differentials.

Problem 4. Time periods for testing have seldom, if ever, been free of at least some government interference in the trade process.

Exchange Rate Indices: Real and Nominal

Any single country in the current global market trades with numerous partners. This requires tracking and evaluating its individual currency value against all other currency values in order to determine relative purchasing power, that is, whether it is "overvalued" or "undervalued" in terms of PPP. One of the primary methods of dealing with this problem is the calculation of exchange rate indices. These indices are formed by trade-weighting the bilateral exchange rates between the home country and its trading partners.

The *nominal effective exchange rate index* calculates, on a weighted average basis, the value of the subject currency at different points in time. It does not really indicate anything about the "true value" of the currency, or anything related to PPP. The nominal index simply calculates how the currency value relates to some arbitrarily chosen base period. The *real effective exchange rate index* indicates how the weighted average purchasing power of the currency has changed relative to some arbitrarily selected base period.

A number of exchange rate indices are published on a frequent basis, such as the widely used International Monetary Fund Index, which is shown in Exhibit 5.3. It illustrates the degree to which PPP has held for four of the most important currencies during the period 1985 to 1993. If changes in exchange rates just offset differential inflation rates, all the real effective exchange rate indices would stay at 100. If an exchange rate strengthened more than was justified by differential inflation, its index would rise above

Exhibit 5.3 International Monetary Fund's Nominal and Real Effective Exchange Rate Indices

	United States		Germany		Japan		United Kingdom	
Year	Nominal[1]	Real[2]	Nominal[1]	Real[2]	Nominal[1]	Real[2]	Nominal[1]	Real
1982	85.5	87.2	97.4	101.9	83.0	97.1	113.7	107.9
1983	89.7	89.6	101.1	103.7	91.8	101.7	105.3	101.9
1984	96.8	96.3	100.0	100.8	97.9	102.7	100.6	99.3
1985	100.0	100.0	100.0	100.0	100.0	100.0	100.0	100.0
1986	80.2	79.5	108.8	110.4	124.4	123.7	91.6	92.8
1987	70.3	68.6	115.4	119.9	133.2	128.4	90.1	91.9
1988	65.9	64.7	114.6	120.8	147.4	135.7	95.5	97.7
1989	69.3	66.9	113.6	120.0	142.0	129.4	92.7	97.1
1990	65.0	61.4	119.1	127.3	126.0	114.8	91.3	99.2
1991	64.4	60.0	117.8	128.0	137.0	124.3	91.7	102.0
1992[3]	62.8	56.3	121.2	133.0	142.9	131.0	88.4	102.1

Source: International Monetary Fund, *International Financial Statistics,* monthly, Washington, D.C.

[1]Nominal effective exchange rate indexes (line *neu* in the IMF statistics) are derived from trade in manufactured goods with that country's major trading partners in 1980. The weights are based on relative proportions of trade for the base year of 1980, and the index is calculated for a base year of 1985 = 100.0. IMF.

[2]Real effective exchange rate indexes (line *reu* in the IMF statistics) are compiled from the nominal effective exchange rate index and a cost indicator of relative normalized unit labor costs in manufacturing. The reference base is 1985 = 100 in accordance with all indexes published by the IFS. However, it should be borne in mind that 1985 was a year in which the U.S. dollar was particularly strong in terms of other major currencies. IMF.

    Author's note: For example, the real effective exchange rate index for the U.S. dollar, $E_R^\$$, is found by multiplying the nominal effective exchange rate index, $E_N^\$$, by the ratio of U.S. dollar costs, $C^\$$, over foreign currency costs, C^{FC} (both in index form):

$$E_R^\$ = E_N^\$ \times \frac{C^\$}{C^{FC}}.$$

[3]Index values for 1992 are period averages for the first three quarters.

100, and it would be considered "overvalued" from a competitive perspective. An index value below 100 would suggest an "undervalued" currency.

As Exhibit 5.3 shows, the real effective exchange rate has varied considerably from year to year for some currencies, but the data lend some support to the concept that PPP may hold for the long run. For example, the index of the real effective exchange rate for the U.S. dollar rose from an undervalued level of 87.2 in 1982 to a value level of 100.0 in 1985, only to fall continually in value through 1992. The Japanese yen suddenly became overvalued in 1986, peaked in 1988, fell in 1989 and 1990, only to once again return to an upward path in 1991 and 1992. Germany and the United Kingdom showed only modest deviations from purchasing parity between 1982 and 1986, with the mark becoming increasingly overvalued after 1986.

Apart from measuring deviations from PPP, a country's real effective exchange rate is an important tool for predicting upward or downward pressure on its balance of payments and exchange rate, as well as an indicator of the desirability to produce for export from that country. The latter question is analyzed in Chapter 8 as part of a discussion of operating exposure.

Exchange Rate Pass-Through

Incomplete *exchange rate pass-through* is one reason a country's real effective exchange rate index can deviate for lengthy periods from its PPP-equilibrium level of 100. The degree to which the prices of imported and exported goods change as a result of exchange rate changes is termed pass-through.[3] Although PPP implies all exchange rate changes are passed on through equivalent changes in prices to trading partners, empirical research has questioned this long held assumption. For example, the sizable current account deficits of the United States in the 1980s did not respond to changes in the value of the dollar.

To illustrate exchange rate pass-through, assume BMW produces an automobile in Germany and pays all production expense in marks. When exporting the auto to the United States the price of the BMW in the U.S. market should simply be the mark value converted to dollars at the spot exchange rate:

$$P^{\$}_{\text{BMW}} = P^{\text{DM}}_{\text{BMW}} \times \frac{1}{S} \, ,$$

where $P^{\$}_{\text{BMW}}$ is the BMW price in dollars, $P^{\text{DM}}_{\text{BMW}}$ is the BMW price in marks, and S is the number of marks per dollar. If the mark appreciated 10% versus the U.S. dollar, the new spot exchange rate should result in the price of the BMW in the United States rising a proportional 10%. If the price in dollars increases by the same percentage change as the exchange rate, the pass-through of exchange rate changes is complete (or 100%).

However, if the price in dollars rises by less than the percentage change in exchange rates (as is often the case in international trade), the pass-through is *partial,* as illustrated in Exhibit 5.4. The 71% pass-through (U.S. dollar prices rise only 14.29% when the mark appreciated 20%) implies that BMW is absorbing a portion of the adverse exchange rate change. This absorption could result from smaller profit margins, cost reductions, or both. For example, components and raw materials imported to Germany cost less in marks when the mark appreciates. It is also likely that some time may pass before all exchange rate changes are finally reflected in the prices of traded goods, including the period over which previously signed contracts are delivered upon. It is obviously in the interests of BMW to keep the appreciation of the mark from raising the price of its automobiles in major export markets.

---

[3]For a more detailed description of pass-through analysis see Stephen P. Magee, "Currency Contracts, Pass-Through, and Devaluation," *Brookings Papers on Economic Activity,* vol. 1, 1973, pp. 303–325; Stephen P. Magee, "U.S. Import Prices in the Currency-Contract Paper," *Brookings Papers on Economic Activity,* vol. 1, 1974, pp. 117–164. For more recent analyses for the United States see Catherine L. Mann, "Prices, Profit Margins, and Exchange Rates," *Federal Reserve Bulletin,* June 1986, pp. 366–379, and Michael H. Moffett, "The J-Curve Revisited: An Empirical Examination for the United States," *Journal of International Money and Finance,* 1989, pp. 425–444.

Exhibit 5.4   Exchange Rate Pass-Through

Pass-through is the measure of response of imported and exported product prices to exchange rate changes. Assume the price in dollars and marks of a BMW automobile produced in Germany and sold in the United States at the initial spot exchange rate S_1 is:

$$P_{BMW}^{DM} = DM59,500 \qquad S_1 = DM1.7000/\$ \qquad P_{BMW}^{\$} = \$35,000$$

If the mark were to appreciate 20% versus the U.S. dollar, from DM1.7000/\$ to DM1.4167/\$, the price of the BMW in the U.S. market should theoretically be \$41,999 (DM59,500 ÷ DM1.4167/\$). But if the price of the BMW in the United States does not rise by 20%, for example to only \$40,000, then the degree of pass-through is only *partial:*

$$\frac{P_2^{\$}}{P_1^{\$}} = \frac{\$40,000}{\$35,000} = 1.1429, \text{ or a } 14.29\% \text{ increase.}$$

The degree of pass-through is measured by the proportion of the exchange rate change reflected in dollar prices. In this example, the dollar price of the BMW rose only 14.29%, while the DM appreciated 20.0% against the U.S. dollar. The degree of pass-through is partial, 14.29% ÷ 20.00%, or approximately .71 (71% pass-through). The remaining 5.71% of the exchange rate change (20.0% − 14.29%) has been absorbed by BMW.

The concept of price elasticity of demand is useful when determining the desired level of pass-through.[4] A German product that is relatively price inelastic, meaning the quantity demanded is relatively unresponsive to price changes, may often demonstrate a high degree of pass-through. This is because a higher dollar price in the U.S. market would have little noticeable effect on the quantity of the product demanded by consumers, and would, in fact, result in an increase in total dollar sales revenue. However, products that are relatively price elastic would respond in the opposite direction. If the 10% mark appreciation resulted in 10% higher dollar prices, U.S. consumers would decrease the number of BMWs purchased. If price elasticity for BMWs in the United States was greater than one, total dollar sales revenue of BMWs would decline.

Interest Rates and Exchange Rates

We have just seen how prices of goods in different countries should be related through exchange rates. We now consider how interest rates are linked to exchange rates.

---

[4]Recall that the own-price elasticity of demand for any good is the percentage change in quantity of the good demanded as a result of the percentage change in the good's own price:

$$\text{Price elasticity of demand} = E_p = \frac{\%\Delta Q_d}{\%\Delta P},$$

where Q_d is quantity demanded and P is product price. If the absolute value of E_p is less than 1.0 the good is relatively "inelastic," while greater than 1.0 indicates a relatively "elastic" demand.

The Fisher Effect

The *Fisher effect,* named after economist Irving Fisher, states that *nominal interest rates in each country are equal to the required real rate of return plus compensation for expected inflation.* More formally:[5]

$$i = r + \pi + r\pi,$$

where i is the nominal rate of interest, r is the real rate of interest, and π is the expected rate of inflation over the period of time for which funds are to be lent. The final compound term, $r\pi$, is frequently dropped from consideration due to its relatively minor value. The Fisher effect then reduces to:

$$i = r + \pi.$$

The Fisher effect applied to two different countries like the United States and Japan would be:

$$i^\$ = r^\$ + \pi^\$; \; i^¥ = r^¥ + \pi^¥,$$

where the superscripts $\$$ and $¥$ pertain to the respective nominal (i), real (r), and expected inflation (π) components of financial instruments denominated in dollars and yen, respectively. Note that this requires a forecast of the future rate of inflation, not what inflation has been. Predicting the future can be difficult.

Empirical tests using ex-post national inflation rates have shown the Fisher effect to exist particularly for short-maturity government securities such as Treasury bills and notes. Comparisons based on longer maturities suffer from the increased financial risk inherent in fluctuations of the market value of the bonds prior to maturity. Comparisons of private sector securities are influenced by unequal creditworthiness of the issuers. All the tests are inconclusive to the extent that the ex-post rate of inflation does not correctly measure the ex-ante expected rate of inflation.[6]

The International Fisher Effect

The relationship between the percentage change in the spot exchange rate over time and the differential between comparable interest rates in different national capital markets is known as the *international Fisher effect.* "Fisher-open," as it is often termed, states that *the spot exchange rate should change in an equal amount but in the opposite direction to the difference in interest rates between two countries.* More formally:

---

[5]This is derived from $(1 + r)(1 + \pi) - 1$.

[6]Some relevant studies of the Fisher effect, the international Fisher effect, and interest rate parity are Robert E. Cumby and Maurice Obstfeld, "A Note on Exchange-Rate Expectations and Nominal Interest Differentials: A Test of the Fisher Hypothesis," *Journal of Finance,* June 1981, pp. 697–703; Frederick S. Mishkin, "Are Real Interest Rates Equal across Countries? An Empirical Investigation of International Parity Conditions," *Journal of Finance,* December 1984, pp. 1345–1357; and Fred R. Kaen, Evangelos O. Simos, and George A. Hachey, "The Response of Forward Exchange Rates to Interest Rate Forecasting Errors," *Journal of Financial Research,* Winter 1984, pp. 281–290.

$$\frac{S_1 - S_2}{S_2} \times 100 = i^{\$} - i^{\yen},$$

where $i^{\$}$ and $i^{\yen}$ are the respective national interest rates, and S is the spot exchange rate using indirect quotes at the beginning of the period (S_1) and the end of the period (S_2). This is the approximation form commonly used in industry. The precise formulation using indirect quotes on the U.S. dollar would be the following (see appendix to this chapter for the complete mathematical derivation):

$$\frac{S_1 - S_2}{S_2} = \frac{i^{\$} - i^{\yen}}{1 + i^{\yen}}.$$

Justification for the international Fisher effect is that investors must be rewarded or penalized to offset the expected change in exchange rates. For example, if a dollar-based investor buys a 10-year yen bond earning 4% interest, compared to 6% interest available on dollars, the investor must be expecting the yen to appreciate vis-à-vis the dollar by at least 2% per year during the 10 years. If not, the dollar-based investor would be better off remaining in dollars. If the yen appreciates 3% during the 10-year period, the dollar-based investor would earn a bonus of 1% higher return. However, the international Fisher effect predicts that with unrestricted capital flows, an investor should be indifferent between investing in dollar or yen bonds, since investors worldwide would see the same bonus opportunity and compete it away.

Empirical tests lend some support to the relationship postulated by the international Fisher effect, although considerable short-run deviations occur. However, a more serious criticism has been posed by recent studies that suggest the existence of a foreign exchange risk premium for most major currencies. Thus the expected change in exchange rates might not consistently equal the difference in interest rates.

Interest Rate Parity (IRP)

The theory of interest rate parity (IRP) provides the linkage between the foreign exchange markets and the international money markets: *The difference in the national interest rates for securities of similar risk and maturity should be equal to, but opposite in sign to, the forward rate discount or premium for the foreign currency, except for transaction costs.* Unlike the international Fisher effect, the theory is applicable only to securities with maturities of one year or less, since forward contracts are not routinely available for periods longer than one year.

Exhibit 5.5 illustrates the theory. Assume an investor has $1,000,000 and several alternative but comparable Swiss franc (SF) monetary investments. If the investor chooses to invest in a dollar money market instrument, the investor would earn the dollar rate of interest. This results in $(1 + i^{\$})$ at the end of the period, where $i^{\$}$ is the dollar rate of interest in decimal form. The investor may, however, choose to invest in a Swiss franc money market instrument of identical risk and maturity for the same period. This would require the investor to exchange the dollars for Swiss francs at the spot rate of exchange, invest the Swiss francs in a money market instrument, and at the end of the period convert the resulting proceeds back to dollars.

Exhibit 5.5   Interest Rate Parity (IRP)

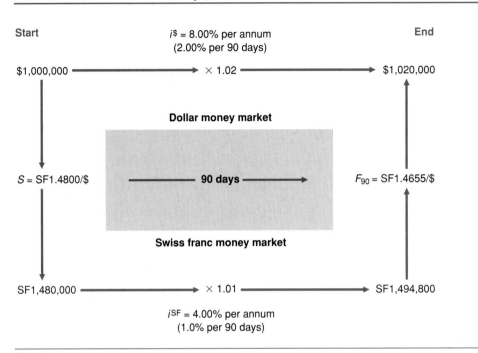

A dollar-based investor would evaluate the relative returns of starting in the top left corner and investing in the dollars (straight across the top of the box) compared to investing in the Swiss franc market (going around the box to the top right corner). The comparison of returns would be:

$$(1 + i^\$) = S^{SF/\$} \times (1 + i^{SF}) \times \frac{1}{F^{SF/\$}},$$

where S = the spot rate of exchange and F = the forward rate of exchange. Substituting in the spot rate (SF1.4800/\$) and forward rate (SF1.4655/\$) and respective interest rates ($i^\$ = 0.02$, $i^{SF} = 0.01$) from Ex. 5.5, the interest rate parity condition is:

$$(1 + .02) = 1.4800 \times (1 + .01) \times \frac{1}{1.4655}.$$

The left-hand side of the equation is the gross return the investor would earn by investing in dollars. The right-hand side is the gross return the investor would earn by exchanging dollars for Swiss francs at the spot rate, investing the Swiss franc proceeds in the Swiss franc money market, and simultaneously selling the principal plus interest in Swiss francs forward for dollars at the current 90-day forward rate.

Ignoring transaction costs, if the returns in dollars are equal between the two alternative money market investments, the spot and forward rates are considered to be at *interest rate parity* (IRP). The transaction is "covered" because the exchange rate back to dollars is guaranteed at the end of the 90-day period. Therefore, as in Exhibit 5.5, in order for the two alternatives to be equal, any differences in interest rates must be offset by the difference between the spot and forward exchange rates (in approximate form):

$$\frac{F}{S} = \frac{(1 + i^{SF})}{(1 + i^{\$})}, \quad \text{or} \quad \frac{\text{SF1.4655/\$}}{\text{SF1.4800/\$}} = \frac{1.01}{1.02} = 0.9902 \approx 1\%.$$

Covered Interest Arbitrage (CIA)

The spot and forward exchange markets are not, however, constantly in the state of equilibrium described by interest rate parity. When the market is not in equilibrium, the potential for "riskless" or arbitrage profit exists. The arbitrager who recognizes such an imbalance will move to take advantage of the disequilibrium by investing in whichever currency offers the higher return on a covered basis. This is called *covered interest arbitrage* (CIA).

Exhibit 5.6 describes the steps a currency trader, most likely working in the arbitrage division of a large international bank, would implement to perform a CIA transaction. The currency trader, William Wong, may utilize any of a number of major Eurocurrencies that his bank possesses to conduct arbitrage investments. The morning conditions indicate to William Wong that a CIA transaction which exchanges U.S. dollars for Japanese yen, invested in a six-month Euroyen account and sold forward back to dollars, will yield a profit of $4,638 over and above that available from a Eurodollars investment. Conditions in the exchange markets and Euromarkets change rapidly, however, so if William Wong waits even a few minutes, the profit opportunity may disappear.[7]

This process of covered interest arbitrage drives the international currency and money markets toward the equilibrium described by interest rate parity. Slight deviations from equilibrium provide opportunities for arbitragers to make small riskless profits. Such deviations provide the supply and demand forces that will move the market back toward parity (equilibrium).

Covered interest arbitrage should continue until interest rate parity is reestablished, because the arbitragers are able to earn risk-free profits by repeating the cycle as often as possible. Their actions, however, nudge the foreign exchange and money markets back toward equilibrium for the following reasons:

1. Purchase of yen in the spot market and sale of yen in the forward market narrows the premium on the forward yen. This is because the spot yen strengthens from the extra demand and the forward yen weakens because of the extra sales. A narrower premium on the forward yen reduces the foreign exchange gain previously captured by investing in yen.

---

[7]Note that all profits are stated in terms of the currency in which the transaction was initialized, but that a trader (in this case in Hong Kong) may conduct investments denominated in U.S. dollars, Swiss francs, or any other major convertible currency.

Exhibit 5.6   Covered Interest Arbitrage (CIA)

Morning. William Wong, an arbitrager for Hong Kong & Shanghai Banking Corporation, Hong Kong, arrives at work Tuesday morning to be faced with the currency quotations shown in the "Morning Quotation Box" below. He has access to several major Eurocurrencies for arbitrage trading. On the basis of the quotations below he decides to execute the following CIA transaction:

Step 1:   Convert $1,000,000 at the spot rate of ¥106.00/$ to ¥106,000,000 (see "START").

Step 2:   Invest the proceeds, ¥106,000,000, in a Euroyen account for six months, earning 4.00% per annum, or 2% for 180 days.

Step 3:   Simultaneously sell the proceeds (¥108,120,000) forward for dollars at the 180-day forward rate of ¥103.50/$. This "locks in" gross dollar revenues of $1,044,638 (see "END").

Step 4:   Calculate the cost (opportunity cost) of funds used at the Eurodollar rate of 8.00% per annum, or 4% for 180 days, with principal and interest then totaling $1,040,000. Profit on CIA at the "END" is:

$1,044,638 (proceeds) − $1,040,000 (cost) = $4,638.

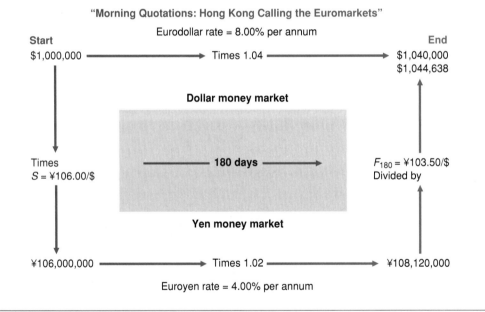

"Morning Quotations: Hong Kong Calling the Euromarkets"

2.   The demand for yen-denominated securities causes yen interest rates to fall, while the higher level of borrowing in the United States causes dollar interest rates to rise. The net result is a wider interest differential in favor of investing in the dollar.

Equilibrium Between Interest Rates and Exchange Rates

Exhibit 5.7 illustrates the conditions necessary for equilibrium between interest rates and exchange rates using the values from the previous William Wong example. The

Exhibit 5.7 Interest Rate Parity and Equilibrium

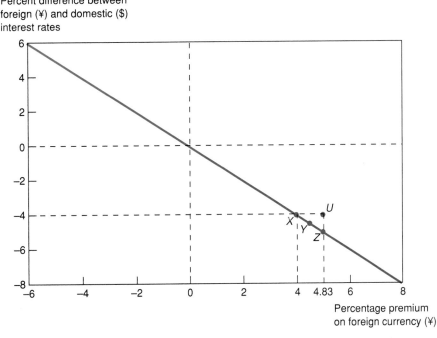

vertical axis shows the percentage difference between foreign (yen-denominated) and domestic (dollar-denominated) interest rates, and the horizontal axis shows the forward premium or discount on the yen. The *interest rate parity line* shows the equilibrium state, but transaction costs cause the line to be a band rather than a thin line.[8] Point X shows one possible equilibrium position, where a −4% interest differential on yen securities would be offset by a 4% premium on the forward yen.

The disequilibrium situation, which encouraged the interest rate arbitrage activity of William Wong in the previous CIA example, is illustrated by point U. It is located off the interest rate parity line because the percentage differential in interest rates is −4%

---

[8]Transaction costs arise from foreign exchange and investment brokerage costs on buying and selling securities. Typical transaction costs in recent years have been in the range of 0.18% to 0.25% on an annual basis. For individual transactions like William Wong's arbitrage activity in the previous example, there is no explicit transaction cost per trade; rather the costs of the bank in supporting Wong's activities are the transaction costs.

(annual basis), whereas the premium on the forward yen is slightly over 4.8% (annual basis). Using the forward premium calculation presented earlier, the actual premium on the yen is:

$$\frac{¥106.00/\$ - ¥103.50/\$}{¥103.50/\$} \times \frac{360 \text{ days}}{180 \text{ days}} \times 100 = 4.83\%.$$

The situation depicted by point U is unstable because all investors have an incentive to execute the same covered interest arbitrage. Except for a bank failure, the arbitrage gain is virtually risk free.

Some observers have suggested political risk does exist, since one of the governments might apply capital controls that would prevent execution of the forward contract. This risk is fairly remote for covered interest arbitrage between major financial centers of the world, especially since a large portion of funds used for covered interest arbitrage is in Eurodollars. The concern may be valid for pairings with countries not noted for political and fiscal stability.

The net result of the disequilibrium is that fund flows will narrow the gap in interest rates and/or decrease the premium on the forward yen. In other words, market pressures will cause point U in Exhibit 5.7 to move toward the interest rate parity band. Equilibrium might be reached at point Y, or at any other locus between X and Z, depending on whether forward market premiums are more or less easily shifted than interest rate differentials.

Forward Rate as an Unbiased Predictor of the Future Spot Rate

Some forecasters believe that for the major floating currencies, foreign exchange markets are "efficient" and forward exchange rates are unbiased predictors of future spot exchange rates.[9]

Exhibit 5.8 demonstrates what this concept of "unbiased prediction" means in terms of how the forward rate performs in estimating future spot exchange rates. If the forward rate is an unbiased predictor of the future spot rate, the expected value of the future spot rate at time 2 equals the present forward rate for time 2 delivery, available at time 1 (now), $E(S_2) = F_1$.

Intuitively this means the distribution of possible actual spot rates in the future is centered on the forward rate. An unbiased predictor, however, does not mean the future

---

[9]For example, see Ian H. Giddy and Gunter Dufey, "The Random Behavior of Flexible Exchange Rates," *Journal of International Business Studies,* Spring 1975, pp. 1–32. Also see Dennis E. Logue, Richard J. Sweeney, and Thomas D. Willett, "The Speculative Behavior of Foreign Exchange Rates during the Current Float," *Journal of Business Research,* vol. 6, no. 2, 1978, pp. 159–173; Richard M. Levich, "Tests of Forecasting Models and Market Efficiency in the International Money Market," in Jacob A. Frenkel and Harry G. Johnson, eds., *The Economics of Exchange Rates,* Reading, Mass.: Addison-Wesley, 1978, pp. 129–158.

Exhibit 5.8   Forward Rate as an Unbiased Predictor of Future Spot Rate

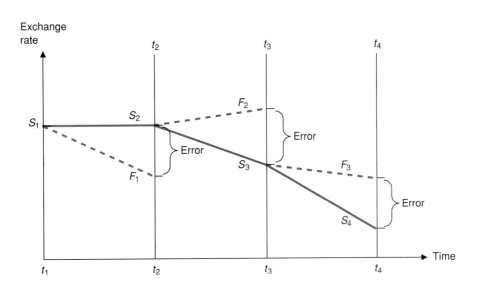

The forward rate available today ($F_{t,t+1}$), time t, for delivery at future time $t + 1$, is used as a "predictor" of the spot rate of exchange which will exist on that day in the future. The forecasted spot rate for time t_2 is F_1; the actual spot exchange rate turns out to be S_2. The vertical distance between the forward rate prediction — F_1 — and the actual spot rate which does exist on that date — S_2 — is the forecast error.

When the forward rate is termed an "unbiased predictor of the future spot rate," it means the forward rate overestimates and underestimates the future spot rate with relatively equal frequency and amount. It therefore "misses the mark" in a regular and orderly manner. The sum of the errors equals zero. The authors would like to thank Gunter Dufey for the original version of this clear presentation of unbiased prediction.

spot rate will actually be equal to what the forward rate predicts. Unbiased prediction simply means the forward rate will, on average, overestimate and underestimate the actual future spot rate in equal frequency and degree. The forward rate may, in fact, never actually equal the future spot rate.

The rationale for this relationship is based on the hypothesis that the foreign exchange market is reasonably efficient. Market efficiency assumes that (1) all relevant information is quickly reflected in both the spot and forward exchange markets, (2) transaction costs are low, and (3) instruments denominated in different currencies are perfect substitutes for one another.

Empirical studies of the efficient foreign exchange market hypothesis have yielded conflicting results. Nevertheless, a consensus is developing that rejects the efficient market hypothesis. It appears the forward rate is not an unbiased predictor of the future spot rate and that it does pay to use resources in an attempt to forecast exchange rates.

Early studies after exchange rates were floated in 1973 seemed to favor the efficient market hypothesis.[10] For example, Giddy and Dufey tested five different forecasting methods against foreign exchange quotations for the Canadian dollar, British pound, and French franc for the 1973–1974 period. Their results were consistent with the notion that the foreign exchange market is efficient and exchange rate forecasting is not profitable. Their major tests were on the so-called weak form of the random walk hypothesis, which asserts that successive changes in prices are independent of the sequence of past prices. Their conclusion was that "for short periods, one is able to detect a low degree of market inefficiency in the foreign exchange market. But the longer the forecasting horizon, the more evident is the inaccuracy of the time series forecasting of exchange rate changes."[11]

Kohlhagen attempted to determine whether the forward exchange market is a low-cost means of hedging exchange risks. He examined 90-day forward rates and subsequent spot rates for six countries (Canada, Denmark, France, West Germany, Switzerland, the United Kingdom) for the period of floating rates from April 1973 through December 1974, as well as for an earlier period of fixed exchange rates.[12] Among his findings was the observation that any difference between the forward rate and subsequent spot rate at the maturity of the forward contract could be attributed to random variations. Stated differently, any profit or loss from taking a consistently long or short position in the forward market was due to random forces, and the forward rates themselves were unbiased predictors of future spot rates.

Fama, who also studied the early floating rate period, concluded;

> When adjusted for variation through time in expected premiums, the forward rates of interest that are implicit in Treasury Bill prices contain assessments of expected future spot rates of interest that are about as good as those that can be obtained from the information in past spot rates. Moreover, in setting bill prices and forward rates, the market reacts appropriately to the negative autocorrelation in monthly changes in the spot rate and to changes through time in the degree of this autocorrelation. This evidence is consistent with the market

---

[10]A good review of early foreign exchange market efficiency studies is in Stephen W. Kohlhagen, *The Behavior of Foreign Exchange Markets—A Critical Survey of the Empirical Literature,* New York: New York University Monograph Series in Finance and Economics, no. 3, 1978. An excellent summary of all the foreign exchange forecasting and management literature is in Laurent L. Jacque, "Management of Foreign Exchange Risk: A Review Article," *Journal of International Business Studies,* Spring/Summer 1981, pp. 81–101.

[11]Op. cit. Giddy and Dufey, "Random Behavior of Flexible Exchange Rates," p. 27.

[12]Stephen W. Kohlhagen, "The Performance of the Foreign Exchange Markets: 1971–1974," *Journal of International Business Studies,* Fall 1975, pp. 33–39.

efficiency proposition that in setting bill prices, the market correctly uses the information in past spot rates.[13]

If these conclusions are correct, a financial executive cannot expect to profit in any consistent manner from forecasting future exchange rates because current quotations in the forward market reflect all that is presently known about likely future rates. While future exchange rates may well differ from the expectation implicit in the present forward market quotation, one cannot know today which way actual future quotations will differ from today's forward rate. The expected mean value of deviations is zero. The forward rate is therefore an "unbiased" estimator of the future spot rate.

More recent tests of foreign exchange market efficiency, using longer time periods of analysis, challenge the earlier findings and conclude that either exchange market efficiency is untestable or, if it is testable, the market is not efficient. Furthermore, the existence and success of foreign exchange forecasting services suggest that managers are willing to pay a price for forecast information even though they can use the forward rate as a forecast at no cost.[14] If the exchange market is not efficient, it would pay for a firm to spend resources on forecasting exchange rates. This is the opposite conclusion to the one in which exchange markets are deemed efficient.

Prices, Interest Rates, and Exchange Rates in Equilibrium

Exhibit 5.9 illustrates all of the fundamental parity relations simultaneously using the Japanese yen. The yen is expected to strengthen 4% versus the dollar. The spot exchange rate, ¥104/$, is forecasted to change to ¥100/$ one year from now using PPP (relation A), the international Fisher effect (relation C), and the forward rate (relation E). The forecasted inflation rates for Japan (1.0%) and the United States (5.0%) result in a forecast of ¥100/$ (relative version of purchasing power parity). If the difference in nominal interest rates is used (international Fisher effect), the forecasted spot rate is also ¥100/$. Finally, the one-year forward rate on the Japanese yen, ¥100/$, if assumed to be an unbiased predictor of the future spot rate, also forecasts ¥100/$.

---

[13]Eugene F. Fama, "Forward Rates as Predictors of Future Spot Rates," *Journal of Financial Economics,* October 1976, pp. 361–377.

[14]Three such studies are reported in the following articles: Stephen Goodman, "Foreign Exchange Forecasting Techniques: Implications for Business and Policy," *Journal of Finance,* May 1979, pp. 415–427; Richard M. Levich, "Analyzing the Accuracy of Foreign Exchange Forecasting Services: Theory and Evidence," in Clas Wihlborg and Richard Levich, eds., *Exchange Risk and Exposure: Current Developments in International Financial Development,* Lexington, Mass.: Heath, 1980; John F. O. Bilson, "The Evaluation and Use of Foreign Exchange Rate Forecasting Services," in R. J. Herring, ed., *Management of Foreign Exchange Risk,* Cambridge, England: Cambridge University Press, 1983, pp. 149–179.

Exhibit 5.9   International Parity Relations in Equilibrium

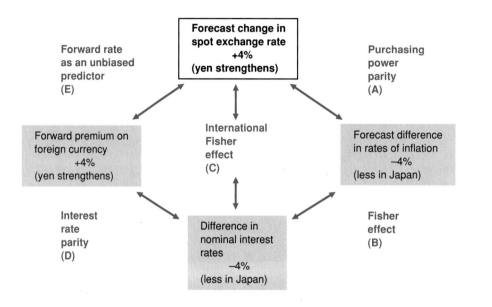

1. **Exchange Rates:**
   a. Current Spot Rate: $S_1 = ¥104/\$$
   b. Forward Rate (one year): $F = ¥100/\$$
   c. Expected Spot Rate: $S_2 = ¥100/\$$
   d. Forward Premium on yen:

$$f^{¥} = \frac{S_1 - F}{F} \times 100 = \frac{104 - 100}{100} \times 100 = +4\%$$

   e. Forecast Change in Spot Rate:

$$\%\Delta S = \frac{S_1 - S_2}{S_2} \times 100 = \frac{104 - 100}{100} \times 100 = +4\%$$

2. **Forecast Rate of Inflation:**
   a. Japan   1%
   b. United States   5%
   c. Difference   −4%

3. **Interest on One-Year Government Security:**
   a. Japan   4%
   b. United States   8%
   c. Difference   −4%

Exchange Rate Forecasting

Having completed the discussion of the parity conditions that tie together currencies, prices, and interest rates on world markets, we next identify forecasting needs of the multinational firm. We then provide an overview of the methods of exchange rate forecasting, including examples of how exchange rate forecasts may be generated in practice.

Forecasting Needs of the Multinational Firm

A multinational firm needs exchange rate forecasts for one or more of the following purposes:

- Accounts payable and receivable. Existing and expected foreign currency-denominated payables and receivables are exposed to foreign exchange losses when converted to a firm's reporting currency. Exchange rate forecasts are helpful in deciding whether or not to protect against these potential losses. Protection is covered in detail in Chapter 7.

- International price lists. To quote a product price in a foreign currency requires the firm to estimate what exchange rate will be in effect at the time of sale and remittance. These forecasts may extend from one day to one year into the future.

- Working capital management. A multinational firm is constantly managing cash flows among the parent and foreign affiliates. Correct exchange rate forecasts allow the most efficient timing of the movements of these cash flows (see Chapter 22).

- International investment analysis. The evaluation of international capital projects and portfolio investments requires exchange rate forecasts well out into the future (1, 2, 5, or even 10 years). These decisions are covered in Chapters 19 and 20.

Each firm's forecasting needs are characterized by a similar set of dimensions: point in time, frequency of forecast revision, and available resources for forecast construction. Exchange rate forecasts that must be continually regenerated and implemented, for example in working capital management, must be available on a short-term basis and require few resources. Long-term forecast needs, such as for multinational capital budgeting, are worthy of more in-depth analysis.

Fundamental Versus Technical Analysis

Forecasting exchange rates includes elements common to all forecasting applications. The primary methodological question is whether to construct forecasts on the basis of financial and economic theories, *fundamental analysis,* or to derive forecasts from the trend of the data series itself, *technical analysis.*

Forecasters who favor fundamental analysis are split into two schools of thought. The balance of payments approach emphasizes analysis of a country's balance of payments as an indicator of pressure on a managed exchange rate. The asset market approach postulates that the relative attractiveness of a currency for investment purposes is the main force driving exchange rates.

The Balance of Payments Approach. If a country spends more abroad in combined purchases and investments than it earns or otherwise acquires from abroad over a sustained period of time, the probability of devaluation of its currency increases. Foreigners will be building up, on balance, monetary claims against the country. If foreigners are willing to hold these claims in monetary form, the subject currency need not devalue. However, if foreigners convert these monetary claims to a different currency, pressure for devaluation will increase. A country's currency might, on the other hand, appreciate if that country runs a large surplus on current account and foreigners are eager to hold its currency.

The facts and figures watched most frequently by fundamental analysts are summarized in the "User's Guide" in Exhibit 5.10. Although economic forces are often difficult to distinguish from political forces, we have segmented the more regulatory-related factors from the economic and financial factors. Note that certain macroeconomic factors that at first glance may seem far removed from exchange rate analysis are included. The interpretation of their impacts on exchange rates usually returns to basic supply and demand factors for currencies. Many of these factors (for example, government spending or money supply growth) translate into inflation.

Asset Market Approach. Whether or not foreigners are willing to hold claims in monetary form depends partly on relative real interest rates and also on a country's outlook for economic growth and profitability. For example, during the period 1981 to 1985 the U.S. dollar strengthened despite growing current account deficits. This strength was due partly to relatively high real interest rates in the United States. Another factor, however, was the heavy inflow of foreign capital into the U.S. stock market and real estate, motivated by good long-run prospects for growth and profitability in the United States.

Bruno Solnik summarizes why some forecasters believe exchange rates are more influenced by economic prospects than by the balance of payments as follows:

> The asset market approach. Many economists reject the view that the short-term behavior of exchange rates is determined in flow markets. Exchange rates are asset prices traded in an efficient financial market. Indeed, an exchange rate is the relative price of two currencies and therefore is determined by the willingness to hold each currency. Like other asset prices, the exchange rate is determined by expectations about the future, not current trade flows.
>
> A parallel with other asset prices may illustrate the approach. Let's consider the stock price of a winery traded on the Bordeaux stock exchange. A frost in late spring results in a poor harvest, in terms of both quantity and quality. After the harvest the wine is finally sold, and the income is much less than the previous year. On the day of the final sale there is no reason for the stock price to be influenced by this flow. First, the poor income has already been discounted for several months in the winery stock price. Second, the stock price is affected by future, in addition to current, prospects. The stock price is based on expectations of future earnings, and the major cause for a change in stock price is a revision of these expectations.
>
> A similar reasoning applies to exchange rates: Contemporaneous international flows should have little effect on exchange rates to the extent they have already been expected. Only news about future economic prospects will affect exchange rates. Since economic

Exhibit 5.10   User's Guide to Long-Term Exchange Rate Fundamental Analysis

Political Exchange Rate Factors

Capital Controls	Government restrictions on the use of foreign currency for business transactions is an obvious control of exchange rates. Although governments intentionally do not publicize the imposition or removal of these restrictions, signals such as increased spreads in black market rates are often visible.
Exchange Rate Spreads	Currencies that are not traded freely (government restrictions) will still be sold "unofficially" through external or internal black markets. An increasing spread between the official (government) exchange rate and the black market (unrestricted) rate indicates potential pressures leading to eventual devaluation or depreciation.

Macroeconomic Fundamentals

Balance of Payments	The BOP is in effect the supply and demand for foreign currencies. Indicators of imbalances such as the current account balance and the trade balance are helpful in tracking forces pushing on exchange rates. A significant increase (decrease) in the current account balance or trade balance is interpreted as an early sign of a currency appreciation (depreciation).
Foreign Exchange Reserves	A government that is intervening in the foreign exchange markets will be using its foreign currency reserves to either push up or push down the value of its domestic currency. Efforts to support the domestic currency will result in the loss of foreign currency reserves; efforts to depreciate the domestic currency will result in the accumulation of foreign currency reserves.
GNP or GDP Growth	Economic growth is the largest single force affecting imports and exports. If the domestic economy is growing relatively rapidly compared to major trade partners, the level of imports is likely to rise faster than exports, trade deficits ensue, and currency depreciation is likely. A possible mixed signal is if the more rapid economic growth attracts large capital inflows, possibly offsetting the negative trade effects.
Government Spending	Although most countries worldwide possess large government sectors, a rapid increase in government spending, particularly if financed through deficit spending, results in increased inflationary pressures on the economy. Inflation infers possible depreciation.
Relative Inflation	As described previously, a country suffering relatively higher inflation rates will, as a result of PPP forces, see its currency depreciate.
Money Supply Growth	One of the primary causes of inflation is the rapid growth of the money supply. Many countries choose to stave off recession by increasing money supply growth to lower domestic interest rates. This usually results in a higher domestic inflation rate; currency depreciation follows.

expectations are potentially volatile and influenced by many variables, especially variables of a political nature, the short-run behavior of exchange rates is volatile.[15]

We are left with an obvious dilemma as to which theory to follow. As do others, we compromise. The consensus of opinion is that short-run exchange rate movements are determined by asset markets, interest rates, and the expectations of market participants. In the long term, however, equilibrium exchange rates are determined by PPP.

[15]Bruno Solnik, *International Investments*, Addison-Wesley, 1991, p. 89. Reprinted with permission.

Technical Analysis. Technical analysts, traditionally referred to as chartists, focus on price and volume data to determine past trends that are expected to continue into the future. The single most important element of time-series analysis is that future exchange rates are based on the current exchange rate. Exchange rate movements, similar to equity price movements, can be subdivided into periods: (1) day-to-day movement that is seemingly random; (2) short-term movements extending from several days to trends lasting several months; and (3) long-term movements that are characterized by up and down long-term trends. Long-term technical analysis has gained new popularity as a result of recent research into the possibility that long-term "waves" in currency movements exist under floating exchange rates.[16]

The longer the time horizon of the forecast, the more inaccurate the forecast is likely to be. Whereas forecasting for the long run must depend on economic fundamentals of exchange rate determination, many of the forecast needs of the firm are short- to medium-term in their time horizon and can be addressed with less theoretical approaches. Time-series techniques infer no theory or causality, but simply predict future values from the recent past. Forecasters freely mix fundamental and technical analysis, presumably because forecasting is like horseshoes and hand grenades: Getting close is all that counts!

Forecasting in Practice

Numerous foreign exchange forecasting services exist, many of which are provided by banks and independent consultants. In addition, some multinational firms have their own in-house forecasting capabilities. Predictions can be based on elaborate econometric models, technical analysis of charts and trends, intuition, and a certain measure of gall.

Whether any of the forecasting services are worth their cost depends partly on the motive for forecasting as well as the required accuracy of the forecast. For example, long-run forecasts may be motivated by a multinational firm's desire to initiate a direct foreign investment in Japan, or perhaps to raise long-term funds denominated in Japanese yen. Or a portfolio manager may be considering diversifying for the long term in Japanese securities. The longer the time horizon of the forecast, the more inaccurate but also the less critical the forecast is likely to be. The forecaster will typically use annual data to display long-run trends in such economic fundamentals as Japanese inflation, growth, and the balance of payments.

Short-term forecasts are typically motivated by a desire to hedge a receivable, payable, or dividend for perhaps a period of three months. In this case the long-run economic fundamentals may not be as important as technical factors in the marketplace, government intervention, news, and passing whims of traders and investors. Accuracy of the forecast is critical, since most of the exchange rate changes are relatively small even though the day-to-day volatility may be high.

Forecasting services normally undertake fundamental economic analysis for long-term forecasts, and some base their short-term forecasts on the same basic model.

---

[16]Charles Engel and James D. Hamilton, "Long Swings in the Dollar: Are They in the Data and Do Markets Know It?" *American Economic Review,* September 1990, pp. 689–713.

Others base their short-term forecasts on technical analysis similar to that conducted in security analysis. They attempt to correlate exchange rate changes with various other variables, regardless of whether there is any economic rationale for the correlation. The chances of these forecasts being consistently useful or profitable depends on whether one believes the foreign exchange market is efficient. The more efficient the market is, the more likely it is that exchange rates are "random walks," with past price behavior providing no clues to the future. The less efficient the foreign exchange market is, the better the chance that forecasters may get lucky and find a key relationship that holds, at least for the short run. If the relationship is really consistent, however, others will soon discover it and the market will become efficient again with respect to that piece of information.

Exhibit 5.11 summarizes the various forecasting periods, regimes, and the authors' opinions on the preferred methodologies. Opinions, like the future, are subject to change without notice!

Exhibit 5.11   Exchange Rate Forecasting in Practice

Forecast Period	Regime	Recommended Forecast Methods
SHORT RUN	*Fixed Rate*	1. Assume the fixed rate is maintained 2. Indications of stress on fixed rate? 3. Capital controls; black market rates 4. Indicators of government's capability to maintain fixed rate? 5. Changes in official foreign currency reserves

	Floating Rate	1. Technical methods that capture trend
		2. Forward rates as forecasts
		  a. < 30 days, assume a random walk
		  b. 30–90 days, forward rates
		  c. 90–360 days, combine trend with fundamental analysis
		3. Fundamental analysis of inflationary concerns
		4. Government declarations and agreements regarding exchange rate goals
		5. Cooperative agreements with other countries

LONG RUN	*Fixed Rate*	1. Fundamental analysis 2. Balance of payments management 3. Ability to control domestic inflation 4. Ability to generate hard currency reserves to use for intervention 5. Ability to run trade surpluses
	Floating Rate	1. Focus on inflationary fundamentals and PPP 2. Indicators of general economic health such as economic growth and stability 3. Technical analysis of long-term trends; new research indicates possibility of long-term technical "waves"

Summary

- Under conditions of freely floating rates the expected rate of change in the spot exchange rate, differential rates of national inflation and interest, and the forward discount or premium are all directly proportional to each other and mutually determined. A change in one of these variables has a tendency to change all of them with a feedback on the variable that changes first.

- If the identical product or service can be sold in two different markets, and there are no restrictions on its sale or transportation costs of moving the product between markets, the product's price should be the same in both markets. This is called the law of one price.

- The absolute version of the theory of purchasing power parity states that the spot exchange rate is determined by the relative prices of similar baskets of goods.

- The relative version of the theory of purchasing power parity states: If the spot exchange rate between two countries starts in equilibrium, any change in the differential rate of inflation between them tends to be offset over the long run by an equal but opposite change in the spot exchange rate.

- The Fisher effect, named after economist Irving Fisher, states that nominal interest rates in each country are equal to the required real rate of return plus compensation for expected inflation.

- The international Fisher effect, "Fisher-open" as it is often termed, states that the spot exchange rate should change in an equal amount but in the opposite direction to the difference in interest rates between two countries.

- The theory of interest rate parity (IRP) states that the difference in the national interest rates for securities of similar risk and maturity should be equal to, but opposite in sign to, the forward rate discount or premium for the foreign currency, except for transaction costs.

- When the spot and forward exchange markets are not in equilibrium as described by interest rate parity, the potential for "riskless" or arbitrage profit exists. This is called covered interest arbitrage (CIA).

- Some forecasters believe that for the major floating currencies, foreign exchange markets are "efficient" and forward exchange rates are unbiased predictors of future spot exchange rates.

- Time-series techniques or simple use of the forward rate are forecast alternatives. Longer term forecasting, over one year, requires a return to the basic analysis of exchange rate fundamentals such as balance of payments, relative inflation rates, relative interest rates, and the long-run properties of purchasing power parity.

Questions

1.   Wheat Trading
Two countries, the United States and Australia, produce just one good, wheat. Suppose the price of wheat in the United States is US$2.80 per bushel and in Australia is A$3.70 per bushel.

    a.   According to purchasing power parity, what should be the U.S./Australian dollar spot rate of exchange?

    b.   Suppose the price of wheat over the next year is expected to rise to US$3.10 in the United States and to A$4.65 in Australia. What should be the one-year forward U.S./Australian dollar exchange rate?

    c.   Given your answers to (a) and (b), and given the current interest rate in the United States is 10% for notes of a one-year maturity, what would you expect current Australian interest rates to be?

2.   McDonald's Hamburger Standard and the Law of One Price
Exhibit 5.1, *The Economist*'s hamburger standard, demonstrated one measure of what the purchasing power parity exchange rate would be if the Big Mac was considered a standardized product around the world.

    a.   What does it mean when the value of a currency is "overvalued" or "undervalued"?

    b.   Explain precisely, using the appropriate rates from Exhibit 5.1, whether the Russian rouble is undervalued or overvalued.

3.   Austrian Exchange Rate and Tyrolean Rents
You have just rented a castle in the Tyrolean Alps for a vacation 12 months hence. Your landlord wants to preserve his real income in Austrian schillings, and so the present monthly rent of AS24,000/month will be adjusted upward or downward for any change in the Austrian cost of living between now and then.

    You expect Austrian inflation to be 2% and U.S. inflation to be 8% over the coming year. You believe implicitly in the theory of purchasing power parity, and you note from the *Wall Street Journal* that the current spot rate is AS12.00/$. How many U.S. dollars will you need one year hence to pay your first month's rent?

4.   Japan and Germany
Money and foreign exchange markets in Japan and Germany are quite efficient. You have the following information:

	Japan	*Germany*
Spot exchange rate	¥100.00/DM	DM0.0100/¥
Expected inflation rate	2.00% p.a.	5.00% p.a.
One-year "T-bill" rate	Unknown	8.00% p.a.

    a. What is your estimate of the one-year T-bill rate in Japan?

    b. What is your estimate of the one-year forward exchange rate between Japanese yen and German marks?

5.   Borrowing Mexican Pesos

Suppose that on January 1 a firm in the United States borrows 500,000 pesos for one year at 20% interest. During the year, U.S. inflation is 4% and Mexican inflation is 15%. Over the one year period the exchange rate changes from Ps3.00/$ to Ps3.40/$. At the end of the year the firm exchanges dollars for pesos to repay the peso loan.

    a. What is the cost to the U.S.-based firm, in dollar-terms, of borrowing the pesos for one year?

    b. What is the real interest cost to the U.S.-based firm, in dollar-terms, of borrowing the pesos for one year?

6.   Ecuadorian Debt for Development

Jack Van de Water is still nervous (you remember Jack from Chapter 3). Assume Jack did complete the Debt for Development swap as described in the DFD case, yielding a massive amount of cash: sucre 107,777,778.

    Jack cannot, however, figure out what to do with the cash. Only one-half of the total cash in hand is needed now, the rest to be spent in six months on rent and educational travel expenses. He is still worried about inflation, which is running at about 40% per annum. He has considered depositing the balance in an interest-bearing account that is guaranteed to yield the rate of inflation.

    a. What do you recommend Jack do with his excess cash in the six months preceding when it is needed?

    b. How do individuals and firms operating in high-inflation environments typically deal with the continuing problem of losses in purchasing power?

7.   Foreign Currency Pricing at K2

Katja Seizinger is assistant V.P. for marketing for K2's ski sales. K2 is not only based in Germany, but does all its manufacturing in Germany and then distributes worldwide through sales offices. One of Seizinger's primary responsibilities is establishing prices for all of the foreign sales offices. She is now looking at the price lists for all U.S. sales offices, and needs prices set for the coming year.

    The current spot rate is DM1.7358/$, with a one-year forward rate of DM1.7613/$. The one-year Eurocurrency deposit rates for Deutschemarks and dollars are 5.2500% and 3.8125%, respectively. The largest selling downhill ski, the K2 Lillehammer, is currently priced at $475 to U.S. retailers. Current inflation estimates for Germany and the United States are both at about 3%. K2 has a standard policy of trying to absorb about 50% of all exchange rate-induced price increases, but pass along 100% of all exchange rate price decreases if possible. The business is competitive.

    Katja calls you in on Friday afternoon and explains she is involved in extensive product testing this weekend and you will therefore be responsible for setting the U.S. dollar prices for the coming year. Your price list is due Monday morning at 10 A.M.

8. Covered Interest Arbitrage in Japan (C05A.WK1)

Yume Tanaka is a currency arbitrager for C.Itoh and Company, Tokyo. The spot rate this morning is ¥111.22/$, and early indications are that short-term interest rates in the United States, 90-day rates, are about to rise from their current level of 3.1250%. The central bank of the United States, the Fed, is worried about rising inflation and has been publicly considering raising interest rates 25 basis points (1/4%). The 90-day forward rate quoted to Yume by local banks like Daichi Kangyo are all about the same, ¥111.14/$. The current 90-day yen Eurodeposit rate of interest is 2.1560%. Yume has ¥250 million at her disposal.

    a.   How can Yume make a profit through covered interest arbitrage? How much in yen can she hope to make in profit in 90 days?

    b.   If future spot exchange rates were determined by interest differentials alone (i.e., if the forward rate was a very good forecast of future spot exchange rates), what would Yume expect the spot rate to be in 90 days if the U.S. Federal Reserve does the expected?

    c.   If Yume's expectation of the future spot rate is that of part b, what profit could she expect to make from uncovered interest arbitrage (not signing a forward contract)?

9. Percentage Changes in Exchange Rates

If the following currencies change in value relative to the dollar as indicated, calculate the ending exchange rate in terms of local currency units per dollar:

Currency	Initial exchange rate	Change relative to U.S. dollar
Chilean peso	Ps312.50/$	devalues 20%
Singapore dollar	S$1.7000/US$	appreciates 6%

10. CIA in Montreal

Harry Johnson, an arbitrager with Bank of Montreal, faces the following Canadian dollar/U.S. dollar quotes:

Spot rate	C$1.1520/$
Six-month forward rate	C$1.1635/$
Six-month Canadian dollar interest rate	10.00% per annum
Six-month U.S. dollar interest rate	7.50% per annum

Harry is authorized to use C$10,000,000 or its U.S. dollar equivalent. Transaction costs would be $1,700 paid at the end of six months. The ending profit, if any, should be held in Canadian dollars. Assuming Harry can borrow or invest at the interest rates quoted here, how can he complete a covered interest arbitrage? What is his profit?

11. William Wong: CIA Back in Hong Kong

Your favorite Hong Kong-based foreign exchange trader, William Wong, thinks he sees a chance to make a risk-free profit from covered interest arbitrage, rather than doing his normal speculation. He faces the following rates:

Spot rate:	¥125.00/$
Six-month forward rate:	¥124.00/$
Six-month interest rate on U.S. dollars:	8.00% per annum
Six-month interest rate on Japanese yen:	6.00% per annum

Explain, using words, numbers, and diagrams, how he can make a risk-free profit. He wants to end up with his profit in U.S. dollars. He can borrow $5,000,000 or its yen equivalent for the purpose of speculation. Ignore transaction costs.

12. Indian Rupiah

The foreign exchange rate between India and the United States one year ago was Rps.26.0/$. At that time, the price index in both India and the United States was 100.0. Between last year and this year the rupee depreciated by 20% against the dollar, the price index in the United States remained the same, and the price index in India rose to 128.

    a.   What is the nominal exchange rate today?

    b.   What should have been the exchange rate today, based on purchasing power parity, if you use last year as a base?

    c.   Did the rupee depreciate or appreciate in real terms, relative to the U.S. dollar? By what percentage?

13. Nations of Alpine and Bayshore

Alpine and Bayshore are both large countries with efficient capital and money markets. Alpine's currency is the *alp* (Å) and Bayshore's currency is the *wave* (≈). For both countries the Fisher effect, purchasing power parity, and interest rate parity are currently in equilibrium and are expected to remain so.

    Recently, the *Financial Times* (London) published the following data:

	For Alpine	*For Bayshore*
Spot foreign exchange quote	Å 8.00/≈	≈0.1250/Å
12-month T-bill rate	10%	not available
Expected inflation rate	5% p.a.	11% p.a.

As chief financial officer for your company you are asked to determine and/or forecast the following, using an algebraic approach.

    a.   The 12-month T-bill rate in Bayshore.

    b.   The 12-month forward exchange quotation, direct basis, for both Alpine and Bayshore.

Bibliography

Abuaf, Niso, and Philippe Jorion, "Purchasing Power Parity in the Long Run," *Journal of Finance,* March 1990, pp. 157–174.

Adler, Michael, and Bernard Dumas, "Portfolio Choice and the Demand for Forward Exchange," *American Economic Review,* May 1976, pp. 332–339.

Aggarwal, Raj, "Distribution of Spot and Forward Exchange Rates: Empirical Evidence and Investor Valuation of Skewness and Kurtosis," *Decision Sciences,* Summer 1990, pp. 588–595.

———, "The Distribution of Exchange Rates and Forward Risk Premia," *Advances in Finan-*

cial Planning and Forecasting, vol. 4, 1990, pp. 43–54.

Ang, James S., and Ali M. Fatemi, "A Test of the Rationality of Forward Exchange Rate," *Advances in Financial Planning and Forecasting,* vol. 4, 1990, pp. 3–22.

Baillie, Richard T., and Tim Bollerslev, "Common Stochastic Trends in a System of Exchange Rates," *Journal of Finance,* March 1989, pp. 167–181.

Bilson, John F.O., "The Evaluation and Use of Foreign Exchange Rate Forecasting Services," in *Management of Foreign Exchange Risk,* R. J. Herring, ed., Cambridge, England: Cambridge University Press, 1983, pp. 149–179.

Blake, David, Michael Beenstock, and Valerie Brasse, "The Performance of U.K. Exchange Rate Forecasters," *The Economic Journal,* December 1986, pp. 986–999.

Chen, T.J., K.C. John Wei, "Risk Premiums in Foreign Exchange Markets: Theory and Evidence," *Advances in Financial Planning and Forecasting,* vol. 4, 1990, pp. 23–42.

Chiang, Thomas C., "Empirical Analysis on the Predictors of Future Spot Rates," *Journal of Financial Research,* Summer 1986, pp. 153–162.

Choi, Jongmoo Jay, and Richard Ajayi, "The Effect of Foreign Debt on Currency Values," *Journal of Economics and Business,* 45, August/ October 1993, pp. 331–340.

Cornell, Bradford, and J. K. Dietrich, "Inflation, Relative Price Changes, and Exchange Risk," *Financial Management,* Autumn 1980, pp. 30–34.

Cosset, Jean-Claude, "Forward Rates as Predictors of Future Interest Rates in the Eurocurrency Market," *Journal of International Business Studies,* Winter 1982, pp. 71–83.

Cumby, Robert E., and Maurice Obstfeld, "A Note on Exchange-Rate Expectations and Nominal Interest Differentials: A Test of the Fisher Hypothesis," *Journal of Finance,* June 1981, pp. 697–703.

Darby, Michael R., "Movements in Purchasing Power Parity: The Short and Long Runs," in *The International Transmission of Inflation,* Michael R. Darby and James R. Lothian, eds., Chicago: University of Chicago Press, 1983.

Dornbusch, Rudiger, "Flexible Exchange Rates and Interdependence," *International Monetary Fund Staff Papers,* March 1983, pp. 3–30.

Dufey, Gunter, and Ian H. Giddy, "International Financial Planning: The Use of Market-Based Forecasts," *California Management Review,* Fall 1978, pp. 69–81; reprinted in Heide V. Wortzel and Lawrence Wortzel, eds., *Strategic Management of Multinational Corporations: The Essentials,* 2nd ed. New York: Wiley, 1991.

———, "Forecasting Foreign Exchange Rates: A Pedagogical Note," *Columbia Journal of World Business,* Summer 1981, pp. 53–61.

Edison, Hali J., "Purchasing Power Parity in the Long Run: A Test of the Dollar/Pound Exchange Rate (1890–1978), *Journal of Money, Credit, and Banking,* August 1987, pp. 376–387.

Eun, Cheol S., "Global Purchasing Power View of Exchange Risk," *Journal of Financial and Quantitative Analysis,* December 1981, pp. 639–650.

Everett, Robert M., Abraham M. George, and Aryeh Blumberg, "Appraising Currency Strengths and Weaknesses: An Operational Model for Calculating Parity Exchange Rates," *Journal of International Business Studies,* Fall 1980, pp. 80–91.

Fama, Eugene F., "Forward Rates as Predictors of Future Spot Rates," *Journal of Financial Economics,* October 1976, pp. 361–377.

Fama, Eugene F., "Forward and Spot Exchange Rates," *Journal of Monetary Economics,* 14, 1984, pp. 319–338.

Finnerty, Joseph E., James Owers, and Francis J. Crerar, "Foreign Exchange Forecasting and Leading Economic Indicators: The U.S. Canadian Experience," *Management International Review,* Vol. 27, no. 2, 1987, pp. 59–70.

Folks, William R., and Stanley R. Stansell, "The Use of Discriminant Analysis in Forecasting

Exchange Risk Movements," *Journal of International Business Studies,* Spring 1975, pp. 33–50.

Frankel, Jeffrey, and Alan MacArthur, "Political Vs. Currency Premia in International Real Interest Rate Differentials: A Study of Forward Rates for 24 Countries," *European Economic Review,* vol. 32, no. 5, June 1988, pp. 1083–1114.

Frenkel, Jacob A., and Richard M. Levich, "Covered Interest Arbitrage: Unexploited Profits?" *Journal of Political Economy,* April 1975, pp. 325–338.

———, "Transaction Costs and Interest Arbitrage: Tranquil versus Turbulent Periods," *Journal of Political Economy,* November-December 1977, pp. 1209–1226.

Giddy, Ian H., "An Integrated Theory of Exchange Rate Equilibrium," *Journal of Financial and Quantitative Analysis,* December 1976, pp. 863–892.

———, and Gunter Dufey, "The Random Behavior of Flexible Exchange Rates," *Journal of International Business Studies,* Spring 1975, pp. 1–32.

Goodwin, Barry K., Thomas Grennes, and Michael K. Wohlgenant, "Testing the Law of One Price When Trade Takes Time," *Journal of International Money and Finance,* March 1990, pp. 21–40.

Hilley, John L., Carl R. Beidleman, and James A. Greenleaf, "Does Covered Interest Arbitrage Dominate in Foreign Exchange Markets?" *Columbia Journal of World Business,* Winter 1979, pp. 99–107.

———, "Why There Is No Long Forward Market in Foreign Exchange," *Euromoney,* January 1981, pp. 94–103.

Huang, Roger D., "Expectations of Exchange Rates and Differential Inflation Rates: Further Evidence on Purchasing Power Parity in Efficient Markets," *Journal of Finance,* March 1987, pp. 69–79.

Kaen, Fred R., Evangelos O. Simos, and George A. Hachey, "The Response of Forward Exchange Rates to Interest Rate Forecasting Errors," *Journal of Financial Research,* Winter 1984, pp. 281–290.

Kohlhagen, Stephen W., *The Behavior of Foreign Exchange Markets—A Critical Survey of the Empirical Literature,* New York: New York University Monograph Series in Finance and Economics, no. 3, 1978.

Koveos, Peter, and Bruce Seifert, "Purchasing Power Parity and Black Markets," *Financial Management,* Autumn 1985, pp. 40–46.

Kwok, Chuck C.Y., and LeRoy D. Brooks, "Examining Event Study Methodologies in Foreign Exchange Markets," *Journal of International Business Studies,* Second Quarter 1990, pp. 189–224.

Levich, Richard M., "Tests of Forecasting Models and Market Efficiency in the International Money Market," in *The Economics of Exchange Rates,* Jacob A. Frenkel and Harry G. Johnson, eds., Reading, Mass.: Addison-Wesley, 1978, pp. 129–158.

———, "Are Forward Exchange Rates Unbiased Predictors of Future Spot Rates?" *Columbia Journal of World Business,* Winter 1979, pp. 49–61.

Lewis, Karen K., "Can Learning Affect Exchange Rate Behavior? The Case of the Dollar in the Early 1980s," *Journal of Monetary Economics,* vol. 23, 1989, pp. 79–100.

Magee, Stephen P., "Currency Contracts, Pass-Through, and Devaluation," *Brookings Papers on Economic Activity,* vol. 1:1973, pp. 303–325.

———, "Contracting and Spurious Deviations from Purchasing Power Parity," in *The Economics of Exchange Rates,* Jacob A. Frenkel and Harry G. Johnson, eds., Reading, Mass.: Addison-Wesley, 1978, pp. 67–74.

Mahajan, Arvind, and Dileep Mehta, "Swaps, Expectations, and Exchange Rates," *Journal of Banking and Finance,* March 1986, pp. 7–20.

Manzur, Meher, "An International Comparison of Prices and Exchanges Rates: A New Test of Purchasing Power Parity," *Journal of Inter-*

national Money and Finance, March 1990, pp. 75–91.

Maldonado, Rita, and Anthony Saunders, "Foreign Exchange Restrictions and the Law of One Price," *Financial Management,* Spring 1983, pp. 19–23.

Meese, Richard, and Kenneth Rogoff, "Was It Real? The Exchange Rate-Interest Differential Relation over the Modern Floating-Rate Period," *Journal of Finance,* September 1988, pp. 933–948.

Melvin, Michael, and David Bernstein, "Trade Concentration, Openness, and Deviations from Purchasing Power Parity," *Journal of International Money and Finance,* December 1984, pp. 369–376.

Mishkin, Frederick S., "Are Real Interest Rates Equal Across Countries? An Empirical Investigation of International Parity Conditions," *Journal of Finance,* December 1984, pp. 1345–1357.

Moffett, Michael H., "The J-Curve Revisited: An Empirical Examination for the United States," *Journal of International Money and Finance,* 1989, pp. 425–444.

Officer, Lawrence H., "The Purchasing Power-Parity Theory of Exchange Rates: A Review Article," *IMF Staff Papers,* March 1976, pp. 1–60.

Officer, Lawrence H., Edward I. Altman, and Ingo Walter, eds., *Purchasing Power Parity and Exchange Rates: Theory, Evidence, and Relevance,* Contemporary Studies in Economic and Financial Analysis, vol. 35, London: JAI Press, 1982.

Ohno, Kenichi, "Exchange Rate Fluctuations, Pass-Through, and Market Share," *IMF Staff Papers,* vol. 37, no. 2, June 1990, pp. 294–310.

Oxelheim, Lars, *International Financial Market Fluctuations,* Somerset, N.J.: Wiley, 1985.

———, and Clas G. Wihlborg, "Corporate Strategies in a Turbulent World Economy," *Management International Review,* vol. 31, no. 4, 1991, pp. 293–315.

———, and Clas Wihlborg, *Macroeconomic Uncertainty: International Risks and Opportunities for the Corporation,* Chichester, U.K.: Wiley, 1987.

Popper, Helen, "Long-Term Covered Interest Parity: Evidence from Currency Swaps," *Journal of International Money and Finance,* August 1993, pp. 439–448.

Roll, Richard W., and Bruno H. Solnik, "A Pure Foreign Exchange Asset Pricing Model," *Journal of International Economics,* May 1977, pp. 161–179.

Wihlborg, Clas, "Interest Rates, Exchange Rate Adjustments, and Currency Risks: An Empirical Study, 1967–1975," *Journal of Money, Credit and Banking,* February 1982, pp. 58–75.

Williamson, John, *Equilibrium Exchange Rates: An Update,* Washington, D.C.: Institute for International Economics, 1990.

Wolff, Christian C. P., "Forward Foreign Exchange Rates, Expected Spot Rates, and Premia: A Signal Extraction Approach," *Journal of Finance,* June 1987, pp. 395–406.

Chapter 5 Appendix
An Algebraic Primer to International Parity Conditions

The following is a purely algebraic presentation of the parity conditions explained in this chapter. It is offered to provide those who wish additional theoretical detail and definition-ready access to the step-by-step derivation of the various conditions.

The Law of One Price

The *law of one price* refers to the state in which, in the presence of free trade, perfect substitutability of goods, and costless transactions, the equilibrium exchange rate between two currencies is determined by the ratio of the price of any commodity i denominated in two different currencies. For example,

$$S_t = \frac{P_{i,t}^\$}{P_{i,t}^{SF}},$$

where $P_i^\$$ and P_i^{SF} refer to the prices of the same commodity i, at time t, denominated in U.S. dollars and Swiss francs, respectively. The spot exchange rate, S_t, (U.S. dollars/Swiss franc) is simply the ratio of the two currency prices.

Purchasing Power Parity

The more general form in which the exchange rate is determined by the ratio of two price indexes is termed the absolute version of *purchasing power parity (PPP)*. Each price index reflects the currency cost of the identical "basket" of goods across countries. The exchange rate that equates purchasing power for the identical collection of goods is then stated:

$$S_t = \frac{P_t^\$}{P_t^{SF}},$$

where $P_t^\$$ and P_t^{SF} are the price index values in U.S. dollars and Swiss francs at time t, respectively. If the Greek letter π (pi) represents the rate of inflation in each country, the spot exchange rate at time $t + 1$ would be:

$$S_{t+1} = \frac{P_t^{\$}(1 + \pi^{\$})}{P_t^{SF}(1 + \pi^{SF})} = S_t \left[\frac{(1 + \pi^{\$})}{(1 + \pi^{SF})} \right].$$

The change from period t to $t + 1$ is then:

$$\frac{S_{t+1}}{S_t} = \frac{\dfrac{P_t^{\$}(1 + \pi^{\$})}{P_t^{SF}(1 + \pi^{SF})}}{\dfrac{P_t^{\$}}{P_t^{SF}}} = \frac{S_t \left[\dfrac{(1 + \pi^{\$})}{(1 + \pi^{SF})} \right]}{S_t} = \frac{(1 + \pi^{\$})}{(1 + \pi^{SF})}.$$

Isolating the percentage change in the spot exchange rate between periods t and $t + 1$:

$$\frac{S_{t+1} - S_t}{S_t} = \frac{S_t \left[\dfrac{(1 + \pi^{\$})}{(1 + \pi^{SF})} \right] - S_t}{S_t} = \frac{(1 + \pi^{\$}) - (1 + \pi^{SF})}{(1 + \pi^{SF})}.$$

This equation is often approximated by dropping the denominator of the right-hand side if it is considered to be relatively close to 1. It is then stated as:

$$\frac{S_{t+1} - S_t}{S_t} = (1 + \pi^{\$}) - (1 + \pi^{SF}) = \pi^{\$} - \pi^{SF}.$$

Forward Rates

The *forward exchange rate* is that contractual rate which is available to private agents through banking institutions and other financial intermediaries who deal in foreign currencies and debt instruments. The annualized percentage difference between the forward rate and the spot rate is termed the *forward premium:*

$$f^{SF} = \left[\frac{F_{t,t+1} - S_t}{S_t} \right] \times \left[\frac{360}{n_{t,t+1}} \right],$$

where f^{SF} is the forward premium on the Swiss franc, $F_{t,t+1}$ is the forward rate contracted at time t for delivery at time $t + 1$, S_t is the current spot rate, and $n_{t,t+1}$ is the number of days between the contract date (t) and the delivery date $(t + 1)$. This is the formula for direct quotes (American Terms).

Covered Interest Arbitrage (CIA) and Interest Rate Parity (IRP)

The process of *covered interest arbitrage* is when an investor exchanges domestic currency for foreign currency in the spot market, invests that currency in an interest-bearing instrument, and signs a forward contract to "lock in" a future exchange rate at which to convert the foreign currency proceeds (gross) back to domestic currency. The net return on CIA is:

$$\text{Net Return} = \left[\frac{(1 + i^{SF}) \, F_{t,t+1}}{S_t} \right] - (1 + i^{\$})$$

where S_t and $F_{t,t+1}$ are the spot and forward rates (\$/SF), i^{SF} is the nominal interest rate (or yield) on a Swiss franc-denominated monetary instrument, and $i^{\$}$ is the nominal return on a similar dollar-denominated instrument.

If they possess exactly equal rates of return, that is, if CIA results in zero riskless profit, *interest rate parity* (IRP) holds, and appears as

$$(1 + i^{\$}) = \left[\frac{(1 + i^{SF}) \, F_{t,t+1}}{S_t} \right],$$

or alternatively

$$\frac{(1 + i^{\$})}{(1 + i^{SF})} = \frac{F_{t,t+1}}{S_t}.$$

If the percent difference of both sides of this equation is found (the percentage difference between the spot and forward rate is the forward premium), then the relationship between the forward premium and relative interest rate differentials is:

$$\frac{F_{t,t+1} - S_t}{S_t} = f^{SF} = \frac{i^{\$} - i^{SF}}{1 + i^{SF}}$$

If these values are not equal (thus the markets are not in equilibrium) there exists a potential for riskless profit. The market will then be driven back to equilibrium through CIA by agents attempting to exploit such arbitrage potential, until CIA yields no positive return.

Fisher Effect

The *Fisher effect* states that all nominal interest rates can be decomposed into an implied real rate of interest (return) and an expected rate of inflation:

$$i^{\$} = [(1 + r^{\$}) (1 + \pi^{\$})] - 1$$

where $r^{\$}$ is the real rate of return and $\pi^{\$}$ is the expected rate of inflation, for dollar-denominated assets. The subcomponents are then identifiable:

$$i^{\$} = r^{\$} + \pi^{\$} + r^{\$}\pi^{\$}.$$

As with PPP, there is an approximation of this function that has gained wide acceptance. The cross-product term of $r^{\$}\pi^{\$}$ is often very small, and therefore dropped altogether:

$$i^{\$} = r^{\$} + \pi^{\$}.$$

International Fisher Effect

The *international Fisher effect* is the extension of this domestic interest rate relationship to the international currency markets. If capital, by way of covered interest arbitrage (CIA), attempts to find higher rates of return internationally resulting from current interest rate differentials, the real rates of return between currencies are equalized (e.g., $r^\$ = r^{SF}$),

$$\frac{S_{t+1} - S_t}{S_t} = \frac{(1 + i^\$) - (1 + i^{SF})}{(1 + i^{SF})} = \frac{i^\$ - i^{SF}}{(1 + i^{SF})}.$$

If the nominal interest rates are then decomposed into their respective real and expected inflation components, the percentage change in the spot exchange rate is

$$\frac{S_{t+1} - S_t}{S_t} = \frac{(r^\$ + \pi^\$ + r^\$\pi^\$) - (r^{SF} + \pi^{SF} + r^{SF}\pi^{SF})}{1 + r^{SF} + \pi^{SF} + r^{SF}\pi^{SF}}.$$

The international Fisher effect has a number of additional implications, if the following requirements are met: (1) capital markets can be freely entered and exited; (2) capital markets possess investment opportunities that are acceptable substitutes; and (3) market agents have complete and equal information regarding these possibilities.

Given these conditions, international arbitragers are capable of exploiting all potential riskless profit opportunities, until real rates of return between markets are equalized ($r^\$ = r^{SF}$). Thus the expected rate of change in the spot exchange rate reduces to the differential in the expected rates of inflation:

$$\frac{S_{t+1} - S_t}{S_t} = \frac{\pi^\$ + r^\$\pi - \pi^{SF} - r^{SF}\pi^{SF}}{1 + r^{SF} + \pi^{SF} + r^{SF}\pi^{SF}}.$$

If the approximation forms are combined (both the elimination of the denominator and the elimination of the interactive terms of r and π), the change in the spot rate is simply

$$\frac{S_{t+1} - S_t}{S_t} = \pi^\$ - \pi^{SF}.$$

Note the similarity (identical in equation form) of the approximate form of the international Fisher effect to purchasing power parity discussed previously (the only potential difference is that between ex-post and ex-ante (expected) inflation.

Chapter 6
Foreign Currency Options

Global View

French Bank Stages Mock Options Market on Super Bowl to Teach Businesses How to Hedge Their Risks

'Skins Up by 10? You Make the Call: Punt or Put?

Move over, Jimmy the Greek. Make way for Société Generale. The French bank is throwing a Super Bowl party today at which 80 top corporate executives will speculate continuously on the game's outcome in a mock, Wall Street trading pit — complete with computer monitors, hustling clerks and big TV screens to watch the game in progress.

The bank hopes that the exercise will cast light on the real-life options market, a fast-growing but little-known corner of the financial markets in which corporations, investors and speculators trade the rights to buy everything from Japanese yen and IBM stock to gold.

After every big plunge on Wall Street, public critics charge that the options market, centered in this country mainly at the Chicago Board Options Exchange, is nothing but a den of gamblers and speculators. The impression may not exactly be dispelled by Société Generale's football bash. But supporters say the options market is an invaluable aid to banks and businesses seeking to "hedge," or limit, their risks in a highly volatile, interconnected global economy. And like a real options market, there will be the usual "calls" and "puts" — the two basic types of options that represent the right to buy and to sell, respectively.

Given the risks, some say that the most speculative thing an international company such as International Business Machines Corp. can do is not to buy and sell options, since it is then completely exposed to the fluctuations of currencies.

Although Société Generale would prefer the public to focus only on worthy causes such as foreign currency hedging, it and other banks with large options operations are among the biggest speculators in options. Such speculation, while not strictly gambling, can lead to very big profits or very big losses, depending on whether one correctly anticipates the direction of foreign exchange or interest rates.

Source: Adapted from Robert J. McCartney, "Skins Up by 10?," *The Washington Post,* 1/26/92, H1, H5. © 1992 The Washington Post. Reprinted with permission.

Foreign currency options are instruments that have assumed increasing importance in the marketplace in recent years. They can be used to hedge the foreign exchange risk that results from commercial transactions, and they can be used for speculative purposes. Use of foreign currency options to hedge commercial transactions is covered in Chapter 7.

This chapter is presented in two parts. The first half provides a basic description of currency options, of the markets in which they are traded, and of their use for investment or speculation purposes. The second half of the chapter provides a deeper look into the forces determining option values (pricing), and how option values change with these forces.

Vocabulary

- A *foreign currency option* is a contract giving the option purchaser (the buyer) the right, but not the obligation, to buy or sell a given amount of foreign exchange at a fixed price per unit for a specified time period (until the expiration date). In many ways buying an option is like buying a ticket to a Rolling Stones concert. The buyer has the right to attend the concert, but does not have to (after all, Mick Jagger is over 50 years old). The buyer of the concert ticket risks nothing more than what was paid for the ticket. Similarly, the buyer of an option cannot lose anything more than what was paid for the option. If the buyer of the ticket decides later not to attend the concert, prior to the day of the concert, the ticket can be sold to someone else who does wish to go (someone interested in the music of aging rock stars).

- There are two basic types of options: calls and puts. A *call* is an option to buy foreign currency, and a *put* is an option to sell foreign currency.

- The buyer of an option is termed the *holder;* the seller of an option is referred to as the *writer* or *grantor.*

- Every option has three different price elements: (1) the exercise or strike price, the exchange rate at which the foreign currency can be purchased (call) or sold (put); (2) the premium, the cost, price, or value of the option itself; and (3) the underlying or actual spot exchange rate in the market.

- An *American option* gives the buyer the right to exercise the option at any time between the date of writing and the expiration or maturity date. *European options* can be exercised only on their expiration date, not before.

- The premium or option price is the cost of the option, usually paid in advance by the buyer to the seller. In the over-the-counter market (options offered by banks), premiums are quoted as a percentage of the transaction amount. Premiums on exchange-traded options are quoted as a domestic currency amount per unit of foreign currency.

- An option whose exercise price is the same as the spot price of the underlying currency is said to be *at-the-money (ATM)*. An option that would be profitable (ignoring the premium) if exercised immediately is said to be *in-the-money (ITM)*. An option that would not be profitable if exercised immediately is referred to as *out-of-the-money (OTM)*.

Foreign Currency Options Markets

In the past decade the use of foreign currency options as a hedging tool and for speculative purposes has blossomed into a major foreign exchange activity. A number of banks in the United States and other capital markets offer flexible foreign currency options on transactions of $1 million or more. The bank market, or over-the-counter market as it is called, offers custom-tailored options on all major trading currencies for any time period up to several years. These provide a useful alternative to forward and futures contracts (discussed in chapter 4) for firms interested in hedging foreign exchange risk on commercial transactions.

In December 1982, the Philadelphia Stock Exchange introduced trading in standardized foreign currency option contracts in the United States. The Chicago Mercantile Exchange and other exchanges in the United States and abroad have followed suit. Exchange-traded contracts are particularly appealing to speculators and individuals who do not normally have access to the over-the-counter market. Banks also trade on the exchanges because this is one of several ways they can offset the risk of options they have transacted with clients or other banks.

Increased use of foreign currency options is a reflection of the explosive growth in the use of other kinds of options and the resultant improvements in option pricing models. The original option pricing model was developed by Black and Scholes in 1973.[1] It has been extended by others to apply to foreign currency options.[2] Several commercial programs are available for option writers and traders to utilize.

---

[1] Fisher Black and Myron Scholes, "The Pricing of Options and Corporate Liabilities," *Journal of Political Economy,* May/June 1973, pp. 637–659.

[2] Mark Garman and Steven Kohlhagen, "Foreign Currency Option Values," *Journal of International Money and Finance,* December 1983, pp. 231–237; J. Orlin Grabbe, "The Pricing of Call and Put Options on Foreign Exchange," *Journal of International Money and Finance,* December 1983, pp. 239–253; and Nahum Biger and John Hull, "The Valuation of Currency Options," *Financial Management,* Spring 1983, pp. 24–28.

Options on the Over-the-Counter Market

Over-the-counter (OTC) options are most frequently written by banks for U.S. dollars against British pounds, German marks, Swiss francs, Japanese yen, and Canadian dollars. They are usually written in round lots of $5 to $10 million in New York and $2 to $3 million in London.

The main advantage of over-the-counter options is that they are tailored to the specific needs of the firm. Financial institutions are willing to write or buy options that vary by amount (notional principal), strike price, and maturity. Although the over-the-counter markets were relatively illiquid in the early years, the market has grown to such proportions that liquidity is now considered quite good. On the other hand, the buyer must assess the writing bank's ability to fulfill the option contract. Termed *counterparty risk,* the financial risk associated with the counterparty is an increasing issue in international markets as a result of recent failures, such as the Bank of New England and Drexel-Burnham Lambert, and legal risks associated with certain semi-sovereign parties in the United Kingdom (Chapter 14 provides an expanded discussion of counterparty risk). However, firms buying and selling currency options as part of their risk management program (as detailed in Chapter 7), do so primarily in the over-the-counter market. Exchange-traded options are more the territory of the financial institutions themselves.

A firm wishing to purchase an option in the over-the-counter market normally places a call to the currency option desk of a major money center bank, specifies the currencies, maturity, strike rate(s), and asks for an *indication,* a bid-offer quote. The bank normally takes a few minutes to a few hours to price the option and return the call.

Options on Organized Exchanges

Options on the physical (underlying) currency are traded on a number of organized exchanges worldwide, one of which is the Philadelphia Stock Exchange. Exchange-traded options are settled through a clearinghouse. Buyers do not deal directly with sellers. The clearinghouse is the counterparty to every option contract and it guarantees fulfillment. Clearinghouse obligations are in turn the obligation of all members of the exchange, including a large number of banks.

Foreign currency options on seven major currencies are traded on the Philadelphia Stock Exchange (each against the U.S. dollar): Australian dollar, British pound, Canadian dollar, Deutschemark, French franc, Japanese yen, and Swiss franc. It also trades the European Currency Unit (ECU). The Philadelphia Stock Exchange has recently introduced cross-currency options (STG/DEM, DEM/YEN)[3] and end-of-month contract maturities in addition to the current mid-month maturity. Both American and European options are available for each of the currencies, except for European Currency Units (ECUs), which trade only an American option. Options on exchanges are traded in standardized amounts per option contract. For example, on the Philadelphia Stock Exchange each option on Deutschemarks is for DM62,500. If a

---

[3]Note that the Philadelphia Stock Exchange uses the three-letter computer symbols for the British pound sterling, STG, and the Deutschemark, DEM, rather than the traditional symbols utilized throughout this book of £ and DM, respectively.

company wishes to buy options on DM1,000,000, the company would purchase 16 contracts, because DM1,000,000/ DM62,500 per contract = 16 contracts.

Each foreign currency option is introduced for trading with one, two, three, six, nine, and twelve months to run until expiration. Expiration months are March, June, September, and December, with trading also available in two additional near-term consecutive months. Thus in November, trading would occur in November, December, January, March, June, and September maturities. Finally, each mid-month option contract expires at 11:59 P.M. on the Friday preceding the third Wednesday of the expiration month. All end-of-month (EOM) options expire at 11:59 P.M. on the last Friday of the expiration month.[4]

Currency Option Quotations and Prices

Quotes in the *Wall Street Journal* for options on German marks are shown in Exhibit 6.1. The *Journal's* quotes refer to transactions completed on the Philadelphia Stock Exchange on the previous day. Quotations are usually available for more combinations of strike prices and expiration dates than were actually traded and thus reported in the newspaper.

Exhibit 6.1 illustrates the three different prices that characterize any foreign currency option. The three prices that characterize an "August 58 1/2 call option" (highlighted in Exhibit 6.1) are the following:[5]

1. **Spot rate.** In Exhibit 6.1, "option and underlying" means that 58.51 cents, or $0.5851, is the spot dollar price of one German mark at the close of trading on the preceding day. This spot rate is sometimes omitted from the *Wall Street Journal* quotations.

2. **Exercise price.** The exercise price, or "strike price" listed in Exhibit 6.1, means the price per mark that must be paid if the option is exercised. The August call option on marks of 58 1/2 means $0.5850/DM. Exhibit 6.1 lists nine different strike prices, ranging from $0.5600/DM to $0.6000/DM, although more were available on that date than listed here.[6]

3. **Premium.** The premium is the cost or price of the option. The price of the August 58 1/2 call option on German marks is 0.50 U.S. cents per mark, or $0.0050/DM. There was no trading of the September and December 58 1/2 call on that day. The premium is the market value of the option, and therefore the

---

[4]Expiration dates on the Philadelphia Stock Exchange were traditionally the Saturday following the third Wednesday of the expiration month, not Friday. The change to Friday was made effective on June 13, 1993, in an attempt to better accommodate trading in a 24-hour marketplace.

[5]Currency option strike prices and premiums on the U.S. dollar are quoted throughout this chapter as direct quotations ($/DM, $/¥, etc.) as opposed to the more common usage of indirect quotations used throughout the rest of the book. This is standard practice with option prices as quoted on major option exchanges like the Philadelphia Stock Exchange.

[6]Options are available at fixed strike prices, the prices reflecting current market prices of the underlying currency at the time that option was first offered.

Exhibit 6.1   Foreign Currency Option Quotations (Philadelphia Stock Exchange)

Option and Underlying	Strike price	Calls—Last			Puts—Last		
		Aug.	Sept.	Dec.	Aug.	Sept.	Dec.
62,500 German marks-cents per unit.							
58.51	56	—	—	2.76	0.04	0.22	1.16
58.51	56 1/2	—	—	—	0.06	0.30	—
58.51	57	1.13	—	1.74	0.10	0.38	1.27
58.51	57 1/2	0.75	—	—	0.17	0.55	—
58.51	58	0.71	1.05	1.28	0.27	0.89	1.81
58.51	58 1/2	0.50	—	—	0.50	0.99	—
58.51	59	0.30	0.66	1.21	0.90	1.36	—
58.51	59 1/2	0.15	0.40	—	2.32	—	—
58.51	60	—	0.31	—	2.32	2.62	3.30

Source: Adapted from *The Wall Street Journal,* Tuesday, August 3, 1993; quotes are for close of Monday, August 2, 1993.

terms *premium, cost, price,* and *value* are all interchangeable when referring to an option.[7]

The August 58 1/2 call option premium is 0.50 cents per mark, and in this case, the August 58 1/2 put's premium is also 0.50 cents per mark. Since one option contract on the Philadelphia Stock Exchange consists of 62,500 marks, the total cost of one option contract for the call (or put in this case) is DM62,500 × $0.0050/DM = $312.50.

Foreign Currency Speculation

Speculation is an attempt to profit by trading on expectations about prices in the future. In the foreign exchange markets, one speculates by taking an open (unhedged) position in a foreign currency and then closing that position after the exchange rate has moved— one hopes—in the expected direction. In the following section we analyze the way speculation is undertaken in spot, forward, and options markets. It is important to understand this phenomenon because it has a major impact on our inability to accurately forecast future exchange rates.

Speculating in the Spot Market

Willem Koopmans is a currency speculator in Amsterdam. He is willing to risk money on his own opinion about future currency prices. Willem Koopmans may speculate in

---

[7]All option premiums are expressed in cents per unit of foreign currency on the Philadelphia Stock Exchange except for the French franc, which is expressed in tenths of a cent per franc, and the Japanese yen, which is expressed in hundredths of a cent per yen.

the spot, forward, or options markets. To illustrate, assume the German mark is currently quoted as follows:

Spot rate:	$0.5851/DM
Six-month forward rate:	$0.5760/DM

Willem Koopmans has $100,000 with which to speculate, and he believes in six months the spot rate for the mark will be $0.6000/DM. Speculation in the spot market requires only that the speculator believe the foreign currency will appreciate in value. He should take the following steps:

1. Today use the $100,000 to buy DM170,910.96 spot at $0.5851/DM.

2. Hold the DM170,910.96 indefinitely. Although the mark is expected to rise to the target value in six months, the speculator is not committed to that time horizon.

3. When the target exchange rate is reached, sell DM170,910.96 at the new spot rate of $0.6000/DM, receiving DM170,910.96 × $0.6000/DM = $102,546.57.

4. Profit = $2,546.57, or 2.5% on the $100,000 committed for six months (5.0% per annum). This ignores interest income on the Deutschemarks and opportunity cost on the dollars for the moment.

The potential maximum gain is unlimited; the maximum loss will be $100,000 if the marks purchased in step 1 drop in value to zero. Having initially undertaken a spot market speculation for six months, Koopmans is nevertheless not bound by that target date. He may sell the marks earlier or later if he wishes.

Speculating in the Forward Market

Forward market speculation occurs when the speculator believes the spot price at some future date will differ from today's forward price for that same date. Success does not depend on the direction of movement of the spot rate, but on the relative position of the future spot rate and the current forward rate. Given the data and expectations just described, Willem Koopmans should take the following steps:

1. Today buy DM173,611.11 forward six months at the forward quote of $0.5760/DM. Note that this step requires no outlay of cash.

2. In six months, fulfill the forward contract, receiving DM173,611.11 at $0.5760/DM for a cost of $100,000.

3. Simultaneously sell the DM173,611.11 in the spot market, receiving DM173,611.11 × $0.6000/DM = $104,166.67.

4. Profit: $4,166.67.

The profit of $4,166.67 cannot be related to an investment base to calculate a return on investment because the dollar funds were never needed. On the six-month anniversary Willem Koopmans simply crosses the payment obligation of $100,000 with receipts of $104,166.67, and accepts a net $4,166.67. Nevertheless, some financial institutions might require him to deposit collateral as margin to assure his ability to complete the trade.

In this particular forward speculation, the maximum loss is $100,000, the amount needed to buy marks via the forward contract. This loss would be incurred only if the value of the spot mark in six months were zero. The maximum gain is unlimited, since marks acquired in the forward market can in theory rise to an infinite dollar value.

Forward market speculation cannot be extended beyond the maturity date of the forward contract. However, if the speculator wants to close out the speculative operation before maturity, that speculator may buy an offsetting contract. In our example, after, say, four months, Willem Koopmans could sell DM173,611.11 forward two months at whatever forward price then existed. Two months after that he would close the matured six-month contract to purchase marks against the matured two-month contract to sell marks, pocketing any profit or paying up any loss. The amount of profit or loss would be fixed by the price at which Willem Koopmans sold forward two months.

The example just presented is only one of several possible types of forward speculations. Note that the examples given in this discussion have ignored any interest earned. In a spot speculation, the speculator can invest the principal amount in the foreign money market to earn interest. In the various forward speculations, a speculator who is holding cash against the risk of loss can invest those funds in the home money market. Thus relative profitability will be influenced by interest differentials.

Speculating in Option Markets

Options differ from all other types of financial instruments in the patterns of risk they produce. The option owner has the choice of exercising the option or allowing it to expire unused. The owner will exercise it only when exercising is profitable, which means only when the option is in the money. In the case of a call option, as the spot price of the underlying currency moves up, the holder has the possibility of unlimited profit. On the down side, however, the holder can abandon the option and walk away with a loss never greater than the premium paid.

Buyer of a Call

The position of Willem Koopmans as a buyer of a call is illustrated in the upper half of Exhibit 6.2. Assume that Koopmans purchases the August call option on German marks described previously, the one with a strike price of 58 1/2 ($0.5850/DM) and a premium of $0.005/DM. The vertical axis measures profit or loss for the option buyer, at each of several different spot prices for the mark up to the time of maturity.

At all spot rates *below* the strike price of $0.585, Koopmans would choose not to exercise his option. This is obvious, since at a spot rate of $0.585, for example, Koopmans would prefer to buy a German mark for $0.580 on the spot market rather than exercising his option to buy a mark at $0.585. If the spot rate remains below $0.580 until August when the option expired, Koopmans would not exercise the option. His total loss would be limited to only what he paid for the option, the $0.005/DM purchase price. At any lower price for the mark, his loss would similarly be limited to the original $0.005/DM cost.

Alternatively, at all spot rates *above* the strike price of $0.585, Koopmans would exercise the option, paying only the strike price for each German mark. For example, if the spot rate were $0.595 cents per mark at maturity, Koopmans would exercise his call

Exhibit 6.2   Profit and Loss Position for the Buyer and Writer of a Call Option on German Marks with a Premium of $0.005/DM

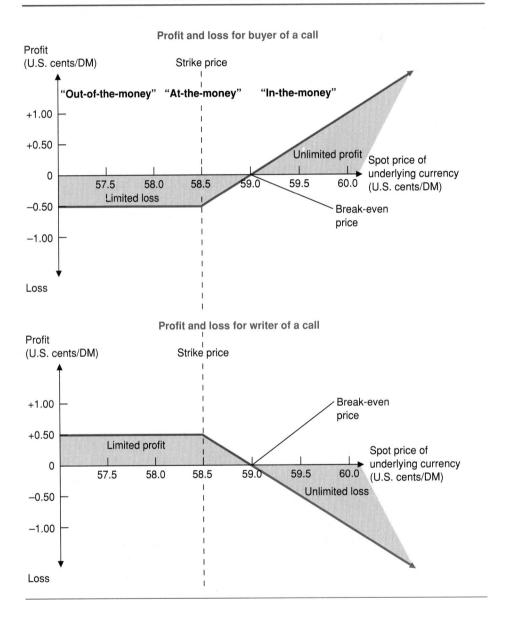

option, buying German marks for $0.585 each instead of purchasing them on the spot market at $0.595 each. The German marks could be sold immediately in the spot market for $0.595 each, pocketing a gross profit of $0.010/DM, or a net profit of $0.005/DM after deducting the original cost of the option of $0.005/DM. The profit to Koopmans, if the spot rate is greater than the strike price, with strike price $0.585, a premium of $0.005, and a spot rate of $0.595, is:

$$\text{Profit} = \text{Spot Rate} - (\text{Strike Price} + \text{Premium})$$
$$= \$0.595/\text{DM} - (\$0.585/\text{DM} + \$0.005/\text{DM})$$
$$= \$0.005/\text{DM}.$$

More likely, Koopmans would realize the profit through executing an offsetting contract on the options exchange rather than taking delivery of the currency. Because the dollar price of a mark could rise to an infinite level (off the upper right-hand side of the page in Exhibit 6.2), maximum profit is unlimited. The buyer of a call option thus possesses an attractive combination of outcomes: limited loss and unlimited profit potential.

The *break-even price* of $0.590/DM is the price at which Koopmans neither gains nor loses on exercise of the option. The premium cost of $0.005, combined with the cost of exercising the option of $0.585, is exactly equal to the proceeds from selling the marks in the spot market at $0.590. Note that Koopmans will still exercise the call option at the break-even price. This is because by exercising it Koopmans at least recoups (pardon the pun) the premium paid for the option. At any spot price above the exercise price but below the break-even price, the gross profit earned on exercising the option and selling the underlying currency covers part (but not all) of the premium cost.

Writer of a Call

The position of the writer (seller) of the same call option is illustrated in the bottom half of Exhibit 6.2. If the option expires when the spot price of the underlying currency is below the exercise price of $0.585, the option holder does not exercise. What the holder loses, the writer gains. The writer keeps as profit the entire premium paid of $0.005/DM. Above the exercise price of $0.585, the writer of the call must deliver the underlying currency for $0.585/DM at a time when the value of the mark is above $0.585. If the writer wrote the option naked, that is, without owning the currency, that writer will now have to buy the currency at spot and take the loss. The amount of such a loss is unlimited and increases as the price of the underlying currency rises. Once again, what the holder gains, the writer loses, and vice versa. Even if the writer already owns the currency, the writer will experience an opportunity loss, surrendering against the option the same currency that could have been sold for more in the open market.

For example, the profit to the writer of a call option of strike price $0.585, premium $0.005, a spot rate of $0.595/DM is:

$$\text{Profit} = \text{Premium} - (\text{Spot Rate} - \text{Strike Price})$$
$$= \$0.005/\text{DM} - (\$0.595/\text{DM} - \$0.585/\text{DM})$$
$$= -\$0.005/\text{DM}$$

but **only** if the spot rate is greater than or equal to the strike rate. At spot rates less than the strike price, the option will expire worthless and the writer of the call option will keep the premium earned. The maximum profit the writer of the call option can make is limited to the premium. The writer of a call option would have a rather unattractive combination of potential outcomes: limited profit potential and unlimited loss potential, but there are ways to limit such losses through other techniques.

Buyer of a Put

The position of Koopmans as buyer of a put is illustrated in Exhibit 6.3. The basic terms of this put are similar to those we just used to illustrate a call. The buyer of a put option, however, wants to be able to sell the underlying currency at the exercise price when the market price of that currency drops (not rises as in the case of a call option). If the spot price of a mark drops to, say, $0.575/DM, Koopmans will deliver marks to the writer and receive $0.585/DM. The marks can now be purchased on the spot market for $0.575 each and the cost of the option was $0.005/DM, so he will have a net gain of $0.005/DM.

Explicitly, the profit to the holder of a put option if the spot rate is less than the strike price, with a strike price $0.585/DM and premium of $0.005/DM, and a spot rate of $0.575/DM is:

$$\text{Profit} = \text{Strike Price} - (\text{Spot Rate} + \text{Premium})$$
$$= \$0.585/DM - (\$0.575/DM + \$0.005/DM)$$
$$= \$0.005/DM.$$

The break-even price for the put option is the strike price less the premium, or $0.580/DM in this case. As the spot rate falls further and further below the strike price, the profit potential would continually increase, and Koopmans' profit could be unlimited (up to a maximum of $0.580/DM, when the price of a DM would be zero). At any exchange rate above the strike price of $0.585, Koopmans would not exercise the option, and so would lose only the $0.005/DM premium paid for the put option. The buyer of a put option has an almost unlimited profit potential with a limited loss potential. Like the buyer of a call, the buyer of a put can never lose more than the premium paid up front.

Writer of a Put

The position of the writer of the put sold to Koopmans is shown in the lower half of Exhibit 6.3. Note the symmetry of profit/loss, strike price, and break-even prices between the buyer and the writer of the put as was the case of the call option. If the spot price of marks drops below $0.585 per mark, the option will be exercised by Koopmans. Below a price of $0.585 per mark, the writer will lose more than the premium received from writing the option ($0.005/DM), falling below break even. Between $0.580/DM and $0.585/DM the writer will lose part, but not all, of the premium received. If the spot price is above $0.585/DM, the option will not be exercised, and the option writer

Exhibit 6.3 Profit and Loss Position for the Buyer and Writer of a Put Option on German Marks with a Premium of $0.005/DM

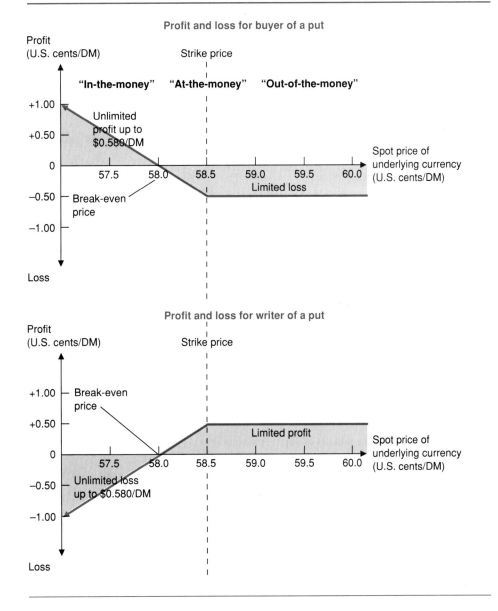

pockets the entire premium of $0.005/DM. The profit earned by the writer of a $0.585 strike price put, premium $0.005, at a spot rate of $0.575, is:

$$\text{Profit} = \text{Premium} - (\text{Strike Price} - \text{Spot Rate})$$
$$= \$0.005/\text{DM} - (\$0.585/\text{DM} - \$0.575/\text{DM})$$
$$= -\$0.005/\text{DM},$$

but **only** for spot rates that are less than or equal to the strike price. At spot rates that are greater than the strike price, the option expires out-of-the-money and the writer keeps the premium earned up front. The writer of the put option has the same basic combination of outcomes available to the writer of a call: limited profit potential and unlimited loss potential.

Option Pricing and Valuation

Exhibit 6.4 illustrates the profit/loss profile of a European-style call option on British pounds. The call option allows the holder to buy British pounds (£) at a strike price of $1.70/£. The value of this call option is actually the sum of two components:

$$\text{Total Value (premium)} = \text{Intrinsic Value} + \text{Time Value}.$$

Intrinsic value is the financial gain if the option is exercised immediately. It is shown by the solid line in Exhibit 6.4, which is zero until reaching the strike price, then rises linearly 1 cent for each 1 cent increase in the spot rate. Intrinsic value will be zero when the option is out-of-the-money, that is, when the strike price is above the market price, since no gain can be derived from exercising the option. When the spot price rises above the strike price, the intrinsic value becomes positive because the option is always worth at least this value if exercised.

In Exhibit 6.4, when the spot rate is $1.72/£ the option has an *intrinsic value* of $1.72 less $1.70/£, or 2 cents per pound. At a spot rate below $1.70/£, the option is out-of-the-money and has no intrinsic value (and only a fool would exercise it instead of buying pounds more cheaply on the spot market).

The *time value* of an option exists because the price of the underlying currency, the spot rate, can potentially move further and further in-the-money between the present time and the option's expiration date. Time value is shown in Exhibit 6.4 as the area between the total value of the option and its intrinsic value. At a spot rate of $1.72/£, the option's total value is composed of the 2 cents per pound intrinsic value and 2.39 cents per pound in time value, for a total value of 4.39 cents per pound.

An investor will pay something today for an out-of-the-money option (i.e., zero intrinsic value) on the chance the spot rate will move far enough before maturity to move the option in-the-money. Consequently, the price of an option is always somewhat greater than its intrinsic value, since there is always some chance the intrinsic value will rise between the present and the expiration date.

Components of Option Pricing

The total value of an option is the sum of its intrinsic value, which is easy to calculate, and its time value, which depends on the market's expectations about the likelihood the

Exhibit 6.4   Intrinsic Value, Time Value, and Total Value of a Call Option on
                  British pounds

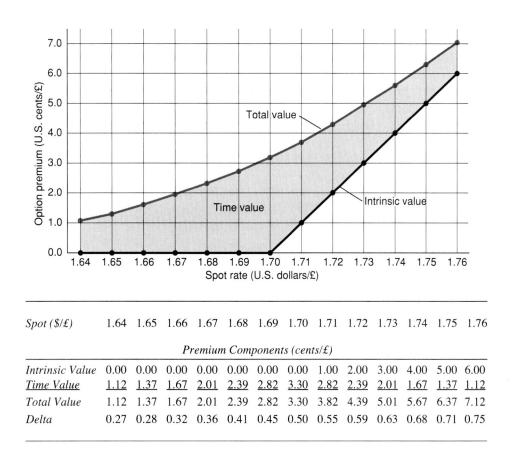

Spot ($/£)	1.64	1.65	1.66	1.67	1.68	1.69	1.70	1.71	1.72	1.73	1.74	1.75	1.76
Premium Components (cents/£)													
Intrinsic Value	0.00	0.00	0.00	0.00	0.00	0.00	0.00	1.00	2.00	3.00	4.00	5.00	6.00
Time Value	1.12	1.37	1.67	2.01	2.39	2.82	3.30	2.82	2.39	2.01	1.67	1.37	1.12
Total Value	1.12	1.37	1.67	2.01	2.39	2.82	3.30	3.82	4.39	5.01	5.67	6.37	7.12
Delta	0.27	0.28	0.32	0.36	0.41	0.45	0.50	0.55	0.59	0.63	0.68	0.71	0.75

underlying currency will rise in value (for a call option) prior to maturity. On the date of maturity an option will have a value equal to its intrinsic value (zero time remaining means zero time value).

The pricing of a currency option combines six elements. For example, the European style call option on British pounds depicted in Exhibit 6.4 has a premium of $0.033/£ at a spot rate of $1.70/£. This premium is based on the following assumptions:

1. present spot rate, $1.70/£;

2. time to maturity, 90 days;

3. forward rate for matching maturity (90 days), $1.70/£;

4. U.S. dollar interest rate, 8.00% per annum;

5. British pound sterling interest rate, 8.00% per annum;

6. volatility, the standard deviation of daily spot price movement, 10.00% per annum.

These assumptions are all that are needed to calculate the option premium. This base case numerical example, which we continue to use through the remainder of the chapter, assumes both currency interest rates are the same. This means the forward rate equals the spot rate. In the following section we demonstrate how the value of the option—the option premium—changes as these six components change. This chapter's appendix describes the theoretical specification of currency option pricing and demonstrates the numerical calculation of the call option just described.

Currency Option Pricing Sensitivity

If currency options are to be used effectively, either for the purposes of speculation or risk management (covered in the coming chapters), the individual trader needs to know how option values—premiums—react to their various components. The following section analyzes these six basic sensitivities:

1. the impact of changing forward rates;

2. the impact of changing spot rates;

3. the impact of time to maturity;

4. the impact of changing volatility;

5. the impact of changing interest differentials;

6. the impact of alternative option strike prices.

1. Forward Rate Sensitivity

Although rarely noted, standard foreign currency options are priced around the forward rate. This is because the current spot rate and both the domestic and foreign interest rates (home currency and foreign currency rates) are included in the option premium calculation.[8] Regardless of the specific strike rate chosen and priced, the forward rate is central to valuation. The option-pricing formula calculates a subjective probability distribution centered on the forward rate. This does not mean the market expects the forward rate to be equal to the future spot rate, it is simply a result of the arbitrage-pricing structure of options.

---

[8]Recall from Chapter 4 that the forward rate is calculated from the current spot rate and the two subject currency interest rates for the desired maturity. For example, the 90-day forward rate for the call option on British pounds just described is calculated as follows:

$$F_{90} = \$1.70/\pounds \times \left[\frac{1 + .08\left(\frac{90}{360}\right)}{1 + .08\left(\frac{90}{360}\right)} \right] = \$1.70/\pounds.$$

The forward rate focus also provides helpful information for the trader managing a position. When the market prices a foreign currency option, it does so without any bullish or bearish sentiment on the direction of the foreign currency's value relative to the domestic currency. If the trader has specific expectations about the future spot rate's direction, those expectations can be put to work. A trader will not be inherently betting against the market. In a following section we also describe how a change in the interest differential between currencies, the theoretical foundation of forward rates, also alters the value of the option.

2. Spot Rate Sensitivity (Delta)

The call option on British pounds depicted in Exhibit 6.4 possesses a premium that exceeds the intrinsic value of the option over the entire range of spot rates surrounding the strike rate. As long as the option has time remaining before expiration, the option will possess this time value element. This is one of the primary reasons why an American-style option, which can be exercised on any day up to and including the expiration date, is seldom actually exercised prior to expiration. If the option holder wishes to liquidate it for its value, it would normally be sold, not exercised, so any remaining time value can also be captured by the holder. If the current spot rate falls on that side of the option's strike price which would induce the option holder to exercise the option upon expiration, the option also has an intrinsic value. The call option illustrated in Exhibit 6.4 is in-the-money (ITM) at spot rates to the right of the strike rate of $1.70/£, at-the-money (ATM) at $1.70/£, and out-of-the-money (OTM) at spot rates less than $1.70/£.

The vertical distance between the market value and the intrinsic value of a call option on pounds is greatest at a spot rate of $1.70/£. At $1.70/£ the spot rate equals the strike price (at-the-money). This premium of 3.30 cents per pound consists entirely of time value.[9] The further the option's strike price is out-of-the-money, the lower the value or premium of the option. This is because the market believes the probability of this option actually moving into the exercise range prior to expiration is significantly less than one that is already at-the-money. If the spot rate were to fall to $1.68/£, the option premium falls to 2.39 cents/£, again, entirely time value. If the spot rate were to rise above the strike rate to $1.72/£, the premium rises to 4.39 cents/£. In this case the premium represents an intrinsic value of 2.00 cents ($1.72/£ − $1.70/£) plus a time value element of 2.39 cents. Note the symmetry of time value premiums (2.39 cents) to the left and to the right of the strike rate.

The symmetry of option valuation about the strike rate is seen by decomposing the option premia into their respective intrinsic and time values. Exhibit 6.5 illustrates how varying the current spot rate by ± $0.05 about the strike rate of $1.70/£ alters each option's intrinsic and time values.

The sensitivity of the option premium to a small change in the spot exchange rate is called the *delta*. For example, the delta of the $1.70/£ call option, when the spot rate

---

[9]In fact, the value of any option that is currently out-of-the-money (OTM) is made up entirely of time value.

Exhibit 6.5   Decomposing Call Option Premiums: Intrinsic Value and Time Value

Strike Rate ($/£)	Spot Rate ($/£)	Money	Call Premium = (cents/£)	Intrinsic Value + (cents/£)	Time Value (cents/£)	Delta (0 to 1)
1.70	1.75	ITM	6.37	5.00	1.37	.71
1.70	1.70	ATM	3.30	0.00	3.30	.50
1.70	1.65	OTM	1.37	0.00	1.37	.28

changes from $1.70/£ to $1.71/£, is simply the change in the premium divided by the change in the spot rate:

$$\text{delta} = \frac{\Delta \text{ Premium}}{\Delta \text{ Spot Rate}} = \frac{\$0.038/£ - \$0.033/£}{\$1.71/£ - \$1.70/£} = 0.5.$$

If the delta of the specific option is known, it is easy to determine how the option's value will change as the spot rate changes. If the spot rate changes by one cent ($0.01/£), given a delta of 0.5, the option premium would change by 0.5 × $0.01, or $0.005. If the initial premium was $0.033/£, and the spot rate increased by 1 cent (from $1.70/£ to $1.71/£), the new option premium would be $0.033 + $0.005 = $0.038/£. Delta varies between +1 and 0 for a call option, and −1 and 0 for a put option.

Traders in options categorize individual options by their delta rather than in-the-money, at-the-money, or out-of-the-money.[10] As an option moves further in-the-money, like the in-the-money option in Exhibit 6.5, delta rises toward 1.0 (in this case to .71). As an option moves further out-of-the-money, delta falls toward zero. Note that the out-of-the-money option in Exhibit 6.5 has a delta of only .28.[11]

> **Rule of Thumb:** The higher the delta (deltas of .7 or .8 and up are considered high) the greater the probability of the option expiring in-the-money.

3. Time to Maturity: Value and Deterioration (Theta)

Option values increase with the length of time to maturity. The expected change in the option premium from a small change in the time to expiration is termed *theta*.

Theta is calculated as the change in the option premium over the change in time. If the $1.70/£ call option were to age one day from its initial 90-day maturity, the theta of

---

[10]The full range of delta values at the bottom of Exhibit 6.4 illustrate how a call option's delta changes as the spot rate moves from out-of-the-money to far in-the-money.

[11]The expected change in the option's delta resulting from a small change in the spot rate is termed *gamma*. It is often used as a measure of the stability of a specific option's delta. Gamma is utilized in the construction of more sophisticated hedging strategies that focus on deltas (delta-neutral strategies).

the call option would be the difference in the two premiums, 3.30 cents/£ and 3.28 cents/£ (assuming a spot rate of \$1.70/£):

$$\text{Theta} = \frac{\Delta \text{ premium}}{\Delta \text{ time}} = \frac{\text{cents } 3.30/\pounds - \text{cents } 3.28/\pounds}{90 - 89} = .02.$$

Theta is based not on a linear relationship with time, but rather the square root of time. Exhibit 6.6 illustrates the time value deterioration for our same \$1.70/£ call option on pounds. The at-the-money strike rate is \$1.70/£, and the out-of-the-money and in-the-money spot rates are \$1.67/£ and \$1.73/£, respectively. Option premiums deteriorate at an increasing rate as they approach expiration. In fact, the majority of the option premium—depending on the individual option—is lost in the final 30 days prior to expiration.

This exponential relationship between option premium and time is seen in the ratio of option values between the three-month and the one-month at-the-money maturities. The ratio for the at-the-money call option is not 3 to 1 (holding all other components constant), but rather

$$\frac{\text{Premium of 90 day ATM call}}{\text{Premium of 30 day ATM call}} = \frac{\text{cents } 3.30/\pounds}{\text{cents } 1.93/\pounds} = 1.71.$$

The three-month option's price is only 1.71 times that of the one month, not 3 times the price.

The rapid deterioration of option values in the last days prior to expiration is seen by

Exhibit 6.6   Theta: Option Premium Time Value Deterioration

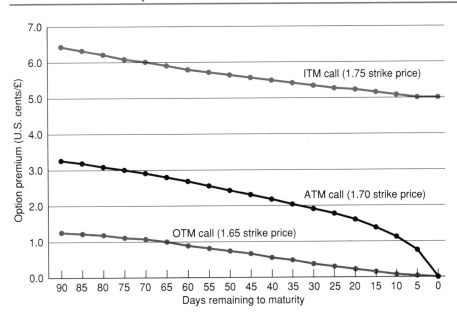

once again calculating the theta of the $1.70/£ call option, but now as its remaining maturity moves from 15 days to 14 days:

$$\text{Theta} = \frac{\Delta \text{ premium}}{\Delta \text{ time}} = \frac{\text{cents } 1.37/£ - \text{cents } 1.32/£}{15 - 14} = .05.$$

A decrease of one day in the time to maturity now reduces the option premium by .05 cents/£, rather than only .02 cents/£ as it did when the maturity was 90 days.

Exhibit 6.6 also illustrates the basic spot rate-option premium relations noted previously. The out-of-the-money call option's premium is logically smaller than the at-the-money option throughout its life, but deteriorates at a slower rate due to having an initially smaller level to fall from. The in-the-money option is of greater value throughout its time-life relative to the at-the-money, falling toward its intrinsic value (5 cents/£) at expiration. The at-the-money option, however, falls particularly quickly in the final periods prior to expiration. As any specific option ages, moving continually toward expiration, the time value will constantly decrease (assuming nothing else has changed). This would be illustrated by the total value line of the call option initially shown in Exhibit 6.4 collapsing inward toward the strike price of $1.70.

The implications of time value deterioration for traders are quite significant. A trader purchasing an option with only one or two months until expiration will see the option's value deteriorate rapidly. If the trader were then to sell the option, it would have a significantly smaller market value in the periods immediately following its purchase.

At the same time, however, a trader who is buying options of longer maturities will pay more, but not proportionately more, for the longer maturity option. A 6-month option's premium is approximately 2.45 times more expensive than the one month; the 12-month option would be only 3.46 times more expensive than the one month. This implies that two 3-month options do not equal one 6-month option.[12]

> **Rule of Thumb:** A trader will normally find longer maturity options better values, giving the trader the ability to alter an option position without suffering significant time value deterioration.

4. Sensitivity to Volatility (Vega)

There are few words in the financial field that are more used and abused than *volatility*. *Option volatility* is defined as the standard deviation of daily percentage changes in the underlying exchange rate. Volatility is important to option value because of an exchange rate's perceived likelihood to move either into or out of the range in which the option would be exercised. If the exchange rate's volatility is rising, and therefore the risk of the option being exercised increasing, the option premium would be increasing.

---

[12]A common error among beginning option traders is to purchase short-dated options that are then continually replaced with expiration to maintain their portfolio positions. The purchase of a longer dated option, for example a six-month or even twelve-month option, is significantly cheaper for the basic option position.

Volatility is stated in percent per annum. For example, an option may be described as having a 12.6% annual volatility. The percentage change for a single day can be found as follows:

$$\frac{12.6\%}{\sqrt{365}} = \frac{12.6\%}{19.105} = 0.66\% \text{ daily volatility.}$$

The sensitivity of the option premium to a unit change in volatility is termed *vega* (also termed *kappa*). For our $1.70/£ call option, an increase in annual volatility of 1 percentage point, for example from 10.0% to 11.0%, will increase the option premium from $0.033/£ to $0.036/£.

$$\text{Vega} = \frac{\Delta \text{ premium}}{\Delta \text{ volatility}} = \frac{\$0.036/£ - \$0.033/£}{.11 - .10} = 0.30.$$

The primary problem with volatility is that it is *unobservable;* it is the only input into the option pricing formula that is judgmentally based by the trader pricing the option. There is no single correct method for its calculation. The problem is one of fore-casting; the historical volatility is not necessarily an accurate predictor of the future volatility of the exchange rate's movement, yet there is little to go on except historical data.

Volatility is viewed three ways: *historic,* where the volatility is drawn from a recent period of time; *forward looking,* where the historic volatility is altered to reflect expecta-tions about the future period over which the option will exist; and *implied,* where the volatility is backed out of the market price of the option itself.

Historic volatility is normally measured as the percentage movement in the spot rate on a daily, 6, or 12-hour basis over the previous 10, 30, or even 90 days. If option traders believe the immediate future will be the same as the recent past, the historic volatility will equal the forward-looking volatility. If, however, the future period is expected to experience greater or lesser volatility, the historic measure must be altered for option pricing. Implied volatility is equivalent to having the answers to the test; implied volatil-ities are calculated by being backed out of the market option premium values traded. Since volatility is the only unobservable element of the option premium price, after all other components are accounted for, the residual value of volatility that is *implied* by the price is used.

Option premia are highly sensitive to volatility. As illustrated in Exhibit 6.7, the at-the-money call premium on the British pound rises linearly with currency volatility. That is, a doubling of volatility translates into a doubling of the option value. The out-of-the-money call option also gains value rapidly with rising volatility. Even though the out-of-the-money option may possess no intrinsic value at this point in time, the higher the volatility the greater the chance the spot rate could move enough to move the option in-the-money. The in-the-money call option on pounds, although possessing a positive premium even at 0% volatility due to its intrinsic value, also rises in value with increased volatility due to the potential for further movements of the spot rate in-the-money.

Exhibit 6.7   Vega: Option Premium Sensitivity to Volatility

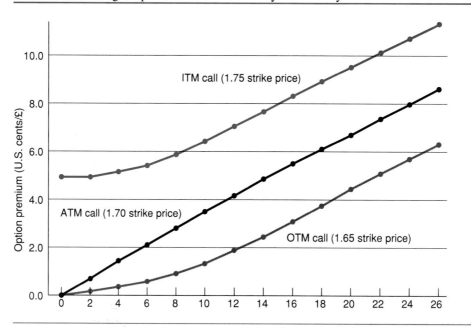

Like all futures markets, option volatilities react instantaneously and negatively to unsettling economic and political events (or rumor). Most currency option traders focus their activities on predicting movements of currency volatility in the short run, for they will move price the most. For example, option volatilities rose significantly in the months preceding the Persian Gulf War of 1991, in September 1992 when the European Monetary System was in crisis, and in July 1993 when the EMS once again was in crisis and was eventually restructured. In all instances option volatilities for major cross-currency combinations such as the DM/$ rose to nearly 20% for extended periods.

Sample implied volatilities for a number of currency pairs in February 1993 are listed in Exhibit 6.8. Volatilities are the only judgmental component that the option writer contributes, and yet they play a critical role in the pricing of options. Volatilities are typically expressed in bid/offer form, reflecting whether the trader wishes to buy or sell (write) the specific option. Note also that the implied volatilities do vary over maturity (3, 6, or 12 months in Exhibit 6.8). All currency pairs have historical series that contribute to the formation of the expectations of option writers. There is a noticeable difference in relative implied volatilities, with the SFR/DM at 3 months at 5.5%/6.0% at the low end, and the $/£ at 3 months at 13.3%/13.5% at the high end.

> **Rule of Thumb:** Traders who believe volatilities will fall significantly in the near term will sell (write) options now, hoping to buy them back for a profit immediately after volatilities fall causing option premia to fall.

Exhibit 6.8 Implied Volatilities in February 1993 (percent per annum)

Cross	3 months	6 months	12 months
DM/$	12.3/12.5	12.3/12.5	12.4/12.6
¥/$	10.2/10.45	10.2/10.35	10.1/10.3
SFR/$	13.5/13.7	13.5/13.7	13.6/13.8
$/£	13.3/13.5	13.3/13.5	13.4/13.6
C$/$	5.3/5.8	5.8/6.3	5.8/6.3
US$/A$	9.4/9.8	9.0/9.4	8.4/8.7
DM/¥	11.3/11.55	11.2/11.45	11.1/11.3
SFR/DM	5.5/6.0	5.5/6.0	5.6/6.1
£/DM	7.5/8.0	7.6/8.1	7.6/8.1

Source: *Finance & Treasury Risk Advisor*, Economic Intelligence Unit, June 21, 1993, p.7.

5. Sensitivity to Changing Interest Rate Differentials (Rho and Phi)

At the start of this section we pointed out that currency option prices and values are focused on the forward rate. The forward rate is in turn based on the theory of interest rate parity discussed in Chapter 5. According to option-pricing theory, the premium on an option (European style) must be greater than or equal to the difference between the strike rate and the forward rate:[13]

Premium ≥ (Strike rate − Forward rate).

Interest rate changes in either currency will alter the forward rate, which in turn will alter the option's premium or value. The expected change in the option premium from a small change in the domestic interest rate (home currency) is termed *rho*. The expected change in the option premium from a small change in the foreign interest rate (foreign currency) is termed *phi*.

For example, throughout the early 1990s U.S. dollar (domestic currency) interest rates were substantially lower than other currency (foreign currency) interest rates. This meant foreign currencies consistently sold forward at a discount versus the U.S. dollar. If these interest differentials were to widen (either from U.S. interest rates falling or foreign currency interest rates rising, or some combination of both), the foreign currency would sell forward at a larger discount. An increase in the forward discount is the same as a decrease in the forward rate (in U.S. dollars per unit of foreign currency). The option premium condition just described states that the premium must increase as interest rate differentials increase (assuming spot rates remain unchanged).

Exhibit 6.9 demonstrates how European call option premiums change with interest differentials. Using the same option value assumptions as before, an increase in U.S.

---

[13]For American-style options, which may be exercised on any date up to and including the expiration date, the condition is slightly different: If the difference between the strike rate and forward rate is greater than the difference between the strike rate and spot rate, the premium will be the larger difference. The premium must, however, be at least the difference between the strike rate and spot rate.

Exhibit 6.9   Rho and Phi: Interest Differentials and Option Premiums

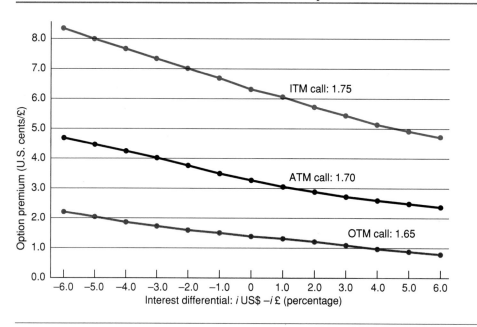

dollar interest rates relative to British pound interest rates results in a decline in call option premia.

For the option trader, an expectation on the differential between interest rates can obviously help in the evaluation of where the option value is headed. For example, when foreign interest rates are higher than domestic interest rates, the pound sells forward at a discount. This results in relatively higher call option premia (and lower put option premia).

> **Rule of Thumb:** A trader who is purchasing a call option on foreign currency should do so before the foreign interest rate rises or the domestic interest rate falls. This allows the trader to purchase the option before its price rises.

6. Alternative Strike Prices and Option Premiums

The sixth and final element that is important in option valuation (but thankfully has no Greek alias) is the selection of the actual strike price. Although we have conducted all of our sensitivity analysis using the strike price of $1.70/£ (a forward at-the-money strike rate), a firm purchasing an option in the over-the-counter market may choose its own strike rate. The question is how to choose?

Exhibit 6.10 illustrates call option premiums required for a series of alternative strike rates above and below the forward at-the-money strike rate of $1.70/£ using

Exhibit 6.10   Option Premiums for Alternative Strike Rates

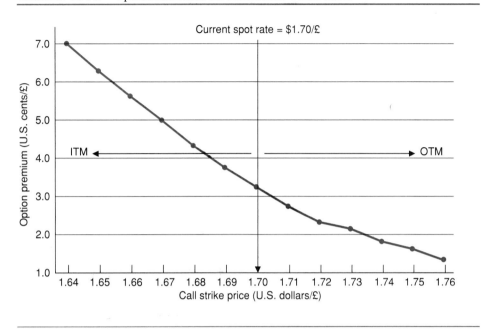

our benchmark example. The option premium for the call option used throughout, the $1.70/£, is 3.3 cents/£. Call options written with strike prices less than $1.70/£, when the present spot rate is $1.70/£, are already profitable or in-the-money. For example, a call option with a strike rate of $1.65/£ would have an intrinsic value of 5.0 cents/£ ($1.70/£−$1.65/£), which the option premium must cover. The call option premium for the $1.65/£ strike rate is 6.3 cents/£, which is higher than the benchmark.

Similarly, call options on pounds at strike rates above $1.70/£ are increasingly cheap because the underlying spot rate, which is presently $1.70/£, will have to move further to make them profitable. At present they have no intrinsic value. For example, a call option on pounds with a strike rate of $1.75/£ possesses a premium of only 1.5 cents/£ because the option is at present very much out-of-the-money. The option has no intrinsic value but time value only.

Exhibit 6.11 briefly summarizes the various "Greek" elements and impacts discussed in the previous sections. The option premium is one of the most complex concepts in financial theory, and the application of option pricing to exchange rates does not make it any simpler. Only with a considerable amount of time and effort can you expect to attain a "second sense" in the management of currency option positions.

Exhibit 6.11   Summary of Option Premium Components

Greek	Definition	Interpretation
Delta	Expected change in the option premium for a small change in the **spot rate**	Higher the delta the more likely the option will move in-the-money
Theta	Expected change in the option premium for a small change in **time to expiration**	Premiums are relatively insensitive until the final 30 or so days
Vega	Expected change in the option premium for a small change in **volatility**	Premiums rise with increases in volatility
Rho	Expected change in the option premium for a small change in the **domestic interest rate**	Increases in domestic interest rates cause falling call option premiums
Phi	Expected change in the option premium for a small change in the **foreign interest rate**	Increases in foreign interest rates cause increasing call option premiums

Summary

- Foreign currency options are financial contracts that give the holder the right, but not the obligation, to buy (in the case of calls) or sell (in the case of puts) a specified amount of foreign exchange at a predetermined price on or before a specified maturity date.

- The use of a currency option as a speculative device for the buyer of an option arises from the fact that an option gains in value as the underlying currency rises (for calls) or falls (for puts). Yet the amount of loss when the underlying currency moves opposite to the desired direction is limited to the cost of the option.

- The use of a currency option as a speculative device for the writer (seller) of an option arises from receiving an option premium at the start. If the option, either a put or call, expires out-of-the-money (valueless), the writer of the option has earned the premium.

- Speculation is an attempt to profit by trading on expectations about prices in the future. In the foreign exchange market, one speculates by taking a position in a foreign currency and then closing that position after the exchange rate has moved; a profit results only if the rate moves in the direction that the speculator expected.

- Currency option valuation, the determination of the option's premium, is a complex calculation based on the current spot rate, the specific strike rate, the forward rate (which itself is dependent on the current spot rate and interest differentials), currency volatility, and time to maturity.

Questions

1. Currency Option Premiums and Alternative Strike Prices

Use Exhibit 6.1 to answer the following questions.

    a.   If the current spot rate is 58.51 (cents/DM) and the first option strike price listed is a "56," is the Aug 56 put in- or out-of-the-money?

    b.   As the strike price of the put option rises from 56 upward to 60, how does the Aug maturity put option premium change? Why?

    c.   What is the break-even rate for the Sep maturity put option with a strike price of 59 1/2?

2. Willem Koopmans and Call Option Speculation (C06A.WK1)

Willem Koopmans is considering a different call option on German marks than what he bought previously (see Exhibit 6.2). He can also buy an August call option with a strike price of 59.0 cents per Deutschemark. The premium for this call option is 0.30 cents per Deutschemark.

    a.   Diagram the profit and loss potential for this call option as seen by Willem Koopmans.

    b.   What is the break-even price for Koopmans?

    c.   What would Koopmans expect as the profit or loss on this call option if by August the spot exchange rate is $0.6000/DM?

3. Willem Koopmans and Put Option Speculation (C06B.WK1)

Willem Koopmans is considering a different put option on German marks than what he bought previously (see Exhibit 6.3). He can also buy a September put option with a strike price of 58.5 cents per Deutschemark. The premium for this option is much higher, 0.99 cents per Deutschemark.

    a.   Diagram the profit and loss potential for this put option as seen by Willem Koopmans.

    b.   What is the break-even price for Koopmans?

    c.   What would Koopmans expect as the profit or loss on this put option if by December the spot exchange rate is $0.5700/DM?

4. Pricing Your Own Options: Calls on British pounds (OPTION.WK1)

The set of assumptions used throughout the second half of this chapter assumed a spot rate of $1.70/£, a 90-day period, U.S. dollar and British pound 90-day interest rates of 8.00% per annum, and a $/£ volatility for 90 days of 10.0%.

Using these assumptions and the OPTION.WK1 spreadsheet, answer the following questions after plugging in the values as shown to make sure your results (option prices and Greeks) are consistent with what is shown here. Note that the exchange rates of $1.70/£ are entered as "170.00 cents/£". Use only the European option prices and Greeks in all questions.

Simple Options Valuation Program

PARAMETERS	INPUT	AMERICAN MODEL	
		Price	3.289
		Delta	0.5030
Current Spot Rate	170.0000	Gamma	0.0481
Foreign Interest Rate (5% as .05)	8.000%	Theta	6.6954
Domestic Interest Rate (10% as .1)	8.000%		
Option (1, CALL, −1 PUT)	1	EUROPEAN MODEL	
Strike Rate	170.0000	Price	3.302
Days to Maturity	90	Delta	0.4999
Annual Volatility (10% as .1)	10.00%	Gamma	0.0463
		Theta	6.4294

Source: Professor James N. Bodurtha, Jr., The University of Michigan. Reprinted with permission.

    a. If the spot rate suddenly changed, the pound falling to $1.65/£, what would be the new 90-day call option premium?

    b. If the British government responded to the falling pound by raising British interest rates to 8.50% per annum, what would the value of the call option be?

    c. As a result of the falling pound and the policy decision to raise interest rates, the British prime minister is thought to be about to lose his support. The volatility rises to 12.0%. What is the new 90 day call option premium?

5. Pricing Your Own Options: Puts on Deutschemarks (OPTION.WK1)

You now consider a put option on Deutschemarks, with an initial volatility of 12.0%, Euro-$ deposit interest rate of 4.2500%, Euro-DM deposit interest rate of 9.6500%, and maturity of 90 days. The strike price of the put is $0.6000/DM.

    a. Calculate the premium and record the option delta for the following spot rates:

Spot ($/DM):	0.55	0.56	0.57	0.58	0.59	0.60	0.61	0.62	0.63	0.64
P_m ($/DM):	___	___	___	___	___	___	___	___	___	___
Delta:	___	___	___	___	___	___	___	___	___	___

    b. Using the data derived in part a, graph the premiums and spot rates, separating out time value from intrinsic value similar to that of Exhibit 6.4.

6. Option Volatilities and Premiums

Using the volatilities listed in Exhibit 6.8, answer the following questions:

    a. Which of the currency crosses is the most volatile at any maturity?

    b. Which of the currency crosses is the least volatile at any maturity?

    c. Do the volatilities per currency cross generally increase or decrease as maturity lengthens?

7. Option Volatilities and Trader's Expectations

As discussed in the chapter, many option traders who believe option volatilities are about to fall will write (sell) options now, expecting to be able to close out their position (buy their option back) in a matter of days at a substantial profit.

    a. Calculate the price of a 90-day call option on Swiss francs (put option on U.S. dollars) with a strike price of SF1.4823/$, if the spot rate is currently SF1.4796, the 90-day Euro-$ and Euro-SF interest rates are 3.1250% and 3.9375%, and the SF/$ 90-day volatility is 13.6%.

    b. If this same call option was repriced the following day, and everything had remained the same except the volatility had fallen to 12.5%, what would be the new price?

    c. If a currency trader sold SF5,000,000 in notional principal of these call options on the first day, and bought them back on the second day at the lower volatility (and one-day shorter maturity), what would be the net profit in U.S. dollars?

8. Speculating on the Movement of the Dutch Guilder

The current spot rate for Dutch guilders is: NGL 1.9200/$.
The three-month forward quote is: NGL 1.9000/$.

You believe that the spot Dutch guilder in three months will be NGL 1.8800/$, and you have $100,000 with which to speculate for three months. Any bank with which you conduct a forward market transaction will want 100% initial margin; that is, you will be required to deposit the amount of any transaction in a certificate of deposit.

Illustrate two different ways of speculating, and calculate the dollar profit to be made by each method. Assume the three-month rate of interest for deposits or lending in guilders is 4% per annum and in U.S. dollars is 8% per annum. For each way of speculating, explain the risks involved.

9. Allied-Lyons: Option Hedging Run Amok

Allied-Lyons (A-L), the British conglomerate that owns a number of American fast-food chains including Roy Rogers, Dunkin Donuts, and Hardees, had a relatively profitable treasury as a result of its aggressive management of currency exposures and its willingness to write options and predict market movements. In the first quarter of 1991, however, A-L reported a loss of £150 million (approximately $268 million) on foreign exchange transactions.

A-L's finance director, Clifford Hatch Jr., and his chief financial strategist, Michael Bartlett, had actively pursued a number of currency option speculation strategies. The strategy employed by Allied-Lyons in the early months of 1991 was not in any fashion simplistic. The strategies combined both *rate views,* expectations regarding the direction of a specific exchange rate, and *volatility views,* expectations regarding the size of the daily movements of the exchange rate. A combination of rate views and volatility views could work as follows:

    ■ First, if A-L believed in January 1991 that the U.S. dollar had risen as far as likely against the British pound sterling, it could write call options.

- Second, if A-L believed option volatilities were as high as they were going to go, they should sell options now and buy them back (if necessary) after volatilities had dropped substantially (or not at all if it looked like their first assumption was correct).

   a. What would be the premium earnings by A-L if they sold 30-day call options on 10 million U.S. dollars on Friday January 11, when the spot rate was $1.9000/£, option volatilities were about 14.5%, and 30 day Euro-$ and Euro-£ interest rates were 6.00% and 8.00%, respectively?

   b. What would be the losses incurred by A-L on these options 21 days later (February 1) if the spot rate were now $1.9755/£, and volatilities were 16.0% and climbing?

Bibliography

Abuaf, Niso, "Foreign Exchange Options: The Leading Hedge," *Midland Corporate Finance Journal,* Summer 1987, pp. 51–58.

Adams, Paul D., and Steve B. Wyatt, "On the Pricing of European and American Foreign Currency Call Options," *Journal of International Money and Finance,* vol. 6, no. 3, September 1987, pp. 315–338.

Amin, Kaushik, and Robert A. Jarrow, "Pricing Foreign Currency Options Under Stochastic Interest Rates," *Journal of International Money and Finance,* September 1991, pp. 310–329.

Biger, Nahum, and John Hull, "The Valuation of Currency Options," *Financial Management,* Spring 1983, pp. 24–28.

Black, Fischer, and Myron Scholes, "The Pricing of Options and Corporate Liabilities," *Journal of Political Economy,* May/June 1973, pp. 637–659.

Bodurtha, James N., Jr., and Georges R. Courtadon, "Efficiency Tests of the Foreign Currency Options Market," *Journal of Finance,* March 1986, pp. 151–162.

————, "Tests of an American Option Pricing Model on the Foreign Currency Options Market," *Journal of Financial and Quantitative Analysis,* June 1987, pp. 153–168.

Briys, Eric, and Michel Crouhy, "Creating and Pricing Hybrid Foreign Currency Options," *Financial Management,* Winter 1988, pp. 59–65.

Chesney, Marc, and Louis Scott, "Pricing European Currency Options: A Comparison of the Modified Black-Scholes Model and a Random Variance Model," *Journal of Financial and Quantitative Analysis,* September 1989, pp. 267–284.

Choi, Jongmoo Jay and Shmuel Hauser, "The Effects of Domestic and Foreign Yield Curves on the Value of American Currency Call Options," *Journal of Banking and Finance,* 14, March 1990, pp. 41–53.

Choi, Jongmoo Jay and Shmuel Hauser, "Forward Foreign Exchange in Continuous-Time Derivative Asset Framework," *Research in Finance,* JAI Press, 1994.

Choi, Jongmoo Jay and Shmuel Hauser, "The Value of Foreign Currency Options and the Term Structure of Interest Rates," *Recent Developments in International Banking and Finance.* Vol. 3, Probus, 1989.

Cox, J.C., and S.A. Ross, "The Valuation of Options for Alternative Stochastic Processes," *Journal of Financial Economics,* 3, 1976, pp. 145–166.

Cox, J.C., S.A. Ross, and M. Rubinstein, "Option Pricing: A Simplified Approach," *Journal of Financial Economics,* 7, 1979, pp. 229–263.

European Bond Commission, *The European Options and Futures Markets: An Overview and Analysis for Money Managers and Traders,"* Chicago, IL: Probus, 1991.

Feiger, George, and Bertrand Jacquillat, "Currency Option Bonds, Puts and Calls on Spot Exchange and the Hedging of Contingent Foreign Earnings," *Journal of Finance,* December 1979, pp. 1129–1139.

Garman, Mark B., and Steven W. Kohlhagen, "Foreign Currency Option Values," *Journal of International Money and Finance,* December 1983, pp. 231–237.

Giddy, Ian H., "Foreign Exchange Options," *Journal of Futures Markets,* Summer 1983, pp. 143–166.

———, "The Foreign Exchange Option as a Hedging Tool," *Midland Corporate Finance Journal,* Fall 1983, pp. 32–42.

Grabbe, J. Orlin, "The Pricing of Call and Put Options on Foreign Exchange," *Journal of International Money and Finance,* December 1983, pp. 239–253.

Hull, John, and Alan White, "Hedging the Risks from Writing Foreign Currency Options," *Journal of International Money and Finance,* June 1987, pp. 131–152.

Jorion, Philippe, and Neal M. Stoughton, "An Empirical Investigation of the Early Exercise Premium of Foreign Currency Options," *Journal of Futures Markets,* October 1989, pp. 365–375.

Philadelphia Stock Exchange, "Controlling Risk with Foreign Currency Options," *Euromoney,* February 1985. (Supplementary issue; the entire issue is devoted to foreign currency options.)

Shastri, Kuldeep, and Kishore Tandon, "Valuation of Foreign Currency Options: Some Empirical Tests," *Journal of Financial and Quantitative Analysis,* June 1986, pp. 145–160.

Shastri, Kuldeep, and Kulpatra Wethyavivorn, "The Valuation of Currency Options for Alternate Stochastic Processes," *Journal of Financial Research,* vol. 10, no. 4, Winter 1987, pp. 283–294.

Stoll, Hans R., and Robert E. Whaley, *Futures and Options: Theory and Applications, Current Issues in Finance,* Cincinnati: Southwestern, 1993.

Sutton, W. H., *Trading in Currency Options,* New York: New York Institute of Finance, 1988.

Tucker, Alan, "Foreign Exchange Option Prices as Predictors of Equilibrium Forward Exchange Rates," *Journal of International Money and Finance,* vol. 6, no. 3, September 1987, pp. 283–294.

Wyatt, Steve B., "On the Valuation of Puts and Calls on Spot, Forward, and Future Foreign Exchange: Theory and Evidence," *Advances in Financial Planning and Forecasting,* vol. 4, 1990, pp. 81–104.

Chapter 6 Appendix A
Currency Option Pricing Theory

The foreign currency option model presented here, the European-style option, is the result of the work of Black and Scholes (1972), Cox and Ross (1976), Cox, Ross, and Rubinstein (1979), Garman and Kohlhagen (1983), and Bodurtha and Courtadon (1987). Although we do not explain the theoretical derivation of the following option-pricing model, the original model derived by Black and Scholes is based on the formation of a riskless hedged portfolio composed of a long position in the security, asset, or currency, and a European call option. The solution to this model's expected return yields the option premium.

The basic theoretical model for the pricing of a European call option is:

$$C = e^{-r_f T}SN(d1) - Ee^{-r_d T}N(d2)$$

where

C	premium on a European call
e	continuous time discounting
S	spot exchange rate ($/fc)
E	exercise or strike rate
T	time to expiration
N	cumulative normal distribution function
r_f	foreign interest rate
r_d	domestic interest rate
σ	standard deviation of asset price (volatility)
ln	natural logarithm

The two density functions, $d1$ and $d2$, are defined:

$$d1 = \frac{\ln\left(\dfrac{S}{E}\right) + \left(r_d - r_f + \dfrac{\sigma^2}{2}\right)T}{\sigma\sqrt{T}},$$

and

$$d2 = d1 - \sigma\sqrt{T}$$

This can be rearranged so the premium on a European call option is written in terms of forward rates:

$$C = e^{r_f T}FN(d1) - e^{r_d T}EN(d2),$$

where the spot rate and foreign interest rate have been replaced with the forward rate, F, and both the first and second terms are discounted over continuous time, e. If we now slightly simplify, we find the option premium is the present value of the difference between two cumulative normal density functions:

$$C = [FN(d1) - EN(d2)] \, e^{rdT}.$$

The two density functions are now defined:

$$d1 = \frac{\ln\left(\dfrac{F}{E}\right) + \left(\dfrac{\sigma^2}{2}\right) T}{\sigma\sqrt{T}},$$

and

$$d2 = d1 - \sigma\sqrt{T}.$$

Solving each of these equations for d1 and d2 allows the determination of the European call option premium. The premium for a European put option, P, is similarly derived:

$$P = [F(N(d1) - 1) - E(N(d2) - 1)] \, e^{rdT}.$$

The European Call Option: Numerical Example

The actual calculation of the option premium is not as complex as it appears from the preceding set of equations. Assuming the following basic exchange rate and interest rate values, computation of the option premium is relatively straightforward:

Spot rate	= \$1.7000/£
90-day forward	= \$1.7000/£
Strike rate	= \$1.7000/£
U.S. dollar interest rate	= 8.00% (per annum)
Pound sterling interest rate	= 8.00% (per annum)
Time (days)	= 90
Standard deviation (volatility)	= 10.00 %
e (infinite discounting)	= 2.71828

The value of the two density functions are first derived:

$$d1 = \frac{\ln\left(\dfrac{F}{E}\right) + \left(\dfrac{\sigma^2}{2}\right) T}{\sigma\sqrt{T}} = \frac{\ln\left(\dfrac{1.7000}{1.7000}\right) + \dfrac{.1000^2}{2} \dfrac{90}{365}}{.1000\sqrt{\dfrac{90}{365}}} = .025,$$

and

$$d2 = .025 - .1000 \sqrt{\frac{90}{365}} = -.025.$$

The values of d1 and d2 are then found in the cumulative normal probability table (see Appendix 6B),

$$N(d1) = N(.025) = .51; \quad N(d2) = N(-.025) = .49.$$

The premium of the European call with a "forward at-the-money" strike rate is

$$C = [(1.7000)(.51) - (1.7000)(.49)]\, 2.71828^{-.08(90/.365)} = \$0.033/\pounds.$$

This is the call option premium shown in Exhibit 6.4 and used throughout the second half of the chapter in the sensitivity analyses.

Chapter 6 Appendix B
Cumulative Normal Probability Tables

The probability that a drawing from a unit normal distribution will produce a value less than the constant d is

$$\text{Prob}\,(\tilde{z} < d) = \int_{-\infty}^{d} \frac{1}{\sqrt{2\pi}} e^{-z^2/2} dz = N(d).$$

Range of d: $-2.49 \leq d \leq 0.00$

d	-0.00	-0.01	-0.02	-0.03	-0.04	-0.05	-0.06	-0.07	-0.08	-0.09
-2.40	0.00820	0.00798	0.00776	0.00755	0.00734	0.00714	0.00695	0.00676	0.00657	0.00639
-2.30	0.01072	0.01044	0.01017	0.00990	0.00964	0.00939	0.00914	0.00889	0.00866	0.00842
-2.20	0.01390	0.01355	0.01321	0.01287	0.01255	0.01222	0.01191	0.01160	0.01130	0.01101
-2.10	0.01786	0.01743	0.01700	0.01659	0.01618	0.01578	0.01539	0.01500	0.01463	0.01426
-2.00	0.02275	0.02222	0.02169	0.02118	0.02068	0.02018	0.01970	0.01923	0.01876	0.01831
-1.90	0.02872	0.02807	0.02743	0.02680	0.02619	0.02559	0.02500	0.02442	0.02385	0.02330
-1.80	0.03593	0.03515	0.03438	0.03362	0.03288	0.03216	0.03144	0.03074	0.03005	0.02938
-1.70	0.04457	0.04363	0.04272	0.04182	0.04093	0.04006	0.03920	0.03836	0.03754	0.03673
-1.60	0.05480	0.05370	0.05262	0.05155	0.05050	0.04947	0.04846	0.04746	0.04648	0.04551
-1.50	0.06681	0.06552	0.06426	0.06301	0.06178	0.06057	0.05938	0.05821	0.05705	0.05592
-1.40	0.08076	0.07927	0.07780	0.07636	0.07493	0.07353	0.07215	0.07078	0.06944	0.06811
-1.30	0.09680	0.09510	0.09342	0.09176	0.09012	0.08851	0.08691	0.08534	0.08379	0.08226
-1.20	0.11507	0.11314	0.11123	0.10935	0.10749	0.10565	0.10383	0.10204	0.10027	0.09853
-1.10	0.13567	0.13350	0.13136	0.12924	0.12714	0.12507	0.12302	0.12100	0.11900	0.11702
-1.00	0.15866	0.15625	0.15386	0.15150	0.14917	0.14686	0.14457	0.14231	0.14007	0.13786
-0.90	0.18406	0.18141	0.17879	0.17619	0.17361	0.17106	0.16853	0.16602	0.16354	0.16109
-0.80	0.21186	0.20897	0.20611	0.20327	0.20045	0.19766	0.19489	0.19215	0.18943	0.18673
-0.70	0.24196	0.23885	0.23576	0.23270	0.22965	0.22663	0.22363	0.22065	0.21770	0.21476
-0.60	0.27425	0.27093	0.26763	0.26435	0.26109	0.25785	0.25463	0.25143	0.24825	0.24510
-0.50	0.30854	0.30503	0.30153	0.29806	0.29460	0.29116	0.28774	0.28434	0.28096	0.27760
-0.40	0.34458	0.34090	0.33724	0.33360	0.32997	0.32636	0.32276	0.31918	0.31561	0.31207
-0.30	0.38209	0.37828	0.37448	0.37070	0.36693	0.36317	0.35942	0.35569	0.35197	0.34827
-0.20	0.42074	0.41683	0.41294	0.40905	0.40517	0.40129	0.39743	0.39358	0.38974	0.38591
-0.10	0.46017	0.45620	0.45224	0.44828	0.44433	0.44038	0.43644	0.43251	0.42858	0.42465
0.00	0.50000	0.49601	0.49202	0.48803	0.48405	0.48006	0.47608	0.47210	0.46812	0.46414

Range of d: $0.00 \le d \le 2.49$

d	0.00	0.01	0.02	0.03	0.04	0.05	0.06	0.07	0.08	0.09
0.00	0.50000	0.50399	0.50798	0.51197	0.51595	0.51994	0.52392	0.52790	0.53188	0.53586
0.01	0.53983	0.54380	0.54776	0.55172	0.55567	0.55962	0.56356	0.56749	0.57142	0.57535
0.20	0.57926	0.58317	0.58706	0.59095	0.59483	0.59871	0.60257	0.60642	0.61026	0.61409
0.30	0.61791	0.62172	0.62552	0.62930	0.63307	0.63683	0.64058	0.64431	0.64803	0.65173
0.40	0.65542	0.65910	0.66276	0.66640	0.67003	0.67364	0.67724	0.68082	0.68439	0.68793
0.50	0.69146	0.69497	0.69847	0.70194	0.70540	0.70884	0.71226	0.71566	0.71904	0.72240
0.60	0.72575	0.72907	0.73237	0.73565	0.73891	0.74215	0.74537	0.74857	0.75175	0.75490
0.70	0.75804	0.76115	0.76424	0.76730	0.77035	0.77337	0.77637	0.77935	0.78230	0.78524
0.80	0.78814	0.79103	0.79389	0.79673	0.79955	0.80234	0.80511	0.80785	0.81057	0.81327
0.90	0.81594	0.81859	0.82121	0.82381	0.82639	0.82894	0.83147	0.83398	0.83646	0.83891
1.00	0.84134	0.84375	0.84614	0.84850	0.85083	0.85314	0.85543	0.85769	0.85993	0.86214
1.10	0.86433	0.86650	0.86864	0.87076	0.87286	0.87493	0.87698	0.87900	0.88100	0.88298
1.20	0.88493	0.88686	0.88877	0.89065	0.89251	0.89435	0.89617	0.89796	0.89973	0.90147
1.30	0.90320	0.90490	0.90658	0.90824	0.90988	0.91149	0.91309	0.91466	0.91621	0.91774
1.40	0.91924	0.92073	0.92220	0.92364	0.92507	0.92647	0.92785	0.92922	0.93056	0.93189
1.50	0.93319	0.93448	0.93574	0.93699	0.93822	0.93943	0.94062	0.94179	0.94295	0.94408
1.60	0.94520	0.94630	0.94738	0.94845	0.94950	0.95053	0.95154	0.95254	0.95352	0.95449
1.70	0.95543	0.95637	0.95728	0.95818	0.95907	0.95994	0.96080	0.96164	0.96246	0.96327
1.80	0.96407	0.96485	0.96562	0.96637	0.96712	0.96784	0.96856	0.96926	0.96995	0.97062
1.90	0.97128	0.97193	0.97257	0.97320	0.97381	0.97441	0.97500	0.97558	0.97615	0.97670
2.00	0.97725	0.97778	0.97831	0.97882	0.97932	0.97982	0.98030	0.98077	0.98124	0.98169
2.10	0.98214	0.98257	0.98300	0.98341	0.98382	0.98422	0.98461	0.98500	0.98537	0.98574
2.20	0.98610	0.98645	0.98679	0.98713	0.98745	0.98778	0.98809	0.98840	0.98870	0.98899
2.30	0.98928	0.98956	0.98983	0.99010	0.99036	0.99061	0.99086	0.99111	0.99134	0.99158
2.40	0.99180	0.99202	0.99224	0.99245	0.99266	0.99286	0.99305	0.99324	0.99343	0.99361

Source: *Futures and Options*, by Hans R. Stoll and Robert E. Whaley, Southwestern Publishing, 1993, pp. 242–243. Reprinted with permission.

Chapter 7
Transaction Exposure:
Measurement and Management

Global View
Sony's Hedging is More Profitable Than Its Sales

Tokyo—Sony Corp. reported a 31% jump in first-quarter group pretax profit on falling sales, a result that largely reflected its success in hedging against the yen's recent rise. The company's group pretax profit in the quarter ended June 30 rose to 38.63 billion yen ($379.7 million) from 29.48 billion yen a year earlier. Its group sales fell 10% over the same period, to 828.71 billion yen, from 924.39 billion yen.

Company officials blamed the fall in sales on the strengthening yen, which has risen 22% against the dollar since the beginning of the year. A stronger yen usually weakens Japanese export sales by making products more expensive overseas. Sony attributed the rise in pretax profit—the company's first year-to-year quarterly increase, excluding extraordinary items, in 2 1/2 years—mainly to its successful anticipation of the yen's appreciation. Sony's winning gamble led it to report 20.36 billion yen in income from foreign-exchange gains during the first quarter, nearly 10 times what it reported on such gains a year earlier. Sony derives about 72% of its revenue from markets outside of Japan.

What Sony's currency gains don't do, as evidenced by its big drop in operating profit, is change its underlying difficulties. The company's sales have been hit hard not only by the high yen, but also by the stagnant Japanese economy and a prolonged slump in its mainstay consumer electronics business brought on by market saturation. Even now, many analysts agree that without new hit products, Sony will have a hard time regaining its once-impressive rates of growth.

Source: Adapted from David P. Hamilton, "Sony's Hedging Helps Lift Earnings 31% for Quarter," 8/20–21/93. Reprinted by permission of *The Wall Street Journal Europe*, © 1993 Dow Jones & Co., Inc. All rights reserved worldwide.

Foreign exchange exposure is a measure of the potential for a firm's profitability, net cash flow, and market value to change because of a change in exchange rates. An important task of the financial manager is to measure foreign exchange exposure and to manage it in such a way as to maximize the profitability, net cash flow, and market value of the firm.

Types of Foreign Exchange Exposure

What happens to a firm when foreign exchange rates change? The effect can be measured in several ways. Exhibit 7.1 shows schematically the three main types of foreign exchange exposure: **transaction, operating,** and **accounting.**

Transaction Exposure

Transaction exposure measures changes in the value of outstanding financial obligations incurred prior to a change in exchange rates but not due to be settled until after the exchange rates change. Transaction exposure thus deals with changes in cash flows that result from existing contractual obligations. This chapter analyzes how transaction exposure is measured and managed.

Operating Exposure

Operating exposure, also called **economic exposure, competitive exposure,** or **strategic exposure,** measures the change in the present value of the firm resulting from any change in the future operating cash flows of the firm caused by an *unexpected* change in exchange rates. The change in value depends on the effect of the exchange rate change on future sales volume, prices, or costs. Chapter 8 analyses operating exposure.

Exhibit 7.1   Conceptual Comparison of Difference Between Operating, Transaction, and Accounting Foreign Exchange Exposure

Moment in time when exchange rate changes

Accounting exposure
Accounting-based changes in consolidated financial statements caused by a change in exchange rates

Operating exposure
Change in expected cash flows arising because of an unexpected change in exchange rates

Transaction exposure
Impact of settling outstanding obligations entered into before change in exchange rates but to be settled after change in exchange rates

Time 0

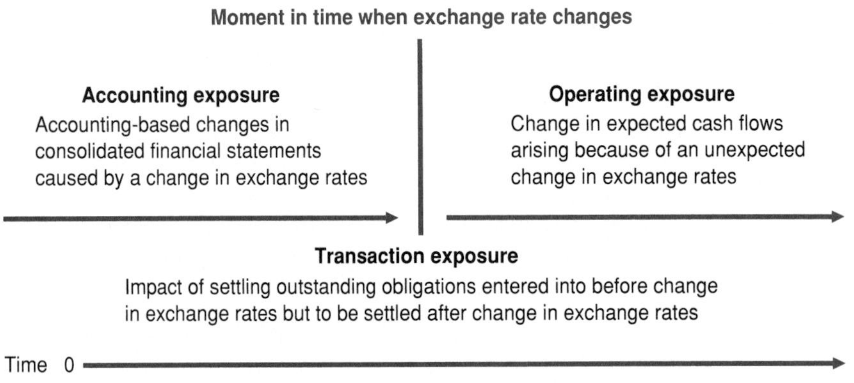

Both transaction exposure and operating exposure exist because of unexpected changes in future cash flows. The difference is that transaction exposure is concerned with preexisting cash flows that will occur in the near future, whereas operating exposure is concerned with expected future cash flows that are potentially impacted by changing international competitiveness.

Accounting Exposure

Accounting exposure, also called **translation exposure,** is the potential for accounting-derived changes in owners' equity that occur because of the need to "translate" foreign currency financial statements of foreign affiliates into a single reporting currency to prepare worldwide consolidated financial statements. Chapter 9 is about accounting exposure.

Tax Exposure

The tax consequence of foreign exchange exposure varies by country, but as a general rule only *realized* foreign exchange losses are deductible for purposes of calculating income taxes. Similarly, only realized gains create taxable income. "Realized" means the loss or gain involves cash flows.

Losses from transaction exposure usually reduce taxable income in the year in which they are realized. Losses from operating exposure reduce taxable income over a series of future years. As we explain in Chapter 9, losses from accounting exposure are not cash losses and so are not deductible. Some steps taken to minimize one or another of the types of exposure, such as entering into a forward exchange contract, create taxable income or loss. Other steps taken to obtain the same protection have no income tax implications. Because tax exposure is determined by the country of domicile of each affiliate, a multinational firm needs to plan its foreign exchange management policies to minimize the worldwide after-tax consequences of foreign exchange losses and to maximize after-tax gains.

Why Hedge?

Multinational firms produce a multitude of cash flows that are sensitive to changes in exchange rates, interest rates, and commodity prices. These three financial price risks are the subject of the growing field of *financial risk management.*[1] Here we focus on the sensitivity of the individual firm's future cash flows to exchange rates alone. Chapter 14 expands the subject of risk management to interest rates.

Many firms attempt to manage their currency exposures through *hedging.* A firm hedges by taking a position, such as acquiring a cash flow or an asset or a contract (including a forward contract), that will rise (fall) in value and offset a drop (rise) in value of an existing position. Hedging therefore protects the owner of the existing asset

---

[1]For an excellent overview of the developing field of financial risk management see *Managing Financial Risk* by Clifford W. Smith, Charles W. Smithson, and D. Sykes Wilford, Harper-Business, Ballinger, 1990.

from loss.[2] But this does not really answer the question of what the firm gains from hedging.

The value of a firm according to financial theory is the net present value of all expected future cash flows. The fact they are *expected* cash flows emphasizes that nothing about the future is certain. If the reporting currency value of many of these cash flows is altered as a result of changes in exchange rates, a firm that hedges its currency exposures reduces some of the variance in the value of its future expected cash flows. *Currency risk* can therefore be defined roughly as variance in expected cash flows arising from exchange rate changes.

Exhibit 7.2 illustrates the distribution of expected net cash flows of the individual firm. Hedging these cash flows narrows the distribution of the cash flows about the mean of the distribution. Currency hedging reduces risk. Reduction of risk is not, however, the same thing as adding value or return. The value of the firm depicted in Exhibit 7.2 would only be increased if hedging actually shifted the mean of the distribution to the right. Is the reduction in the variability of cash flows then sufficient reason for currency risk management?

This is actually a continuing debate in multinational financial management. Opponents of currency hedging commonly make the following arguments:[3]

- Stockholders are much more capable of diversifying currency risk than is management of the firm. If stockholders do not wish to accept the currency risk of any

Exhibit 7.2   Impact of Hedging on the Expected Cash Flows of the Firm

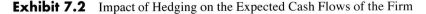

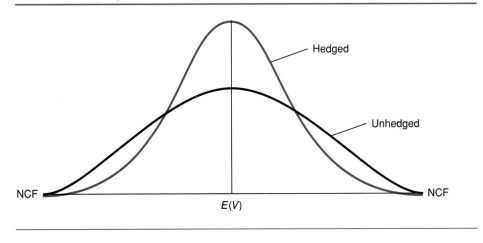

[2]It is always important to note that a hedge protects the purchaser against loss or gain resulting from changes in exchange rates on the value of the exposure.

[3]This discussion draws on the article entitled "Why Hedge?", *Intermarket,* July 1989, pp. 12–16, by Clifford W. Smith, Charles W. Smithson, and D. Sykes Wilford. Other good overviews of the why hedge debate include Stulz (1984), Smith and Stulz (1985), and Levi and Sercu (1991).

specific firm they can diversify their portfolios to manage the currency risk in a way that matches their individual preferences and risk tolerance.

- As we noted, currency risk management does not add value to the firm. It does, however, use precious resources of the firm that leads to a net reduction in value.

- Management often conducts hedging activity that benefits management at the expense of the stockholder. The field of finance called *agency theory* frequently argues that management is generally more risk averse than stockholders. If the firm exists only for the maximization of stockholder wealth (and this may not be the case), then hedging activity is probably not in the best interest of the stockholder.

- Managers cannot outguess the market. If and when markets are in equilibrium with respect to parity conditions, the expected net present value of hedging is zero.

- Management's motivation to reduce variability is sometimes driven by accounting reasons. Management may believe it will be criticized more severely for incurring foreign exchange losses in its financial statements than for incurring similar or even higher costs in avoiding the foreign exchange loss. Foreign exchange losses appear in the income statement as a highly visible separate line item or as a foot-note, but the higher costs of protection are buried in operating or interest expenses.

- Efficient market theorists believe that investors can see through the "accounting veil" and therefore have already factored the foreign exchange effect into a firm's market valuation.

Proponents of hedging cite the following reasons:

- Reduction of risk in future cash flows improves the planning capability of the firm. If the firm can more accurately predict future cash flows, it may be able to under-take specific investments or activities that it might otherwise not consider.[4]

- Reduction of risk in future cash flows reduces the likelihood the firm's cash flows will fall below a necessary minimum. A firm must generate sufficient cash flows to make debt-service payments in order for it to continue to operate. This minimum cash flow point, often referred to as the point of *financial distress,* lies to the left of the center of the distribution of expected cash flows. Hedging reduces the likelihood of the firm's cash flows falling to this level.

- Management has a comparative advantage over the individual stockholder in know-ing the actual currency risk of the firm.[5] Regardless of the level of disclosure pro-vided by the firm to the public, management always possesses an advantage in the depth and breadth of knowledge concerning the real risks and returns inherent in any firm's business.

---

[4]See Froot, Scharfstein, and Stein (1993).

[5]See Rene M. Stulz, "Optimal Hedging Policies," *Journal of Financial and Quantitative Analysis,* vol. 19, no. 2, June 1984, p. 127.

- Markets are usually in disequilibrium because of structural and institutional imperfections, as well as unexpected external shocks (such as an oil crisis or war). Management is in a better position than stockholders to recognize disequilibrium conditions and to take advantage of onetime opportunities to enhance firm value through *selective hedging*.[6]

As is the case with any managerial dimension of business, the conclusion to the "why hedge?" debate will vary with the individuals—both stockholder and management—involved. If there is any indication of who is winning the debate, it would be that more and more firms worldwide are undertaking greater study and active management of their currency exposures.

Measurement of Transaction Exposure

Transaction exposure measures gains or losses that arise from the settlement of existing financial obligations whose terms are stated in a foreign currency. Transaction exposure arises from the following:

1. Purchasing or selling on credit goods or services whose prices are stated in foreign currencies,

2. Borrowing or lending funds when repayment is to be made in a foreign currency,

3. Being a party to an unperformed foreign exchange forward contract, and

4. Otherwise acquiring assets or incurring liabilities denominated in foreign currencies.

The most common example of transaction exposure arises when a firm has a receivable or payable denominated in a foreign currency. Exhibit 7.3 demonstrates how this exposure is born. The total transaction exposure consists of quotation, backlog, and

Exhibit 7.3   The "Life Span" of a Transaction Exposure

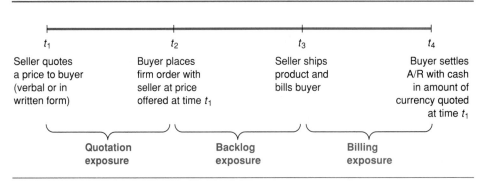

---

[6]*Selective hedging* usually refers to the hedging of large, singular, exceptional exposures, or the occasional use of hedging when management has a strong expectation on the direction of exchange rates.

billing exposures. A transaction exposure is actually created at the first moment the seller quotes a price in foreign currency terms to a potential buyer (t_1). The quote can be either verbally, as in a telephone quote, or in the form of a written bid or even a printed price list. When the buyer places an order (t_2), the potential exposure created at the time of the quotation (t_1) is converted into that of an actual transaction exposure, which now constitutes a currency exposure to the seller. The transaction exposure exists until actual payment is received by the seller (t_4).

Purchasing or Selling on Open Account

Suppose a U.S. firm sells merchandise on open account to a Belgian buyer for Bf700,000, payment to be made in 60 days. The current exchange rate is Bf35/$, and the U.S. seller expects to exchange the Bf700,000 for $20,000 when payment is received.

Transaction exposure arises because of the risk that the U.S. seller will receive something other than $20,000. For example, if the exchange rate was Bf38/$ when payment was received, the U.S. seller would receive only Bf700,000 ÷ Bf38/$ = $18,421, some $1,579 less than anticipated. Had the exchange rate gone to Bf33/$, however, the seller would have received $21,212, an increase of $1,212 over the amount expected. Thus exposure is the chance of either a loss or a gain.

The U.S. seller might have avoided transaction exposure by invoicing the Belgian buyer in dollars. Of course, if it attempted to sell only in dollars it might not obtain the sale in the first place. Avoiding transaction exposure by not having sales is counterproductive to the well-being of the firm! Even if the Belgian buyer agrees to pay in dollars, transaction exposure is not eliminated. Instead it is transferred to the Belgian buyer, whose dollar account payable has an unknown cost in Belgian francs 60 days hence.

Borrowing and Lending

A second example of transaction exposure arises when funds are borrowed or loaned and the amount involved is denominated in a foreign currency. For example, Britain's Beecham Group borrowed SF100 million in 1971 at a time when that amount of Swiss francs was worth £10.13 million. When the loan came due five years later, the cost of repayment of principal was £22.73 million—more than double the amount borrowed. The London *Sunday Times,* August 22, 1976, termed this transaction loss "an expensive lump of lolly!"

Other Causes of Transaction Exposure

When a firm buys a forward exchange contract, it creates transaction exposure on purpose. This is usually done in order to hedge an existing transaction exposure. For example, a U.S. firm might want to offset an existing obligation to purchase DM1 million to pay for an import from Germany in 90 days. As we show in more detail in the next section, one way to offset this payable is to purchase DM1 million in the forward market for delivery in 90 days. In this manner any change in value of the mark relative to the dollar will be neutralized. If the mark increases in value, the account payable will have cost more dollars, a transaction loss; but the forward contract has already fixed the number of dollars needed to buy the DM1 million. Thus the potential transaction loss, or gain, on the account payable has been offset by the transaction gain or loss on the forward contract.

Note that cash balances do not create transaction exposure, even though their foreign exchange value changes immediately with a change in exchange rate. This is because no legal obligation exists to move the cash from one country and currency to another. If such an obligation did exist, it would show on the books as a payable (e.g., dividends declared and payable) or receivable and then be counted as part of transaction exposure. Nevertheless, the foreign exchange value of cash balances does change when exchange rates change.

Contractual Hedges

Foreign exchange transaction exposure can be managed by *contractual, operating,* and *financial hedges*. The main contractual hedges employ the forward, money, futures, and options markets. Operating and financial hedges (also commonly termed *natural hedges*) employ the use of risk-sharing agreements, leads and lags in payment terms, swaps, and other strategies discussed in Chapter 8.

Dayton Manufacturing's Transaction Exposure

To illustrate how contractual hedging techniques may be used to protect against transaction exposure, consider an example in which Dayton, a U.S. manufacturing firm, sells a gas turbine generator to Crown, a British firm, in March for £1,000,000. Payment is due three months later, in June. Dayton's cost of capital is 12%. The following quotes are available:

- Spot exchange rate: $1.7640/£

- Three-month forward rate: $1.7540/£ (a 2.2676% per annum discount on the British pound)

- U.K. three-month borrowing interest rate: 10.0% (or 2.5%/quarter)

- U.K. three-month investment interest rate: 8.0% (or 2.0%/quarter)

- U.S. three-month borrowing interest rate: 8.0% (or 2.0%/quarter)

- U.S. three-month investment interest rate: 6.0% (or 1.5%/quarter)

- June put option in the over-the-counter (bank) market for £1,000,000; strike price $1.75 (nearly at-the-money); 1.5% premium

- June put option in the over-the-counter (bank) market for £1,000,000; strike price $1.71 (out-of-the-money); 1.0% premium

- Dayton's foreign exchange advisory service forecasts that the spot rate in three months will be $1.76/£.

Like many manufacturing firms, Dayton operates on relatively narrow margins. Although Dayton would of course be very happy if the pound appreciated versus the dollar, its concerns center on the possibility that the pound will fall. When

Dayton budgeted this specific contract, it determined that its minimum acceptable margin was at a sales price of $1,700,000. The *budget rate,* the lowest acceptable dollar per pound exchange rate, was therefore established at $1.70/£. Any exchange rate below this budget rate would result in Dayton actually losing money on the transaction.

Four alternatives are available to Dayton:

1. Remain unhedged.
2. Hedge in the forward market.
3. Hedge in the money market.
4. Hedge in the options market.

Unhedged Position

Dayton may decide to accept the transaction risk. If the firm believes its foreign exchange adviser, it expects to receive £1,000,000 × $1.76 = $1,760,000 in three months. However, that amount is at risk. If the pound should fall to, say, $1.65, Dayton would receive only $1,650,000. Exchange risk is not one-sided, however; if the transaction was left uncovered and the pound strengthened even more than forecast by the adviser, Dayton could receive considerably more than $1,760,000.

The essence of an unhedged approach is as follows:

(Today)   (Three months hence)

Do nothing   Receive £1,000,000
                                                                Sell £1,000,000 spot and receive
                                                                dollars at spot rate existing then

Forward Market Hedge

A "forward hedge" involves a forward (or futures) contract and a source of funds to fulfill that contract. The forward contract is entered into at the time the transaction exposure is created. In Dayton's case, that would be in March, when the sale to Crown was booked as an account receivable. Funds to fulfill the contract will be available in June, when Crown pays £1,000,000 to Dayton. If funds to fulfill the forward contract are on hand or are due because of a business operation, the hedge is considered "covered," "perfect," or "square" because no residual foreign exchange risk exists. Funds on hand or to be received are matched by funds to be paid.

In some situations funds to fulfill the forward exchange contract are not already available or due to be received later, but must be purchased in the spot market at some future date. Such a hedge is "open" or "uncovered." It involves considerable risk because the hedger must take a chance on purchasing foreign exchange at an uncertain future spot rate in order to fulfill the forward contract. Purchase of such funds at a later date is referred to as "covering." There is an old financial saying that is appropriate for an uncovered forward obligation:

He who sells what isn't his'n
Must buy it back or go to prison![7]

Should Dayton wish to hedge its transaction exposure in the forward market, it will sell £1,000,000 forward today at the three-month forward quotation of $1.7540 per pound. This is a "covered transaction" in which the firm no longer has any foreign exchange risk. In three months the firm will receive £1,000,000 from the British buyer, deliver that sum to the bank against its forward sale, and receive $1,754,000. This certain sum is $6,000 less than the uncertain $1,760,000 expected from the unhedged position because the forward market quotation differs from the firm's three-month forecast.

The essence of a forward hedge is as follows:

(Today)

Sell £1,000,000
forward @ $1.7540/£

(Three months hence)

Receive £1,000,000
Deliver £1,000,000
    against forward sale
Receive $1,754,000

If Dayton's forecast of future rates was identical to that implicit in the forward quotation, that is, $1.7540, expected receipts would be the same whether or not the firm hedges. However, realized receipts under the unhedged alternative could vary considerably from the certain receipts when the transaction is hedged. Belief that the forward rate is an unbiased estimate of the future spot rate does not preclude use of the forward hedge to eliminate the risk of an unexpected change in the future spot rate.

Money Market Hedge

Like a forward market hedge, a money market hedge also involves a contract and a source of funds to fulfill that contract. In this instance the contract is a loan agreement. The firm seeking the money market hedge borrows in one currency and exchanges the proceeds for another currency. Funds to fulfill the contract—that is, to repay the loan—may be generated from business operations, in which case the money market hedge is "covered." Alternatively, funds to repay the loan may be purchased in the foreign exchange spot market when the loan matures. In this instance the money market hedge is "uncovered" or "open."

A money market hedge can cover a single transaction, such as Dayton's £1,000,000 receivable, or repeated transactions. Hedging repeated transactions is called *matching*. It requires the firm to match the expected foreign currency cash inflows and outflows by currency and maturity. For example, if Dayton had numerous sales denominated in pounds to British customers over a long period of time, it would have somewhat predictable British pound cash inflows. The appropriate money market hedge technique would be to borrow British pounds in an amount matching the typical size and maturity

---

[7]This quotation is attributed to Daniel Drew, in Bouck White, *The Book of Daniel Drew,* New York: Doran, 1910, p. 180.

of expected pound inflows. Then, if the pound depreciated or appreciated, the foreign exchange effect on cash inflows in pounds would be approximately offset by the effect on cash outflows in pounds from repaying the pound loan plus interest.

The structure of a money market hedge resembles that of a forward hedge. The difference is that the cost of the money market hedge is determined by differential interest rates, whereas the cost of the forward hedge is a function of the forward rate quotation. In efficient markets interest rate parity should ensure that these costs are nearly the same, but not all markets are efficient at all times. Furthermore, the difference in interest rates facing a private firm borrowing in two separate national markets may be different than the difference in risk-free government bill rates or Eurocurrency interest rates in these same markets. It is the latter differential that is relevant for interest rate parity.

To hedge in the money market, Dayton will borrow pounds in London at once, immediately convert the borrowed pounds into dollars, and repay the pound loan in three months with the proceeds from the sale of the generator. How much should Dayton borrow? It will need to borrow just enough to repay both the principal and interest with the sale proceeds. The borrowing interest rate will be 10% per annum, or 2.5% for three months. Therefore, assuming that x is the amount of pounds to borrow, we obtain

$$1.025x = £1,000,000$$

$$x = £975,610.$$

Dayton should borrow £975,610 and in three months repay that amount plus £24,390 of interest from the sale proceeds. Dayton should exchange the £975,610 loan proceeds for dollars at the current spot exchange rate of $1.7640/£, receiving $1,720,976 at once.

In order to compare the forward hedge with the money market hedge, it is necessary to analyze how Dayton's loan proceeds will be utilized for the next three months. Remember that the loan proceeds are received today but the forward contract proceeds are received in three months. Therefore one needs to calculate either the future value in three months of the loan proceeds or the present value of the forward contract proceeds. We use future value for pedagogical reasons, but correct use of present value would give the same comparative results.

Since both the forward contract proceeds and the loan proceeds are relatively certain, it is possible to make a clear choice between the two alternatives based on the one that yields the higher dollar receipts. This result, in turn, depends on the assumed rate of investment of the loan proceeds.

At least three logical choices exist for an assumed investment rate for the loan proceeds for the next three months. First, if Dayton is cash rich, the loan proceeds might be invested in U.S. dollar money market instruments that have been assumed to yield 6% per annum. Second, Dayton might simply use the pound loan proceeds to substitute for an equal dollar loan that it would otherwise have undertaken at an assumed rate of 8% per annum. Third, Dayton might invest the loan proceeds in the general operations of the firm, in which case the cost of capital of 12% per annum would be the appropriate rate. The future value of the loan proceeds at the end of three months under each of these three investment assumptions would be as follows:

Received today	Invested at	Future value in three months
$1,720,976	6%/yr or 1.5%/quarter	$1,746,791
$1,720,976	8%/yr or 2.0%/quarter	$1,755,396
$1,720,976	12%/yr or 3.0%/quarter	$1,772,605

Since the proceeds in three months from the forward hedge would be $1,754,000, the money market hedge would be superior to the forward hedge if Dayton used the loan proceeds to replace a dollar loan (8%) or to conduct general business operations (12%). The forward hedge would be preferable if Dayton merely invested the pound loan proceeds in dollar-denominated money market instruments at 6% annual interest.

A break-even investment rate can be calculated that would make Dayton indifferent between the forward hedge and the money market hedge. Assume that r is the unknown three-month investment rate, expressed as a decimal, that would equalize the proceeds from the forward and money market hedges. We have

$$(\text{Loan proceeds}) \times (1 + \text{rate}) = (\text{forward proceeds}),$$
$$\$1,720,976 \times (1 + r) = \$1,754,000,$$
$$r = 0.0192.$$

One can convert this three-month (90 days) investment rate to an annual whole percentage equivalent, assuming a 360-day financial year, as follows:

$$0.0192 \times \frac{360}{90} \times 100 = 7.68\%.$$

In other words, if Dayton can invest the loan proceeds at a rate higher than 7.68% per annum, it would prefer the money market hedge. If Dayton can only invest at a lower rate than 7.68%, it would prefer the forward hedge.

The essence of a money market hedge is as follows:

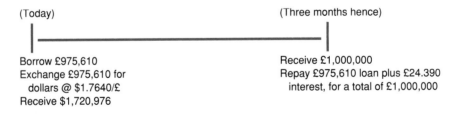

(Today)

Borrow £975,610
Exchange £975,610 for
  dollars @ $1.7640/£
Receive $1,720,976

(Three months hence)

Receive £1,000,000
Repay £975,610 loan plus £24.390
  interest, for a total of £1,000,000

Options Market Hedge

Dayton could also cover its £1,000,000 exposure by purchasing a put option. This technique allows Dayton to speculate on the upside potential for appreciation of the pound while limiting downside risk to a known amount.

Given the two quotes shown earlier, Dayton could purchase from its bank a three-month put option on £1,000,000 at either (1) an at-the-money (ATM) strike price of $1.75/£ (and a premium cost of 1.50%), or (2) an out-of-the-money (OTM) strike price of $1.71/£ (and a premium cost of 1.00%). The cost of the first option with strike price of $1.75, a strike price which would be considered close to forward-at-the-money, is:[8]

$$(\text{Size of option}) \times (\text{premium}) \times (\text{spot rate}) = (\text{cost of option}),$$
$$\pounds 1,000,000 \times 0.015 \times \$1.7640 = \$26,460.$$

Since we are using future value to compare the various hedging alternatives, it is necessary to project the premium cost of the option forward three months. Once again one could justify several investment rates. We use the cost of capital of 12% per annum or 3% per quarter. Therefore the premium cost of the put option as of June would be $26,460 × (1.03) = $27,254. This is equivalent to $0.0273 per pound ($27,254 ÷ £1,000,000).

When the £1,000,000 is received in June, the value in dollars depends on the spot rate at that time. The upside potential is unlimited, the same as in the unhedged alternative. At any exchange rate above $1.75/£ Dayton would allow its option to expire unexercised and would exchange the pounds for dollars at the spot rate. If the expected rate of $1.76/£ materialized, for example, Dayton would exchange the £1,000,000 in the spot market for $1,760,000. Net proceeds would be $1,760,000 minus the $27,254 cost of the option, or $1,732,746.

In contrast to the unhedged alternative, downside risk is limited with an option. If the pound depreciated below $1.75/£, Dayton would exercise its option to sell (put) £1,000,000 at $1.75/£, receiving $1,750,000 gross, but $1,722,746 net of the $27,254 cost of the option. Although this downside result is worse than the downside of the forward or money market hedges, the upside potential is not limited the way it is with those hedges. Thus whether the option strategy is superior to a forward or money market hedge depends on the degree to which management is risk averse.

The essence of the at-the-money (ATM) option market hedge is as follows:

(Today)   (Three months hence)

Buy put option to   Receive £1,000,000
   sell pounds @ $1.75/£   Either deliver £1,000,000 against put,
Pay $26,460 for put option   receiving $1,750,000; or sell £1,000,000
                                                             spot if current spot rate is > $1.75/£

We can calculate a trading range for the pound that defines the break-even points for the option compared with the other strategies. The upper bound of the range is determined by comparison with the forward rate. The pound must appreciate enough above the $1.7540 forward rate to cover the $0.0273/£ cost of the option. Therefore the break-even upside spot price of the pound must be $1.7540 + $0.0273 = $1.7813. If the spot pound appreciates above $1.7813, proceeds under the option strategy will be greater than under the forward hedge. If the spot pound ends up below $1.7813, the forward hedge would be superior in retrospect.

---

[8]Recall from Chapter 6 that currency options are priced on the basis of the forward rate. An option that possesses a strike price which is the same as the forward rate is called *forward at-the-money*.

The lower bound of the range is determined by a comparison with the unhedged strategy. If the spot price falls below $1.75, Dayton will exercise its put option and sell the proceeds at $1.75. The net proceeds per pound will be $1.75 less the $0.0273 cost of the option, or $1.7221. If the spot rate falls below $1.7221, the net proceeds from exercising the option will be greater than the net proceeds from selling the unhedged pounds in the spot market. At any spot rate above $1.7221, the spot proceeds from the unhedged alternative will be greater.

The same basic calculations, costs, and break-even points can be determined for the second option, the one with a strike price of $1.71/£. It has a smaller premium cost because it is out-of-the-money (OTM). The resulting comparison of the two alternative over-the-counter options appears as follows:[9]

Put Option Strike Price	ATM Option $1.75/£	OTM Option $1.71/£
Option cost (future value)	$27,254	$18,169
Proceeds if exercised	$1,750,000	$1,710,000
Minimum net proceeds	$1,722,746	$1,691,831
Maximum net proceeds	Unlimited	Unlimited
Break-even spot rate	$1.7813	$1.7722

Comparison of Alternatives

The four alternatives available to Dayton are shown in Exhibit 7.4. The forward hedge yields a certain $1,754,000 in three months. This would be equivalent to a money market hedge if the loan proceeds are invested at 7.68% per annum. At any higher rate, such as the 12% cost of capital, the money market hedge is preferable, but at any lower rate the forward hedge is preferable.

If Dayton does not hedge, it can "expect" $1,760,000 in three months. However, this sum is at risk and might be greater or smaller. Under conditions when the forward rate is accepted as the most likely future spot rate, the expected results from an unhedged position are identical to the certain results from the forward hedge. Under such circumstances the advantage of hedging over remaining unhedged is the reduction of uncertainty.

The two put options offer a unique alternative. If the exchange rate moves in Dayton's favor, both options have nearly the same upside potential as the unhedged alternative except for their up-front costs. If, however, the exchange rate moves against Dayton, the put options limit the downside risk to net receipts of either $1,722,746 for the $1.75 strike, or $1,691,831 for the $1.71 strike put.

Foreign currency options have a variety of hedging uses beyond the one illustrated by Dayton. A put option is useful to construction firms or other exporters when they must submit a fixed price bid in a foreign currency without knowing until some later

---

[9]The cost of the $1.71 strike put option = £1,000,000 × 0.010 × $1.7640 = $17,640. In future value terms, $17,640 × 1.03 = $18,169.20, or $0.018169 per pound. The break-even rate versus the forward contract rate is $1.7540 + $0.0182 = $1.7722/£.

Exhibit 7.4   Comparison of Alternative Hedging Strategies for Dayton

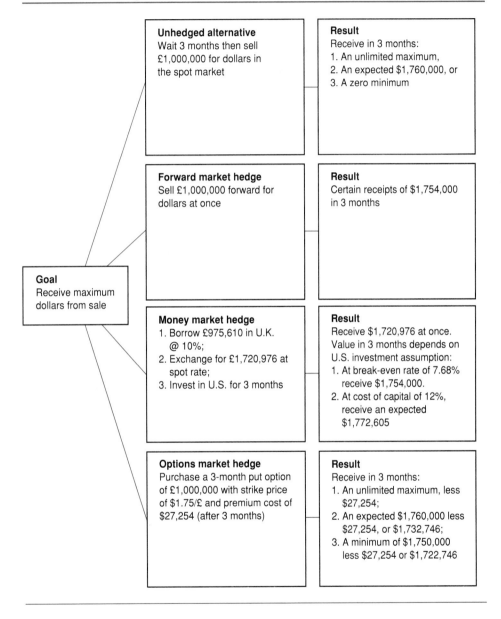

date whether their bid is successful. A put option can be used to hedge the foreign exchange risk either for the bidding period alone or for the entire period of potential exposure if the bid is won. If the bid is rejected, the loss is limited to the cost of the option. In contrast, if the risk is hedged by a forward contract and the bid is rejected, the forward contract must be reversed or eventually fulfilled at an unknown potential loss or gain. The bidder has an uncovered forward contract.

Strategy Choice and Outcome

The preceding section provided a comparison of the hedging alternatives available to Dayton. Dayton, like all firms attempting to hedge transaction exposure, must decide on a strategy before the exchange rate changes occur. Exhibit 7.5 provides an evaluation of each potential strategy open to Dayton over a range of exchange rates that may occur at the end of the three-month period.

On what basis is Dayton to choose among the alternative hedging strategies? Answer: on the basis of two decision criteria: (1) the *risk tolerance* of Dayton; and (2) Dayton's *view,* or expectation of which direction (and how far) the exchange rate will move over the coming three-month period.

Dayton's *risk tolerance* is a combination of management's philosophy toward transaction exposure and the specific goals of treasury activities. Many firms believe currency risk is simply a part of doing business internationally, and therefore start their analysis from an unhedged baseline. Other firms, however, view currency risk as unacceptable, and either start their analysis from a full forward contract cover baseline,

Exhibit 7.5   Valuation of Cash Flows Under Various Hedging Alternatives
for Dayton

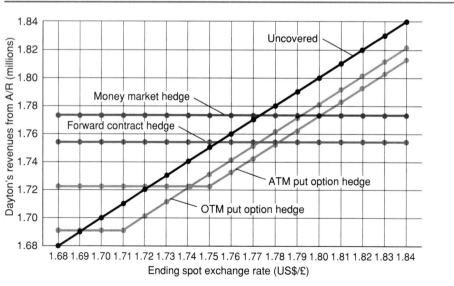

or simply mandate that all transaction exposures be fully covered by forward contracts regardless of the value of other hedging alternatives. The treasury in such firms operates as a cost or service center for the firm. On the other hand, if the treasury operates as a profit center, it might tolerate taking more risks.

If management is willing to consider all alternatives, the firm's *view* of likely exchange rate changes aids in the hedging choice. As is evident from Exhibit 7.5, if the exchange rate is expected to move against Dayton—to the left of $1.76/£—the money market hedge is the clearly preferred alternative. At a guaranteed value of $1,772,605, the money market hedge is by far the most profitable choice. If the exchange rate is expected to move in Dayton's favor, to the right of $1.76/£, the choice of the hedge is more complex. Consider the following points:

- If the spot rate is expected to move to the right of $1.77, the unhedged alternative always provides the highest U.S. dollar value for the receivable.

- If, however, Dayton is worried its expectations may prove incorrect, the decision to remain unhedged does not assure it of meeting its budgeted exchange rate of $1.70. This is an outcome the firm cannot afford. The possibility always exists of a major unexpected political or economic event disrupting international currency markets.

- If the spot rate is expected to move to the *right* of $1.77, but not far to the right, for example $1.78, the expected benefits of remaining unhedged versus the risks of remaining unhedged are probably not worth it. The money market hedge is still the preferred choice.

- If the spot rate is expected to move far to the right of $1.76 such as $1.84, the put option would potentially allow Dayton to enjoy the upside movement and simultaneously provide a safety net of a minimum value if the puts are exercised.

- If the spot rate is expected to move so far to the right that Dayton considers both put options, the choice is one of trade-offs. The $1.71 strike put option is significantly cheaper, but also provides a lower level of protection ($1,691,831 minimum net proceeds as opposed to the $1,722,746 assured by the $1.75 strike put). You get what you pay for. The decision in this case is simplified for Dayton by the fact that the OTM put option does not assure Dayton, after premium expenses, of meeting its budgeted exchange rate of $1.70/£ (or minimum net proceeds of $1,700,000).

The final choice among hedges if Dayton does expect the pound to appreciate combines both the firm's risk tolerance, its view, and its confidence in its view. Transaction exposure management with contractual hedges requires managerial judgment.

Management of an Accounts Payable

The Dayton Manufacturing case used throughout this chapter assumes a foreign currency denominated receivable. The management of an account payable, where the firm would be required to make a foreign currency payment at a future date, is similar but not identical in form.

If Dayton had a £1,000,000 **account payable** in 90 days, the hedging choices would appear as follows:

1. *Remain unhedged.* Dayton could wait 90 days, exchange dollars for pounds at that time, and make its payment. If Dayton expects the spot rate in 90 days to be $1.7600/£, the payment would be expected to cost $1,760,000. This amount is, however, uncertain; the spot exchange rate in 90 days could be very different from that expected.

2. *Forward market hedge.* Dayton could **buy** £1,000,000 forward, locking in a rate of $1.7540/£, and a total dollar cost of $1,754,000. This is $6,000 less than the expected cost of remaining unhedged, and therefore clearly preferable over alternative 1.

3. *Money market hedge.* The money market hedge is distinctly different for a payable as opposed to a receivable. To implement a money market hedge in this case, Dayton would exchange U.S. dollars spot and invest them for 90 days in a pound-denominated interest-bearing account. The principal and interest in British pounds at the end of the 90-day period would be used to pay the £1,000,000 account payable.

In order to assure that the principal and interest exactly equal the £1,000,000 due in 90 days, Dayton would discount the £1,000,000 by the pound investment interest rate of 8% for 90 days in order to determine the pounds needed today:

$$\frac{£1,000,000}{1 + \left(.08 \times \dfrac{90}{360}\right)} = £980,392.16.$$

This £980,392.16 needed today would require $1,729,411.77 at the current spot rate of $1.7640/£:

$$£980,392.16 \times \$1.7640/£ = \$1,729,411.77.$$

Finally, in order to compare the money market hedge outcome with the other hedging alternatives, the $1,729,411.77 cost today must be carried forward 90 days to the same future date as the other hedge choices. If the current dollar cost is carried forward at Dayton's WACC of 12%, the total cost of the money market hedge is $1,781,294.12:

$$\$1,729,411.77 \times \left[1 + \left(.12 \times \frac{90}{360}\right)\right] = \$1,781,294.12.$$

This is higher than the forward hedge and therefore unattractive.

4. *Option hedge.* Dayton could cover its £1,000,000 account payable by purchasing a call option on £1,000,000. A June call option on British pounds with a near at-the-money strike price of $1.75/£ would cost 1.5% (premium) or

$$£1,000,000 \times 0.015 \times \$1.7640/£ = \$26,460.$$

This premium, regardless of whether the call option is exercised or not, will be paid up-front. Its value carried forward 90 days at the WACC of 12%, as it was in the receivable example, would raise its end of period cost to $27,254.

If the spot rate in 90 days is less than $1.75/£, the option would be allowed to expire and the £1,000,000 for the payable purchased on the spot market. The total cost of the call option hedge if the option is not exercised is theoretically smaller than any other alternative (with the exception of remaining unhedged, because the option premium is still paid and lost).

If the spot rate in 90 days is greater than $1.75/£, the call option would be exercised. The total cost of the call option hedge if exercised is as follows:

Exercise call option (£1,000,000 × $1.75/£) $1,750,000

Call option premium (carried forward 90 days)   27,254

Total maximum expense of call option hedge $1,777,254

The four hedging methods of managing a £1,000,000 account payable for Dayton are summarized as follows:

Hedging Alternative	Cost to Dayton	Degree of Risk
1. Remain unhedged	$1,760,000	Uncertain
2. Forward hedge	$1,754,000	Certain
3. Money market hedge	$1,781,294	Certain
4. Call option hedge	$1,777,254	Maximum

As with Dayton's account receivable, the final hedging choice depends on the confidence of firm exchange rate expectations, and Dayton's willingness to bear risk. The forward hedge provides the lowest cost of making the account payable payment which is certain. If the dollar were to strengthen against the pound, ending up at a spot rate less than $1.75/£, the call option could potentially be the lowest cost hedge. Given an expected spot rate of $1.76/£, however, the forward hedge appears the preferred alternative.

Foreign Exchange Contractual Hedging in Practice

As many different approaches to transaction exposure management exist as there are firms. A variety of surveys of corporate risk management practices in recent years in the United States, the United Kingdom, Australia, Belgium, the Netherlands, and Germany indicates that no real consensus exists about an optimal approach.[10] The following is our attempt to assimilate the basic results of these surveys and combine them with our own personal experiences in industry.

Which Goals?

The treasury function of most private firms, the group typically responsible for transaction exposure management, is usually considered a cost center. It is not expected to add

---

[10]A partial listing of published research surveys on the foreign exchange management practices of firms would include the following: Batten, Mellor, and Wan (1993), Australia; Edelshain (1992), United Kingdom; Belk and Glaum (1990), United Kingdom; Aggarwal and Soenen (1989), United Kingdom, Belgium, and the Netherlands; Khoury and Chan (1988), United States.

profit to the firm's bottom line (which is not the same thing as saying it is not expected to add value to the firm). Currency risk managers are expected to err on the conservative side when managing the firm's money.

One of the most interesting recent studies is by David Edelshain of the London Business School.[11] Corporate risk managers were asked a series of questions and asked to repond affirmatively or negatively. Approximately 40% of survey respondents agreed with this statement: "Our strategy is to try to smooth out the impact on our business of currency related influences." The statement "Our objective is to make profit from the sale of our products and services, and we do not consciously seek to profit from supporting or non-trading activities" was confirmed by 47% of survey respondents. Although this is a relatively large number, the implication is nevertheless that over 50% of the firms in this sample believe at least part of their overall objective is to profit from treasury activities.

Which Exposures?

Transaction exposures exist before they are actually booked as foreign currency-denominated receivables and payables. However, many firms do not allow the hedging of quotation exposure or backlog exposure as a matter of policy. The reasoning is straightforward: Until the transaction exists on the accounting books of the firm, the probability of the exposure actually occurring is considered to be less than 100%. Conservative hedging policies dictate that contractual hedges be placed only on existing exposures.

An increasing number of firms, however, are actively hedging not only backlog exposures, but also selectively hedging quotation and *anticipated* exposures. Anticipated exposures are transactions for which there are — at present — no contracts or agreements between parties, but are anticipated on the basis of historical trends and continuing business relationships. Although on the surface this would appear to be overly speculative behavior on the part of these firms, it may be that hedging expected foreign currency payables for future periods is the most conservative approach to protect the firm's future operating revenues against unexpected exchange rate changes.[12]

Which Contractual Hedges?

As might be expected, transaction exposure management programs are generally divided along an "option line": those that use options and those that do not. Firms that do not use currency options rely almost exclusively on forward contracts and money market hedges. A few firms with appreciable quantities of transaction exposure actually do no hedging at all. Edelshain's 1992 survey of British currency risk managers found a surprisingly high utilization rate of currency options (see Exhibit 7.6), as well as mandatory proportional exposure hedging.

---

[11]David Edelshain, *British Corporate Currency Exposure and Foreign Exchange Risk Management,* Ph.D. thesis (unpublished), London Business School, Sussex Place, Regents Park, London, 1992. Edelshain's survey was conducted in December 1991 yielding usable survey responses from 116 firms with operations in Great Britain.

[12]Anticipatory hedging programs have been the focus of considerable debate in recent years, particularly the accounting principles that apply to their use.

Exhibit 7.6 Use of Contractual Strategies for Currency Risk in the
United Kingdom

Percentage of Survey Respondents That Use:

Forward contracts	78%
Futures contracts	15%
Currency options	51%
Proportional hedging	46%

Source: David Edelshain, *British Corporate Currency Exposure and Foreign Exchange Risk Management,* Ph.D. thesis (unpublished), London Business School, 1992.

Proportional Hedges. Many multinational firms have established rather rigid transaction exposure risk management policies that mandate proportional hedging. These policies generally require the use of forward contract hedges on a percentage (e.g., 50, 60, or 70%) of existing transaction exposures. As the maturity of the exposures lengthens, the percentage forward-cover required decreases. The remaining portion of the exposure is then selectively hedged on the basis of the firm's risk tolerance, view of exchange rate movements, and confidence level.

As the Lufthansa case at the end of this chapter highlights, the logic of a partial cover strategy is somewhat questionable. If a firm is required to cover 50% of all transaction exposures with forwards, and then selectively chose to leave the remaining 50% of the exposure completely unhedged because of an expected currency movement, the two legs of the same exposure management program are internally inconsistent, and the financial results are generally unsatisfactory. Note, however, that mandatory forward-cover programs are constructed on the basis of conservative exposure management, and may have nothing really to do with expected exchange rate movements.

Although rarely acknowledged by the firms themselves, the continual use of selective hedging programs—as in the Dayton case in which the firm may choose a hedge partially on the basis of its view of exchange rate movements—is essentially speculation against the markets. Significant theoretical questions remain as to whether a firm or a financial manager can consistently predict the future direction of exchange rate movements. One observer has noted, "It may occasionally be possible to find money lying in the street, but I would not expect to make a living at it."[13]

Forward Points. In addition to having required minimum forward-cover percentages, many firms also require full forward-cover when forward rates "pay them the points." The *points on the forward rate* is the forward rate's premium or discount. For example, in the Dayton Manufacturing case, the forward rate of $1.7540/£ could be the result of

---

[13]Gunter Dufey, the University of Michigan, undated.

the following 90-day Eurocurrency interest rates on U.S. dollars (6.80% per annum) and British pounds (9.12% per annum):

$$\text{Forward}_{90} = \$1.7640/\pounds \times \left[\frac{1 + \left(.0680 \times \dfrac{90}{360}\right)}{1 + \left(.0912 \times \dfrac{90}{360}\right)} \right] = \$1.7540/\pounds.$$

Because British pound interest rates are higher than U.S. dollar interest rates, the pound is selling forward at a discount. A firm such as Dayton purchasing a forward contract to sell pounds forward would itself be *paying the points*.

If, however, U.S. dollar interest rates (6.80% per annum) were higher than British pound interest rates (6.00% per annum), the pound would be selling forward at a premium:

$$\text{Forward}_{90} = \$1.7640/\pounds \times \left[\frac{1 + \left(.0680 \times \dfrac{90}{360}\right)}{1 + \left(.0600 \times \dfrac{90}{360}\right)} \right] = \$1.7675/\pounds.$$

A forward rate of $1.7675/£ would allow Dayton to lock in an exchange rate for 90 days in the future that is better than the exchange rate which would be realized even if Dayton received the British pounds today.

Many firms require that when the firm earns the forward points (as shown in this example) that full forward-cover be put in place. Not only is the exchange rate in the firm's favor, it also allows the firm to earn a U.S. dollar effective rate that meets its budget exchange rate and a hedge choice which is independent of the firm's exchange rate view. Although the favorable forward rate is a result only of interest rate differences, many firms view this as riskless profit.

Bought Currency Options. A further distinction in practice can be made between those firms that buy currency options (buy a put or buy a call) and those that both buy and write currency options. Those firms that do use currency options are generally more aggressive in their tolerance of currency risk. This is a generalization, however, and in many cases firms that are extremely conservative and risk intolerant may be hedging all existing exposures with forwards and then additionally hedging a variety of backlog and anticipated exposures with options. The currency options used by multinational firms are nearly exclusively over the counter in origin and European in pricing style.

Hedgers with some degree of settlement risk may find it in their best interest to purchase protective options with maturities longer than the expected exposure maturity. This allows the hedger to at least recapture some of the option premium investment through resale if the exposure cash flow does indeed not occur as expected. The hedger must then determine if the added benefits of a longer maturity and security in settlement risk coverage are worth the added expense.

Written Currency Options. Since the writer of an option has a limited profit potential with unlimited loss potential, the risks associated with writing options can be substantial. Firms that write options usually do so to finance the purchase of a second option. For example, a firm such as Dayton, which is long British pounds, may write an out-of-the-money call option on pounds to partially offset the expense of purchasing an at-the-money put option on the same quantity of British pounds. These so-called *complex options* are gaining ever wider use in industry. Chapter 23 provides a detailed description of many of these complex options.[14]

If the hedger was actually writing options as part of its exposure management program (as we describe in later sections), the writer will find it beneficial to write relatively short-term options with rapidly deteriorating prices. This technique allows the writer to gain the benefits of the sale, the initial premium, yet in most cases rest assured that time value deterioration will cause the value of the option to drop precipitously soon after sale, making any possible repurchase of the option affordable.

Limitations of Contractual Hedges

As sophisticated as the range of contractual hedges and financial derivatives have become, they only provide temporary protection against medium to longer term exchange rate movements. Contractual hedges are not long-term solutions. As the introductory Global View states in the case of Sony, "What Sony's currency gains don't do, as evidenced by its big drop in operating profit, is change its underlying difficulties." Transaction exposure management is only the first step in the measurement and management of a firm's currency exposure. The following chapters on operating and accounting exposure measurement and management address many of the more fundamental sources of exposure that in reality give rise to transaction exposure.

Summary

- Three types of currency exposure are encountered by multinational firms: (1) transaction exposure, (2) operating exposure, and (3) accounting exposure.

- Transaction exposure measures gains or losses that arise from the settlement of financial obligations whose terms are stated in a foreign currency. Transaction exposure arises from (1) purchasing or selling on credit goods or services whose prices are stated in foreign currencies; (2) borrowing or lending funds when repayment is to be made in a foreign currency; (3) being a party to an unperformed forward foreign exchange contract; and (4) otherwise acquiring assets or incurring liabilities denominated in foreign currencies.

- There is considerable theoretical debate as to whether firms should hedge currency risk. Theoretically, hedging reduces the variability of the cash flows to the firm.

---

[14]The most frequently used complex options are *range forwards*, *participating forwards*, *break forwards*, and *average rate options*, which are discussed in Chapter 23.

Hedging does not increase the net cash flows to the firm. In fact, the costs of hedging may potentially lower them.

- Transaction exposure can be managed by contractual techniques and certain operating strategies. Contractual hedging techniques include forward, futures, money market, and option hedges.

- The choice of which contractual hedge to use depends on the individual firm's currency risk tolerance and its expectation of the probable movement of exchange rates over the transaction exposure period.

- In general, if an exchange rate is expected to move in a firm's favor, the preferred contractual hedges are probably those that allow it to participate in some up-side potential (remaining unhedged or using a currency option), but protect it against significant adverse exchange rate movements.

- In general, if the exchange rate is expected to move against the firm, the preferred contractual hedge is one that locks in an exchange rate, such as the forward contract hedge or money market hedge.

Decision Case
Lufthansa[15]

It was February 14, 1986, and Herr Heinz Ruhnau, chairman of Lufthansa (Germany) was summoned to meet with Lufthansa's board. The board's task was to determine if Herr Ruhnau's term of office should be terminated. Herr Ruhnau had already been summoned by Germany's transportation minister to explain his supposed speculative management of Lufthansa's exposure in the purchase of Boeing aircraft.

In January 1985 Lufthansa (Germany), under the chairmanship of Herr Heinz Ruhnau, purchased twenty 737 jets from Boeing (U.S.). The agreed upon price was $500,000,000, payable in U.S. dollars on delivery of the aircraft in one year (January 1986). The U.S. dollar had been rising steadily and rapidly since 1980, and was approximately DM3.2/$ in January 1985. If the dollar were to continue to rise, the cost of the jet aircraft to Lufthansa would rise substantially by the time payment was due.

---

[15]Michael H. Moffett, Oregon State University, August 1993. Reprinted with permission. The author thanks David Eiteman and Arthur Stonehill for significant contributions. This case draws on several major sources including, "Where Options Would Have Made a Difference," *Intermarket* (November Supplement, 1986), pp. 20, 22; *Trading in Currency Options*, by William Sutton, New York Institute of Finance (1988), pp. 82–83, and *The Financial Times*, London (February 24, 1986).

Herr Ruhnau had his own *view* or expectations regarding the direction of the exchange rate. Like many others at the time, he believed the dollar had risen about as far as it was going to go, and would probably fall by the time January 1986 rolled around. But then again, it really wasn't his money to gamble with. He compromised. He covered half the exposure ($250,000,000) at a rate of DM3.2/$, and left the remaining half ($250,000,000) uncovered.

Evaluation of the Hedging Alternatives

Lufthansa and Herr Ruhnau had the same basic hedging alternatives available to all firms:

1. Remain uncovered;

2. Cover the entire exposure with forward contracts;

3. Cover some proportion of the exposure, leaving the balance uncovered;

4. Cover the exposure with foreign currency options;

5. Obtain U.S. dollars now and hold them until payment is due.

Although the final expense of each alternative could not be known beforehand, each alternative's outcome could be simulated over a range of potential ending exchange rates. Exhibit 7.7 illustrates the final net cost of the first four alternatives over a wide range of potential end-of-period (January 1986) spot exchange rates.

Exhibit 7.7   Lufthansa's Net Cost by Hedging Alternative

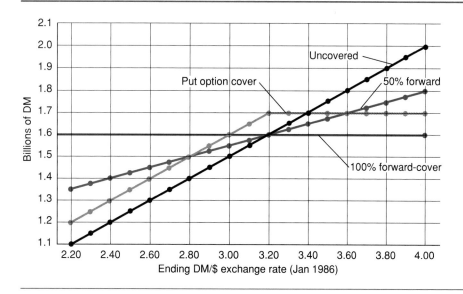

1: Remain Uncovered

Remaining uncovered is the maximum risk approach. It therefore represents the greatest potential benefits (if the dollar weakens versus the Deutschemark), and the greatest potential cost (if the dollar continues to strengthen versus the Deutschemark). If the exchange rate were to drop to DM2.2/$ by January 1986, the purchase of the Boeing 737s would be only DM 1.1 billion. Of course if the dollar continued to appreciate, rising to perhaps DM4.0/$ by 1986, the total cost would be DM 2.0 billion. The uncovered position's risk is therefore shown as that value line which has the steepest slope (covers the widest vertical distance) in Exhibit 7.7. This is obviously a sizable level of risk for any firm to carry. Many firms believe the decision to leave a large exposure uncovered for a long period of time to be nothing other than *currency speculation.*

2: Full Forward Cover

If Lufthansa were very risk averse and wished to eliminate fully its currency exposure, it could buy forward contracts for the purchase of U.S. dollars for the entire amount. This would have locked in an exchange rate of DM3.2/$, with a known final cost of DM 1.6 billion. This alternative is represented by the horizontal value line in Exhibit 7.7; the total cost of the Boeing 737s no longer has any risk or sensitivity to the ending spot exchange rate. Most firms believe they should accept or tolerate risk in their *line of business,* not in the process of payment. The 100% forward cover alternative is often used by firms as their benchmark, their comparison measure for actual currency costs when all is said and done.

3: Partial Forward Cover

This alternative would cover only part of the total exposure leaving the remaining exposure uncovered. Herr Ruhnau's expectations were for the dollar to fall, so he expected Lufthansa would benefit from leaving more of the position uncovered (as in alternative 1). This strategy is somewhat arbitrary, however, in that there are few objective methods available for determining what the proper balance (20/80, 40/60, 50/50; etc.) between covered/uncovered should be. Exhibit 7.7 illustrates the total ending cost of this alternative for a partial cover of 50/50: $250 million purchased with forward contracts of DM3.2/$, and the $250 million remaining purchased at the end-of-period spot rate. Note that this value line's slope is simply half that of the 100% uncovered position. Any other partial cover strategy would similarly fall between the unhedged and 100% cover lines.

Two principal points can be made regarding partial forward cover strategies such as this. First, Herr Ruhnau's total potential exposure is still unlimited. The possibility that the dollar would appreciate to astronomical levels still exists, and $250 million could translate into an infinite amount of Deutschemarks. The second point is that the first point is highly unlikely to occur. Therefore, for the immediate ranges of potential exchange rates on either side of the current spot rate of DM3.2/$, Herr Ruhnau has reduced the risk (vertical distance in Exhibit 7.7) of the final Deutschemark outlay over a range of ending values and the benchmark value of DM3.2/$.

4: Foreign Currency Options

The foreign currency option is unique among the hedging alternatives due to its kinked-shape value line. If Herr Ruhnau had purchased a put option on marks at DM3.2/$, he could have obtained what many people believe is the best of both worlds. If the dollar had continued to strengthen above DM3.2/$, the total cost of obtaining $500 million could be locked in at DM1.6 billion plus the cost of the option premium, as illustrated by the flat portion of the option alternative to the right of DM3.2/$.[16] If, however, the dollar fell as Herr Ruhnau had expected, Lufthansa would be free to let the option expire and purchase the dollars at lower cost on the spot market. This alternative is shown by the falling value line to the left of DM3.2/$. Note that the put option line falls at the same rate (same slope) as the uncovered position, but is higher by the cost of purchasing the option.

In this instance Herr Ruhnau would have had to buy put options for DM 1.6 billion given an exercise price of DM3.2/$. In January 1985 when Herr Heinz Ruhnau was thinking over these alternatives, the option premium on Deutshemark put options was about 6%, equal to DM96,000,000 or $30,000,000! The total cost of the purchase in the event the put option was exercised would be DM1,696,000,000 (exercise plus premium).

It is important to understand what Herr Ruhnau would be hoping to happen if he had decided to purchase the put options. He would be expecting the dollar to weaken (ending up to the left of DM3.2/$ in Exhibit 7.7), therefore he would expect the option to expire without value. In the eyes of many corporate treasurers, DM96,000,000 is a lot of money for the purchase of an instrument that the hedger expects or hopes not to use!

5: Buy Dollars Now

The fifth alternative is a money market hedge for an account payable: Obtain the $500 million now and hold those funds in an interest-bearing account or asset until payment was due. Although this would eliminate the currency exposure, it required that Lufthansa have all the capital in hand now. The purchase of the Boeing jets had been made in conjunction with the ongoing financing plans of Lufthansa, and these did not call for the capital to be available until January 1986. An added concern (and what ultimately eliminated this alternative from consideration) was that Lufthansa had several relatively strict covenants in place that limited the types, amounts, and currencies of denomination of the debt it could carry on its balance sheet.

Herr Ruhnau's Decision

Although Herr Ruhnau truly expected the dollar to weaken over the coming year, he believed remaining completely uncovered was too risky for Lufthansa. Few would argue this, particularly given the strong upward trend of the DM/$ exchange rate as seen in Exhibit 7.8. The dollar had shown a consistent three-year trend of appreciation versus the Deutschemark, and that trend seemed to be accelerating over the most recent year.

Because he personally felt so strongly the dollar would weaken, Herr Ruhnau chose to go with partial cover. He chose to cover 50% of the exposure ($250 million) with

---

[16]Interest expenses on the option premium are ignored in this case for simplicity of calculation.

Exhibit 7.8   What Herr Ruhnau Could See: The Rise

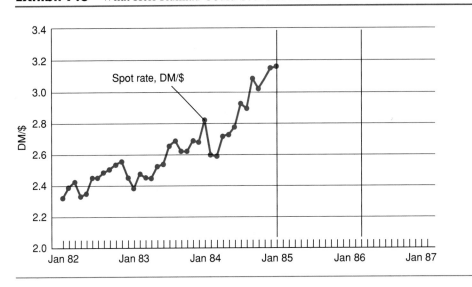

forward contracts (the one-year forward rate was DM3.2/$) and to leave the remaining 50% ($250 million) uncovered. Because foreign currency options were as yet a relatively new tool for exposure management by many firms, and because of the sheer magnitude of the up-front premium required, the foreign currency option was not chosen. Time would tell if this was a wise decision.

How It Came Out

Herr Ruhnau was both right and wrong. He was definitely right in his expectations. The dollar appreciated for one more month, and then weakened over the coming year. In fact, it did not simply *weaken,* it plummeted. By January 1986 when payment was due to Boeing, the spot rate had fallen to DM2.3/$ from the previous year's DM3.2/$ as shown in Exhibit 7.9. This was a spot exchange rate movement in Lufthansa's favor.

The bad news was that the total Deutschemark cost with the partial forward cover was DM1.375 billion, a full DM225,000,000 more than if no hedging had been implemented at all! This was also DM129,000,000 more than what the foreign currency option hedge would have cost in total. The total cost of obtaining the needed $500 million for each alternative at the actual ending spot rate of DM2.3/$ would have been:

Alternative	Relevant Rate	Total DM Cost
1: Uncovered	DM2.3/$	1,150,000,000
2: Full Forward Cover (100%)	DM3.2/$	1,600,000,000
3: Partial Forward Cover	1/2(DM2.3) + 1/2(DM3.2)	1,375,000,000
4: DM Put Options	DM3.2/$ strike	1,246,000,000

Exhibit 7.9   What Herr Ruhnau Couldn't See: The Fall

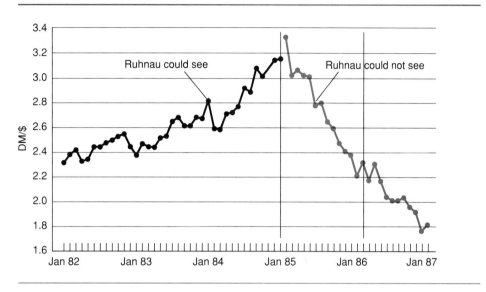

Herr Ruhnau's political rivals, both inside and outside of Lufthansa, were not so happy. Ruhnau was accused of recklessly speculating with Lufthansa's money, but the *speculation* was seen as the forward contract, not the amount of the dollar exposure left uncovered for the full year. It is obvious that the term *speculation* holds an entirely new meaning when perfect hindsight is used to evaluate performance.

Case Questions

Herr Ruhnau was accused of making the following four mistakes:

1. Purchasing the Boeing aircraft at the wrong time. The U.S. dollar was at an all-time high at the time of the purchase in January 1985.

2. Choosing to hedge half the exposure when he expected the dollar to fall. If he had gone through with his instincts or expectations, he would have left the whole amount unhedged (which some critics have termed "whole hog").

3. Choosing to use forward contracts as his hedging tool instead of options. The purchase of put options would have allowed Herr Ruhnau to protect himself against adverse exchange rate movements while preserving the flexibility of exchanging DM for U.S. dollars spot if the market moved in his favor.

4. Purchasing Boeing aircraft at all. Germany, as well as the other major European Economic Community countries, has a vested interest in the conglomerate Airbus. Airbus's chief rival was Boeing in the manufacture of large long-distance civil aircraft.

Given these criticisms, should the board of Lufthansa retain Herr Heinz Ruhnau as chairman? How should Ruhnau justify his actions and so justify his further employment?

Questions

1. Yount Aircraft Parts of Phoenix

Yount Aircraft Parts, headquartered in Phoenix, Arizona, is completing a new parts facility in Alicante, Spain. The final construction payment is due in six months in the amount of Pta16,000,000. Foreign exchange and interest rate quotations are as follows:

Present spot rate	Pta138.20/$
Six-month forward rate	Pta145.50/$
Spanish peseta six-month interest rate	12.00% per annum
U.S. dollar six-month interest rate	8.00% per annum

The treasury manager suggests that in six months the following spot rates can be expected:

Highest expected rate	Pta145.00/$
Most likely rate	Pta140.00/$
Lowest expected rate	Pta130.00/$

Yount Parts has no excess cash at present, but it expects to receive adequate dollars from recovery of a facility liquidation (already overdue) in six months. Yount's weighted average cost of capital is 20% per annum.

  a. What are the realistic alternatives available to Yount for making payment?
  b. How are the financing of the payment and the hedging of the payment related?
  c. Which of the available alternatives will probably minimize Yount's expense for making the final construction payment?

2. Dayton Manufacturing (C07A.WK1)

Dayton Manufacturing (the same U.S. manufacturer used throughout the chapter) has changed its forecast of the spot exchange rate in 90 days to $1.8050/£.

  a. If all other interest and exchange rates remain the same, evaluate the hedging alternatives available to Dayton. Dayton's international treasurer wants all analysis to differentiate hedging alternatives which *control* the exchange rate risk from alternatives which *eliminate* the risk.
  b. Dayton has concluded a second sale of two additional gas turbines to Crown (U.K.). Total payment of £2,000,000 is due in 90 days. Dayton has discovered that it will only be able to borrow in the United Kingdom at 15% per annum. Although all other interest rates have remained the same, the spot rate has changed to $1.7620/£, and the three-month forward rate is now $1.7550/£.

Dayton now forecasts a spot rate of $1.7850/£ in 90 days. Which transaction exposure hedge is now in Dayton's best interest?

3. Sony's Successful Hedging (C07B.WK1)

The *Global View* that opened this chapter described the success of Sony in its hedging program in the second quarter of 1993. The currency hedging program was so successful that Sony reaped substantial profits from hedging alone (enough in fact to offset substantial declines in sales). Using the following end-of-month exchange rates (or the C07B.WK1 template) answer the following questions.

Month	¥/$	¥/DM	Month	¥/$	¥/DM
January	125.01	77.37	April	112.45	70.46
February	120.96	73.68	May	110.40	68.74
March	117.07	71.06	June	107.34	64.97

a. If Sony (Japan) is generally *long* most foreign currencies as a result of the successful operations of its foreign subsidiaries, what must Sony have been doing in its hedging program to generate such sizable profits in 1993?

b. As a shareholder in Sony, how dependable would these profits be in estimating the future earnings of Sony shares?

4. Eli Lily and Treasury's Hedging Policy

Eli Lily, the U.S.-based pharmaceutical firm, long ago did away with selective hedging by its treasury staff. All foreign currency-denominated cash flows, if the date of the transaction is known with certainty, must follow the following mandatory forward contract cover formula (remaining amounts may be left uncovered):

	Exposure Coverage Required by Maturity		
If Eli Lily is:	*0–90 days*	*91–180 days*	*>180 days*
"paying the points forward"	75%	50%	40%
"receiving the points forward"	100%	80%	50%

- If Lily was expecting to receive a Norwegian krone payment of NK1,500,000 in four months, the spot rate was NK7.4503/$, and the forward rate NK7.6000/$:

  a. What would be the amount of forward cover required?

  b. If at the same time the spot rate in four months was expected to be NK7.2000/$, what would be the amount in krone covered and uncovered?

  c. What would be the expected total end-of-period U.S. dollar value of the position taken in part b?

- If Lily was to make a Norwegian krone payment of NK1,000,000 in two months, the spot rate was NK7.4503/$, and the forward rate NK7.2500/$:

  a. What would be the amount of forward cover required?

  b. If the spot rate in two months was expected to be NK7.4000/$, what would be the amount sold forward (NK) and the amount (NK) left uncovered?

  c. What would be the expected total end-of-period U.S. dollar value of the position taken in part b?

5. Ford in Hungary

Ford of North America's (NA) Electric Fuel Handling Division of Ypsilanti, Michigan, is co-financing with Ford's German subsidiary the construction of a new fuel-injection assembly plant in Hungary. Ford NA is providing the equity for the project—paying for the project's construction and setup, while Ford of Germany is providing all project debt—to be used for working capital and operating expenses.

The construction contract has been awarded to Strabag of Austria on a competitive bid basis. Since Strabag is Austrian and not Hungarian, the contract calls for all construction payments to be denominated in Austrian shillings, not Hungarian forints. (Ford also has a standard policy of paying all foreign contractors in their own home currency.) The Austrian shilling, currently trading at AST12.05/US$, is a managed float against the Deutschemark.

The construction contract calls for payments on completion of stages (3), in the following amounts beginning 3 months from now:

Stage I	May 1	AST645,000,000
Stage II	August 1	122,000,000
Stage III	November 1	83,000,000
Total		AST850,000,000

The debt, totaling DM68,484,000 at the current spot rate of DM1.7121/$, is to be serviced by the Hungarian plant once under operation by its sales (100%) to Ford's German subsidiary. The first and foremost exposure is therefore the construction itself. The Austrian shilling can be bought or sold forward at a regulated forward rate of 3% annual premium (the shilling is always more "expensive" to outsiders at forward rates). Because of the narrow trading and regulated market for the Austrian shilling, options on the shilling are not yet readily available.

    a. Diagram the cash flows and individual parties to the Hungarian project.

    b. What should Ford NA use as a budgeted cost of the project?

    c. What should Ford NA do in order to protect itself against currency exposure during construction?

    d. What would happen to the hedge chosen in part c if the construction completion payments are postponed due to delays in construction?

    e. How could Ford NA use the Deutschemark as a "proxy" currency to hedge its exposure if the Deutschemark was currently selling forward at the following rates?

$$F_{90} = DM1.7237/\$ \qquad F_{180} = DM1.7316/\$ \qquad F_{360} = DM1.7389/\$$$

    f. How would Ford NA's and Ford of Germany's respective exposures change if the construction contract was a cost-plus contract allowing up to 10% cost overruns?

6. Utah International and Tokyo Power & Electric (C07C.WK1)

Utah International (US) is shipping 200,000 tons of low sulfur bituminous coal from its deep mines in the Wasatch Plateau of northern Utah to Tokyo Power (Japan). The current market price of this premium coal is about $28.50/ton in the United States. Given the current spot rate of ¥108.33/$, Utah has agreed to accept a purchase price of ¥617.5 million. Payment will be made in 90 days.

Utah, although not accustomed to a lot of foreign currency-denominated sales, does have an expert treasury staff capable of using (and allowed to use) currency forwards or options. Utah's treasury staff collects the following market information, including a recently published consensus forecast that the spot rate will be moving to about ¥110/$ in the coming two to three months.

F_{90} = ¥108.02/$ S^e_{90} = ¥110.00/$

90-day Eurodollar rate	3.3750%
90-day Euroyen rate	2.3125%
90-day Dollar borrowing rate	8.0000%
90-day Yen borrowing rate	9.5000%
90-day Yen option volatilities	11.80%

a. What would be the value of the receivable in 90 days if expectations are correct and the exposure is left uncovered?

b. What would be the value of the receivable in 90 days if expectations are correct and the yen proceeds had been sold forward?

c. What is the total premium cost for a forward ATM put option on yen?

d. What is the expected dollar value of the receivable if a forward ATM put option was purchased as protection?

e. What is the expected value of a money market hedge on the yen receivable?

f. Which is the best hedge, and why?

7. Shell Showa and Forward Contracts

Shell Showa (Japan) is the Japanese subsidiary of Royal Dutch Shell (Netherlands). Shell Showa's treasury had become a leader in the late 1980s and early 1990s in the practice of *zaiteku,* the use of financial derivatives to increase the value of business operations.

In 1989, however, the traders in Shell Showa's treasury center repeatedly missed the movement of the yen versus the dollar and Deutschemark. They had been selling enormous quantities of yen forward (buying dollars forward) in the hope of profit. Instead, they were now facing substantial losses on the forward positions (speculations, not hedges).

With the expectation that things would eventually turn in their favor, the traders continually "rolled forward" the positions over the next three years. This meant that instead of actually paying off or "realizing" the value of the positions as they matured, they recontracted at current forward rates further into the future. This was legal under Japanese financial instrument accounting practices at the time.

When the actual values of these financial speculation positions were realized by Shell Showa in 1992, the firm had book losses of ¥125 billion ($1.05 billion). These losses would be totally realized over the 1993–1995 period.

a. How appropriate is it for the corporate treasury division of a major multinational corporation to undertake speculation?
b. How appropriate is it that current accounting practices allow these types of financial losses to be "unrecognized and unrealized" over such an extended period of time?
c. Much of the problem at Shell Showa has been blamed on senior management's lack of vigilance and control over currency trading activity. How could this be improved?

8. L.A. Lever, Inc.

L.A. Lever, Inc., of Marina Del Rey has just purchased a French company that manufactures a line of sports shoes for children. These shoes provide a special bounce for kids who want a playground advantage in basketball or who are just plain reckless. The purchase price is FF60,000,000, with payment due the selling shareholders in six months. The spot rate is FF5.4635/$, and the 6 month forward rate is FF5.6155/$. Additional data are:

6-month French interest rate:	9.00% p.a.
6-month U.S. interest rate:	4.00% p.a.
6-month call option on francs at 5.45:	3.0% premium
6-month put option on francs at 5.45:	2.4% premium

Assume that L.A. Lever can invest at the given interest rates, or borrow at 1% p.a. above the investment rates. L.A. Lever's weighted average cost of capital is 24%.

a. Compare alternate ways that L.A. Lever might deal with its foreign exchange exposure.
b. What do you recommend and why?

9. Compaq's Hedging Policies

Compaq Computer Corporation (US) considers itself a very conservative firm. For example, at least 80% of each individual transaction exposure must be covered (mostly with forwards, occasionally with options). In fact, Compaq's FX manager has been quoted as saying that the 80% cover may be increased to 110% of the exposure if it is deemed prudent.

a. What would it mean to cover 110% of a transaction exposure?
b. What would be considered the most conservative transaction exposure management policy by a firm? How does that of Compaq compare?

10. Gulliver Radio, Inc.

On March 1, Gulliver Radio of Los Angeles sold a shipment of garage door radios to Smeltzer, GmbH, of Heilbronn, Germany, for DM500,000, payable DM250,000 on June 1, and DM250,000 on September 1. Gulliver had offered to sell the radios on February 1 for DM500,000, payable in Deutschemarks, after calculating this price by multiplying its U.S. sales price of $312,500 by the then current spot rate of DM1.6000/$.

When the order was received and booked on March 1, the mark was at DM1.5625/$, so the sale was in fact worth DM500,000 ÷ 1.5625 = $320,000. Gulliver had already gained an extra $7500 from favorable exchange rate movements! Nevertheless Jonathan Swift, Gulliver's director of finance, now wondered if he should protect the firm against a possible future weakening of the mark. Four approaches were possible:

1. Hedge in the forward market. The 3-month forward exchange quote is DM1.5900/$ and the 6-month forward quote is DM1.5800/$.

2. Hedge in the money market. Gulliver can borrow marks in Germany, from the German correspondent of its U.S. bank, at one percentage point above the current German bank prime rate of 6.8% p.a.

3. Hedge with foreign currency options. Deutschemark options are available in multiples of DM62,500 per contract. June put options with a strike price of 62 (cents per mark) can be purchased for a price of 1.17 cents (e.g., $0.0117) per mark, and September put options at 62 are available at 1.12 cents per mark. June call options at 62 can be purchased for 1.60 cents per mark, and September call options at 62 can be purchased for 1.88 cents per mark.

4. Do nothing. Swift can decide to wait until the sales proceeds are received in June and September and at that time sell the marks received for dollars in the spot market.

Gulliver can borrow dollars from its U.S. bank at 7.2% per annum. Swift estimates Gulliver's cost of equity capital to be 24% per annum; as a small firm, Gulliver cannot sell long-term debt. U.S. T bills yield 4.6% per annum. What should Swift do?

11. Dole Pineapple: Hedging a Note Payable
The Dole Company (U.S.) has just purchased a Canadian food distributor for C$6,000,000. Payment is due in six months. Dole's cost of capital is 12.0%. The following quotes are current in the market:

	United States	Canada
Six-month interest rate for borrowing	6.00% p.a.	10.0% p.a.
Six-month interest rate for investing	4.00% p.a.	8.00% p.a.
Spot exchange rate	$1.00=	C$1.20
Six-month forward exchange rate	$1.00=	C$1.22

Six-month call option on C$6,000,000 at an exercise price of C$1.20/$, premium of 1%
Six-month put option on C$6,000,000 at an exercise price of C$1.20/$, premium of 2%

   a. Compare the alternative ways that Dole can hedge the foreign exchange transaction exposure.
   b. Show all your calculations and explain the advantages and disadvantages of each alternative. Which do you recommend?

12. Tektronix: Hedging an Account Receivable
Tektronix, Inc. of Beaverton, Oregon, has sold graphics systems to Daimler-Benz of Germany for DM2,000,000 with payment due in three months. The following quotes are available:

Three-month interest rate (borrowing or investing) on U.S. dollars: 6.00% per annum

Three-month interest rate (borrowing or investing) on Deutschemarks: 8.00% per annum

Spot exchange rate: DM1.6000/$

Three-month forward exchange rate: DM1.6120/$

Three-month options from Bank of America:

    call option on DM2,000,000 at exercise price of DM1.6000/$ and a 1% premium

    put option on DM2,000,000 at exercise price of DM1.6000/$ and a 3% premium

Tek's cost of capital is 10.0%, and it wishes to protect the dollar value of this receivable.

  a. What are the costs and benefits of each alternative?
      Which is the best alternative?

  b. What is the break-even reinvestment rate when comparing forward and money market alternatives?

Bibliography

Aggarwal, Raj, and Luc A. Soenen, "Corporate Use of Options and Futures in Foreign Exchange Management," *Journal of Cash Management,* November/December 1989, pp. 61–66.

Aubey, R. T., and R. H. Cramer, "Use of International Currency Cocktails in the Reduction of Exchange Rate Risk," *Journal of Economics and Business,* Winter 1977, pp. 128–134.

Babbel, David F., "Determining the Optimum Strategy for Hedging Currency Exposure," *Journal of International Business Studies,* Spring/Summer 1983, pp. 133–139.

Batra, Raveendra N., Shabtai Donnenfeld, and Josef Hadar, "Hedging Behavior by Multinational Firms," *Journal of International Business Studies,* Winter 1982, pp. 59–70.

Batten, Jonathan, Robert Mellor, and Victor Wan, "Foreign Exchange Risk Management Practices and Products Used by Australian Firms," *Journal of International Business Studies,* Third Quarter 1993, pp. 557–573.

Beidleman, Carl R., John L. Hillary, and James A. Greenleaf, "Alternatives in Hedging Long-Date Contractual Foreign Exchange Exposure," *Sloan Management Review,* Summer 1983, pp. 45–54.

Belk, P.A, and M. Glaum, "The Management of Foreign Exchange Risk in UK Multinationals: An Empirical Investigation," *Accounting and Business Research,* vol. 21, no.81, 1990, 3–13.

Bishop, Paul, and Don Dixon, *Foreign Exchange Handbook: Managing Risk and Opportunity in Global Currency Markets,* New York: McGraw-Hill, 1992.

Booth, Laurence D., "Hedging and Foreign Exchange Exposure," *Management International Review,* vol. 22, no. 1, 1982, pp. 26–42.

Buckley, Adrian, *Multinational Finance,* 2nd ed., London: Prentice Hall, 1992.

Chang, Jack S. K., and Latha Shanker, "A Risk-Return Measure on Hedging Effectiveness: A Comment," *Journal of Financial and Quantitative Analysis,* vol. 22, no. 3, September 1987, pp. 373–376.

Controlling Risk with Foreign Currency Options: supplement to *Euromoney,* February 1985.

David, Edward, Jeff Coates, Paul Collier, and Steven Longden, *Currency Risk Management in Multinational Companies,* Research Studies in Accounting, London: Prentice Hall International, 1991.

DeRosa, David F., *Managing Foreign Exchange Risk,* Chicago: Probus, 1991.

Dufey, Gunter, and S.I. Srinivasulu, "The Case for Corporate Management of Foreign Exchange

Risk," *Financial Management,* Winter 1983, pp. 54–62.

Eaker, Mark R., "Denomination Decision for Multinational Transactions," *Financial Management,* Autumn 1980, pp. 23–29.

———, "The Numeraire Problem and Foreign Exchange Risk," *Journal of Finance,* May 1981, pp. 419–427.

———, and Dwight M. Grant, "Cross-Hedging Foreign Currency Risk," *Journal of International Money and Finance,* March 1987, pp. 85–105.

Edelshain, David, *British Corporate Currency Exposure and Foreign Exchange Risk Management,* Ph.D. thesis (unpublished), London Business School, Sussex Place, Regents Park, London, 1992.

Evans, Thomas G., William R. Folks, Jr., and Michael Jilling, *The Impact of Statement of Financial Accounting Standards No.8 on the Foreign Exchange Management Practices of American Multinationals: An Economic Impact Study,* Stamford, Conn.: Financial Accounting Standards Board, November 1978.

Folks, William R., Jr., "Decision Analysis for Exchange Risk Management," *Financial Management,* Winter 1972, pp. 101–112.

———, "The Optimal Level of Forward Exchange Transactions," *Journal of Financial and Quantitative Analysis,* January 1973, pp. 105–110.

Froot, Kenneth A., David S. Scharfstein, and Jeremy C. Stein, "Risk Management: Coordinating Corporate Investment and Financing Policies," *Journal of Finance,* vol. 48, No. 5, December 1993, pp. 1629–1658.

Giddy, Ian H., "Why It Doesn't Pay to Make a Habit of Forward Hedging," *Euromoney,* December 1976, pp. 96–100.

———, "The Foreign Exchange Option as a Hedging Tool," *Midland Corporate Finance Journal,* Fall 1983, pp. 32–42.

Griffiths, Susan, and Paul S. Greenfield, "Foreign Currency Management: Part I—Currency Hedging Strategies," *Journal of Cash Management,* July/August 1989, pp. 24–26.

Howard, Charles T., and Louis J. D'Antonio, "A Risk-Return Measure of Hedging Effectiveness: A Reply," *Journal of Financial and Quantitative Analysis,* vol. 22, no. 3, September 1987, p. 377.

Jacque, Laurent, "Management of Foreign Exchange Risk: A Review Article," *Journal of International Business Studies,* Spring/Summer 1981, pp. 81–100.

Jones, Eric T., and Donald L. Jones, *Hedging Foreign Exchange: Converting Risk to Profit,* New York: Wiley, 1987.

Kaufold, Howard, and Michael Smirlock, "Managing Corporate Exchange and Interest Rate Exposure," *Financial Management,* Autumn 1986, pp. 64–72.

Kerkvliet, Joe, and Michael H. Moffett, "The Hedging of an Uncertain Future Foreign Currency Cash Flow," *Journal of Financial and Quantitative Analysis,* vol. 26, no. 4, December 1991, pp. 565–578.

Khouri, Sarkis J., and K. Hung Chan, "Hedging Foreign Exchange Risk: Selecting the Optimal Tool," *Midland Corporate Finance Journal,* Winter 1988, pp. 40–52.

Kohlhagen, Steven W., "A Model of Optimal Foreign Exchange Hedging without Exchange Rate Projections," *Journal of International Business Studies,* Fall 1978, pp. 9–19.

Korsvold, Paul, "The Futility of Currency Hedging Models," in Göran Bergendahl, ed., *International Financial Management,* Stockholm: Norstedts, 1982, pp. 104–127.

Levi, Maurice D., and Piet Sercu, "Erroneous and Valid Reasons for Hedging Foreign Exchange Rate Exposure," *Journal of Multinational Financial Management,* vol. 1, no. 2, 1991, pp. 25–37.

Lewent, Judy C., and A. John Kearney, "Identifying, Measuring, and Hedging Currency Risk at Merck," *Journal of Applied Corporate Finance,* vol. 2, no. 4, Winter 1990, pp. 19–28.

Luehrman, Timothy A., "The Exchange Rate Exposure of a Global Competitor," *Journal of*

International Business Studies, Second Quarter, 1990, 225–242.

Maloney, Peter J., "Managing Currency Exposure: The Case of Western Mining," *Journal of Applied Corporate Finance,* vol. 2, no. 4, Winter 1990, pp. 29–34.

Moffett, Michael H., and Jan Karl Karlsen, "Managing Foreign Exchange Rate Economic Exposure," *Journal of International Financial Management and Accounting,* vol. 5, no. 2, June 1994, pp. 157–175

Nance, Deana R., Clifford W. Smith Jr., and Charles W. Smithson, "On the Determinants of Corporate Hedging," *Journal of Finance,* March 1993, pp. 267–284.

Remmers, H. L., *FORAD: International Financial Management Simulation* (Players' Manual, Release 2.4), Fontainebleau, France: INSEAD, 1990.

Rodriguez, Rita M., "Corporate Exchange Risk Management: Theme and Aberrations," *Journal of Finance,* May 1981, pp. 427–439.

Ruesch, Otto J., "Protecting Your Profits with Foreign Exchange Procedures," *Journal of European Business,* May/June 1992, pp. 34–36.

Smith, Clifford W., Jr., Charles W. Smithson, and D. Sykes Wilford, *Managing Financial Risk,* The Institutional Investor Series in Finance, New York: Harper Business, 1990.

———, "Financial Engineering: Why Hedge?," in *The Handbook of Financial Engineering,* Clifford W. Smith, Jr., and Charles W. Smithson, eds., New York: Harper Business, 1990.

Smith, Clifford W., and Rene M. Stulz, "The Determinants of Firms' Hedging Policies," *Journal of Financial and Quantitative Analysis,* vol. 20, December 1985, pp. 391–405.

Soenen, Luc A., and E. G. F. van Winkel, "The Real Costs of Hedging in the Forward Exchange Market," *Management International Review,* vol. 22, no. 1, 1982, pp. 53–59.

Stulz, Rene M., "Optimal Hedging Policies," *Journal of Financial and Quantitative Analysis,* vol. 19, no. 2, June 1984, p. 127.

Swanson, Peggy E., and Stephen C. Caples, "Hedging Foreign Exchange Risk Using Forward Foreign Exchange Markets: An Extension," *Journal of International Business Studies,* Spring 1987, pp. 75–82.

Wheelwright, Steven, "Applying Decision Theory to Improve Corporate Management of Currency-Exchange Risks," *California Management Review,* Summer 1975, pp. 41–49.

Wunnicke, Diane B., David R. Wilson, and Brooke Wunnicke, *Corporate Financial Risk Management,* New York: Wiley, 1992.

Chapter 8
Operating Exposure

Global View
Daring to Hedge the Unhedgeable

Eastman Kodak, the U.S. photography-to-chemicals giant, recently put its exchange rate risk management policy under review. The result of the overhaul is that Kodak will shortly adopt a completely new strategy to control its foreign exchange risks. The company found that its existing policy did not take account of its "competitive" currency risks.

Competitive currency risk represents the exposure of a company's competitive position in a market to currency fluctuations. Most big companies try to hedge transaction exposure—the exposure of overseas income, expenditure and cross-border flows to foreign exchange moves. But few look at how long-term currency moves affect a company's relative position in the marketplace.

All that is changing. More and more companies are using competitive currency risk analysis to re-examine their exchange rate exposures. The result has led many to change dramatically the currencies they hedge, and the size and term structure of hedges. Some companies are dumping their old currency risk management policies completely. Kodak's new exchange rate risk management policy is based on the net currency exposure of its perceived translation, transaction and competitive risks. "What we're talking about is no longer the simple job of hedging balance-sheet or transaction exposures," says a senior Kodak treasury manager. "We're talking about overall corporate performance in the long term. Balance-sheet and transaction risks are merely subsets of overall currency risk."

But hedging competitive currency risk is both complex and controversial. Only a handful of corporates have dared to adopt competitive hedging strategies. And even fewer admit it. Competitive hedging is an integral part of a company's long term package of production, pricing and marketing plans for the goods or services it sells. And the adoption of competitive currency positions is done only at the most senior—often board—level.

It is a process that is time-consuming and expensive: Kodak spent months developing its new currency strategy. "Quantifying economic risk is not easy. But it can be done," says Touche Ross consultant Derek Ross. "It's easier in industries where costs and competitors are easily identified."

It can take several years before a significant exchange rate move can eat away market share and profits. Most competitive currency hedges span three to five years, though Bankers Trust has done seven- and 10-year hedges for corporate clients. Such hedges range in face value from $10 million–$20 million to $1 billion. The average is $100 million–$200 million, say bankers. The hedges are almost exclusively constructed with options. Buying options is more flexible and less risky than straight forward contracts. And banks are prepared to make a price in currency options with a longer maturity than with forwards.

Source: Adapted from "Daring to Hedge the Unhedgeable," *Corporate Finance*, August 1988, pp. 11–13. Reprinted with permission.

This chapter extends the concept of transaction exposure, described in Chapter 7, further into time and across the multitudes of cash flows that comprise the value of any multinational firm. *Operating exposure*, also called *economic exposure, competitive exposure,* or *strategic exposure,* measures any change in the present value of a firm resulting from changes in future operating cash flows caused by any unexpected change in exchange rates. Operating exposure *analysis* assesses the impact of changing exchange rates over coming months and years on a firm's own operations and on its competitive position vis-à-vis other firms. The goal is to identify strategic moves or operating techniques the firm might wish to adopt to enhance its value in the face of unexpected exchange rate changes.

Operating exposure and transaction exposure are related in that they both deal with future cash flows. They differ in terms of which cash flows are observed and why those cash flows change when exchange rates change.

Transaction Exposure to Operating Exposure

Operating exposure of the firm requires forecasting and analyzing all of the firm's future individual transaction exposures together with the future exposures of all of the firm's competitors and potential competitors worldwide. A simple example may clarify the point.

An Example: Eastman Kodak (U.S.)

A firm like Eastman Kodak (U.S.) possesses a number of transaction exposures at any point in time. Kodak has sales in the United States, Japan, and Europe, and therefore possesses a continuing series of foreign currency receivables (and payables). Sales and expenses that are already contracted for are traditional *transaction exposures*. Sales that are highly probable based on Kodak's historical business line and market shares, but have no legal basis yet, are *anticipated transaction exposures*.

What if the analysis of the firm's exposure to exchange rate changes is extended even further into the future? What are the longer term exposures of Kodak to exchange rate changes? The impact on the firm's cash flows from future exchange rate changes will not only alter the domestic currency *value* (U.S. dollars in this case) of foreign currency cash flows, it will change the *quantity* of foreign currency cash flows generated. The changes in Kodak's cash flows in the future will depend on how competitive it is in various markets. Kodak's international competitiveness will in turn be affected by the operating exposures of its major competitors like Fuji (Japan) and Agfa (Germany). It is the analysis of this longer term—where exchange rate changes are unpredictable and therefore unexpected—which is the goal of operating exposure analysis.

Operating and Financing Cash Flows

The cash flows of the multinational firm can be divided into operating cash flows and financing cash flows. *Operating cash flows* arise from interfirm (between unrelated firms) and intrafirm (between units of the same firm) receivables and payables, rent and lease payments for the use of facilities and equipment, royalty and license fees for the use of technology and intellectual property, and assorted management fees for services provided. *Financing cash flows* are payments for the use of interfirm and intrafirm loans (principal and interest) and stockholder equity (new equity investments and dividends). Each of these cash flows can occur at different time intervals, in different amounts, in different currencies of denomination, and have a different predictability of occurrence.

Operating Exposure Defined

Operating exposure is far more important for the long-run health of a business entity than changes caused by transaction or accounting exposure. However, operating exposure is inevitably subjective because it depends on estimates of future cash flow changes over an arbitrary time horizon. Thus operating exposure does not spring from the accounting process but rather derives from operating analysis. Planning for operating exposure is a total management responsibility because it involves the interaction of strategies in finance, marketing, purchasing, and production.

An *expected* change in foreign exchange rates is not included in the definition of operating exposure because both management and investors should have factored this information into their evaluation of anticipated operating results and market value. From a management perspective, budgeted financial statements already reflect information about the effect of an expected change in exchange rates. For example, under equilibrium conditions the forward rate might be used as an unbiased predictor of the future spot rate. In such a case management would use the forward rate when preparing the operating budgets, rather than assume the spot rate would remain unchanged.

Another example is that expected cash flow to amortize debt should already reflect the international Fisher effect. The level of expected interest and principal repayment should be a function of expected exchange rates rather than existing spot rates.

From an investor's perspective, if the foreign exchange market is efficient, information about expected changes in exchange rates should be widely known and thus reflected in a firm's market value. Only unexpected changes in exchange rates, or an inefficient foreign exchange market, should cause market value to change.

Measuring the Impact of Operating Exposure

An unexpected change in exchange rates impacts a firm's expected cash flows at four levels, depending on the time horizon used.[1]

Short Run

The first-level impact is on expected cash flows in the one-year operating budget. The gain or loss depends on the currency of denomination of expected cash flows. The currency of denomination cannot be changed for existing obligations, such as those defined by transaction exposure, or even for implied obligations such as purchase or sales commitments. Apart from real or implied obligations, in the short run it is difficult to change sales prices or renegotiate factor costs. Therefore realized cash flows will differ from those expected in the budget. However, as time passes, prices and costs can be changed to reflect the new competitive realities caused by a change in exchange rates.

Medium Run: Equilibrium Case

The second-level impact is on expected medium-run cash flows, such as those expressed in two- to five-year budgets, assuming parity conditions hold among foreign exchange rates, national inflation rates, and national interest rates. Under equilibrium conditions the firm should be able to adjust prices and factor costs over time to maintain the expected level of cash flows. In this case the currency of denomination of expected cash flows is not as important as the countries in which cash flows originate. National monetary, fiscal, and balance of payments policies determine whether equilibrium conditions will exist and whether firms will be allowed to adjust prices and costs.

If equilibrium exists continuously, and a firm is free to adjust its prices and costs to maintain its expected competitive position, its operating exposure may be zero. Its expected cash flows would be realized and therefore its market value unchanged, since the exchange rate change was anticipated. However, it is also possible that equilibrium conditions exist but the firm is unwilling or unable to adjust operations to the new competitive environment. In such a case the firm would experience operating exposure

---

[1]This four-level approach is developed more fully in theory and with an extended case (Novo Industri A/S) in Arthur I. Stonehill, Niels Ravn, and Kåre Dullum, "Management of Foreign Exchange Economic Exposure," in *International Financial Management*, Göran Bergendahl, ed., Stockholm: Norstedt & Soners, 1982, pp. 128–148.

because its realized cash flows would differ from expected cash flows. As a result, its market value might also be altered.

Medium Run: Disequilibrium Case

The third-level impact is on expected medium-run cash flows assuming disequilibrium conditions. In this case the firm may not be able to adjust prices and costs to reflect the new competitive realities caused by a change in exchange rates. The firm's realized cash flows will differ from its expected cash flows. The firm's market value may change because of the unanticipated results.

Long Run

The fourth-level impact is on expected long-run cash flows, meaning those beyond five years. At this strategic level a firm's cash flows will be influenced by the reactions of existing and potential competitors to exchange rate changes under disequilibrium conditions. In fact, all firms that are subject to international competition, whether they are purely domestic or multinational, are exposed to foreign exchange operating exposure in the long run whenever foreign exchange markets are not continuously in equilibrium.

Illustration of Operating Exposure

To illustrate the consequences of operating exposure in the short and medium run cases, we develop a hypothetical example of a multinational firm, Washington Controls. Exhibit 8.1 shows possible cash flows for Washington Controls, Inc., a U.S.-based multinational firm, and its wholly owned affiliates, Instruments Napoleon, S.A. (France), and Canadian Instruments, Ltd. The parent firm trades directly with other firms in Mexico. In addition to the obvious transaction exposures arising from the U.S. parent importing from Mexico, it has both operational and financial cash flows with its French and Canadian subsidiaries. From the perspective of Washington Controls, dollars invested in the French and Canadian subsidiaries have a 20% required rate of return after taxes.

Instruments Napoleon manufactures in France from French material and labor. Half of production is sold within France and half is exported to other EEC countries. All sales are invoiced in French francs, and accounts receivable are equal to one-fourth of annual sales. In other words, the average collection period is 90 days. Inventory is also equal to one-fourth of annual sales and is carried at direct cost, which equals 75% of sales price. Instruments Napoleon can expand or contract production volume without any significant change in unit direct costs or in overall general and administrative expenses. Depreciation on plant and equipment is FF240,000 per year, and the corporate income tax rate in France is 50%. The December 31, 1995, balance sheet is as shown in Exhibit 8.2.

In the examples of Exhibit 8.2, we assume that on January 1, 1996, before any commercial activity begins, the French franc unexpectedly drops 20% in value, from FF6.40/$ to FF8.00/$. If no devaluation had occurred, Instruments Napoleon was expected to perform in 1996 as shown in Exhibit 8.2.

Exhibit 8.1   Cash Flows of a U.S.-Based Multinational Firm with French and
Canadian Subsidiaries and Trade with Mexico

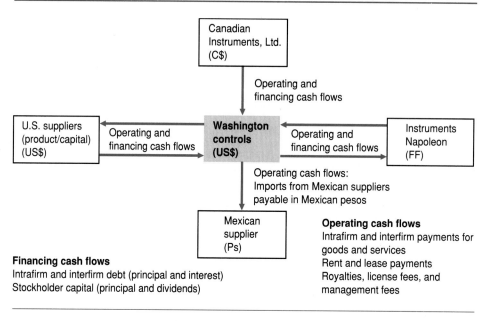

Operating exposure depends on whether an unexpected change in exchange rates causes unanticipated changes in sales volume, sales prices, or operating costs. Following a devaluation of the French franc, Instruments Napoleon might choose to maintain its domestic sales prices constant in terms of French francs or try to increase domestic prices because competing imports might now be priced higher. The firm might choose to maintain export prices constant in terms of foreign currencies, or in terms of francs, or somewhere in between. The strategy followed depends to a large measure on price elasticity of demand. On the cost side, Instruments Napoleon's costs might rise because of more expensive imported raw materials or components, or simply because all domestic prices in France have risen and labor is now demanding higher wages to compensate for domestic inflation.

Instruments Napoleon's domestic sales and costs might also be partly determined by the effect of a French devaluation on demand. To the extent that the devaluation stimulates purchases of French goods in import-competing sectors of the economy as well as greater exports of French goods, both caused by initially more competitive prices of French goods, French national income should increase. This statement assumes that the favorable effect of a French devaluation on comparative prices is not immediately offset by higher French inflation. Thus Instruments Napoleon might be able to sell more goods domestically because of price and income effects and internationally because of price effects.

Exhibit 8.2   Instruments Napoleon, S.A., Beginning Balance Sheet and Expected Cash Flows

Balance Sheet, December 31, 1995

Cash	FF1,600,000	Accounts payable	FF800,000
Accounts receivable	3,200,000	Short-term bank loan	1,600,000
Inventory	2,400,000	Long-term debt	1,600,000
Net plant and equipment	4,800,000	Common stock	1,800,000
		Retained earnings	6,200,000
	FF12,000,000		FF12,000,000

Expected Cash Flow, No Devaluation, 1996

Sales (1,000,000 units @ FF12.8/unit)	FF12,800,000
Direct costs (1,000,000 units @ FF9.6/unit)	9,600,000
Cash operating expenses (fixed)	1,200,000
Depreciation	240,000
Pretax profit	FF1,760,000
Income tax expense (50%)	880,000
Profit after tax	FF880,000
Add back depreciation	240,000
Cash flow from operations, in francs	FF1,120,000
Existing exchange rate: FF6.40/$	
Cash flow from operations, in dollars	$175,000

Expected Cash Flow, with Devaluation (Case 1)

Cash flow from operations, in francs (as above)	FF1,120,000
New exchange rate: FF8.00/$	
Cash flow from operations, in dollars	$140,000

To illustrate the effect of various postdevaluation scenarios on Instruments Napoleon's operating exposure, we consider three simple cases:

Case 1:   no change in any variable;
Case 2:   increase in sales volume, other variables remain constant; and
Case 3:   increase in sales price, other variables remain constant.

To calculate the net change in present value under each of these scenarios, we assume a five-year time horizon for any change in cash flow induced by the change in the franc/dollar exchange rate.

Case 1: No Change in Any Variable

Assume that in the five years ahead no changes occur in sales volume, sales price, or operating costs. Profits for the coming year in francs will be as expected, and cash flow from operations will be FF1,120,000. With a new exchange rate of FF8.00 per dollar, next year's cash flow measured in dollars will be FF1,120,000/8 = $140,000. The difference in first-year cash flow if a devaluation occurs at once will be:

Expected first-year cash flow, no devaluation	$175,000
Realized first-year cash flow, with devaluation	140,000
Decrease in first-year cash flow	$35,000

Instruments Napoleon thus experiences a drop of $35,000 in the dollar value of its French franc cash flow, and if this drop continues over the five-year time horizon, the total reduction in net cash flow will be $35,000 × 5 = $175,000. The discounted present value of this series of diminished dollar value cash flows is considered later in this chapter.

Case 2: Volume Increases, Other Variables Remain Constant

Assume that sales within France double following the devaluation because French-made instruments are now more competitive with imports. Additionally, export volume doubles because French-made instruments are now cheaper in countries whose currencies have not weakened. The sales price is kept constant in French franc terms because management of Instruments Napoleon has not observed any change in local French operating costs.

Expected cash flow for the following year would be as described in Exhibit 8.3. The cash flow shown in the first year, however, is not available because a doubling of sales volume will require additional investment in accounts receivable and in inventory. Although a portion of this additional investment might be financed by increasing accounts payable, we assume additional working capital is financed by cash flow from operations.

At the end of the first year, accounts receivable would be equal to one-fourth of annual sales, or FF6,400,000. This amount is twice receivables of FF3,200,000 at the end of the prior year, and the incremental increase of FF3,200,000 must be financed from available cash. Year-end inventory would be equal to one-fourth of annual direct costs, or FF4,800,000, an increase of FF2,400,000 over the year-beginning level. At the end of five years these incremental cash outflows will be recaptured because any investment in current assets eventually rolls over into cash.

Assuming no further change in volume, price, or costs, cash inflows for the five years would be as described in Exhibit 8.3. In this instance the devaluation causes a major drop in first-year cash flow from the $175,000 anticipated in the first year without devaluation to a negative flow of $360,000. However, in the remaining four years cash flow is substantially enhanced by the operating effects of the devaluation. Over time Instruments Napoleon generates significantly more cash for its owners. The devaluation produced an operating **gain** over time, rather than an operating **loss**.

The reason Instruments Napoleon is better off in Case 2 following the devaluation is that sales volume doubled while the per unit dollar-equivalent sales price fell

Exhibit 8.3 Instruments Napoleon, S.A.; Case 2: Volume Increases

Sales (2,000,000 units @ FF12.8/unit)	FF25,600,000
Direct costs (2,000,000 units @ FF9.6/unit)	19,200,000
Cash operating expenses (fixed)	1,200,000
Depreciation	240,000
Pretax profit	FF4,960,000
Income tax expense (50%)	2,480,000
Profit after tax	FF2,480,000
Add back depreciation	240,000
Cash flow from operations, in francs	FF2,720,000

New exchange rate: FF8.00/$

Cash flow from operations, in dollars	$340,000

Projected Cash Flows for Five Years

Year	Item	Francs	Dollars @FF8.00/$
1	Cash flow from operations	FF2,720,000	
	Less new investment in working capital	−5,600,000	
		FF2,880,000	−$360,000
2	Cash flow from operations	2,720,000	340,000
3	Cash flow from operations	2,720,000	340,000
4	Cash flow from operations	2,720,000	340,000
5	Cash flow from operations	2,720,000	340,000
	Incremental working capital recapture in last year	5,600,000	700,000

only 20%. In other words, the product faced a price elasticity of demand greater than one.

Case 3: Sales Price Increases, Other Variables Remain Constant

Assume the franc sales price is raised 25%, from FF12.8 to FF16.0 per unit, in order to preserve the original dollar-equivalent unit sales price of $2.00/unit. Assume further that volume remains constant in spite of this price increase; that is, customers expect to pay the same dollar-equivalent price, and local costs do not change.

The situation would be as described in Exhibit 8.4. In this instance Instruments Napoleon is better off following the devaluation than it was before because the sales price, pegged to the international price level, increased but volume did not drop. The new level of accounts receivable would be one-fourth of the new sales level of FF16,000,000, or FF4,000,000, an increase of FF800,000. No additional investment in inventory would be necessary.

Hence cash flow for the first five years would be as shown in Exhibit 8.4. Expected cash flow in every year exceeds the cash flow of $175,000 that had been

Exhibit 8.4   Instruments Napoleon, S.A.; Case 3: Sales Price Increase

Sales (1,000,000 units @ FF16.0/unit)	FF16,000,000
Direct costs (1,000,000 units @ FF9.6/unit)	9,600,000
Cash operating expenses (fixed)	1,200,000
Depreciation	240,000
Pretax profit	FF4,960,000
Income tax expense (50%)	2,480,000
Profit after tax	FF2,480,000
Add back depreciation	240,000
Cash flow from operations, in francs	FF2,720,000

New exchange rate: FF8.00/$

Cash flow from operations, in dollars	$340,000

Projected Cash Flows for Five Years

Year	Item	Francs	Dollars @FF8.00/$
1	Cash flow from operations	FF2,720,000	
	Less new investment in working capital	−800,000	
		FF1,920,000	$240,000
2	Cash flow from operations	2,720,000	340,000
3	Cash flow from operations	2,720,000	340,000
4	Cash flow from operations	2,720,000	340,000
5	Cash flow from operations	2,720,000	340,000
	Incremental working capital recapture in last year	800,000	100,000

anticipated with no devaluation. The increase in working capital causes net cash flow to be only $240,000 in the first year, but thereafter the cash flow is $340,000 per year.

The key to this improvement is in operating leverage. If costs are incurred in francs and do not increase after a devaluation, an increase in the sales price by the amount of devaluation will lead to sharply higher profits.

Other Possibilities

If any portion of sales revenues were incurred in other currencies, the situation would be different. The firm might leave the foreign sales price alone, in effect raising the French-franc-equivalent price; or it might leave the French-franc-equivalent price alone, in effect lowering the foreign sales price in an attempt to gain volume. Or, of course, it could position itself between these two extremes. Depending on elasticities and the proportion of foreign to domestic sales, total sales revenue might rise or fall.

Similarly, if some or all raw materials or components were imported and paid for in harder currencies, after-devaluation franc operating costs would increase with a drop in the value of the franc. Another possibility is that local franc costs rise after a devaluation. One cannot generalize for all countries of the world; nevertheless, local costs usually rise with some time lag following a devaluation. In each individual country, therefore, management must estimate how devaluation will affect the firm's sales revenue, sales volume, and local costs over a period of time.

Measurement of Loss

Exhibit 8.5 summarizes the change in expected cash flows for the three cases, and compares them with the cash flow expected should no devaluation occur (base case). The top portion of the exhibit restates the expected cash flows (CF) for the three cases. CF in the lower portion shows the change in cash flow compared to the nondevaluation situation. ΔCF shows the gain or loss from these changes in future cash flows. This should be determined by their present value using a discount rate of 20%, Washington Controls' required rate of return.

In case 1, in which nothing changes after the franc is devalued, Washington Controls incurs an operating loss with a present value of $104,800. In case 2, in which volume doubled with no price change after the devaluation, Washington Controls experiences an operating gain with a present value of $191,700. In case 3, in which the franc sales price was increased and volume did not change, the present value of

Exhibit 8.5 Summary of Operating Loss Following Devaluation for Instruments Napoleon, S.A.: Three Separate Cases (thousands of U.S. dollars)

Assumptions	No Devaluation	Case 1	Case 2	Case 3
Exchange rate (FF/$)	6.4	8.0	8.0	8.0
Sales units (millions)	1.0	1.0	2.0	1.0
Price per unit (FF)	12.8	12.8	12.8	16.0
Cost per unit (FF)	9.6	9.6	9.6	9.6

Year	No Devaluation	CF^1	ΔCF^2	CF^1	ΔCF^2	CF^1	ΔCF^2
1 (1996)	175	140	−35	−360	−535	240	65
2 (1997)	175	140	−35	340	165	340	165
3 (1998)	175	140	−35	340	165	340	165
4 (1999)	175	140	−35	340	165	340	165
5 (2000)	175	140	−35	340	165	340	165
5 working capital	0	0	0	700	700	100	100
Operating Loss: Incremental Present Value at 20% discount rate[3]			−104.8		+191.7		+450.3

[1]Cash flow (CF) in thousands of U.S. dollars resulting from new set of operating assumptions.

[2]Change in cash flows (CF) from base case of no devaluation.

[3]Present value of change in cash from stream from base case.

operating gain from devaluation was $450,300. An almost infinite number of combinations of volume, price, and cost could follow a devaluation, and any or all of them might become effective soon after a devaluation or only after the passage of some time.

Managing Operating Exposure at the Strategic Level Through Diversification

The objective of both operating and transaction exposure management is to anticipate and influence the effect of unexpected changes in exchanges rates on a firm's future cash flows, rather than merely hoping for the best. To meet this objective, management can *diversify the firm's operating and financing base*. Management can also *change the firm's operating and financing policies* through techniques we discuss later in this chapter.

The key to managing operating exposure at the strategic level is for management to recognize a disequilibrium in parity conditions when it occurs and to be prepositioned to react in the most appropriate way. This task can best be accomplished if a firm diversifies internationally both its operating and its financing bases. Diversifying operations means diversifying sales, location of production facilities, and raw material sources. Diversifying the financing base means raising funds in more than one capital market and in more than one currency.

Depending on management's risk preference, a diversification strategy permits the firm to react either actively or passively to opportunities presented by disequilibrium conditions in the foreign exchange, capital, and product markets. Such a strategy does not require management to predict disequilibrium but only to *recognize* it when it occurs. It does require management to consider how *competitors* are prepositioned with respect to their own operating exposures. This knowledge should reveal which firms would be helped or hurt competitively by alternative disequilibrium scenarios.

Diversifying Operations

If a firm's operations are diversified internationally, management is prepositioned both to recognize disequilibrium when it occurs and to react competitively. Consider the case where purchasing power parity is temporarily in disequilibrium. Although the disequilibrium may have been unpredictable, management can often recognize its symptoms as soon as they occur. For example, management might notice a change in comparative costs in the firm's own plants located in different countries. It might also observe changed profit margins or sales volume in one area compared to another, depending on price and income elasticities of demand and competitors' reactions.

Recognizing a temporary change in worldwide competitive conditions permits management to make changes in operating strategies. Management might make marginal shifts in sourcing raw materials, components, or finished products, such as described in the Global View: Sourcing From Thailand. If spare capacity exists, production runs can be lengthened in one country and reduced in another. The marketing effort can be strengthened in export markets where the firm's products have become more price competitive because of the disequilibrium condition.

Global View
Sourcing From Thailand

Japanese carmakers look at sourcing from Thailand—
where the currency is cheaper, and moves with the U.S. dollar

There has been some talk of late about the significance of Thailand as a regional manufacturing hub for Japanese carmakers. Some firms predict domestic sales will exceed 400,000 units this year, and exports of components hit $350 million in 1992—up from $63 million in 1987. These trends, along with the high yen, have led Toyota and others to consider moving production to southeast Asia. A shift of this nature would appear to mitigate the firms' currency exposure, because the Thai baht is cheap and correlated to the U.S. dollar.

Hedging With Production Changes

For most firms, such a move is fraught with pitfalls, including the difficulty of maintaining world-class levels of quality and productivity. Japanese carmakers investing in Thailand are not immune to these problems. Automobile consumers in most OECD countries have come to expect total quality. According to one analyst, the Japanese plants in Thailand produce work that is approximately 97–98% defect-free (vs 99% or above in Japan). Another issue is productivity: A plant for light pick-ups in Japan is said to be two and a half times as efficient as a plant in Thailand (based on trucks per minute).

The ultimate success of Japanese offshore production in Thailand, however, rests with Japanese suppliers of parts and components: They must move offshore as well, because the level of integrated manufacturing capabilities in Thailand is relatively low.

Don't Panic Yet

"No carmaker sourcing production in Thailand seems confident at the moment that these vehicles can be exports to the rest of the world," a Thai analyst notes. Some compact and light truck models, however, with higher price sensitivity, may be produced in Thailand for global consumption—probably in three to five years for OECD markets. In the interim, Japanese producers are probably planning to experiment with component manufacturing in Thailand, and elsewhere in Asia, for final assembly in Japan. In theory, component sourcing can be diversified, and an optimal assembly point determined on the basis of costs, including those associated with productivity, quality and currency exposure. Also to be factored in are the generous tax incentives offered by host governments in the region and the purchasing power of the yen.

Source: *Finance and Treasury,* "A Change in Currency?," 10/18/93, p. 1, the Economist Intelligence Unit. Reprinted with permission.

Even if management does not actively distort normal operations when exchange rates change, the firm should experience some beneficial portfolio effects. The variability of its cash flows is probably reduced by international diversification of its production, sourcing, and sales because exchange rate changes under disequilibrium conditions are likely to increase the firm's competitiveness in some markets while reducing it in others. In that case operating exposure would be neutralized.

In contrast to the internationally diversified multinational firm, a purely domestic firm might be subject to the full impact of foreign exchange operating exposure even though it does not have foreign currency cash flows. For example, it could experience intense import competition in its domestic market from competing firms producing in countries with undervalued currencies. Domestic and Japanese personal computer manufacturers were both made aware of this problem when Korean personal computers captured a share of the U.S. market in the late 1980s. The Korean won was probably undervalued relative to both the U.S. dollar and the Japanese yen.

A purely domestic firm does not have the option to react to an international disequilibrium condition in the same manner as a multinational firm. In fact, a purely domestic firm will not be positioned to recognize that a disequilibrium exists because it lacks comparative data from its own internal sources. By the time external data are available from published sources, it is often too late to react. Even if a domestic firm recognizes the disequilibrium condition, it cannot quickly shift production and sales into foreign markets in which it has had no previous presence.

Diversifying Financing

If a firm diversifies its financing sources, it will be prepositioned to take advantage of temporary deviations from the international Fisher effect. If interest rate differentials do not equal expected changes in exchange rates, opportunities to lower a firm's cost of capital will exist. However, to be able to switch financing sources, a firm must already be well known in the international investment community, with banking contacts firmly established. Once again, this is not an option for a domestic firm that has limited its financing to one capital market.

Although we recommend diversification as a strategy for foreign exchange risk management, such a strategy has a potentially favorable impact on other risks as well. In particular, it could reduce the variability of future cash flows due to domestic business cycles, provided these are not perfectly correlated with international cycles. It could increase the availability of capital, also reducing its cost, by diversifying such risks as restrictive capital market policies or government borrowing competition in the capital market. It could diversify political risks such as expropriation, war, blocked funds, or just unfavorable changes in laws that reduce or eliminate profitability. The list of advantages from international diversification can even be extended to such areas as spreading the risk of technological obsolescence and reducing portfolio risk in the context of the capital asset pricing model—but now we are preempting the diversification strategy theme that appears throughout the rest of this book.

Constraints exist that may limit the feasibility of a diversification strategy for foreign exchange risk management or one of the other risks just mentioned. For example, the technology of a particular industry may require such large economies of scale that it is not economically feasible to diversify production locations. Firms in this industry could still diversify sales and financing sources, however. On the other hand, the firm may be too small or too unknown to attract international equity investors or lenders. Yet it could at least diversify its sales internationally. Thus a diversification strategy can only be implemented as far as is feasible.

Managing Operating Exposure By Changing Operating Policies

Operating and transaction exposures can be partially managed by adopting operating policies that deviate from normal domestic-oriented policies but have the virtue of reducing foreign exchange exposure. The cost of adopting such policies is less obvious than the cost of contractual arrangements because operations may become less efficient, but sometimes rethinking operating procedures leads to new efficiencies that were previously not discovered. Three of the operating policies commonly employed to manage operating and transaction exposures are these:

1.   Using leads and lags;
2.   Requiring customers to share the risk through currency clauses;
3.   Using a reinvoicing center.

Leads and Lags: Retiming the Transfer of Funds

Firms can reduce both operating and transaction exposure by accelerating or decelerating the timing of payments that must be made or received in foreign currencies. *To lead* is to pay early. A firm holding a "soft currency" or that has debts denominated in a "hard currency" will lead by using the soft currency to pay the hard currency debts as soon as possible. The object is to pay the currency debts before the soft currency drops in value. *To lag* is to pay late. A firm holding a hard currency and having debts denominated in a soft currency will lag by paying those debts late, hoping that less of the hard currency will be needed. If possible, firms will also lead and lag their collection of receivables, collecting soft foreign currency receivables early and collecting hard foreign currency receivables later.

Leading and lagging may be done between affiliates or with independent firms. Assuming payments will be made eventually, leading or lagging always results in changing the cash and payables position of one firm, with the reverse effect on the other firm.

Interfirm Leads and Lags. Leading or lagging between independent firms requires the time preference of one firm to be imposed to the detriment of the other firm. For example, a German firm may wish to lead in collecting its Italian accounts receivable that are denominated in lira because it expects the lira to drop in value compared with the Deutschemark. But why should the Italian customers prepay their accounts payable? Credit was part of the inducement for them to purchase from the German firm. The only way the Italians would willingly lead their accounts payable would be for the German creditor to offer them a discount about equal to the forward discount on the lira or, in equilibrium, the difference between Italian and German interest rates for the period of prepayment. Of course, this "discount" may eliminate the benefit of collecting the "soft" currency earlier!

Intrafirm Leads and Lags. Leading and lagging between related firms is more feasible because they presumably embrace a common set of goals for the consolidated group. Furthermore, periodic payments are often made between units of a multinational firm, providing the opportunity for many types of leads or lags. Because opportunities for leading or lagging payments depend on the requirement for payments of this nature, the device is more readily adaptable to a company that operates on an integrated worldwide basis. If each unit functions as a separate and self-sufficient entity, the motivation for leading or lagging diminishes. In the case of financing cash flows with foreign affiliates, there is an additional motivation for early or late payments to position funds for liquidity reasons.

The use of leads and lags in conjunction with intrafirm family receivables is feasible only with 100% ownership of the various affiliates because the economic effect of extended payment terms alters the relative rate of return of the various units. This practice is unfair if each unit has minority stockholders separate from the corporate family, since they do not necessarily benefit from practices that benefit the multinational firm as a whole. Inequities may also arise between various profit centers in a group of wholly owned affiliates unless adjustments are made to reflect a particular center's sacrifice. A necessary condition for efficient use of leads and lags is the ability of the parent to adjust its techniques for measuring profit or controlling investment in assets by its various affiliates so the performance rating of units and managers is not changed when one unit "helps" another for the good of the overall enterprise.

Because the use of leads and lags is an obvious technique for minimizing foreign exchange exposure and for shifting the burden of financing, many governments impose limits on the allowed range. Terms allowed by governments are often subject to negotiation when a good argument can be presented. Thus some limits are subject to exceptions. For example, in the past Italy has placed no limit on export and import lags on trade payments with other OECD countries. However, a 180-day limit on export lags and a five-year limit on import lags was applied to trade with non-OECD countries.

Currency Clauses: Risk Sharing

An alternative arrangement for managing a long-term cash flow exposure between firms with a continuing buyer-supplier relationship is *risk sharing*. Risk sharing is a contractual arrangement in which the buyer and seller agree to "share" or split currency movement impacts on payments between them. If the two firms are interested in a long-term relationship based on product quality and supplier reliability, and not on the occasional unpredictable and potentially painful whims of the currency markets, a cooperative agreement to share the burden of currency risk management may be in order.

If Ford's North American operations import automotive parts from Mazda (Japan) every month, year after year, major swings in exchange rates can benefit one party at the expense of the other. If the exchange rate movement became too large, one or the other of the two parties might choose to terminate the relationship. One potential solution would be for Ford and Mazda to agree that all purchases by Ford will be made in Japanese yen at the current exchange rate, as long as the spot rate on the date of invoice is between, say, ¥115/$ and ¥125/$. If the exchange rate is between these values on the payment dates, Ford agrees to accept whatever transaction exposure exists (because it is paying in a foreign currency). If, however, the exchange rate falls outside of this range on the payment date, Ford and Mazda will *share* the difference equally.

For example, Ford has an account payable of ¥25,000,000 for the month of March. If the spot rate on the date of invoice is ¥110/$, the Japanese yen would have appreciated versus the dollar causing Ford's costs of purchasing automotive parts to rise. Since this rate falls outside the contractual range, Mazda would agree to accept a total payment in Japanese yen, which would result from a difference of ¥5/$ (¥115 − ¥110). The payment made by Ford would be

$$\left[\frac{¥25,000,000}{¥115.00/\$ - \dfrac{¥5.00/\$}{2}} \right] = \frac{¥25,000,000}{¥112.50/\$} = \$222,222.22.$$

Ford's total payment in Japanese yen would be calculated using an exchange rate of ¥112.50/$, and saves Ford $5,050.50.[2] Both parties therefore incur costs and benefits from exchange rate movements outside of the specified band. Note that the movement could just as easily have been in Mazda's favor if the spot rate had moved to ¥130/$.

The risk-sharing arrangement is intended to smooth the impact on both parties of volatile and unpredictable exchange rate movements. Of course a sustained appreciation of one currency versus the other would require the negotiation of a new sharing agreement, but the ultimate goal of the agreement is to alleviate currency pressures on the continuing business relationship. Risk-sharing agreements like these have been in use for nearly 50 years on world markets. They became something of a rarity during the 1950s and 1960s when exchange rates were relatively stable under the Bretton Woods Agreement. But with the return to floating exchange rates in the 1970s, firms with long-term customer-supplier relationships across borders have returned to some old ways of maintaining mutually beneficial long-term trade.

Reinvoicing Centers

A reinvoicing center is a separate corporate subsidiary that manages in one location all transaction exposure from intracompany trade. Manufacturing affiliates sell goods to distribution affiliates of the same firm only by selling to a reinvoicing center, which in turn resells to the distribution affiliate. Title passes to the reinvoicing center, but the physical movement of goods is direct from manufacturing plant to distribution affiliate. Thus the reinvoicing center handles paperwork but has no inventory.

---

[2]At a spot rate of ¥110/$, Ford's cost for the month of March would be $227,272.73. The risk-sharing agreement between Ford and Mazda allows Ford to pay $222,222.22, a savings of $5,050.50 over the cost without risk sharing (i.e., this "savings" is a reduction in an increased cost, not a true cost reduction).

As depicted in Exhibit 8.6, the Korean manufacturing unit of a multinational firm invoices the firm's reinvoicing center in Singapore in Korean won. The reinvoicing center in turn invoices the firm's Japanese sales affiliate in yen. Consequentially, all operating units deal only in their own currency, and all transaction exposure lies with the reinvoicing center.

To avoid accusations of profit shifting through transfer pricing, most reinvoicing centers "resell" at cost plus a small commission for their services. The resale price is frequently the manufacturer's price times the forward exchange rate for the date on which payment from the distribution affiliate is expected, although other combinations are possible. The commission covers the cost of the reinvoicing center, but does not shift profits away from operating affiliates.

The reinvoicing center should avoid doing business with suppliers or customers in the country of location so it will be able to establish nonresident status. Although the exact definition of and benefits of nonresident status vary from country to country, in general a finance subsidiary not doing any local business may be free of some taxes, such as interest withholding taxes or capital formation taxes. Nonresident firms may have greater access to external foreign exchange markets than local operating firms; they may be freer to deal in external currency markets, including Euromarkets; and they may be allowed to own bank accounts in foreign countries when that is restricted for domestic firms. Nonresident firms are usually not restricted in either borrowing from or investing with foreign banks.

Exhibit 8.6   Reinvoicing Center Structure

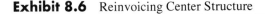

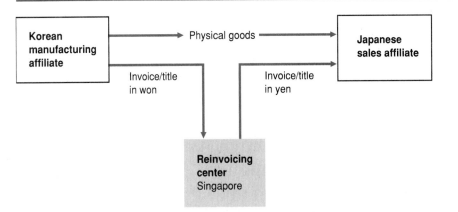

Korean manufacturing unit ships goods directly to the Japanese sales affiliate. The invoice by the Korean unit, which is denominated in Korean won, is passed on to the reinvoicing center located in Singapore. The Singapore reinvoicing center takes legal title to the goods. It subsequently invoices the Japanese sales affiliate in the Japanese unit's own currency, Japanese yen.

There are three basic benefits arising from the creation of a reinvoicing center:

1. The formation of the center allows the management of all foreign exchange transaction exposure for intracompany sales to be located in one place. Reinvoicing center personnel can develop a specialized expertise in choosing which hedging technique is best at any moment, and they are likely to obtain more competitive foreign exchange quotations from banks because they are dealing in larger transactions.

2. By guaranteeing the exchange rate for future orders, the reinvoicing center can set firm local currency costs in advance. This enables distribution affiliates to make firm bids to unrelated final customers, and to protect against the exposure created by a backlog of unfilled orders. Backlog exposure does not appear on the corporate books because the sales are not yet recorded. Sales subsidiaries can focus on their marketing activities and their performance can be judged without distortion because of exchange rate changes.

3. The center can manage intra-affiliate cash flows, including leads and lags of payments. With a reinvoicing center all affiliates settle intracompany accounts in their local currencies. The reinvoicing center need only hedge residual exposure.

The main disadvantage is one of cost relative to benefits received. One additional corporate unit must be created, and a separate set of books must be kept. The initial setup cost can be high because existing order-processing procedures must be reprogrammed. The center will have an impact on the tax status and customs duties of all affiliates, as well as on the amount of foreign exchange business directed to local banks in each country. Establishment of a reinvoicing center is likely to bring increased scrutiny by tax authorities to be sure it is not functioning as a tax haven. Consequently a variety of professional costs will be incurred for tax and legal advice, in addition to the costs of personnel operating the center.

Managing Operating Exposure By Changing Financing Policies

Operating and transaction exposures can be partially managed by adopting financing policies that offset anticipated foreign exchange exposures. Three of the financing policies commonly employed are these:

1. Use of natural hedges by matching currency cash flows;
2. Back-to-back or parallel loans;
3. Currency swaps.

Natural Hedging: Matching Currency Cash Flows

One way to offset an anticipated continuous long exposure to a particular currency is to acquire debt denominated in that currency. Exhibit 8.7 depicts the exposure of a U.S. firm with continuing export sales to Canada. In order to compete effectively in Canadian markets all export sales are invoiced in Canadian dollars. This policy results in a continuing receipt of Canadian dollars month after month. If the export sales are part of a

Exhibit 8.7   A U.S.-Based Firm and Matching of Canadian Dollar Cash Flows

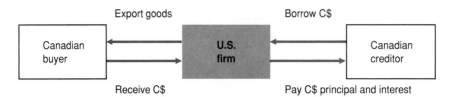

A U.S.-based firm with continuing inflows of Canadian dollars could offset, or *match* these cash flows, by creating a matching outflow. If the firm were to borrow Canadian dollar-denominated debt, it could then service this debt with the Canadian dollars earned through exports.

continuing supplier relationship, the long Canadian dollar position is relatively predictable and constant. This endless series of transaction exposures could of course be continually hedged with forward contracts or other contractual hedges as discussed in the previous chapter.

But what if the firm sought out a continual use, that is, an outflow, for its continual inflow of Canadian dollars? If the U.S. firm were to acquire part of its debt capital in the Canadian dollar markets it could use the relatively predictable Canadian dollar cash inflows from export sales to service the principal and interest payments on Canadian dollar debt and be *naturally hedged.* The U.S.-based firm has hedged an operational cash inflow by creating a financial cash outflow, and so does not have to actively manage the exposure with contractual financial instruments such as forward contracts. This form of natural hedge, sometimes referred to as *matching,* is effective in eliminating currency exposed when the exposure cash flow is relatively constant and predictable over time.

The list of potential matching strategies is nearly endless. A second alternative would be for the U.S. firm to seek out potential suppliers in Canada as a substitute for raw materials or components being supplied by U.S. or other foreign firms. A third alternative, often referred to as *currency switching,* would be to pay foreign suppliers with Canadian dollars. For example, if the U.S. firm imported components from Mexico, it is possible that the Mexican firms themselves may be short Canadian dollars in their multinational cash flow network.

Back-to-Back Loans

A *back-to-back loan,* also referred to as a *parallel loan* or *credit swap* loan, involves two business firms in separate countries arranging to borrow each other's currency for a specific period of time. At an agreed terminal date they return the borrowed currencies. The operation is conducted outside the foreign exchange markets, although spot quotations may be used as the reference point for determining the amount of funds to be swapped.

Such a swap creates a covered hedge against exchange loss, since each company, on its own books, borrows the same currency it repays. Back-to-back loans are also used at a time of actual or anticipated legal limitations on the transfer of investment funds to or from either country.

The structure of a typical back-to-back loan is illustrated in Exhibit 8.8. A British parent firm wanting to invest funds in its Dutch affiliate locates a Dutch parent firm that wants to invest funds in the United Kingdom. Avoiding the exchange markets entirely, the British parent lends pounds to the Dutch affiliate in the United Kingdom; the Dutch parent lends guilders to the British affiliate in the Netherlands. The two loans would be for equal values at the current spot rate and for a specified maturity. At maturity the two separate loans would each be repaid to the original lender, again without any need to use the foreign exchange markets. Neither loan carries any foreign exchange risk, and neither loan normally needs the approval of any governmental body regulating the availability of foreign exchange for investment purposes.

Parent company guarantees are not needed on the back-to-back loans because each loan carries the right of offset in the event of default of the other loan. A further agreement can provide for maintenance of principal parity in case of changes in the spot rate between the two countries. For example, if the pound dropped by more than, say, 6% for as long as 30 days, the British parent might have to advance additional pounds to the Dutch affiliate so as to bring the principal value of the two loans back to parity. A similar provision would protect the British if the guilder should weaken. Although this parity provision might lead to changes in the amount of home currency each party must lend during the period of the agreement, it does not increase foreign exchange risk because at maturity all loans are repaid in the same currency loaned.

There is one fundamental impediment to widespread use of the back-to-back loan: It is difficult for a firm to find a partner, termed a *counterparty,* for the currency, amount,

Exhibit 8.8   Creation of a Back-to-Back Loan

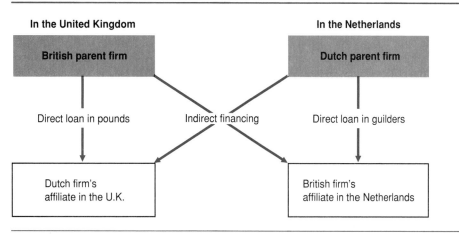

and timing desired.[3] This disadvantage has led to the rapid development and wide use of the currency swap, which we describe next.

Currency Swaps

A *currency swap* resembles a back-to-back loan except that it does not appear on a firm's balance sheet. As noted in Chapter 4, the term *swap* is widely used to describe a foreign exchange agreement between two parties to exchange a given amount of one currency for another and, after a period of time, to give back the original amounts swapped. Care should be taken to clarify which of the many different swaps is being referred to in a specific case.

In a currency swap, a firm and a swap dealer or swap bank agree to exchange an equivalent amount of two different currencies for a specified period of time. Currency swaps can be negotiated for a wide range of maturities up to at least 10 years. If funds are more expensive in one country than another, a fee may be required to compensate for the interest differential. The swap dealer or swap bank acts as a middleman in setting up the swap agreement.

A typical currency swap first requires two firms to borrow funds in the markets and currencies in which they are best known. For example, a Japanese firm would typically borrow yen on a regular basis in its home market. If, however, the Japanese firm were exporting to the United States and earning U.S. dollars, it might wish to construct a natural hedge that would allow it to use the U.S. dollars earned to make regular debt service payments on U.S. dollar debt. If, however, the Japanese firm is not well known in the U.S. financial markets, it may have no ready access to U.S. dollar debt. One way in which it could, in effect, borrow dollars, is to participate in a currency swap (see Exhibit 8.9). The Japanese firm could swap its yen-denominated debt service payments with another firm that has U.S. dollar debt service payments. The Japanese firm would then have dollar debt service without actually borrowing U.S. dollars.

Swap dealers arrange most swaps on a "blind basis," meaning the firm does not know what firm is on the other side of the swap arrangement. The firm views the dealer or bank as its counterparty. Because the swap markets are dominated by the major money center banks worldwide, the counterparty risk is thought to be acceptable. Because the swap dealer's business is arranging swaps, the dealer can generally arrange for the currency, amount, and timing of the desired swap.

Accountants in the United States treat the currency swap as a foreign exchange transaction rather than as debt and treat the obligation to reverse the swap at some later date as a forward exchange contract. Forward exchange contracts can be matched against assets, but they are entered in a firm's footnotes rather than as balance sheet items. The result is that both accounting and operating exposures are avoided, and neither a long-term receivable nor a long-term debt is created on the balance sheet. The risk of changes in currency rates to the implied collateral in a long-term currency swap can

---

[3]Another source of concern is that of *counterparty risk,* the risk that the other party to such an agreement will not fulfill their obligations in a timely manner.

Exhibit 8.9   Creation of a Currency Swap Through a Swap Dealer

A Japanese firm can swap its U.S. dollar-denominated debt payments for the Japanese yen-denominated debt payments of a U.S. firm through a swap dealer. The swap dealer searches out matching currency exposures and plays the role of a middleman, providing a valuable currency management service for both firms.

be treated with a clause similar to the maintenance-of-principal clause in a back-to-back loan. If exchange rates change by more than some specified amount, say 10%, an additional amount of the weaker currency might have to be advanced.

After being introduced on a global scale in the early 1980s, currency swaps have grown to be one of the largest financial derivative markets in the world. Chapter 14 provides a detailed explanation of the theory and application of currency swaps in the context of interest rate risk management.

Operating Exposure Management in Practice

Which of the broad array of operating and financing techniques just described are actually popular in practical use? Surveys of practice are periodically published but quickly become obsolete in this dynamic field. Nevertheless, it is useful to look at a few recent ones.

In addition to diversifying and using changes in operating and financing strategies, multinational firms often try to hedge their operating exposures with contractual strategies such as those described in Chapter 7.

Industry Use: Survey Results

Exhibit 8.10 reports results of operating strategies employed by British firms. The survey results indicate a relatively wide use of most of the operating strategy techniques. Of special note is the frequent use of currency matching (61%), acquisition of local currency debt for foreign affiliate financing (60%), and the use of currency swaps (40%). Although every multinational firm will have differing currency exposures and exposure management needs, these operating strategies—most of which have been used by industry for decades—are solid practices for the management of reoccurring transaction exposures, anticipated transaction exposures, and even helpful in the management of the firm's competitive long-run operating exposure.

Exhibit 8.10   Use of Operating Strategies by Firms in the United Kingdom

Percentage of Firms Using

Contract indexing (risk sharing)	21%
Currency switching	34%
Leading and lagging	20%
Matching	61%
Parallel loans	17%
Acquiring local currency debt	60%
Reinvoicing	5%
Swaps	40%

Source: David Edelshain, *British Corporate Currency Exposure and Foreign Exchange Risk Management,* Ph.D. thesis (unpublished), London Business School, 1992.

Contractual Approaches: Hedging the Unhedgeable

As described in the Global View opening this chapter, many multinational firms now attempt to hedge their operating exposure with contractual strategies. Firms like East-man Kodak (US) and Merck (US) have undertaken long-term currency option hedges designed to offset lost earnings from adverse exchange rate changes.[4] This hedging of what many of these firms refer to as *strategic exposure* or *competitive exposure* seemingly flies in the face of traditional theory.

The ability of firms to hedge the "unhedgeable" is dependent on *predictability:* (1) the predictability of the firm's future cash flows; and (2) the predictability of the firm's competitors' responses to exchange rate changes. Although many firms may believe they are capable of predicting their own cash flows, few in practice feel capable of accurately predicting competitor response.

Merck is an example of a firm that feels capable of both. The company possesses relatively predictable long-run revenue streams due to the product-niche nature of the pharmaceuticals industry. As a U.S.-based exporter to foreign markets, markets in which sales levels by product are relatively predictable and prices are often regulated by government, Merck believes it can accurately predict net long-term cash flows in foreign currencies five and ten years into the future. Because of Merck's relatively undiversified operating structure (it is highly centralized in terms of where research, development, and production costs are located), it feels it has no real alternatives but contractual hedging if it is to weather long-term unexpected exchange rate changes. Merck has purchased over-the-counter (OTC) long-term put options on foreign currencies versus the U.S. dollar as insurance against potential lost earnings from exchange rate changes. In the case of Merck, the predictability of competitor response to

---

[4]For a detailed explanation of Merck's operating exposure program see Judy C. Lewent and A. John Kearney, "Identifying, Measuring, and Hedging Currency Risk at Merck," *Continental Bank Journal of Applied Corporate Finance,* 1990, pp. 19–28.

exchange rate changes is less pertinent given the niche-market nature of pharmaceutical products.

Eastman Kodak, the subject of the opening Global View, is another multinational firm that undertakes contractual hedging of its operating exposure. Kodak believes its markets are largely price driven, and is aware that its major competitor, Fuji, has a Japanese cost base. If the U.S. dollar were to strengthen in the medium to long term, Kodak's market share in the United States and in foreign markets would decline. Kodak also believes that whatever sales it loses, its competitors will gain. Kodak has therefore also purchased long-term put options on foreign currencies that would replace long-term earnings if the value of the U.S. dollar, its home currency, rose unexpectedly.[5]

A significant question remains as to the true effectiveness of hedging operating exposure with contractual hedges. The fact remains that even after feared exchange rate movements and put option position payoffs have occurred, the firm is competitively disadvantaged. The capital outlays required for the purchase of such sizable put option positions is capital not used for the potential diversification of operations that would likely have in the long run more effectively maintained the firm's global market share and international competitiveness.

Summary

- Operating exposure, also called economic exposure, competitive exposure, and even strategic exposure on occasion, measures any change in the present value of a firm resulting from changes in future operating cash flows caused by any unexpected change in exchange rates.

- Strategies for the management of operating exposure emphasize the structuring of firm operations in order to create matching streams of cash flows by currency. This is termed natural hedging.

- Natural hedging strategies frequently used in industry include matching, risk sharing, currency swaps, as well as a variety of structural changes that allow more control over cash flows in the long run such as reinvoicing centers.

- Operating exposure measures the change in value of the firm that results from changes in future operating cash flows caused by an unexpected change in exchange rates.

- An unexpected change in exchange rates impacts a firm's expected cash flow at four levels: (1) short run; (2) medium run, equilibrium case; (3) medium run, disequilibrium case; and (4) long run.

- The objective of operating exposure management is to anticipate and influence the effect of unexpected changes in exchange rates on a firm's future cash flow, rather than being forced into passive reaction to such changes as we described in the

---

[5]The magnitude of the option position depends on what the desired replacement consists of. For example, if Kodak wished only to insure the lost net earnings from exchange rate-induced losses, the option position would obviously be considerably smaller than one attempting to replace gross sales revenues. Given the premium expenses associated with long-term put option positions of this type, the former is generally favored over the latter.

Instruments Napoleon case. This task can best be accomplished if a firm diversifies internationally both its operations and its financing base.

Illustrative Case
An Example of Operating Exposure Management: Statoil of Norway

Statoil is the state-owned oil and gas company of Norway. It is one of the largest oil companies in the world, as well as the leading trader of North Sea oil. Statoil is active in all of the vertical industries associated with the petrochemical industry. Although headquartered in Norway and having the Norwegian krone as its home currency, Statoil's primary revenues, petroleum and petroleum products, are priced and sold on world markets in U.S. dollars. Even when payment is accepted in a nondollar currency, the price is based on the spot rate of a U.S. dollar petrochemical price. Costs, however, are dominated by the servicing of its outstanding debt. The petrochemical industry is an extremely capital-intensive industry, and Statoil needs large quantities of capital.

Exhibit 8.11   Long-Term Debt of the Statoil Group Analyzed by Currency (in millions)

Debt	Long-term debt	Currency swap agreemts	Residual currency position	Average rate of exchange	Book value in Norwegian kroner
Norwegian kroner (NOK)	308	—	308	—	308
U.S. dollars (USD)	1,224	775	1,999	6.65	13,287
German marks (DEM)	684	(307)	377	367.25	1,385
Japanese yen (JPY)	65,640	(44,640)	21,000	4.44	932
French francs (FRF)	750	(400)	350	104.74	367
Swiss francs (CHF)	250	(100)	150	442.42	664
Pounds sterling (GBP)	3	(2)	1	10.96	8
Danish kroner (DKK)	400	(200)	200	90.96	182
European Currency Units (ECU)	100	(100)	0	—	—
Long-term provisions					340
Total Statoil					17,473

1. The majority of long-term loans expire over the period 1992–1998 inclusive, while a minor share runs until 2008.

2. Average rate of interest on long-term loans in 1991 was 7.6%. Average rate of exchange in foreign currency/NOK. USD and GBP are NOK per one unit. All other currencies are per 100 units.

3. Half of the loans are subject to a fixed rate of interest throughout their term.

4. The unused share of long-term loan agreements converts to NOK 5,055 million.

5. Long-term liabilities include provisions for site restoration and removal costs, NOK 281 million.

Source: *Statoil Annual Report and Accounts 1991*, p. 20.

Statoil is a large firm domiciled in a small country. Although sophisticated in structure, the Norwegian capital markets alone cannot feed the voracious capital appetite of such a firm. Statoil must therefore acquire large quantities of capital on world markets.

As illustrated in Exhibit 8.11, Statoil has acquired a large quantity of its capital on world markets denominated in U.S. dollars. But Statoil has also raised capital in other major currency markets such as the Japanese yen and the German mark. To enable the cash flows coming into Statoil as revenues to service the financial outflows in each currency in which it has borrowed, Statoil has swapped large proportions of its debt into U.S. dollar payments. Note in Exhibit 8.11 how the total "currency position" of U.S. dollars is the only currency position that is increased as a result of currency swap agreements. This is a prime example of the use of currency matching to manage the operating exposure of the firm.

Questions

1. Instruments Napoleon (C08A.WK1)
For Instruments Napoleon (see facts in the chapter), assume the domestic sales price remains the same, because of local price controls or competition in France. Assume the export price (in francs) rises by 25%, from FF12.8 to FF16.0, and thus preserves the original foreign-currency-equivalent sales price of $2.00/unit. Assume further that volume in both markets remains the same, because no buyer perceives the price has changed.

    a. What are the impacts on cash flow?
    b. What are the impacts on working capital?
    c. What are the valuation consequences?

2. Instruments Napoleon (C08A.WK1)
For Instruments Napoleon, assume that both domestic and foreign sales prices in francs increase 25% to FF16.0. Assume further that direct costs and cash operating costs also increase by 25%, possibly because of local inflation and because imported raw materials and components rise in franc terms as a result of the franc's depreciation. Volume remains the same.

    a. What are the impacts on cash flow?
    b. What are the impacts on working capital?
    c. What are the valuation consequences?

3. Operating Gains and Currency Depreciation
The interrelationships between transaction exposure and operating exposure are sometimes quite complex. Explain why it is possible to have an operating gain when the currency in which a foreign affiliate operates drops in value.

4. Eastman Kodak: Hedging the Unhedgeable
The Global View that opened this chapter described the exposure analysis problems and efforts of Eastman Kodak. Kodak, like a number of other major firms, is attempting to understand their own operating exposure better, so that they may consider various

operating or contractual hedges to protect firm value. Use the following assumptions to analyze and prescribe potential exposure management solutions:

1. Kodak considers Fuji (Japan) as its primary competitor in the U.S. market and the Japanese consumer market, while Agfa (Germany) is its primary European competitor;

2. Kodak, Fuji, and Agfa produce entirely at home and then export their products to the individual foreign markets;

3. The photographic products produced by all three are essentially identical; therefore price is the basis for all competitive sales and market shares.

    a. How would the direction of the yen/dollar and Deutschemark/dollar exchange rates affect the net profits earned by Eastman Kodak?

    b. What are some of the potential operating strategies Kodak could employ to manage this operating exposure?

    c. What are some of the potential contractual strategies Kodak could employ to manage this operating exposure?

    d. If Kodak were to hedge the exposure using financial contracts, what "value" of Kodak's business (sales, net profits, dividends, etc.) would Kodak need to attempt to cover?

    e. Using the OPTION.WK1 spreadsheet, what would be the premium on the appropriate option on Japanese yen, assuming a $50 million notional principal, 5-year maturity, a strike price of ¥100.00/$, a spot rate of ¥100.00/$, volatility of 10.0%, and 5-year Euro-¥ and Euro-$ interest rates of 5%? How would Kodak's treasury finance this purchase?

5. Sourcing from Thailand

The Global View midway through this chapter described how a number of Japanese automakers such as Toyota have considered using Thailand as a "natural hedge" for their U.S. dollar exposures.

    a. Explain, using boxes and arrows as units and cash flows, respectively, how this would work in principle.

    b. What assumption is critical to this strategy working effectively as a hedge?

    c. How dependable is this assumption over the long run?

6. Statoil of Norway

Statoil, the national oil company of Norway (and a major sponsor of the Lillehammer Olympic games), has acquired debt capital in a variety of foreign currencies (see Exhibit 8.11). After borrowing the capital, however, they swapped their currency obligations in order to hedge their currency exposure. As described in Exhibit 8.11, the residual currency position in most major currencies is relatively small. Why do you think Statoil has chosen to reduce its long-term currency position in some currencies to near zero, while leaving other currency positions essentially untouched?

7. Hedging Hogs: Risk Sharing at Harley Davidson (C08B.WK1)

Harley-Davidson (US) is one firm that reportedly uses risk-sharing agreements with its own foreign subsidiaries and with independent foreign distributors. Since the foreign units typically sell in local markets, earning local currency, Harley would like to ease their individual currency exposure problems by allowing them to pay for merchandise from Harley (US) in their local functional currency.

- *Harley-Davidson, Australia.* The spot rate between the U.S. dollar and the Australian dollar on January 1 is $0.7152/A\$. Assume that Harley uses this rate as the basis for setting the *central rate* or base exchange rate for the year of $0.7150/A\$. Harley agrees to price all contracts to Australian distributors at this exact exchange rate as long as the current spot rate on the order date is within ±5% of this rate. If the spot rate falls outside of this range, but is still within ±10% of the central rate, Harley will "share" (50/50) the exchange rate change with the distributor.

  a. What are the specific exchange rates at the boundaries of the neutral and risk-sharing zones?
  b. If Harley (US) ships a motorcycle, a "hog," with an invoice of $7,500 to Australia, and the exchange rate on the order date is $0.6350/A\$, what is the price in Australian dollars to the foreign distributor?
  c. If Harley (US) ships the same hog to Australia, and the exchange rate on the order date is $0.8600/A\$, what is the price in Australian dollars to the foreign distributor?
  d. Does a risk-sharing agreement like this shift the currency exposure from one party of the transaction to the other?
  e. Does a risk-sharing agreement like this increase or decrease the pricing stability of Harley's product in foreign markets?
  f. How does the date of verification, the order date in this case, alter the exposure? What if the date for exchange rate determination was the shipping date or merchandise receipt date instead?

8. Operating Exposure: Merck

Merck Pharmaceuticals is a multinational firm with an enormous operating exposure problem. Assume Merck does all of its product research and development and manufacturing in the United States. Because of the capital and technical requirements of the pharmaceutical industry, diversification of its operations is not financially practical. Once all pharmaceutical products are produced, they are distributed and sold worldwide in over 60 countries through local sales agents, offices, or affiliates. Because all local markets pay in local currencies, Merck (US) ends up long in a multitude of currencies.

Pharmaceutical prices are typically regulated by host-country governments. Because most individual drug companies have their own niche products, complete with patents and licenses, individual market volume sales are relatively predictable. Competition between companies is focused in the R&D stage, not in the marketplace for existing products.

  a. How would you describe the operating exposure of Merck? (Use boxes for units and arrows for cash flows.)
  b. What potential operating or contractual hedging strategies might be appropriate for Merck's long positions in foreign currencies?
  c. How far out into the future would these hedges need to be placed in order for Merck to yield true benefits? How effective are these strategies likely to be in the long run?

9. Local Currency Financing as a Hedge

Many multinational firms provide most of the capital structure for the establishment of their new foreign subsidiaries themselves. This is common because a new subsidiary has no financial credit worth (or record) of its own, and the parent firm can acquire capital much more cheaply. As soon as the subsidiary is operating, however, the parent company always encourages (or requires) the subsidiary to acquire as much local currency financing as possible. How would this serve as a natural hedge for most subsidiaries?

10. Mismatched Freddie Laker

Laker Airways (UK), spearheaded by the self-made entrepreneur Sir Freddie Laker, was forced into bankruptcy in 1982. Laker Airways pioneered a railroadlike system called *Skytrain,* in which passengers could not make reservations or purchase tickets prior to 4 A.M. on the date of the flight. The idea was to fill all the seats at the same consistently low price, with no frills service. (Sir Freddie was once quoted that he would start serving fancy meals when restaurants started flying!)

Laker Airways, like many start-up enterprises, was heavily laden with debt. Between 1979 and 1982 Laker took on an enormous amount of new debt in order to purchase the aircraft needed to service promising routes such as the Gatwick Airport (UK) link to Kennedy Airport (US). The debt came in three major segments:

1. Mitsui of Japan extended a loan of approximately $59 million in 1979 for the purchase of two DC-10 aircraft, at 8.5% fixed interest for 20 years.

2. The Export-Import Bank of the United States, in conjunction with the Private Export Funding Corporation and assorted banks, extended a total loan of $228 million at rates ranging from 6% to 9% over 9 years for the purchase of five new McDonald Douglas DC-10-30s in 1979.

3. Midland Bank (UK), in 1981, led a syndicate of European banks in extending a loan of $131 million for the purchase of three new Airbus A300-B4s. The interest rate was also fixed by the British government as long as Laker Airways agreed to (a) not sell any of the aircraft; and (b) accept the loan proceeds and payments in U.S. dollars. Because the British pound was quite strong against the dollar at this time, this resulted in a lower subsidy cost to the British government.

The problem was that although two-thirds of Laker Airways revenues were denominated in British pounds, its entire debt structure and its major operating cost—jet fuel—were all denominated or priced on the basis of U.S. dollars. As the pound fell against the U.S. dollar from 1979 to 1982, so did Laker Airways.

a. Diagram the cash flow structure by currency of denomination. How would a falling pound cause difficulties for Laker Airways?

b. Prior to the financial distress resulting in bankruptcy, what would be some of the solutions which most likely were attempted?

c. In the international financial world of the 1990s, in which there are a variety of techniques for managing currency exposure, what could be done now to solve Sir Freddie Laker's mismatched currency cash flows?

Bibliography

Abuaf, Niso, "The Nature and Management of Foreign Exchange Risk," *Midland Corporate Finance Journal,* Fall 1986, pp. 30–44.

Adler, Michael, and Bernard Dumas, "Exposure to Currency Risk: Definition and Measurement," *Financial Management,* Spring 1984, pp. 41–50.

Booth, Laurence, and Wendy Rotenberg, "Assessing Foreign Exchange Exposure: Theory and Application Using Canadian Firms," *Journal of International Financial Management and Accounting,* vol. 2, no. 1, Spring 1990, pp. 1–22.

Carter, Joseph R., Shawnee K. Vickery, and Michael P. D'Itri, "Currency Risk Management Strategies for Contracting with Japanese Suppliers," *International Journal of Purchasing & Materials Management,* vol. 29, no. 3, Summer 1993, pp. 19–25.

Dickins, Paul, "Daring to Hedge the Unhedgeable," *Corporate Finance,* August 1988, pp. 11–13.

Dufey, Gunter, "Corporate Finance and Exchange Rate Variations," *Financial Management,* Summer 1972, pp. 51–57.

———, "Funding Decisions in International Companies," in *International Financial Management,* Göran Bergendahl, ed., Stockholm: Norstedts, 1982, pp. 29–53.

Dufey, Gunter, and S. L. Srinivasulu, "The Case for Corporate Management of Foreign Exchange Risk," *Financial Management,* Winter 1983, pp. 54–62.

Eaker, Mark R., and Dwight Grant, "Optimal Hedging of Uncertain and Long-Term Foreign Exchange Exposure," *Journal of Banking and Finance,* June 1985, pp. 222–231.

Flood, Eugene, Jr., and Donald R. Lessard, "On the Measurement of Operating Exposure to Exchange Rates: A Conceptual Approach," *Financial Management,* Spring 1986, pp. 25–36.

Giddy, Ian H., "Exchange Risk: Whose View?" *Financial Management,* Summer 1977, pp. 23–33.

Glaum, Martin, "Strategic Management of Exchange Rate Risks," *Long Range Planning,* vol. 23, no. 4, 1990, pp. 65–72.

Grant, Robert, and Luc A. Soenen, "Conventional Hedging: An Inadequate Response to Long-Term Foreign Exchange Exposure," *Managerial Finance,* vol. 17, no. 4, 1991, pp. 1–4.

Hekman, Christine R., "Don't Blame Currency Values for Strategic Errors," *Midland Corporate Finance Journal,* Fall 1986, pp. 45–55.

———, "A Financial Model of Foreign Exchange Exposure," *Journal of International Business Studies,* Summer 1985, pp. 83–99.

———, "Measuring Foreign Exchange Exposure: A Practical Theory and Its Application," *Financial Analysts Journal,* September/October 1983, pp. 59–65.

Jacque, Laurent L., *Management of Foreign Exchange Risk: Theory and Practice,* Lexington, Mass.: Heath, 1978.

———, "Management of Foreign Exchange Risk: A Review Article," *Journal of International Business Studies,* Spring/Summer 1981, pp. 81–101.

Jorion, Philippe, "The Exchange-Rate Exposure of U.S. Multinationals," *Journal of Business,* vol. 63, no. 3, July 1990, pp. 331–345.

Kohn, Ken, "Futures and Options: Are You Ready for Economic-Risk Management?" *Institutional Investor,* September 1990, pp. 203–204, 207.

Kwok, Chuck C. Y. "Hedging Foreign Exchange Exposures: Independent vs. Integrative Approaches," *Journal of International Business Studies,* Summer 1987, pp. 33–52.

Lessard, Donald R., and S. B. Lightstore, "Volatile Exchange Rates Can Put Operations at Risk," *Harvard Business Review,* July/August 1986, pp. 107–114.

Levi, Maurice D., and Piet Serçu, "Erroneous and Valid Reasons for Hedging Foreign Exchange Rate Exposure," *Journal of Multinational Financial Management,* vol 1, no. 2, 1991, pp. 19–28.

Levich, Richard M., and Clas G. Wihlborg, eds., *Exchange Risk and Exposure,* Lexington, Mass.: Lexington Books, 1980.

Lewent, Judy C., and A. John Kearney, "Identifying, Measuring, and Hedging Currency Risk at Merck," *Journal of Applied Corporate Finance,* Winter 1990, pp. 19–28.

Luehrman, Timothy A., "The Exchange Rate Exposure of a Global Competitor," *Journal of International Business Studies,* vol. 21, no. 2, 1990, pp. 225–242.

Millar, William, and Brad Asher, *Strategic Risk Management,* New York: Business International, January 1990.

Moffett, Michael H., and Jan Karl Karlsen, "Managing Foreign Exchange Rate Economic Exposure," *Journal of International Financial Management and Accounting.* vol. 5, no. 2, June 1994, pp. 157–175.

Oxelheim, Lars, and Clas Wihlborg, "Corporate Strategies in a Turbulent World Economy," *Management International Review*, Vol. 31, no. 4, 1991, pp. 293–315.

———, and Clas Wihlborg, *Macroeconomic Uncertainty: International Risks and Opportunities for the Corporation*, Chichester, U.K.: Wiley, 1987.

Pringle, John J., "Managing Foreign Exchange Exposure," *Journal of Applied Corporate Finance,* vol. 3, no. 4, Winter 1991, pp. 73– 82.

Rawls, S. Waite, III, and Charles W. Smithson, "Strategic Risk Management," *Journal of Applied Corporate Finance,* Winter 1990, pp. 6–18.

Shapiro, Alan C., and David P. Rutenberg, "Managing Exchange Risks in a Floating World," *Financial Management,* Summer 1976, pp. 48–58.

Soenen, Luc A., and Jeff Madura, "Foreign Exchange Management—A Strategic Approach," *Long Range Planning,* vol. 24, no. 5, October 1991, pp. 119–124.

Stonehill, Arthur I., Niels Ravn, and Kåre Dullum, "Management of Foreign Exchange Economic Exposure," in *International Financial Management,* Göran Bergendahl, ed., Stockholm: Norstedts, 1982, pp. 128–148.

Wihlborg, Clas, "Economics of Exposure Management of Foreign Subsidiaries of Multinational Corporations," *Journal of International Business Studies,* Winter 1980, pp. 9–18.

Chapter 9
Accounting Exposure

Global View
Rethinking Functional Currencies

Economic reality for many multinationals, especially in the U.S., has changed dramatically since the early '80s. International business accounts for an increasingly bigger piece of total earnings. Intensifying competition means pricing strategies must be more flexible. Currency market volatility has become a constant headache for multinationals, especially when corporate earnings are squeezed as they are now.

One fallout from these new pressures is that MNCs are being forced to review what functional currency they use for accounting purposes. Back in the early '80s, most U.S. MNCs chose the dollar. Now many, especially in the high-tech industry, are taking a close look at the decision to keep the U.S. dollar as their functional currency.

"This is a different world than it was in the '80s," says Fred Cohen, national practice leader, Treasury Management Services at KPMG Peat Marwick. "Companies are looking at business more globally, not just from a U.S. perspective. International accounted for a smaller percentage of their business back when the original decision to pick a functional currency was made. But now that overseas earnings may account for close to 50% of revenues, international is of greater importance."

Some MNCs Choose Not to Change
While many MNCs are rethinking the question, only some are choosing to actually switch, since the decision does entail a major overhaul of the accounting system and in some cases, many internal procedures. Also, the decision has to be based on a set of economic facts set forth by the FASB in FAS 52. Although, in most cases, an MNC can meet the requirements for both and choose which facts to use in order to get the desired result.

Pricing procedures and currency of sale would also have to be rethought, as well as credit terms offered, says Peat Marwick's Cohen. On the sub level, changing functional currencies may entail a complete revision of performance measurement criteria, he says.

Digital Equipment Corp, for example, decided to stick with the dollar. "We have rethought our original decision and decided to stay with the dollar as the functional currency," says Dick Stewart, manager of accounting research at the MNC. "Our approach has been to attempt to measure the cash flow in dollars and local currency and go with the dominant one as the functional currency. Most of our subsidiaries have net cash flows in dollars, since most use the dollar as their currency of billing." The sales subsidiaries also pay in dollars for DEC products.

Source: Adapted from *Business International Money Report,* "New Economic Reality Forces MNCs to Rethink Functional Currencies," Nilly Landau, 8/13/90, pp. 314–315, the Economist Intelligence Unit. Reprinted with permission.

Accounting exposure, also called *translation exposure,* arises because foreign currency financial statements of foreign affiliates must be restated in the parent's reporting currency if the parent is to prepare consolidated financial statements. Foreign affiliates of U.S. companies must restate, for example, local mark, franc, or sterling statements into U.S. dollars so the foreign values can be added to the parent's U.S. dollar-denominated balance sheet and income statement. This accounting process is called "translation."

Although the main purpose of translation is to prepare consolidated statements, translated statements are also used by management to assess the performance of foreign affiliates. Such assessment might be performed from the local currency statements, but restatement of all affiliate statements into the single "common denominator" of one currency facilitates management comparison.

Accounting exposure is defined as the potential for an increase or decrease in the parent's net worth, and reported net income, caused by a change in exchange rates since the last translation. Two basic procedures for translation are currently used in most of the world: the *current rate method* and the *monetary/nonmonetary method.* Another procedure, termed the *temporal method,* is similar to the monetary/nonmonetary method under most circumstances and is sometimes regarded as a variation of that method. Still other methods have been used in times past.

Current Rate Method

The current rate method is the most prevalent in the world today. Under this method, all assets and liabilities are translated at the current rate of exchange, that is, at the rate of exchange in effect on the balance sheet date. Income statement items, including depreciation and cost of goods sold, are translated at either the actual exchange rate on the dates the various revenues, expenses, gains, and losses were incurred or at an appropriately weighted average exchange rate for the period. Dividends paid are translated at the exchange rate in effect on the date of payment.

Common stock and paid-in capital accounts are translated at historical rates. Year-end retained earnings consist of the original year-beginning retained earnings plus or minus any income or loss for the year. However, gains or losses caused by translation adjustments are *not* included in the calculation of net income, and thus the change in retained earnings does not reflect translation gains or losses. Rather, translation gains or losses are reported separately and accumulated in a separate equity reserve account with a title such as "cumulative translation adjustment" (CTA).

If a foreign affiliate is sold or liquidated, translation gains or losses of past years accumulated in the CTA account are reported as one component of the total gain or loss on sale or liquidation. The total gain or loss is reported as net income or loss for the time period in which the sale or liquidation occurs.

The current rate method became official U.S. practice with the December 1981 issuance of *Statement of Financial Accounting Standards Number 52* (FAS #52, also called SFAS #52 and FASB #52) by the Financial Accounting Standards Board. This is the authority in the United States that determines accounting policy for U.S. firms and certified public accountants.

The biggest advantage of the current rate method is that the gain or loss on translation does not pass through the income statement but goes directly to a reserve account. This eliminates the variability of reported earnings due to foreign exchange gains or losses. A second advantage of the current rate method is that the relative proportions of individual balance sheet accounts remain the same. Hence the process of translation does not distort such balance sheet ratios as the current ratio or the debt-to-equity ratio. The main disadvantage of the current rate method is that it violates the accounting principle of carrying balance sheet accounts at historical cost. Foreign assets purchased with dollars and then recorded on an affiliate's statements at their foreign currency historical cost are translated back into dollars at a different rate. Thus they are reported in the consolidated statement in dollars at something other than their historical dollar cost.

Monetary/Nonmonetary Method

Under the monetary/nonmonetary method, monetary assets (primarily cash, marketable securities, accounts receivable, and long-term receivables) and monetary liabilities (primarily current liabilities and long-term debt) are translated at current exchange rates, while all other assets and liabilities are translated at historical rates.

Income statement accounts are translated at the average exchange rate for the period, except for items such as depreciation and cost of goods sold that are directly associated with nonmonetary assets or liabilities. These accounts are translated at their historical rate.

The basic advantage of the monetary/nonmonetary method is that foreign nonmonetary assets are carried at their original costs in the parent's consolidated statement. In most countries this approach is consistent with the original cost treatment of domestic assets of the parent firm. In practice, however, if some foreign accounts are translated at one exchange rate while others are translated at different rates, the resulting translated balance sheet will not balance! Hence there is a need for a "plug" to remove what has been called the "dangling debit or credit."[1] The true nature of the gain or loss created by use of such a "plug" is open to question. Unrealized foreign exchange gains or losses are included in quarterly primary earnings per share (EPS), thus increasing variability of reported earnings.

Temporal Method

As we mentioned earlier, the temporal method is often regarded as a variation of the monetary/nonmonetary method. If the foreign affiliate keeps all of its accounts on a historical cost basis, the temporal method is identical to the monetary/nonmonetary method. However if the foreign affiliate restates any unexposed assets (such as inventory or net plant and equipment) to market value, the temporal method provides for their translation at the current exchange rate. Such restatement to market value is not uncommon in countries such as Argentina or Israel that are experiencing hyperinflation.

The temporal method was required in the United States when *Statement of Financial Accounting Standards Number 8* (FAS #8) was adopted in October 1975. It remained in effect until replaced by FAS #52 in December 1981.

Technical Aspects of Translation

Most countries have an accounting authority or legal system that prescribes whether or not foreign operations must be consolidated into a parent's statements and, if so, what translation method must be used. Terms such as *functional currency* and *reporting currency* must be defined. Rules must be established for deciding when and how gains or losses will be recognized in the income statement, and exceptions allowed for special circumstances.

Functional Versus Reporting Currency

A foreign affiliate's *functional currency* is the currency of the primary economic environment in which the affiliate operates and in which it generates cash flows. In other words, it is the dominant currency used by that foreign affiliate in its day-to-day operations. A *reporting currency* is the currency used by the parent to present its own financial statements. Normally the reporting currency is the parent's home currency.

Management must evaluate the nature and purpose of its foreign operations to decide on the appropriate functional currency. The procedure for deciding when to

---

[1]Gerhard G. Mueller, Helen Gernon, and Gary Meek, *Accounting: An International Perspective*, Homewood, Ill.: Richard D. Irwin, 1987, p. 93.

translate and what currency to use is summarized in Exhibit 9.1. If the financial statements of foreign affiliates of U.S. companies are maintained in U.S. dollars, translation is not required. If maintained in the local currency and the local currency is the functional currency, they are translated by the current rate method. If, however, they are maintained in the foreign currency but that currency is not the functional currency, then a choice must be made how to translate into U.S. dollars. If the dollar is the functional currency, the statements are translated into U.S. dollars by the temporal method. If some other

Exhibit 9.1   Translation Procedure Flow Chart

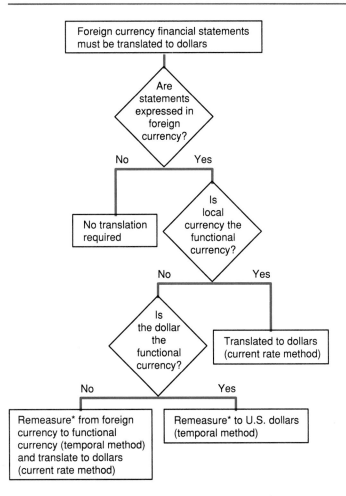

Source: Frederick D. S. Choi and Gerhard G. Mueller, *International Accounting,* 2nd ed., Englewood Cliffs, N.J.: Prentice Hall, 1992, p. 169.

*The term *remeasure* means to translate so as to change the unit of measure from a foreign currency to the functional currency.

currency (say, francs, marks, or pesos) is the functional currency, then the statement is first translated into the functional currency by the temporal method, and then translated into dollars by the current rate method.

In effect, if a foreign affiliate's operations are relatively self-contained and integrated within a particular country, its functional currency is the local currency of that country. Thus the German affiliates of Ford and General Motors, which do most of their manufacturing in Germany and sell most of their production for Deutschemarks, use the Deutschemark as their functional currency.

If the foreign affiliate's operations are in fact an extension of, say, its U.S. parent's operations, the functional currency becomes the U.S. dollar. U.S.-owned *maquiladora* assembly plants across the Mexican border from such U.S. cities as San Diego and El Paso receive all of their raw material from their U.S. parent and export all of their production back to the U.S. parent. Their functional currency is the U.S. dollar, and their financial statements are translated by the temporal method. Although such companies use the temporal method for affiliates where the dollar is the functional currency, they simultaneously use the current rate method for other affiliates. When the temporal method is used, translation gains or losses flow directly to the income statement; they are not charged to a cumulative translation adjustment (CTA) account.

Time of Recognizing Gains or Losses

Translation by any of the methods usually produces an accounting gain or loss when exchange rates have changed. This gain or loss measures a change in valuation according to accounting rules; it is not a cash out-of-pocket gain or loss. A remaining accounting question is whether such gain or loss should be *recognized* in the current income statement, deferred to a later reporting period, or closed directly into retained earnings or an equity reserve account without ever passing through the income statement.

In the United States, translation gains or losses determined by the current rate method do not increase or decrease net income, but are instead accumulated in a cumulative translation adjustment (CTA) account within the consolidated stockholders' equity section until substantial or complete liquidation of the assets or the firm occurs. In other words, these unrealized translation gains or losses are held in abeyance until the gain or loss is actually realized. In the case of fixed assets this realization might well be decades into the future. Only when realized is the gain or loss reported as net income or loss for that period. Note, however, that *transaction* gains or losses, as distinguished from *translation* gains or losses, have an immediate impact on income for the current period.

Under the temporal method used in the United States from 1975 to 1981, translation gains and losses passed through the quarterly income statement, increasing or decreasing both quarterly and annual net income and earnings per share. Equity reserves were not permitted. This "flow through" requirement existed at a time when the value of the U.S. dollar fluctuated widely. Because of the whipsaw effect on reported quarterly earnings, this reporting rule was very unpopular with corporate executives who wanted to emphasize stable growth of reported earnings. In many multinational firms foreign exchange risk management policies were dominated by the desire to manage quarterly earnings so they appeared to be stable—and rising. Many firms engaged in costly efforts to hedge foreign activities so quarterly earnings would not fluctuate unduly because of noncash translation gains or losses.

Hyperinflation Countries

FAS #52 has a special provision for translating statements of foreign affiliates of U.S. companies operating in countries where cumulative inflation has been approximately 100% or more over a three-year period. Financial statements of these affiliates must be translated into the reporting currency using the temporal method.

The rationale for special treatment of hyperinflation countries is to correct the distortion that occurs when depreciation at historical cost is subtracted from revenue at current prices. Translating plant, equipment, and depreciation expenses at the historical exchange rate yields a higher asset value in the reporting currency than would use of the current (depreciated) exchange rate. This, in turn, leads to a less distorted income statement and balance sheet. If the current rate were used, depreciation would be understated relative to replacement costs, profits would be overstated in real terms, and the book value of plant and equipment would eventually nearly disappear from the balance sheet as its value diminished in reporting currency terms. In effect, FAS #52 declares the functional currency of affiliates in hyperinflation countries to be the reporting currency (U.S. dollars for U.S. firms).

Although the hyperinflation standard is somewhat controversial, it has some precedence in business practice. Russell Taussig has stated it very well:

> When a country is plagued with hyperinflation, it often uses the U.S. dollar or other hard currency as its de facto functional currency for actual transactions regardless of accounting standards. For example, most Israeli retailers in 1982 priced their merchandise in U.S. dollars, not shekels. In the face of triple-digit inflation, they cannot change their prices every other day. The U.S. dollar becomes the unit of account. Also, when an Israeli holds U.S. dollars and the shekel is devalued, his holding in dollars remains the same, whereas if he holds currency in shekels and the shekel is devalued, his holding declines in purchasing power. The U.S. dollar becomes the storehouse of value. Consistent with the mercantile practice of businessmen in highly inflationary economies, the FASB promulgates the accounting standard that the home currency becomes the functional currency when inflation is rampant; otherwise the local currency is the functional currency. Accounting standards-setting simply is patterned after accepted business practice.[2]

Current Rate and Monetary/Nonmonetary Translation Example

We illustrate use of the current rate method of translation by continuing the example of Instruments Napoleon, S.A., from Chapter 8. This example is supplemented with an illustration of translation by the monetary/nonmonetary method in order to show the very arbitrary nature of a translation gain or loss. Selection of the accounting method is

---

[2]Russell A. Taussig, "Impact of SFAS No. 52 on the Translation of Foreign Financial Statements of Companies in Highly Inflationary Economies," *Journal of Accounting, Auditing, and Finance,* Winter 1983, pp. 145–146. Reprinted with permission.

the major factor in determining the magnitude of gain or loss. The example that follows deals with balance sheet translation only. The somewhat more complex procedures for translating income statements are described in international accounting texts.[3]

The functional currency of Instruments Napoleon, S.A., is the French franc, and the reporting currency of its parent, Washington Controls, is the U.S. dollar. Assume the following:

1. Plant and equipment, long-term debt, and common stock were acquired by Instruments Napoleon some time in the past when the exchange rate was FF6.00/$.

2. Inventory currently on hand was purchased or manufactured during the immediately prior quarter when the average exchange rate was FF6.25/$.

3. At the close of business on Friday, December 29, 1995, the current spot exchange rate was FF6.40/$.

4. When business reopens on January 2, 1996, after the New Year holiday, the franc had dropped 20% in value to a new exchange rate of FF8.00/$.

The example also looks at the consequences had the franc strengthened overnight to FF5.00/$.

Current Rate Method

The top half of Exhibit 9.2 illustrates translation loss using the current rate method. Assets and liabilities on the predevaluation balance sheet are translated at the current rate of FF6.40/$. Capital stock is translated at the historical rate of FF6.00/$, and retained earnings are translated at a composite rate that is equivalent to having each past year's addition to retained earnings translated at the exchange rate in effect in that year.

As shown in the top half of Exhibit 9.2, the "just before devaluation" dollar translation reports an accumulated translation loss from prior periods of $50,000. This balance is the cumulative gain or loss from translating franc statements into dollars in prior years, and has been carried separately in the cumulative translation adjustment (CTA) account.

After the 20% depreciation, assets and liabilities are all translated at the new exchange rate of FF8.00/$. Equity accounts, including retained earnings, are translated just as they were before devaluation, and as a result the cumulative translation loss increases to $300,000. The increase of $250,000 in this account (from a cumulative loss of $50,000 to a cumulative loss of $300,000) is the translation loss measured by the current rate method.

This translation loss is a decrease in equity, measured in the parent's reporting currency, of "net exposed foreign assets." An "exposed asset" is an asset the value of which drops with a devaluation of the functional currency and rises with an appreciation of that currency. "Net" exposed assets in this context means exposed assets minus exposed liabilities. Net exposed assets are positive (that is, "long") if exposed assets exceed exposed liabilities, and are negative ("short") if exposed assets are smaller than exposed liabilities.

Exposure can be measured by creating a "before" and "after" translated balance sheet, as was done in Exhibit 9.2. A simpler method is to multiply "net exposed assets" by the

---

[3]See, for example, Frederick D.S. Choi and Gerhard G. Mueller, *International Accounting,* 2nd ed., Englewood Cliffs, N.J.: Prentice Hall, 1992, pp. 170–175.

Exhibit 9.2 Translation Loss Just After a Devaluation of the French Franc. Instruments Napoleon, S.A.

	French francs	FF/$	December 29, 1995 Just Before Devaluation Dollars	FF/$	January 2, 1996 Just After Devaluation Dollars
Current Rate Method					
Cash	1,600,000	6.4	250,000	8.0	200,000
Accounts receivable	3,200,000	6.4	500,000	8.0	400,000
Inventory	2,400,000	6.4	375,000	8.0	300,000
Net plant and equipment	4,800,000	6.4	750,000	8.0	600,000
Total	12,000,000		1,875,000		1,500,000
Accounts payable	800,000	6.4	125,000	8.0	100,000
Short-term bank debt	1,600,000	6.4	250,000	8.0	200,000
Long-term debt	1,600,000	6.4	250,000	8.0	200,000
Capital stock	1,800,000	6.0	300,000	6.0	300,000
Retained earnings	6,200,000	(a)	1,000,000	(b)	1,000,000
Cumulative translation adjustment (CTA)			<50,000>		<300,000>
Total	12,000,000		1,875,000		1,500,000
Monetary/Nonmonetary Method					
Cash	1,600,000	6.4	250,000	8.0	200,000
Accounts receivable	3,200,000	6.4	500,000	8.0	400,000
Inventory	2,400,000	6.25	384,000	6.25	384,000
Net plant and equipment	4,800,000	6.0	800,000	6.0	800,000
Total	12,000,000		1,934,000		1,784,000
Accounts payable	800,000	6.4	125,000	8.0	100,000
Short-term bank debt	1,600,000	6.4	250,000	8.0	200,000
Long-term debt	1,600,000	6.4	250,000	8.0	200,000
Capital stock	1,800,000	6.0	300,000	6.0	300,000
Retained earnings	6,200,000	(a)	1,009,000	(b)	1,009,000
Translation gain or loss					<25,000>
Total	12,000,000		1,934,000		1,784,000

aDollar-retained earnings before devaluation are the cumulative sum of additions to retained earnings of all prior years, translated at exchange rates in effect in each year.

bTranslated into dollars at the same rate as before devaluation. However, under the monetary/nonmonetary method the translation loss of $25,000 would be closed into retained earnings, via the income statement, rather than left as a separate line item. Hence under the monetary/nonmonetary method ending retained earnings would actually be $1,009,000 minus $25,000 = $984,000.

percentage amount of devaluation. This has been done for the current rate method in the left column of Exhibit 9.3, which illustrates a 20% depreciation of the French franc means that net exposed assets of $1,250,000 lose 20% of their value, a translation loss of $250,000.

Suppose instead that the franc had appreciated. If, by the end of the year, the French franc had appreciated from FF6.40/$ to FF5.00/$, the appreciation would be 28%. The

Exhibit 9.3   Calculation of Translation Loss Just After 20% Devaluation of the French franc, from FF6.40/$ to FF8.00/$. Instruments Napoleon, S.A.

	Current Rate Method	*Monetary/ Nonmonetary Method*
Exposed assets		
Cash	$250,000	$250,000
Accounts receivable	500,000	500,000
Inventory	375,000	not exposed
Net plant and equipment	750,000	not exposed
Total exposed assets ("A")	$1,875,000	$750,000
Exposed liabilities		
Accounts payable	$125,000	$125,000
Short-term bank debt	250,000	250,000
Long-term debt	250,000	250,000
Total exposed liabilities ("L")	$625,000	$625,000
Loss if franc depreciates 20%		
Net exposed assets ("A" − "L")	$1,250,000	$125,000
times amount of		
devaluation (as decimal)	× .20	× .20
Translation loss	$250,000	$25,000

Exhibit 9.4   Calculation of Translation Gain After 28% Appreciation of the French Franc, from FF6.40/$ to FF5.00/$ for Instruments Napoleon, S.A.

Gain If Franc Appreciates 28%	*Current Rate Method*	*Monetary/ Nonmonetary Method*
Net exposed assets ("A" − "L")	$1,250,000	$125,000
times amount of		
appreciation (as decimal)	× .28	× .28
Translation gain	$350,000	$35,000

effect of this is seen in Exhibit 9.4, which starts with the same net exposed assets calculated in Exhibit 9.3. Under the current rate method, the U.S. parent would have a translation gain of $350,000.

Monetary/Nonmonetary Method

Translation of the same accounts under the monetary/nonmonetary method shows the arbitrary nature of any gain or loss from translation. This is illustrated in the bottom half of Exhibit 9.2: monetary assets and monetary liabilities in the predevaluation French franc balance sheet are translated at the current rate of exchange; other assets and the equity accounts are translated at their historic rates. For Instruments Napoleon, the historic rate for inventory differs from that for net plant and equipment because inventory was acquired more recently.

Under the temporal version of the monetary/nonmonetary method, translation losses were not accumulated in a separate equity account but passed directly through each quarter's income statement. Thus in the dollar balance sheet translated before devaluation, retained earnings were the cumulative result of earnings from all prior years translated at historical rates in effect each year, plus translation gains or losses from all prior years. In Exhibit 9.2, no translation loss appears in the predevaluation dollar balance sheet because any losses would have been closed to retained earnings.

The effect of the 20% devaluation is to create an immediate translation loss of $25,000. This amount is shown as a separate line item in Exhibit 9.2 in order to focus attention on it for this textbook example. Under the temporal method, this translation loss of $25,000 would pass through the income statement, reducing reported net income and reducing retained earnings. In our example, then, ending retained earnings would in fact be $984,000, that is, $1,009,000 minus $25,000. Other countries using the monetary/nonmonetary method do not necessarily require gains and losses to pass through the income statement.

When translation loss is viewed in terms of changes in the value of exposed accounts, the loss of $25,000 under the monetary/nonmonetary method is 20% of net exposure of $125,000, as calculated in the right half of Exhibit 9.3. With a 28% appreciation of the French franc, the translation gain to the U.S. parent would be $35,000, as shown at the bottom of the right column in Exhibit 9.4.

Managerial Implications

In Exhibits 9.3 and 9.4, translation loss or gain is larger under the current rate method because inventory and net plant and equipment, as well as all monetary assets, are deemed exposed. When net exposed assets are larger, gains or losses from translation are also larger.

The managerial implications of this fact are very important. If management expects a foreign currency to devalue, it should minimize accounting exposure by reducing net exposed assets. If management anticipates an appreciation of the foreign currency, it should increase net exposed assets to benefit from a gain.

Depending on the accounting method of the moment, management might select different assets and liabilities for reduction or increase. Thus "real" decisions about investing and financing might be dictated by which accounting technique is required, when in fact the method of reporting should be neutral in its influence on operating and financing decisions.

Comparison of Accounting Exposure with Operating Exposure

Translation gains or losses in the event of devaluation are compared with the operating gains or losses from Chapter 8 in Exhibit 9.5. Obviously translation gains or losses can

Exhibit 9.5   Comparison of Accounting Exposure with Operating Exposure, Devaluation of French Franc from FF6.4/$ to FF8.0/$. Instruments Napoleon, S.A.

Exposure	Amount of Loss or Gain
Accounting Exposure (source: Exhibits 9.2 and 9.3)	
Current rate method	$ 250,000 loss on translation
Monetary/nonmonetary method	25,000 loss on translation
Operating Exposure (in present value terms; source: Exhibit 8.5, Chapter 8)	
Case 1	$ 104,800 loss on operations
Case 2	191,700 gain on operations
Case 3	450,300 gain on operations

be quite different from operating gains or losses, not only in magnitude but also in sign. A manager focusing only on translation losses, in a situation such as Instruments Napoleon, might avoid France because of the likelihood of such a loss. Such a manager might fear loss of a bonus tied to reported profits, or possibly loss of a job if the investment in France were made and subsequently the translated income statement reported severe translation losses back to the home office.

Operating exposure presents an entirely different view of the same situation. As summarized in Exhibit 9.5, France became a more (not less) desirable location for investment because of the *operating* consequences that followed devaluation in two of the three cases. This illustrates the importance of focusing decisions primarily on the operating consequences of changes in exchange rates, and only secondarily (if at all) on accounting measurements.

Consolidation of Accounts

Translation of statements is necessary to prepare a consolidated balance sheet and income statement. It is also the first step in preparing corporatewide exposure reports for management use. Assume that on December 29, 1995, the various spot exchange rates are as shown in Exhibit 9.6.

Balance sheets for Washington Controls, Inc., the U.S. parent, and its two wholly owned affiliates, Instruments Napoleon, S.A., and Canadian Instruments, Ltd., are shown in Exhibit 9.7. The unconsolidated balance sheet of the parent is shown in column 1; column 2 shows the balance sheet of Instruments Napoleon; and column 3 shows the balance sheet of Canadian Instruments. All balance sheets are for December 31, 1995, before any changes in exchange rates. The symbol C$ is used to designate Canadian dollars; $ by itself means U.S. dollars.

Footnotes to Exhibit 9.7 explain details of the financial situation. The U.S. parent has £100,000 on deposit in a London bank; Canadian Instruments owes its U.S. parent C$600,000; the parent carries its investments in Instruments Napoleon and Canadian

Exhibit 9.6   Assumed Exchange Rates, Friday, December 29, 1995

Spot Rates

$1.00 = FF6.40 or FF1.00 = $0.15625

$1.00 = C$1.25 or C$1.00 = $0.80

$1.00 = £0.6667 or £1.00 = $1.50

Cross Rates

C$1.00 = £0.5333 or £1.00 = C$1.8750

FF1.00 = C$0.1953 or C$1.00 = FF5.1200

Exhibit 9.7   Unconsolidated Balance Sheets for Washington Controls, Inc., and Its French and Canadian Affiliates, December 31, 1995 (in thousands of currency units)

	Washington Controls (parent only)	Instruments Napoleon	Canadian Instruments
Assets			
Cash	$ 800[a]	FF 1,600	C$ 600
Accounts receivable	2,400[b]	3,200	2,000
Inventory	3,000	2,400	1,800
Net plant and equipment	5,000	4,800	3,000
Investment in Instruments Napoleon, S.A.	1,250[c]		
Investment in Canadian Instruments, Ltd.	3,340[d]		
	$15,790	FF12,000	C$7,400
Liabilities and Net Worth			
Accounts payable	$ 2,000	FF 800	C$1,400[b]
Short-term bank loan	2,000[e]	1,600	825[f]
Long-term debt	3,000	1,600	1,000[g]
Capital stock	4,000	1,800	1,200
Retained earnings	4,790	6,200	2,975
	$15,790	FF12,000	C$7,400

[a]U.S. parent has £100,000 in a London bank, carried on its books as $150,000. This amount is part of the total cash balance of $800,000 shown on the parent's books.

[b]Canadian Instruments owes the U.S. parent C$600,000, included in accounts payable and carried on the U.S. books at $480,000. Remaining accounts receivable (parent books) and accounts payable (Canadian Instrument's books) are in U.S. and Canadian dollars, respectively.

[c]The U.S. parent carries its 100% ownership of Instruments Napoleon at $1,250,000, this being the sum of capital stock ($300,000) and retained earnings ($1,000,000), minus translation adjustment ($50,000), before devaluation, as shown in Exhibit 9.2 under the current rate method of translation.

[d]The U.S. parent carries its 100% ownership of Canadian Instruments at $3,340,000, this being the sum of capital stock (C$1,200,000) and retained earnings (C$2,975,000), the sum times $0.80/C$. (C$4,175,000 × .80 = $3,340,000).

[e]The U.S. parent has borrowed, on a short-term basis, £200,000 from a London bank, carried on its books as $300,000. Remaining parent short-term bank debt is denominated in U.S. dollars.

[f]Canadian Instruments' short-term bank loan consists of £440,000, carried on Canadian books as C$825,000. (C$825,000 = $660,000.)

[g]Canadian Instruments' long-term debt consists of FF5,120,000 in Eurofrancs, carried on Canadian books as C$1,000,000.

Instruments at $1,000,000 and $3,340,000, respectively; the U.S. parent has borrowed £200,000 from a London bank; and Canadian Instruments has long-term debt denominated in French francs of FF5,120,000.

The process of creating a consolidated balance sheet from affiliate statements is shown in Exhibit 9.8. Intracompany accounts are canceled. Then remaining foreign currency accounts are translated into U.S. dollars; and the dollar amounts are added horizontally to create, in the right-hand column, the consolidated balance sheet. In this example, translation has been accomplished by the current rate method. Details of the translation for intracompany accounts are given in the notes to Exhibit 9.8.

Exhibit 9.8   Consolidated Balance Sheet for Washington Controls, Inc., December 31, 1995 (accounts translated into thousands of U.S. dollars with intracompany accounts removed)

	Washington Controls (parent)	Instruments Napoleon	Canadian Instruments	Consolidated Balance Sheet
ASSETS				
Cash	$ 800[a]	$ 250	$ 480	$1,530
Accounts receivable	1,920[b]	500	1,600	4,020
Inventory	3,000	375	1,440	4,815
Net plant and equipment	5,000	750	2,400	8,150
Investment in Instruments Napoleon, S.A.	0[c]			
Investment in Canadian Instruments, Ltd.	0[c]			
				$18,515
LIABILITIES AND NET WORTH				
Accounts payable	$2,000	$125	$640[e]	$2,765
Short-term bank loan	2,000[d]	250	660[f]	2,910
Long-term debt	3,000	250	800[g]	4,050
Capital stock	4,000	0[c]	0[c]	4,000
Retained earnings	4,790	0[c]	0[c]	4,790
				$18,515

[a]The U.S. parent has £100,000 on deposit in a London bank, carried on its books as $150,000. This amount is part of the total cash balance of $800,000 shown on the parent's books.

[b]$2,400,000 − $480,000 intracompany debt = $1,920,000.

[c]Investments in affiliates cancel with the equity of the affiliates in consolidation. If the carrying value on the books of the parent is not equal to the translated equity value of the affiliate, the difference is closed to retained earnings.

[d]Includes £200,000 carried at $300,000.

[e]Original company balance sheet amount   C$1,400,000
    less intracompany debt   − 600,000
                                                C$ 800,000
    times exchange rate ($0.80/C$)   × .80
    U.S. dollar amount $ 640,000

[f]Consists of £440,000 carried as C$825,000. C$825,000 × 0.80 = $660,000. (Alternatively, £440,000 × 1.50 = $660,000.)

[g]Consists of FF5,120,000 carried as C$1,000,000. C$1,000,000 × 0.80 = $800,000. (Alternatively, FF5,120,000/6.4 = $800,000.)

The net effect of consolidation is to create a worldwide consolidated balance sheet that reports, in U.S. dollar terms, assets of $18,515,000, liabilities of $9,725,000, and shareholders' equity of $8,790,000. As we stated earlier, the main purpose of translation is to create such a consolidated balance sheet.

Managing Accounting Exposure

The main technique to minimize accounting exposure is called a *balance sheet hedge*. At times some firms have attempted to hedge accounting exposure in the forward market. Such action amounts to speculating in the forward market in the hope a cash profit will be realized to offset the noncash loss from translation. Success depends on a precise prediction of future exchange rates, for such a hedge will not work over a range of possible future spot rates. In addition, the profit from the forward "hedge" (i.e., speculation) is taxable, but the translation loss does not reduce taxable income.

Balance Sheet Hedge Defined

A balance sheet hedge requires an equal amount of *exposed* foreign currency assets and liabilities on a firm's consolidated balance sheet. If this can be achieved for each foreign currency, net accounting exposure will be zero. A change in exchange rates will change the value of exposed liabilities in an equal but opposite direction to the change in value of exposed assets. If a firm translates by the monetary/nonmonetary method, a zero net exposed position is called *monetary balance*.

The cost of a balance sheet hedge depends on relative borrowing costs. If foreign currency borrowing costs, after adjusting for foreign exchange risk, are higher than parent currency borrowing costs, the balance sheet hedge is costly, and vice versa. Normal operations, however, already involve decisions about the magnitude and currency denomination of specific balance sheet accounts. Thus balance sheet hedges are a compromise in which the denomination of balance sheet accounts is altered, perhaps at a cost in terms of interest expense or operating efficiency, to achieve some degree of foreign exchange protection.

Balance Sheet Hedge Illustrated

To illustrate a balance sheet hedge, let us return again to the accounting exposure previously identified for Instruments Napoleon and its parent, Washington Controls. Earlier data from Exhibit 9.3 is restated in a different format in Exhibit 9.9.

Instruments Napoleon expects the French franc to drop 20% in value from its year-beginning value to a new exchange rate of FF8.00/$. Under the current rate method, the expected loss is 20% of the exposure of FF8,000,000, or FF1,600,000. At FF6.40/$, this equals the $250,000 identified in Exhibit 9.2. Under the monetary/nonmonetary method, the expected loss is 20% of the exposure of FF800,000, or FF160,000. This equals $25,000.

Exhibit 9.9   Balance Sheet Exposure: Instruments Napoleon, S.A.

	Balance Sheet Accounts	Current Rate Exposure	Monetary/ Nonmonetary Exposure
Assets			
Cash	FF1,600,000	FF1,600,000	FF1,600,000
Accounts receivable	3,200,000	3,200,000	3,200,000
Inventory	2,400,000	2,400,000	
Net plant and equipment	4,800,000	4,800,000	
Total assets	FF12,000,000		
Exposed assets		FF12,000,000	FF4,800,000
Liabilities and Capital			
Accounts payable	FF800,000	FF800,000	FF800,000
Short-term bank debt	1,600,000	1,600,000	1,600,000
Long-term debt	1,600,000	1,600,000	1,600,000
Capital stock	1,800,000		
Retained earnings	6,200,000		
Total liabilities and net worth	FF12,000,000		
Exposed liabilities		FF4,000,000	FF4,000,000
Net exposed assets in francs		FF8,000,000	FF800,000
Divide by exchange rate (FF/$)		6.4	6.4
Net exposed assets in dollars		$1,250,000	$125,000
Times amount of devaluation		× .20	× .20
Expected translation loss		$250,000	$25,000

To achieve a balance sheet hedge, Washington Controls must reduce exposed French franc assets without also reducing franc liabilities. One way to do this is to exchange existing franc cash for dollars. If Instruments Napoleon does not have large franc cash balances, it can borrow francs and exchange the borrowed francs for dollars.

Current Rate Method. Under the current rate method, up to FF8,000,000 should be borrowed. The initial effect of this first step is to increase both an exposed asset (cash) and an exposed liability (notes payable) on the balance sheet of Instruments Napoleon, with no immediate effect on *net* exposed assets. The required follow-up step can take two forms: (1) Instruments Napoleon could exchange the acquired French francs for U.S. dollars and hold those dollars itself, or (2) it could transfer the borrowed francs to Washington Controls, perhaps as a franc dividend or as repayment of intracompany debt. Washington Controls could then exchange the French francs for dollars. In some countries, of course, local monetary authorities will not allow their currency to be so freely exchanged.

Another possibility would be for Washington Controls or a sister affiliate to borrow the French francs, thus keeping the French franc debt entirely off Instrument Napoleon's books. However, the second step is still essential to eliminate French franc exposure; the borrowing entity must exchange the francs for dollars or other unexposed assets. Any such borrowing should be coordinated with all other franc borrowings to avoid the possibility that one affiliate is borrowing French francs to reduce accounting exposure at the same time as another affiliate is repaying French franc debt. (Note that francs can be "borrowed" by simply delaying repayment of existing franc debt; the goal is to increase franc debt, not borrow in a literal sense.)

Monetary/Nonmonetary Method. If translation is by the monetary/nonmonetary method, up to FF800,000 can be borrowed. As before, Instruments Napoleon could use the proceeds of the loan to acquire U.S. dollars. However, Instruments Napoleon could also use the proceeds to acquire inventory or fixed assets in France, for under the monetary/nonmonetary method these assets are not regarded as exposed and do not drop in dollar value when the franc devalues.

When Is a Balance Sheet Hedge Justified?

If a firm's subsidiary is using the local currency as the functional currency, the following circumstances could justify using a balance sheet hedge:

1. when the foreign affiliate is about to be liquidated, so the value of its CTA would be realized;
2. when the firm has debt covenants or bank agreements which state that the firm's equity/debt ratios will be maintained in specific limits;
3. when management is evaluated on the basis of certain income statement and balance sheet measures which are affected by translation losses and gains;
4. when the foreign affiliate is operating in a hyperinflationary environment.

If a firm is using the parent's home currency as the functional currency of the foreign affiliate, all translation gains/losses are passed through to the income statement. Hedging this consolidated income to reduce its variability may be important to investors and bond rating agencies.

Choice Between Minimizing Transaction or Accounting Exposure

Management will find it almost impossible to offset both accounting and transaction exposure at the same time. Reduction of one exposure usually changes the amount of the other exposure. For example, the easiest way to offset accounting exposure is to require the parent and all affiliates to denominate all exposed assets and liabilities in the parent's reporting currency. For U.S. firms and their affiliates, all assets and liabilities would be held in dollars. Such a firm would have no accounting exposure, but each affiliate would have its own transaction exposure.

To illustrate, assume a U.S. parent instructs its Japanese affiliate to bill an export to the parent in dollars. The account receivable on the Japanese affiliate's books is shown as the yen equivalent of the dollar amount, and yen profit is recorded at the time of sale. If, before the parent pays dollars to the Japanese affiliate, the yen appreciates 5%, the parent still pays only the contracted dollar amount. The Japanese affiliate receives 5% fewer yen than were expected and booked as profit. Hence the Japanese affiliate will experience a 5% foreign exchange loss on its dollar-denominated accounts receivable. Lower yen profit will eventually be translated into lower dollar profit when the affiliate's income statement is consolidated with that of the parent. Eventually the consolidated U.S.-based multinational firm will show a foreign exchange loss—on dollars!

Similar reasoning will show that if a firm chooses to eliminate transaction exposure, accounting exposure might even be increased. The easiest way to be rid of transaction exposure is to require the parent and all affiliates to denominate all accounts subject to transaction exposure in local currency. Thus every affiliate would avoid transaction gains or losses. However, each affiliate would be creating net accounting exposure by being either long or short in terms of local currency exposed assets or liabilities. The consolidated financial statement of the parent firm would show accounting exposure in each local currency.

As a general matter, firms seeking to reduce both types of exposure usually reduce transaction first, then recalculate accounting exposure (which may have changed), and then decide if any residual accounting exposure can be reduced without creating more transaction exposure. Taxes complicate the decision to seek protection against transaction or accounting exposure. Transaction losses are normally considered "realized" losses and are therefore deductible from pretax income. However, accounting losses are only "paper" losses, involve no cash flows, and are not deductible from pretax income. It is highly debatable whether protective techniques that necessitate cash payments, and so reduce net cash flow, should be incurred to avoid noncash losses.

Summary

- Accounting exposure results from translating foreign currency-denominated statements of foreign affiliates into the parent's reporting currency so the parent can prepare consolidated financial statements. Accounting exposure is the potential for loss or gain from this translation process.

- The two basic procedures for translation used in most countries today are the current rate method and the monetary/nonmonetary method. FASB 52's use of the current rate method has the advantage of insulating the firm's income statements from translation impacts (assuming foreign currency functional). The primary disadvantage is valuing fixed assets at current rates. The temporal method does value fixed assets at historical rates. Many analysts believe that what is eventually needed is a mix—a hybrid—of these two translation methods.

- Technical aspects of translation include questions of when to recognize gains or losses in the income statement, the distinction between functional and reporting currency, and the treatment of affiliates in hyperinflation countries.

- The main technique for managing accounting exposure is a balance sheet hedge. This calls for having an equal amount of exposed foreign currency assets and liabilities on a firm's balance sheet.

- Even if management chooses to follow an active policy of hedging accounting exposure, it is nearly impossible to offset both transaction and translation exposure simultaneously. If forced to choose, most managers will protect against transaction losses because these are realized cash losses, rather than protect against accounting losses, which are only book losses.

Decision Case
Computer International, Inc.[4]

William Dodenhoff had just returned from a trip to his company's corporate headquarters in the United States. Dodenhoff is the general manager of Computer International, Inc's (CI) German subsidiary. Both CI and its German subsidiary are involved in the manufacture and distribution of computer parts.

Not only is Dodenhoff suffering from jet lag, but he had received some disturbing news from his U.S. boss, Wallace Smith, that was giving him more of a headache than the jet lag. Smith had informed him that upon the advice of the firm's independent accountants, management was considering a change in the functional currency of the German subsidiary from the U.S. dollar to the German mark.

Corporate management had originally selected the U.S. dollar as the functional currency for several reasons. First, approximately 36 percent of the subsidiary's sales were intercompany sales to other subsidiaries located in Europe. Moreover, all of these sales were denominated in U.S. dollars under company policy that called for all intercompany transactions to be U.S. dollar-denominated. Second, royalty payments, which represented approximately 22 percent of the subsidiary's total expenses, were paid to various research and development divisions of the company located worldwide. Again, these payments are denominated in U.S. dollars under existing company policy. Third, the subsidiary generally remits about 15 percent of its profits to headquarters. When dividends and royalties are combined, a significant portion of the subsidiary's cash outflows are in U.S. dollars. Last, and perhaps the most important reason, management was used to reporting under the requirements of FASB Statement No. 8 and was happy with the results. If the U.S. dollar were the functional currency, their reported results would be essentially the same as under FASB Statement No. 8. Management was uncertain how the change in functional currency would affect reported results, and consequently internal performance measures. In particular, they were concerned how the change would affect trends in expenses measured in U.S. dollars. The company had recently adopted a total quality management (TQM) approach to improve profits. TQM focuses on reducing expense while improving the quality of a company's products.

Management was not concerned about the unexpected swings in income that could result from exchange gains and losses when the functional currency is the U.S. dollar. It was not anticipated that these gains and losses would have a material effect on the consolidated income because corporate headquarters hedged against such currency exposures. Even if the functional currency were the foreign currency and the translation gains and losses not recognized in income, headquarters would probably hedge the exposures because should

---

[4]Copyright 1992, Barbara L. Reed, American Graduate School of International Management, all rights reserved. This case is based on a large U.S. multinational company (i.e., a Fortune 100 company). To protect the anonymity of the firm, the industry setting and details of the case have been changed; however, the substantive issues raised are accurately portrayed.

the company decide to sell part or all of its foreign operations, the cumulative translation gain or loss would be recognized in consolidated income at the time of the sale.

While still in the United States, Dodenhoff had called Friedrich Sauer, his assistant in Germany, and asked him to prepare a report that would show how the proposed change in the functional currency would affect the subsidiary's financial statements. He had just finished reading the report and the results were worse than he had anticipated.

Dodenhoff's thoughts were interrupted by the buzzer on his desk. It was his secretary informing him his call to the United States had been completed and that Wallace Smith was on the line. He picked up the phone: "Hi, Wally; I'm glad I was able to reach you. I realize it is still early morning in the States."

"Good to hear from you; I hope the return trip to Germany was not too exhausting. What can I do for you?"

"Well, ever since I left headquarters I have been mulling over this idea about changing the functional currency, and the more I contemplate the change the more I feel confident that it is not the best way to go."

"I am interested in hearing your thoughts about the change because earlier today I talked with our independent auditors and they are pushing for the change. To be quite honest, Bill, some of the points they brought up were very convincing."

"Wally, I was just reviewing FASB Statement No. 52, and as you know, it lists several economic indicators to be used when determining the functional currency of a foreign subsidiary. According to these indicators the functional currency should be the currency of the country in which a subsidiary primarily generates and expends cash. And, as you well know, a substantial portion of our sub's operations involve intercompany sales to our other affiliates located throughout Europe. Moreover, our firm-wide policy is that the transfer price for all intercompany sales is to be denominated in U.S. dollars. In addition, we maintain extensive research and development divisions located around the world that do fundamental and advanced research in computer technology. Royalty payments made to the research and development divisions are denominated in U.S. dollars; and these royalty payments represent a substantial share of the German subsidiary's total expenses. Also, all of the dividends that we remit to headquarters are in U.S. dollars. Although we retain about 85 percent of our profits for future growth in Germany, when we do send cash to headquarters it is company policy that the cash be denominated in U.S. dollars."

"What you say may be true, Bill; however, the auditors contend that FASB No. 52 concludes that the functional currency should be the foreign currency when the foreign operations are relatively self-contained and integrated within a particular country. You may make sales to entities outside of Germany, but 45 percent of the subsidiary's sales are within Germany; and generally the sales outside of Germany are denominated in marks except for intercompany sales. Moreover, 90 percent of the piece parts and raw materials used by your subsidiary are supplied by German companies. And, as a final point, all labor and most costs—with the exception of those you mentioned—are denominated in marks, which is a key point since the subsidiary generates enough marks to cover all of its expenses and debt obligations. All in all, these factors have convinced the auditors that the German subsidiary is relatively self-contained, and consequently, that the functional currency should be the mark." (See Exhibit 9.10 for a list of the FASB's economic indicators to be used in determining the functional currency of a foreign subsidiary.)

Exhibit 9.10 Economic Indicators for Determining the Functional Currency

a. Cash flow indicators

    (1) Foreign Currency—Cash flows related to the foreign entity's individual assets and liabilities are primarily in the foreign currency and do not impact the parent company's cash flows.

    (2) Parent's Currency—Cash flows related to the foreign entity's individual assets and liabilities directly impact the parent's cash flows on a current basis and are readily available for remittance to the parent company.

b. Sales price indicators

    (1) Foreign Currency—Sales prices for the foreign entity's products are not primarily responsive on a short-term basis to changes in exchange rates but are determined more by local competition or by local government regulation.

    (2) Parent's Currency—Sales prices for the foreign entity's products are primarily responsive on a short-term basis to changes in exchange rates; for example, sales prices are determined more by worldwide competition or by international prices.

c. Sales market indicators

    (1) Foreign Currency—There is an active local sales market for the foreign entity's products, although there might also be significant amounts of exports.

    (2) Parent's Currency—The sales market is mostly in the parent's country or sales contracts are denominated in the parent's currency.

d. Expense indicators

    (1) Foreign Currency—Labor, materials, and other costs for the foreign entity's products or services are primarily local costs, even though there might also be imports from other countries.

    (2) Parent's Currency—Labor, materials and other costs for the foreign entity's products or services, on a continuing basis, are primarily costs for components obtained from the country in which the parent company is located.

e. Financing indicators

    (1) Foreign Currency—Financing is primarily denominated in foreign currency, and funds generated by the foreign entity's operations are sufficient to service existing and normally expected debt obligations.

    (2) Parent's Currency—Financing is primarily from the parent or other dollar-denominated obligations, or funds generated by the foreign entity's operations are not sufficient to service existing and normally expected debt obligations without the infusion of additional funds from the parent. Infusion of additional funds from the parent for expansion is not a factor, provided funds generated by the foreign entity's expanded operations are expected to service that additional financing.

f. Intercompany transactions and arrangements indicators

    (1) Foreign Currency—There is a low volume of intercompany transactions and there is not an extensive interrelationship between the operations of the foreign entity and the parent company. However, the foreign entity's operations may rely on the parent's affiliates' competitive advantages, such as patents and trademarks.

    (2) Parent's Currency—There is a high volume of intercompany transactions and there is an extensive interrelationship between the foreign entity and the parent company. Additionally, the parent's currency generally would be the functional currency if the foreign entity is a device or shell corporation for holding investments, obligations, intangible assets, etc., that could readily be carried on the parent's or an affiliate's books.

Source: From FASB Statement No. 52, *Foreign Currency Translation,* copyrighted by the Financial Accounting Standards Board, Norwalk, CT. Reprinted with permission.

"Nonetheless, Wally, it is our prerogative to determine the functional currency of our subsidiaries. Statement No. 52 clearly indicates that management's judgment is paramount in determining the functional currency of a subsidiary in those instances in which the indicators are mixed and the functional currency is not obvious. My best judgment is that the functional currency should be the U.S. dollar! Besides, in the past, we have used the U.S. dollar as the functional currency and the auditors have given us a clean opinion! Statement No. 52 states that once a determination of the functional currency is made, the decision should not be changed unless there are significant changes in economic facts and circumstances. And, in my opinion, there haven't been any significant changes. To switch the functional currency now could lead to the erroneous inference that we were wrong in the past, and that our previously issued financial statements were misleading—a fact that could very likely lead to a shareholder lawsuit against the company, as well as the auditors!"

"You've brought up some good points, Bill, and I promise to discuss them with the auditors. I'm having a meeting with them next week, and one of the topics on the agenda is changing the functional currency of the German subsidiary. I will present your arguments to them and, after the meeting, I'll give you a call to let you know their reaction. In the meantime, if you think of anything else you would like for me to discuss with them, give me a call."

"Thanks for being so open to my suggestions, and I will certainly give you a call if there is anything else I feel should be brought to their attention."

Dodenhoff slowly put down the phone and began reflecting on the events of the past three years. It was almost three years ago that he had been promoted to general manager of the German subsidiary. Corporate management in the United States had been dissatisfied with the prior financial performance of the German subsidiary. He had been given the charge to reduce costs since they were higher than comparable costs in any of the company's other manufacturing facilities around the world. Headquarters had also indicated that they thought the German subsidiary had the potential to generate higher sales. They had realized that it would take some time to get things turned around and had given him five years to accomplish this task.

For the past three years, Dodenhoff and his staff had worked hard to improve the sales and the cost structure of the German subsidiary. Finally, this year, it appeared that all of their efforts were going to pay off. The budgeted results indicated that profits were to be at an all time high due to increased sales and reduced costs from a more efficient use of fixed assets. (See Exhibit 9.11 for last year's actual and budgeted (pro forma) balance sheets in marks and Exhibit 9.12 for the budgeted (pro forma) income statement prepared in marks.)

In addition, return on assets (ROA)—a key performance indicator used by top management to evaluate subsidiary performance—was anticipated to be much higher than previous years. Management defined ROA as income before transaction gains and losses divided by average total assets minus current liabilities. Transaction exposures were eliminated from the calculation since headquarters hedges these exposures.

Dodenhoff was aware that the company's top executives used ROA for a variety of decision-making purposes, including the determination of bonuses for all of the firm's

Exhibit 9.11   Computer International, Inc., German Subsidiary (marks in thousands) Balance Sheets (*), 19X1

	Beginning Actual (DM)	Ending Pro Forma (DM)
Cash	50	95
Accounts Receivable, Net	201	198
Inventories	81	72
Prepaid Expenses	62	65
Total Current Assets	394	430
Property, Plant, and Equipment	390	405
Other Assets	240	240
Total Assets	1,024	1,075
Accounts Payable	88	90
Accrued Liabilities	294	290
Total Current Liabilities	382	380
Long-Term Debt	163	163
Other Liabilities	50	54
Common Stock	88	88
Retained Earnings	341	390
Total Liabilities and Stockholder Equity	1,024	1,075

*See Exhibit 9.12 for footnotes.

managerial level employees. For the first time in many years, the management of the German subsidiary was anticipating decent bonuses, and consequently, morale was high.

When Dodenhoff called his assistant Friedrich Sauer, from the United States, he had asked him to survey the firm's international bankers to obtain a forecast of expected movements in the exchange rate between the mark and the U.S. dollar for the coming year. He had instructed Sauer to use these estimates to prepare U.S. dollar pro forma financial statements for the German subsidiary under various scenarios: (1) that the U.S. dollar was the functional currency and the value of the U.S. dollar would appreciate relative to the mark; (2) that the U.S. dollar was the functional currency and the value of the U.S. dollar would depreciate relative to the mark; (3) that the mark was the functional currency and the value of the U.S. dollar would appreciate relative to the mark; and (4) that the mark was the functional currency and the value of the U.S. dollar would depreciate relative to the mark (see Exhibit 9.13). In each scenario that Sauer had developed, he found that the net income of the German subsidiary was higher when the functional currency was the U.S. dollar, largely due to the lower costs. Also, the ROA was considerably higher, as was the gross margin and return on sales percentages when the functional currency was the dollar!

Dodenhoff was concerned that the morale of his employees would be adversely affected if their bonuses were lower than anticipated. He was also concerned about the

Exhibit 9.12   Computer International, Inc., German Subsidiary Pro Forma
(Budgeted) Income Statement,* (thousands of DM)

Sales	600
Cost of sales	252
Gross profits	348
Selling, general, and administrative expenses	200
Depreciation expense	52
Operating income	96
Income taxes	38
Net income	58

Average Net Assets = ((1024–382)/(1075–380)) divided by 2 = 668.5
ROA = 58/668.5 = 8.68%

---

*Statements in Exhibits 9.12 and 9.13 were prepared according to the following assumptions:

1. Dividends—DM9,000, paid evenly over the year.

2. Fixed assets—DM67,000, purchased evenly over the year. It is company policy to take no depreciation in the year an asset is purchased and take a full year's depreciation in the year an asset is sold or scrapped. No assets were sold or scrapped this year.

3. Manufacturing costs—DM243,000; assume all costs incurred evenly over the year.

4. Beginning inventory—DM81,000; all purchased at the beginning exchange rate.

5. Ending inventory—DM72,000; all purchased at the ending exchange rate.

6. Included in selling general and administrative expenses are DM64,000 of prepaid expenses. These resulted from beginning prepaid (62,000) + purchased prepaid (67,000) − ending prepaid (65,000) = DM64,000.

7. Inventories and prepaid expenses assume a FIFO flow of costs and were purchased evenly over the year.

8. Assume no beginning and ending raw materials and work-in-process inventories.

effect that the change in functional currency would have on costs. One of his primary responsibilities had been to reduce costs, and he felt that he would have a harder time convincing top management that the cost structure had significantly improved if the functional currency were the mark. When the functional currency is the dollar, many of the subsidiary's costs are remeasured using historical exchange rates and are unaffected by exchange rate fluctuations; but when the functional currency is the foreign currency, all costs are remeasured using current exchange rates and, thus, tend to fluctuate more. In the past, top management's philosophy was that they were primarily concerned about the impact that foreign operations had on the consolidated financial statements. Therefore, their main emphasis in the evaluation process was on the financial results of the foreign subsidiaries in dollars and very little, if any, attention was devoted to the financial results calculated in the foreign currency. Dodenhoff doubted that this philosophy would change in the future. Hence, any change that affected the financial results in dollars could potentially have a large effect on the evaluation of foreign subsidiaries and their managers, and, based on Sauer's report, a change in the functional currency would not bode well for the evaluation of the German subsidiary.

In addition, management was used to evaluating him and the subsidiary when the functional currency was the dollar and he was comfortable with things as they

Exhibit 9.13 Computer International Inc., Exchange Rate Scenarios

| Case | Functional Currency | Rate Scenario | Exchange Rates | | |
			Beginning (DM/$)	Average (DM/$)	Ending (DM/$)
1	U.S. dollar	Dollar appreciates	1.58	1.70	1.90
2	U.S. dollar	Dollar depreciates	1.58	1.35	1.32
3	Deutschemark	Dollar appreciates	1.58	1.70	1.90
4	Deutschemark	Dollar depreciates	1.58	1.35	1.32

were. Sauer's report illustrated how the choice of functional currency affected the anticipated financial statements for the coming year. He also felt unsure how the change would affect the overall evaluation of the subsidiary. Currently, headquarters was responsible for hedging the transaction exposures related to the income statement. If the functional currency were the mark, a large portion of these gains and losses would be reported as translation gains and losses in stockholders' equity. Would headquarters continue to hedge the exposures if they were not reported on the income statement? If they were not hedged, would the translation gains and losses be used in the evaluation of foreign subsidiaries? These questions and others needed to be answered before Dodenhoff could feel comfortable with the change in the functional currency.

Dodenhoff decided to contact Sauer to inform him of the meeting between Smith and the auditors. Sauer and his staff could surely generate some additional arguments for not changing the functional currency. Perhaps one argument they could emphasize was that the choice of the functional currency did not really affect cash flows or the economic consequences of the underlying transactions. Any differences were simply the result of bookkeeping gains and losses. So why not use the choice that gives the subsidiary the best reported results? Dodenhoff decided to discuss this argument, and others, with his staff before calling Smith.

He looked at his watch. It was later than he thought and he had to prepare for his next appointment. He wanted to brief his staff as soon as possible about the proposed accounting change and get their feedback. He decided to have his secretary set up a meeting for the next morning.

Case Questions

1. Based on the economic indicators listed in Exhibit 9.10 and the information given in the case, according to FASB #52, should the functional currency of CI's German subsidiary be the U.S. dollar or the German mark?

2. If you were advising Dodenhoff, would you recommend he confront the auditors with the argument that any differences in net income and ROA which result from the choice of functional currency are nothing more than bookkeeping gains and losses,

and, therefore, a company is justified in choosing the functional currency that gives the best reported results?

3.   Assume the functional currency is the U.S. dollar. Using the exchange rates listed in Exhibit 9.13, calculate the expected net income of the German subsidiary in U.S. dollars (use the pro forma statements in Exhibits 9.11 and 9.12 as a starting point). Assuming the German subsidiary does not include transaction gains and losses in calculating its return on net assets, calculate the expected ROA.

You will also need the following assumed rates: purchased PP&E on beginning balance sheet, DM2.40/$; issued common stock, DM3.60/$; purchased other assets, DM2.10/$; purchased beginning prepaid expenses, ending exchange rate; purchased prepaid expenses during year, average exchange rate; ending prepaid expenses, average exchange rate.

4.   Assume the functional currency is the German mark. Using the exchange rates listed in Exhibit 9.13, calculate the expected net income of the German subsidiary in U.S. dollars as you did in question 3.

Questions

1. Instruments Napoleon (C09A.WK1)
For Instruments Napoleon (see facts in the chapter), assume the exchange rate on January 2, 1966, in Exhibit 9.2 is FF7.2/$ rather than FF8.0/$. Either on paper or using spreadsheet template C09A.WK1, recalculate Instruments Napoleon's translated balance sheet for January 2, 1996 with the new exchange rate, using both the current rate method and monetary/nonmonetary method.

   a.   Current rate method: What is the value of the CTA account now?
   b.   Monetary/nonmonetary method: What is the translation gain/loss now?
   c.   If the French franc had actually appreciated versus the U.S. dollar, say to FF4.0/$, what would the current rate's CTA value and the monetary/nonmonetary method's translation gain/loss be?

2. Instruments Napoleon (C09B.WK1)
Exhibits 9.6 and 9.7 combine to create the consolidated balance sheet for Washington Controls, Inc. Answer the following questions using the following assumed exchange rates: FF6.8/$; C$1.4$; $1.60/£.

   a.   Recalculate the entries for Exhibit 9.8's consolidated balance sheet for Washington Controls, Inc., for December 31, 1995.
   b.   How have the *values* of Instruments Napoleon and Canadian Instruments changed in the eyes of Washington Controls compared to the chapter case?

3. Functional Currency Determination
The Global View that opened this chapter described the issue of functional currency determination for U.S. multinationals and the decision of Digital to stay with the dollar.

Why do so many U.S.-based firms continue to use the U.S. dollar as the functional currency of their foreign subsidiaries although there may be economic justification for changing it?

4. Operating Exposure at Compaq Computer

Compaq, like many U.S.-based multinationals, has traditionally used the dollar as the functional currency for all of its foreign subsidiaries and sales offices. Organizationally, the U.S. parent sells the product to its foreign sales offices, billing them in U.S. dollars. The foreign sales offices in turn sell the product in the local market in local currency.

The use of the dollar as the functional currency, however, exposes Compaq's consolidated income statement to exchange rate-induced volatility. This in turn puts a lot of pressure on the treasury staff of Compaq to "smooth out" these exchange rate related fluctuations. What would you recommend a company like Compaq do to manage this problem?

5. Bayonne, S.A.

Bayonne, S.A., is the French manufacturing subsidiary of a U.S. corporation. Bayonne's balance sheet, in thousands of French francs, is as follows:

Cash	FF6,000	Accounts payable	FF9,000
A/R	8,400	Notes payable in $[b]	12,000
A/R in $[a]	9,600	Long-term debt (in FF)	10,800
Inventory	12,000		
Net plant	15,000	Shareholders' equity	19,200
Total	FF51,000	Total	FF51,000

[a]$1,600,000 (equals FF9,600,000 at current spot rate) of receivables denominated in dollars. $1,000,000 is due from unaffiliated foreign customers of Bayonne, and $600,000 is due from Bayonne's U.S. parent.

[b]All $2,000,000 (equals FF12,000,000 at current spot rate) is borrowed from a Japanese branch bank in London at 6% p.a. interest for six months. The debt can be repaid in whole or part at any time, or extended beyond the nominal six-month maturity.

Current spot exchange rate:	FF6.00/$.
Six-month forward exchange rate:	FF6.30/$.
Management's forecast of spot rate in six months:	FF6.60/$.

    a. What is Bayonne's accounting/translation exposure by the current rate method? That is, what are its net exposed assets?

    b. If the franc depreciates as expected by management, what will Bayonne contribute to its parent's accounting/translation loss or gain?

    c. What transaction exposure exists on the books of Bayonne, and what will be Bayonne's transaction loss or gain should the French franc depreciate as expected?

    d. Bayonne can borrow French francs in France at 9% per annum interest. What might it do to reduce transaction exposure to exactly zero with a refinancing? Assuming the franc depreciates as management expects, what is the cash consequence (cost or saving) of this alternative?

    e. Would Bayonne be better off to hedge its net transaction exposure in the forward market (rather than engage in a franc refinancing)? Explain, and show benefit of one over the other.

f. Assume that Bayonne hedges its net transaction exposure with a franc refinancing. After such a hedge, what is Bayonne's remaining accounting (translation) exposure?

6. Hyperinflation and FAS #52

Why does FAS #52 allow firms with operating subsidiaries in currencies of countries experiencing a cumulative 100% inflation rate to use the temporal method? Why does FAS #52 use inflation as the determinate, and not the percentage change in the exchange rate?

7. Vivaldi Spice, BHD

Vivaldi Spice, BHD, purchases, processes, and packages spices at its plantation in Java. Vivaldi is the wholly owned subsidiary (100%) of Four Seasons Spice, Inc., of Los Angeles.

Vivaldi's functional currency is the Indonesian rupiah, which currently sells at Rp2,000 per U.S. dollar. Four Seasons's reporting currency is the U.S. dollar. Nonconsolidated financial statements for Vivaldi and Four Seasons are as follows:

	Four Seasons	Vivaldi, BHD
Cash	$80,000	Rp200,000,000
Accts receivable[a]	120,000	400,000,000
Inventory	80,000	300,000,000
Net plant	160,000	80,000,000
Investment in Vivaldi	90,000	
	$530,000	Rp980,000,000
Current liabilities[a]	$200,000	Rp400,000,000
Five-year term loan[b]		400,000,000
Common stock	80,000	100,000,000
Retained earnings	250,000	80,000,000
	$530,000	Rp980,000,000

[a]Four Seasons owes its Vivaldi subsidiary Rp 300,000,000 on open account for imports. The debt is denominated in rupiahs, and is carried on Four Seasons's books at $150,000.

[b]The entire term loan is for $200,000 and is denominated in U.S. dollars. The loan is from a London bank, and is not guaranteed by Four Seasons.

a. Prepare a consolidated balance sheet for Four Seasons and its Vivaldi subsidiary.

b. What is Four Seasons's translation exposure in its Indonesian subsidiary? Use the current rate method of calculation.

c. Before any business activities take place, the Indonesian rupiah depreciates 10% in value relative to the dollar. What is the new spot rate?

d. What is Four Seasons's translation loss or gain, if any, after the devaluation? Four Seasons uses the current rate method.

e. How would this be reported on Four Seasons's current balance sheet and income statement under FASB #52?

f. From a financial policy point of view, what (if anything) is Four Seasons/Vivaldi doing well, vis-à-vis any type of foreign exchange exposure?

g. From a financial policy point of view, what (if anything) is Four Seasons/Vivaldi doing poorly, vis-à-vis any type of foreign exchange exposure?

Bibliography

Adler, Michael, "Translation Methods and Operational Foreign Exchange Risk Management," in *International Financial Management,* Göran Bergendahl, ed., Stockholm: Norstedt & Soners, 1982, pp. 87–103.

———, and Bernard Dumas, "Should Exposure Management Depend on Translation Accounting Methods?" *Euromoney,* June 1981, pp. 132–138.

Aliber, R. Z., and C. P. Stickney, "Accounting Measures of Foreign Exchange Exposure: The Long and Short of It," *Accounting Review,* January 1975, pp. 44–57.

Arnold, Jerry L., and William W. Holder, *Impact of Statement 52 on Decisions, Financial Reports, and Attitudes,* Morristown, N.J.: Financial Executives Research Foundation, 1986.

Choi, Frederick D. S., Howard D. Lowe, and Reginald G. Worthley, "Accountors, Accountants, and Standard No. 8," *Journal of International Business Studies,* Fall 1978, pp. 81–87.

Choi, Jong Moo Jay, "Accounting Valuation and Economic Hedging of Foreign Inventory Under Exchange and Inflation Risk," in *Advances in Working Capital Management,* vol. 2, JAI Press, 1991.

Collier, Paul A., E.W. Davis, J.B. Coates, and S.G. Longden, "Policies Employed in the Management of Currency Risk: A Case Study Analysis of US and UK," *Managerial Finance,* vol. 18, no. 3, 1992, pp. 41–52.

Eaker, M. R., "The Numeraire Problem and Foreign Exchange Risk," *Journal of Finance,* May 1981, pp. 419–426.

Evans, Thomas G., and Timothy S. Doupnik, *Determining the Functional Currency Under Statement 52,* Stamford, Conn.: Financial Accounting Standards Board, 1986.

———, *Foreign Exchange Risk Management Under Statement 52,* Stamford, Conn.: Financial Accounting Standards Board, 1986.

Evans, Thomas G., William R. Folks, Jr., and Michael Jilling, *The Impact of Statement of Financial Accounting Standards No. 8 on the Foreign Exchange Management Practices of American Multinationals: An Economic Impact Study,* Stamford, Conn.: Financial Accounting Standards Board, November 1978.

Financial Accounting Standards Board, *Accounting for the Translation of Foreign Currency Transactions and Foreign Currency Financial Statements, Statement of Financial Accounting Standards No. 8,* October 1975, Stamford, Conn.: Financial Accounting Standards Board, 1975. Reprinted, except for Appendix D, in *Journal of Accountancy,* December 1975, pp. 78–89.

———, *Foreign Currency Translation, Statement of Financial Accounting Standards No. 52,* December 1981, Stamford, Conn.: Financial Accounting Standards Board, 1981.

Garlicki, T. Dessa, Frank J. Fabozzi, and Robert Fonfeder, "The Impact of Earnings Under FASB 52 on Equity Returns," *Financial Management,* Autumn 1987, pp. 36–44.

Harris, Trevor S., "Foreign Currency Transactions and Translation," Chapter 16 in *Handbook of International Accounting,* Frederick D. S. Choi, ed., New York: Wiley, 1991.

Houston, Carol Olson, "Translation Exposure Hedging Post SFAS No. 52," *Journal of International Financial Management and Accounting,* vol. 2, nos. 2 and 3, Summer and Autumn 1990, pp. 145–170.

Ijiri, Yuji, "Foreign Currency Accounting and Its Transition," in *Management of Foreign Exchange Risk,* R. J. Herring, ed., Cambridge, England: Cambridge University Press, 1983.

Malindretos, John, Edgar Norton, and Demetri Tsanacas, "Hedging Considerations Under FAS #52," *Mid-Atlantic Journal of Business,* vol. 29, no. 2, June 1993, pp. 199–211.

Newhausen, Benjamin S., "Consolidated Financial Statements and Joint Venture Accounting," Chapter 15 in *Handbook of International Accounting,* Frederick D. S. Choi, ed., New York: Wiley, 1991.

Rayburn, Frank R., and G. Michael Crooch, "Currency Translation and the Funds Statement: A New Approach," *Journal of Accountancy,* October 1983, pp. 51–62.

Rezaee, Zabihollah, R.P. Malone, and Russell F. Briner, "Capital Market Response to SFAS Nos. 8 and 52; Professional Adaptation," *Journal of Accounting, Auditing & Finance,* vol. 8, no. 3, Summer 1993, pp. 313–332.

Rosenfield, Paul, "Accounting for Foreign Operations," *Journal of Accountancy,* August 1987, pp. 103–112.

Ross, Derek, "Investors: For or Against Translation Hedging?," *Accountancy,* vol. 109, no. 1182, February 1992, p. 100.

Ruland, Robert G., and Timothy S. Doupnik, "Foreign Currency Translation and the Behavior of Exchange Rates," *Journal of International Business Studies,* Fall 1988, pp. 461–476.

Sapy-Mazello, Jean-Pierre, Robert M. Woo, and James Czechowicz, *New Directions in Managing Currency Risk: Changing Corporate Strategies and Systems Under FAS No. 52,* New York: Business International, 1982.

Sheikholeslami, Mehdi, "A Profile Analysis of the Predictability of Accounting Earnings Numbers After FAS 52," *Journal of Applied Business Research,* vol. 8, no. 2, Spring 1992, pp. 31–35.

Taussig, Russell A., "Impact of SFAS No. 52 on the Translation of Foreign Financial Statements of Companies in Highly Inflationary Economies," *Journal of Accounting, Auditing and Finance,* Winter 1983, pp. 142–156.

Chapter 10
Internationalizing the Cost of Capital

Global View
Foreign Firms Tap U.S. Capital Markets

New York—Foreign companies are falling in love with American finance.

The latest illustration of the widespread appeal of U.S. capital markets is Daimler-Benz AG's decision to list its shares on the New York Stock exchange, beginning today. To qualify for listing, the diversified German auto maker had to undertake a costly, excruciating revision of its accounting practices that 2 1/2 weeks ago caused a $592 million first-half loss, the company's first since World War II.

American investment bankers who stand to profit by arranging financing for foreign companies are understandably gleeful. That Daimler was willing to subject itself to America's rigorous accounting rules to get on the Big Board makes a fundamental shift in the way U.S. financial markets are viewed abroad, they say.

With all the foreign interest in listing stock on U.S. markets, why the hoopla about Daimler's decision? As with other German and Swiss giants, Daimler's long history of steady profits can be attributed partly to its ability to massage its financial statements through off-the-books "hidden reserves." Whenever product demand slackens and operating losses develop, these companies tap the reserves, built up from earlier earnings, to offset the loss and show a modest profit.

But "hidden reserves" are anathema to the SEC, which has steadfastly maintained that the only way Daimler or any other German or Swiss company could get a Big Board listing was to disclose the reserves and their effects on profits. For three acrimonious years, that issue had stalemated negotiations between the SEC and several big German companies. Finally, last March, Daimler broke, pushed by its need for capital.

Arthur Levitt Jr. [SEC Chairman] . . . says he is concerned about the enormous costs that foreign companies face when translating their financial data to the U.S.

format. "I regard foreign listings as one of my top two priorities," says Mr. Levitt, who also hopes to increase public confidence in the debt markets.

If Mr. Levitt doesn't make it easier for foreign companies to enter the U.S. markets, they will go elsewhere, some observers say. "There are some 200 global companies with multibillion-dollar sales, which would easily qualify for listing on the New York Stock Exchange—and that is where they belong," says William Freund, a former chief economist at the Big Board. "But unless they have a financial reason like Daimler-Benz, I don't think they will. And if they don't, the New York Stock Exchange will be consigned to a secondary role among world markets."

Source: Adapted from Anita Raghavan and Michael R. Sesit, "Financing Boom: Foreign Firms Raise More and More Money in the U.S. Markets," 10/5/93, A1, A9. Reprinted by permission of *The Wall Street Journal*, © 1993 Dow Jones & Co., Inc. All rights reserved worldwide

How can firms take advantage of the rapidly developing global capital market in order to lower their cost of capital and increase its availability? That is the subject of the next five chapters.

The purpose of this chapter is to explain the theoretical arguments for expecting firms to benefit from gaining access to global capital markets. The two main arguments are based on improving *market liquidity* and taking advantage of opportunities arising from *capital market segmentation*. Chapter 11 analyzes how a firm can design an optimal financial structure given access to global markets. Chapters 12 and 13 explain exactly how a firm can source equity and debt in global markets. Chapter 14, which concludes Part 4, analyzes how a firm can manage its interest rate risk on a global scale.

The approach taken in this chapter assumes you have a basic understanding of the theory of a weighted average cost of capital. A brief review of the theory is provided in the appendix to this chapter for those in need of a refresher.

It is also assumed in this chapter that the main beneficiaries of access to global capital markets are multinational firms. They usually enjoy the necessary size and worldwide operational visibility to attract foreign investors to buy and trade in their securities. Large, purely domestic firms can theoretically achieve the same benefits from global sourcing of capital, but lack of a physical presence abroad is sometimes a barrier to attracting foreign investors.

Improving Market Liquidity

Although no consensus exists about the definition of *market liquidity*, it can be observed by noting the degree to which a firm can issue a new security without depressing the existing market price, as well as the degree to which a change in price of its securities elicits a substantial order flow.

Exhibit 10.1   Availability of Funds and the Cost of Capital

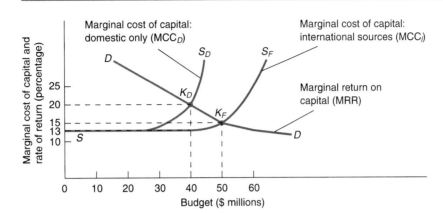

If the multinational firm has access to additional sources of capital outside an illiquid domestic capital market, the marginal cost of capital shifts to the right, and the firm can raise more capital at lower cost.

In the domestic case an underlying assumption is that total availability of capital to a firm is determined at any time by supply and demand in the domestic capital markets. A firm should always expand its capital budget by raising funds in the same proportion as its optimal financial structure, but as its budget expands in absolute terms, its marginal cost of capital will eventually increase. In other words, a firm can only tap the capital market for some limited amount in the short run before suppliers of capital balk at providing further funds, even if the same optimal financial structure is preserved. In the long run this may not be a limitation, depending on market liquidity.

In the multinational case a firm is able to improve market liquidity by raising funds in the Euromarkets (money, bond, and equity), by directed security issues in individual national capital markets, and by tapping local capital markets through foreign affiliates.[1] Such activity should logically expand the capacity of a multinational firm to raise funds in the short run over what might have been raised if the firm were limited to its home capital market. This situation assumes the firm's optimal financial structure is preserved. Exhibit 10.1 shows how the availability of capital in international markets helps the multinational firm obtain a lower marginal cost of capital and a larger budget than might otherwise have been the case.

Exhibit 10.1 shows that the multinational firm has a given marginal return on capital at different budget levels, represented in the line DD. This demand is determined by ranking potential projects according to net present value or internal rate of return. Percentage rate of return to both users and suppliers of capital is shown on the vertical scale. If the

[1]The full menu of possible sources of funds and the means to tap them are the subject of Chapters 12 and 13.

firm is limited to raising funds in its domestic market, the line SS_D shows the marginal domestic cost of capital (vertical axis) at various budget levels (horizontal axis). Remember that the firm continues to maintain the same debt ratio as it expands its budget, so that financial risk does not change. The optimal budget in the domestic case is $40 million, where the marginal return on capital (MRR) just equals the marginal cost of capital (MCC_D). At this budget the marginal domestic cost of capital, K_D, would be equal to 20%.

If the multinational firm has access to additional sources of capital outside an illiquid domestic capital market, the marginal cost of capital should shift to the right, as shown by line SS_F in Exhibit 10.1. In other words, foreign markets can be tapped for long-term funds at times when the domestic market is saturated because of heavy use by other borrowers or equity issuers, or is unable to absorb another issue of the multinational firm in the short run. Exhibit 10.1 shows that by a tap of foreign capital markets the marginal international cost of capital, K_F, has been reduced to 15%, even while an additional $10 million is raised. This assumes that about $20 million is raised abroad, since only about $30 million could be raised domestically at a 15% cost of capital.

Overcoming Market Segmentation

Capital market segmentation is a major imperfection. Firms resident in a segmented market need to source capital abroad to lower their cost of capital and improve their market liquidity.

Definition of Market Segmentation

A national capital market is segmented if the required rate of return on securities in that market differs from the required rate of return on securities of comparable expected return and risk that are traded on other national securities markets (New York and London, for example). On the other hand, if all capital markets are fully integrated, securities of comparable expected return and risk should have the same required rate of return in each national market after adjusting for foreign exchange risk and political risk. This definition applies to both equity and debt, although it often happens that one or the other may be more integrated than its counterpart.

Market Efficiency in a Segmented Market

A national securities market can be efficient in a domestic context and yet segmented in an international context. According to finance theory, a market is efficient if security prices in that market reflect all available relevant information and adjust quickly to any new relevant information. Therefore the price of an individual security reflects its "intrinsic value," and any price fluctuations will be "random walks" around this value. This statement assumes transaction costs are low, many participants are in the market, and these participants have sufficient financial strength to move security prices. Empirical tests of market efficiency have been conducted on most of the major European securities markets, Japan, Canada, and, of course, the United States. The results show that most of these markets are reasonably efficient.

An efficient national securities market might very well "correctly price" all securities traded in that market on the basis of information available to the investors who participate in that market. However, if that market is segmented, foreign investors would not be participants. Thus securities in the segmented market would be priced on the basis of domestic rather than international standards.

What Causes a National Capital Market to Be Segmented?

Market segmentation is a financial market imperfection caused by government constraints and investor perceptions. The most important imperfections are as follows:

1. information barriers
2. regulatory barriers
3. transaction costs
4. foreign exchange risk
5. takeover defenses
6. small country bias
7. political risk

Information Barriers. The main information barriers are language, accounting principles, and quality of disclosure. In order to tap international equity and debt markets, a selling prospectus must normally be prepared in English. Any unusual local accounting principles must be reconciled with international norms, such as U.K. or U.S. standards, or standards of the market in which the securities will be sold. The level of disclosure that will give comfort to foreign investors is often higher than would normally be required for a purely domestic issue.

Regulatory Barriers. Taxation of capital gains and losses varies dramatically from country to country. Some countries have no capital gains tax; others, such as the United States, have taxes as high as 28%.

Restrictions on the amount of shares foreigners can own still exist in a number of countries, even highly developed ones such as Sweden, Norway, Switzerland, and Finland. Virtually no restrictions on capital movements exist any longer in the industrial countries, but do exist in the second- and third-tier markets, such as South Korea, Taiwan, Indonesia, and most of Latin America.

Transaction Costs. Taxes imposed on securities transactions are a quick way to segment a market. Both Germany and Sweden recently discovered this painful lesson. When taxes were imposed the securities business simply fled to other capital markets, usually London, thereby impoverishing the German and Swedish brokerage business. The taxes were soon rescinded or modified.

High quotation spreads or fixed brokerage commissions, and lack of competition among brokers, are another way to segment a local market. The business simply is transacted in other markets.

Foreign Exchange Risk. An exceptionally volatile exchange rate, or one that always depreciates, is not conducive to attracting long-term foreign investors. Lack of a liquid forward market, or derivative markets, makes such a market even less attractive and thus more segmented.

Takeover Defenses. As explained in Chapter 1, the non-Anglo-American markets are not characterized by the one-share-one-vote rule and they have numerous other takeover defenses. Normally it is the "B" shares, one with less voting rights, which are sold to the public, including foreigners. This means that any "takeover premium," which might have shown up in an Anglo-American market's valuation of "A" shares, will not be part of the B share's valuation.

Small Country Bias. Small country capital markets lack economies of scale and scope. International institutional investors are interested in being able to make block purchases, but even more important, they want to be able to liquidate them easily. The small country markets are usually too illiquid to handle these transaction sizes easily. Furthermore, there are often not enough investment grade securities to warrant the attention of the international institutional investors. There are too few publicly traded firms in attractive industries, too many government-owned firms that would be privatized elsewhere, and the best firms are often still privately held.

Political Risk. Fear of government intervention or other unpredictable political behavior is a sure way to segment a capital market. Capital market laws are just now evolving in the former Eastern Bloc countries as they try to leap to a market economy. The judicial systems to enforce these laws lag a bit, even on such simple matters as enforcing a contract. Until the legal and political infrastructure is in place, and believable, these markets will remain the most segmented of all today. However, they appear to be moving in the right direction.

Effect of Market Segmentation on the Cost of Capital

The degree to which capital markets are segmented may have an important influence on a firm's cost of capital. At one extreme, if a firm is sourcing its capital in a fully segmented market, it is likely to have a higher cost of capital than if it had access to other capital markets. However, as we show later, a firm may be able to overcome this disadvantage by adopting financial policies that give it access to other capital markets.[2]

---

[2]The corporate financial policy implications for firms residing in segmented capital markets were investigated by Stapleton and Subrahmanyam. They concluded:

> In most cases, the effect of segmenting capital markets is to depress security prices and also to produce an incentive for corporations to increase the diversification opportunities available to investors. Three corporate financial policies that effectively reduce the effects of segmented markets are:
> a. Foreign portfolio/direct investment by firms.
> b. Mergers with foreign firms.
> c. Dual listing of the securities of the firm on foreign capital markets.

Richard C. Stapleton and Marti G. Subrahmanyam, "Market Imperfections, Capital Market Equilibrium, and Corporation Finance," *Journal of Finance*, May 1977, p. 317.

From a managerial perspective the difference between sourcing capital in a segmented versus integrated capital market can be shown diagrammatically by using the same example as we used in Exhibit 10.1. Exhibit 10.2 shows how escaping from dependence on a segmented capital market can lower a firm's cost of capital. The line $S'S_U$ represents the decreased marginal cost of capital for a firm that has gained access to other capital markets. As a result of the combined effects of greater availability of capital and international pricing of the firm's securities, the marginal cost of capital, K_U, declines to 13%, and the optimal capital budget climbs to $60 million.

Most of the tests of market segmentation suffer from the usual problem for model builders, namely, the need to abstract from reality in order to have a testable model. In our opinion a realistic test would be to observe what happens to a single security's price when it has been traded only in a domestic market, is "discovered" by foreign investors, and then is traded in a foreign market. Arbitrage should keep the market price equal in both markets. However, if during the transition one observes a significant change in the security's price uncorrelated with price movements in either of the underlying securities markets, one may infer the domestic market was segmented.

In academic circles tests based on case studies are often considered to be "casual empiricism," since no theory or model exists to explain what is being observed. Nevertheless, something may be learned from such cases, just as scientists learn from observing nature in an uncontrolled environment. Furthermore, case studies that preserve real

Exhibit 10.2   Market Segmentation and the Cost of Capital

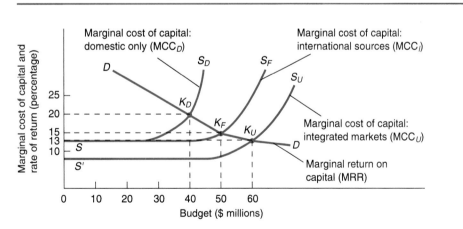

A firm that raises capital on international markets shifts the marginal cost of capital from SS_D to SS_F due to the favorable effect on the liquidity of its securities (see Exhibit 10.1). If, however, the firm not only escapes the illiquid domestic capital market but also is successful in having its securities integrated and priced on international markets, the marginal cost of capital shifts down and further right to $S'S_U$. The firm now has access to lower cost capital over the entire budget range.

world complications may illustrate specific kinds of barriers to market integration and ways in which they might be overcome.

Unfortunately, few case studies have been documented where a firm has "escaped" from a segmented capital market. In practice, escape usually means listing on a foreign stock market such as New York or London and/or selling securities in foreign capital markets. We illustrate what can be learned from a case study by using the example of Novo Industri A/S, a Danish firm.

Novo Industri A/S (Novo)[3]

Novo is a Danish multinational firm that produces industrial enzymes and pharmaceuticals (mostly insulin). In 1977, Novo's management decided to internationalize its capital structure and sources of funds. This decision was based on the observation that the Danish securities market was both illiquid and segmented from international markets. In particular, the lack of availability and the high cost of equity capital in Denmark resulted in Novo having a higher cost of capital than its main multinational competitors, Eli Lilly (United States), Miles Laboratories (United States, owned by Bayer, Germany), and Gist Brocades (the Netherlands).

Apart from the cost of capital, Novo's projected growth opportunities signaled an eventual need to raise new long-term capital beyond what could be raised in the limited Danish market. Since Novo is a world technology leader in its specialties, planned capital investments in plant, equipment, and research could not be postponed until internal financing from cash flow became available. Novo's competitors would preempt any markets not served by Novo.

Even if an equity issue of the size required could have been raised in Denmark, the required rate of return would have been unacceptably high. For example, Novo's price/earnings ratio was typically around 5; that of its foreign competitors was well over 10. Yet Novo's business and financial risk appeared to be about equal to that of its competitors. A price/earnings ratio of 5 appeared appropriate for Novo only within a domestic Danish context when Novo was compared with other domestic firms of comparable business and financial risk.

If Denmark's securities market were integrated with world markets, one would normally expect foreign investors to rush in and buy "undervalued" Danish securities. In that case firms like Novo would enjoy an international cost of capital comparable to that of their foreign competitors. Strangely enough, no Danish government restrictions existed that would have prevented foreign investors from holding Danish securities.

---

[3]The Novo case material is a condensed version of Arthur Stonehill and Kåre B. Dullum, *Internationalizing the Cost of Capital in Theory and Practice: The Novo Experience and National Policy Implications*, Copenhagen: Nyt Nordisk Forlag Arnold Busck, 1982; and New York: Wiley, 1982. Reprinted with permission. Novo Industri A/S acquired its main European competitor, Nordisk Insulin (also Danish), after this book was written. The name was changed to Novo-Nordisk. It is today the largest producer of insulin and industrial enzymes in the world. It has sold successfully several more equity issues in the United States at higher prices.

Therefore one must look for investor perception as the main cause of market segmentation in Denmark at that time.

At least six characteristics of the Danish securities market were responsible for market segmentation:

1. Disparity in the information base of Danish and foreign investors.

2. Taxation.

3. Alternative sets of feasible portfolios.

4. Financial risk.

5. Foreign exchange risk.

6. Political risk.

Disparity in the Information Base

Certain Danish institutional characteristics caused Danish and foreign investors to be uninformed about each other's equity securities. The most important information barrier was the Danish regulation that prohibited Danish investors from holding foreign private sector securities. Therefore Danish investors had no incentive to follow developments in foreign securities markets or to factor such information into their evaluation of Danish securities. As a result, Danish securities might have been priced correctly in the efficient market sense relative to each other, considering the Danish information base, but priced incorrectly considering the combined foreign and Danish information base. Another detrimental effect of this regulation was that foreign securities firms did not locate offices or personnel in Denmark, since they had no product to sell. Lack of a physical presence in Denmark reduced the ability of foreign securities analysts to follow Danish securities.

A second information barrier was lack of enough security analysts who followed Danish securities. Only one professional Danish securities analysis service was published (Børsinformationen), and that was in the Danish language. A few Danish institutional investors employed in-house analysts, but their findings were not available to the public. Almost no foreign security analysts followed Danish securities because they had no product to sell and the Danish market was too small (small country bias).

Other information barriers included language and accounting principles. Naturally financial information was normally published in Danish, using Danish accounting principles. A few firms, such as Novo, published English versions, but almost none used U.S. or British accounting principles or attempted to show any reconciliation with such principles.

Taxation

Danish taxation policy had all but eliminated investment in common stock by individuals. Until a tax law change in July 1981, capital gains on shares held for over two years were taxed at a 50% rate. Shares held for less than two years, or for "speculative" purposes, were taxed at personal income tax rates, with the top marginal rate being 75%. In contrast, capital gains on bonds were tax free. This situation resulted in bonds being issued at deep discounts because the redemption at par at maturity was considered a capital gain. Thus most individual investors held bonds rather than stocks. This factor reduced the liquidity of the stock market and increased the required rate of return on stocks if they were to compete with bonds.

Feasible Set of Portfolios

Because of the prohibition on foreign security ownership at the time, Danish investors had a very limited set of securities from which to choose a portfolio. In practice, Danish institutional portfolios were composed of Danish stocks, government bonds, and mortgage bonds. Since Danish stock price movements are closely correlated with each other, Danish portfolios possessed a rather high level of systematic risk. In addition, government policy had been to provide a relatively high real rate of return on government bonds after adjusting for inflation. The net result of taxation policies on individuals and attractive real yields on government bonds was that required rates of returns on stocks were relatively high by international standards.

From a portfolio perspective Danish stocks provide an opportunity for foreign investors to diversify internationally. If Danish stock price movements were not closely correlated with world stock price movements, inclusion of Danish stocks in foreign portfolios should reduce their systematic risk. Furthermore, foreign investors are not subject to the high Danish income tax rates, since they are normally protected by tax treaties, which typically limit their taxes to 15% on dividends and capital gains. As a result of the international diversification potential, foreign investors might require a lower rate of return on Danish stocks than Danish investors, other things being equal. However, other things may not be equal because foreign investors may perceive Danish stocks to carry more financial, foreign exchange, and political risk than their own domestic securities.

Financial, Foreign Exchange, and Political Risks

Financial leverage utilized by Danish firms is relatively high by U.S. and U.K. standards but not abnormal for Scandinavia, Germany, Italy, and Japan. In addition, most of the debt is short term, with variable interest rates. Just how foreign investors would view financial risk in Danish firms depends on what norms they follow in their home countries. We know from Novo's experience in tapping the Eurobond market in 1978 that Morgan Grenfell, their British investment bankers, were eager for Novo to maintain a debt ratio (debt/total capitalization) closer to 50% rather than the traditional Danish 65 to 70%.

Foreign investors in Danish securities are subject to foreign exchange risk. Whether this is a plus or a minus factor depends on the investor's home currency, perception about the future strength of the krone, and its impact on a firm's operating exposure. Through personal contacts with foreign investors and bankers, Novo's management did not believe foreign exchange risk was a factor in Novo's stock price because their operations were perceived as being well diversified internationally.

From the same interviews, with respect to political risk, Denmark was perceived as a stable Western democracy but with the potential to cause periodic problems for foreign investors. In particular, Denmark's national debt was regarded as too high for comfort, although this judgment had not yet shown up in the form of risk premiums on Denmark's Eurocurrency syndicated loans. The other threat perceived by foreign investors was that Denmark would move toward implementing "economic democracy" in a more substantial manner. Economic democracy would result in a mandatory profit-sharing plan whereby a central fund, governed by labor unions, would eventually become a major shareholder in private sector firms. Despite these general concerns about Denmark's political situation, investors in Novo in particular indicated that their evaluation of Novo's prospects was not influenced by political risk.

The Road to Internationalization

Although Novo's management in 1977 wished to escape from the shackles of Denmark's segmented and illiquid capital market, many barriers had to be overcome. It is worthwhile to describe some of these, since they typify the barriers faced by other firms from segmented markets that wish to internationalize their capital sources.

Closing the Information Gap. Novo had been a family-owned firm from its founding in the 1920s by the two Petersen brothers until 1974, when it went public and listed its "B" shares on the Copenhagen Stock Exchange. (The "A" shares were held by the Novo Foundation; the "A" shares were sufficient to maintain voting control.) However, Novo was essentially unknown in investment circles outside Denmark. To overcome this disparity in the information base, Novo increased the level of its financial and technical disclosure in both Danish and English versions. This procedure was aided in late 1977 by Grieveson, Grant and Company, a British stock brokerage firm, which had started to follow Novo's stock and issued the first professional securities analysis report about Novo in English.

The Eurobond Issue. The information gap was further closed when Morgan Guaranty Trust Company of New York, Novo's main foreign commercial banker, was consulted about alternative strategies to tap international capital markets. Its advice was to try a Eurobond issue. It then introduced Novo to Morgan Grenfell, a leading U.K. investment bank, which confirmed the recommended strategy. In 1978, Morgan Grenfell successfully organized a syndicate to underwrite and sell a $20 million convertible Eurobond issue for Novo. In connection with this offering Novo listed its shares on the London Stock Exchange to facilitate conversion and to gain visibility. These twin actions were the keys to dissolving the information barrier, and, of course, they also raised a large amount of long-term capital on favorable terms, which would have been unavailable in Denmark.

Despite the favorable impact of the Eurobond issue on availability of capital, Novo's cost of capital actually increased when Danish investors reacted negatively to the potential dilution effect of the conversion right. During 1979 Novo's share price declined from around DKr300 per share to around DKr200–225 per share.

The Biotechnology Boom. During 1979 a fortuitous event occurred. Biotechnology began to attract the interest of the U.S. investment community, with several sensationally oversubscribed stock issues by such start-up firms as Genentech and Cetus. Thanks to the aforementioned information gap, Danish investors were unaware of these events and continued to value Novo at a low price/earnings ratio of 5, compared with over 10 for its established competitors and 30 or more for these new potential competitors.

At this point Novo felt it had to position itself with its customers in the U.S. market as a firm that had a proven track record in biotechnology, in contrast to the "blue sky" promises of the recent start-up firms. A failure to do so could lead to the faulty conclusion that Novo was not at the forefront in technology. Therefore, to protect its customer base, Novo organized a seminar in New York City on April 30, 1980. About 40 journalists and financial analysts attended the seminar. Soon after the seminar a few sophisticated individual U.S. investors began buying Novo's shares and convertibles through the London Stock Exchange. Danish investors were only too happy to supply this foreign demand. Therefore, despite relatively strong demand from U.S. and British investors, Novo's share price increased only gradually, reaching back to the DKr300 level by midsummer. However, during the following months foreign interest began to snowball, and by the end of 1980 Novo's share price had reached the DKr600 level. Moreover, foreign investors had increased their proportion of share ownership from virtually nothing to around 30%. Novo's price/earnings ratio had risen to around 16, which was now in line with those of its international competitors but not with those of the Danish market. At this point one must conclude that Novo had succeeded in internationalizing its cost of capital. Other Danish securities remained locked in a segmented capital market. Exhibit 10.3 shows that the movement in the Danish stock market in general did not parallel the rise in Novo's share price, nor could it be explained by movement in the U.S. or U.K. stock markets as a whole.

Improving Liquidity: Sponsoring the ADR System. To improve the liquidity of its shares held by U.S. investors and to increase the availability of capital by tapping the U.S. new issues market, Novo decided to sponsor an American depositary receipts (ADR) system in the United States, have its shares quoted on the over-the-counter market (NASDAQ), and retain a U.S. investment banker to advise it about a U.S. share issue. Goldman Sachs was selected for this purpose. Morgan Guaranty Trust Company of New York established the ADR system in April 1981. Novo's shares were split five for one in the U.S. market by issuing five times as many American depositary shares as there were underlying Danish kroner shares held in the bank.

A Directed Share Issue in the United States. During the first half of 1981, under the guidance of Goldman Sachs and with the assistance of Morgan Grenfell and Copenhagen Handelsbank, Novo prepared a prospectus for SEC registration of a U.S. share offering and eventual listing on the New York Stock Exchange. The main barriers encountered in this effort, which would have general applicability, were connected with preparing financial statements that could be reconciled with U.S. accounting principles and the higher level of disclosure required by the SEC. In particular, industry segment reporting was a problem both from a disclosure perspective and an accounting perspective because the accounting data were not available internally in that format. As it turned out, the investment barriers in the United States were relatively tractable, although expensive and time consuming to overcome.

The more serious barriers were caused by a variety of institutional and government regulations in Denmark. The latter were never designed so firms could issue shares at

Exhibit 10.3   Nova's B-Share Prices Compared to Stock Market Indices

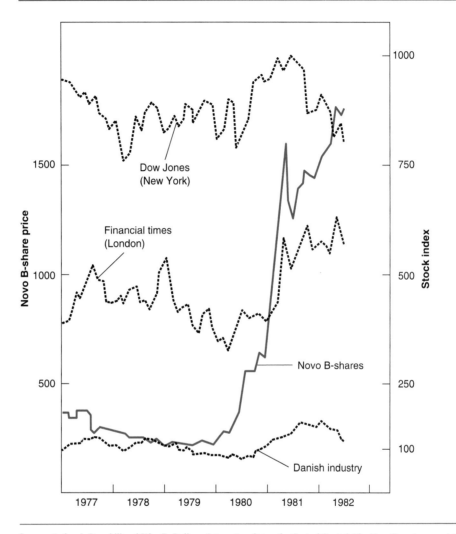

Source: Arthur I. Stonehill and Kåre B. Dullum, *Internationalizing the Cost of Capital: The Novo Experience and National Policy Implications*, John Wiley, London, 1982, p. 73. Reprinted with permission.

market value, since Danish firms typically issued shares at par value with preemptive rights. Even Novo's own shareholders had to be educated about the value of giving up their preemptive rights, but by this time Novo's share price, driven by continued foreign buying, was so high that virtually nobody in Denmark thought it was worth the price foreigners were willing to pay. In fact, prior to the time of the share issue in July 1981, Novo's share price had risen to over DKr1,500, before settling down to a level around DKr1,400. Foreign ownership had increased to over 50% of the shares outstanding!

Market segmentation was very apparent during the first half of 1981. Published and unpublished reports by Danish security analysts, bankers, and the popular press consistently claimed Novo was seriously overvalued while their foreign counterparts were consistently touting Novo as undervalued. The difference in views was based partly on investor perceptions of the importance of biotechnology and Novo's role in this field.

Stock Market Reactions. One final piece of evidence on market segmentation can be gleaned from the way Danish and foreign investors reacted to the announcement of the proposed $61 million U.S. share issue on May 29, 1981. Novo's share price dropped 156 points in Copenhagen, equal to about 10% of its market value. As soon as trading started in New York six hours later, the share price immediately recovered all its loss. The Copenhagen reaction was typical for an illiquid market. Investors worried about the dilution effect of the new share issue, since it would increase the number of shares outstanding by about 8%. They did not believe Novo could invest the new funds at a rate of return that would not dilute future earnings per share. They also feared the U.S. shares would eventually flow back to Copenhagen if biotechnology lost its glitter.

The U.S. reaction to the announcement of the new share issue was consistent with what one would expect in a liquid and efficient market. U.S. investors viewed the new issue as creating additional demand for the shares as Novo became more visible because of the selling efforts of a large aggressive syndicate. Furthermore, the marketing effort was directed at institutional investors who were previously underrepresented among Novo's U.S. investors. They had been underrepresented because U.S. institutional investors want to be ensured of a liquid market so they may get out, if desired, without depressing the share price. The wide distribution effected by the new issue, plus SEC registration and a New York Stock Exchange listing, all added up to more liquidity and an international cost of capital.

Novo Postscript.   Segmented capital markets do not last forever. Partly as a result of the Novo experience, Denmark soon removed any remaining regulatory barriers, especially the restriction on Danes owning foreign securities. The Danish stock market was reformed with its own "big bang" in the mid-1980s. As a result, Danish investors became much more sophisticated and their investment portfolios became internationalized. Foreign share issues by Danish firms in the 1990s have had no favorable effect on share price. This provides anecdotal evidence that the Danish equity market is now integrated with other world capital markets.

Are Capital Markets Segmented Today?

No national capital market has always been fully segmented or fully integrated with world markets at all times. The capital markets of most industrial countries, including Japan, Hong Kong, and Singapore, are much more integrated today than they were even

10 years ago.[4] A second tier of markets, including Latin America, the Middle East, and Southeast Asia, is moving rapidly toward capital market integration with the industrial countries. Even China, the republics of the former Soviet Union, and eastern Europe are moving from nearly complete segmentation toward eventual integration.

The Daimler Benz Experience

Although Denmark's small capital market is no longer segmented, other capital markets, even large and liquid ones, still show some signs of residual capital market segmentation today. For example, Daimler Benz's share price increased 30% following its announcement on October 5, 1993 that it intended to list on the NYSE (see *Global View*). This was a far greater increase than experienced by either the German or U.S. stock market indexes during the same time period. It could only have happened if the German and U.S. stock markets were partly segmented from each other, because U.S. and other foreign investors could always have bought Daimler Benz on the Frankfurt Stock Exchange where it was listed. Investors must have anticipated that by listing on the NYSE the shares would be more liquid, more convenient to trade, and subject to fuller disclosure of Daimler Benz's operating results.

Media Coverage

Further anecdotal evidence can be gleaned from the vastly increased amount of media coverage of foreign stock, bond, and derivative markets, and the impressive increase in international portfolio investment (see Chapter 20). Examples of expanded media coverage can be found daily in the financial press and on such television stations as CNN, Skynews, and the BBC. Investors can now easily follow events and stock market indexes in a variety of foreign markets rather than just their domestic markets. For example, Exhibit 10.4 shows the daily report entitled "Stock Market Indexes" that is published in the *Wall Street Journal*.

Summary

- Gaining access to global capital markets should allow a firm to lower its cost of capital. This can be achieved by increasing the market liquidity of its shares and, where relevant, escaping from a capital market that is segmented.

---

[4]Some recent tests concluding that capital markets are becoming more integrated are reported in the following: M. Wayne Marr, John L. Trimble, and Raj Varma, "On the Integration of International Capital Markets: Evidence from Euro-equity Offerings," *Financial Management*, Winter 1991, pp. 11–21; S. Wheatley, "Some Tests of International Equity Integration," *Journal of Financial Economics*, September 1989, pp. 177–212; Alan Alford and William R. Folks, Jr., "A Test for Increased Capital Market Integration," *Financial Review*, forthcoming; Mustafa N. Gultekin, N. Bulent Gultekin, and Alessandro Penati, "Capital Controls and International Capital Market Segmentation: The Evidence from the Japanese and American Stockmarkets," *Journal of Finance*, Sept. 1989, pp. 849–869.

Exhibit 10.4   Stock Market Indexes

Exchange	1/13/94 Close	Net Chg	Pct Chg
Tokyo Nikkei 225 Average	18577.26	−216.62	−1.15
Tokyo Nikkei 300 Index	277.07	−1.79	−0.64
Tokyo Topix Index	1503.47	−7.96	−0.53
London FT 30-share	2577.4	+3.2	+0.12
London 100-share	3360	−12	−0.36
London Gold Mines	242.9	−17.9	−6.86
Frankfurt DAX	2164.66	−44.52	−2.02
Zurich Swiss Market	2949.6	−50.3	−1.68
Paris CAC 40	2252.19	−29.17	−1.30
Milan Stock Index	968	−2	−0.21
Amsterdam ANP-CBS General	282.9	−1.0	−0.35
Stockholm Affarsvarlden	1487.5	+5.4	+0.36
Brussels Bel-20 Index	1473.32	−16.59	−1.11
Australia All Ordinaries	2175.2	−20.4	−0.93
Hong Kong Hang Seng	10176.51	−536.22	−5.01
Singapore Straits Times	2194.86	−65.45	−2.90
Johannesburg J'burg Gold	2060	−98	−4.54
Madrid General Index	331.26	+0.42	+0.13
Mexico I.P.C.	2535.58	−29.75	−1.16
Toronto 300 Composite	4479.90	+25.21	+0.57
Euro, Aust, Far East MSCI-p	973.5	−12.0	−1.22

p = Preliminary

Source: *Wall Street Journal*, January 14, 1994, p. C12.

- A firm is able to increase its market liquidity by raising funds in the Euromarkets, by directed security issues in individual national capital markets, and by tapping local capital markets through foreign affiliates. Increased market liquidity causes the marginal cost of capital line to "flatten out to the right." This results in the firm being able to raise more capital at the same low marginal cost of capital, and thereby justify investing in more capital projects.

- A national capital market is segmented if the required rate of return on securities in that market differs from the required rate of return on securities of comparable expected return and risk that are traded on other national securities markets.

- A national securities market might be "efficient" in a domestic context but segmented from other national markets if foreign investors are not participants.

- Capital market segmentation is a financial market imperfection caused by government constraints and investor perceptions. The most important imperfections are (1) information barriers, (2) regulatory barriers, (3) transaction costs, (4) foreign exchange risk, (5) takeover defenses, (6) small country bias, and (7) political risk.

- If a firm is resident in a segmented capital market it can still escape from this market by sourcing its debt and equity abroad. The result should be a lower marginal cost of capital, improved liquidity for its shares, and a larger capital budget.

- Novo, a Danish multinational firm, was able to escape the shackles of its segmented national capital market. Its strategy was to close the information gap by becoming more visible to foreign investors. It also sponsored an ADR system for its U.S. shareholders. Novo eventually reaped the full benefit of its dramatic share price increase by selling an equity issue in the United States at a high price, and listing on the New York and London Stock Exchanges.

- Segmented capital markets do not stay segmented forever. Although the Daimler Benz listing on the NYSE in 1983 suggested that the German and U.S. stock markets are segmented from each other, today anecdotal and research evidence indicates that markets are indeed becoming more integrated.

Questions

1. Suislaw Corporation

Suislaw Corporation, a large U.S. manufacturing firm, wants to finance an $80 million expansion. Suislaw wants a capital structure that is 50% debt and 50% equity. Its corporate combined federal and state income tax rate is 40%.

Suislaw finds that it can finance in the U.S. domestic market at the following rates. Both debt and equity would have to be sold in multiples of $10 million, and these cost figures show the component costs in increments of $5 million, raised half by equity and half by debt.

	Cost of Domestic Equity	Cost of Domestic Debt
Up to $20 million of new capital:	12%	8%
$21 to $40 million of new capital:	16%	12%
$41 to $60 million of new capital:	22%	16%

A London bank advises Suislaw that funds could be raised in London in the Eurodollar market at the following costs, in multiples of $5 million and the 50/50 capital structure preserved.

	Cost of Euro-equity	Cost of Euro-debt
Up to $20 million of new capital:	14%	6%
$21 to $40 million of new capital:	14%	10%
$41 to $60 million of new capital:	24%	18%

Each increment of cost would be influenced by the total amount of capital raised. That is, if Suislaw first borrowed $10 million in the Eurodollar market at 6% and matched this with an additional $10 million of equity, additional debt would cost 12% in the United States and 10% in Europe. The same relationship holds for equity financing.

    a.   Calculate the lowest average cost of capital for each increment of $20 million of new capital, where Suislaw raises $10 million in the equity market and an additional $10 million in the debt market at the same time.

    b.   If Suislaw plans an expansion of $40 million, how should that expansion be financed? What will be the weighted average cost of capital for the expansion?

2. Segmented Capital Markets

Pick a country that you believe has a segmented capital market. Explain why you believe this market is segmented. Are there any firms within this country that have a chance to internationalize their cost of capital by raising capital outside of this country? If so, how should they proceed?

3. Japanese Cost of Capital

Some critics claimed the Japanese capital market was not well integrated with other capital markets during the 1980s. Yet it was also claimed that Japanese firms enjoyed a lower cost of capital than their foreign competitors. Explain this apparent "anomaly."

4. South Korea and Multinational Firms

South Korea is home to a number of large multinational firms such as Daewoo, Samsung, and Lucky Goldstar. Although restrictions may be loosening, up until now foreign investors cannot purchase common stock in Korean companies, including these well-known multinationals. On the other hand, foreign investors can purchase shares of the Korea Fund, which is an officially sanctioned mutual fund of Korean shares. The Korea Fund has typically sold at a substantial premium over the market value of its underlying shares.

    a.   Explain how the restrictions on foreign ownership probably influence the cost of capital of Daewoo, Samsung, and Lucky Goldstar.

    b.   What needs to be done by these firms to lower their cost of capital?

    c.   What needs to be done by South Korea to unsegment their equity market?

    d.   Why do you think South Korea prevented direct foreign ownership in the first place?

5. Corporate Taxation and the WACC

Governments set tax rates and determine what cash flows and expenditures of firms are tax deductible and which are not. Interest expenses on debt are nearly universally accepted as deductible expenses of the firm. How could a particular government alter their tax rates or their tax deductibility policies to aid lower domestic firms' cost of capital and in some ways then aid these firms' international competitiveness?

6. Cost of Capital for Emerging Markets

Firms resident in emerging capital markets, such as South Korea, Thailand, and Indonesia, could be candidates for lowering their cost of capital. What needs to be done by these firms and their countries of origin in order for them to achieve this result?

7. Valdivia Vineyards

Valdivia Vineyards of Chile was recently acquired by Sauvignon Winery of Napa, California. At present Valdivia is paying 50% p.a. interest on Ps100 million of five-year, balloon maturity, peso debt; but it would be possible to refinance this into dollar debt costing only 10% p.a., saving some 40 percentage points over the cost of peso debt.

All Valdivia's wine is exported to the United States, where it is sold for dollars. Valdivia is allowed by Chilean regulations to use hard currency earned to pay hard currency expenses, including interest.

The current exchange rate is Ps32/$, and both Chile and the United States have a 35% corporate income tax. Because of Chile's high inflation, you expect the exchange rate to drop to Ps48/$ one year from now, and to continue to deteriorate thereafter at the same rate.

a. As assistant financial manager of Sauvignon Winery in charge of the Latin American Beverage Division, you wonder if you should refinance Valdivia's Chilean peso debt into dollars.

b. Would your answer be different if all of Valdivia's sales were within Chile? (Explain and show calculation.)

Bibliography

Abbott, Ashok B., and K. Victor Chow, "Cointegration Among European Equity Markets," *Journal of Multinational Financial Management,* vol. 2, no. 3/4, 1993, pp. 167–184.

Adler, Michael, "The Cost of Capital and Valuation of a Two-Country Firm," *Journal of Finance,* March 1974, pp. 119–132.

———, and Bernard Dumas, "International Portfolio Choice and Corporation Finance: A Synthesis," *Journal of Finance,* June 1983, pp. 925–984.

Bonser-Neal, Catherine, Greggory Brauer, Robert Neal, and Simon Wheatley, "International Investment Restrictions and Closed-End Country Fund Prices," *Journal of Finance,* June 1990, pp. 523–548.

Booth, Laurence David, "Taxes, Funds Positioning, and the Cost of Capital for Multinationals," *Advances in Financial Planning and Forecasting,* vol. 4, part B, 1990, pp. 245–270.

Choi, Jongmoo Jay, "Diversification, Exchange Risk, and Corporate International Investment," *Journal of International Business Studies,* Spring 1989, pp. 145–155.

———, "A Model of Firm Valuation with Exchange Exposure," *Journal of International Business Studies,* Summer 1986, pp. 145–152.

Choi, Jongmoo Jay and Alan Severn, "On the Effects of International Risk, Segmentation and Diversification on the Cost of Equity Capital: A Critical Review and Synthesis," *Journal of Multinational Financial Management,* vol. 1, Issue 3, 1991, 1–19.

Cohn, Richard A., and John J. Pringle, "Imperfections in International Financial Markets: Implications for Risk Premia and the Cost of Capital to Firms," *Journal of Finance,* March 1973, pp. 59–66.

Constand, Richard L., Lewis P. Freitas, and Michael J. Sullivan, "Factors Affecting Price Earnings

Ratios and Market Values of Japanese Firms," *Financial Management*, Winter 1991, pp. 68–79.

Doukas, John, and Nickolaos G. Travlos, "The Effect of Corporate Multinationalism on Shareholders' Wealth: Evidence from International Acquisitions," *Journal of Finance*, December 1988, pp. 1161–1175.

Errunza, Vihang R., and Lemma W. Senbet, "The Effects of International Operations on the Market Value of the Firm: Theory and Evidence," *Journal of Finance*, May 1981, pp. 401–417.

———, "International Corporate Diversification, Market Valuation, and Size-Adjusted Evidence," *Journal of Finance*, July 1984, pp. 727–743.

Fatemi, Ali M., "The Effect of International Diversification on Corporate Financing Policy," *Journal of Business Records*, vol. 16, no. 1, January 1988, pp. 17–30.

Frankel, J. A., "The Japanese Cost of Finance: A Survey," *Financial Management*, Spring 1991, pp. 95–127.

Friend, Irwin, and Ichiro Tokutsu, "The Cost of Capital to Corporations in Japan and the U.S.A.," *Journal of Banking and Finance*, vol. 11, no. 2, June 1987, pp. 313–328.

Gultekin, Mustafa N., N. Bulent Gultekin, and Alessandro Penati, "Capital Controls and International Capital Market Segmentation: The Evidence from the Japanese and American Stock Markets," *Journal of Finance*, September 1989, pp. 849–869.

Hodder, James E., and Adrian E. Tschoegl, "Some Aspects of Japanese Corporate Finance," *Journal of Financial and Quantitative Analysis*, June 1985, pp. 173–191.

Hughes, John S., Dennis E. Logue, and Richard J. Sweeney, "Corporate International Diversification and Market Assigned Measures of Risk and Diversification," *Journal of Financial and Quantitative Analysis*, November 1975, pp. 627–637.

Jacque, Laurent, and Gabriel Hawawini, "Myths and Realities of the Global Market for Capital: Lessons for Financial Managers," *Journal of Applied Corporate Finance*, vol. 6, no. 3, 1993, pp. 81–90.

Kester, W. Carl, "Capital and Ownership Structure: A Comparison of United States and Japanese Manufacturing Corporations," *Financial Management*, Spring 1986, pp. 5–16.

Lee, W. Y., and K. S. Sachdeva, "The Role of the Multinational Firm in the Integration of Segmented Capital Markets," *Journal of Finance*, May 1977, pp. 479–492.

Lessard, Donald R., "Finance and Global Competition: Exploiting Financial Scope and Coping with Volatile Exchange Rates," *Midland Corporate Finance Journal*, Fall 1986, pp. 6–29.

Marr, M. Wayne, John L. Trimble, and Raj Varma, "On the Integration of International Capital Markets: Evidence from Euro-equity Offerings," *Financial Management*, Winter 1991, pp. 11–21.

McCauley, R. N., and S. A. Zimmer, "Explaining International Differences in the Cost of Capital," *Federal Reserve Bank of New York Quarterly Review*, Summer 1989, pp. 7–28.

Stapleton, Richard C., and Marti Subrahmanyam, "Market Imperfections, Capital Asset Equilibrium, and Corporation Finance," *Journal of Finance*, May 1977, pp. 307–319.

Stonehill, Arthur, and Kåre B. Dullum, *Internationalizing the Cost of Capital in Theory and Practice: The Novo Experience and National Policy Implications*, Copenhagen: Nyt Nordisk Forlag Arnold Busck, 1982; and London: Wiley, 1982.

Stulz, Rene M., "On the Effects of Barriers to International Investment," *Journal of Finance*, September 1981, pp. 923–933.

Wheatley, S., "Some Tests of International Equity Integration," *Journal of Financial Economics*, September 1989, pp. 177–212.

Chapter 10 Appendix
Weighted Average Cost of Capital

A firm's weighted average cost of capital is normally found by combining the cost of equity with the cost of debt in proportion to the relative weight of each in the firm's optimal long-term financial structure. More specifically,

$$K_{\text{wacc}} = K_e \frac{E}{V} + K_d (1 - t) \frac{D}{V},$$

where K_{wacc} = weighted average after-tax cost of capital,
  K_e = risk-adjusted cost of equity,
  K_d = before-tax cost of debt,
  t = marginal tax rate,
  E = market value of the firm's equity,
  D = market value of the firm's debt,
  V = total market value of the firm's securities $(E + D)$.

Cost of Equity

The cost of equity for a firm can be measured in at least two different ways. The traditional approach, called the dividend capitalization model, measures the cost of equity by the following formula:

$$K_e = \frac{D_1}{P_0} + g,$$

where K_e = required return on equity,
  D_1 = expected dividends per share during year 1,
  P_0 = market value per share at time zero (beginning of year 1),
  g = expected growth rate of dividends or market price of a share of stock.

The traditional approach assumes the required return on equity is determined by the market's preferred trade-off between risk and return. Risk is typically defined as either the standard deviation, σ, of returns on a share or the coefficient of variation, γ, of returns on a share.

The capital asset pricing model approach is to define the cost of equity for a firm (security) by the following formula:

$$K_e = K_{rf} + \beta (K_m - K_{rf}),$$

where K_e = expected (required) rate of return on equity,
  K_{rf} = rate of interest on risk-free bonds (Treasury bills, for example),
  β = coefficient of systematic risk for the firm,

K_m = expected (required) rate of return on the market portfolio of stocks (Standard & Poor's 500 Index, for example).

The main difference between the two approaches to cost of equity is that the dividend capitalization model emphasizes the total risk of expected returns, whereas the capital asset pricing model emphasizes only the systematic risk of expected returns. As detailed in Chapter 20, systematic risk is a function of the total variability of expected returns of the firm relative to the market index and the degree to which the variability of expected returns of the firm is correlated to the expected returns on the market index. Empirical studies show that both approaches to the cost of equity have some validity, depending on the sample and time period tested. In any case, the important point is that the cost of equity is some function of the market's preference for return and risk, however risk is defined.

Cost of Debt

The normal procedure for measuring the cost of debt for a domestic firm requires a forecast of domestic interest rates for the next few years, the proportions of various classes of debt the firm expects to use, and the domestic corporate income tax rate. The interest costs of the different debt components are then averaged according to their proportion in the debt structure. This before-tax average, K_d, is then adjusted for corporate income taxes by multiplying it by the expression [1 − the tax rate], that is, $K_d(1 - t)$, to find the weighted average after-tax cost of debt.

The weighted average cost of capital is normally used as the risk-adjusted discount rate whenever a firm's new projects are in the same general risk class as its existing projects. On the other hand, a project-specific required rate of return should be used as the discount rate if a new project differs from existing projects in business or financial risk.

Taxation and the Cost of Retained Earnings and Depreciation

A multinational firm is subject to taxation both in the home market and in each host country in which it has affiliates or a commercial presence. Tax planning is the subject of Chapter 21, but for the moment we are interested in how it affects the calculation of cost of capital.

The way in which a parent firm's country of domicile taxes the firm's foreign-source income may have an effect on the cost of equity. Normally the cost of funds from retained earnings and depreciation is considered to be about equal to the cost of equity from new issues of common stock, if we ignore the transactions costs involved in underwriting new issues. In the U.S. multinational case, however, earnings retained in foreign subsidiaries are not subject to U.S. corporate income tax, foreign withholding taxes, or transfer costs until those earnings are repatriated. Walter Ness has pointed out that this tax deferral privilege should therefore reduce the cost of equity for retained earnings of subsidiaries by the value of the tax deferral.[5] (This should also logically include funds

---

[5]Walter L. Ness, Jr., "U.S. Corporate Income Taxation and the Dividend Remittance Policy of Multinational Corporations," *Journal of International Business Studies*, Spring 1975, pp. 67–77.

retained due to the depreciation tax shield.) Thus Ness feels the overall cost of equity for a U.S. multinational firm should be adjusted downward to reflect the advantage of tax deferral on retained earnings in subsidiaries.

One can contest this viewpoint on the grounds that U.S. multinational firms have many methods other than dividends of repatriating funds or repositioning them abroad. These methods, which are discussed in Chapter 22, include transfer pricing, fees and royalties, intracompany loans, and leads and lags. In most cases they do not involve payment of either the U.S. corporate income tax or foreign withholding tax on dividends. Therefore little difference exists between retained earnings and any other form of equity from the consolidated firm's viewpoint. Investors have already taken the tax deferral advantage into consideration when setting their required return on a multinational firm's equity. What is true, however, is that the U.S. multinational firm may in fact enjoy an effective overall tax rate that is lower than 35% as long as payment of the U.S. corporate income tax is deferred by efficient positioning of funds. Theoretically, of course, these funds might someday be returned to the parent and eventually the shareholders as a "final liquidating dividend," but in the meantime the U.S. Treasury is making an interest-free loan on the deferred taxes.

Taxation and the Cost of Debt

Determining the effective tax impact on the cost of debt for a multinational firm is complicated. First, the tax manager must forecast tax rates in each market in which the firm intends to borrow. Second, the deductibility of interest by each national tax authority must be determined. In some countries, such as the United Kingdom, interest paid to related foreign affiliates is not tax deductible. Third, a determination must be made of which legal entities are most cost effective as borrowers. Fourth, any tax deferral privilege must be considered, although this has the same counterargument as we made for tax deferral on retained earnings. Fifth, foreign exchange gains and losses must be anticipated when interest and loan repayments are made.

Chapter 11
Designing the Financial Structure

Global View
Capital and Ownership Structure

After adjusting for accounting reserves and liquid assets, Japanese manufacturing is not as highly leveraged as it might first appear. Indeed, on a market value basis there is no significant country difference in leverage between U.S. and Japanese manufacturing after controlling for characteristics such as growth, profitability, risk, size and industry classification.

While a significant country difference exists when leverage is measured on a book value basis, this result is concentrated among the mature, capital-intensive industries. It does not appear to be a general characteristic common to all Japanese manufacturing.

The foregoing notwithstanding, it must still be recognized that the composition of Japanese capital and ownership structure is quite different from that commonly observed in the United States. Moreover, it is different in ways that could result in a competitive advantage for Japanese corporations even if the overall degree of leverage is not significantly different. By blunting incentives to engage in asset substitution or to underinvest, the rolling over of short-term bank loans and the substantial ownership of equity by major lenders are effective means of promoting optimal investment while funding heavily with debt.

Source: Excerpted from W. Carl Kester, "Capital and Ownership Structure: A Comparison of United States and Japanese Manufacturing Corporations," *Financial Management*, Spring 1986, p. 15. Reprinted with permission.

The theory of optimal financial structure must be modified considerably to encompass the multinational firm. A number of new variables must be taken into account:

1. How does international availability of capital affect the optimal debt ratio of a multinational firm?

2. Can financial risk for a multinational firm be reduced through international diversification of cash flows?

3. What should be the finance structures of foreign affiliates, taking into consideration varying country norms, availability of funds, foreign exchange risk, political risk, and tax minimization?

After a brief review of the domestic theory of optimal financial structure, we treat each of these questions in order.

Theory of Optimal Financial Structure

After many years of debate, finance theorists still disagree on whether or not an optimal financial structure exists for a firm, and if so, how it can be determined. The great debate between the so-called traditionalists and the Modigliani and Miller school of thought has apparently ended in a compromise theory. When taxes and bankruptcy costs are considered, a firm has an optimal financial structure determined by that particular mix of debt and equity that minimizes the firm's cost of capital for a given level of business risk. If the business risk of new projects differs from the risk of existing projects, the optimal mix of debt and equity would change to recognize tradeoffs between business and financial risks.

Exhibit 11.1 illustrates how the cost of capital varies with the amount of debt employed. As the debt ratio, defined as total debt divided by total assets, increases, the overall cost of capital (K_{wacc}) decreases because of the heavier weight of low-cost debt $[K_d(1 - t)]$ compared to high-cost equity (K_e). The low cost of debt is, of course, due to the tax deductibility of interest shown by the term $(1 - t)$.

Partly offsetting the favorable effect of more debt is an increase in the cost of equity (K_e), because investors perceive greater financial risk. Nevertheless, the overall weighted average after-tax cost of capital (K_{wacc}) continues to decline as the debt ratio increases, until financial risk becomes so serious that investors and management alike perceive a real danger of insolvency. This result causes a sharp increase in the cost of new debt and equity, thus increasing the weighted average cost of capital. The low point on the resulting U-shaped cost of capital curve, which is at 14% in Exhibit 11.1, defines the debt ratio at which the cost of capital is minimized.

Most theorists believe the low point is actually a rather broad flat area encompassing a wide range of debt ratios, 30% to 60% in Exhibit 11.1, where little difference exists in the cost of capital. They also believe that, at least in the United States, the range of the flat area and the location of a particular firm's debt ratio within that range are determined by a variety of noncost variables. Two such variables have an important effect on the financial structure of multinational firms, namely, availability of capital and financial risk. These are discussed in the next two sections.

Exhibit 11.1   Cost of Capital and Financial Structure

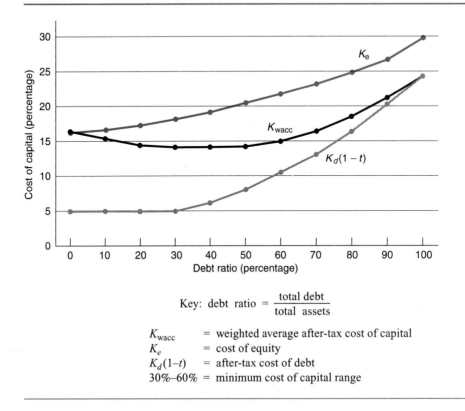

Key: debt ratio $= \dfrac{\text{total debt}}{\text{total assets}}$

K_{wacc} = weighted average after-tax cost of capital
K_e = cost of equity
$K_d(1-t)$ = after-tax cost of debt
30%–60% = minimum cost of capital range

Availability of Capital

We saw in Chapter 10 that international availability of capital to a multinational firm may allow it to lower its cost of equity and debt compared with most domestic firms. In addition, international availability permits a multinational firm to maintain its desired debt ratio, even when significant amounts of new funds must be raised. In other words, a multinational firm's marginal cost of capital is constant for considerable ranges of its capital budget. This statement is not true for most small domestic firms because they do not have access to the national equity or debt markets. They must either rely on internally generated funds or borrow short and medium term from commercial banks.

Multinational firms domiciled in countries that have illiquid equity markets are in almost the same situation as small domestic firms. They must rely on internally generated funds and bank borrowing, although the larger non-U.S. multinationals also have access to Eurobond and foreign bond markets. If they need to raise significant amounts of new funds to finance growth opportunities, they may need to borrow more than would be optimal from the viewpoint of minimizing their cost of capital. This is equivalent to saying that their marginal cost of capital is increasing at higher budget levels.

As an illustration of the effect of availability of capital on optimal financial structure and the marginal cost of capital, Exhibit 11.2 presents a graphic comparison between a U.S. multinational firm and either a non-U.S. multinational firm that faces an illiquid equity market at home or a small domestic U.S. firm.

In Exhibit 11.2(a) a U.S. multinational firm is depicted as enjoying a constant marginal cost of capital at all levels of its likely capital budget. Thus it is able to raise funds in the proportion desired for minimizing its cost of capital (K_{wacc}). In this example it can minimize its cost of capital by choosing any debt ratio between 30% and 60%, which is the lowest (flat) part of its cost of capital curve. If it chooses 45%, for example, it can raise all the funds it needs in the proportion of 45% debt and 55% equity without raising the cost of these funds. Even if internally generated funds are insufficient to maintain this proportion,

Exhibit 11.2   Cost of Capital and Financial Structure: Constant Versus Rising
Marginal Cost of Capital

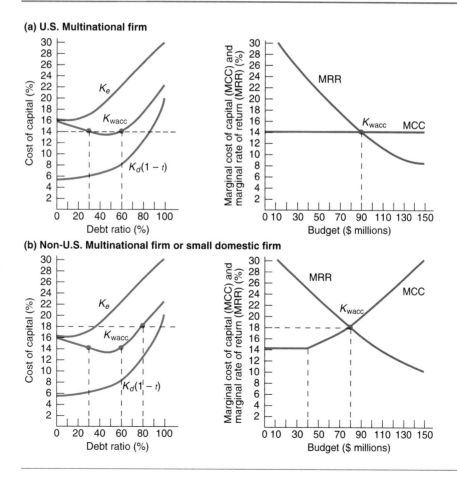

it can sell new equity at about the same price as its existing equity. The optimal capital budget for the U.S. multinational firm in this example happens to be $90 million (Exhibit 11.2a). This is the point where its marginal return on capital just equals its marginal cost of capital. In other words, if it ranks all capital budgeting projects according to their internal rate of return (IRR), the last project to be accepted would be the one whose IRR just equals the firm's 14% marginal weighted average after-tax cost of capital (K_{wacc}).

Neither the non-U.S. multinational firm, which is assumed not to have access to a liquid national equity market, nor the small U.S. domestic firm can raise funds in the proportions desired to minimize their cost of capital (K_{wacc}). Yet they are assumed to have the same relationship between their cost of capital (K_{wacc}) and their debt ratios as the U.S. multinational firm. In other words, the left-hand graphs are identical (Exhibits 11.2a and 11.2b). Furthermore, all three firms are assumed to face the same opportunities, represented by the marginal return on capital curves (MRR). The difference is that the non-U.S. multinational firm and small U.S. domestic firm can maintain their optimal debt ratio range (30% to 60%) only for capital budgets up to $40 million (Exhibit 11.2b, right side). At that point they have committed all their internally generated funds plus the optimal proportion of additional debt. If they wish to reach their optimal budget, which is $80 million, they must borrow all the remaining $40 million. Neither firm can raise $40 million in its national equity markets, except perhaps at exorbitant rates or with unacceptable loss of control. Nevertheless, despite increasing their debt ratios to 80%, and thus their cost of capital (K_{wacc}) to 18%, both firms should borrow the additional $40 million in order to realize their profit potential. Their profit potential is maximized at the point in the capital budget where the marginal return on capital (MRR) equals the marginal cost of capital (MCC) (Exhibit 11.2b, right side).

Note that not only do the non-U.S. multinational firm and the U.S. domestic firm have a higher cost of capital, which is 18% compared to 14% for the U.S. multinational firm, but their optimal capital budget is lower, $80 million compared to $90 million for the U.S. multinational firm. Thus it is not surprising that financial market imperfections have been cited frequently in this book as factors that give U.S. multinational corporations an advantage over U.S. domestic firms or non-U.S. multinationals that do not have access to liquid equity markets. It should also be noted, however, that a number of large non-U.S. multinational firms do indeed have access to U.S. equity markets for new issues and are also listed on U.S. stock markets. Furthermore, the equity markets in the United Kingdom are considered to be fairly liquid, and equity markets in the European Union and Japan are rapidly improving.

Financial Risk Reduction Through International Diversification of Cash Flows

The theoretical possibility exists that multinational firms are in a better position than domestic firms to support higher debt ratios because their cash flows are diversified internationally. The probability of a firm covering fixed charges under varying conditions in product, financial, and foreign exchange markets should improve if the variability of its cash flows is minimized.

By diversifying cash flows internationally, the multinational firm might be able to achieve the same kind of reduction in cash flow variability as portfolio investors receive from diversifying their security holdings internationally. The same argument applies, namely, that returns are not perfectly correlated between countries. For example, in 1993 the economies of Germany and Japan were in recession, but the United States was experiencing acceptable growth. Therefore one might have expected returns, on either a cash flow or an earnings basis, to be depressed in Germany and Japan while being favorable in the United States. A multinational firm with operations located in all three of these countries could rely on its strong U.S. cash inflow to cover debt obligations, even if the German and Japanese affiliates produced weak net cash inflows.

In contrast, a domestic German firm would not enjoy the benefit of cash flow international diversification but would have to rely entirely on its own depressed net cash inflow from domestic operations. Perceived financial risk for the German firm would have been greater than for a multinational firm because the variability of its German domestic cash flows could not be offset by positive cash flows elsewhere in the world.

Despite the theoretical elegance of these arguments, a study by Kwang Lee and Chuck Kwok came to the opposite conclusion.[1] They found that, after adjusting for size, multinational firms actually have a lower debt ratio than their domestic equivalents.[2] Despite international diversification of cash flows, bankruptcy risk was about the same for multinational and domestic firms. However, agency costs of debt were higher for the multinational firms as a result of political risks, market imperfections, and the complexity of international operations. These costs led to a lower debt ratio for multinational firms.

Financial Structure of Foreign Affiliates

If one accepts the theory that minimizing the cost of capital for a given level of business risk and capital budget is an objective that should be implemented from the perspective of the consolidated multinational firm, then the financial structure of each affiliate is relevant only to the extent that it affects this overall goal. In other words, an individual affiliate does not really have an independent cost of capital, and therefore its finance structure should not be based on an objective of minimizing its own independent cost of capital.

On the other hand, market imperfections and national institutional constraints dictate that variables other than minimizing the cost of capital are often major determinants

---

[1] Kwang Chul Lee and Chuck C. Y. Kwok, "Multinational Corporations vs. Domestic Corporations: International Environmental Factors and Determinants of Capital Structure," *Journal of International Business Studies*, Summer 1988, pp. 195–217. This article summarizes Lee's doctoral dissertation, which was supervised by Kwok at the University of South Carolina and won the Academy of International Business's outstanding dissertation award for 1986.

[2] The fact that multinational firms have a lower debt ratio than equivalent domestic firms was also a conclusion of an article by Allen Michel and Israel Shaked, "Multinational Corporations vs. Domestic Corporations: Financial Performance and Characteristics," *Journal of International Business Studies*, Fall 1986, pp. 89–100.

of debt ratios for firms in many capital markets. A question is thus raised about whether a multinational firm should consider these country norms that are not related to cost when it establishes finance structures for its foreign affiliates. In order to answer this question, we present some empirical findings that describe financial structure norms in representative countries. Then we analyze whether a multinational firm should attempt to conform to these country norms within the broader constraint of minimizing their cost of capital on a consolidated worldwide basis.

Country Debt Ratio Norms

Financial structure norms for firms vary widely from one country to another but cluster together for firms domiciled in the same country. This is the conclusion of a long line of empirical studies that have investigated this question from 1969 to the present time.[3]

In our opinion the most definitive study has been by William Sekely and J. Markham Collins.[4] They compared debt ratios for 677 firms in 9 industries in 23 countries. Their results, presented in Exhibit 11.3, confirm most previous studies, which also concluded that cultural factors, related to each host country's political, legal, social, institutional, and tax environments, cause debt ratios to cluster by country rather than by industry or size. Sekely and Collins have gone a step further, however, and identified seven "cultural realms." These are groupings of countries with similarities in financial structure norms. The realms and countries grouped in each one are as follows.[5]

Anglo-American: Australia, Canada, South Africa, United Kingdom, and United States

Latin American: Argentina, Brazil, Chile, and Mexico

West Central Europe: Benelux, Switzerland, and West Germany

Mediterranean Europe: France, Italy, and Spain

Scandinavia: Denmark, Finland, Norway, and Sweden

Indian Peninsula: India and Pakistan

Southeast Asia: Malaysia and Singapore

Low debt ratios were typical of the Southeast Asian, Latin American, and Anglo-American groups. High debt ratios were found in the Scandinavian, Mediterranean, and Indian Peninsula groups. The West Central Europe group had debt ratios in the middle of the seven groups.

---

[3]See the following references in the bibliography at the end of this chapter: Stonehill and Stitzel (1969), Remmers et al. (1974), Toy et al. (1974), Stonehill et al. (1975), Shapiro (1978), Errunza (1979), Aggarwal (1981), Stanley (1981), Collins and Sekely (1983), Sarathy and Chatterjee (1984), Wright and Suzuki (1985), Kester (1986), Sekely and Collins (1988), Lee and Kwok (1988), and Hodder and Senbet (1990).

[4]William S. Sekely and J. Markham Collins, "Cultural Influences on International Capital Structure," *Journal of International Business Studies*, Spring 1988, pp. 87–100.

[5]Ibid., pp. 92 and 95.

Exhibit 11.3 Debt Ratio for Selected Industries and Countries (arranged in order of increasing use of debt)[1]

	Alcoholic Beverages	Automobiles	Chemicals	Electrical	Foods	Iron & Steel	Nonferrous Metals	Paper	Textiles	Country Mean
Singapore	0.20	0.22		0.57	0.28	0.28	0.38			0.34
Malaysia		0.60	0.41		0.30	0.38	0.30	0.77	0.69	0.37
Argentina	0.29	0.42		0.44	0.35	0.32				0.38
Australia		0.50	0.52	0.51	0.45	0.53	0.34	0.48	0.54	0.46
Chile	0.18		0.33	0.28	0.70	0.48	0.50	0.47		0.46
Mexico			0.47	0.57	0.59	0.53	0.47	0.47		0.47
South Africa	0.59	0.50	0.51		0.46	0.53	0.32	0.42	0.69	0.50
Brazil		0.66	0.48	0.53	0.57	0.61		0.37		0.54
United Kingdom	0.45	0.73	0.50	0.60	0.55	0.51	0.57	0.56	0.52	0.55
United States	0.51	0.58	0.55	0.54	0.56	0.54	0.58	0.58	0.50	0.55
Benelux	0.41	0.62	0.60	0.51	0.64	0.61	0.49	0.65	0.54	0.56
Canada	0.55		0.45	0.52			0.61	0.68		0.58
India	0.08	0.75	0.55	0.52		0.69	0.69	0.74	0.48	0.60
Switzerland				0.63	0.54	0.49				0.60
West Germany	0.66	0.57	0.56	0.66	0.49	0.64	0.70	0.70	0.65	0.62
Denmark			0.47	0.74	0.69	0.60	0.61	0.74		0.63
Spain	0.79	0.59	0.64	0.45	0.66	0.52	0.70	0.85	0.43	0.64
Sweden	0.56	0.75	0.67	0.67	0.63	0.82	0.64	0.61	0.60	0.68
France	0.56	0.67	0.72	0.72	0.78	0.67	0.67	0.74	0.74	0.71
Finland	0.40	0.82	0.71	0.73	0.77	0.73	0.72	0.76	0.82	0.72
Pakistan		0.87	0.87			0.73	0.71	0.66	0.70	0.72
Norway			0.76	0.67	0.79	0.62		0.82	0.75	0.74
Italy	0.49	0.49	0.65	0.79	0.85	0.87	0.86	0.77	0.83	0.76
Industry Mean	0.49	0.58	0.56	0.59	0.62	0.61	0.58	0.63	0.70	

[1] Debt ratios are defined as total debt divided by total assets at book value. Data are for the period 1979–1980. Data were obtained from *Moody's Industrial Manual* for the United States and *Moody's International Manual* for all other firms. Data represent 677 firms in 9 industries in 23 countries.

Source: William S. Sekely and J. Markham Collins, "Cultural Influences on International Capital Structure," *Journal of International Business Studies*, Spring 1988, p. 91. Reprinted with permission.

Within a country neither industry nor size were important determinants of debt ratios. This finding was also true for earlier international studies, but contradicts the U.S.-based theory that industry is a determinant.

Other comparative international studies also concluded that country-specific environmental variables are key determinants of debt ratios. Janette Rutterford studied debt ratios in the United States, United Kingdom, France, Germany, and Japan. She concluded as follows:

> Accounting variations across countries appear to exaggerate the differences in debt-equity ratios between countries but, if these variations are allowed for, the essential differences still remain.
>
> Tax factors, whether assuming a Modigliani and Miller model or an investor clientele model such as that proposed by Miller, do not appear to be able to explain cross-sectional differences. A relatively high tax advantage to debt or likely demand for debt in a particular country is not related to a high aggregate leverage ratio.
>
> Agency costs of debt, on the other hand, do seem to be able to explain why Japanese, French and German corporations continue to rely heavily on debt finance, a dependence which dates in most cases from post–World War II reorganization and central government encouragement. The close relationships established between the banks and their client firms reduce both moral hazard risk and the cost associated with information asymmetry. Firms in these countries have therefore not needed to rely heavily on the more expensive (in agency cost terms) external finance.
>
> U.S. and U.K. corporations have had lower agency costs of equity relative to those for debt, since banks, at least in the U.K., appear to have restricted their lending and the agency costs of debt securities are higher than for bank finance. As a result, both countries have well-developed equity markets, with efficient information dissemination, stringent auditing and monitoring procedures and low issue costs which keep the agency costs of equity to a minimum.[6]

Carl Kester compared a large sample of U.S. and Japanese manufacturing firms. His conclusions are presented in the Global View at the beginning of this chapter.

An earlier study by an international consortium of researchers conducted interviews with financial executives of 87 firms in four industries in five countries (France, Japan, the Netherlands, Norway, and the United States).[7] These executives responded that in determining the optimal financial structure for their firms the following factors were more important than minimizing the cost of capital:

1. risk: defined as the degree of cash flow coverage of fixed charges under varying market conditions,

---

[6]Janette Rutterford, "An International Perspective on the Capital Structure Puzzle," *Midland Corporate Finance Journal*, Fall 1985, p. 72. Reprinted with permission.

[7]Arthur Stonehill, Theo Beekhuisen, Richard Wright, Lee Remmers, Norman Toy, Antonio Parés, Alan Shapiro, Douglas Egan, and Thomas Bates, "Financial Goals and Debt Ratio Determinants: A Survey of Practice in Five Countries," *Financial Management*, Autumn 1975, pp. 27–41. Since this survey was conducted in 1973, it is likely that some of the results no longer apply. However, the survey is still illustrative of the noncost factors that are important to financial executives in choosing a financial structure.

2. availability of capital, and

3. international factors related to financing foreign operations, and reacting to foreign exchange and political risks. A number of institutional, cultural, and historical reasons explain why these noncost factors are important debt ratio determinants for both U.S. and non-U.S. firms.

Localized Financial Structures for Foreign Affiliates

Within the given constraint of minimizing its consolidated worldwide cost of capital, should a multinational firm take differing country debt ratio norms into consideration when determining its desired debt ratio for foreign affiliates?

For definition purposes the debt considered here should be only what is borrowed from sources outside the multinational firm. This debt would include local and foreign currency loans as well as Eurocurrency loans. The reason for this definition is that parent loans to foreign affiliates are often regarded as equivalent to equity investment both by host countries and by investing firms. A parent loan is usually subordinated to other debt and does not create the same threat of insolvency as an external loan. Furthermore, the choice of debt or equity investment is often arbitrary and subject to negotiation between host country and parent firm.

The main advantages of a finance structure for foreign affiliates that conforms to local debt norms are as follows:

1. A localized financial structure reduces criticism of foreign affiliates that have been operating with too high a proportion of debt (judged by local standards), often resulting in the accusation that they are not contributing a fair share of risk capital to the host country. At the other end of the spectrum, it would improve the image of foreign affiliates that have been operating with too little debt and thus appear to be insensitive to local monetary policy.

2. A localized financial structure helps management evaluate return on equity investment relative to local competitors in the same industry. In economies where interest rates are relatively high as an offset to inflation, the penalty paid reminds management of the need to consider price level changes when evaluating investment performance.

3. In economies where interest rates are relatively high because of a scarcity of capital, the penalty paid for borrowing local funds reminds management that unless return on assets is greater than the local price of capital—that is, negative leverage—they are probably misallocating scarce domestic resources. This factor may not appear to be relevant to management decisions, but it will certainly be considered by the host country in making decisions with respect to the firm.

The main disadvantages of localized financial structures are as follows:

1. A multinational firm is expected to have a comparative advantage over local firms in overcoming imperfections in national capital markets through better availability of capital and the ability to diversify risk. Why should it throw away these important

competitive advantages to conform to local norms that are established in response to imperfect local capital markets, historical precedent, and institutional constraints that do not apply to the multinational firm?

2. If each foreign affiliate of a multinational firm localizes its financial structure, the resulting consolidated balance sheet might show a financial structure that does not conform to any particular country's norm. The debt ratio would be a simple weighted average of the corresponding ratio of each country in which the firm happened to operate. This feature could increase perceived financial risk and thus the cost of capital for the multinational firm, but only if two additional conditions are present:

    a. The consolidated debt ratio must be pushed completely out of the discretionary range of acceptable debt ratios in the flat area of the cost of capital curve, shown previously in Exhibit 11.1.

    b. The multinational firm must be unable to offset high debt in one foreign affiliate with low debt in other foreign or domestic affiliates at the same cost. If the international Fisher effect is working, replacement of debt should be possible at an equal after-tax cost after adjusting for foreign exchange risk. On the other hand, if market imperfections preclude this type of replacement, the possibility exists that the overall cost of debt, and thus the cost of capital, could increase for the multinational firm if it attempts to conform to local norms.

3. The debt ratio of a foreign affiliate is in reality only cosmetic, since lenders ultimately look to the parent and its consolidated worldwide cash flow as the source of repayment. In many cases, debt of affiliates must be guaranteed by the parent firm. Even if no formal guarantee exists, an implied guarantee usually exists because almost no parent firm would dare to allow an affiliate to default on a loan. If it did, repercussions would surely be felt with respect to the parent's own financial standing, with a resulting increase in its cost of capital.

In our opinion a compromise position is possible. Both multinational and domestic firms should try to minimize their overall weighted average cost of capital for a given level of business risk and capital budget, as finance theory suggests. However, if debt is available to a foreign affiliate at equal cost to that which could be raised elsewhere, after adjusting for foreign exchange risk, then localizing the foreign affiliate's financial structure should incur no cost penalty and yet would also enjoy the advantages just listed.

Naturally, if a particular foreign affiliate has access to local debt at a lower cost, after adjusting for foreign exchange risk, than other sources of debt available to the multinational firm, the multinational firm should borrow all it can through that foreign affiliate. The reverse would be true if the foreign affiliate only had access to higher cost debt than available elsewhere. Nothing should be borrowed externally through that foreign affiliate.

These disequilibrium situations for a foreign affiliate can only occur in imperfect or segmented markets because otherwise the international Fisher effect should eliminate any such opportunities. The fact that opportunities to lower the cost of debt do exist is simply evidence of market imperfections or segmentation.

In summary, a multinational firm should probably follow a policy of borrowing at lowest cost, after adjusting for foreign exchange risk, anywhere in the world without regard to the cosmetic impact on any particular affiliate's financial structure. This policy assumes that local regulations permit this practice. The objective for a multinational firm is the same as that for a domestic firm, namely, to minimize its consolidated cost of capital for a given level of business risk and capital budget. On the other hand, if conforming to host country debt norms does not require a cost penalty, but merely replaces debt in one affiliate by debt in another, worthwhile advantages can be realized. These advantages include better public relations with host country monetary authorities and more realistic evaluation of performance of foreign affiliates relative to competition with host country firms.

Choosing Among Sources of Funds to Finance Foreign Affiliates

In addition to resolving the issue of choosing an appropriate financial structure for foreign affiliates, financial managers of multinational firms need to choose among alternative sources of funds to finance foreign affiliates.

Potential Sources of Funds

Sources of funds available to foreign affiliates can be classified as shown in Exhibit 11.4. In general terms they include the following:

- Funds generated internally by the foreign affiliates.
- Funds from within the corporate family.
- Funds from sources external to the corporate family.

The choice among the sources of funds ideally involves simultaneously minimizing the cost of external funds after adjusting for foreign exchange risk, choosing internal sources in order to minimize worldwide taxes and political risk, and ensuring that managerial motivation in the foreign affiliates is geared toward minimizing the firm's consolidated worldwide cost of capital, rather than the foreign affiliate's cost of capital. Needless to say, this task is almost impossible, and the tendency is to place more emphasis on one of the variables at the expense of others.

Minimizing the cost of new long-term external funds, after adjusting for foreign exchange risk, was already analyzed earlier from the viewpoint of minimizing the cost of debt and equity to the consolidated worldwide firm. This is a more appropriate perspective than analyzing external funds from the viewpoint of a foreign affiliate.

The political risk implications of various strategies for financing foreign affiliates is treated in Chapter 18. Political risk needs to be integrated with other considerations of cost, taxes, foreign exchange risk, and managerial motivation, but so far this integration has not been accomplished in theory or practice.

At least a portion of the financing problem is to provide short-term financing when and where it is needed by the affiliates. This problem can best be analyzed as an exercise in optimal positioning of funds within the multinational family group; that is the subject

Exhibit 11.4   Potential Sources of Capital for Financing a Foreign Affiliate

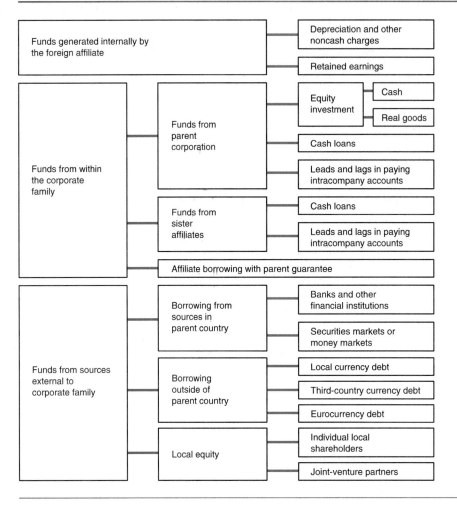

of Chapter 22. However, one issue that often arises in connection with short-term financing—and is not related to optimal positioning—is the question of parent guarantees of bank borrowing by foreign affiliates.

Parent Guarantees of Bank Loans to Foreign Affiliates

A large portion of bank lending to foreign affiliates is based on formal or informal guarantees by the parent firm. Parent guarantees can take a variety of forms. The strongest type is an "unlimited guarantee" in which the lender is protected on all loans to the affiliate without regard to amount or time limit. Other guarantees are limited to a single loan agreement between a lender and an affiliate and constitute only part of the specific loan agreement.

Yet another type of guarantee is a purchase agreement under which the parent commits itself to purchase the affiliate's promissory note from the lender in case the affiliate defaults. A weaker version of this is a "collection guarantee" in which the parent guarantees only that the lender will be able to collect the note. The lender must first try to collect the note from the affiliate before turning to the guarantor-parent. An even weaker arrangement, which is not a true guarantee, is for the parent to subordinate its own claims on the affiliate to those of the lender.

When a parent is willing to guarantee a loan, that parent will often want the guarantee effective only under the home country legal jurisdiction. This policy ensures that any litigation will take place under a known set of laws and that the parent will not become a political whipping boy in a foreign court system.

If a direct parent guarantee to a bank is involved, that guarantee will often be to an entity in the home country. For example, the Italian affiliate of a U.S. manufacturing firm borrows in Italy with a parent guarantee. If the loan is from the Milan branch of a U.S. bank, the guarantee will be made to the U.S. parent bank. If the loan is from the parent office of an Italian bank, the guarantee will be made to the U.S. branch of that Italian bank.

Parents are not the only source of guarantees. A given affiliate's loans may also be guaranteed by sister affiliates, perhaps for reasons of legal jurisdiction or perhaps to put a smaller limit on the effective amount of the guarantee.

Summary

- The theory of optimal financial structure must be modified considerably to encompass the multinational firm. Access to international capital markets permits it to maintain its desired debt ratio even when significant amounts of new funds must be raised. Its marginal cost of capital is constant for much wider ranges of its capital budget compared to a domestic competitor that does not have access to international capital markets.

- Multinational firms are in a better position than domestic firms to support higher debt ratios because their cash flows are diversified internationally. This gives them the same kind of reduction in variability that portfolio investors receive from diversifying their security holdings internationally.

- Offsetting the diversification effect, agency costs of debt might be higher for multinational firms because of political risks, market imperfections, and the complexity of international operations.

- Empirical studies show that multinational firms do not have a higher debt ratio, after adjusting for size and industry.

- The multinational firm should choose a capital structure that minimizes its cost of capital from the perspective of the consolidated firm. The financial structure of each affiliate is relevant only to the extent it affects this overall goal. An individual affiliate does not have an independent cost of capital.

- Debt ratio norms vary considerably by country. Should a multinational firm structure its affiliates' capital structures to conform to local norms, if that action does not increase its consolidated cost of capital?

- The main advantage of localizing the financial structures would be as follows:
  — reduce criticism of foreign affiliates that have been operating with too high a proportion of debt (judged by local standards), suggesting a lack of confidence in the local economy, or conversely, too little debt, suggesting insensitivity to local monetary policy.
  — help management evaluate return on equity investment relative to local competitors, especially where interest rates are relatively high to offset local inflation.
  — remind management that unless return on assets is greater than the local price of capital, the multinational firm is probably misallocating scarce domestic resources.

- The main disadvantages of localizing the financial structures would be as follows:
  — the multinational firm might be throwing away its comparative advantage in overcoming imperfection in national capital markets through better availability of capital and the ability to diversify risk.
  — the consolidated debt ratio of the multinational firm might become distorted, but only if it is unable to offset a distortion in one market with opposite distortions in other markets.
  — the debt ratio of a foreign affiliate is only cosmetic, since lenders ultimately look to the parent as the source of repayment, a fact reinforced by guarantees.

- Potential sources of funds to finance foreign affiliates include the following:

  — funds generated internally by the foreign affiliates
  — funds from within the corporate family
  — funds from sources external to the corporate family.

- The choice of funds involves simultaneously minimizing the cost of external funds after adjusting for foreign exchange risk, choosing internal sources in order to minimize worldwide taxes and political risk, and ensuring that managerial motivation in the foreign affiliates is geared toward minimizing the firm's consolidated worldwide cost of capital, rather than the foreign affiliate's cost of capital.

Questions

1. Optimal Financial Structure

U.S.-based multinational Beaver Products, Inc., has a wholly owned subsidiary in Milan, Italy. It is considering the proper debt ratio for the Italian subsidiary. Beaver's optimal debt ratio is 45%. What are the possible considerations in determining the Italian subsidiary's capital structure?

2. Japanese Leverage Ratios
Japanese industrial firms typically have a higher debt to equity ratio (leverage ratio) than U.S., U.K., and Canadian firms in the same industries. Explain why this occurs.

3. Multinational Firms and Leverage Ratios
It has been suggested that multinational firms are able to support higher debt ratios than their domestic competitors. Explain why this is or is not true.

4. Debt and the Subsidiary
It is commonly argued that multinational firms wish to capitalize their foreign subsidiaries with as little of their own equity as possible, preferring instead to provide most of the capitalization in the form of intrafirm debt. Because debt has a set debt service payment schedule, the parent is assured of more predictable cash flows returning from the foreign subsidiary than it does from the equity portion of the investment. Dividends are dependent on profitability, distribution decisions, and government allowances for dividend distributions.

   a. If you are senior management of a foreign subsidiary, how, if at all, would the capitalization of your unit affect the profitability of your unit?
   b. As subsidiary management, what would you do any differently in your active management as a result of being more heavily leveraged than some of your local competitors?

Bibliography

Aggarwal, Raj, "International Differences in Capital Structure Norms: An Empirical Study of Large European Companies," *Management International Review*, 1981/1, pp. 75–88.

Baldwin, Carliss Y., "Competing for Capital in a Global Environment," *Midland Corporate Finance Journal*, Spring 1987, pp. 43–64.

Boris, C. E. V., "Leverage and Financing of Non-Financial Companies: An International Perspective," *BIS Economic Papers*, no. 27, May 1990.

Collins, J. Markham, "A Market Performance Comparison of U.S. Firms Active in Domestic, Developed and Developing Countries," *Journal of International Business Studies*, Second Quarter 1990, pp. 271–287.

Collins, J. Markham, and William S. Sekely, "The Relationship of Headquarters, Country, and Industry Classification to Financial Structure," *Financial Management*, Autumn 1983, pp. 45–51.

Dodd, Mikel T., and James A. Millar, "Financial Structure in Japanese and American Firms: An Indirect Test of Agency Relationships," *Journal of International Financial Management and Accounting*, vol. 2, nos. 2 and 3, Summer and Autumn 1990, pp. 131–144.

Errunza, Vihang R., "Determinants of Financial Structure in the Central American Common Market," *Financial Management*, Autumn 1979, pp. 72–77.

———, "Financing MNC Subsidiaries in Central America," *Journal of International Business Studies*, Fall 1979, pp. 88–93.

Hodder, James E., and Lemma W. Senbet, "International Capital Structure Equilibrium," *Journal of Finance*, December 1990, pp. 1495–1516.

Kester, W. Carl, "Capital and Ownership Structure: A Comparison of United States and Japanese Manufacturing Corporations," *Financial Management*, Spring 1986, pp. 5–16.

Lee, Kwang Chul, and Chuck C. Y. Kwok, "Multinational Corporations vs. Domestic Corporations: International Environmental Factors and Determinants of Capital Structure," *Journal of International Business Studies*, Summer 1988, pp. 195–217.

Lin, James Wuh, and Jeff Madura, "Optimal Debt Financing for Multinational Projects," *Journal of Multinational Financial Management*, vol. 3, nos. 1 and 2, 1993, pp. 63–73.

Michel, Allen, and Israel Shaked, "Multinational Corporations vs. Domestic Corporations: Financial Performance and Characteristics," *Journal of International Business Studies*, Fall 1986, pp. 89–100.

Remmers, Lee, Arthur Stonehill, Richard Wright, and Theo Beekhuisen, "Industry and Size as Debt Ratio Determinants for Manufacturing Internationally," *Financial Management*, Summer 1974, pp. 24–32.

Remolona, E. M., "Why International Trends in Leverage Have Been So Different," New York: Federal Reserve Bank of New York (Working Paper No. 9002), February 1990.

Rutterford, Janette, "An International Perspective on the Capital Structure Puzzle," *Midland Corporate Finance Journal*, Fall 1985, p. 72.

Sarathy, Ravi, and Sangit Chatterjee, "The Divergence of Japanese and U.S. Corporate Financial Structure," *Journal of International Business Studies*, Winter 1984, pp. 75–89.

Sekely, William S., and J. Markham Collins, "Cultural Influences on International Capital Structure," *Journal of International Business Studies*, Spring 1988, pp. 87–100.

Shapiro, Alan C., "Evaluating Financing Costs for Multinational Subsidiaries," *Journal of International Business Studies*, Fall 1975, pp. 25–32.

———, "Financial Structure and Cost of Capital in the Multinational Corporation," *Journal of Financial and Quantitative Analysis*, June 1978, pp. 211–226.

Stanley, Marjorie T., "Capital Structure and Cost of Capital for the Multinational Firm," *Journal of International Business Studies*, Spring/Summer 1981, pp. 103–120.

Stonehill, Arthur, Theo Beekhuisen, Richard Wright, Lee Remmers, Norman Toy, Antonio Parés, Alan Shapiro, Douglas Egan, and Thomas Bates, "Financial Goals and Debt Ratio Determinants: A Survey of Practice in Five Countries," *Financial Management*, Autumn 1975, pp. 27–41.

Stonehill, Arthur, and Thomas Stitzel, "Financial Structure and Multinational Corporations," *California Management Review*, Fall 1969, pp. 91–96.

Thomadakis, Stavros, and Nilufer Usmen, "Foreign Project Financing in Segmented Capital Markets: Equity Versus Debt," *Financial Management*, Winter 1991, pp. 42–53.

Toy, Norman, Arthur Stonehill, Lee Remmers, Richard Wright, and Theo Beekhuisen, "A Comparative International Study of Growth, Profitability and Risk as Determinants of Corporate Debt Ratios in the Manufacturing Sector," *Journal of Financial and Quantitative Analysis*, November 1974, pp. 875–886.

Wright, Richard, and Sadahiko Suzuki, "Financial Structure and Bankruptcy Risk in Japanese Companies," *Journal of International Business Studies*, Spring 1985, pp. 97–110.

Chapter 12
Sourcing Equity Internationally

Global View
Privatization and ADRs

It's being trumpeted as the asset sale of the century—and you're invited. From Italy to Taiwan, scores of governments, caught up in a free-market frenzy and needing cash, are selling shares of state-run companies to the public. This sweeping global privatization movement, involving more than 50 nations and expected to raise some $300 billion over five years, should provide opportunities for individual investors. "Privatizations tend to be good long-term plays," says Vikram Pandit, managing director for equity capital markets at Morgan Stanley. "These are often the largest companies in their countries and thus blue chips in basic industries."

Privatization's popularity stems partly from Britain's success in the 1980s and early 1990s unloading everything from water utilities to airlines. Mexico, Chile, and a handful of developing countries have also done well. Now, as foreign governments sell off most or all their holdings in nationalized companies, investors hope to get in on the ground floor of the next British Telecom or Compañía de Teléfonos de Chile, whose share price has increased almost sevenfold since its initial offering in 1990.

Of course, not all privatizations are hits. Sometimes, a government overprices shares or a newly privatized company falters because of an industry-wide slump, as was the case with British Steel in the 1980s. However, according to a study done for the Global Privatization Fund, a new closed-end fund managed by Alliance Capital, anyone who invested the same amount in the major privatization issues as they came to market during the five years ended in December [1993] would have earned a 174% return, vs. an 85% gain for Standard & Poor's 500-stock index.

Privatized Companies with ADRs

Company	Issue Date	Issue Price	Price 4/4/94
YPF (Argentina)	6/28/93	19.00	22.25
Telefonica De Argentina	12/1/91	24.00	57.50
British Steel	12/5/88	23.38	19.625
British Telecommunications	12/1/84	15.50	56.25
Compañía de Teléfonos de Chile	7/1/90	16.13	86.00
Elf Aquitaine (France)	6/13/91	29.37	31.25
Rhone-Poulenc (France)	2/3/93	23.48	23.50
Telefonos de Mexico	5/1/91	27.25	57.00
Telecom Corp. of New Zealand	7/1/91	22.58	44.00
Banco Comercial Portugues	6/11/92	15.44	15.125
REPSOL (Spain)	5/10/89	14.35	29.00
Telefonica de Espana (Spain)	6/1/87	20.88	35.125

Data: Global Investing, Bridge Information Systems, Inc., Montgomery Asset Management, Bank of New York.

We established in Chapter 10 that gaining access to global capital markets should lower a firm's cost of capital because of improved market liquidity and by overcoming market segmentation. This chapter explains exactly how sourcing equity internationally con- tributes to this objective.

Sourcing equity internationally is defined here to mean both crosslisting shares abroad to improve the secondary market liquidity for a firm's existing shares and selling new shares to foreign investors. The first part of the chapter analyzes whether to crosslist abroad, and if so, where? The second part analyzes alternative ways to sell new shares to foreign investors.

Why Crosslist on Foreign Stock Exchanges?

By crosslisting its shares on foreign stock exchanges a firm hopes to achieve one or more of the following six objectives:

1. Improve the liquidity of its existing shares by making it easier for foreign sharehold- ers to trade in their home markets and currencies.

2. Increase its share price by overcoming mispricing in a segmented, illiquid, home capital market.

3. Provide a liquid secondary market to support a new equity issue in the foreign market.

4. Establish a secondary market for shares used to acquire local firms.

5. Increase the firm's visibility and political acceptance to its customers, suppliers, creditors, and host governments.

6. Create a secondary market for shares that will be used to compensate local management and employees in foreign affiliates.[1]

Improving the Liquidity for Existing Foreign Shareholders: The Use of Depositary Receipts

Quite often foreign investors have acquired a firm's shares through normal brokerage channels, even though the shares are not listed in the investors' home market, or maybe are not traded in the investors' preferred currency. Crosslisting is a way to encourage such investors to continue to hold and trade these shares, thus marginally improving secondary market liquidity.

Crosslisting is usually accomplished by *depositary receipts*. In the United States, foreign shares are usually traded through *American depositary receipts*, or ADRs. These are negotiable certificates issued by a U.S. bank in the United States to represent the underlying shares of stock, which are held in trust at a custodian bank. ADRs are sold, registered, and transferred in the United States in the same manner as any share of stock, with each ADR representing some multiple of the underlying foreign share. This permits ADRs to trade in an appropriate price range for the U.S. market even if the price of the foreign share is inappropriate when converted to U.S. dollars.

ADRs can be exchanged for the underlying foreign shares, or vice versa, so arbitrage activities keep foreign and U.S. prices of any given share the same. For example, investor demand in one market will cause a price rise there, which will cause an equivalent price in the other market even when investors there are not as bullish on the stock.

ADRs convey certain technical advantages to U.S. shareholders. Dividends paid by a foreign firm are passed to its custodial bank and then to the bank that issued the ADR. The issuing bank exchanges the foreign currency dividends for U.S. dollars and sends the dollar dividend to the ADR holders. ADRs are in registered form, rather than in bearer form. Transfer of ownership is facilitated because it is done in the United States in accordance with U.S. laws and procedures. In the event of death of a shareholder the estate need not go through probate in a foreign court system.

ADRs are either "sponsored" or "unsponsored." Sponsored ADRs are created at the request of a foreign firm wanting its shares traded in the United States. The firm applies to the Securities and Exchange Commission and a U.S. bank for registration and issuance of ADRs. The foreign firm pays all costs of creating such sponsored ADRs. If a foreign firm does not seek to have its shares traded in the United States but U.S.

---

[1]Research studies on the motivation for foreign listings are reported in Shahrokh M. Saudagaran, "An Empirical Study of Selected Factors Influencing the Decision to List on Foreign Stock Exchanges," *Journal of International Business Studies*, Spring 1988, pp. 101–128; J. David Siltz and Sie Ting Lau, "An Empirical Investigation of Factors That Influence U.S. Firms to Become Inter-Listed on the New York and Tokyo Stock Exchanges," University of Texas at Arlington, August 1992; Hikent Baker, "Why U.S. Companies List on the London, Frankfurt and Tokyo Stock Exchanges," American University, 1992.

investors are interested, a U.S. securities firm may initiate creation of the ADRs. Such an ADR would be unsponsored.

Favorable Effect on Share Price?

Does merely crosslisting on a foreign stock exchange have a favorable impact on share prices? It depends on the degree to which markets are segmented.

If a firm's home capital market is segmented it could theoretically benefit by crosslisting in a foreign market if that market values the firm or its industry more than does the home market. This was certainly the situation experienced by Novo Industri A/S when it listed on the New York Stock Exchange (NYSE) in 1981 (see Chapter 10), and by Daimler Benz when it listed on the NYSE in 1993 (see Chapter 10). However, as detailed in Chapter 10, most capital markets are becoming more integrated with global markets.

There has been a flurry of empirical research in recent years to study the actual, rather than theoretical, impact of foreign crosslistings on share prices. The results are mixed. Howe and Kelm (1987) reported a negative effect on share price for a sample of 161 U.S. firms that listed on stock exchanges in Basel, Frankfurt, or Paris.[2] On the other hand, McGoun (1987) found a positive share price reaction to announcements by U.S. firms of intentions to list on the Tokyo, Toronto, or London stock exchanges.[3] Alexander, Eun, and Janakiramanan (1988) found a positive share price effect for 34 foreign firms listing on the NYSE, American Stock Exchange, or Nasdaq during the period 1969 to 1982, when markets were presumably more segmented than today.[4]

Supporting a New Equity Issue

Firms domiciled in countries with small illiquid capital markets have often outgrown that market and are forced to raise new equity abroad. Listing on a stock exchange in the market in which these funds are to be raised is typically required by the underwriters to ensure post-issue liquidity in the shares.

An empirical study of 481 multinational firms by Shahrokh Saudagaran found that the relative size of a firm within its domestic capital market has a significant influence on its decision to list abroad.[5] The larger the firm relative to its domestic capital market, the more likely it is to list abroad. He also found that this tendency was even more pronounced for firms with a relatively large degree of multinationality. This reasoning

---

[2]John S. Howe and Katherine Kelm, "The Stock Price Impacts of Overseas Listings," *Financial Management*, Autumn 1987, pp. 51–56.

[3]George E. McGoun, *The Value of American Stock Listing on Foreign Stock Exchanges*, Ph.D. thesis (unpublished), Indiana University, 1987.

[4]Gordon J. Alexander, Cheol S. Eun, and S. Janakiramanan, "International Listings and Stock Returns: Some Empirical Evidence," *Journal of Financial and Quantitative Analysis*, June 1988, pp. 135–151.

[5]Shahrokh M. Saudagaran, "An Empirical Study of Selected Factors Influencing the Decision to List on Foreign Stock Exchange," *Journal of International Business Studies*, Spring 1988, pp. 101–127.

certainly was a major factor in Novo Industri's decision to list on the NYSE in 1981, simultaneously with its U.S. equity issue (Chapter 10).

Even firms domiciled in a large capital market might need to raise equity and list in a foreign market to finance a very large capital investment, such as a factory, in that market. This motive, plus a desire to enhance its corporate image, were the forces behind Daimler Benz's agonizing decision to list on the NYSE in October 1993 (see Chapter 10).

Potential for Share Swaps with Acquisitions

Firms that follow a strategy of growth by acquisition are always looking for creative ways to fund these acquisitions rather than just pay cash. Offering their shares as partial payment is considerably more attractive if those shares have a liquid secondary market. In that case the target's shareholders have an easy way to convert their acquired shares to cash if they do not prefer a share swap. However, a share swap is often attractive as a tax-free exchange.

Increasing Visibility and Political Acceptance to Customers, Suppliers, Creditors, and Host Governments

Multinational firms list in markets where they have substantial physical operations. Commercial objectives are to enhance their corporate image, advertise trademarks and products, get better local press coverage, and become more familiar with the local financial community in order to raise working capital locally.

Political objectives might include the need to meet local ownership requirements for a multinational firm's foreign joint venture. Local ownership of the parent firm's shares might provide a forum for publicizing the firm's activities and how they support the host country.

Compensating Management and Employees

If a multinational firm wishes to use stock options and share purchase compensation plans for local management and employees, local listing would enhance the perceived value of such plans. It should reduce transaction and foreign exchange costs for the local beneficiaries.

Barriers to Crosslisting

Although a firm may decide to crosslist abroad, certain barriers exist. The most serious barriers are the future commitment to providing full disclosure of operating results and balance sheets, as well as a continuous program of investor relations.

The Commitment to Disclosure and Investor Relations

A decision to crosslist must be balanced against the implied increased commitment to full disclosure and a continuing investor relations program. For firms resident in the Anglo-American markets, listing abroad might not appear to be much of a barrier. For example, the Securities and Exchange Commission's (SEC) disclosure rules for listing in the United States are so stringent and costly that any other market's rules are mere child's play. Reversing the logic, however, non-U.S. firms must really think twice before listing in the United States. Not only are the disclosure requirements breathtaking, but a continuous demand for timely quarterly information is required by U.S. investors. This means the foreign firm must supply a costly continuous investor relations program for its U.S. shareholders, including frequent "road shows" and the personal time consuming involvement of top management.

Disclosure Is a Two-Edged Sword

The U.S. school of thought is that the worldwide trend toward requiring fuller and more standardized financial disclosure of operating results and balance sheet positions may have the desirable effect of lowering the cost of equity capital. Frederick D. S. Choi has presented a strong theoretical argument for this policy. He concludes:

> Increased firm disclosure tends to improve the subjective probability distributions of a security's expected return streams in the mind of an individual investor by reducing the uncertainty associated with the return stream. For firms which generally outperform the industry average, it is also argued that improved financial disclosure will tend to increase the relative weighting which an investor will place on favorable firm statistics relative to the firm. Both of the foregoing effects will entice an individual to pay a larger amount for a given security than otherwise, thus lowering a firm's cost of capital.[6]

The other school of thought is that the U.S. level of required disclosure is an onerous, costly burden. It chases away many potential listers, thereby narrowing the choice of securities that are available to U.S. investors at reasonable transaction costs. As a result only 153 foreign firms are listed on the NYSE, whereas 508 foreign firms are listed on the London Stock Exchange. Getting Daimler Benz to list on the NYSE in 1993 was considered a great victory worthy of front page news in the United States, but it would only have been a routine event in London.

A recently completed study of 203 internationally traded shares concluded there is a statistically significant relationship between the level of financial disclosure required and on which markets the firms chose to list.[7] The higher the level of disclosure required, the less likely a firm would list in that market.

Where to Crosslist

Having decided to crosslist, despite disclosure and reporting costs, the next question is where to do it. This depends on the motive for listing. If it is to support a new equity issue or to establish a market for share swaps, the target market should also be the listing

---

[6]Frederick D. S. Choi, "Financial Disclosure in Relation to a Firm's Capital Costs," *Accounting and Business Research*, Autumn 1973, p. 279.

[7]Shakrokh M. Saudagaran and Gary C. Biddle, "Financial Disclosure Levels and Foreign Stock Exchange Listing Decisions," *Journal of International Financial Management and Accounting*, Volume 4, Number 2, Summer 1992, pp. 106–148.

market. If it is to increase the firm's commercial and political visibility or to compensate local management and employees, it should be the markets in which the firm has significant physical operations. If it is to improve the liquidity of existing shares or to achieve a higher share price, it should be a major liquid stock market. In practice the major liquid markets are London, New York, Tokyo, Frankfurt, and Paris. Between them they account for 68% of the world's stock market capitalization.

The choice among these five markets depends on whether their unique institutional characteristics can increase the market liquidity of a specific firm's shares.[8] There needs to be a good match of the firm with its listing markets. The most important characteristics that should bear on each firm's decision are the size of the market and the sophistication of market-making activities, including competitive transaction costs, and competent crisis management.

Size of Market

Exhibit 12.1 is a size comparison of the stock exchanges in New York, London, Tokyo, Germany (mainly Frankfurt), and Paris. The New York Stock Exchange (NYSE) is the largest in market capitalization, value of trading (turnover), and number of listed firms. London (LSE) is second largest in the value of trading and number of listed firms. Tokyo (TSE) is second in market capitalization in 1993, although a few years earlier it had temporarily moved ahead of the NYSE. The Federation of German Stock Exchanges (FGSE) and Paris Stock Exchange (PSE) are considerably smaller and less liquid than the top three.

At the moment, Paris and Frankfurt (most of FGSE) do not appear to be large enough or have enough trading volume to justify consideration to be the primary crosslisting market for foreign firms. However, a number of foreign firms crosslist in Paris and Frankfurt as secondary choices once they have listed in London, New York, or Tokyo. Paris and Frankfurt also enjoy a lot of listings from other European Union (EU) countries. The EU Commission is striving to improve the integration of the continental stock markets with each other and with London. This should eventually increase the trading volume in both domestic and foreign shares in all the European markets.

The London Stock Exchange is first with respect to the number of listed foreign firms (508) and their trading value, which was $434.2 billion (Seaq International) in 1993. The New York Stock Exchange was second with respect to trading value which was $200 billion in ADRs in 1993, but the NYSE has fewer listed foreign firms (153) than London, Frankfurt, or Paris. The major reason for this is the more stringent disclosure and reporting requirements imposed by the U.S. Securities and Exchange Commission.

Although the number of listed foreign firms on the New York Stock Exchange is relatively small, their individual trading volume is typically quite large relative to their

---

[8]For a very readable description of the institutional characteristics of these five markets (and Toronto) see Roger D. Huang and Hans R. Stoll, *Major World Equity Markets: Current Structure and Prospects for Change*, New York: New York University Salomon Center; Monograph Series in Finance and Economics, no. 3, 1991.

Exhibit 12.1   Size Comparison of the Five Major Stock Exchanges

Market	Market Capitalization (bill US$) Dec 31, 1993	Value of Trading (bill US$) 1993	Number of Listed Domestic Firms Dec 31, 1993	Number of Listed Foreign Firms Dec 31, 1993
New York Stock Exchange (NYSE)[1]	4,540.8	2,283.4	2,361	153
London Stock Exchange (LSE)[2]	1,133.6	857.3	1,927	508
Tokyo Stock Exchange (TSE)[3]	2,906.3	793.0	1,667	110
Federation of German Stock Exchanges (FGSE)[4]	443.5	594.9	864	345
Paris Stock Exchange (PSE)	457.1	171.8	726	208

[1]Foreign firms' shares are listed in ADR form. The 1993 value of trading in ADRs of foreign companies on the NYSE was $200 billion. This is about 80% of total trading in ADRs in the United States, the rest being on the American Stock Exchange and over-the-counter.

[2]The value of trading on the LSE was composed of $434.2 billion on Seaq International (foreign firms) and $423.2 on Seaq Domestic (domestic British firms).

[3]The TSE figures include both the First Section (about 80% of trading value) and the Second Section (about 20% of trading value).

[4]The FGSE includes all 8 stock exchanges in Germany, but the biggest one by far is Frankfurt.

Sources: *New York Stock Exchange Annual Report 1993*, New York: NYSE, 1993; *Federation Internationale des Bourses de Valeurs (FIBV) Statistics 1993*, Paris, FIBV, 1993; New York Stock Exchange Research Department: Edward Lucas and Jean Tobin (interviews April 1994).

home markets. For example, Telefonos de Mexico (Mexican Telephone) was the fourth most actively traded stock on the NYSE in 1993. Glaxso (British) was the second most actively traded on the NYSE in 1992.

Market-Making Activities, Transaction Costs, and Crisis Management

The liquidity of a market is very much influenced by professional market-making activities, transaction costs, and crisis management. At one end of the spectrum is the NYSE, where assigned specialists are responsible for ensuring a *liquid, low cost, fair, and orderly* market. At the other end of the spectrum is the London Stock Exchange, where *market makers*, formerly called *jobbers*, voluntarily make an active market in some but not all listed shares. The Tokyo Stock Exchange lies somewhere in the middle.

The New York Stock Exchange

The NYSE has 1,366 members (December 31, 1993) who are allowed to trade on the floor of the exchange. Out of the total membership, 432 members are *specialists*, organized into 40 groups. Each specialist group is assigned exclusively a certain number of the listed shares.

Market-Making Activities. It is the specialists' *affirmative obligation* to ensure that their assigned shares enjoy a liquid, low cost, fair, and orderly market at all times, even when a crisis arises. In order to ensure a *liquid market*, the specialists must risk their own capital to buy shares when the public wants to sell and sell shares when the public wants to buy.

Transaction Costs. In order to guarantee low transaction costs the spread between one transaction and the next one should normally be no more than one-eighth of a point (12.5 cents) for active shares, or one-quarter of a point (25 cents) for less active shares.[9] The specialists do not act as brokers for the public in their assigned shares, but they trade with other floor members who represent the public. Negotiated commissions are the lowest in the world.

Fairness. Fairness is guaranteed in several ways. Orders from the public are executed chronologically. About 75% of the orders come in through a computerized system but are executed by the responsible specialist. About 35% of the time the specialist can arrange a better price for both buyer and seller than they would receive if their orders were just matched automatically by the computer. Large orders (the other 25%) come to the specialist manually through the other floor brokers. These orders are executed during the day by the specialist dealing with other floor brokers, professional floor traders, and the specialist's own capital account. Fairness is also enhanced by a 200-person staff whose function is surveillance. A very sophisticated computer-based surveillance system searches continually for evidence of insider trading.

Limit Orders. Although the specialist groups have a quasi monopoly on their assigned stocks, they experience competition from professional floor traders and from limit orders. A *limit order* is an order to buy or sell a share at a specified price. For example, a public investor wants to buy 1,000 shares of IBM at a price no higher than $50 per share at a time when IBM is selling at $55 per share. If and when IBM ever falls to $50 a share, that investor's order will be executed by the specialist in chronological sequence, and of course, ahead of any purchase at that price by the specialist.

Crisis Management. In deciding where to list to improve share liquidity, a firm should not just consider how a market functions under normal conditions but also if liquidity remains even during a stock market crisis. Unfortunately, the world experienced major stock market crises in 1987 and 1989. Most analysts believe the specialist-driven NYSE system did a better job of crisis management during these episodes than did competing dealer-driven markets.

For example, on "Black Monday," October 19, 1987, the Dow Jones Industrial Average (DJIA) fell by 22.6%. This was the largest single-day drop in history. The DJIA fell an additional 12% the following day. This stock market crash (or what could be termed the largest technical correction in history) seemingly originated in the United States and then spread around the globe. By the end of the crash week, the U.S. Standard & Poor's 500 had fallen 12.2%, the Tokyo Stock Exchange index had fallen 12%, the London Financial Times ordinary share index was down 23%, and the Frankfurt FAZ general

---

[9]The actual allowable spread for a share is a function of its normal volume, the price of the share, and special circumstances.

index was down 11.7%. The Hong Kong market had closed for that week on Tuesday. The Australian, Singapore, and Taiwan markets had fallen 20.3%, 20.8%, and 18.5%, respectively.

Although the specialists on the NYSE were not obligated to offset the overwhelming surge of public sell orders, they were able to maintain a liquid and orderly auction market. The NYSE share prices declined but not with the huge spreads between transactions experienced in the world's dealer-driven markets, including London and NASDAQ in the United States. In those markets there is no affirmative obligation to ensure an orderly market with low transaction costs. Many of the market makers "disappeared" or offered huge spreads between bid and ask quotes.

A similar divergence in crisis management was experienced on Friday, October 13, 1989, when a mini-crash occurred with worldwide repercussions. Once again the NYSE outperformed the other stock markets with respect to maintaining an orderly market.

The London Stock Exchange

London experienced its "Big Bang" in October 1986, an event which moved trading from the floor of the London Stock Exchange upstairs to computer screens in a dealer-driven market. The former distinction between brokers and jobbers (market makers) was abolished, along with fixed commissions. Entry restrictions were removed, opening securities firms up to foreign ownership and greatly increased competition.

Market-Making Activities. Competing dealer/brokers trade with the help of a screen quotation system modeled after the NASDAQ system in the United States. Foreign shares are grouped together on the International Stock Exchange (ISE) in London but quoted on SEAQ International (Stock Exchange Automated Quotation System). Domestic British firms are quoted on SEAQ Domestic.

In contrast to the NYSE, there are no assigned specialists, but market makers voluntarily make a liquid market in the shares of their choice. Since there are competing market makers for many of the active shares, nobody has an exclusive "affirmative obligation" to ensure a liquid, low cost, fair, or orderly market. It is expected these attributes will evolve from the level of competition.

Limit Orders. One competitive element that is missing is official limit orders. The public can give limit orders to their broker but there is no guarantee these will actually be executed chronologically or even at the exact limit order price.

A Comparison of London to New York. Comparing the London Stock Exchange to the NYSE, liquidity in the most actively traded shares is comparable, but the NYSE specialist system results in a more liquid market for the less popular shares. Transaction costs as measured by spreads are definitely lower on the NYSE. The London Stock Exchange spreads are about comparable to the spreads on NASDAQ. In terms of fairness, the NYSE is superior because orders are executed chronologically, whereas in London one has to shop from dealer to dealer. As mentioned previously, crisis management in practice has been more effective on the NYSE than any other exchanges including London.

Despite the more favorable liquidity attributes of the NYSE, more foreign firms list in London and the trading volume in those shares is twice as high as foreign listed shares on the NYSE. One must conclude that ease and cost of listing, lower required disclosure levels, and less frequent reporting requirements have tilted the scale toward London for firms that might have trouble overcoming these barriers. However, for those firms who are willing to pay the price, a listing on the NYSE should improve the liquidity of their shares more than could be achieved with a London listing.

The Tokyo Stock Exchange

Foreign stocks are listed in a special foreign section of the Tokyo Stock Exchange (TSE). Foreign securities firms can also now be members of the TSE. Trading of the most active shares (Section 1) takes place on the TSE floor, but most of the listed securities are traded via an automated screen-based quotation system (Section 2). Orders are matched by "Saitori" members who also maintain limit order books. However, unlike the NYSE specialists, the Saitori have no affirmative obligation to be market makers and are not even allowed to trade for their own accounts. Commissions are still fixed but declining gradually. They remain higher than either New York or London.

About 110 foreign firms are listed in Tokyo (December 31, 1993), but their motivation is more likely to be image driven rather than liquidity driven. The actual trading volume in foreign shares is often so low that some foreign firms that listed when they could first do so in the early 1980s have already dropped their listings on the TSE. The requirements for listing, disclosure, and reporting are about as onerous as those on the NYSE. This has proven to be a big barrier to foreign firms that might otherwise have listed in Tokyo.

Compared to New York or London, Tokyo is presently an "also ran" in terms of being an attractive location for foreign listings. However, as the world's second most richly capitalized stock market, its impressive overall turnover of shares, and its gradual evolution into a modern market, means a listing on the TSE may be in the future plans for many of the world's multinational firms.

Sourcing New Equity Shares in International Markets

In addition to crosslisting on multiple stock exchanges, a firm can lower its cost of capital and increase its liquidity by selling its shares to foreign investors through a new share issue or resale of existing shares. Four alternative ways to accomplish this are as follows:

- Sale of a *directed* share issue to investors in one particular foreign equity market.
- Sale of a *Euro-equity* share issue to foreign investors simultaneously in more than one market, including both foreign and domestic markets.
- Sale of a foreign subsidiary's shares to investors in its host country.
- Sale of shares to a foreign firm as part of a strategic alliance.

Directed Share Issues

A *directed* share issue is defined as one targeted at investors in a single country and underwritten in whole or in part by investment institutions from that country. The issue might or might not be denominated in the currency of the target market. The shares might or might not be listed on a stock exchange in the target market.

Improving Liquidity. The $61 million U.S. share issue by Novo Industri A/S in 1981 (Chapter 10) was a good example of a successful directed share issue that both improved the liquidity of Novo's shares and lowered its cost of capital. Novo repeated this success in 1983 with a $100 million share issue at $53 per share (ADR), compared to $36 per share two years earlier.

Funding Acquisitions or Capital Investments. A directed share issue might be motivated by a need to fund acquisitions or major capital investments in a target foreign market. This is an especially important source of equity for firms resident in smaller capital markets which have outgrown that market. A foreign share issue, plus crosslisting, can provide it improved liquidity for its shares and the means to use those shares to pay for acquisitions.

Hafslund Nycomed, a small but well-respected Norwegian pharmaceutical firm, is an example of this type of motivation for a directed share issue combined with crosslisting. Its commercial strategy for growth is to leverage its sophisticated knowledge of certain market niches and technologies within the pharmaceutical field by acquiring other promising firms that possess relevant technologies, personnel, or market niches. Europe and the United States have provided fertile hunting grounds. The acquisitions are paid for partly with cash and partly with shares. Norway is too small a home capital market to fund these acquisitions for cash or to provide a liquid enough market to minimize Hafslund Nycomed's marginal cost of capital.

Hafslund Nycomed has responded to the challenge by selling two successful directed share issues abroad. In June 1989 they listed on the London Stock Exchange (quoted on SEAQ International) and raised the equivalent of about $100 million in equity from foreign investors there. Then in June 1992 they listed on the NYSE and raised about $75 million with a share issue directed at U.S. investors.

Private Placements. One type of directed issue that has a long history as a source of both equity and debt is the private placement market. A *private placement* is the sale of a security to a small set of qualified institutional buyers. The investors are traditionally insurance companies and investment companies. Since the securities are not registered for sale to the public, investors have typically followed a "buy and hold" policy. In the case of debt instruments terms are often custom designed on a negotiated basis. On the other hand, equities are usually the same as the publicly traded versions except they are unregistered. Private placement markets exist in most countries.

In April 1990, the Securities and Exchange Commission (SEC) approved SEC Rule 144A. This permits qualified institutional buyers (QIBs) to trade privately placed securities without the previous holding period restrictions and without requiring SEC registration.[10] Simultaneously, the SEC modified its Regulation S to permit foreign issuers to tap the U.S. private placement market through an SEC Rule 144A issue, also without SEC registration. A screen-based automated trading system called PORTAL was established by the National Association of Securities Dealers (NASD) to support the distribution of primary issues and to create a liquid secondary market for these unregistered private placements.

Since SEC registration has been identified as the main barrier to foreign firms wishing to raise funds in the United States, SEC Rule 144A placements are proving attractive to foreign issuers of both equity and debt securities. Atlas Copco, the Swedish multinational firm, was the first foreign firm to take advantage of SEC Rule 144A. It raised $49 million in the United States through an ADR equity placement as part of its larger $214 million Euro-equity issue in 1990. Since then, several billion dollars a year have been raised by foreign issuers with private equity placements in the United States.

A similar private placement market in Europe has also developed historically, but is now reinventing itself to encourage more crossborder issues.

Euro-Equity Issues

The gradual integration of the world's capital markets and increased international portfolio investment has spawned the emergence of a very viable *Euro-equity* market. This has come to mean that a firm can issue equity which is underwritten and distributed in multiple foreign equity markets, sometimes simultaneously with distribution in the domestic market. The same financial institutions that had previously created an infrastructure for the Euronote and Eurobond markets were responsible for the Euro-equity market.[11] The term *Euro* does not imply the issuers or investors are located in Europe. It is a generic term for international equity issues originating and sold anywhere in the world.

The Euro-equity market has been able to absorb single equity issues ranging in size from less than $10 million to over $3 billion. It has also accepted B shares (low vote), preference shares, equity warrants, and hybrid instruments.

The largest and most spectacular recent issues have been in conjunction with a wave of privatizations of government-owned enterprises (see Global View at the beginning of this chapter). The Thatcher government in the United Kingdom created the model when it privatized British Telecom in December 1984. That issue was so large it was necessary and desirable to sell "tranches" to foreign investors in addition to the sale to domestic investors. A *tranche* means an allocation of shares, typically to underwriters that are expected to sell to investors in their designated geographic markets. The objective is both to raise the funds and to ensure postissue worldwide liquidity. Unfortunately, in the

---

[10]A qualified institutional buyer (QIB) is an entity (except banks and savings and loans) that owns and invests on a discretionary basis $100 million in securities of nonaffiliates. Banks and savings and loans must meet this test but also have a minimum net worth of $25 million. The SEC has estimated that about 4,000 QIBs exist, composed mainly of investment advisers, investment companies, insurance companies, pension funds, and charitable institutions.

[11]The Euronote and Eurobond markets are described in the next chapter.

Exhibit 12.2 Tombstone for YPF Sociedad Anónima

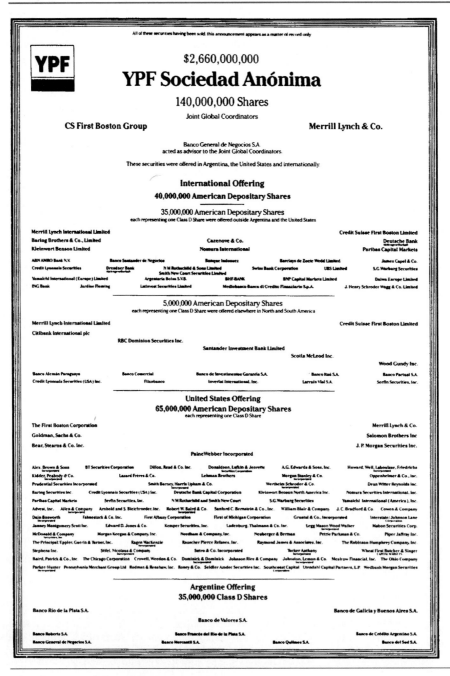

Source: YPF Sociedad Anónima. Reprinted with permission.

case of British Telecom the issue, in retrospect, was underpriced. Most of the foreign shares, especially those placed in the United States, flowed back to London, leaving a nice profit behind for the U.S. underwriters and investors. Nevertheless, other large British privatization issues followed British Telecom, most notably British Steel in 1988.

Euro-equity privatization issues have been particularly popular with international portfolio investors because most of the firms are very large, with excellent credit ratings and profitable quasi-government monopolies at the time of privatization. Thus business risk was initially fairly low and postissue liquidity of the shares was expected to be high because of the size of the issue and its international distribution.

The British privatization model has been so successful that numerous others have followed and many more are expected in the second half of the 1990s. Even government-owned firms in newly developing capital markets have implemented privatization with the help of foreign tranches. One example is Teléfonos de Mexico, the giant Mexican telephone company, which had a $2 billion Euro-equity issue in 1991. It now has U.S.-based Southwest Bell as a 10% shareholder, numerous other foreign institutional and individual investors, and a very liquid listing on the NYSE.

One of the world's largest Euro-equity offerings was the 1993 sale of shares for $3.04 billion by YPF Sociedad Anónima, Argentina's state-owned oil company. About 75% of its shares were placed in tranches outside of Argentina, with 46% in the United States alone. Exhibit 12.2 is a copy of the "tombstone" announcing this immense underwriting. It represents a virtual who's who of the world's leading investment banks.

Sale of a Foreign Subsidiary's Shares to Investors in Its Host Country

Sale of a foreign subsidiary's shares to investors in its host country can lower a firm's cost of capital if investors in the host country award a higher capitalization rate on the subsidiary's earnings than investors award on the parent firm's earnings. Levi Strauss has successfully implemented such a sale of shares in its Japanese subsidiary to Japanese investors. An even stranger case was the sale of U.S.-based Shaklee to Japanese investors. The following Global View describes what happened.

Global View
"A New Kind of Arbitrage"

Minneapolis Raider Irwin Jacobs, discovering a new form of global arbitrage, made a nice bundle off Shaklee (*Forbes*, June 12). He noticed that Shaklee's partly owned Japanese subsidiary was trading in Tokyo at a price that made the parent's stake in it worth more than the entire value of the parent on the New York Stock Exchange. Not surprising, given the huge price/earnings multiples Japanese investors are comfortable with.

Jacobs, who made his first money selling distressed merchandise, knows how to turn a dollar. He bought shares in the whole company and induced it to sell its Japanese subsidiary to a Japanese drug company for more than the whole company was worth when he got in. Then he got the Japanese to buy the rest, and doubled his money in five months.

Says William Jacques, a partner at Martingale Asset Management in Boston: "The Shaklee story really emphasized the valuation discrepancies in various markets."

Is there another Shaklee out there? Evidently nothing that juicy, but we have turned up a list of companies with valuable Japanese operations. If a Japanese company's earnings are worth 40 times earnings, why shouldn't an American company's Japanese earnings be worth that much instead of the multiples of 10 to 15 routinely given U.S. stocks?

The *Weekly Tokyo Keizai* publishes an annual directory listing the pretax incomes of Japanese subsidiaries of U.S. multinationals. These profit figures are public in Japan, even though the parents generally don't disclose them to their U.S. stockholders.

Next, we assumed a 58% tax rate for the subsidiary, the top rate in Japan, and a multiple for the Japanese operation of 40, which is on the low side. (The average P/E in Tokyo is 55.) We compared the resulting hypothetical valuation of the Japanese operation with the market valuation of the U.S. parent. In the table [see Exhibit 12.3] we list 10 multinationals that have 100% owned Japanese subsidiaries potentially worth at least 10% of the parent's market value.

Are these genuinely hidden values? Or is this just amusing arithmetic? Impossible to say. A first step to realizing the values might be a decision by the parent to make a public offering of its Japanese subsidiary. Considering how cheap equity capital is over there, that could become a common tactic over the next decade.

Shinichi Fuki is an associate of New York City-based Jafco America Ventures Inc., an advisory firm to companies considering making public offerings in Japan. He suggests another motivation for a Tokyo offering: in Japan, public companies have prestige that can lead to higher revenues, alliances with better banks and improved recruiting prospects.

Lisle, Ill.-based Molex, a manufacturer of cables and connectors, has a subsidiary potentially worth nearly $800 million, or 98% of the recent value of shares in the U.S. parent traded over the counter. You don't have to bank on a raid by Jacobs to see a buy here. Think of it this way: the non-Japanese operations, which probably earned about $1.30 a share last year, are trading pretty cheap.

Beyond all this lies an intriguing question: Are U.S.-based stocks undervalued? Or is the Tokyo Stock Exchange overvalued? The world seems happy to capitalize Matsushita's substantial U.S. earnings at Japanese multiples, while capitalizing IBM's Japanese earnings at U.S. multiples. To be sure, Matsushita's growth record is better than IBM's; nonetheless, the nearly twofold difference in both price/earnings and price/cash flow multiples is striking. The question arises because the speculative arithmetic above depends entirely on arbitrage between two markets that are very much out of line.

Source: Reprinted by permission of *Forbes*, July 10, 1989, p. 128. © Forbes Inc., 1989.

Exhibit 12.3   What if U.S. Stocks Had Japanese Multiples?

U.S. companies can capitalize on the high P/E multiples of the Tokyo market by taking their Japanese subsidiaries public over there. A handful of U.S. multinationals have done this. Here are some that haven't—yet. They all have Japanese subsidiaries that could be worth a large fraction of their U.S. market capitalizations.

Company	Recent Price	Pretax Profit Japanese Sub at 150 Yen/Dollar ($ million)	Hypothetical Value of Subsidiary* ($ million)	Per U.S. Share	Subsidiary Value as % of Parent Co. Value
Molex	32	$47	$800	31 1/4	98
Applied Materials	27 3/4	13	210	13	36
IBM	109 1/2	1,391	23,400	39 1/2	36
Nordson	48	7	120	12 1/2	26
AMP	42 1/4	62	1,040	9 1/2	23
Coca-Cola	56 1/8	270	4,540	12 3/4	23
Mobil	49	179	3,020	7 1/4	15
Digital Equipment	91 3/8	95	1,600	13 1/4	14
Sun Microsystems	16 3/4	10	170	2 1/2	11
Tandem	17 7/8	11	190	2	11

*Assuming an aftertax price/earnings multiple of 40 and a 58% tax rate.

Strategic Alliance: The Philips Alliance with Bang & Olufsen

Strategic alliances are normally formed by firms that expect to gain synergies from one or more of the following joint efforts. They might share the cost of developing technology or pursue complementary marketing activities. They might gain economies of scale or scope or a variety of other commercial advantages. However, one synergy that may sometimes be overlooked is the possibility for a financially strong firm to help a financially weak firm to lower its cost of capital by providing attractively priced equity or debt financing.

One excellent example of financial synergy was provided by the crossborder strategic alliance of Philips N.V. of the Netherlands with Bang & Olufsen (B & O) of Denmark in 1990. Philips N.V. is one of the largest multinational firms in the world and the leading consumer electronics firm in Europe. B & O is a small European competitor but with a nice market niche at the high end of the audiovisual market.

Philips' Motivation. Philips was a major supplier of components to B & O, which it wished to continue. It also wished to join forces with B & O in the upscale consumer electronics market where Philips did not have the quality image enjoyed by B & O. Philips was also concerned that financial pressure might force B & O to choose a Japanese competitor for a partner. That would be very unfortunate. B & O had always supported Philips's political efforts to gain EU support to make the few remaining European-owned consumer electronics firms more competitive vis-à-vis their strong Japanese competitors.

B & O's Motivation. B & O was interested in an alliance with Philips to gain more rapid access to its new technology and assistance in converting that technology into B & O product applications. B & O wanted assurance of timely delivery of components at large volume discounts from Philips itself, as well as access to Philips's large network of suppliers under terms enjoyed by Philips. Equally important, B & O wanted to get an equity infusion from Philips to strengthen its own shaky financial position. Despite its commercial artistry, in recent years B & O had been only marginally profitable and its publicly traded shares were considered too risky to justify a new public equity issue either in Denmark or abroad. It had no excess borrowing capacity.

The Strategic Alliance. A strategic alliance was agreed upon that would give each partner what they desired commercially. Philips agreed to invest Dkr342 million (about $50 million) to increase the equity of B & O's main operating subsidiary. In return it received a 25% ownership of the expanded subsidiary.

When B & O's strategic alliance was announced to the public on May 3, 1990, the share price of B & O Holding, the listed company on the Copenhagen Stock Exchange, jumped by 35% during the next two days. It remained at that level until the Gulf War crisis temporarily depressed B & O's share price. The share price has since recovered and the expected synergies are starting to materialize.

In evaluating what happened, it is obvious that an industrial purchaser might be willing to pay a higher price for a firm that will provide it some synergies than would a portfolio investor that does not receive these synergies. Portfolio investors are only pricing firm's shares based on the normal risk versus return trade-off. They cannot normally anticipate the value of synergies that might accrue to the firm from an *unexpected* strategic alliance partner. The same conclusion should hold for a purely domestic strategic alliance but this example happens to be a cross border alliance.[12]

---

[12]A favorable impact on the share price of firms receiving equity infusions was also the conclusion of a study of a large sample of strategic alliances by firms resident in the United States as reported in Su Han Chan, John W. Kensinger, Arthur J. Keown, and John D. Martin, "Shareholder Wealth Effects of Investments in Strategic Alliances," San Francisco: Financial Management Association Meetings, October 24, 1992.

Summary

A firm crosslists its shares on foreign stock exchanges for one or more of the following reasons:

- Improve the liquidity of its existing shares.
- Increase its share price by overcoming mispricing by a segmented, illiquid home capital market.
- Support a new equity issue sold in a foreign market.
- Establish a secondary market for shares used in acquisitions.
- Increase the firm's visibility and political acceptance to its customers, suppliers, creditors, and host governments.
- Create a secondary market for shares that will be used to compensate local management and employees in foreign affiliates.

Barriers to listing include an increased commitment to full disclosure and a continuing investor relations program.

The choice of where to crosslist depends on the motive for listing.

- If it is to support a new equity issue or to establish a market for share swaps, the target market should also be the listing market.
- If it is to increase the firm's commercial and political visibility or to compensate local management and employees, it should be the markets in which the firm has significant operations.
- If it is to improve the liquidity of its shares, it should crosslist on a major liquid stock market. The major liquid stock markets are New York, London, Tokyo, Frankfurt, and Paris.
- The choice among these five markets depends on its size and the sophistication of its market-making activities, including competitive transaction costs and competent crisis management.

A firm can lower its cost of capital and increase its liquidity by selling its shares to foreign investors in one or more of four alternative ways:

- Sale of a directed share issue to investors in one particular foreign equity market.
- Sale of a Euro-equity share issue to foreign investors simultaneously in more than one market, including both foreign and domestic markets.
- Sale of a foreign subsidiary's shares to investors in its host country.
- Sale of shares to a foreign firm as part of a strategic alliance.

Questions

1. Growth of Japanese Equities

What are the factors contributing to the rapid growth of the Japanese equity markets? How has the appreciation of the yen affected this growth in valuation and turnover?

2. Equity Market Integration Versus Market Correlation

The terms *integration* and *correlation* are often used interchangeably, although they have very different meanings.

    a.   In reference to stock markets and market activity around the world, differentiate the two terms.

    b.   Would computers and other technological advancements be expected to increase the degree of integration and correlation between markets?

    c.   What evidence exists that the world's markets are increasingly correlated or integrated?

3. Unilever: Motives for Crosslisting

Unilever (UK) is one of the largest multinational firms in the world, and also one of the most crosslisted firms in the world in equity markets.

    a.   What specifically do you think the motives of Unilever were when it listed its shares on equity exchanges around the world?

    b.   Are there specific exchanges that are more important to Unilever than others?

4. European Union and Equity Market Integration

The European Union is attempting to integrate and harmonize the equity markets of its member countries. What are the barriers that need to be overcome? Which stock markets will be the winners and which the losers?

5. Danish Segmentation: J. Lauritzen Holding & Carlsberg

During the early 1990s, J. Lauritzen Holding (a Danish shipping and transport company) and Carlsberg (Danish breweries—Carlsberg and Tuborg beer) raised equity through successful Euro-equity issues. However, unlike Novo Industri in 1981, they experienced a modest drop in their share prices following the announcement of their impending issues.

    a.   Based on the experience of these two firms, do you think the Danish equity market is still segmented? If not, what do you think has happened since 1981 to change the situation?

    b.   What can these two firms do now to further internationalize their cost of capital?

6. Equities: Life After Issuance

Firms issue stock to raise capital, capital needed for the operation and growth of their business. If the firm wishes to raise the most capital per share issued (at the lowest cost possible), management often believes it is the share price at issuance that is important, not what happens to the share price after issued.

    a.   Assuming you are an existing stockholder of the firm, and the firm issues new equity, how do you feel? What determines your rate of return on your investment?

    b.   Assuming you are one of the buyers of the new shares of equity in the firm, what determines the rate of return on your investment?

c. Assuming you are management of the firm, what do you want to see the stock price do in the periods following a new equity issuance?

7. 1987 Stock Market Crash and Contagion

This chapter stated the following: "On Monday, October 19, 1987, the Dow Jones Industrial Average of the New York Stock Exchange fell by 22.6%. The following day it fell an additional 12%. By the end of the week the Japanese SE "new" index had fallen 12%, the London Financial Times ordinary share index was down 23%, and the Frankfurt FAZ general index was down 11.7%. The Hong Kong stock exchange had been closed on Tuesday for the entire week. The Australian, Singapore, and Taiwan markets had fallen 29.3%, 30.8%, and 18.5%, respectively."

The question, however, is not only why the DJIA fell, but why all other markets seemingly fell in sympathy.

a. What business and economic fundamentals should cause the stock price of one firm to fall?

b. What business and economic fundamentals should cause a "market," for example the London Stock Exchange, to fall?

c. Given your answers to parts a) and b), what would link falling equity prices in one market with all markets worldwide?

d. How would the growth of crosslisting affect the linkage between stock markets and stock market movements around the globe?

Bibliography

Adhikari, Ajay, and Rasoul H. Tondkar, "Environmental Factors Influencing Accounting Disclosure Requirements of Global Stock Exchanges," *Journal of International Financial Management and Accounting*, vol. 4, no. 2, Summer 1992, pp. 75–105.

Aggarwal, Reena, Ricardo Leal, and Leonardo Hernandez, "The Aftermarket Performance of Initial Public Offerings in Latin America," *Financial Management*, Spring 1993, pp. 42–53.

Alexander, G., C. Eun, and S. Janakiramanan, "Asset Pricing and Dual Listing on Foreign Capital Markets: A Note," *Journal of Finance*, March 1987, pp. 151–158.

Alexander, Gordon J., Cheol S. Eun, and S. Janakiramanan, "International Listings and Stock Returns: Some Empirical Evidence," *Journal of Financial and Quantitative Analysis*, vol. 23, no. 2, June 1988, pp. 135–151.

Bank for International Settlements, Annual Report, annual issues, Basle.

Baumol, William J. and Burton G. Malkiel, "Redundant Regulation of Foreign Security Trading and U.S. Competitiveness," *Journal of Applied Corporate Finance*, Winter 1993, pp. 19–27.

Biddle, Gary C., and Shahrokh M. Saudagaran, "The Effects of Financial Disclosure Levels on Firms' Choices Among Alternative Foreign Stock Exchange Listings," *Journal of International Financial Management and Accounting*, vol. 1, no. 1, Spring 1989, pp. 55–87.

Bodurtha, James N., D. Chinhyung Cho, and Lemma W. Senbet, "Economic Forces in the Stock Market: An International Perspective," *Global Finance Journal*, Fall 1989, pp. 21–46.

Choi, Frederick D.S., and Arthur Stonehill, "Foreign Access to U.S. Securities Markets: The Theory, Myth and Reality of Regulatory Barriers," *The Investment Analyst*, July 1982, pp. 17–26.

Cochrane, James L., "Helping to Keep U.S. Capital Markets Competitive: Listing World-Class Non-U.S. Firms on U.S. Exchanges," *Journal of International Financial Management and Accounting*, vol. 4, no. 2, Summer 1992, pp. 163–170.

Edwards, Franklin R., "Listing of Foreign Securities on U.S. Exchanges," *Journal of Applied Corporate Finance*, Winter 1993, pp. 28–36.

Eun, Cheol S., and S. Janakiramanan, "Bilateral Cross-Listing and the Equilibrium Security Prices," *Advances in Financial Planning and Forecasting*, vol. 4, part B, 1990, pp. 59–74.

Freund, William C., "Current Issues: International Markets, Electronic Trading and Linkages in International Equity Markets," *Financial Analysts Journal*, May/June 1989, pp. 10–15.

Fry, Clifford, Insup Lee and Jongmoo Jay Choi, "International Listing and Valuation: The Case of the Tokyo Stock Exchange," *Review of Quantitative Finance and Accounting*, March 1994.

Hawawini, Gabriel, and Eric Rajendra, *The Transformation of the European Financial Services Industry: From Fragmentation to Integration*, New York: New York University Salomon Center; Monograph Series in Finance and Economics, no. 4, 1989.

Howe, John S., and Kathryn Kelm, "The Stock Price Impacts of Overseas Listings," *Financial Management*, Autumn 1987, pp. 51–56.

Huang, Roger D., and Hans R. Stoll, *Major World Equity Markets: Current Structure and Prospects for Change*, New York: New York University Salomon Center; Monograph Series in Finance and Economics, no. 3, 1991.

Jacque, Laurent, and Gabriel Hawawini, "Myths and Realities of the Global Capital Market: Lessons for Financial Managers," *Journal of Applied Corporate Finance*, Fall 1993, pp. 81–90.

Marr, M. Wayne, John L. Trimble, and Raj Varma, "On the Integration of International Capital Markets: Evidence from Euroequity Offerings," *Financial Management*, Winter 1991, pp. 11–21.

———, "Innovation in Global Financing: The Case of Euroequity Offerings," *Journal of Applied Corporate Finance*, Spring 1992.

Meek, G. K., and S. J. Gray, "Globalization of Stock Markets and Foreign Listing Requirements: Voluntary Disclosures by Continental European Companies Listed on the London Stock Exchange," *Journal of International Business Studies*, Summer 1989, pp. 315–336.

Meek, Gary K, "U.S. Securities Market Responses to Alternate Earnings Disclosures of Non-U.S. Multinational Corporations," *The Accounting Review*, April 1983, pp. 394–402.

Muscarella, Chris, and Michael Vetsuypens, "The British Petroleum Stock Offering: An Application of Option Pricing," *Journal of Applied Corporate Finance*, Winter 1989, pp. 74–80.

Roll, Richard, "The International Crash of 1987," *Financial Analysts Journal*, September-October 1988, pp. 19–35.

Saudagaran, Shahrokh M., "An Investigation of Selected Factors Influencing Multiple Listing and the Choice of Foreign Stock Exchanges," *Advances in Financial Planning and Forecasting*, vol. 4, part B, 1990, pp. 75–122.

———, "An Empirical Study of Selected Factors Influencing the Decision to List on Foreign Stock Exchanges," *Journal of International Business Studies*, Spring 1988, pp. 101–128.

———, and Gary C. Biddle, "Financial Disclosure Levels and Foreign Stock Exchange Listing Decisions," *Journal of International Financial Management and Accounting*, vol. 4, no. 2, Summer 1992, pp. 106–148.

Solnik, Bruno H., *International Investments*, 2nd ed., Reading, Mass.: Addison-Wesley, 1991.

Stoll, Hans R., *Major World Equity Markets: Current Structure and Prospects for Change*, New York: New York University Salomon Center; Monograph Series in Finance and Economics, no. 3, 1991.

Torabzadeh, Khalil M., William J. Bertin, and Terry L. Zivney, "Valuation Effects of International Listings," *Global Finance Journal*, vol. 3, no. 2, 1992, pp. 159–170.

Tsetsekos, George P., "Multinationality and Common Stock Offering Dilution," *Journal of International Financial Management and Accounting*, vol. 3, no. 1, Spring 1991, pp. 1–16.

Wahab, Mahmoud, and Malek Lashgari, "Stability and Predictability of the Comovement Structure of Returns in the American Depositary Receipts Market," *Global Finance Journal*, vol. 4, no. 2, 1993, pp. 141–169.

Walter, Ingo, and Roy C. Smith, *Investment Banking in Europe: Restructuring for the 1990s*, Cambridge, Mass.: Basil Blackwell, 1990.

Chapter 13
Sourcing Debt Internationally

Global View
Foreign Companies Borrow in Cheap U.S. Markets

London—Foreign companies are piling into U.S. debt markets to borrow funds they would have trouble raising at home or in the offshore, London-based markets. They are attracted by low U.S. interest rates and the fact that American money managers are groping for higher returns and more diversified portfolios.

"As interest rates decline, people are scrambling to replace yields wherever they can," says John E. Cartland, a vice president at Travelers Asset Management International Corp. in Hartford, Connecticut. "There has been an enormous amount of money going into bonds and bond funds; this money has to be invested, and there's a scarcity of product." The upshot, says R. Edward Chambliss, a managing director at SBCI, the New York investment banking unit of Swiss Bank Corp., is that "U.S. investors will have an opportunity to buy the bonds of corporations that haven't issued debt in the U.S. before and in longer-term maturities than they have been able to get."

A prime example, he and others say, is triple-B-rated Philips Electronics NV's recent $500 million offering of so-called Yankee bonds, which are foreign companies' debt sold in the U.S. In a two-part underwriting led by Goldman, Sachs & Co., the big Dutch consumer electronics company sold $250 million in 10-year notes and $250 million in 20-year bonds. Because Philips has a low credit rating—although still investment grade—from Standard & Poors and was able to borrow large sums at long maturities in a public bond offering, Mr. Chambliss calls the issue "a watershed deal."

U.S. capital markets, the world's largest, offer foreign companies, especially European concerns, a chance to diversify their funding sources and borrow at longer maturities than those usually available in either the Euromarket or their home markets. By contrast, roughly 95% of all Eurobonds mature in 10 years or less, according to Securities Data Co. In addition, many European companies, including Philips, have traditionally relied on bank borrowing for most of their funding.

Source: Adapted from Michael R. Sesit, "Foreign Companies Borrow in Cheap, Hungry U.S. Markets," 9/14/93, C1, C15. Reprinted by permission of *The Wall Street Journal*, © 1993 Dow Jones & Co., Inc. All Rights Reserved Worldwide.

Cross-border financial markets are an increasingly important source of debt capital for multinational firms. Chapters 10 and 11, which opened this part, described the theoretical and practical dimensions of a multinational firm's financial structure and its desired financing in the future. Chapter 12 described the issues and methods by which a multinational firm can go outside its home country for equity capital. Assuming the multinational firm has determined its desired capital structure, this chapter explores the methods and choices the multinational firm may use to raise long-term debt on international markets.

The first part of this chapter details the common financial guidelines which firms follow when acquiring long-term debt. In addition to the normal concerns, however, debt capital that is denominated in foreign currency poses specific problems for the firm (although these may not always be bad). The second part of the chapter provides a cursory overview of the major debt markets and instruments available to the multinational firm, the *menu* of choices. The third and final section provides a short but detailed analysis of the financial decision making that goes into the selection of a specific debt issue when it may be sourced in three different currency markets.

Debt Management and Funding Goals

The multinational firm raising debt capital on the international markets must—as it must always do in a domestic market—determine the quantity of funds needed per issuance, the maturity of the issuance, and the type of repayment stream to be used. In addition to these customary domestic dimensions of debt issuance is the question of currency of denomination. So how does the firm determine what types of debt it wants?

Maturity Matching

The most common method for structuring the firm's debt portfolio is *matching*. A firm typically wants to finance current assets with current liabilities and permanent or long-term assets with long-term liabilities. This *matching of maturity* prevents the firm from being exposed to significant interest rate and funding risks as differing categories of assets turn over with time.

Exhibit 13.1   The Financing of Assets: Short-Term Versus Long-Term Funding

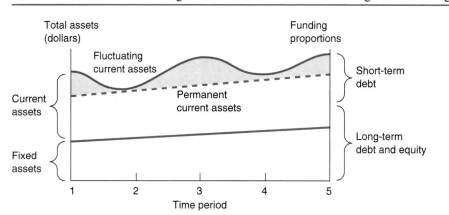

Fixed assets and current assets grow over time as the firm grows. Current assets, however, fluctuate over seasonal and business cycles, but typically do not fall below some minimum level. This minimum level of current assets is called *permanent current assets*. The firm must determine what proportion of fixed assets and current assets are to be financed with long-term sources of capital or short-term sources of debt. Typically, all fixed assets and some proportion of current assets, for example the permanent current assets, are financed with long-term capital. The remaining current assets, *fluctuating current assets*, are financed with short-term debt.

Exhibit 13.1 illustrates the changing financing needs of a firm as it grows over time. The firm's *current assets* and *fixed assets* must be financed.[1] The financial manager must choose the proportions of long-term debt versus short-term debt to use in this funding. The choice, however, requires the manager to weigh the trade-off between having the flexibility of short-term financing versus the risks of potentially higher financial expenses.

For example, as the firm grows in its financing needs from period 2 to period 3, current assets can be seen to fluctuate over time. Current assets can therefore be subdivided into permanent current assets and fluctuating current assets. *Permanent current assets* is the name given to that level of current assets below which total current assets never falls. The remaining current assets, those current assets over and above this minimal permanent level, are termed *fluctuating current assets*. Many firms experience a buildup of inventories in periods leading up to the high points in seasonal sales, followed by drawdowns of inventories as the peak sales period passes.

---

[1] Current assets include cash, securities, accounts receivable, and inventories. Fixed assets typically include fixed plant and equipment, land, and building structures for operations.

The financial manager has then the opportunity of financing three different asset categories in total: fixed assets, permanent current assets, and fluctuating current assets. So which would the financial manager prefer, short-term or long-term financing? What are the corresponding costs and benefits of short-term financing?

A firm that knows its short-term funding requirements can borrow funds just for the period needed, therefore not committing to debt levels and interest expenses over and above its basic needs. If, however, it finds it needs the funding for longer than previously expected, the firm must renew or replace some of these short-term funds. If the firm has difficulty in renewing this funding, or renewing it at the same price (called *refunding risk*), it might have serious problems.

To avoid the possibility of not having sufficient funds the firm may choose to finance most of its current assets with longer term debt. Although this would assure the firm of sufficient funding at known cost, the firm may be committing itself to levels of debt and interest expense that it may not need in the long run. The choice is obviously not an easy one, but it is the burden of all financial managers.

Currency Matching

The multinational firm possesses a continuing series of foreign currency-denominated assets. The firm may wish to fund these assets with liabilities of not only the same maturity structure, but also the same currency of denomination. This is the basic *operating strategy* for transaction exposure management first discussed in Chapter 8.

The question is whether it is the currency of denomination of assets and liabilities (the balance sheet) that is of critical significance, or the currency of denomination of cash flows (the income statement) of the firm. A firm that is acquiring debt denominated in a specific currency for asset/liability matching is focusing on *accounting exposures* (Chapter 9). A firm focusing on the matching of currency of denomination of cash flows *arising* from assets and liabilities is focusing on potential *transaction and operating exposures* (Chapters 7 and 8). As we concluded in Part 3, the primary emphasis of multinational financial management should be on cash flow-based value, and not on accounting conventions and practices that have no real cash flow impact.

As Chapters 10 and 11 emphasized, however, there are potential benefits to diversifying the sources of long-term debt in terms of capital cost. If the firm intentionally diversifies debt sourcing across currencies (for example like that shown for Statoil of Norway at the end of Chapter 8), care must be taken that these cost benefits gained initially from diversification do not disappear as the debt is repaid. As the following section describes, the currency risks associated with foreign currency-denominated debt are significant and must be managed from the time of the debt issuance.

Foreign Exchange Risk and the Cost of Debt

When a firm issues foreign currency-denominated debt, its effective cost equals the after-tax cost of repaying the principal and interest in terms of the firm's own currency. This amount includes the nominal cost of principal and interest in foreign currency terms, adjusted for any foreign exchange gains or losses.

For example, if a U.S.-based firm borrows Sfr1,500,000 for one year at 5.00% interest, and during the year the franc appreciates from an initial rate of Sfr1.5000/$ to Sfr1.4400/$, what is the dollar cost of this debt $(k_d^\$)$?

The dollar proceeds of the initial borrowing are calculated at the current spot rate of Sfr1.5000/$:

$$\frac{Sfr1,500,000}{Sfr1.5000/\$} = \$1,000,000.$$

At the end of one year the U.S.-based firm is responsible for repaying the Sfr1,500,000 principal plus 5.00% interest, or a total of Sfr1,575,000. This repayment, however, must be made at an ending spot rate of Sfr1.4400/$:

$$\frac{Sfr1,500,000 \times 1.05}{Sfr1.4400/\$} = \$1,093,750.$$

The actual dollar cost of the loan's repayment is not simply 5.00%, which was paid in Swiss franc interest, but 9.375%.

$$\frac{\$1,093,750}{\$1,000,000} = 1.09375.$$

The dollar cost is higher than expected due to appreciation of the Swiss franc against the U.S. dollar.

This total home currency cost is actually the result of the combined percentage cost of debt and percentage change in the foreign currency's value. The total cost of borrowing Swiss francs by a U.S. dollar-based firm, $k_d^\$$, can be found by multiplying one plus the Swiss franc interest expense, k_d^{Sfr}, by one plus the percentage change in the Sfr/$ exchange rate, s:

$$k_d^\$ = \left[(1 + k_d^{Sfr}) \times (1 + s)\right] - 1$$

where $k_d^{Sfr} = 5.00\%$ and $s = 4.1667\%$.[2] The total expense is:

$$k_d^\$ = \left[(1 + .0500) \times (1 + .041667)\right] - 1 = .09375.$$

The total percentage cost of capital is 9.375%, not simply the foreign currency interest payment of 5%. The after-tax cost of this Swiss franc-denominated debt, when the U.S. income tax rate is 34%, is:[3]

---

[2]The percentage change in the value of the Swiss franc versus the U.S. dollar, when the home currency is the U.S. dollar is:

$$\frac{S_1 - S_2}{S_2} \times 100 = \frac{Sfr1.5000/\$ - Sfr1.4400/\$}{Sfr1.4400/\$} \times 100 = +4.1667\%.$$

[3]The added 4.1667% cost of this debt in terms of U.S. dollars would be reported as a foreign exchange transaction loss, and it would be deductible for tax purposes.

Exhibit 13.2   Costs of Borrowing in Foreign Currency-Denominated Bonds (percentage)

Issuer (parent)	Date of issue	(A) Cost of Funds at time of issue, mark-denominated (%)	(B) Cost of Funds at time of issue, dollar-denominated (%)	(C) Effective Cost of DM-issue adjusted for currency changes as of Oct 1973 (%)	(D) Effective Cost of DM-issue adjusted for currency changes as of maturity (%)
National Lead	5-26-67	6.58	7.08	12.38	12.56
General Instrument	5-29-68	7.08	8.33	13.17	14.52
Gulf Oil	9-05-68	6.57	7.51	12.01	12.93
Occidental Petroleum	10-08-68	6.70	7.70	12.20	13.20
Tenneco	12-17-68	6.88	8.13	12.35	13.61
Chrysler	7-10-69	7.14	7.49	13.40	14.50
Studebaker-Worthington	7-31-69	7.65	8.81	14.00	16.60
Int. Standard Electric	9-01-69	7.14	8.40	13.38	14.36
TRW	10-15-69	7.82	8.70	13.17	14.74

Source: Steven M. Dawson, "Eurobond Currency Selection: Hindsight," *Financial Executive*, November 1973, p. 73. Column A presents expected cost to maturity of issue given coupon, new issue price, maturity, and sinking fund requirements. Column B makes similar calculation assuming the issue were denominated in U.S. dollars. Columns C and D present costs to maturity after coupons are adjusted by Morgan Guaranty. Adjustments in columns C and D include the dollar devaluation and mark revaluations subsequent to debt issuance. Each principal and coupon payment is adjusted for U.S. bank transfer rate in effect at time of payment. All payments after October 1, 1976, are assumed made at the October 1 exchange rate.

$$k_d^\$(1 - t) = 9.375\% \times 0.66 = 6.1875\%.$$

Multinational firms have discovered that borrowing foreign currency debt on a long-term basis creates considerable exposure to transaction gains or losses. For example, U.S. firms that borrowed long-term Deutschemarks prior to December 1971 rue that day. In an article appropriately titled "Eurobond Currency Selection: Hindsight," Steven Dawson calculated what happened to the nine Deutschemark-denominated bonds that were issued by U.S. firms during the fixed exchange rate period May 1967 to October 1969.[4] Exhibit 13.2 shows that in each case the borrower would have been much better off to have borrowed in dollars. This is despite the fact that the initial nominal interest rate would have been higher for a dollar-denominated issue than for a Deutschemark-denominated one. Exhibit 13.2, column C, shows that most of the damage must have been done during the transition to floating exchange rates (December 1971 to October 1973). Column D shows that the large transaction losses continued right up to maturity.

Debt sourced internationally, however, need not end up being more expensive. As Chapter 14 on interest rate risk management explains, there are a variety of strategies and methods for managing foreign currency-denominated debt.

---

[4]Steven M. Dawson, "Eurobond Currency Selection: Hindsight," *Financial Executive*, November 1973, pp. 72–73, updated by Steven M. Dawson, February 1991.

International Debt Markets: Instrument Choices

The international debt markets offer the borrower a variety of different maturities, repayment structures, and currencies of denomination. Once the international financial manager knows the quantities of debt needed, as well as the currency of denomination and maturity, a look at the menu of choices is more meaningful. Exhibit 13.3 provides an overview of the three major sources of debt funding on the international markets: *international bank loans*, the *Euronote market*, and the *international bond market*.

A multinational firm will normally need debt in a variety of maturities, payment structures, and currencies, therefore often using all three markets—in addition to their traditional domestic funding base. The following sections describe the basic attributes of these markets and instruments, as well as their relative advantages and disadvantages for meeting the funding needs of the individual firm.

Exhibit 13.3   Raising Debt Capital in the International Markets

Markets and Instruments	Maturities	Pricing	Market Size[1]
International Bank Loans			
Short to Medium Term Bank Loans	1 yr–5 yrs	Floating rate	
Syndicated Credits (Eurocredits)	2 yrs–10 yrs	Floating rate	
Gross international bank credit[2]			7,351.6
Less interbank redepositing[3]			3,691.6
Net international bank credit			$3,660.0
Euronote Market			
Euronotes	3 yrs–7 yrs	Floating rate	37.0
Euro-Commercial Paper (ECP)	30 days–365 days/1–5 yrs	Fixed rate	78.7
Euro-Medium Term Notes (EMTN)	2 yrs–6 yrs	Fixed rate	61.1
Net Euronote market credit			$ 176.9
International Bond Market			
Straight Fixed Rate Issues	2 yrs–20 yrs	Fixed	1,211.4
Floating Rate Notes (FRNs)	2 yrs–20 yrs	Floating	221.6
Equity-Related Issues	2 yrs–10 yrs	Fixed, equity dependent	254.2
Net international bond market credit			$1,687.2
Less double-counting between bank and creditors[4]			(584.1)
Total net international debt financing			$4,940.0

[1]Stocks at current exchange rates, end-of-year 1992, in billions of U.S. dollars.

[2]Bank and syndicated credits combined. Gross cross-border claims of reporting banks and local claims in foreign currency.

[3]Excluding, on an estimated basis, redepositing between reporting banks.

[4]International bonds taken up by reporting banks, to the extent they are included in the banking statistics as claims on nonresidents; bonds issued by the reporting banks mainly for the purpose of underpinning their international lending activities.

Source: Constructed by authors from Bank for International Settlements, *63rd Annual Report*, Basle, 14 June 1993, pp. 100–117.

International Bank Loans

International bank loans have traditionally been sourced in the Eurocurrency markets that were described in Chapter 2. Eurodollar bank loans are also called "Eurodollar credits" or simply "Eurocredits." The latter title is broader because it encompasses nondollar loans in the Eurocurrency market. We use the term "Eurodollar" throughout this chapter as a proxy for all Eurocurrencies in order to simplify the exposition.

The key factor attracting both depositors and borrowers to the Eurocurrency loan market is the narrow interest rate spread within that market. The difference between deposit and loan rates is often less than 1%. The narrower spread of the Euromarkets, compared to domestic markets, is illustrated in Exhibit 13.4 for Eurodollars.

Interest spreads in the Eurodollar market are small for a number of reasons. Low lending rates exist because the Eurodollar market is a "wholesale" market, where deposits and loans are made in amounts of $500,000 or more on an unsecured basis. Borrowers are usually large corporations or government entities that qualify for low rates because of their credit standing and because the transaction size is large. In addition, overhead assigned to the Eurodollar operation by participating banks is small.

Deposit rates are higher in the Eurodollar market than in the U.S. domestic market because banks need not comply with U.S. reserve requirements. These reserve requirements, although significantly smaller than in the past, require that a certain percentage of funds be held in noninterest earning form. This raises the cost of banking operations. A second cost avoided in the Eurocurrency and Eurodollar markets is the payment of

Exhibit 13.4 Comparative Spreads Between Lending and Deposit Rates: The Eurodollar Market

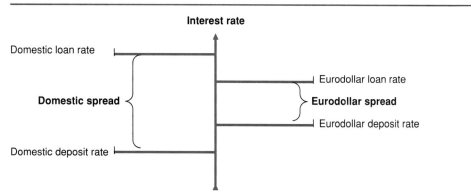

Eurodollar deposit rates are higher and Eurodollar loan rates are lower than their corresponding domestic deposit and loan rates due to the absence of banking restrictions such as reserve requirements and depositor insurance fees, and the wholesale nature of the market.

deposit insurance fees, such as Federal Deposit Insurance Corporation (FDIC) assessments paid on deposits in the United States.

Eurocredits

Eurocredits are bank loans to business firms, sovereign governments, international institutions, and to other banks, denominated in Eurocurrencies and extended by banks in countries other than the country in whose currency the loan is denominated. Because of the large size of these loans, the lending banks form a syndicate (group) in order to diversify their risk.

The basic borrowing interest rate for Eurodollar loans has long been tied to the London Interbank Offered Rate (LIBOR), which is the deposit rate applicable to interbank loans within London. In the early 1980s, however, use of this LIBOR base was supplemented by use of a U.S. money market rate base. Consequently, both rates serve as the base for different credits. Borrowers usually pay a premium over the base rate determined by their creditworthiness and the terms of the credit.

Eurodollars are lent for both short- and medium-term maturities, with transactions for six months or less regarded as routine. Most Eurodollar loans are for a fixed term with no provision for early repayment.

Standby Eurodollar credits are of two types: a Eurodollar line of credit and a Eurodollar revolving commitment. Under a *Eurodollar line of credit*, a bank promises to lend Eurodollars up to the credit limit, with the interest rate determined by market conditions when the loan is made. Because the line of credit can be canceled by the bank at any time, the arrangement is essentially one of preparing for borrowing in advance.

Under a *Eurodollar revolving commitment*, a bank agrees to lend for a period of perhaps three to five years by accepting a series of sequential notes of short maturity. For example, the borrower may renew a series of 180-day notes at each maturity at the interest rate then in effect. Banks charge a fee of about 0.5% per annum on the unused portion of such a revolving, nonrevocable commitment.

Structure of a Syndicated Credit

The syndication of loans has enabled banks to spread the risk of very large loans among a number of banks. Syndication has been particularly important because many large multinational firms need credit in excess of a single bank's loan limit.

A syndicated bank credit is arranged by a lead bank on behalf of its client. Before finalizing the loan agreement, the lead bank seeks the participation of a group of banks, with each participant providing a portion of the total funds needed. The lead bank will work with the borrower to determine the amount of the total credit, the floating-rate base and spread over the base rate, maturity, and fee structure for managing the participating banks. The syndicated loan may or may not be totally underwritten by the participating banks. In the case of loans that are undersubscribed, the amount of credit may be altered to reflect market demand. When oversubscribed, allotment is required. The periodic expenses of the syndicated credit are composed of two elements:

1. the actual interest expense of the loan, normally stated as a spread in basis points over a variable-rate base such as LIBOR;

2. the commitment fees paid on any unused portions of the credit. The spread paid by the borrower is considered the *risk premium*, reflecting the general business and financial risk applicable to the borrower's repayment capability.

Spreads in the syndicated loan market have typically varied from as little as 1/16% to over 2 1/2% (paid by the government of Brazil in 1981 and 1982 on what were then termed "Jumbo Loans" of $1 billion or more). The size and nature of the commitment fees paid depends on whether the syndicated loan is a revolving credit or term credit. If a term credit, the borrower has a specified drawdown time schedule for the loan, and there is usually no associated commitment fee. If, however, the credit is in the form of a revolving credit, the participating banks have "theoretically" set aside capital that must be paid for if unused. Exhibit 13.5 illustrates the structure and pricing of a syndicated credit for Irish Aerospace concluded in 1989.

The Euronote Market

The Euronote market is the collective term used to describe short- to medium-term debt instruments sourced in the Eurocurrency markets. Although there are a multitude of differentiated financial products, they can be divided into two major groups: underwritten facilities and nonunderwritten facilities. The *underwritten facilities* are used for the sale of Euronotes in a number of different forms. The *nonunderwritten facilities* are used for the sale and distribution of *Euro-Commercial Paper* (ECP) and *Euro-Medium-Term Notes* (EMTNs).

Facilities for Euronotes

A major development in international money markets was the establishment of facilities for sales of short-term, negotiable, promissory notes—*Euronotes*. Among the facilities for their issuance were revolving underwriting facilities (RUFs), note issuance facilities (NIFs), and standby note issuance facilities (SNIFs). These facilities were provided by international investment and commercial banks. They reflected the movement toward securitization that hit both domestic and international financial markets after the onset of the debt crisis in the early 1980s.

The RUFs, NIFs, and SNIFs all constitute medium-term (three- to seven-year) commitments by commercial and investment banks to underwrite and distribute the Euronotes. A typical structure would include between one and three arranger banks that would organize a group of participating banks to take shares of the total commitment. The arranger banks would keep relatively small shares for themselves, and earn fees for their services. The arrangers and participating banks stand ready to buy the borrower's notes in the event the notes could not be placed in the market at previously guaranteed

Exhibit 13.5 Pricing and Structure of a Syndicated Eurocredit

Borrower:	Irish Aerospace, GPA Airbus, GPA Fokker, GPA Jetprop, GPA Rolls
Amount:	US$1.25 billion; Revolving loans/guarantees/letters of credit
Terms:	8 years at 93.75 basis points over LIBOR, with a margin of 7/8% for GPA Airbus drawings
Arranger:	Citicorp Investment Bank
Lead Managers & Underwriters:	Citibank, Chase Investment Bank, Toronto-Dominion Bank, Citibank (Channel Islands) for a syndicate of Japanese leasing companies, Credit Suisse, Societe Generale (London), Amsterdam-Rotterdam Bank, Bank of Nova Scotia, Bank of Tokyo International, Daiwa Bank, IBJ, Irish Inter-continental Bank/Kredeitbank International Group, Mitsubishi Trust & Banking, National Westminster Bank, Swiss Bank, Tokai Bank

A typical syndicated loan of this type would have up-front fees totaling 1.5% of the principal. The fees would be divided between three groups: (1) the lead arranger bank(s), which organizes the loan and participants; (2) the lead managing and underwriting banks, which aid in the syndication of the loan; and (3) the participating banks, which actually provide the capital.

If the 1.5% total fee was subdivided equally among the three groups, the proceeds of the loan after expenses of issuance and arrangement are:

$1,250,000,000 - [(0.005 + 0.005 + 0.005) \times $1,250,000,000] = $1,231,250,000.

The debt service payments over the 8-year period prior to principal repayment are LIBOR + 93.75 basis points; assuming an initial LIBOR rate of 9.00% (reset every six months for semi-annual debt service payments):

$$\left[\frac{0.0900 + 0.009375}{2}\right] \times \$1,250,000,000 = \$62,109,375.$$

The effective annual cost is thus:

$$\left[\frac{\$62,109,375}{\$1,231,250,000}\right] \times 2 \times 100 = 10.09\%.$$

Source: Adapted from "Syndicated Loans," *Euromoney*, November 1989, p. 165.

rates (usually stated as a maximum interest expense). The Euronote was a substantially cheaper source of short-term funds than syndicated loans, since the notes were placed directly with the investor public, and the securitized and underwritten form allowed the ready establishment of liquid secondary markets. The banks received substantial fees initially for their underwriting and placement services.[5]

---

[5]The Euronote market essentially died in the late 1980s, amounting to only $6.6 billion in gross new issues in 1989. The demise of the underwritten Euronote has been mostly due to competition from Euro-commercial paper, Euro-medium-term notes, and growth in newly established, non-underwritten, domestic commercial paper markets in many countries.

Euro-Commercial Paper (ECP)

Euro-commercial paper (ECP), like the commercial paper (CP) issued in domestic markets around the world, is a short-term debt obligation of a corporation or bank. Maturities are typically one, three, and six months. The paper is sold normally at a discount or occasionally with a stated coupon. Although the market is capable of supporting issues in any major currency, over 90% of issues outstanding are denominated in U.S. dollars. Exhibit 13.6 shows typical yield calculations for ECP, along with a number of factors relevant to specific ECP currency issues.

The typical ECP issue has changed from completely underwritten issues in the early years to the recent movement toward nonunderwritten issues similar to commercial paper issued in the United States. Unlike domestic commercial paper markets, the ECP market did not place much importance on quality of issuer as measured by ratings until recently. As of 1989 only about 50% of all outstanding ECP issues were rated; the increase in the number of defaults caused a significant change in market concern regarding quality.

The ECP market is in competition with domestic markets of the same instrument. The increasing concern for quality ratings of issuers in the ECP market has reduced the comparative advantage of some borrowers to issue internationally (ECP) rather than in their domestic market. For example, the U.S. domestic commercial paper market has always been considered less cosmopolitan because domestic borrowers normally raise funds at lower cost than foreign issuers in the United States. This is changing. As

Exhibit 13.6   Pricing and Structure of Euro-Commercial Paper (ECP)

The proceeds of the issuance of Euro-commercial paper (ECP) at a discount by corporate borrowers is calculated as follows:

$$\text{Market Price} = \frac{\text{Face Value}}{1 + \left[\left(\frac{N}{360}\right) \times \left(\frac{Y}{100}\right)\right]}$$

where   Y = yield in annual percent
        N = days remaining until maturity.

For example, the market price (proceeds) of the sale of a $1,000 face-value 90-day ECP priced to yield 8.0% annually (reflecting current market yields on similar debt securities for comparable credit ratings) would be:

$$\text{Market Price} = \frac{\$1,000}{1 + \left[\left(\frac{90}{360}\right) \times \left(\frac{8.0}{100}\right)\right]} = \$980.39.$$

The calculation of the market price varies by the currency of denomination's day-count convention. For example, the British pound sterling-denominated ECP market uses a 365-day financial year instead of the U.S. dollar's 360-day year.

financial deregulation continues in both Japan and Europe, domestic commercial paper markets may increasingly constitute effective competition for ECP. Lower quality borrowers may now find their domestic market their most reasonably priced source of such debt.

Euro-Medium-Term Notes (EMTNs)

The Euro-medium-term note is the latest major entrant on the world's debt markets. It began in 1986 with two major issues, a $160 million facility for First Interstate Bank (U.S.) and a $200 million facility established for Nordic Investment Bank. The EMTN effectively bridges the maturity gap between ECP and the longer term and less flexible international bond. Although many of the notes were initially underwritten, most EMTNs are now nonunderwritten.

The rapid initial growth of the EMTN market followed directly on the heels of the same basic instrument that began in the U.S. domestic market in 1982. With SEC Rule #415 instituted in 1982, the SEC allowed a U.S. corporation to obtain a *shelf registration*

Exhibit 13.7   Structure and Pricing of a Euro-Medium-Term Note (EMTN)

EMTNs, because they are shelf registered with fixed coupon and maturity dates, result in some rather awkward valuations. For example, let us assume an EMTN is issued on November 1, 1994, in the denomination of US$1000. The note matures on June 15, 1996, with set coupon dates of May 1 and November 1 each year. The coupon is 7.0% per annum and is paid semiannually to the bearer.

Since the note is issued on November 15, 1994, and the next scheduled coupon payment is on May 1 of 1995, the first coupon period is only 165 days and therefore the buyer will not receive the full coupon payment (only 165/180% of the $35.00 semiannual coupon). The full valuation of this specific issue off-the-shelf appears as follows:

Cash Flow	Date	Number of Days Since Prev. Date	Days as Percentage of 180 Days	Amount of Cash Flow
First coupon	1 May 95	165	92%	$ 32.08
Second coupon	1 Nov 95	180	100%	$ 35.00
Third coupon	1 May 96	180	100%	$ 35.00
Final coupon	15 June 96	45	25%	$ 8.75
Principal	15 June 96	45	25%	$1000.00

Note that the final time period, the one following the third coupon payment, is only 45 days. This results in a final coupon payment of $8.75 (45/180 × $35.00). The principal of US$1000 is also fully repaid upon the specified maturity date.

The market price (P) or present value of the EMTN on November 15, 1994—the date of issuance—yielding 6% annually (a 3.0% semiannual discount factor) would be calculated in the following way:

$$P = \frac{\$32.08}{(1 + 0.3)^{0.92}} + \frac{\$35.00}{(1 + .03)^{1.92}} + \frac{\$35.00}{(1 + .03)^{2.92}} + \frac{\$8.75}{(1 + .03)^{3.17}} + \frac{\$1000}{(1 + .03)^{3.17}} = \$1,008.31.$$

This amount, net of any issuance fees (if any), would constitute the proceeds of the issue to the firm.

for debt issues. What this meant was that once the registration was obtained, the corporation could issue notes on a continuous basis without having to obtain new registrations for each additional issue. This in turn allowed a firm to sell short- and medium-term notes through a much cheaper and more flexible issuance facility than ordinary bonds. Although the European version does not, of course, have the problem of registration like that of the U.S. domestic note, its success to date has been a result of the same basic features that have given the MTN in the United States its advantages over the traditional bond.

The EMTN's basic characteristics are similar to a bond, with principal, maturity, and coupon structures and rates being comparable. The EMTN's typical maturities range from as short as 9 months to a maximum of 10 years. Coupons are typically paid semiannually, and coupon rates are comparable to similar bond issues. The EMTN does, however, have three unique characteristics. First, the EMTN is a facility, allowing continuous issuance over a period of time, unlike a bond issue that is essentially sold all at once. Second, because EMTNs are sold continuously, in order to make debt service (coupon redemption) manageable, coupons are paid on set calendar dates regardless of the date of issuance. Finally, EMTNs are issued in relatively small denominations, from $2 million to $5 million, making medium-term debt acquisition much more flexible than the large minimums customarily needed in the international bond markets. Exhibit 13.7 details the pricing and structure of a sample EMTN issue.

The International Bond Market

The international bond market sports a rich array of innovative instruments created by imaginative investment bankers, who are unfettered by the usual controls and regulations governing domestic capital markets. Indeed, the international bond market rivals the international banking market in terms of the quantity and cost of funds provided to international borrowers.

All international bonds fall within two generic classifications, *Eurobonds* and *foreign bonds*. The distinction between categories is based on whether the borrower is a domestic or a foreign resident, and whether the issue is denominated in the local currency or a foreign currency.

A Eurobond is underwritten by an international syndicate of banks and other securities firms, and is sold exclusively in countries other than the country in whose currency the issue is denominated. For example, a bond issued by a firm resident in the United States, denominated in U.S. dollars, but sold to investors in Europe and Japan (not to investors in the United States), would be a Eurobond.

A foreign bond is underwritten by a syndicate composed of members from a single country, sold principally within that country, and denominated in the currency of that country. The issuer, however, is from another country. A bond issued by a firm resident in Sweden, denominated in dollars, and sold in the United States to U.S. investors by U.S. investment bankers, would be a foreign bond. Foreign bonds have nicknames: Foreign bonds sold in the United States are "Yankee bonds"; foreign bonds sold in Japan are "Samurai bonds"; and foreign bonds sold in the United Kingdom are "Bulldogs."

Eurobond Market

Eurobonds are issued by multinational corporations, large domestic corporations, sovereign governments, governmental enterprises, and international institutions. They are offered simultaneously in a number of different national capital markets, but not in the capital market or to residents of the country in whose currency the bond is denominated. Almost all Eurobonds are in bearer form with call provisions and sinking funds.

The syndicate that offers a new issue of Eurobonds might be composed of underwriters from a number of countries, including European banks, foreign subsidiaries of U.S. banks, banks from offshore financial centers, investment and merchant banks, and nonbank securities firms. In the United States, commercial banks may not underwrite corporate securities, but their foreign subsidiaries may do so. This distinction does not exist in most of the world, where commercial banks also act as major underwriters and distributors of new issues of securities.

The Straight Fixed-Rate Issue

The straight fixed-rate issue is structured like most domestic bonds, with a fixed coupon, set maturity date, and full principal repayment upon final maturity. Coupons are normally paid annually, rather than semiannually, primarily because the bonds are bearer bonds and annual coupon redemption is more convenient for the holders.

The Floating-Rate Note (FRN)

The floating-rate note (FRN) was the new instrument of fashion on the international bond scene in the early 1980s. The FRN normally pays a semiannual coupon that is determined using a variable-rate base. A typical coupon would be set at some fixed spread over LIBOR. This structure, like most variable-rate interest-bearing instruments, was designed to allow investors to shift more of the interest rate risk of a financial investment to the borrower. It was a popular instrument in the early 1980s when world markets were characterized by relatively high and unpredictable interest rates. Although many FRNs have fixed maturities, a number of major issues since 1985 are perpetuities. The principal will never be repaid. Thus they serve many of the same financial functions as equity.

The Equity-Related Issue

The most recent major addition to the international bond markets is the equity-related issue (convertible bond). The equity-related international bond resembles the straight fixed-rate issue in practically all price and payment characteristics, with the added feature that it is convertible to stock prior to maturity at a specified price per share (or alternatively, number of shares per bond). The borrower is able to issue debt with lower coupon payments due to the added value of the equity conversion feature.

The rapid development of this instrument over the past eight years has been largely a result of Japanese borrowers. The increase of Japanese stock prices in the late 1980s allowed Japanese borrowers to issue substantial equity-related debt at low interest rates. Investors were attracted to the potential capital gains from such instruments, particularly since a large portion of issues were dollar denominated with detachable warrants. This allowed the separate development of a market for the warrants, the equivalent of long-dated call options on Japanese yen equities. The market outlook, however, is at present uncertain given the introduction of a registration requirement by the Japanese Ministry of Finance and the collapse of the Japanese stock market. Exhibit 13.8 provides a sample

Exhibit 13.8 A New Issuance of Glaxo Holdings p.l.c. International Convertible Bonds

<u>**Shelf Sale**</u>

¥20 Billion, Japanese Yen, Convertible Bonds, First Series   Rating: Aaa

Offering Price:	100
Underwriters:	A syndicate led by The Nomura Securities Co., Ltd.
Yield:	Current: 4.30% Maturity: 4.30%
Interest:	4.30% annually.
Interest Payment Dates:	March 28 and September 28, commencing September 28, 1991.
Maturity:	28 September 1998.
Call Features:	The bonds may be called in the twelve-month period beginning September 28, 1994, at 103. Thereafter, the price declines 1.0 annually, to 100 on or after September 28, 1997. The bonds may be redeemed in whole, not in part. Further, in the event of a change in the laws of the United Kingdom, or a subdivision thereof, which would require the company to make additional payments for tax reasons, the company may redeem the bonds in whole at 100.
Conversion Feature:	The initial conversion price will be ¥1,299 per share, but will be subject to adjustment for certain events. The initial number of ordinary shares to be issued upon conversion will be determined by dividing the Japanese yen principal amount of the bond by the fixed exchange rate of ¥236 = £1. The pound sterling principal amount will then be divided by the conversion price per share. The shares may be converted at any time between August 1, 1991, and September 22, 1998.
Purpose:	General corporate purposes. The proceeds will be used for investment in or loans to an affiliate of the company in Japan.
Form:	Bearer form, with coupons.
Denomination:	¥1 million.
Governing Law:	Japanese law.
Tax Treatment:	U.K. taxation.
Security:	The bonds are unsecured obligations of the company, ranking pari passu with all other unsecured, unsubordinated obligations of the company.
Proceeds to Company:	Approximately ¥19.6 billion.
Remaining Shelf Balance:	¥80 billion.

Source: Adapted from *Moody's Bond Survey*, August 19, 1991, p. 4644.

Exhibit 13.9   International Corporate Bonds: ABB Finance

ABB Finance Inc[1]	(1) Coupon (percentage)	(2) Maturity (year)	(3) S & P's Rating	(4) Moody's Rating	(5) Interest Dates	(6) Amount (Mill$)	(7) When Issued	(8) Currency
Euronotes	10.50	1992	AA	Aa2	Dec 3	100	12-3-90	ECU
Euronotes	11.50	1992	AA	Aa2	Dec 18	100	12-18-90	C$
Euronotes	10.125	1994	AA	Aa2	Apr 1	125	4-1-91	C$
Euronotes	9.25	1994	AA	Aa2	Jun 27	100	6-27-91	ECU
Euronotes	12.375	1995	AA	Aa2	May 22	100	4-15-91	Lira
Euronotes	13.75	1995	AA	Aa2	Oct 18	100	10-12-90	A$
Euronotes	10.50	1996	AA	Aa2	Jun 20	750	6-20-91	SKr
Euronotes	11.00	1996	AA	Aa2	Jun 28	300	6-28-91	FIM

[1]Asea Brown Boveri, Incorporated, guarantees the issues of ABB Finance. Individual issues are characterized by their guaranteed interest payment and maturity date. For example, ABB's first issue listed.

Source: *Moody's Bond Record*, October 1991, p. 178, and *Standard & Poor's International Creditweek*, February 3, 1992, p. 25.

of the structure of a convertible bond issue in Japanese yen by a British firm, Glaxo Holdings, plc.

As noted at the beginning of this section, the multinational firm has a wide range of funding needs and will typically acquire debt in all three major markets in a variety of maturities, pricing structures, and currencies of denomination. Exhibit 13.9 illustrates the major international debt issues outstanding for one firm, ABB Finance Inc., the Swiss financial subsidiary of Asea Brown Boveri (ABB), a large Swedish-Swiss engineering firm.

Unique Characteristics of Eurobond Markets

Although the Eurobond market evolved at about the same time as the Eurodollar market, the two markets exist for different reasons, and each could exist independently of the other. The Eurobond market owes its existence to several unique factors, some of which have changed recently. Three of the original factors still of importance are absence of regulatory interference, less stringent disclosure practices, and favorable tax treatment.

Absence of Regulatory Interference. National governments often impose tight controls on foreign issuers of securities denominated in the local currency and sold within their national boundaries. However, governments in general have less stringent limitations for securities denominated in foreign currencies and sold within their markets to holders of those foreign currencies. In effect, Eurobond sales fall outside the regulatory domain of any single nation.

Less Stringent Disclosure. Disclosure requirements in the Eurobond market are much less stringent than those of the Securities and Exchange Commission (SEC) for sales within the United States. U.S. firms often find that the registration costs of a

Eurobond offering are less than those of a domestic issue and that less time is needed to bring a new issue to market. Non-U.S. firms often prefer Eurodollar bonds over bonds sold within the United States because they do not wish to undergo the costs, and disclosure, needed to register with the SEC. However, the SEC has recently relaxed disclosure requirements for certain private placements (Rule #144A), which is expected to improve the attractiveness of the U.S. domestic bond and equity markets (see Chapter 12 for more details).

Favorable Tax Status. Eurobonds offer tax anonymity and flexibility. Interest paid on Eurobonds is generally not subject to an income withholding tax. As one might suspect, Eurobond interest is not always reported to tax authorities. Prior to June 1984, U.S. corporations issuing Eurobonds were required to withhold up to 30% of each interest payment to foreigners for U.S. income taxes. The rate depended on the foreigner's country of residence and the bilateral tax treaty between that country and the United States. U.S. corporations wishing to issue Eurobonds had to do so through offshore finance affiliates, typically in the Netherlands Antilles, in order to avoid this tax. In 1984, however, the U.S. tax laws were revised to exempt foreign holders of bonds issued by U.S. corporations from any withholding tax. U.S. corporations found it feasible for the first time to sell Eurobonds directly to foreigners. Repeal of the U.S. withholding tax caused other governments, including those of France, Germany, and Japan, to liberalize their tax rules as a defensive measure to avoid an outflow of capital from their markets.

As noted earlier, Eurobonds are usually issued in bearer form, meaning the name and country of residence of the owner is not on the certificate. To receive interest, the bearer cuts an interest coupon from the bond and turns it in at a banking institution listed on the issue as a paying agent. European investors are accustomed to the privacy provided by bearer bonds and are very reluctant to purchase registered bonds, which require holders to reveal their names before they receive interest. Bearer bond status, of course, is also tied to tax avoidance.

Rating of Eurobonds and Other International Issues

Purchasers of Eurobonds do not only rely on bond-rating services or on detailed analyses of financial statements. General reputation of the issuing corporation and its underwriters has been a major factor in obtaining favorable terms. For this reason, larger and better known multinational firms, state enterprises, and sovereign governments are able to obtain the lowest interest rates. Firms whose names are better known to the general public, possibly because they manufacture consumer goods, are often believed to have an advantage over equally qualified firms whose products are less widely known.

Rating agencies, such as Moody's and Standard & Poor's (S&P's), provide ratings for selected international bonds for a fee.[6] S&P's ratings for international bonds imply

---

[6]A detailed description of Standard & Poor's procedure for determining credit ratings for all securities, including international securities, is given in their booklet, *Credit Overview, Corporate and International Ratings*, Standard & Poor's Corporation, 25 Broadway, New York, NY 10004.

the same creditworthiness as for domestic bonds of U.S. issuers. S&P's limits its evaluation to the issuer's ability to obtain the necessary currency to repay the issue according to the original terms of the bond, and excludes any assessment of risk to the investor caused by changing exchange rates. Exhibit 13.10 lists S&P's sovereign (country) ratings for January 1992.

S&P's rates international bonds on request of the issuer. Based on supporting financial statements and other material obtained from the issuer, a preliminary rating is made. The issuer is then informed and given an opportunity to comment. After S&P's determines its final rating, the issuer may decide not to have the rating published. Consequently, a disproportionately large number of published international ratings fall into the highest categories, since issuers about to receive a lower rating often decide not to have the rating published.

S&P's review of political risk includes study of the government system, the social environment, and the nation's external relations. Its review of economic risk looks at debt burden, international liquidity, balance of payments flexibility, economic structure,

Exhibit 13.10   Standard & Poor's Sovereign Ratings and Assessments

Country	Long-term[1]	Short-term[2,3,4]	Country	Long-term	Short-term
Australia	AA	A–i+	Luxembourg	N.R.	A–1+i
Austria	AAA	A–1+	Malaysia	A	A–1i
Belgium	AA+i	A–1+i	Netherlands	AAAi	A–1+i
Canada	AAA	A–1+	New Zealand	AA–	A–1+
China	N.R.	N.R.	Norway	AAA	A–1+
Denmark	AA+	A–1+	Portugal	A+i	A–1+i
Finland	AAA	A–1+i	Singapore	AA+i	A–1+i
France	AAA	A–1+	South Korea	A+i	A–1+i
Germany	AAA	A–1+i	Spain	AA	A–1+
Greece	BBB–i	A–3i	Sweden	AAA	A–1+
Hong Kong	Ai	A–1i	Switzerland	AAAi	A–1+i
Iceland	Ai	A–1	Taiwan	AA+i	A–1+i
India	BB+i	Bi	Thailand	A–	A–1
Ireland	AA–	A–1+	Turkey	N.R.	N.R.
Israel	BBB–i	A–3i	United Kingdom	AAA	A–1+
Italy	AA+i	A–1+i	United States	AAAi	A–1+i
Japan	AAA	A–1+	Venezuela	BB	Bi

[1]Long-term debt are bonds having an original maturity of more than 365 days. Long-term debt of an *investment grade* includes ratings of AAA, AA, A, and BBB. *Speculative grade* ratings are BB, CCC, CC, C, CI, and D.

[2]Short-term debt has an original maturity of no more than one year and encompasses commercial paper and short-term CD programs. *Investment grade* short-term debt categories are A–1, A–2, A–3. *Speculative grade* short-term debt categories are B, C, and D.

[3]The letter i indicates the rating is implied. Such ratings are assigned to governments that have not requested explicit ratings for specific debt issues. Implied ratings represent the sovereign ceiling or upper limit for ratings on specific debt issues of entities domiciled in the country.

[4]+/– show relative standing within the major rating categories. N.R. indicates no public rating has been requested, that there is insufficient information on which to base a rating, or that S&P's does not rate a particular type of obligation as a matter of policy.

Source: "International Ratings," *Standard & Poor's International Creditweek*, New York: McGraw-Hill, February 3, 1992, p. F21.

growth performance, economic management, and economic outlook. S&P's also evaluates the bonds of sovereign-supported entities by looking first at their creditworthiness on a stand-alone basis, and then looking at the extent to which sovereign support either enhances or diminishes the borrower's financial strength.

Credit ratings are critical to borrowers and investors alike. A multinational firm's credit rating determines its cost of funds. For example, for the week ending January 22, 1992, the composite yields for Eurodollar and Euroyen denominated bonds by category were as follows:

S&P's Composite Rating[7]

Bond Issues	AAA	AA	A
Eurodollar Bonds	5.30%	6.44%	7.39%
Euroyen Bonds	6.62%	6.85%	6.98%

A firm issuing long-term debt with a rating of "A" was on average paying 209 basis points (2.09%) more for every dollar raised, and 36 basis points (0.36%) more for every yen raised over that paid by a "AAA"-rated firm. A higher cost of obtaining debt capital such as this one would not only add significantly to the annual financial expenses of the firm, but over the long term could form the basis for a continuing source of international competitive weakness.

Summary

- Cross-border financial markets are an increasingly important source of capital for multinational firms, sovereign entities, and international institutions.

- The main components of the international debt markets are bank syndicated loans, Euronotes, and Eurobonds.

- Syndicated loans, known as Eurocredits, are bank loans to business firms, sovereign entities, international institutions, and other banks.

- The basic borrowing rate on syndicated loans is a variable rate of interest based on LIBOR.

- The Euronote market is the collective term used to describe short- to medium-term debt instruments sourced in the Eurocurrency markets.

- Euro-commercial paper is a short-term debt obligation similar to domestic commercial paper but sourced in the Eurocurrency markets.

---

[7]"Bond Indexes," *Standard & Poor's International Creditweek*, July 1, 1991, p. 7. *Composite bond yields* include both corporate sector and public sector borrowers. S&P's Eurodollar and Euroyen bond indexes for each rating category represent the average yield to maturity, calculated on an annual basis, for a sample group of fixed rate Eurobonds carrying ratings. The indexes are calculated using price data supplied by the Association of International Bond Dealers.

- Euro-medium-term notes bridge the maturity gap between Euro-commercial paper and Eurobonds. Their terms of repayment are similar to bonds but they have a shorter maturity.

- A Eurobond is underwritten by an international syndicate of financial institutions and is sold exclusively in countries other than the country in whose currency the bond is denominated.

- Eurobonds can be straight fixed-rate issues, floating-rate notes, or equity-related issues.

- Eurobonds are attractive because of the absence of regulatory interference, less stringent disclosure requirements, and a favorable tax status due to their bearer form.

- The cost of foreign currency-denominated debt includes the nominal cost of principal and interest in foreign currency terms, adjusted for any foreign exchange gains or losses. This creates transaction exposure that can be risky.

Questions

1. Federal Republic of Brazil

The Federal Republic of Brazil acquired much of its debt in the late 1970s and early 1980s through large international syndicated loans. By 1980 the Brazilian government had borrowed so frequently from the markets that what was known as "Brazilian pricing" became standard for many such syndicated credits:

Principal	US$500,000,000
Maturity	8.0 years
Base interest rate	LIBOR
Spread	2½%
Syndication fees	1½%

    a. What would be the actual loan proceeds from such a syndicated credit?
    b. What would the effective annual cost of funds be for the first year?

2. The BOC Group, plc

The BOC Group, plc, is a multinational manufacturer of carbon-based industrial gas products, health-care products and services, and specialty graphite industrial products. Although it is incorporated in the United Kingdom, a large portion of its cash flows are in dollars. It now wishes to access the international debt markets for short-term capital, which will be hopefully cheaper than bank credit and acquired at current low interest rates.

    If The BOC Group issues a total principal of US$500,000,000 in Euro-commercial paper (ECP) at a discount, with the following characteristics, what are the total proceeds to BOC of the issues?

Issue	Notional Principal	Yield
90-day ECP	US$300,000,000	8.20%
180-day ECP	US$200,000,000	8.40%

3. Cache la Poudre Products of Colorado

Cache la Poudre Products (ClPP) of Colorado seeks to borrow $800,000 to finance working capital needs. ClPP finds it can borrow from a Denver bank for 8% per annum. Because ClPP has an ongoing subsidiary in Switzerland, it has an established credit position there and so can also borrow Swiss francs at 5% per annum. The Swiss francs would be exchanged for dollars at the spot rate, and dollars would later be used to acquire Swiss francs spot to repay the loan. La Poudre believes the Swiss franc will appreciate at 4% per annum during the period of the loan. Where should Cache la Poudre borrow?

4. Norwegian Transport

Norwegian Transport of Bergen needs NKr10,000,000 for one year to finance a special project. It can borrow Norwegian kroner in Oslo at 14%, or it can borrow Eurodollars in London at 8%. At present, NKr6.75 = $1.00. Assume no forward market exists. What kroner/dollar exchange rate one year hence would cause the firm to be indifferent as to its financing source?

5. Spich Corporation (C13A.WK1)

Spich Corporation wishes to raise $2,000,000 in U.S. dollars with debt financing. The funds, needed to finance working capital, will be repaid with interest in one year. Spich's treasurer is considering three sources:

- **a.** Borrow U.S. dollars from Bank of America at 8%.
- **b.** Borrow British pounds from National Westminster Bank at 14%.
- **c.** Borrow Japanese yen from Sanwa Bank at 5%.

If Spich borrows a foreign currency, it will remain uncovered; that is, it will simply change foreign currency for dollars at today's spot rate and buy foreign currency back one year later at the spot rate then in effect. Spich Corporation has no operations in either the United Kingdom or Japan.

Spich estimates the pound will depreciate 5% relative to the dollar and the yen will appreciate 3% relative to the dollar during the next year. Corporate income tax rates are 35% in the United States, 36% in the United Kingdom, and 40% in Japan.

From which bank should Spich borrow and what is its projected after-tax cost of borrowing (in dollars) from each source?

6. Ford Motor Company (C13B.WK1)

Ford Motor Company wants to borrow $50,000,000 for five years to finance modernization of its Dearborn, Michigan, factories. A five-year bond with a fixed coupon rate of 8% can be sold in the United States at par. Ford can also borrow in the Eurocurrency market, as follows:

1. Borrow Eurodollars for five years at 1% above dollar LIBOR. Dollar LIBOR is currently 7%. The interest rate would be floating, and would be readjusted once each year.

2. Borrow Euromarks for five years at 1% above mark LIBOR. Deutschemark LIBOR is currently 5%. The interest rate would be floating, and would be readjusted annually.

Describe the benefits and risks for Ford of borrowing in the Eurocurrency market instead of in the U.S. domestic market.

7. Gekko & Fox Investment Banking

You work for a U.S. investment company, Gekko & Fox, that seeks U.S. dollar returns, but which is also quite willing to take foreign exchange risks.

You are negotiating the dollar purchase of a new Euro-yen bond issue of Hakone Corporation. The issue is for one billion yen (¥1,000,000,000), has a maturity of five years, is to be issued at par today, and will pay 80 million yen (¥80,000,000) interest annually starting one year from today. You forecast the yen to appreciate 2% per year against the dollar, starting from the current spot rate of ¥108.00/$.

    a. What is the current yield-to-maturity in Japan on yen bonds of this risk and maturity?

    b. What dollar price would you be willing to pay for the issue today, if you wanted to obtain an identical yield-to-maturity in dollars, and if you were positive of your foreign exchange forecasts?

    c. If the dollar price you would pay today (answer to question (b) above) is not equal to one billion yen at today's exchange rate, explain briefly why you would be willing to pay more or would be able to buy the issue for less than its par value in Japanese yen.

8. Platz-Ho, Inc. (C13C.WK1)

Platz-Ho wants to borrow $50 million or the foreign currency equivalent for five years. These alternatives are available:

    a. Borrow in U.S. dollars: Borrow dollars at 7% per annum with bonds sold at par. Expenses of the issue will be 2.5% of amount borrowed.

    b. Borrow in Deutschemarks: Borrow Deutschemarks at 8% per annum with bonds sold at "99." Expenses of the issue will be 3.0% of amount borrowed. The current exchange rate is DM1.7000/$, and the mark is expected to depreciate against the dollar by 1% per annum.

    c. Borrow in Japanese yen: Borrow yen at 4% per annum, bonds sold at par, and 3.0% off the face value for expenses. The current exchange rate is ¥114.00/$. The yen is expected to appreciate against the dollar by 2% per annum.

Evaluate the cost of each alternative and make a recommendation to the chief financial officer (CFO) regarding the source of capital that is likely to be cheapest for the five-year period.

9. Teknekron's Euro-Medium-Term Notes

Teknekron (Belgium) issues US$10,000,000 in Euro-medium-term notes on September 1, 1994. Although the EMTNs are officially "issued" on that date, they are shelf registered and will be actually sold on continuing dates over the period. All the notes possess 9% per annum coupons paid semiannually.

The first issue is sold on September 1, 1994, and is set to mature on May 1, 1996. What is the market price of this $1,000 EMTN on November 1, 1994, if similar issues are yielding 8% per annum at that time?

10. Ex-Post Cost of a Foreign Currency Bond

Find a bond denominated in a foreign currency that has been issued by a U.S. firm and has been outstanding at least five years. Then answer the following questions:

a. Track the annual interest cost of servicing this bond after considering exchange rate changes but not considering taxes. Compare this cost to what the cost would have been if the U.S. firm had issued a dollar-denominated bond at the time it issued the foreign currency-denominated bond.

b. Assume the bond is retired at the end of this year so the gain or loss on principal will be counted in your calculations. Assume no further changes in exchange rates before the end of this year and that the interest is paid at the end of each year. Did the firm end up paying more or less for this capital?

Bibliography

Bradley, Finbarr, "An Analysis of Call Strategy in the Eurodollar Bond Market," *Journal of International Financial Management and Accounting*, vol. 2, no. 1, Spring 1990, pp. 23–46.

Bullock, Gareth, *Euronotes and Euro-Commercial Paper*, London: Butterworths, 1987.

Chang, Rosita P., Peter E. Koveos, and S. Ghon Rhee, "Financial Planning for International Long-Term Debt Financing," *Advances in Financial Planning and Forecasting*, vol. 4, part B, 1990, pp. 33–58.

Chuppe, Terry M., Hugh R. Haworth, and Marvin G. Watkins, "Public Policy Toward the International Bond Markets in the 1980s," *Advances in Financial Planning and Forecasting*, vol. 4, part B, 1990, pp. 3–32.

de Caires, Bryan, ed., *The Guide to International Capital Markets*, London: Euromoney Publications, 1988.

Doukas, John, "Syndicated Euro-Credit Sovereign Risk Assessments, Market Efficiency and Contagion Effects," *Journal of International Business Studies*, Summer 1989, pp. 255–267.

Fisher, F. G., III, *Eurobonds*, London: Euromoney Publications, 1987.

Folks, W. R., Jr., "Optimal Foreign Borrowing Strategies with Operations in Forward Exchange Markets," *Journal of Financial and Quantitative Analysis*, June 1978, pp. 245–254.

Heller, Lucy, *Eurocommercial Paper*, London: Euromoney Publications, 1988.

International Capital Markets: Developments and Prospects, Washington, D.C.: IMF, 1990.

Jadlow, Janice Wickstead, "Market Assessment of the Eurodollar Default Risk Premium," *Advances in Financial Planning and Forecasting*, vol. 4, part A, 1990, pp. 105–122.

Jennergren, L. Peter, and Bertil Nëslund, "Models for the Valuation of International Convertible Bonds," *Journal of International Financial Management and Accounting*, vol. 2, nos. 2 and 3, Summer and Autumn 1990, pp. 93–110.

Krol, Robert, "The Term Structure of Eurodollar Interest Rates and Its Relationship to the U.S. Treasury-Bill Market," *Journal of International Money and Finance*, vol. 6, no. 3, September 1987, pp. 339–354.

Marr, M. Wayne, Robert W. Rogowski, and John L. Trimble, "The Competitive Effects of U.S. and Japanese Commercial Bank Participation in

Eurobond Underwriting," *Financial Management*, Winter 1989, pp. 47–54.

Remmers, H. Lee, "A Note on Foreign Borrowing Costs," *Journal of International Business Studies*, Fall 1980, pp. 123–134.

Rhee, S. Ghon, Rosita P. Chang, and Peter E. Koveos, "The Currency-of-Denomination Decision for Debt Financing," *Journal of International Business Studies*, Fall 1985, pp. 143–150.

Robichek, Alexander A., and Mark R. Eaker, "Debt Denomination and Exchange Risk in International Capital Markets," *Financial Management*, Autumn 1976, pp. 11–18.

Shapiro, Alan C., "The Impact of Taxation on the Currency-of-Denomination Decision for Long-Term Borrowing and Lending," *Journal of International Business Studies*, Spring/Summer 1984, pp. 15–25.

Chapter 14
Interest Rate Risk Management

Global View
Interest Rate Risk Management at Apple

An important but overlooked part of Apple's new business strategy is its treasury's role in managing a cash portfolio of over $1 billion. As Apple's gross margins have declined, it has become more important to maximize income from its investments. Hedging strategies implemented by Apple have increased the yield on its portfolio by over 100 basis points, while three-month LIBOR has fallen from 8% in October 1990 to 4 1/8% in February 1992.

Daniel Kayphagian, Apple's capital markets manager, made these assets go a little further by managing interest rate risk. "Our profits are around $500 million per year, so what [the treasury does] doesn't make or break the company. On the other hand, we want to show that treasury has real strategic value to the company and isn't just a general administration expense."

Interest income might account for 10–15% of Apple's overall profits in good economic times, Kayphagian estimates. But the treasury was afraid this might not be possible were rates to fall too sharply in a prolonged recession. "We used different types of derivatives, including swaps and options, to protect our cash portfolio," says Kayphagian.

Overall, Apple is pleased with its success in applying its forex hedging expertise to cash management. "Most companies watch foreign exchange risk very closely, since it is marked every month," Kayphagian concludes. "Cash management is viewed in quite the opposite way—no one seems to blame you, so long as you don't lose money. That may have been our previous attitude, but now we want to manage cash exposures as prudently as foreign exchange exposures."

Source: Adapted from "Silicon Enhancements," by William Falloon, *Risk*, March 1992, Vol. 5, No. 3, 57–58. Reprinted with permission.

The management of financial risk is a rapidly expanding area of multinational financial management. *Financial risk management* includes foreign exchange (FX) exposure, interest rate (I/R) exposure, and the firm's sensitivity to commodity prices. The general rise in inflation rates and interest rates in the 1970s, coupled with the considerable volatility of these same rates in the 1980s, forced the issue of interest rate risk management to the attention of corporate treasurers. Identification, measurement, and management of interest rate risk now receives the same level of management attention and effort focused on foreign exchange risk just a few years ago. In this chapter we provide an overview of interest rate risk management as practiced by international treasurers today. Many of the same basic functional, managerial, and even financial instrument relations used in foreign currency exposure management are also used in interest rate risk management.[1]

Growing Need for Interest Rate Risk Management

We can attribute two main reasons for increased attention to interest rate risk management. First, interest rate volatility has increased significantly. Although firms develop strategies to save 20 to 30 basis points in a spread over a base rate, little attention has been placed on the volatility of the underlying rate itself.

The second major reason to pay attention to interest rate risk management is the increasing use of shorter maturity debt or variable rate debt. More firms are funding greater proportions of their total liabilities with these more interest-sensitive liabilities. The expanded use of securitized debt in the 1980s made more firms conscious of the impact of interest rate changes on their cost of capital and resulted in a greater emphasis on managing the risks of debt service.

Defining Interest Rate Risk

All firms, domestic or multinational, small or large, leveraged or nonleveraged, are sensitive to interest rate movements in one way or another. There are two basic types of interest rate risk: basis risk and gap risk.

Basis risk is the mismatching of interest rate bases for associated assets and liabilities. One of the basic tenets of balance sheet management is to match the maturity of assets and liabilities. Even if assets and liabilities have the same maturity (and same currency of denomination for the multinational firm), they may have a different interest rate base. If a particular asset's value is sensitive to U.S. dollar six-month LIBOR, while the corresponding liability is based on U.S. dollar prime, a movement in interest rates will possibly alter the spread between the interest bases. Financial institutions, whose primary revenues and costs consist of interest rate payment flows, often define their interest rate

---

[1]The authors would like to thank Torben Juul Andersen of Unibank A/S, Copenhagen, for his constructive comments on this section.

risk and exposure as the net interest income (NII) of the firm. *Net interest income* is the difference between interest income from assets and the net interest expense of liabilities.

Gap risk is more typical of a nonfinancial firm. *Gap risk* arises from mismatched timing in repricing interest-rate-sensitive assets and liabilities. The typical nonfinancial firm possesses a relatively small amount of interest-sensitive assets, while funding may consist of a relatively large amount of interest-bearing debt. Whereas the financial firm's exposure arises from small differences in relative interest rate movements, the nonfinancial firm faces a significantly larger problem of interest-sensitive funding with relatively little matching interest-sensitive asset values. All firms have some form of interest-rate-sensitive liabilities. Even those firms with no appreciable securitized debt or bank debt still extend trade credit to customers. The cost of this trade credit is in fact based on interest rates.

Two additional characteristics of debt service must be noted for management purposes. First, most firms possess relatively predictable debt service cash flows. This results from the scheduling of principal and interest payments on any specific debt obligation. Hence cash outflows occur at regular time intervals and in fairly predictable amounts. Second, the terms *short term* and *long term* are deceptive when defining the firm's interest rate exposure. In reality it is not the maturity of the obligation that is of immediate importance, but rather the frequency at which the interest rate itself is either reset or rolled over.

This chapter focuses on interest rate risk management practices of nonfinancial firms. A nonfinancial firm typically experiences at least two of the following three interest rate exposures:

1. Short-term floating-rate borrowing.

2. Short-term floating-rate investment (or reinvestment).

3. Medium- to long-term floating-rate borrowing.

The first two are single-period interest rate exposures. The measurement of exposures is straightforward, with the rate of interest on a specific cash flow, either a near-term borrowing or investment, being managed. These exposures are similar in nature to those of foreign exchange transaction exposure.

The third exposure is typical of longer term floating-rate exposures for firms worldwide. Although these three exposures are obviously not all-inclusive of the interest rate risks of firms, they do cover the majority of present efforts in interest rate risk management.

Interest Rate Practices

The way interest rates are calculated or referenced varies significantly across countries depending on currency and country practice. Exhibit 14.1 provides a brief overview of the three major approaches used. The so-called *international practice* is the one most commonly used today, but we must still pay special attention to the traditional British and Swiss calculation methods.

Exhibit 14.1   International Interest Rate Practices

Practice Employed	Day Count	Days/Year
International	Exact number of days	360 days
British	Exact number of days	365 days
Swiss	30 days/month	360 days

Source: "Hedging Instruments for Foreign Exchange, Money Market, and Precious Metals," *Union Bank of Switzerland*, pp. 41–42.

The impact of a small change in the day count of a period or the day definition of a year can have a major impact on the calculation of interest expenses or earnings. For example, a one-month money market deposit in the amount of $10,000,000, with a term from February 1 to February 28 (actual day count 28 days) and earning 5 1/2% per annum, produces three different incomes depending on the calculation method employed. The first of several methods, *international practice*, uses actual day counts as a proportion of a 360-day year:

$$\text{International: } \$10,000,000 \times .0550 \times \frac{28}{360} = \$42,777.78.$$

The second method, the traditional *British practice*, also uses the exact number of days in the numerator, but as a proportion of a 365-day year:

$$\text{British: } \$10,000,000 \times .0550 \times \frac{28}{365} = \$42,191.78.$$

The third method, *Swiss practice* or *Eurobond practice*, assumes 30-day months as proportions of a 360-day year.

$$\text{Swiss: } \$10,000,000 \times .0550 \times \frac{30}{360} = \$45,833.33.$$

Obviously, those receiving interest would not select the same method as those paying interest! A lender or borrower unaware of the three possible methods may find itself exploited. All investors should take the time to verify what method is being utilized for the specific agreement at hand. Interest rate computation methods vary not only across currencies but also across instruments within the same currency or country.

The second noteworthy interest rate practice is the use of reference rates. A *reference rate*, for example U.S. dollar LIBOR, is the rate of interest used in a standardized quotation, loan agreement, or financial derivative valuation. LIBOR, the London Inter-Bank Offered Rate, is officially defined by the British Bankers Association (BBA). U.S. dollar LIBOR is the mean of 16 multinational banks' interbank offered rates as sampled by the BBA at approximately 11 A.M. London time in London. Similarly, the Japanese yen LIBOR and Deutschemark LIBOR rates are calculated at the same time in London by the BBA from samples of 8 banks and 16 banks, respectively. LIBOR rates are quoted in percentages (e.g., 7 3/8%).[2]

Finally, the interbank interest rate market is not always focused on London. Most major domestic financial centers construct their own interbank offer rates for domestic loan agreements. These would include PIBOR (Paris Interbank Offer Rate), MIBOR (Madrid Interbank Offer Rate), FIBOR (Frankfurt Interbank Offer Rate), HELIBOR (Helsinki Interbank Offer Rate), SIBOR (Singapore Interbank Offer Rate), and CIBOR (Copenhagen Interbank Offer Rate). These more commonly refer to rates of interest on domestic currency agreements in the individual domestic market (Danish kroner in Copenhagen, for example).

Management of Interest Rate Risk

Managing interest rate risk requires not only identifying the type and size of interest rate exposure, but also the goals of management. In order for the firm to achieve the agreed upon managerial goals, treasury must form a view of future interest rate movements and select the appropriate tool or technique for management. The chosen solution must fit both the exposure and the management goals of the firm. This step typically generates the most interest among financial managers and treasurers.

Corporate Treasury Goals and Interest Rate Risk

Treasurers have always worked to manage or reduce interest rate expenses, but this is simply an extension of other financial tasks, such as the proper timing and pricing of new debt issues or loans. Treasury has traditionally been considered a cost center to the firm, not a contributor to the bottom line, although less costs are better. Treasury management practices are predominantly conservative, but opportunities to reduce costs or actually earn profits are not ignored.

Forming a View of Interest Rate Movements

Foreign exchange and interest rate risk management should focus on hedging existing or anticipated cash flow exposures of the firm. As in foreign exchange exposure management, the firm cannot undertake informed management or hedge strategies without

---

[2]A second set of interest settlement rates that are commonly used in international financial agreements are termed *BBA settlement rates*. Like LIBOR, the British Bankers Association (BBA) collects Eurocurrency deposit offer rates from a consistent sample of high credit-quality banks in London on a weekly basis (Fridays at approximately 11 A.M. London time), and officially publishes them on Telerate page 3750/3740 at 2 P.M. that same day. Unlike LIBOR, the BBA drops the two highest and lowest offer rates and averages the remaining rates, rounding the final rate to five decimal places. Regardless of which reference rate is used, however, the ability of banks and firms worldwide to reference a simple set of common interest rates such as LIBOR or BBA settlement rates greatly increases the compatibility of international financial practices.

forming expectations about the direction and volatility of interest rate movements. Forecasting of interest rates begins with the market's own implied forecast—the series or strip of forward interest rates.

Forward interest rates, also called *forward spot rates*, are interest rates for specified time periods beginning at future dates. Forwards are useful for a number of instruments used in obtaining contractual or hedge commitments for interest rate obligations of the firm (debts or investments) that begin at future dates. Forwards are calculated from yield curves. Any currency that possesses interest-bearing instruments of varying maturities at the same level of risk can be used as a base for forward interest rates.

For example, a Canadian investor has C$1,000,000 to invest for six months. The investor considers two alternatives: (1) invest for the entire six months at current Euro-Canadian dollar rates of 5.0625% (per annum); or (2) invest the funds for three months at 4.8750% (per annum), and then roll the funds over at the end of the three-month period for a second three months.

1. Invest for six months at 5.0625% p.a.

```
├──────────────────────────┼──────────────────────────┤  R₆ = 5.0625% p.a.
0                      3 months                   6 months
```

2. Invest for three months at 4.8750%, then reinvest for a second three-month period.

The problem is the investor does not know at time $t = 0$ the second three-month interest rate, the one starting three months from time 0.

```
├──────────────────────────┤  R₃ = 4.8750% p.a.
0                      3 months
                       ├──────────────────────────┤  R₃,₆ = ? % p.a.
                                               6 months
```

Because financial markets are generally efficient, the two investments should actually have the same rate of return (in the absence of a liquidity premium or risk premium for the second rollover alternative). If it is assumed the same rate of return should be achieved by either path, the two alternatives can be set equal in order to solve for the *implied forward spot interest rate:*

$$\left[1 + \left(.048750 \times \frac{90}{360}\right)\right] \times (1 + R_{3,6}) = \left[1 + \left(.050625 \times \frac{180}{360}\right)\right].$$

This creates a "3 against 6 forward spot rate" of

$$R_{3,6} = \left[\frac{1.0253125}{1.0121875} - 1\right] = .012967.$$

This is 1.2967% for three months, or 5.1868% per annum for the second three-month period.

Exhibit 14.2 The Euro-Canadian Dollar Yield Curve

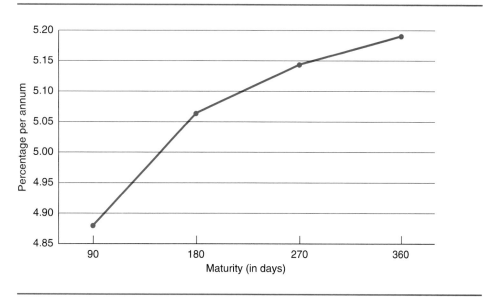

Exhibit 14.2 illustrates this Euro-Canadian dollar yield curve for these shorter money market maturities, and the implicit forward spot interest rates. It is possible to construct an entire "strip" of implied forward rates of interest from any yield curve. These implied forward rates can be considered the market's implicit forecasts of future short-term interest rates.

Selecting the Appropriate Tool or Technique

Once management has formed expectations about future interest rate levels, it must choose the appropriate instrument or technique for managing that exposure. A variety of methods exist for the actual management and hedging of interest rate risk. The list of alternatives combines both general funding management strategies, such as borrowing short term or long term with frequent rate resets, with the use of financial instruments or engineered products such as *forward rate agreements* (FRAs) and *interest rate caps* and *floors*. The choice of appropriate instrument depends on the firm and the individual circumstances. In the following sections we provide overviews of the various hedging or management alternatives, their structure, cost, and typical usage. The following discussion separates the techniques and instruments on the basis of *outright* (standard interest management instruments) versus *option-based* instruments. Exhibit 14.3 provides an overview of the various tools and techniques for interest rate risk management.

Exhibit 14.3 Overview of I/R Risk Management Tools and Techniques

Outright Techniques	Definition and Description
Mismatched Maturities	A combined position of lending and borrowing the same principal at different maturities to take advantage of yield curve slope.
	Traded in OTC. Maturities: typically 1–5 years
FX Forward Mismatching	A combined position of selling one currency forward at one maturity while buying the same currency forward at a different maturity to lock in a future interest rate on the foreign currency.
	Traded in OTC. Maturities: 30, 60, 90, 120, 180, 360 days
Forward Rate Agreement	An agreement between two parties locking in an interest rate for a future period. The agreement is based on a notional loan or deposit, one party agreeing to make a compensating payment to the other on the basis of a reference rate of interest.
	Traded in OTC. Maturities: typically 90, 180, 270, and 360 days
I/R and Currency Swap	An agreement between two parties to exchange debt service payment streams. The exchange can be a floating-rate payment for a fixed-rate payment, an interest rate swap, or an exchange of currency of denomination of payment, a currency swap.
	Traded in OTC. Maturities: 2 to 10 years
Interest Rate Futures	A contract on the future price of a financial variable, in this case an interest rate. Available only in standardized amounts and maturities.
	Traded on exchange. Maturities: 1, 3, 6, 9, and 12 months
Option-Based Techniques	
Caps, Floors, and Collars	An option that assures the buyer of a maximum interest rate if a future interest rate reaches a specified threshold (a cap) or a minimum interest rate (a floor). A collar is a combined position of buying a cap and selling a floor, or vice versa.
	Traded in OTC. Maturities: 1 to 5 years in total, with 3-, 6-, or 12-month resets
Swaptions	An option to enter into a specified interest rate or currency swap agreement on or before a future date.
	Traded in OTC. Maturities: 2 to 10 years (same as swap market)
Options on I/R Futures	An option on a specific interest rate futures contract.
	Traded on exchange. Maturities: 1, 3, 6, 9, or 12 months

Outright Instruments and Techniques

Techniques and instruments in this first category include some of the oldest and most fundamental relationships in financial markets. The first three techniques, mismatched borrowing, foreign exchange forward swaps, and forward rate agreements, are simply uses of the yield curve shape. The remaining two outright techniques, interest rate swaps and interest rate futures, are a bit more complex derivative-based techniques. Interest rate futures are rarely used by nonfinancial firms, but they are a common technique employed by financial institutions. Due to limitations of time and space, we focus on the nonfutures instruments in the remainder of the chapter.

Mismatched Maturities

The mismatching of maturities, lending long and borrowing short or vice versa, is probably the oldest interest rate management technique around. The premise is very straightforward. If the yield curve is a forecast of future spot interest rates and if it is upward sloping, a firm wishing to lock in a future rate of interest on investments that are more attractive than current rates should borrow short and invest long. The short-term borrowing would provide the funds for the long-term investment, and the repayment of the short-term borrowing would be covered by the inflow of cash to the firm in the medium term. It is this inflow that the firm wishes to invest (or reinvest) at higher rates. With an upward sloping yield curve such as this, a firm wishing to reduce borrowing costs over the long run would be forced to borrow short and continually roll over the debt at market rates of interest.

Although not that common, a negatively sloped yield curve would obviously provide the firm with a set of conditions for relatively low-cost long-term borrowing. If the funds were not needed immediately, short-term loans/investments would allow the firm to cover its cheap long-term debt service expenses.

Foreign Currency Forward Swaps

The foreign currency forward and forward swap were introduced in Chapter 4. Here we show that the combining of two offsetting forwards with different maturities can serve as a method of locking in a future interest rate for a foreign currency investment or loan.

Assume a firm in Germany knows it will need $5,000,000 beginning in six months for a six-month period. Although it could wait six months and borrow the U.S. dollar funds at then current rates, it may wish to reduce the uncertainty of the cost of the funds now. The firm also wishes to take advantage of the fact that U.S. dollar interest rates are relatively low compared to Deutschemark interest rates right now, but might not remain so. This future borrowing of a foreign currency is achieved by simply signing two different forward contracts:

1. Buy $5,000,000 180 days forward at DM1.5400/$,
2. Sell $5,000,000 360 days forward at DM1.5735/$.

The German firm has now assured itself of (1) obtaining $5,000,000 in six months at a certain exchange rate, and (2) six months later of selling the same $5,000,000 for Deutschemarks at a second exchange rate. Because the exchange rate is specified on both ends of the agreement, the cost of the U.S. dollar funds has been locked in. The actual cost of the Eurodollar funds to the German firm is calculated by finding the internal interest rate that equates the amount of DM funds put up at the beginning of the six-month period with the funds returned at the end of the total period:

$$\left[\frac{\$5,000,000 \times DM1.5735/\$}{\$5,000,000 \times DM1.5400/\$}\right] - 1 = \left[\frac{DM7,867,500}{DM7,700,000}\right] - 1 = .02175325,$$

2.175% for six months, or 4.35% per annum. Although the cost of Eurodollar funds could actually be cheaper at maturity of the first forward swap (six months from now), the cost could also be higher. This allows the German firm to eliminate the interest rate uncertainty now, and assure itself of the cost of acquiring the U.S. dollar funds without formally taking out a Eurodollar loan.

Forward Rate Agreements (FRAs)

A *forward rate agreement* (FRA) is an interbank-traded contract to buy or sell interest rate payments on a notional principal. These contracts are settled in cash. The buyer of an FRA obtains the right to effectively lock in an interest rate for a desired term that begins at a future date. The contract specifies that the seller of the FRA will pay the buyer the increased interest expense on a nominal sum (notional principal) of money if interest rates rise above the agreed rate, but the buyer will pay the seller the differential interest expense if interest rates fall below the agreed rate. Maturities are typically 1, 3, 6, 9, and 12 months.

The contract is priced on the basis of the strip of forward interest rates that are calculated from yield curves for the subject interest rate (as described in the previous section). For example, a firm buys a "three against six" FRA for a notional principal of $2,000,000. This means the FRA is for the three-month period beginning three months from now.

To illustrate, assume the agreed rate is 7.50% per annum, with 91 days in the three-month period. Three months from now, at the beginning of the FRA period, the actual three-month rate is 9.00%. Because the actual rate of 9.00% is above the agreed rate of 7.50%, the firm that purchased the FRA (the holder) will receive from the seller of the FRA (the writer) the difference in the interest expenses. This would be a payment of

$$\$2,000,000 \times \left[(.0900 - .0750) \times \left(\frac{91}{360}\right)\right] = \$7,583.33.$$

Because the differential cash flow of the FRA is settled at the beginning of the three-month period (and not at the end as in a normal interest payment), the cash flow must be discounted back the three months of the FRA period. The actual rate of 9.00% is used as the discount factor:

$$\frac{\$7,583.33}{\left[1 + \left(.0900 \times \frac{91}{360}\right)\right]} = \$7,414.65.$$

The actual payment to the buyer of the FRA is therefore $7,414.65.

The impact on the firm's borrowing costs can be seen by isolating the various actual interest and FRA cash flows. The interest expense, independent of the FRA, payable at the end of the six-month period, is

$$\$2,000,000 \times .0900 \times \frac{91}{360} = \$45,500.00.$$

The end-of-period value (six months) of the FRA compensation payment then serves as a cash inflow of $7,583.33. The final net borrowing cost to the firm for the $2,000,000 notional principal is $37,916.67.

Interest payment	($45,500.00)
FRA inflow	7,583.33
Net payment	($37,916.67)

The firm has locked in a borrowing rate of 7.50% per annum, $37,916.67 on $2,000,000.[3]

Forward rate agreements are purchased when a firm intends to borrow in the future or faces a variable rate interest payment in the future, but expects interest rates to rise. If the firm expects interest rates to fall by the date interest is due, it could either remain uncovered or sell (write) the FRA to profit from the expected fall in rates. Similarly, a firm planning to invest funds at a future date, but fearing a fall in market interest rates, can purchase a FRA to lock in an investment (or reinvestment) rate.

Interest Rate and Currency Swaps

Swaps are contractual agreements to exchange or "swap" debt service obligations. If the agreement is for one party to swap its fixed interest rate payment for the floating interest rate payments of another, it is termed an *interest rate swap*. If the agreement is to swap currencies of debt service denomination, for example Swiss franc interest payments in exchange for U.S. dollar interest payments, it is termed a *currency swap*.

What is often termed the "plain vanilla swap" is an agreement between two borrowers to exchange fixed-rate for floating-rate financial obligations. This swap normally requires a borrower with relatively cheap access to fixed-rate funds to exchange the debt

---

[3]The total net borrowing cost of $37,916.67 is 7.50% of the $2,000,000 debt:

$$\$2,000,000 \times .0750 \times \frac{91}{360} = \$37,916.67.$$

service structure with another borrower of slightly lower creditworthiness, who has acquired an obligation at floating rates. Each borrower obtains a payment structure that is "preferred," while still retaining the obligation for the principal repayment.

Interest Rate Swaps

Exhibit 14.4 provides an illustration of how a fixed-for-floating interest rate swap works. First, the two firms, Unilever (U.K.) and MIC (U.S.), have unequal access to capital. Although Unilever can borrow at a fixed rate of 9%, MIC must pay 10% due to its slightly lower credit rating. Both firms can also borrow at floating rates, Unilever at LIBOR + 1/4% and MIC at LIBOR + 3/4%. Each firm has its own comparative advantage in access to capital. Unilever can borrow at a full percentage point less than MIC at fixed rates, but that also means MIC has comparative advantage in borrowing floating-rate funds (as with international trade, a firm cannot possess comparative advantage in both products or processes). Although MIC must pay more for floating-rate funds than Unilever, it only pays 1/2% more floating whereas it must pay a full 1% more fixed. The problem is that Unilever would prefer to borrow at floating rates, but feels that at LIBOR + 1/4%, they are too expensive. Similarly, MIC would prefer fixed-rate borrowing, but at 10% it too feels the funds are too expensive. A solution is the interest rate swap.

Each firm borrows in its advantaged market, Unilever at fixed rates and MIC at floating rates. They then swap debt service obligations, MIC agreeing to make Unilever's fixed interest payments (MIC is termed the "fixed-rate payer") and Unilever covering MIC's floating-rate payments (Unilever is the "fixed-rate receiver"). The final negotiated interest rate swap benefits all three parties. Unilever now makes floating-rate payments at LIBOR + 0% (termed *LIBOR-flat*), which is cheaper than it could acquire on its own (LIBOR + 1/4%). Similarly, MIC now makes fixed-rate payments at 9 7/8%, cheaper than what it could acquire on its own (10%). Citibank receives its own share of 1/8% for facilitating the transaction and accepting some financial risk.

Although interest rate swaps were originally arranged between two independent parties on their own, in the early 1980s a number of international banks became intermediaries in this market. The banks provide the link through which the two parties of the agreement are brought together. Most firms acquiring interest rate swaps today have no idea which other firm may be at the other end of the swap; they are swapping only with the bank or swap dealer. The largest banks dealing in interest rate swaps today run what is called a *book*, in which they provide swaps at market rates as demanded and attempt to cover the other side of the obligation on their own. Note that the bank, for example Citibank in the preceding example, is actually accepting some of the financial risk of the transaction, as the bank is the legal *counterparty* for each individual firm. Banks also swap with one another for the same reasons that firms swap. In addition to the basic "plain vanilla swap," there are a number of different basis swaps. *Basis swaps* are the exchange of variable rate bases such as six-month LIBOR, three-month LIBOR, or six-month U.S. dollar prime.

Interest Rate Swap Quotes and Pricing

Like all major interest rates, swaps are quoted and priced based on yield curves. The first and second columns of the interest rate and currency swap quotations of Exhibit 14.5 list

Exhibit 14.4 Structure and Pricing of an Interest Rate Swap

Unilever (U.K.) and MIC (U.S.) are both in the market for approximately $30 million of debt for a five-year period. Unilever has a AAA credit rating, and therefore has access to both fixed and floating interest rate debt at attractive rates. Unilever would prefer to borrow at floating rates. MIC has an A rating. Although MIC still has access to both fixed- and floating-rate debt, the fixed-rate debt is considered expensive. MIC would prefer to borrow at fixed rates. The firms, through Citibank, could actually borrow in their relatively "advantaged" markets and then swap their debt service payments.

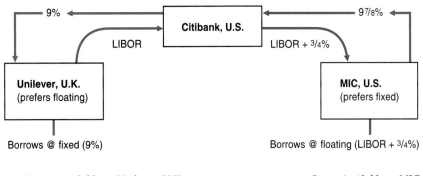

Rates Available to Unilever, U.K.
Fixed: 9%
Float: LIBOR + 1/4%

Rates Available to MIC, U.S.
Fixed: 10%
Float: LIBOR + 3/4%

Implementation of the Interest Rate Swap

1. Unilever borrows at the fixed rate of 9% and swaps the payments to the bank. The bank then agrees to make the debt service payments of fixed rate 9% on behalf of Unilever.

2. Unilever agrees in turn to pay the bank a floating rate of LIBOR, enabling it to make debt service payments on a floating rate basis, which it prefers, as well as at a lower interest rate than it could have acquired on its own.

3. MIC borrows at the floating rate debt of LIBOR + 3/4%, and then swaps the payments to the bank that agrees to service the floating-rate debt payments on behalf of MIC.

4. MIC agrees in turn to pay the bank a fixed rate of 9 7/8%, enabling MIC to make debt service payments on a fixed rate basis, which it prefers. Thus it borrows at lower cost than it could have acquired on its own.

Benefits of the Interest Rate Swap

Each of the borrowers benefits from the interest rate swap by being able to borrow capital in the preferred interest rate structure and at a lower rate than obtainable on their own.

	Unilever, U.K.	MIC, U.S.
If borrowing directly	LIBOR + 0.250%	10.000%
If borrowing through swap	LIBOR + 0.000%	9.875%
Savings	+ 0.250%	+ 0.125%

Exhibit 14.5   Interest Rate and Currency Swap Quotations

	US$ Interest Rate Swaps		Currency Swaps: Fixed Rates Versus US$ LIBOR			
Years	Treasuries price/yield	Spread	Dm/$	Sfr/$	£/$	¥/$
2	100.26/5.302	32–36	9.20–9.25	7.69–7.74	10.40–10.45	5.10–5.15
3	99.07/5.798	49–53	8.92–8.97	7.46–7.51	10.42–10.47	5.44–5.49
4	interpol/6.272	49–53	8.64–8.69	7.27–7.32	10.43–10.48	5.66–5.71
5	100.17/6.746	38–43	8.50–8.55	7.16–7.21	10.45–10.50	5.76–5.81
7	96.02/7.116	43–48	8.26–8.31	7.03–7.08	10.37–10.42	5.81–5.86
10	100.15/7.429	45–49	8.17–8.22	7.00–7.05	10.28–10.32	5.94–5.99

LIBOR six-month US$: 6.4375%

a. Interest rate swaps are quoted bid – offer in spreads over US Treasuries. To pay a floating rate (six-month dollar LIBOR), a swap party would receive the corresponding Treasury yield, plus the bid. To pay a fixed rate (Treasury yield plus the offer), a swap party would receive dollar LIBOR. Interpol is the four-year maturity interpolated from market rates.

b. Currency swaps are quoted bid – offer in terms of foreign currency fixed interest rates. Deutschemark and Swiss franc rates are annual; yen, sterling, and dollar rates are semiannual; and two- and three-year Australian dollar rates are quarterly. To pay six-month dollar LIBOR, firms receive the bid fixed foreign currency rate. To receive dollar LIBOR, firms pay the offered fixed foreign currency rates.

Source: Adapted from *Business International Money Report*, April 9, 1992.

the maturities and yields on U.S. dollar Treasury notes and bonds. These rates represent the risk-free yields that the U.S. government must pay for capital. Private firms wishing to raise capital pay a risk premium above the Treasury yield. The premiums for pricing interest rate swaps on U.S. dollars are listed in column 3, and are derived from top-rated corporate issues in U.S. dollar bond markets. Each is a quotation of a fixed bid and offer interest rate in exchange for the floating six-month LIBOR rate—a rate of 6.4375% on that date. Interpretation of swap quotes is relatively straightforward.

- Swap fixed for floating: Treasury + bid spread
- Swap floating for fixed: Treasury + offer spread

A firm wishing to swap six-month floating LIBOR payments for fixed-interest payments, for a four-year maturity, pays the U.S. Treasury yield + offer spread, or 6.272 + .530 = 6.802%. In the terminology of the swap market the firm would now be the fixed-rate payer and the floating-rate receiver, with the swap dealer/bank being the floating-rate payer and the fixed-rate receiver.

Interest rate swap payments are calculated as a percentage of a stated currency principal, called *notional principal*. Every swap agreement is therefore an exchange of interest payments only on an agreed upon notional principal. The notional principal is not "swapped" between parties because it is denominated in the identical currency and quantity. The notional principal is therefore not at risk if there is a failure of one counterparty to fulfill its swap obligations, only the difference in the interest rate swap payments. For example, the firm in the previous example swapped six-month floating LIBOR payments for a fixed-rate payment of 6.802%. If the swap was arranged on a $10,000,000 notional principal, the fixed interest rate payment, if paid annually, would be the exchange of

$$\$10,000,000 \times .06802 = \$680,200,$$

for two six-month LIBOR payments (assuming LIBOR does not change from the swap date) of 6.4375%; two payments totaling

$$2 \times \left[\$10,000,000 \times \left(.064375 \times \frac{180}{360}\right)\right] = 2 \times \$321,875 = \$643,750.$$

Thus, even if one counterparty fails to pay, the actual cash flows at risk are only the difference between actual interest payments on the agreement over the life of the swap, not the notional principal.

Once it is clear how the price is quoted, understanding the logic of the swap market is much easier. Swaps, like all instruments or tools discussed in this chapter, are not sources of capital. Swaps are contractual arrangements that alter the debt service payments of debt obligations already obtained. In many ways a firm approaching the swap market with a desire to swap floating- for fixed-rate payments is refinancing its debt. Pricing is therefore based on current market conditions. Pricing is the same as if the firm were to go through the process of issuing a new bond, with the pricing of the issue tied to AAA-rated corporate issue spreads above Treasury risk-free rates. A major benefit is that instead of suffering all of the expenses of registration, disclosure, underwriting, and distribution that a new issue would require to come to market, a firm may obtain an alteration of its basic debt service interest payment structure through the swap market much faster and cheaper.

Interest Rate Swap Uses and Strategies

The relatively easy access provided by the interest rate swap to different interest rate structures allows firms to reposition their financial obligations as their expectations on the movements of interest rates change. For example, a firm that has been paying floating rates while interest rates have been falling has enjoyed a reduction in debt service expense. If the firm believes interest rates have fallen as far as they are going to, it can swap from floating rate to fixed rate at little cost. A floating- to fixed-rate swap allows the firm to lock in fixed interest rates at levels the firm's financial managers believe to be in its best interest. The firm has refinanced much of its debt with little expense.

At the time of the initial fixed for floating interest rate swap, the present value of both streams of debt service cash flows are equal. This has to be true in order for both parties to "swap" the two payment streams. However, in the days, weeks, months, and years following the swap agreement, interest rates and market conditions will change. As interest rates change, the relative values of the swap positions change, one party's swap gaining in value while the other loses value. A firm that swaps from floating- to fixed-rate payments at the bottom of interest rate movements will see the value of its swap rise in the following periods when interest rates rise as it expected. This is no different in its impacts on debt value than if the firm had issued a fixed-rate bond when interest rates and corporate coupons were low, and then saw its bonds rise in value—selling at premiums—in the months and years after issuance. This gain or loss on the swap, however, would not be captured by the firm unless it were to liquidate the swap position.

Currency Swaps

Currency swaps enable borrowers to exchange debt service obligations denominated in one currency for the service on similar debt denominated in another currency. By swapping their future cash flow obligations, two parties are able to alter their currency holdings, but do so without incurring increased future currency exposure.

The usual motivation for a currency swap is to replace cash flows scheduled in an *undesired currency* with flows in a *desired currency*. The desired currency is probably that in which the firm's future operating revenue will be generated. Preferential financial terms in a particular currency arise because of market imperfections, which in turn result from a firm's greater access to borrowing in its home currency, the novelty of a particular debt issue, governmental regulations, and investor preference for buying bonds of domestic firms.

Exhibit 14.6 illustrates the currency swap rate yield curve associated with the U.S. dollar interest rate quotations in Exhibit 14.5. The U.S. dollar swap offer rate curve is the series of fixed U.S. dollar interest rates offered in return for the swap dealer/bank to pay the firm six-month U.S. dollar LIBOR. The U.S. dollar offer curve is derived by adding the offer spreads for AAA-rated firms to the appropriate maturity of U.S. Treasury yields.

The firm wishing to swap from floating six-month LIBOR to fixed interest rate payments could, however, swap not only from floating U.S. dollars to fixed U.S. dollars, it could potentially swap into fixed interest payments denominated in any of the other quoted currencies: fixed Deutschemarks, fixed Swiss francs, fixed British pounds, or fixed Japanese yen payments. Just as dollar swap rates reflect the yield required of a AAA-rated firm's new equivalent bond yield offered to the dollar market, a similar credit-quality firm (or potentially the same firm) could issue a bond denominated in marks, francs, pounds, or yen in the international markets.

A firm presently paying floating six-month U.S. dollar LIBOR for seven years could swap into fixed dollar payments of 7.596%, fixed Deutschemark payments of 8.31%, fixed Swiss franc payments of 7.08%, fixed British pound payments of 10.42%, or fixed Japanese yen payments of 5.86%.[4] Each currency swap quote is derived from the risk-free yield plus AAA-equivalent corporate spread rate in the respective currency market.

Each of the fixed foreign currency swap rates could in turn be swapped into floating-rate payments in the respective currencies as well (these rates are not shown in Exhibit 14.5 or 14.6). A multinational firm presently paying Swiss franc payments of 7.51% for three years could swap into fixed dollar payments of 6.328%, or any of the

---

[4]These fixed interest rate offer rates per currency are derived the same way as the U.S. dollar example. In this case, the offer rate by currency is found by reading across the seven-year maturity line (shaded) in Exhibit 14.5.

Exhibit 14.6 U.S. Dollar Currency Swap Rate Yield Curve

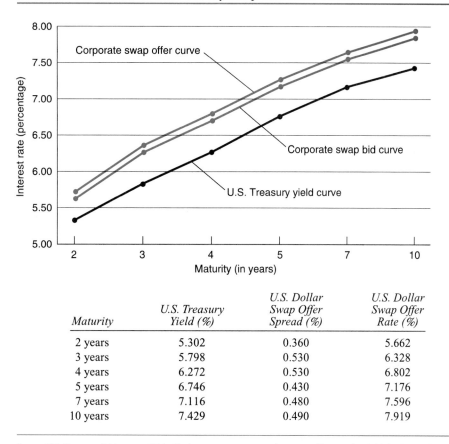

Maturity	U.S. Treasury Yield (%)	U.S. Dollar Swap Offer Spread (%)	U.S. Dollar Swap Offer Rate (%)
2 years	5.302	0.360	5.662
3 years	5.798	0.530	6.328
4 years	6.272	0.530	6.802
5 years	6.746	0.430	7.176
7 years	7.116	0.480	7.596
10 years	7.429	0.490	7.919

Source: U.S. Treasury yield rates and bid-offer interest rate swap spreads as quoted in second and third columns of Exhibit 14.5.

other listed fixed rates for three years. The interest rate and currency swap markets act together to offer the firm with current debt service payments of fixed or floating rates in one currency the ability, with little associated transaction cost, to redenominate both the interest rate payment structure and currency of denomination. It is no surprise the swap markets have grown astronomically in size in the past decade; they offer firms access to worldwide interest rates and currencies with little more than a series of phone calls and telexes/faxes.

An Illustration of a Back-to-Back Currency Swap

The currency swap market was originally used to change the currency of denomination of outstanding debt. A borrower with existing debt obligations in one currency would exchange payment obligations into a second desired currency. The rapid growth and success of the currency swap markets, however, have resulted in the frequent use of the currency swap market in tandem with debt issuance: The debt issuance and swap are arranged simultaneously. An unusual currency swap arrangement of 1991, a three-way back-to-back swap, illustrates both the principle of the currency swap and the flexibility afforded borrowers in the construction of swaps today.

As illustrated in Exhibit 14.7, this swap arrangement is particularly unusual because it involved three borrowers, not just two. The three borrowers, the Finnish Export Credit agency (Finland), the Province of Ontario (Canada), and the Inter-American Development Bank, all possessed ready access to a particular currency market, but wanted their funding to be in another.

- **Finnish Export Credit (FEC) of Finland.** FEC had not raised capital in the Canadian dollar Euromarkets previously, and would be well received if issuing there. FEC, however, had a need for increased debt service payments denominated in U.S. dollars at this time, not Canadian dollars.

- **Province of Ontario, Canada.** The Ontario government needed Canadian dollars, but due to the size of the provincial borrowings over previous periods, further issues by Ontario directly into the Canadian dollar markets would have pushed their cost of borrowing up. The province, however, was considered an attractive borrower by the U.S. dollar Euromarkets.

- **Inter-American Development Bank (IADB).** IADB, like the Finnish Export Credit agency, had a need for additional U.S. dollar funding but had already raised much of its capital in U.S. dollars. It was, however, considered an excellent borrower for the Euro-Canadian dollar market.

As opposed to the more common currency swap arrangement in which one firm contacts a bank or broker who acts as the counterparty to the swap, this particular arrangement required the bank, Goldman Sachs, to act only as a matchmaker in bringing the parties together and aiding in the negotiation of the swap rates.

Exhibit 14.7   Sample Swap: A Three-Way Back-to-Back Currency Swap

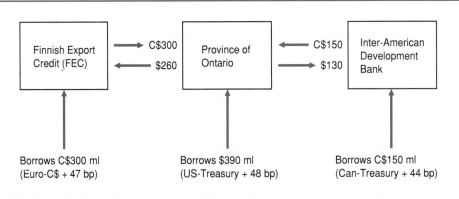

Each borrower determined its initial borrowing amounts and maturities expressly with the needs of the currency swap in mind. The Province of Ontario borrowed $390 million at a rate of Treasury + 48 basis points. Finnish Export Credit borrowed Euro-Canadian dollar debt of C$300 million at the Canadian Treasury bond rate plus 47 basis points, and the Inter-American Development Bank borrowed C$150 million at the Canadian Treasury bond rate plus 44 basis points.

The three parties then immediately swapped the proceeds and debt service payment streams of their borrowings. FEC swapped Euro-C$300 million to the Province of Ontario for Euro-$260 million, and IADB swapped Euro-C$150 million to the Province of Ontario for Euro-$130 million. Each party was therefore able to issue debt in the market in which there was a healthy demand for their issues (which means they paid lower rates of interest to acquire the debt) and then swap the proceeds and debt service payment streams into the currency they needed. All three parties benefited by borrowing where they had a comparative advantage and then swapping into the currency they preferred at a lower rate than they could have achieved by borrowing directly in that currency market.

Option-Based Instruments and Techniques

Interest rate option instruments differ by their market, which may be exchange traded or interbank (over the counter). Interest rate options that are exchange traded are actually options on interest rate futures contracts. Interest rate options that are traded or written over the counter are termed caps, floors, and collars.

Interest Rate Caps and Floors

An *interest rate cap* is an option to fix a ceiling or maximum short-term interest rate payment. The contract is written so the buyer of the cap will receive a cash payment equal to the difference between the actual market interest rate and the cap strike rate on the notional principal, if the market rate rises above the strike rate. Like any option, the buyer of the cap pays a premium to the seller of the cap up front for this right. The premium is normally stated as an annual percentage consistent with that of the strike rate. An *interest rate floor* gives the buyer the right to receive the compensating payment (cash settlement) when the reference interest rate falls below the strike rate of the floor.

Exhibit 14.8 lists interest rate cap and floor quotations for the U.S. dollar three-month LIBOR rate and Deutschemark six-month LIBOR on July 31, 1993. The quotes provide alternative maturities, two, three, or five years, and alternative cap rates for the two shorter maturities, with a single cap and floor rate for the five-year maturity. Each cap and floor has bid and offer quotations so a buyer could either buy or sell (write) the cap or floor.

Maturities and Structure

No theoretical limit exists to the specification of caps and floors. Most currency cap markets are liquid out to 10 years in the over-the-counter market, though the majority of

Exhibit 14.8   Interest Rate Cap and Floor Quotations

	U.S. Dollar Caps vs 3m LIBOR		U.S. Dollar Floors vs 3m LIBOR	
Maturity	Cap Rate	Bid Offer	Floor Rate	Bid Offer
2 years	5.00%	42–46	4.00%	42–47
	6.00%	15–19	5.00%	149–154
3 years	6.00%	69–79	4.00%	54–62
	7.00%	35–42	5.00%	190–200
5 years	7.00%	147–165	5.00%	245–261

	Deutschemark Caps vs 6m LIBOR		Deutschemark Floors vs 6m LIBOR	
Maturity	Cap Rate	Bid Offer	Floor Rate	Bid Offer
2 years	6.00%	35–40	5.50%	57–63
	6.50%	19–24	6.00%	101–107
3 years	6.00%	93–99	5.50%	89–96
	6.50%	60–65	6.00%	156–161
5 years	6.75%	172–185	5.50%	122–145

Source: Adapted from *International Financing Review*, July 31, 1993, Issue 990, p. 83. Bid-offer spreads are stated in basis points. For example, "42–46" is 0.42%–0.46% of the notional principal per annum.

trading falls between 1 and 5 years. There is an added distinction that is important to understanding cap maturity. It is not the total maturity that is singularly important, but the number of interest rate *resets* involved. For example, a common interest rate cap would be a two-year cap on three-month LIBOR. This means the total cap agreement will last for two years, in which there will be a total of seven 3-month LIBOR interest rate reset dates, or *fixings*. No reset exists for the first three-month period. There are two major types of interest rate caps:[5]

1. *Interest Rate Guarantee* (IRG), which provides protection to the buyer for a single period only. Protection is provided to the borrower in the event of a single major variable rate refunding or reinvestment.

2. *Interest Rate Cap*, which provides protection for an extended period of time, for example two to five years, on some interest rate reset. The subperiod reset, for example three-month LIBOR or six-month LIBOR, is called the cap's *tenor*. This protection is discrete, meaning protection is for the interest rate put into effect on a reset date, and not just any day over the period in which the actual market rate may creep up over the strike rate.

The interest rate cap is the more common of the two and is the subject of the following numerical example.

---

[5]Lee Macdonald Wakeman, "Option-Based Rate Risk Management Tools," in *The Handbook of Currency and Interest Rate Risk Management*, Robert J. Schwartz and Clifford W. Smith, Jr., eds., New York Institute of Finance, 1990.

Cap Valuation

A typical cap written over the counter by a bank for a firm would appear as follows:

1. maturity: 3 years
2. strike rate: 6.00%
3. reference rate: 3-month U.S. dollar LIBOR
4. total periods: 12 (4 per year for 3 years)
5. notional principal: $10,000,000
6. premium: 79 basis points (0.79%)
7. fixed borrowing rate: 7.00%

This agreement establishes a cap on all quarterly reset dates for three years. The cap rate is 6.00% per annum. All interest payments made are calculated on the basis of a notional principal of $10,000,000. The up-front cost of the cap, the premium, is 79 basis points. If the firm were to borrow at fixed interest it would pay 7.00%.

The value of a capped interest payment such as this one is actually composed of three different elements: (1) the actual three-month interest payment; (2) the amount of the cap payment to the cap buyer if the reference rate rises above the cap rate; and (3) the annualized cost of the cap. To demonstrate how the cap would work in practice let us assume the three-month LIBOR rate on the reset date (the actual reset rate is normally determined two days prior to the next actual payment date) has risen above the strike rate of 6.00% to 6.50%.

1. **Interest Rate Payment.** Regardless of whether the cap is activated, the buyer of the cap is responsible for making the normal interest payment. The firm owes a payment of three-month U.S. dollar LIBOR of 6.50% on a three-month period of actual 90 days on a notional principal of $10,000,000:

$$\$10{,}000{,}000 \times .0650 \times \frac{90}{360} = \$162{,}500.$$

2. **Receive Cap Cash Flow.** If the three-month LIBOR rate has risen above the cap rate on the reset date, the cap is activated and the buyer of the cap receives a cash payment from the cap seller equal to the difference between the actual three-month LIBOR rate of 6.50% and the cap rate of 6.00%; a cash payment of the following amount:

$$\$10{,}000{,}000 \times \left[(.0650 - .0600) \times \frac{90}{360}\right] = \$12{,}500.$$

3. **Amortized Cap Premium Payment.** But, alas, such flexibility and protection comes at a cost, the premium. The cap premium of 0.79% is a single lump sum payment made at the beginning of the three-year period, and must therefore be annualized in order to calculate the total cost of the capped payment. The fixed rate of interest at which this firm could borrow is 7.00%, and this is therefore the rate of interest used in the amortization of the cap premium over 12 reset periods.

The amortized premium, for 12 periods, discounted at a rate of 7.00% per annum (1.75% per quarter) is found by using the standard loan amortization formula used in calculating mortgage payments of all kinds:

$$\text{Quarterly premium} = \frac{0.7900\%}{\left[\frac{1}{.0175} - \frac{1}{.0175 \times (1.0175)^{12}}\right]} = .07356\%.$$

This is .07356% on a quarterly basis, .2942% on an annual basis.[6]

The resulting total, or all-in-cost (AIC) of the capped interest payment is 6.2942%, or a maximum of $157,356 every three months.

Cap Component	Annualized Interest Cost	Quarterly Cash Payments
1: Interest payment out-flow	6.5000%	$162,500
2: Cap cash payment in-flow	6.0000–6.5000%	−12,500
3: Cap premium payment out-flow	0.2942%	+7,356
Total Cost or All-in-Cost	6.2942%	$157,356

The firm has limited, or *capped* its potential interest payments. If three-month LIBOR is below the cap rate of 6.00% on the next reset date, the firm's all-in-cost would be the actual LIBOR payment plus its quarterly premium payment of 0.294%. The premium payment will be made for the life of the cap regardless of whether the cap is exercised or not.

When the cap is exercised like this, the payment resembles the exchange of a floating for fixed interest payment, a swap. However, unlike a swap, when the reference rate does not rise above the strike rate, the firm continues to make regular interest payments and is not restricted to the swap rate.

In order to understand the motivation of the buyer of the interest rate guarantee or cap, it is useful to see the expected interest payment over a wide range of potential three-month LIBOR rates at the time of the cap agreement initiation. Exhibit 14.9 compares the unhedged interest payment with the cap-hedged interest payment over a range of potential three-month LIBOR rates. Note that although the effective cap interest payment is slightly higher than 6.00% because of the cap premium that must be paid, it is still significantly cheaper than the unhedged interest payment if three-month LIBOR rates were to rise significantly above the strike rate of 6.00%. If LIBOR does not rise

---

[6]This is the calculation formula for amortized loan payments for a fixed rate of interest. The formula itself is

$$\text{Period payment} = \frac{\text{Present Value}}{\left[\frac{1}{r} - \frac{1}{r \times (1 + r)^t}\right]},$$

where the present value is the current loan amount, t is the number of periods, and r is the rate of interest per period. The resulting amortized mortgage payment services both principal and interest in a single constant cash payment per period.

Exhibit 14.9   Profile of an Interest Rate Cap

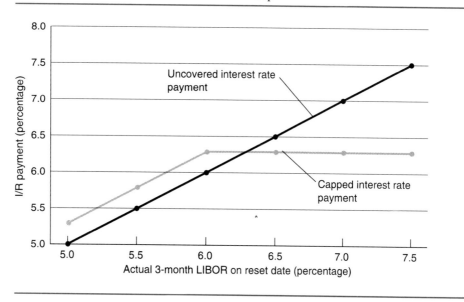

above the cap's strike rate, the presence of the premium of course increases the total cost of debt service above the totally uncovered position.

   If, however, the firm had swapped its three-month LIBOR floating payment for a fixed interest payment of 6.00%, regardless of the actual LIBOR rate on the original reset date it would be locked in to a 6.00% interest payment. The interest rate cap provides the buyer with insurance against a rise in interest rates, while allowing the firm the opportunity to enjoy lower interest payments if actual market rates do not rise. As was the case with the use of foreign currency options in the management of currency transaction exposures in Chapter 7, a firm would only purchase this insurance, this cap, if it expects not to use it. If the firm held a strong expectation that interest rates would rise above 6.00% by the reset date, it would be better off swapping the floating for a fixed-rate payment.

Interest Rate Floors

Interest rate caps are basically call options on an interest rate, and equivalently, interest rate floors are put options on an interest rate. A *floor* guarantees the buyer of the floor option a minimum interest rate to be received (rate of return on notional principal invested) for a specified reinvestment period or series of periods.

   For example, if a firm knows it will receive a cash inflow in three months, which it must invest, it will want to invest at the highest possible rate. If it fears interest rates will fall by that time, it may wish to purchase a floor. The floor will guarantee the firm a minimum effective rate of investment. If when the date of investment arrives the actual market rate of interest is less than the floor rate, the holder of the floor will receive from the writer of the floor a cash settlement equal to the difference between the actual reference rate and the floor rate.

Floor Valuation

The pricing and valuation of an interest rate floor is the same as that of the interest rate cap. Assume a German firm purchases a two-year interest rate floor of 6.00% as listed in Exhibit 14.8. The specifications of the firm and its floor would be as follows:

1. maturity: 2 years
2. strike rate: 6.00%
3. reference rate: 6-month DM LIBOR
4. total periods: 4 (semiannually for 2 years)
5. notional principal: DM5,000,000
6. floor premium: 107 basis points (1.07%)
7. fixed investment rate: 6.50%

The firm does not expect interest rates (investment rates available to it) to fall below 6.00%, but wishes some insurance against the possibility. If at the end of a six-month period, however, the six-month DM LIBOR rate has indeed fallen below the floor rate of 6.00% to 5.80%, the interest rate floor is activated (exercised). The valuation of the floor would be decomposed into the same three basic elements as the cap.

1. **Interest Rate Payment/Yield.** Regardless of whether the floor is activated, the firm that bought the floor will invest its funds at the market rate of interest. The firm therefore will earn 5.80%, the six-month DM LIBOR rate, on a notional principal of DM5,000,000

$$DM5,000,000 \times .0580 \times \frac{180}{360} = DM145,000.$$

2. **Receive Floor Cash Flow.** Since the reference rate (six-month DM LIBOR) has fallen below the floor strike rate, the floor is activated. The buyer of the floor receives the difference between the floor rate and the reference rate in cash of

$$DM5,000,000 \times \left[(.0600 - .0580) \times \frac{180}{360}\right] = DM5,000.$$

3. **Amortized Floor Premium Payment.** Regardless of whether the floor is activated, the firm must pay for the floor option. The single lump sum payment of 1.07% made up front is amortized over the two-year period of six-month reset periods. The rate of interest used for the amortization is the fixed rate of interest available to the firm at the beginning of the period, in this case 6.50%. The premium expense per semiannual period is

$$\text{Semiannual premium} = \frac{1.07\%}{\left[\dfrac{1}{.0325} - \dfrac{1}{.0325 \times (1.0325)^4}\right]} = .2896\%.$$

This is 0.2896% on a semiannual basis, or 0.5792% on an annual basis.

The all-in-yield of the floor-covered interest instrument is then 5.421% per annum, or a minimum return of DM135,520 each six months on a notional principal of DM5,000,000 for the two-year period.

Floor Component	Annualized Interest Yield	Quarterly Cash Flows
1: Interest payment inflow	5.800%	DM145,000
2: Floor cash payment inflow	6.000–5.800%	5,000
3: Floor premium payment outflow	0.579%	−14,480
Total Yield or All-in-Yield	5.421%	$135,520

Exhibit 14.10 illustrates this floor valuation over a range of potential reference rates (six-month DM LIBOR) at the time of the semiannual reset. Note that although the firm had placed a floor of 6.00% on its reinvestment of DM cash flows, its actual effective yield when the reference rate falls below the floor of 6.00% is 5.421% per annum. This is due to the annualized premium expense. Once again, if the firm truly believed interest rates would fall far enough to require the use of the floor, they would be better off investing at the fixed rate of 6.50% at the start of the period, rather than purchasing the floor as protection.

Interest Rate Collars

An *interest rate collar* is the simultaneous purchase (sale) of a cap and sale (purchase) of a floor. The firm constructing the collar earns a premium from the sale of one side to

Exhibit 14.10   Profile of an Interest Rate Floor

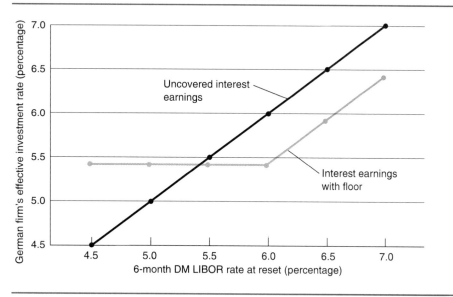

cover in part or in full the premium expense of purchasing the other side of the collar. If the two premiums are equal, the position is often referred to as a *zero-premium collar*.

Interest rate collars allow the firm to retain some of the benefit of declining rates while removing the unpleasantness of paying an up-front option premium for the cap. This unpleasantness can be mitigated, or totally eliminated in the case of a zero-cost collar, by the firm simultaneously selling a floor option of a suitable strike rate. For example, using the cap and floor quotations of Exhibit 14.8, a U.S. firm could fund the purchase of a cap against three-month U.S. dollar LIBOR rising above 5.00% in the next two years (paying a premium of 0.46%) by selling a 4.00% floor on three-month U.S. dollar LIBOR for the same two-year maturity (earning a premium of 0.42%). Although not precisely a zero net cost, the up-front net cost of the position is extremely small (0.46% − 0.42% = 0.04%). This interest rate collar is illustrated in Exhibit 14.11.

The risk of increased rates has been eliminated by forsaking the advantage of rates declining below the floor, at zero cost. It is important to remember that this means *zero initial cost*, for the firm will still be called on to make payments to the collar seller if rates fall below the floor level. Because the firm may be called on to make payments to the seller, each party to the transaction has credit exposure to the other, like a swap. In the extreme case of a zero-cost collar of zero width, the collar becomes a swap. The foreign exchange equivalent of a collar is the simultaneous purchase of a call option and the sale of a put option on the short currency (a synthetic forward for a short foreign currency position).

Exhibit 14.11   Profile of an Interest Rate Collar

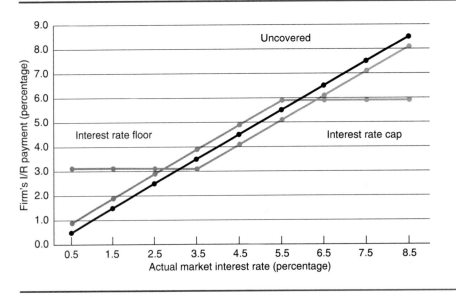

Swaptions

The purchase of a swap option—a *swaption*—gives the firm the right but not the obligation to enter into a swap on a predetermined notional principal at some defined future date at a specified strike rate.[7] The firm's treasurer would typically purchase a *payer's swaption*, giving the treasurer the right to enter a swap in which they pay the fixed rate and receive the floating rate. The treasurer would exercise this option if rates had risen above the strike level of the swaption; otherwise, the treasurer would allow the option to expire and take advantage of the lower rate environment.

If exercised, the swaption may be *swap settled*, settled for cash. In this case, the firm would receive a payment reflecting the intrinsic value of the swap. In the case of cash settlement, this eliminates the ongoing mutual counterparty risk. As with any option, the maximum downside risk for the firm is the initial premium exposure.

Many multinationals increasingly sell swaptions. A U.K.-resident firm would sell a swaption, termed a *receiver's swaption*, struck at an acceptable fixed rate, giving the purchasing bank the right to receive the fixed rate from the firm. The bank would exercise this option if rates had declined below the strike rate.

Summary of Techniques and Expectations

Exhibit 14.12 provides a summary of the techniques and strategies a typical firm could employ in managing debt service payments given expectations about the direction of interest rate movements. The technique choice is also dependent on whether the debt service is short term (where techniques such as interest rate swaps are inappropriate) or long term (where techniques such as forward rate agreements are inappropriate). One

Exhibit 14.12 Summary of Interest Rate Risk Management Techniques and Interest Rate Movement Expectations

Technique	Expect Rates to Rise	Expect Rates to Fall	Impact of Strategy
Mismatched Borrowing	Borrow short, lend long	Borrow long, lend short	Fixes rate of borrowing
FRA	Buy an FRA	Sell an FRA	Fixes future interest rate
Cap	Buy a cap	Sell a cap	Bounds (one-sided) I/R risk
Floor	Sell a floor	Do nothing	Bounds (one-sided) I/R risk
Collar	Buy a collar	Sell a collar	Bounds (two-sided) I/R risk
I/R Swap	Swap floating to fixed	Swap fixed to floating	Borrowing rate positioning

[7]One of the more succinct introductions to swaptions is "Behind the Mirror" by Robert Tompkins, in *From Black-Scholes to Black Holes: New Frontier in Options*, London: Risk Magazine Ltd., 1992, pp. 129–133.

final note should be made: The management of interest rate risk by a firm—for debt service—is not truly symmetrical in design. If expectations are strong for interest rates to fall, the simple logic of leaving floating-rate debt unhedged is dominant.

Swap and Derivative Market Growth

The currency swap market has grown rapidly since the first publicized swap between IBM (U.S.) and the World Bank in 1981. Exhibit 14.13 illustrates the growth of the interest rate and currency swap and derivatives markets from 1986 to end-of-year 1991. The growth in these markets is nothing short of astounding.

First, the total notional principal of outstanding agreements has increased sevenfold between 1986 and 1991 alone, rising from $1.08 trillion to nearly $7.6 trillion. Second, the activity is roughly equally split between exchanges and over-the-counter (OTC) markets. The exchange-traded markets are dominated by interest rate options and futures, with currency options and futures contributing little to the total and indicating no real growth in recent years. The over-the-counter market is dominated by the most important financial derivative of the 1980s, the interest rate swap. The notional principal of interest rate swaps outstanding at end-of-year 1991 was $2.75 trillion alone, accounting for 68% of all over-the-counter traded products, and over 36% of all currency and derivative instruments listed, over the counter or exchange traded. The volumes of over-the-counter traded currency swap and assorted interest rate instruments (caps, floors, collars, swaptions) have all shown rapid growth, representing $700 billion and $630 billion in notional principal at end-of-year 1991, respectively.

The swap market is extremely competitive, with very low profit margins for the financial intermediaries involved. Almost all swaps today involve a major bank as principal in the transaction. Typically, the bank maintains "swap books" in different currencies. For its efforts as principal, a bank will typically earn the present value of from 5 to

Exhibit 14.13   Growth of Interest Rate and Currency Swap and Derivative Instruments

Instruments	Notional principal amounts in billions of US dollars[1]					
	1986	*1987*	*1988*	*1989*	*1990*	*1991*
Exchange-traded instruments	583	724	1,300	1,762	2,284	3,518
I/R options and futures	516	609	1,174	1,588	2,054	3,231
Currency options and futures	49	74	60	66	72	77
Over-the-counter instruments[2]	500	867	1,330	2,402	3,451	4,080
I/R swaps	400	683	1,010	1,503	2,312	2,750
Currency and I/R swaps[3]	100	184	320	449	578	700
Caps, collars, floors, swaptions	—	—	—	450	561	630
Total	1,083	1,591	2,630	4,165	5,735	7,598

[1]Amounts outstanding at year end.

[2]Values for 1991 are estimates as of June.

[3]Adjusted for reporting of both currencies.

Source: Adapted from *Bank for International Settlements 62nd Annual Report*, Basle, Switzerland, June 1992, p. 192.

12 basis points per year, depending on the currency involved (U.S. dollar and Deutschemark swaps earn the least). If a swap is brokered by an intermediary that is not a principal, that broker will earn the present value of one basis point per year per counterparty. The partners to the swap typically save from 5 to 50 basis points per year, compared to their next best alternative for raising the same currency and terms without a swap. Since some commercial risk exists, termed *counterparty risk*, if one of the partners defaults, only firms with quality credit ratings (A or better), or guarantee facilities, can be served by the swap market. We return to the issue of counterparty risk in the final section of this chapter. Furthermore, a standardized swap contract has been designed by the International Swap Dealers Association (ISDA) and adopted by all players to reduce legal disputes.

Counterparty Risk

Counterparty risk is the potential exposure any individual firm bears that the second party to any financial contract will be unable to fulfill their obligations under the contract's specifications. Concern over counterparty risk has recently risen in the interest rate and currency swap markets as a result of a few large and well-publicized swap defaults. The rapid growth in the currency and interest rate financial derivatives markets has actually been accompanied by a surprisingly low default rate to date, although a single default could itself be deemed too much, particularly to managers of the firm experiencing the default.

Counterparty risk has long been one of the major factors that favor the use of exchange-traded rather than over-the-counter derivatives. Most exchanges where financial derivatives are traded are themselves the counterparty to all transactions, thus allowing all firms a high degree of confidence in being able to buy or sell exchange-traded products quickly and with little concern over the credit quality of the exchange itself. Financial exchanges typically require a small fee of all traders on the exchanges to fund insurance funds created expressly for the purpose of protecting all parties. Over-the-counter products, however, are direct credit exposures to the firm because the contract is generally between the buying firm and the selling financial institution. Most financial derivatives in today's world financial centers are sold or brokered only by the largest and generally soundest financial institutions. This does not mean, however, that firms can enter continuing agreements with these financial institutions without some degree of real financial risk and concern.

A firm entering into a currency or interest rate swap agreement retains ultimate responsibility for the timely servicing of its initial debt obligation(s). Although the swap agreement may constitute a contract to exchange U.S. dollar payments for Deutschemark payments, the firm that borrowed the U.S. dollar debt originally still is legally responsible for payment. The original borrowing or debt issuance is still on the borrower's books. In the event the swap counterparty cannot or does not make the payment as agreed, the firm that originally borrowed the debt—the U.S. dollar debt in this instance—is still responsible for debt service.

Exhibit 14.14   Swap Losses by Counterparty (end-of-year 1991)

Counterparty	Percentage of Net Loss (percentage)	Actual Loss (million US$)
ISDA Dealers	0.17	0.60
Non-ISDA Dealers	0.57	2.03
Savings and Loans	5.66	20.28
Other Nondealer Financial Institutions	16.78	60.14
United Kingdom Local Authorities	49.59	177.74
Other Government Entities	0.85	3.04
Corporations	26.38	94.53
Total	100.00	$358.36

Source: ISDA Swap Default Survey, July 1992, *Journal of International Security Markets*, Autumn 1992, pp. 293–296. Swap survey conducted by Arthur Andersen & Company. Survey group covered approximately 70% of the estimated $4.34 trillion outstanding notional principal volume of interest rate swaps, currency swaps, interest rate caps, floors, and collars outstanding at end-of-year 1991.

In the spring of 1992 the International Swap Dealers Association (ISDA) hired Arthur Andersen & Company to conduct a survey of the international interest rate and currency swap market's experience of defaults. The results were published in July 1992 and are summarized in Exhibit 14.14. Total defaults to date involved 513 transactions with 187 counterparties according to the survey of ISDA's 160 members worldwide. General survey results indicated that over 90% of all swap transactions were with investment-grade counterparties. At end-of-year 1991 there were 113,427 swaps in the portfolios of ISDA survey respondents, with an average life of 3.3 years.

According to the ISDA survey, of the $3.1 trillion in total notional swaps outstanding at end-of-year 1991, claims for defaults totaled $9.8 billion, only 0.32% of the total outstanding. Although this may seem a relatively small percentage, a value of $9.8 billion in principal still sounds remarkably high. The problem, however, is that the notional principal on which swap payments are calculated is not actually at risk. In a speech at the Annual Meetings of the International Swap Dealers Association in Hong Kong in March 1993, the chairman of the U.S. Securities and Exchange Commission, Richard Breeden, stated,

> The widespread use of "notional amounts" is the worst thing market participants have done, because the specter of trillions of dollars in "notional amount" has scared many people, including a few members of legislative bodies. . . . While the $1 trillion in contracts that U.S. broker-dealers are booking actually seems large, the amounts actually at risk in these markets do not appear to be unusually large compared with the size of exposures that banks, broker-dealers and insurance companies maintain for their traditional business.[8]

The real exposure of an interest or currency swap is not the total notional principal, but the mark-to-market values of differentials in interest or currency interest payments (replacement cost) since the inception of the swap agreement. This is typically only 2 to

---

[8]"Derivative Instruments, Views on Swap Risks Converge at ISDA Meeting," *International Financing Review*, issue 970, March 13, 1993, p. 109.

Exhibit 14.15   Swap Counterparty Legal Risk: The Hammersmith and
                    Fulham Debacle

Beginning in 1983, the Council of the London borough of Hammersmith and Fulham began using interest rate swaps as part of their debt management program. By the end of March 1987 the total notional principal of interest rate swaps and interest rate option agreements outstanding totaled £112 million. The financial managers of the borough council at that time increased their swap activity in an attempt to add net revenues to the council's budget (the council had recently been capped in its revenue-generating capacities through taxes). The total notional principal of swap and option contracts expanded to over £3.7 billion in the next 15 months.

Fulham Council's auditors found, in July 1988, that the majority of the swap transactions undertaken in recent years were *ultra vires*, beyond the council's legal authority. By the time the annual borrowing report for the council was published in February 1989, the total outstanding swap position had increased to over £6 billion. The magnitude of the speculative position is obvious given that the total outstanding debt of the Fulham borough at end-of-year 1989 was only £390 million! It is estimated that in 1988 the swap trading conducted by the borough of Hammersmith and Fulham alone constituted 1/2% of the global swap market. At this time the Council suspended all payments and receipts of outstanding swap and other interest rate derivatives pending legal findings regarding the legality of the Council entering into the contracts in the first place.

The House of Lords of Great Britain found, in January 1991, that the exotic interest rate transactions entered into by all U.K. municipal authorities between 1983 and 1991 were beyond their legal authority and they were therefore not obligated to pay. The losses to banks both in and outside the United Kingdom were thought to approach £100 million (US$170 million).

3% of the notional principal. Of the $9.8 billion in notional principals in default, gross claims for losses on a mark-to-market basis were only $539 million, of which $126 million was eventually recovered. Total actual net losses therefore totaled only $358 million as reported in Exhibit 14.14, a remarkably low value considering the rapid growth and size of the swap markets. The 1992 survey does, however, indicate a rising rate of defaults. A similar survey in 1988 totaled net losses of only $32 million.

The losses attributed to U.K. local government authorities made up a full 50% of all defaults to date reported by the surveyed dealers and brokers. These defaults are actually the result of *legal risk*, nonpayment resulting from court findings that the municipal authorities of several boroughs of the city of London had no legal authority to enter into hundreds of swap and option agreements between 1983 and 1989 (see Exhibit 14.15).

Summary

- This chapter summarized the definition, measurement, and management of interest rate risk management by firms today. The increasing volatility of world interest rates in recent years combined with the increasing use of short-term and variable-rate debt by firms worldwide has resulted in many firms now actively managing their interest rate risks, particularly debt service, which they only passively managed before.

- There are two major classes of interest rate risk: basis risk and gap risk. Basis risk is most common to financial institutions; gap risk is more commonly experienced by nonfinancial firms.

- The primary sources of interest rate risk to a multinational firm are short-term borrowing and investing, as well as long-term sources of debt.

- Although imperfect, one of the primary sources of interest rate "forecasts" is the shape of the yield curve for a specific currency and risk class.

- The techniques and instruments used in interest rate risk management are in many ways like those in currency risk management: a combination of the old tried and true methods of lending and borrowing with the new method of option-based derivatives.

- The primary outright instruments and techniques for interest rate risk management include the mismatching of asset and liability maturities, forward rate agreements (FRAs), forward swaps, and last but not least, interest rate and currency swaps.

- The interest rate and currency swap markets allow firms that have limited access to specific currencies and interest rate structures to gain access at relatively low costs, and permit these firms to manage their currency and interest rate risks very effectively.

- The option-based instruments and techniques commonly employed for interest rate risk management include interest rate caps, interest rate floors, combined cap and floor positions called collars, and options on future interest rate swaps called swaptions.

- Until recently the risk that parties to a swap or derivative contract would not fulfill their obligations under the contract, counterparty risk, was thought to be negligible. However, recent events such as the Hammersmith and Fulham case have raised new concerns over the counterparty risk of the international financial derivatives markets.

Decision Case
British Columbia Hydro[9]

British Columbia Hydroelectric and Power Authority (BC Hydro) is a provincial crown corporation, a wholly owned subsidiary of the province of British Columbia. BC Hydro is the fifth largest Canadian utility, generating, transmitting, and distributing electricity to more than one million customers in British Columbia. The fact that it is a

---

[9]Michael H. Moffett, University of Michigan, November 1992. Reprinted with permission. The author gratefully acknowledges the helpful comments of David Eiteman. This case is for the purpose of class discussion only, and is not intended to portray either effective or ineffective financial management practices. This case draws heavily on two articles by Terrence Laughlin, "BC Hydro's Discovery," *Intermarket*, September 1989, pp. 26–29, and "Making Ends Meet: BC Hydro Generates a Strategy to Service Debt," *Canadian Business*, April 1990, pp. 97, 99.

government-owned utility does not change its need to manage treasury operations against financial risks.

BC Hydro has substantial exposure to financial risk. Larry Bell, as chairman of BC Hydro, was determined to do something about the financial price risks—the movements of exchange rates, interest rates, and commodity prices—facing the firm. It was now March 1988. The time for discussion had ended and the time for decisions had come.

Financial Exposures

Upon taking over as chairman of BC Hydro in late 1987, Larry Bell started at the ground up in his analysis of the firm's financial exposures. Bell was formerly British Columbia's deputy minister of finance, and therefore not a newcomer to issues in financial management. His first step was to isolate those major business and financial forces driving net income (revenues and operating costs) and the balance sheet (asset and liability component values).

BC Hydro was—at least by financial standards—relatively simple in financial structure. The firm's revenues came from power sales. Power sales were in turn divisible into residential and small business (60%) and transmission sales (40%). Residential power use was extremely stable, so 60% of all revenues of BC Hydro were easily predictable. However, the same could not be said of transmission sales. This was power sold to large industrial users, users who numbered only 80 at that time. The power use of these 80 industrial users was determined by their business needs, and needs were highly cyclical. BC Hydro's sales were predominantly domestic, with only about 5% of all revenues generated from power sales to utilities across the border in the United States. BC Hydro earned Canadian dollars.

The cost structure of BC Hydro was also relatively simple—debt service. Debt service dominated operating expenses, averaging 55% of operating expenses over the mid-1980s. Debt service will rarely constitute 15% of operating expenses in many typical corporate financial structures. Power generation, however, is extremely capital intensive. The requirements for capital are met primarily by debt.

In 1987, BC Hydro had approximately C$8 billion in debt outstanding. Unfortunately, BC Hydro was a victim of its own attractiveness. It had been a direct beneficiary of the need for U.S.-based investors to diversify their exposures in the late 1970s and early 1980s. It had tapped the U.S. dollar debt markets at extremely attractive rates for the time. But now it was faced with the servicing of this U.S. dollar-denominated debt, a full half of its total debt portfolio. Much of the U.S. dollar debt had been acquired when the U.S. dollar was weaker (approximately C$1/$) and both U.S. and Canadian interest rates were higher. As shown in Exhibit 14.16, the appreciation of the U.S. dollar had resulted in an increase in the Canadian dollar debt equivalent of C$750 million. Equity amounted to approximately C$540 million. BC Hydro was *highly leveraged*, to say the least.

BC Hydro had followed the general principles of conservative capital structure management. It financed long-term assets with long-term debt. The match of asset and liability maturities was quite good, but the currency of denomination was not. This constituted an enormous potential exposure to the financial viability of BC Hydro.

Exhibit 14.16   Currency Composition and Exchange Rate Impacts on BC Hydro's Liabilities and Net Worth

Debt and Equity by currency of denomination	Initial values (Canadian dollars)	March 1988 (Canadian dollars)
Debt:		
Canadian dollar-denominated	4,000,000,000	4,000,000,000
U.S. dollar-denominated	3,250,000,000	4,000,000,000
Equity:	540,000,000	540,000,000
Total liabilities and net worth	7,790,000,000	8,540,000,000
Exchange rate related gains (losses)		(750,000,000)

Note: Initial values of debt are Canadian dollar equivalents of debt, regardless of original currency of denomination, on original dates of debt issuance.

Isolating the Issues

In early 1988, Chairman Larry Bell called in Bridgewater Associates, a Connecticut financial consulting firm, for help. Bob Prince and Ray Dalio (president) of Bridgewater, along with senior management of BC Hydro and representatives of the BC Ministry of Finance, met at Whistler Mountain, British Columbia. The purpose of the retreat was to first identify the primary financial risk issues facing BC Hydro, and secondly propose preliminary solutions. Chairman Bell encouraged an open exchange of ideas, but wished all potential solutions to be considered independently of legal and accounting constraints. He felt consideration of these constraints would prevent the analysis from getting to the core issues. The group isolated two questions immediately that had to be addressed prior to moving forward:

1. Does BC Hydro want to *eliminate* all financial risk, or only *manage* it?
2. BC Hydro is in the business of providing power. Is it also in the business of trading or speculating in the financial markets?

Discussion was heated on these points and ended with no clear agreement initially. The participants agreed to move on anyway to a detailed discussion and analysis of BC Hydro's financial exposures.

Financial Price Risks

Financial risk management focuses on how the movement of financial prices (interest rates, exchange rates, and commodity prices) affect the value of the firm. Isolating these impacts on any individual firm requires the evaluation of how revenues and costs, both operational and financial, change with movements in these prices. Bridgewater Associates and BC Hydro's staff conducted a number of statistical studies to find what economic forces were at work in the costs and revenues of the firm.

Revenues. The results were quite clear. The 60% of power sales going to the 1.25 million small business and residential consumers was extremely stable, and was therefore insensitive to movements in interest rates, or other business cycle indicators such as unemployment or inflation. In fact, residential power use was sensitive primarily to population size. The 40% of power sales to the large industrial users was, however, very cyclical. Closer analysis of the industrial users indicated these users were sensitive to basic commodity prices (pulp, paper, chemicals, mining, etc.). Statistically speaking, transmission sales were found to be heavily dependent on movements in commodity prices (positively related) and industrial production (positively related).

Costs. A closer look at the cost structure of BC Hydro also revealed a number of clear economic forces at work. Operating expenses were dominated by debt service, over 55% of the total. The remaining 45% of operating costs possessed little variable content. Although business conditions for industrial users could decline, the nature of the utility industry still required that operations continue with little change in operating expenses achievable.

Secondly, since 55% of operating expenses were debt service, costs could potentially move directly with interest rates. But BC Hydro's practice over the past decade had been to finance long-term assets with long-term debt, and long-term debt at fixed rates obviously did not move with shorter cycle interest rate movements. Long-term interest rates were locked in. And interest rates (short-term and long-term rates) had in general been falling in both the United States and Canada since the early 1980s.

Short-term interest rates move with commodity prices. Because increases in commodity prices frequently lead to more inflation, and interest rates and bond yields must in turn move with changes in inflation, significant commodity price increases translated directly into rising interest rates.

It was now clear that if BC Hydro's revenues and cost structures were to be managed against underlying economic or financial forces, protection would be needed against commodity prices. Exhibit 14.17 illustrates how power sales moved positively with commodity price changes. At the same time it also shows how short-term interest rates moved with commodity price changes, but long-term interest rates did not. Since BC Hydro was financed nearly exclusively with long-term debt, its present debt structure was not enjoying the fruits of these correlated movements (lower commodity prices and interest rates).

Currency Exposure. BC Hydro was facing an enormous foreign currency exposure. The fact that revenues were 95% Canadian dollar denominated, while C$4 billion of total long-term debt was U.S. dollar denominated, meant that debt service was completely exposed to currency risk. The firm earned only 5% of its revenues in U.S. dollars, and therefore had no "natural way" of obtaining the foreign currency it needed to service debt. As Exhibit 14.18 illustrates, the U.S. dollar had been rising against the Canadian dollar until a year earlier.

By 1988 Larry Bell estimated that BC Hydro had realized C$350 million in foreign currency losses on its U.S. dollar debt, all of which passed through current income. The

Exhibit 14.17   BC Hydro's Revenue and Cost Sensitivity to Commodity Price Changes

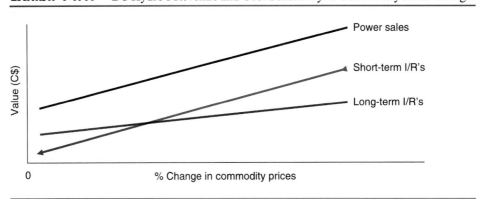

remaining exposure still approached C$400 million depending on the direction of the exchange rate movement. Something had to be done, and done fast. The urgency of the issue was particularly acute when noting that the total equity of BC Hydro only amounted to C$540 million!

The outstanding U.S. dollar debt was to be repaid in single "balloon" payments upon maturity. BC Hydro therefore had an enormous amount of cash flowing into a sinking fund for debt principal repayment. The funds were presently being reinvested in Canadian bonds, yielding short-term current rates on Canadian debt instruments.

Proposed Risk Management Strategies

Several alternative solutions were put forward for both the revenue-cost risks and the foreign currency risks. It seemed the solutions would have to be independently constructed.

The basic revenue-cost mismatch, the fact that BC Hydro held little short-term debt which would parallel the movement of revenues with commodity prices, was attacked first. The obvious solution was to increase the proportion of short-term debt. Although this approach would clearly increase the matching of commodity price cycles, it would do the opposite with regard to asset-liability maturity matching. It was argued that 60% of all power revenues were still very stable, and that the debt structure of the entire utility should not be reworked in order to pursue risk management goals. The critics of the short-term debt approach also emphasized that historical correlations might not hold up in the future. Movements of revenues and short-term interest rates correlated with commodity price movements may not hold true. The debate was heated.

The foreign currency exposure problem was simple, at first glance. The easiest and most risk averse approach would simply be to buy U.S. dollars forward. There was little

Exhibit 14.18 The Canadian Dollar/U.S. Dollar Spot Rate

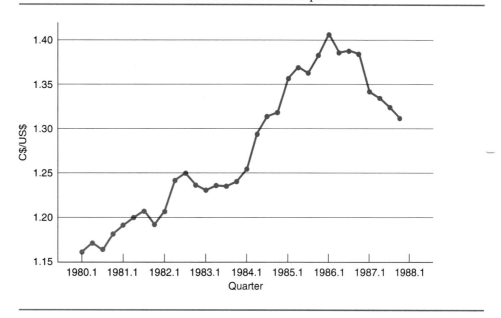

risk in that the debt service schedule was known exactly in terms of amounts and timing, and the resulting forward cover would eliminate the currency risk. Several senior finance ministry officials suggested a currency-interest rate swap instead. All agreed that both would work equally well. However, they were not certain that as a crown corporation they would be allowed to enter into a swap agreement. Late in the final afternoon of the weekend retreat an additional detail was also recognized, that the signing of a forward contract (or series of forward contracts) to cover the U.S. dollar debt service would require BC Hydro to recognize and realize (pass through the income statement) the total currency loss remaining, approximately C$400 million. This was obviously unacceptable.

A second alternative put forward by Ray Dalio of Bridgewater Associates was to move all sinking fund capital out of Canadian dollar bonds into a similar risk category of U.S. dollar-denominated securities. This would result in the security values moving in the opposite direction of the U.S. dollar debt, thus offsetting adverse (or favorable) exchange rate changes, a natural hedge. But, this also meant BC Hydro, a crown corporation, would be intentionally constructing an enormous uncovered foreign currency position. This met with considerable opposition by representatives of the British Columbia Ministry of Finance.

The retreat was over. The participants returned from the beautiful wilderness setting of Whistler Mountain to the hustle and bustle of Vancouver. It was now March 1988, and Larry Bell needed a decision soon.

Case Questions

1. Discuss the pros and cons of each of the following potential solutions to BC Hydro's interest rate and exchange rate exposures:
    a. purchase a series of forward contracts
    b. participate in a cross-currency interest rate swap
    c. replace Canadian dollar investments with U.S. dollar investments in the sinking fund
    d. do nothing

2. It is often stated that sound financial management practices are achieved by focusing on cash flow issues, and not on legal, tax, or accounting-based concerns. How does this statement apply to the case of BC Hydro?

3. What is the logic of increasing the proportion of short-term debt in BC Hydro's debt portfolio at the risk of mismatching the maturity of assets and liabilities?

4. What solutions to the U.S. dollar-denominated debt problem have not been considered? What would a normal private sector firm do to solve a similar exposure problem?

Questions

1. Interest Rate Practices

Many commercial banks now give corporate customers a choice among several different interest rate bases for their bank borrowings, including U.S. prime rates and U.S. dollar LIBOR. Why?

2. Euro-Currency Yield Curves

Closing Eurocurrency deposit interest rates on Friday were the following:

Maturity (days)	Eurodollars (percentage p.a.)	Euro-Swiss francs (percentage p.a.)
30	3.0625	4.5000
90	3.3125	4.4375
180	3.3750	4.2500
360	3.5625	4.0000

a. Calculate the forward spot interest rate for the second half 180-day period for the Swiss franc.
b. Calculate the forward spot interest rate for the second 90-day period of the year for the Euro-dollar deposits.

c. Graph both Eurocurrency yield curves. What conclusions can be drawn about the forward exchange rates between these two currencies without having the actual forward rates?

3. Financial Price Risk and Management Perception

Interest rates and exchange rates are theoretically equivalent in their relative impacts on the value of a firm. Yet interest rate risk is commonly considered by management as a "necessary evil" of doing business, whereas exchange rate risk is perceived as unusual and troublesome.

a. What characteristics of these two risks do you think lead management to perceive these risks in this way?
b. If management handles financial price risks as they perceive them, how will these differing perceptions alter the goals and methods of managing exchange rate and interest rate risk?

4. Yankee Corporation and Kiso Kaido, K.K.

The Yankee Corporation would like to borrow floating-rate dollars, which it can do at LIBOR + 0.5%. It can also borrow fixed-rate yen at 6%. Kiso Kaido, K.K. has a strong preference for fixed-rate yen debt, which will cost it 7.0%. Kiso Kaido, K.K. could borrow floating dollars at LIBOR + 1.0%.

What is the range of possible cost savings to Yankee Corporation from engaging in a combined interest and currency swap with Kiso Kaido, K.K.?

5. Smith and Jones

Smith and Jones corporations both seek funding at the lowest possible cost. They face the following rate structure:

	Smith	*Jones*
Credit rating	AA	BB
Cost of fixed-rate borrowing	10.0%	13.0%
Cost of floating-rate borrowing	LIBOR + 0.5%	LIBOR + 1.0%

a. In what type of borrowing does Smith have a comparative advantage? Why?
b. In what type of borrowing does Jones have a comparative advantage? Why?
c. If a swap were arranged, what is the maximum savings that could be divided between the two parties?
d. Illustrate a transaction that would generate such a savings divided equally between the two firms.

6. Yorkshire Industries and Huron River Salt Company

Yorkshire Industries, a British industrial firm with a U.S. subsidiary, seeks to refinance some of its existing British pound debt to include floating-rate obligations. The best floating rate it can obtain in London is LIBOR + 2.0%. Its current debt is as follows:

$10,000,000 owed to Citibank at 9.3% (fixed) annually.
£5,000,000 owed to Midland Bank at 9.5% (fixed) annually.

Huron River Salt Company wishes to finance exports to Britain with £3,000,000 of pound-denominated fixed-rate debt for six months. Huron River Salt is unable to obtain a fixed interest rate in London for less than 13.5% interest because of its lack of credit history in the United Kingdom. However, Lloyds Bank is willing to extend a floating-rate British pound loan at LIBOR + 2.0%. Huron River Salt, however, cannot afford to pay more than 12.0%.

How can Yorkshire Industries and Huron River Salt help each other via an interest rate swap? Assume that Yorkshire Industries is in a strong bargaining position and can negotiate the best deal possible, but Huron River Salt won't pay over 12%. Transaction costs are zero, and exchange rates do not change.

    a.   Illustrate with boxes and arrows the effective post-swap interest rates of each party.

    b.   What are the interest savings by each party over the six-month period of the swap?

7. Winnemucca's Interest Rate Cap (C14A.WK1)

Winnemucca Properties has just purchased the following interest rate cap agreement:

1. maturity: 2 years
2. strike rate: 7.00%
3. reference rate: 3-month U.S. dollar LIBOR
4. total periods: 8 (4 per year for 2 years)
5. notional principal: $3,600,000
6. premium: 66 basis points (0.66%)
7. fixed borrowing rate: 8.00%

If the actual three-month U.S. dollar LIBOR rate is 7.25% in the time of the next quarterly interest payment, fill in the following cap-payment table values.

Cap Component	Annualized Interest Cost	Quarterly Cash Payments
1: Interest payment outflow	%	$
2: Cap cash payment inflow	%	
3: Cap premium payment outflow	%	
Total Cost or All-in-Cost	%	$

8. Interest Rate Floors at SafeTeNet (C14B.WK1)

SafeTeNet Corporation is a pension fund management firm. It must, by law, hold a minimum percentage of its assets in highly liquid interest-bearing deposits of 360 days maturity or less. Because of the recent continuing decline in market interest rates, SafeTeNet has purchased a floor agreement for the entirety of its money market portfolio, approximately $2,500,000.

1. maturity: 2 years
2. strike rate: 6.00%

3. reference rate: 6-month DM LIBOR

4. total periods: 4 (semiannually for 2 years)

5. notional principal: DM5,000,000

6. floor premium: 107 basis points (1.07%)

7. fixed investment rate: 6.50%

   a.   Calculate the following:

Floor Component	Annualized Interest Yield	Quarterly Cash Flows
1: Interest payment inflow	%	
2: Floor cash payment inflow	%	
3: Floor premium payment outflow	%	
Total Yield or All-in-Yield	%	

   b.   Graphically depict the valuation profile of the interest rate floor.

9. Hammersmith & Fulham Debacle

The Hammersmith & Fulham swap case in the United Kingdom has had widespread impacts on the issue of counterparty risk worldwide. How do swap counterparties protect themselves against the possibility that the courts will, subsequent to the swap agreement, rule the swap counterparty never had the legal right to participate to begin with?

10. Swap or Bond Issuance?

Prior to the initiation of the currency swap market, a firm wishing to raise capital in a foreign currency, or have debt service denominated in a foreign currency, had to issue a foreign currency-denominated bond.

   a.   Using the swap rates listed in Exhibit 14.5, what would a multinational firm (AAA rated) have to pay to issue a five-year bond denominated in British pounds?

   b.   How would you compare the costs, time, and resources required to issue a foreign bond versus a domestic bond swapped into the same foreign currency?

Bibliography

Abken, Peter A., "Interest Rate Caps, Collars, and Floors," *Economic Review*, Federal Reserve Bank of Atlanta, vol. 74, no. 6, November/December 1989, pp. 2–24.

Ahm, Mark J., and William D. Falloon, *Strategic Risk Management*, Chicago: Probus, 1991.

Andersen, Torben Juul, *Currency and Interest Rate Hedging*, 2nd ed., New York: New York Institute of Finance, 1993.

Beidleman, Carl R., *Financial Swaps*, Homewood, Ill.: Dow Jones-Irwin, 1985.

Briys, Eric, Michel Crouhy, and Rainer Schobel, "The Pricing of Default-Free Interest Rate Cap, Floor, and Collar Agreements," *Journal of Finance*, vol. 46, no. 5, December 1991, pp. 1879–1892.

Brown, Keith C., and Donald J. Smith, "Default Risk and Innovations in the Design of Interest

Rate Swaps," *Financial Management*, vol. 22, no. 2, Summer 1993, pp. 94–105.

Cox, John C., Jonathan E. Ingersoll, Jr., and Stephen A. Ross, "Duration and the Measurement of Basis Risk," *Journal of Business*, vol. 52, 1979, pp. 51–61.

Euromoney, "Dictionary of Derivatives," *Euromoney Supplement*, June 1992, London.

Gommo, Richard, "Corporate Treasury: Five Pillars of Wisdom," *Risk*, vol. 4, no. 7, July-August 1991, pp. 14, 16, 19.

Grabbe, J. Orlin, *International Financial Markets*, 2nd ed., New York: Elsevier, 1991.

Howe, Donna M., *A Guide to Managing Interest Rate Risk*, New York: New York Institute of Finance, 1991.

Landau, Nilly, "Riding Interest Rates: How to Time a New Debt Issue," *Business International Money Report*, May 20, 1991, pp. 193–194.

———, "Taking the First Steps Toward Successful Corporate Interest Rate Risk Management," *Business International Money Report*, August 26, 1991, pp. 333–335.

Morgan Guarantee Trust Company, "Swaps: Volatility at Controlled Risk," *World Financial Markets*, April 1991, pp. 1–22.

Quinn, Lawrence R., "How Corporate America Views Financial Risk Management," *Futures*, vol. 18, no. 1, January 1989, pp. 40–41.

Ross, Derek, "Interest Rate Risk Management: Put to the Test," *Accountancy*, vol. 106, no. 1168, December 1990, pp. 109–111.

Smith, Clifford W., Jr., Charles W. Smithson, and Lee MacDonald Wakeman, "The Market for Interest Rate Swaps," *Financial Management*, Winter 1988, pp. 34–44.

———, "The Evolving Market for Swaps," *Midland Corporate Finance Journal*, Winter 1986, pp. 20–32.

Smith, Clifford W., Jr., Charles Smithson, and D. Sykes Wilford, *Managing Financial Risk*, Institutional Investor Series in Finance, New York: Harper & Row, 1990.

Smith, Roy C., and Ingo Walter, *Global Financial Services*, New York: Harper-Business, 1990.

Solnik, Bruno, "Swap Pricing and Default Risk: A Note," *Journal of International Financial Management and Accounting*, vol. 2, no. 1, Spring 1990, pp. 79–91.

Tompkins, Robert, "Behind the Mirror," in *From Black-Scholes to Black Holes: New Frontier in Options*, London: Risk Magazine Ltd, 1992, pp. 129–133.

Wakeman, Lee Macdonald, "Option-Based Rate Risk Management Tools," in *The Handbook of Currency and Interest Rate Risk Management*, Robert J. Schwartz and Clifford W. Smith, Jr., eds., New York: New York Institute of Finance, Simon & Schuster, 1990.

Wunnicke, Diane B., David R. Wilson, and Brooke Wunnicke, *Corporate Financial Risk Management*, New York: Wiley, 1992.

Chapter 15
International Banking

The growth of multinational business since the end of World War II has been accompanied by a parallel development of international financial centers, with international banks acting as the key financial intermediary in these centers. Although our major focus here is on financial management of multinational firms, international banks deserve special attention because they facilitate and support these firms. Furthermore, the banks themselves are usually major multinational enterprises.

International banks facilitate and support multinational firms in the following ways:

- Financing imports and exports (the traditional international banking task).
- Trading foreign exchange and currency options.
- Borrowing and lending in the Eurocurrency market.
- Organizing or participating in international loan syndications.
- Underwriting both Eurobonds and foreign bonds.
- Engaging in project financing.
- Providing international cash management services.
- Soliciting local currency deposits and loans with an intent to operate as a full-service local bank.
- Supplying information and advice to clients, including multinational firms.

Some of the largest world banks attempt to do all of these things. Others have found it advantageous to specialize in a select few of the possible activities. Banks generalize or specialize according to their abilities and size, as well as their perception of what unique services their original home clients need.

In this chapter we first define and identify international financial centers. These are the hubs from which international banks operate. Second, we analyze potential bank strategies under current conditions. Third, we describe the alternative types of banking offices through which international banks implement their strategy. Fourth, we highlight some national differences in the manner that banks offer their services. Fifth, we analyze the risks involved in international lending to developing countries. Sixth, we describe how banks analyze country risk. Finally, we analyze the various strategies and techniques used by both the developing countries and the banks to manage their international debt problems.

International Financial Centers

International banking is concentrated in certain cities that have come to be identified as international financial centers. London, Tokyo, and New York City are the most important, but other locations are also prominent. Four major types of transactions occur in an international financial center that is also an important domestic financial center. These are depicted in Exhibit 15.1.

Any important national financial center depends on the presence of a large body of domestic investors or depositors supplying funds to domestic users (relationship A). Investors supply funds directly to users by purchasing securities such as bonds,

Exhibit 15.1 Schematic View of Transactions in an International Financial Center

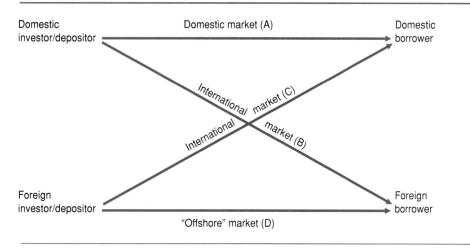

Note: The terms offshore and overseas are often used in the English language as synonyms for "foreign," presumably because England, the home country of the language, is an island. Describing Luxembourg as an "offshore" financial center seems contrary to a literal meaning of the word, since it is England that is "offshore." However, with the completion of the tunnel under the English Channel (or "Chunnel" as it is sometimes called), it is questionable whether anyone is truly offshore!

commercial paper, or shares of stock; depositors supply their funds to financial intermediaries (banks, insurance companies, mutual funds, etc.) that pool these receipts and make loans or equity investments from the pool. Most financial intermediaries guarantee the deposit, so the depositor looks to the intermediary rather than to the ultimate borrower for security.

An international financial center exists when domestic funds are supplied to foreign users or when foreign funds are supplied to domestic users. These are the diagonal relationships B and C. A healthy international financial center will almost always develop business along line D, in which foreign funds are supplied to foreign users.

London, Tokyo, and New York, as the world's most important international financial markets, perform all four of the possible functions. Other cities perform two or three of the four functions quite well and are important regional financial centers. These include Paris, Zurich, Geneva, Amsterdam, Singapore, and Hong Kong.[1]

Still other centers perform only relationship D. They are usually referred to as "offshore" financial centers. They exist by providing a service for nonresidents while (usually)

---

[1]Excellent overall descriptions of international financial centers can be found in Howard C. Reed, *The Preeminence of International Financial Centers,* New York: Praeger, 1981; and Gunter Dufey and Ian H. Giddy, *The International Money Market,* Englewood Cliffs, N.J.: Prentice-Hall, 1978. For a more concise discussion of the development of Asian financial centers, see Howard C. Reed, "The Ascent of Tokyo as an International Financial Center," *Journal of International Business Studies,* Winter 1980, pp. 19–35.

keeping their international business separate from their domestic business. Typical off-shore financial centers are Luxembourg, Cayman Islands, the Bahamas, the Netherlands Antilles, and Bahrain. Jersey, Guernsey, and the Isle of Man function as offshore financial centers for London-based financing.[2] Exhibit 15.2 is the "tombstone" announcing a bond issued by the Bank of Tokyo, Ltd., through its Cayman Islands financial subsidiary.

Exhibit 15.2   The Bank of Tokyo, Ltd.'s "Tombstone" Announcement of Offshore Banking Issue

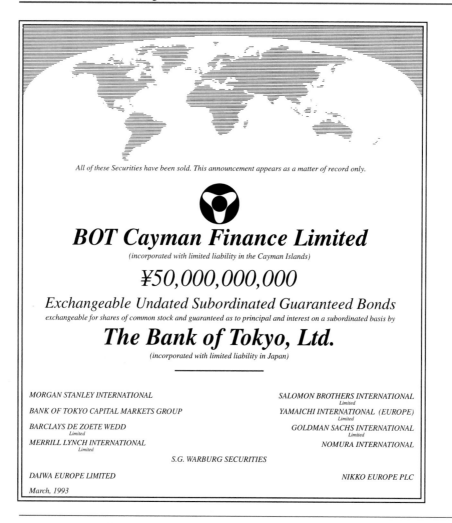

All of these Securities have been sold. This announcement appears as a matter of record only.

BOT Cayman Finance Limited
(incorporated with limited liability in the Cayman Islands)

¥50,000,000,000

Exchangeable Undated Subordinated Guaranteed Bonds
exchangeable for shares of common stock and guaranteed as to principal and interest on a subordinated basis by

The Bank of Tokyo, Ltd.
(incorporated with limited liability in Japan)

MORGAN STANLEY INTERNATIONAL	SALOMON BROTHERS INTERNATIONAL *Limited*
BANK OF TOKYO CAPITAL MARKETS GROUP	YAMAICHI INTERNATIONAL (EUROPE) *Limited*
BARCLAYS DE ZOETE WEDD *Limited*	GOLDMAN SACHS INTERNATIONAL *Limited*
MERRILL LYNCH INTERNATIONAL *Limited*	NOMURA INTERNATIONAL
S.G. WARBURG SECURITIES	
DAIWA EUROPE LIMITED	NIKKO EUROPE PLC

March, 1993

Source: The Bank of Tokyo. Reprinted with permission.

---

[2]R. A. Jones, "The British Isles Offshore Financial Centres," *National Westminster Bank Quarterly Review,* November 1982, pp. 53–65.

The major requirements for success as an offshore financial center are the following:[3]

- Economic and political stability, which gives confidence to nonresidents that fund movements will not be restricted.

- An efficient and experienced financial community, able to carry out necessary technical operations with skill.

- Good communication and support services, so market information can be quickly and efficiently transmitted to participants.

- A regulatory climate that protects investors and depositors but is not unduly restrictive to financial institutions.

Exhibit 15.3 shows how international banking assets were distributed by international financial center at the end of 1992. The most important center—as measured by external

Exhibit 15.3 International Banking Assets, Stock at End-of-Year 1992, by Financial Center (in billions of U.S. dollars)

Positions of Banks	External Assets in Domestic Currency	External Assets in Foreign Currency	Local Assets in Foreign Currency
Europe			
United Kingdom	86.2	933.5	266.2
France	114.1	349.9	75.6
Switzerland	88.0	291.6	18.9
Luxembourg	6.8	325.4	59.4
Germany	205.4	163.2	11.5
Belgium	14.4	182.4	51.3
Italy	11.0	93.8	129.5
Netherlands	29.6	141.0	32.7
Spain	15.1	53.4	36.5
Sweden	3.0	29.1	38.9
Other European	22.3	111.3	58.4
Total European	595.9	2,674.6	778.9
Japan	440.8	438.4	346.2
United States	495.5	62.7	−
Asian Market Centers	10.7[1]	844.9[2]	−
Other Centers[3]	3.5	630.7	28.9[4]
TOTAL	1,546.3	4,651.3	1,154.0

[1]Hong Kong only.

[2]Including Bahrain.

[3]Including Canada.

[4]Canada only.

Source: Abstracted by authors from "Developments in Individual Reporting Market Centres," Bank for International Settlements, *63rd Annual Report*, Basle, June 14, 1993, p. 103.

---

[3]Dufey and Giddy, *The International Money Market,* p. 39.

Exhibit 15.4   Changes of Banks' Net Currency Positions, End-of-Year 1992[1] (in billions of U.S. dollars)

	External Positions in Domestic Currency			External and Local Positions in Foreign Currency		
Currencies[2]	Chg 1991	Chg 1992	Stocks End-1992	Chg 1991	Chg 1992	Stocks End-1992
U.S. dollar	5.4	−52.8	−119.5	−34.4	52.3	63.0
Belgian franc	5.5	−3.9	−6.8	−6.0	1.1	−6.2
Deutschemark	−11.4	−41.4	60.9	0.8	−2.3	−61.4
Dutch guilder	2.3	−11.2	−0.1	−4.8	−3.1	−8.4
French franc	−12.3	37.8	−6.1	2.2	−34.4	−22.3
Italian lira	4.4	2.3	−11.7	4.8	−2.8	16.0
Japanese yen	82.1	45.4	245.8	−8.7	−17.0	2.8
Pound sterling	5.9	14.5	−47.9	−6.7	−0.4	−13.3
Spanish peseta	−0.6	10.8	−1.0	—	—	—
Swedish krona	0.4	−1.0	−2.4	—	—	—
Swiss franc	−6.5	−7.2	25.4	7.9	10.0	−4.5
ECU	—	—	—	4.6	4.6	4.3

[1]Banks in industrial reporting countries only; changes at constant end-quarter exchange rates.

[2]Indicates a decrease in assets, increase in liabilities; for stocks, net liabilities.

Source: Derived by authors from data contained in "Development of Banks' Net Currency Positions," Bank for International Settlements, *63rd Annual Report,* Basle, June 14, 1993, p. 102.

assets in foreign currency—was the United Kingdom (London), followed by Japan (Tokyo). The Japanese market has been the fastest growing segment of the international banking market, especially following the 1986 establishment of a Japanese offshore market. This market is similar in concept to U.S. International Banking Facilities (IBFs) (to be described shortly), in that Japanese banks have a set of segregated accounts that are exempt from certain domestic regulations in order to attract Eurocurrency business. The main depositors and borrowers in this market are the Japanese banks themselves and their foreign branches. The Euroyen is the currency of denomination. The third most important market is the United States, chiefly because of IBFs.

Exhibit 15.4 shows the changes in external positions of reporting banks by the currency of denomination. The most notable change is that of the Japanese yen, being the currency with the largest increase (245.8 billion U.S. dollars) in external positions of *domestic currency*, while the U.S. dollar was the currency of denomination of the largest change (63.0 billion U.S. dollars) at end-of-year 1992 as the currency of denomination of external and local positions in *foreign currency*.

International Strategies of Banks

International strategies of banks are normally evolutionary, with multinational banking being the final step. Currently, bank strategists are wrestling with the opportunities created by the consequences of the Single European Act (1985), the opening of the eastern European markets, and the strengthening of capital adequacy standards.

Stages of Evolution

Ian Giddy has identified three stages of evolution: arm's-length international banking, offshore banking, and host country banking (multinational banking).[4]

Arm's-length international banking exists when the domestic bank carries on its international banking from within its home country, accepting foreign deposits and making foreign loans. This is usually the first phase of a bank's involvement in international activities. It then evolves naturally into a need to develop relationships with correspondent banks in other countries. The international banking department of the home bank functions primarily as a center for clearing international payments and for financing imports and exports. The main customers are importers, exporters, tourists, and foreign banks.

As the needs of their customers become more sophisticated, the next phase for internationalizing the bank's activities is usually to establish an offshore banking presence. In offshore banking, the bank accepts deposits and makes loans and investments in a Eurocurrency and books these transactions in an offshore shell branch location. Examples are Eurodollars held in shell branches in the Bahamas or the Cayman Islands or in International Banking Facilities (IBFs) in the United States. Offshore banks are active in the purchase and placement of short-term funds, in syndicated loans, and in foreign exchange trading. Their depositors and borrowers are usually located in countries other than the home country of the offshore bank. Some offshore banks specialize in taking deposits for relending in their home country.

The ultimate level of international commitment is for a bank to establish itself within other countries. Host country banking typically involves full-service banking in a foreign country through a branch or subsidiary of the parent bank. Deposits and loans are made in the local currency to residents of the host country, in competition with local banks.

Strategic Consequences of the Single European Market

The Single European Market will have a significant impact on the structure of the banking markets of the European Union (EU). The primary provision of the Single European Act of 1985 on banking is the single banking license, which allows banks to operate in all member states without separately licensed and capitalized subsidiaries or branches. These banks can now pursue all banking operations allowed by their own home country license. The single market creates opportunities for previously foreign banks to now be domestic banks.

Although the Single Banking License theoretically allows EU-wide branching, the realities are considerably more restrictive. Many of the country markets in the EU are

---

[4]Ian Giddy, "The Theory and Industrial Organization of International Banking," New York: *Columbia University Graduate School of Business Research Working Paper,* no. 343A, June 30, 1980.

already overbanked, and new branch banking, particularly on the retail level, will not be profitable or likely. In the future, however, the single market will allow many banks to selectively enter foreign niche markets for specialty banking and financial services.[5] Deutsche Bank's acquisition of Banca d'America d'Italia (Italy) and Morgan Grenfell (United Kingdom) is an example of this selective entry approach, gaining entry into retail and investment banking markets, respectively.

In light of this new, more open single banking market, many banks are entering new markets—and protecting domestic markets—through mergers and strategic alliances. These cooperative ventures allow banks to expand into new higher value-added specialty markets abroad, with the cooperation of a locally based bank, while not threatening that bank, and simultaneously protecting its domestic market.

Strategic Consequences of Strengthening Capital Adequacy Standards

The Basle Accord, an agreement among the Group of Ten industrial countries and Luxembourg in 1988, established a framework for the measurement of bank capital internationally and set a standard for minimum capital adequacy. Although the agreement applies only to banks that are internationally active, the same standards are now being adopted by other countries for all their banks.

The Basle Accord divided bank capital into two categories: (1) core capital, which consists of shareholder equity and disclosed reserves; and (2) supplementary capital, consisting of a number of hybrid securities (having characteristics of both debt and equity)—mostly subordinated perpetual notes. The capital needs of the bank are determined by a risk-based weighting of both on- and off-balance-sheet items. The minimum capital adequacy as stated in the Basle Accord is now 4% for each category of bank capital (8% in total).

The strategic implications of these standards is as yet unclear. The most visible impact to date has been the efforts by banks to increase their core capital levels. Many international banks are purported to be shifting assets to low-risk categories, such as the popular asset-backed securities used by U.S. banks. These have already spread in usage to France, Germany, and the United Kingdom. The standards are definitely altering the decisions that banks make regarding the composition of their portfolios, and may have already slowed the expansion of bank balance sheets internationally.

The biggest uncertainty regarding the impacts of the Basle Accord surrounds the competitiveness of banks with nonbanks. The increased financial intermediation costs from higher minimum capital adequacy standards may result in increased use of securitized assets that previously did not meet the credit standards necessary for market trading. There are also early indications of a slowdown in lending as a result of the higher costs. Time will tell.

---

[5]For a thorough description of the many forms of international banking and financial services see Ingo Walter, *Global Competition in Financial Services: Market Structure, Protection, and Trade Liberalization,* Cambridge, Mass.: Ballinger, 1988.

Types of Banking Offices

By combining correspondent banking, offshore banking, and host country banking, a multinational bank can offer a global network to meet the worldwide needs of its client firms. Foreign banking offices of such a global network may be of five types: correspondent banks, representative offices, branch banks, subsidiaries, and affiliates. In addition, U.S. banks now are able to operate International Banking Facilities (IBFs) and Edge Act corporations within the United States. Activities permitted under each form vary somewhat, according to the laws of the various host countries (or, in the case of foreign banks in the United States, according to state laws). The following discussion is necessarily general rather than specific to any single country.

Correspondent Banks

Most major banks of the world maintain correspondent banking relationships with local banks in each of the important foreign cities of the world. The two-way link between banks is essentially one of "correspondence," via fax, cable, and mail, and a mutual deposit relationship. For example, a U.S. bank may have a correspondent bank in Kuala Lumpur, Malaysia, and the U.S. bank will in turn be the correspondent bank for the Malaysian bank. Each will maintain a deposit in the other in local currency.

Correspondent services include accepting drafts, honoring letters of credit, and furnishing credit information. Services are centered around collecting or paying foreign funds, often because of import or export transactions. However, a visiting businessperson can use the home bank's introduction to meet local bankers.

Under a correspondent banking relationship, neither of the correspondent banks maintains its own personnel in the other country. Direct contact between the banks is usually limited to periodic visits between members of the banks' management.

For the businessperson the main advantage of banking at home with a bank having a large number of foreign correspondent relationships is the ability to handle financial matters in a large number of foreign countries through local bankers whose knowledge of local customs should be extensive. The disadvantages are the lack of ability to deposit in, borrow from, or disburse from a branch of one's own home bank, as well as the possibility that correspondents will put a lower priority on serving the foreign banks' customer than on serving their own permanent customers.

Representative Offices

A bank establishes a representative office in a foreign country primarily to help parent bank clients when they are doing business in that country or in neighboring countries. It also functions as a geographically convenient location from which to visit correspondent banks in its region rather than sending bankers from the parent bank at greater financial and physical cost. A representative office is not a "banking office." It cannot accept deposits, make loans, commit the parent bank to a loan, or deal in drafts, letters of credit, or the Eurocurrency market. Indeed, a tourist cannot even cash a travelers check from the parent bank in the representative office.

The basic function of a representative office is to provide information, advice, and local contacts for the parent bank's business clients and to provide a location where business persons from either country can initiate inquiries about the parent bank's services. Representative offices introduce visiting executives to local banks, and they watch over correspondent banking relationships. They put parent bank customers in contact with local business firms interested in supplying, purchasing, or marketing products or services, and they arrange meetings with government officials if that is needed to obtain permissions, approvals, or government help. They provide credit analysis of local firms and economic and political intelligence about the country.

A representative office is usually small, often one executive, two or three assistants, and clerical help, all of whom work in an office that does not resemble a banking office in the physical sense. The representative and the assistants may have come to the office from the home country, but it is equally likely they are citizens or permanent residents of the host country. The major advantage of a representative office is that the local representative will have a more precise understanding of the needs of home country clients than might local correspondents and can thus provide data and advice more suitable to their needs. The local representative will be bilingual, if that is needed, and can advise visitors about local customs and procedures.

If the parent bank eventually decides to open a local general banking office, the existence of a representative office for some prior period usually provides a valuable base of contacts and expertise to facilitate the change. However, representative offices are not necessarily a prelude to a general banking office, nor need an eventual general banking office be the major reason for opening a representative office. In some countries, such as Mexico, foreign banks were precluded from opening new general banking offices. Thus representative offices were the only possible presence in such countries.

The essential disadvantage of the representative office to the business firm is that it cannot conduct general banking activities. Although it can facilitate such transactions with local correspondents, the process may be slower or more cumbersome than a business firm might wish. Because a representative office is usually small, physical limitations do exist on the services that can be supplied to home office clients.

Branch Banks

A foreign branch bank is a legal and operational part of the parent bank, with the full resources of that parent behind the local office. A branch bank does not have its own corporate charter, its own board of directors, or any shares of stock outstanding. Although for managerial and regulatory purposes it will maintain its own set of books, its assets and liabilities are in fact those of the parent bank. However, branch deposits are not subject to reserve requirements or FDIC insurance, in the case of U.S. banks, unless the deposits are reloaned to the U.S. parent bank.

Branch banks are subject to two sets of banking regulations. As part of the parent, they are subject to home country regulations. However, they are also subject to regulations of the host country, which may provide any of a variety of restrictions on their operations.

The major advantage to a business of using a branch bank is that the branch will conduct a full range of banking services under the name and legal obligation of the parent. A deposit in a branch is a legal obligation of the parent. Services to customers are based on the worldwide value of the client relationship rather than just on the relationship to the local office. Legal loan limits are a function of the size of the parent, not of the branch.

From the point of view of a banker, the profits of a foreign branch are subject to immediate taxation at home, and losses of a foreign branch are deductible against taxable income at home. A new office expected to have losses in its early years creates a tax advantage if it is initially organized as a branch, even if eventually the intent is to change it to a separately incorporated subsidiary. From an organizational point of view a foreign branch is usually simpler to create and staff than is a separately incorporated subsidiary.

The major disadvantage of a branch bank is one that accrues to the bank rather than to its customers. The parent bank (not just the branch) may be sued at the local level for debts or other activities of the branch.

Branch banking has been the most important way for U.S. banks to conduct their foreign activities. Foreign branches account for about one-half of all international banking assets held by U.S. banks.[6] Europe is the most important location of U.S. branches with respect to size of assets and historical development. The Caribbean shell branches are also important, but their growth has leveled off in recent years. Asia is growing in importance.[7] Latin America may be reversing a previous decline in importance due to NAFTA and the trend toward privatization of government-owned firms.

Banking Subsidiaries

A subsidiary bank is a separately incorporated bank, owned entirely or in major part by a foreign parent, which conducts a general banking business. As a separate corporation, the banking subsidiary must comply with all the laws of the host country. Its lending limit is based on its own equity capital rather than that of the parent bank. This limits its ability to service large borrowers, but local incorporation also limits the liability of the parent bank to its equity investment in the subsidiary.

A foreign banking subsidiary often appears as a local bank in the eyes of potential customers in host countries and is thus often able to attract additional local deposits. This will especially be true if the bank was independent prior to being purchased by the foreign parent. Management may well be local, giving the bank greater access to the local business community. A foreign-owned bank subsidiary is more likely to be involved in both domestic and international business than is a foreign branch, which is more likely to appeal to the foreign business community but may well encounter difficulty in attracting banking business from local firms.

Sometimes foreign banks are not allowed to operate branches in a host country but are allowed to operate a locally incorporated subsidiary. Tax laws may favor subsidiaries over branches, both from the local perspective and from the parent country perspective.

---

[6]James V. Houpt, "International Trends for U.S. Banks and Banking Markets," *Staff Study of the Board of Governors of the Federal Reserve System*, no. 156, May 1988, p. 3.

[7]Ibid., p. 8.

In the case of U.S. banks, a branch would not be allowed to underwrite corporate securities, since this is not allowed in the United States. However, a foreign subsidiary would be allowed to engage in this activity.

Subsidiaries are the second most important organization form for U.S. banks, with about 20% of all international assets held by U.S. banks located in subsidiaries. Over half of the assets of these subsidiaries are located in Europe, particularly in the United Kingdom.[8]

Affiliates

A banking affiliate is a locally incorporated bank owned in part, but not necessarily controlled, by a foreign parent. The remainder of the ownership may be local, or it may be other foreign banks. The affiliated bank itself may be newly formed, or it may be a local bank in which a foreign bank has purchased a part interest.

The major advantage of an affiliated banking relationship is that which springs from any joint venture between parties of different nationalities. The bank acquires the expertise of two or more sets of owners. It maintains its status as a local institution with local ownership and management, but it has continuing and permanent relations with its foreign part owner, including an ability to draw on the international expertise of that part owner. The major disadvantage is also that common to joint ventures: The several owners may be unable to agree on particular policies important to the viability of the bank.

International Banking Facilities (IBFs)

The Federal Reserve Board of the United States authorized the establishment of U.S.-based International Banking Facilities (IBFs) in 1981 to help U.S. banks capture a larger proportion of the Eurocurrency business. An IBF is not an institution separate from its parent, but is rather a separate set of asset and liability accounts maintained by the parent but segregated from regular bank books. An IBF is thus an accounting entity rather than a legal entity. The establishing entity may be a U.S.-chartered depository institution, a U.S. branch or agency of a foreign bank, or a U.S. office of an Edge Act corporation. Although physically located in the United States, IBFs are not subject to domestic reserve requirements, FDIC insurance premiums, or interest rate ceilings on deposits.

Federal Reserve concern about the possibility of reserve-free transaction accounts "leaking" into the domestic monetary system led to a number of limitations being imposed on IBFs. The limitations do not apply to foreign branches of U.S.-chartered banks. IBF loan and deposit customers are limited to foreign residents, including banks, other IBFs, and the parent bank. IBF time deposits may be offered to foreign banks and to other IBFs. However, nonbank foreign residents are subject to a minimum maturity requirement of two business days.

---

[8]Ibid., p. 11.

Deposits and withdrawals by nonbank customers of IBFs must be at least $100,000 in size, except for transactions to withdraw accumulated interest or close the account. Bank customers, however, are not subject to any minimum transaction amount.

IBFs may not issue negotiable instruments, since such instruments could be transferred to U.S. residents who are not eligible to hold deposits in IBFs. Additionally, IBF loans to foreign nonbank customers are subject to a use-of-proceeds restriction, meaning such funds may not be used to finance the borrower's operations within the United States.

To attract IBFs, several states, including New York, have agreed to exempt them from state and local taxes. U.S.-owned IBFs are already exempt from federal taxes, but foreign-owned IBFs must pay federal taxes.

IBFs have attracted a significant share of Eurodollar business away from other existing centers, especially those located in the Caribbean shell branches. However, they have not replaced the shell branches because the latter can legally lend to U.S. residents, an activity disallowed the IBFs. Since the establishment of IBFs, the offshore shell branches have experienced little or no growth.

A number of reasons explain the growth of IBFs. From a political risk perspective, U.S. residents and firms would prefer to hold their deposits within the political and legal jurisdiction of the United States rather than offshore in the Caribbean. The same motive attracts some foreign funds seeking political safety. Some Eurodollar business has been attracted to the IBFs from London and other European centers because U.S. firms are able to transact business during the normal working day.

One of the main beneficiaries appears to be foreign banks, particularly Japanese, wishing to maintain a presence in the U.S. market to gain easy access to dollars and to conduct certain types of business they are prohibited from doing at home. In fact, almost all the growth in IBFs since 1982 has been in foreign-owned IBFs, which now hold about three times the assets of U.S.-owned IBFs.[9] However, Japan established its own offshore market at the end of 1986 for yen-denominated transactions.

Edge Act and Agreement Corporations

Edge Act and Agreement corporations are subsidiaries of U.S. banks, incorporated in the United States under Section 25 of the Federal Reserve Act as amended, to engage in international banking and financing operations. Not only may such subsidiaries engage in general international banking, they may also finance commercial, industrial, or financial projects in foreign countries through long-term loans or equity participation. Such participation, however, is subject to regulation by the Federal Reserve System.

Edge Act and Agreement corporations are physically located in the United States. Because U.S. banks cannot have branches outside their own state, Edge Act and Agreement corporations are usually located in other states in order to conduct international banking activities. Growth in Edge Act banking was greatly facilitated in 1979 when the Federal Reserve Board issued new guidelines that permitted interstate branching by

[9]Michael H. Moffett and Arthur Stonehill, "International Banking Facilities Revisited," *Journal of International Financial Management and Accounting,* vol. 1, no. 1, Spring 1989, pp. 88–103.

Edge Act corporations. Previously an Edge Act corporation had to be separately incorporated in each state. By increasing their interstate penetration through Edge Act corporations, the large money center banks are establishing a physical presence in most of the important regional financial centers in order to prepare for the day when interstate branching will be permitted also for domestic business.

The International Banking Act of 1978 extended the Edge Act privilege to foreign banks operating in the United States. In return, the previous ability of foreign banks to conduct a retail banking business in more than one state was severely limited. They must pick a single state as home base. In that state they can conduct full-service banking. In all other states they must limit their activities to Edge Act banking in the same manner as U.S. banks. In many cases, however, foreign banks already had retail operations in more than one state. These were accorded "grandfather" protection but are not allowed to expand beyond what they had at the time the act was passed.

Origin. Section 25 of the Federal Reserve Act was amended in 1916 to allow national banks and state banks belonging to the Federal Reserve System and having capital and surplus of $1 million (since increased to $2 million) or more to invest up to 10% of that capital and surplus in a subsidiary incorporated under state or federal law to conduct international or foreign banking. A bank forming such a subsidiary would enter into an "agreement" with the Board of Governors of the Federal Reserve System as to the type of activities in which they would engage—hence the name "Agreement corporation."

In 1919, Congress passed an amendment, proposed by Senator Walter E. Edge of New Jersey, that expanded the original provisions of the act to allow such subsidiaries to be chartered "for the purpose of engaging in international or foreign banking or other international or foreign financial operation either directly or through the agency, ownership, or control of local institutions in foreign countries."[10] Subsidiaries chartered under this amendment, known as Edge Act corporations, can make equity investments abroad, an operation barred to domestic banks.

The major operational difference between the two types of organizations is that Agreement corporations must engage primarily in international or foreign banking, whereas Edge Act corporations may also engage in other foreign financial operations. Edge Act corporations are federally chartered and not subject to the banking laws of the various states. Agreement corporations are normally chartered under state law and operate under state jurisdiction.

Edge Act and Agreement corporations generally engage in two types of activities: direct international banking, including acting as a holding company for the stock of one or more foreign banking subsidiaries, and financing development activities not closely related to traditional banking operations.

International Banking Activities. Edge Act and Agreement corporations may accept demand and time deposits from outside the United States (as well as from within, if such

---

[10]Section 25(a) 1, Federal Reserve Act (12 U.S.C. 611–631).

deposits are incidental to or for the purpose of transactions in foreign countries). Each corporation can also make loans, although commitments to any one borrower cannot exceed 10% of capital and surplus. They can issue or confirm letters of credit; make loans or advances to finance foreign trade, including production loans; create bankers' acceptances; receive items for collection; offer such services as remittance of funds abroad, or buying, selling, or holding securities for safekeeping; issue guarantees; act as paying agent for securities issued by foreign governments or foreign corporations; and engage in spot and forward foreign exchange transactions.

Edge Act subsidiaries whose primary activity is international banking may also function as holding companies by owning shares of foreign banking subsidiaries and affiliates. Domestic banks may have branches abroad, but they may not themselves own shares of foreign banking subsidiaries. Thus the Edge Act route permits U.S. banks to own foreign banking subsidiaries, either as wholly owned subsidiaries via an intermediary Edge Act corporation or as part of a joint venture with foreign or domestic banks or with other nonbanking institutions.

International Financing Activities. Edge Act and Agreement corporations differ from other U.S. banks in their ability to make portfolio-type investments in the equity of foreign commercial and industrial firms, either directly or through the intermediary of official or semiofficial development banks or corporations. Direct investment in a wide variety of local businesses can be made by intermediate-term loans, by purchase of shares of stock, or by a combination of these two methods.

Some longer term development projects are typically initiated in the foreign country by local business and are referred to the Edge Act corporation by the parent bank. Edge Act corporations engaged only in financing may invest up to 50% of their capital and surplus in a single venture. However, if the Edge Act corporation is also engaged in general banking, the limit is 10% of capital and surplus.

Comparing Bank Services

In implementing their strategic plan, banks need to be aware of some differences in the way bank services are offered. Some examples are giro transfer systems, different ways in which banks calculate interest charges, and the range of services available.

Giro Transfer Systems

In the major countries of western Europe, and in parts of Africa and Asia, individuals may make payments through a giro system. The word *giro* itself comes from the Greek *gyros,* meaning circle or turn. A giro system is a money transfer network, usually operated by the post office, intended to facilitate the transfer of a high volume of transactions involving small sums.

Each individual or business has a giro account number. A person wishing to make a payment completes a giro transfer form with his or her own name and account number and the name and account number of the payee. The form is dropped into a postal collection box, and the giro transfer center in the post office reduces the balance in the payer's account, credits the account of the payee, and mails confirmations to both parties. Account holders may deposit directly into their own account at a post office by mailing a check or by having their employer deposit wages or salary directly into the account. Utilities, merchants, or others who normally receive payments from the public may maintain accounts into which their customers pay.

Interest is not paid on giro accounts, and overdrafts or other forms of credit are not a normal part of the system. Postage is free, and the cost of transactions is either free or very nominal.

Several advantages of giro systems over checks are suggested. It is not necessary to verify the presence of sufficient funds, since the credit and debit are simultaneous. If the payer's account is short, no transfer can be made. Hence checks cannot bounce, and payers cannot kite against their future deposits. In addition, a giro is not a negotiable instrument and in fact never passes into the hands of the payee. Thus forgeries and alterations are not possible. Lastly, giro transfer systems are easily computerized, providing for great efficiencies of time and cost. The first giro system, it should be noted, was introduced by the Austrian Post Office Savings Bank in 1883, so the concept predates computers by many decades.

Calculating Interest Charges

Local interest charges can be calculated in various ways. In Europe, banks tend to lend on an "overdraft" basis, with borrowers drawing against a previously established line of credit. Although some commissions or service charges may be imposed for establishment of the overdraft privilege, the basic cost is the interest rate levied on the daily overdraft balance. The borrower pays interest only on funds used, since there is no compensating balance requirement, and only for the period in days for which the funds are taken. For this reason, the effective interest cost of an overdraft "loan" is the nominal or stated interest rate paid on the overdraft balance.

By comparison, U.S. banks normally expect or require compensating balances and may at times loan only on the basis of notes with a specific maturity. Thus the effective cost of a U.S. bank loan is above its nominal cost. Of course, the "cost" of the compensating balance depends on whether such balances would in any event be maintained in the bank for operating purposes. Furthermore, it may be possible to arrange a loan from a branch of a U.S. bank in one country by arranging for compensating balances in another currency at a branch in another country. Thus comparison of effective interest cost is difficult.

Range of Services

Local banks generally have better access to informal contacts among local institutions and individuals, especially in countries in which business contacts are very much a matter of long-established social relationships. Local banks may also be better at dealing with local government red tape or at advising one how to handle situations involving bribery or other forms of corruption.

As a general matter, branches of multinational banks try to offer all services available from local banks, although the quality of such services may vary. Multinational banks are likely, however, to be more sophisticated at financing imports and exports and at handling foreign currency transactions, except when local banks are also involved to a considerable extent in the same activities. Banks with a global network of offices can frequently offer help on collection problems, worldwide credit checks, or advice facilities for worldwide clearing of funds with a minimum of float. Multinational banks are usually more interested, experienced, and aggressive in helping business firms with intermediate- and long-term industrial financing, whereas in many parts of the world local banks are more attuned to short-term financing of sales. Banks from various countries also have reputations for basing loans on different criteria. European bankers are often regarded as "asset lenders" who base their assessment of how much to loan on the existence of physical assets. By comparison, U.S. bankers tend to evaluate expected cash flow and to loan on the prospect that budgeted cash flow will be adequate to repay the loan. Japanese bankers have yet another approach. Although loans may be written for 90 days, Japanese banks see themselves as supplying more or less permanent capital, and what appear to be "short-term" loans are repeatedly rolled over.

Risks in International Lending to Developing Countries

International bank lending involves a more complex approach to assessing risk than that used in domestic banking, primarily because international banking is conducted in a different legal, social, political, and economic environment. The risks of international bank lending may be classified as commercial risk or country risk. Since banks often offer their advice to client firms on matters of commercial and country risk, their effectiveness in assessing risk is important beyond the effect on the bank alone.

Commercial Risk

Commercial risk involves assessing the likelihood that a foreign-based client will be unable to repay its debts because of business reasons. Although this risk has a direct domestic counterpart, differences exist. As in the domestic case, a multinational bank will attempt to judge the quality of a foreign client's products, management, and financial condition. Cultural differences and lack of information may inhibit an assessment of the firm's management, while differing accounting standards and disclosure practices may preclude the type of financial analysis common in the home country. The bank may find it difficult to evaluate foreign economic conditions that might affect the client firm, and may need legal advice to determine its position in any bankruptcy proceedings. In many countries, for example, firms cannot easily dismiss workers whose jobs have been rendered obsolete by a change in competition or the introduction of new technology. The magnitude of payments that must be made to redundant workers may have a significant negative impact on a struggling firm's liquidity, and thus on its ability to repay any bank loans.

Country Risk

Country risk refers to the possibility that unexpected events within a host country will influence a client firm's or a government's ability to repay a loan. Country risk is usually divided into sovereign risk and currency risk. This division is useful when the borrower is a private firm, but when the borrower is the government itself, the distinction between sovereign risk and currency risk becomes blurred.

Sovereign risk, also called political risk, arises because a host government may exercise its sovereign power to unilaterally repudiate foreign obligations, or may prevent local firms from honoring their foreign obligations. The risk may derive from direct government action or from the indirect consequences of ineffective government, as when a government is unable to maintain law and order.

Currency risk, also called foreign exchange risk, arises from the possibility that an unexpected change in exchange rates will alter the home currency value of repayment of loans by foreign clients. If the loan is denominated in the home currency, say U.S. dollars, the risk is shifted to the borrower. However, the bank still runs the currency risk that the borrower cannot obtain dollars to repay the loan. A bank may partially avoid this possibility by sourcing funds for foreign clients in local currencies. Repayment of principal will not then be subject to a currency risk. However, the profit margin between the lending rate and the local cost of sourcing the funds is of value to the parent bank only in terms of its home currency value. This component remains subject to currency risk.

The most serious currency risk is that debtor countries will need to reschedule their external hard currency debts and ration access of local firms to hard currencies. Unfortunately, the "debt crisis" continues to plague both debtor countries and the creditor firms.

Dangers of Lending to Sovereign Nations

With the advantage of hindsight a lively debate also rages over the wisdom of letting the private sector finance developing countries rather than having public sector international institutions, such as the IMF and World Bank, do the financing.

Criticism of bank lending to developing countries runs along the following lines:[11]

1. Evaluation of country risk is extremely complex because it depends on variables that are not normally analyzed by bankers when making domestic commercial loans. The new variables include unfamiliar political, sociological, macroeconomic, and financial variables.

2. Bankers have a poor track record in anticipating dramatic increases in sovereign risk until it is too late. Unexpected events such as wars (Nigeria, Ethiopia, Iraq/Kuwait, the former Yugoslavia, and Lebanon) and social revolutions (Cuba and Iran) are nearly impossible to forecast but are often a prime cause for national default on external debt.

---

[11]The following sources present summaries of the dangers and benefits: Irving S. Friedman, *The Emerging Role of Private Banks in the Developing World,* New York: Citicorp, 1977; Steven I. Davis, "How Risky Is International Lending?" *Harvard Business Review,* January/February 1977, pp. 135–143; Richard S. Dale and Richard P. Mattione, *Mananging Global Debt,* Washington, D.C.: The Brookings Institution, 1983; and Sarkis J. Khoury, "Sovereign Debt: A Critical Look at the Causes and the Nature of the Problem," *Essays in International Business,* University of South Carolina, Center for International Business Studies, July 1985.

3. Some critics believe that bankers relax international credit standards because of weak domestic and commercial demand for loans.

4. In the event a nation's foreign debt needs to be restructured, the fact that so many separate banks and international organizations are involved means coordination is extremely difficult. All creditors must agree for any voluntary restructuring plan to be effective.

5. The concentration of syndicated loans in a relatively few "creditworthy" developing countries, such as Brazil, Argentina, and Mexico, reduces the potential benefit of diversification.

6. Most bank debt is on a variable-interest-rate basis, thus causing the actual burden of interest payments to be uncertain but potentially disastrous to the borrower if interest rates should reach high levels.

7. When countries are unable to service their debt on time, the banks become effectively "locked in" and are forced to reschedule their loans indefinitely to prevent outright defaults. Such rollovers may disguise loans that should be written off and conceal severe depletions of banks' equity capital. Even if eventually repaid, rollovers impair the ability of banks to make new productive loans elsewhere.

8. Some observers have been suspicious of the stability of the whole Eurocurrency interbank structure. If one major bank should fail, that event might have a domino effect on other banks because of the "tiering" of Eurocurrency deposits. The ability of banks of lesser stature to raise Eurocurrencies in the short run at reasonable rates to fund their share of "rollovers" to developing countries would be in jeopardy if confidence in the interbank market waned.

9. The ultimate purpose of some loans is to provide financing for balance of payments deficits. This type of loan does not improve the exporting capability of the borrowing country and therefore does not generate the foreign exchange earnings needed to service the debt. Even some of the so-called project loans are substitutes for other foreign loans, which are then used to finance the deficit.

Benefits of Lending to Sovereign Nations

In spite of the negative criticism of commercial bank lending to developing nations, many positive features do exist for this type of lending, from the viewpoint of both the banks and the recipient countries. The benefits can be summarized as follows:

1. International lending has in the past been a very profitable activity for many of the world's largest banks and has, for example, had a major impact on historical earnings of such giants as Citicorp, Chase Manhattan, Bank of America, and Morgan Guaranty.

2. Diversification of foreign lending by country and by type of customer reduces the risk of catastrophic losses to any one bank.

3. Precisely those banks with the most experience and capability in international

lending are the ones that are most active in international lending. They are at least relatively better qualified to assess country risk than banks.

4. The reason that loans to developing countries have been concentrated in a relatively few countries is that only those select countries have been able to pass the stringent credit test of international bank lenders. For example, India, Pakistan, and Bangladesh have large foreign debts to international public institutions, such as the World Bank and International Monetary Fund, but virtually no debt to private banks. They have not yet passed the credit test.

5. Developing countries badly need foreign banks to meet even relatively modest development plans. Most of the loans are project loans, which are supposed to generate enough new foreign exchange to service the added foreign debt. If the private banking sector does not respond to the legitimate credit needs of responsible developing countries, an even greater burden will be placed on the international development institutions. Their limited funds will inevitably be diverted away from the poorest developing nations, which have no hope of qualifying for loans from private banks.

6. A number of safeguards exist that reduce the risk on a portion of international loans. These include guarantees by export credit insurance programs in the lenders' own countries, guarantees by a parent on loans to its affiliates, and guarantees by host government agencies on loans to private firms within their country. The latter two do not apply to loans to sovereign states but do serve to reduce overall country risk.

7. Foreign governments and central banks have traditionally given highest priority to preserving their own credit standing, even if private firms within the country must default. Therefore lending to sovereign entities at least ensures first priority on whatever foreign exchange is available to repay external debts.

Analysis of Country Risk

Bank managers must develop a better approach to evaluation of both sovereign risk and currency risk of individual countries. Approaches used vary somewhat depending on whether the borrower is the government itself, an industrial firm, or a private commercial bank within the foreign country. The same variables are usually studied for all three client types, but the relative weight given one or another variable may differ substantially. Consideration must also be given to the portfolio effect of loan diversification by country.

Sovereign Risk

Sovereign risk analysis focuses on probable future willingness or ability of a government to honor past obligations or to allow firms and banks within the country to honor their obligations. Variables considered include political stability, since a new government may abrogate obligations incurred by its predecessor. Expected trends in the balance of payments are important because the ability to generate foreign exchange depends on either a favorable current account or a favorable capital account. A third factor is the size of the foreign exchange obligations of the country relative to its GNP and international trade.

Currency Risk

Currency risk is judged primarily from projections of a country's balance of payments surplus or deficit on current account, its present and likely future holdings of foreign exchange reserves, which act as a buffer for a limited period of time in the country's ability to repay foreign debt, and the size and maturity structure of its foreign currency debt. These factors, in turn, are influenced by differential rates of domestic and foreign inflation and whether or not the country's exchange rates are allowed to adjust to the differential. In this context, foreign currency debt includes both governmental debt and the debt of private firms and banks within the country.

A Portfolio Approach

In addition to analyzing the "stand-alone risk" of individual countries, banks have analyzed country risk from a portfolio theory perspective. International loans can be viewed as a portfolio of risky assets whose returns will vary as a result of both commercial and country risks. The total risk of the portfolio will be diminished if the bank successfully diversifies its assets across countries.[12]

International loans are often just part of an ongoing relationship between a bank and its client. The bank may be receiving other compensation from the client, such as fees for foreign exchange transactions or international money management. Denying the loan may bring an end to such fees and may preclude the bank's participation in future loans when the client becomes worthy of credit again. These attributes do not fit neatly into portfolio theory, but they must be remembered in any intuitive application of the concepts of that theory.

Large money center banks cannot easily remove high-risk loans from their portfolios in order to reduce portfolio risk because only a limited secondary market for such loans exists. It is possible to swap a risky loan to one country for a risky loan to another country or for equity. However, when several Latin American governments found themselves unable to repay their debts as scheduled in the 1980s, large money center banks had to increase their risk. They had the choice of extending the maturity of defaulting loans or reporting a loss in earnings for that year. Smaller banks, on the other hand, were able to reduce their risk by refusing to extend the maturities of their Latin American loans. The larger banks were forced to assume the smaller bank's share of the credit to prevent the total loan from going into default.

Portfolio diversification works best if default risk in each country is independent of that in every other country, but often such defaults are closely correlated. For example, default risk for countries in geographical or ideological proximity might be correlated because of a common view of nationalism, as in the case of many Latin American countries; ideologically inspired invasion, as in the case of Kampuchea and Vietnam; drought and starvation, as in the case of East Africa; and civil strife with foreign intervention, as in the case of Nicaragua and El Salvador. Internation dependency complicates the task of

---

[12]The reader already familiar with the fundamentals of portfolio theory will recognize this total risk reduction to be composed of both systematic risk and unsystematic risk. The proper diversification of the portfolio internationally will reduce unsystematic risk.

judging risk in an international loan portfolio, but it does not totally negate the advantages of international loan diversification.

In order to guarantee that international loan portfolios are optimally diversified, most banks set "country loan limits" to restrict exposure in any one country.[13] Limits are established by a country limit committee composed of top bank executives. Country managers and staff analysts present recommendations to the country limit committee, of

Exhibit 15.5   Euromoney's Country Risk Rankings 1993

Top Ten By Rank

March 1993	Sept 1992	Country	Total Score 100	Economic Performance 10	Political Risk 20
1	1	Japan	99.44	9.44	20.00
2	6	United States	99.07	9.07	20.00
3	3	Switzerland	99.01	9.01	20.00
4	5	France	98.46	8.88	19.57
5	2	Netherlands	98.24	8.88	19.36
6	7	Austria	97.94	9.01	18.94
7	4	Germany	97.93	8.57	19.36
8	9	United Kingdom	97.77	8.20	19.57
9	8	Canada	97.77	9.01	19.15
10	10	Belgium	96.68	8.51	18.94

Bottom Ten By Rank

160	152	Tajikistan	13.80	1.12	1.91
161	153	Azerbijan	13.66	1.61	1.28
162	154	Armenia	13.58	1.30	1.28
163	166	Somalia	12.94	0.00	2.13
164	164	Mozambique	12.83	0.99	2.34
165	169	Cambodia	12.15	0.87	1.28
166	158	Afghanistan	12.08	0.81	1.28
167	163	Sudan	9.66	0.43	1.06
168	161	Nicaragua	7.37	1.18	3.62
169	165	Cuba	6.75	0.56	3.19

Euromoney publishes their country risk rankings on a semiannual basis. The assessment uses 10 categories that encompass three broad categories: analytical indicators, credit indicators, and market indicators. The total score (maximum 100) is composed of the following weights: economic performance, 10%; political risk, 20%, debt indicators, 10%; access to bank lending, 10%; access to short-term finance, 10%; access to capital markets, 10%; discount on forfaiting, 10%; credit ratings, 10%; debt in default or rescheduled, 10%. For additional detail for scoring within each individual category see the original source.

Source: Country Risk: Japan Holds on as US Rises, *Euromoney*, March 1993, pp. 92–100. Reprinted with permission.

---

[13]See Stephen V. O. Clarke, *American Banks in the International Interbank Market,* New York: Salomon Brothers Center for the Study of Financial Institutions, *New York University Monograph Series in Finance and Economics,* Monograph 1983, no. 4, p. 28, for a listing of the criteria that bank managements should use in setting limits on lending to other banks in foreign countries.

which they may or may not themselves be members.[14] A country limit decision is typically based on two separate pieces of information. One of these is a country risk analysis study (or ranking as shown in Exhibit 15.5), and the other is a marketing plan presented by the bank official in charge of operations in the country being reviewed.

Strategies for Managing Country Risk

The country risk associated with the continuing developing country debt crisis is being managed by cooperative efforts between debtor countries and creditor banks.

Debtor Country Strategies

The main strategies used by debtor countries to survive the crisis, besides rescheduling the debts, are austerity, overdevaluation of their currencies, encouraging direct foreign investment, and debt-for-equity swaps.

Austerity. The countries themselves have tried to reduce demand for imports and free up capacity for exports by following tighter monetary and fiscal policies. The result has been a slowing of growth rates and a reduction in per capita consumption. Needless to say, this austerity policy is generally unpopular with the voters even though their governments are able to blame the problem on foreign banks and the IMF. In fact, the IMF has usually taken the lead in suggesting austerity as a condition for further loans from both the public agencies and the private banking sector. Nevertheless, some of the governments are too weak politically to endure austerity policies for a prolonged period. Therefore austerity is not the only solution.

Overdevaluation. Most of the indebted countries have tried to become more competitive in nontraditional exports by overdevaluing their currencies. This means their real effective exchange rates will lie well below an index value of 100 on purpose. Creditor countries are willing to tolerate what appears to be a "beggar-thy-neighbor" policy in the interest of encouraging debt repayment.

Encouraging Direct Foreign Investment. Many of the debtor countries have taken steps to encourage more incoming direct foreign investment, including encouraging a reversal of the capital flight problem discussed in Chapter 3. This means removing barriers such as local ownership requirements, work permits for expatriates, local content requirements, and other interferences with the free market. It also means trying to create a more favorable environment for private enterprise in general and perhaps privatizing many of the inefficient public enterprises.

Debt-for-Equity Swaps. A debt-for-equity swap is a technique to encourage a reversal of capital flight by local citizens and an encouragement to banks to convert from debt to equity claims. As discussed in the Ecuadorian Debt-for-Development Case in Chapter 3, creditors are allowed to exchange their loans for equity in local firms. Whether this

---

[14]Briance Mascarenhas and Ole-Christian Sand, "Country-Risk Assessment Systems in Banks: Patterns and Performance," *Journal of International Business Studies*, Spring 1985, pp. 19–35.

approach will be successful depends on the terms of the exchange, that is, how much the debt is discounted, and on the desirability of owning local firms. So far the results have been modest relative to the size of external debt. The most successful programs have been run by Brazil, Chile, and Mexico.

Creditor Bank Strategies

The creditor international banks have also taken steps to reduce their own burden of developing country debt. Many of the banks have increased their equity capital base and their loan loss reserves while greatly reducing any new lending to the debtor countries. Banks have also quietly been selling off some of their exposed loans at big discounts to investors willing to take the risk. For example, in January 1991 the debt of Brazil was selling for as little as 23 cents on the dollar; that of Chile had risen to 75 cents on the dollar. A rise in the secondary market price of this debt reflects the secondary market's assessment of the increased likelihood that Chile will service outstanding debt obligations.

Regulatory Authorities Strategies

Regulatory authorities have also stepped in, both to prevent a recurrence of the developing country debt problem and to prevent any massive bank failures. The Basle Agreement requires international banks to maintain at least 4% core equity in their capital structure, but individual country banking authorities have pressured their own banks to have a considerably higher equity ratio. In addition, the pressure is on banks, at least in the United States, to disclose the composition of their international loan portfolios by geographic area and type of loan.

Summary

- An international financial center exists when domestic funds are supplied to foreign users or when foreign funds are supplied to domestic users. At present, London, Tokyo, and New York City are the leading international financial centers.

- International strategies of banks are normally evolutionary. In the first step, arm's-length international banking, domestic banks accept foreign deposits and make foreign loans. In the second stage, the domestic bank often establishes an offshore banking presence. This offshore bank accepts deposits and makes loans in foreign currencies, for example, Eurocurrencies. The final step is for the bank to establish itself within other countries, usually through subsidiaries and affiliates.

- The Single European Market has had a significant impact on the structure of competition in international banking. The primary provision of the 1992 program for banking was the single banking license, which allows banks incorporated within a member country to branch freely throughout the European Union.

- The Basle Accord of 1988 established a framework for measuring bank capital and setting minimum capital adequacy standards. The Accord requires a total capital requirement of 8%, divided between core capital and supplementary capital.

Multinational Financial Management, vol. 2, no. 3/4, 1993, pp. 11–31.

Goldberg, Lawrence G., "Prospects for Banking Structure and Competition in Europe After 1992," *Journal of Multinational Financial Management,* vol. 2, no. 3/4 1993, pp. 53–71.

Grosse, Robert, "The Debt/Equity Swap in Latin America—In Whose Interest?", *Journal of International Financial Management and Accounting,* vol. 4, no. 1, Spring 1992, pp. 13–39.

———, and Lawrence C. Goldberg, "Foreign Bank Activity in the United States: An Analysis by Country of Origin," *Journal of Banking and Finance,* December 1991, pp. 1093–1112.

Heller, H. Robert, "The Debt Crisis and the Future of International Bank Lending," *American Economic Review,* May 1987, pp. 171–175.

Jain, Arvind K., and Douglas Nigh, "Politics and the International Lending Decisions of Banks," *Journal of International Business Studies,* Summer 1989, pp. 349–359.

Johnson, Ronald A., Venkat Srinivasan, and Paul J. Bolster, "Sovereign Debt Ratings: A Judgmental Model Based on the Analytic Hierarchy Process," *Journal of International Business Studies,* First Quarter 1990, pp. 95–117.

Jones, Geoffrey, editor, *Banks as Multinationals,* London, UK: Routledge, 1990.

Khoury, Sarkis J., *The Deregulation of the World Financial Markets: Myths, Realities, and Impact,* Westport, CT: Quorum Books, 1990.

Lessard, Donald R., *Capital Flight: The Problem and Policy Responses,* Washington, D.C.: Institute for International Economics, 1987.

Mascarenhas, Briance, and Ole C. Sand, "Country-Risk Assessment Systems in Banks: Patterns and Performance," *Journal of International Business Studies,* Spring 1985, pp. 19–35.

Maxwell, Charles E., and Lawrence J. Gitman, "Risk Transmission in International Banking: An Analysis of 48 Central Banks," *Journal of International Business Studies,* Summer 1989, pp. 268–279.

Moffett, Michael H., and Arthur Stonehill, "International Banking Facilities Revisited," *Journal of International Financial Management and Accounting,* vol. 1, no. 1, Spring 1989, pp. 88–103.

Nigh, Douglas, Kang Rae Cho, and Suresh Krishnan, "The Role of Location-Related Factors in U.S. Banking Involvement Abroad: An Empirical Examination," *Journal of International Business Studies,* Fall 1986, pp. 59–72.

Sabi, Manijeh, "An Application of the Theory of Foreign Direct Investment to Multinational Banking in LDCs," *Journal of International Banking Studies,* Fall 1988, pp. 433–447.

Smith, Roy C., and Ingo Walter, *Global Financial Services: Strategies for Building Competitive Strengths in International Commercial and Investment Banking,* New York: Harper Business, 1990.

Tschoegl, Adrian E., "International Retail Banking as a Strategy: An Assessment," *Journal of International Business Studies,* Summer 1987, pp. 67–88.

Walter, Ingo, "Competitive Positioning in International Financial Services," *Journal of International Financial Management and Accounting,* vol. 1, no. 1, Spring 1989, pp. 15–40.

Wright, Richard W., and Gunter A. Pauli, *The Second Wave: Japan's Global Assault on Financial Services,* New York: St. Martin's Press, 1988.

Chapter 16
Import and Export Financing

Global View
The Ukraine's Eximbank's Problems

Ukraine's Eximbank has become rather miserly of late. Although last year the country had a $1.6bn trade surplus with its non-CIS trade partners (imports were $2.1bn and exports $3.7bn), hard-currency holdings are being jealously guarded in the central bank's vaults in Kiev.

Disbursements are made so sparingly that most Ukrainian firms are having a hard time accessing the funds they need for their imports. The lucky companies either have hard currency in the West or manage to get their products on bilateral trade clearing lists. Ukraine has a number of such commercial protocols: with Russia, Hungary, Slovakia, Bulgaria, Poland, Kazakhstan and several other former Comecon states. The problem is that it is usually only the very big companies, like Ukrimpex ($450m worth of exports in 1992), Ukrzovnishpromtechobmin ($300m) or the Nikopol ferro-alloy plant ($170m), that get on these lists.

The only alternative for most others is to get involved in barter or more sophisticated—institutionalized—countertrade deals. But as a trade finance scheme, countertrade isn't too popular with foreign suppliers. It tends to be complicated to put together, and often means involving a big trading firm, such as Ukrbarimex in Kiev. They have the established domestic and international shipping channels; with their considerable commissions and fees, the traders—and their lawyers who draft the delivery contracts and penalty clauses—often make a killing.

Traditionally, such deals involve huge quantities of products, the best way for traders to maximize earnings. One example is the now famous PepsiCo joint venture signed last October [1992]. The American company delivers soft drink concentrate and bottling equipment, and has started setting up Pizza Hut restaurants; the three local partners are supplying freight ships (which are then resold for hard currency in the West) as payment.

More recently, decentralized foreign trade and banking has allowed smaller companies in and outside Ukraine to do countertrade without having to rely on the big traders. Usually on the basis of established business ties, foreign and local companies now turn to commercial banks—such as Ukrsostsbank, the partly foreign-owned First Ukrainian Bank, or the Kiev branches of Agroprombank and Incombank—to help formalize countertrade transactions.

Source: Papp, Bela and Robert Steely, "Trade Finance: Few Options," *Business Central Europe,* July/August 1993, p. 50. © 1993 The Economist Newspaper Group, Inc. Reprinted with permission.

International trade must work around a fundamental dilemma. Imagine an importer and an exporter who would like to do business with each other. Imagine also that they live in different countries located far apart. They have never met. They speak different languages. They operate in different political environments. They worship different Gods (each capitalizes "God" in the home religion and uses a lowercase "god" for foreign religions!). They come from cultures that have different standards for honoring obligations to other persons. They both know that if they default on an obligation, the other party will have a hard time catching up to seek redress. While it might be too harsh to say they don't trust each other, each has perfectly valid reasons for being very cautious in dealing with the other.

Because of the distance between the two, it is not possible to simultaneously hand over goods with one hand and accept payment with the other. The importer would prefer the following:

If done this way, all risk is shifted to the exporter. The exporter's preferences are exactly the opposite, which of course shifts all risk to the importer:

The fundamental dilemma of being unwilling to trust a stranger in a foreign land is solved by using a highly respected bank as intermediary. A greatly simplified view is the following:

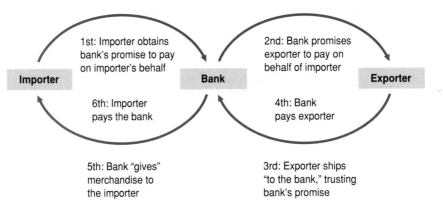

In this simplified view, the importer obtains the bank's promise to pay on its behalf, knowing the exporter will trust the bank. The bank's promise to pay is called a *letter of credit*.

The exporter ships the merchandise to the importer's country. Title to the merchandise is given to the bank on a document called an *order bill of lading*. The exporter asks the bank to pay for the goods, and the bank does so. The document to request payment is a *sight draft*. The bank, having paid for the goods, now passes title to the importer, whom the bank trusts. At that time or later, depending on their agreement, the importer reimburses the bank.

Financial managers of multinational firms must understand these three basic documents, in part because their firms will often trade with unaffiliated parties, but also because the system of documentation provides a source of short-term capital that can be drawn on even when shipments are to sister affiliates.

Benefits of the System

The three key documents and their interaction are described in the following pages. They constitute a system developed and modified over centuries to protect both importer and exporter from the risk of noncompletion and foreign exchange risk, as well as to provide a means of financing.

Risk of Noncompletion

As we stated, once importer and exporter agree on terms the seller usually prefers to maintain legal title to the goods until paid, or at least until assured of payment. The buyer, however, will be reluctant to pay before receiving the goods, or at least before receiving title to them. Each wants assurance that the other party will complete its portion of the transaction. The three key trade documents—letter of credit, draft, and bill of lading—are part of a carefully constructed system to determine who bears the financial loss if one of the parties defaults at any time.

Protection Against Foreign Exchange Risk

In international trade, foreign exchange risk arises from transaction exposure. If the transaction requires payment in the exporter's currency, the importer carries the foreign exchange risk. If the transaction calls for payment in the importer's currency, the exporter has the foreign exchange risk.

Transaction exposure can be hedged by the techniques described in Chapter 7, but in order to hedge the exposed party must be certain that payment of a specified amount will be made on a particular date. The three key documents described in this chapter assure both amount and time of payment, and thus lay the groundwork for effective hedging.

The risk of noncompletion and foreign exchange risk are most important when the international trade is episodic, with no outstanding agreement for recurring shipments and no sustained relationship between buyer and seller. When the import/export relationship is of a recurring nature, as in the case of manufactured goods shipped weekly or monthly to a final assembly or retail outlet in another country, and when it is between countries whose currencies are considered strong, the exporter may well bill the importer on open account after a normal credit check. Banks provide credit information and collection services outside of the system of processing drafts drawn against letters of credit.

Financing the Trade

Most international trade involves a time lag during which funds are tied up while the merchandise is in transit. Once the risks of noncompletion and of exchange rate changes are disposed of, banks are willing to finance goods in transit. A bank can finance goods in transit, as well as goods held for sale, based on the key documents, without exposing itself to questions about the quality of the merchandise or other physical aspects of the shipment.

In the remainder of this chapter we examine the letter of credit, the draft, the bill of lading, and a few additional documents that support these key documents. We also discuss government programs to encourage exports and countertrade, which is a type of barter system.

Exhibit 16.1   Parties to a Letter of Credit

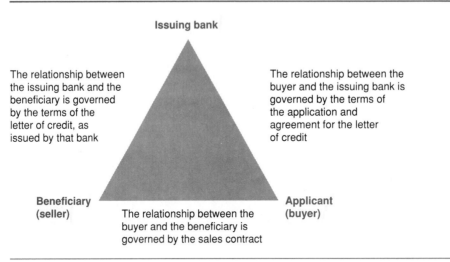

Issuing bank

The relationship between the issuing bank and the beneficiary is governed by the terms of the letter of credit, as issued by that bank

The relationship between the buyer and the issuing bank is governed by the terms of the application and agreement for the letter of credit

Beneficiary (seller)

The relationship between the buyer and the beneficiary is governed by the sales contract

Applicant (buyer)

Source: First National Bank of Chicago, *Financing U.S. Exports*, compiled by Patricia A. Ferris, January 1975, p. 21.

Letter of Credit

A letter of credit, abbreviated L/C, is an instrument issued by a bank at the request of an importer, in which the bank promises to pay a beneficiary upon presentation of documents specified in the letter of credit. In international trade a letter of credit is sometimes referred to as a *commercial letter of credit,* a *documentary letter of credit,* or simply a *credit.* A letter of credit reduces the risk of noncompletion, since the bank agrees to pay against documents rather than actual merchandise. The relationship among the three parties can be seen in Exhibit 16.1.

Typical Transaction

Although details vary, depending on the type of letter of credit and its provisions, the following transaction is typical. An importer (buyer) and exporter (seller) agree on a transaction and the importer applies to its local bank for the issuance of a letter of credit. The importer's bank issues a letter of credit based on its assessment of the importer's creditworthiness, or the bank might require a cash deposit or other collateral from the importer in advance. The importer's bank will want to know the type of transaction, the amount of money involved, and what documents must accompany the draft that will be drawn against the letter of credit.

If the importer's bank is satisfied with the credit standing of the applicant, it will issue a letter of credit guaranteeing to pay for the merchandise if shipped in accordance with the instructions and conditions contained in the credit. Exhibit 16.2 shows a letter of credit issued by Bank of America (Asia), Ltd., in Hong Kong on the application of

Exhibit 16.2   Letter of Credit

---

8 美 國 亞 洲 銀 行
Bank of America (Asia) Ltd.   PAGE   1   Date 02NOV1993

```
CREDIT NUMBER OF ISSUING BANK  YLC35666
CREDIT NUMBER OF ADVISING BANK

ADVISING BANK   BANKAMERICA INTERNATIONAL
                335 MADISON AVENUE
                NEW YORK U.S.A.

BENEFICIARY     ABC ELECTRONICS CORPORATION
                123 GRAND AVENUE
                PALISADES PARK
                NEW JERSEY 07650 U.S.A.

APPLICANT       SHING HING PAPER MERCHANTS LTD.
                168 PRINCE EDWARD ROAD
                KOWLOON HONG KONG

AMOUNT USD*****33,400.00 U.S. DOLLARS THIRTY THREE THOUSAND
                          FOUR HUNDRED ONLY

EXPIRY DATE DECEMBER 29 1993   IN THE COUNTRY OF BENEFICIARY

LATEST SHIPMENT DATE DECEMBER 15 1993

WE HEREBY ISSUE IN YOUR FAVOUR THIS IRREVOCABLE DOCUMENTARY
CREDIT WHICH IS AVAILABLE BY NEGOTIATION OF YOUR DRAFT(S) AT
60 DAYS SIGHT DRAWN ON L/C ISSUING BANK
BEARING THE CLAUSE DRAWN UNDER DOCUMENTARY CREDIT NO. YLC35666
OF BANK OF AMERICA (ASIA) LTD., HONG KONG ACCOMPANIED BY
THE FOLLOWING DOCUMENTS :

SIGNED COMMERCIAL INVOICE IN TRIPLICATE.

PACKING LIST ISSUED BY BENEFICIARY.

FULL SET OF ORIGINAL CLEAN SHIPPED 'ON BOARD' OCEAN BILLS OF
LADING ISSUED BY SHIPPING COMPANY PLUS TWO NON-NEGOTIABLE COPIES
MADE OUT TO ORDER OF BANK OF AMERICA (ASIA) LTD., HONG KONG
MARKED 'FREIGHT PREPAID' AND NOTIFY APPLICANT. FORWARDER'S B/L
NOT ACCEPTABLE.

EVIDENCING SHIPMENT OF
I.P. BLEACHED MF BAG PAPER, DIAMETER : 40'', CORE : 3''
@USD835.00 PER MT COMPRISING :
1)   5MT SUBSTANCE :  81GSM
2) 10MT SUBSTANCE :  98GSM
3) 25MT SUBSTANCE : 114GSM
AS PER SALE CONTRACT NO. IM-228

SHIPMENT FROM U.S.A. TO HONG KONG  C AND F
PARTIAL SHIPMENTS PROHIBITED
TRANSHIPMENT PROHIBITED

SPECIAL INSTRUCTIONS :

ALL BANKING CHARGES OUTSIDE HONG KONG ARE FOR ACCOUNT OF
BENEFICIARY.
```

ORIGINAL FOR BENEFICIARY

                           2   ..... TO BE CONTINUED ON PAGE   2.....
This document consists of   pages.

Bills Department: 31/F, 9 Queen's Road Central, Hong Kong. • SWIFT: SPAB HK HH • Telex: 73471 BOFAA HX • Cable Address: "BOFAAHK" • Fax: 845 307

Exhibit 16.2 *continued*

美 國 亞 洲 銀 行
Bank of America (Asia) Ltd.

PAGE   2   Date 02NOV1993

THIS PAGE IS ATTACHED TO AND FORMS PART OF CREDIT NO   YLC35666

INSURANCE TO BE COVERED BY BUYER.

SHIPMENT DATE PRIOR TO L/C ISSUING DATE NOT ACCEPTABLE.

5 PCT MORE OR LESS BOTH IN QUANTITY OF EACH ITEM OF GOODS
AND CREDIT AMOUNT ACCEPTABLE.

UNLESS OTHERWISE STATED, ALL DOCUMENTS MUST BE MANUALLY SIGNED
AND DOCUMENTS IN PHOTOCOPIES NOT ACCEPTABLE.

THIS CREDIT IS NOT RESTRICTED TO ANY BANK FOR NEGOTIATION.

AT MATURITY, WE SHALL REMIT THE FACE AMOUNT OF DRAFT TO
THE NEGOTIATING BANK ACCORDING TO THEIR INSTRUCTIONS.

ALL DOCUMENTS MUST BE SENT TO BANK OF AMERICA (ASIA) LTD.
HONG KONG BY ONE REGISTERED AIRMAIL.

A DISCREPANCY FEE OF USD30.00 WILL BE DEDUCTED FROM THE
PROCEEDS ON EACH SET OF DOCUMENTS PRESENTED WITH
DISCREPANCY(IES), EVEN IF THE L/C INDICATES THAT ALL BANKING
CHARGES ARE FOR ACCOUNT OF APPLICANT.

WE HEREBY ENGAGE WITH DRAWERS AND/OR BONA FIDE HOLDERS THAT
DRAFTS DRAWN AND NEGOTIATED IN CONFORMITY WITH THE TERMS OF THIS
CREDIT AND SUBSEQUENT AMENDMENT(S) IF ANY WILL BE DULY HONOURED
ON PRESENTATION AND THAT DRAFTS ACCEPTED WITHIN THE TERMS OF THIS
CREDIT WILL BE DULY HONOURED AT MATURITY.
THE AMOUNT OF EACH DRAFT MUST BE ENDORSED ON THE REVERSE OF THIS
CREDIT BY THE NEGOTIATING BANK.   EXCEPT SO FAR AS OTHERWISE
EXPRESSLY STATED, THIS DOCUMENTARY CREDIT IS SUBJECT TO THE
'UNIFORM CUSTOMS AND PRACTICE FOR DOCUMENTARY CREDITS' (1993
REVISION) BY THE INTERNATIONAL CHAMBER OF COMMERCE PUBLICATION
NO. 500.
THE ADVISING BANK IS REQUESTED TO NOTIFY THE BENEFICIARY
WITHOUT ADDING THEIR CONFIRMATION.

AUTHORIZED SIGNATURE(S)

ORIGINAL   FOR BENEFICIARY

SAMPLE COPY

This document consists of   2   pages.

Bills Department: 31/F, 9 Queen's Road Central, Hong Kong • SWIFT: SPAB HK HH • Telex: 73471 BOFAA HX • Cable Address: "BOFAAHK" • Fax: 845 3073

Source: Reprinted with permission of Bank of America (Asia) Ltd.

Shing Hing Paper Merchants, Ltd. The letter of credit is for the importing into Hong Kong of a shipment of I.P. bleached MF bag paper worth US$33,400.00, being purchased from ABC Electronics Corporation in Palisades Park, New Jersey. The letter of credit specifies the documents that must accompany a draft drawn against the credit: commercial invoice in triplicate, packing list issued by beneficiary, a full set of original clean shipped "on board" ocean bills of lading issued by a shipping company, plus two non-negotiable copies made out to the order of Bank of America (Asia), Ltd.

At this point the credit of Bank of America (Asia) has been substituted for that of the Shing Hing Paper Merchants, and the letter of credit becomes a financial contract between Bank of America (Asia) and the designated beneficiary, ABC Electronics Corporation of New Jersey. This financial contract is a separate transaction from the sale of the merchandise. If the terms of the letter of credit are met, any payment problems that develop at a later date are of concern only to the importer and the issuing bank. All other parties to the transaction may rely on the bank's credit without concern about the financial status of the importer.

The importer's bank issuing the letter of credit sends the document to an "advising bank" in the exporter's country, in this case to BankAmerica International in New York City, which will advise the exporter (the beneficiary) of the establishment of a letter of credit in the beneficiary's name. Procedures also exist for letters of credit to be sent by teletransmission. In such cases, the teletransmission is deemed to be the operative letter of credit unless a statement to the contrary is included. Such a contrary statement might be, "Full details to follow."

After shipping the merchandise, the exporter draws a draft against the issuing bank in accordance with the terms of the letter of credit, attaches the required documents, and presents the draft to its own bank for payment. At this point different combinations of events are possible. In the most straightforward case, the exporter's bank will receive the draft and accompanying documents and forward them to the bank of the importer that issued the credit. If all the terms and conditions expressed on the letter of credit have been complied with and the required documents are attached, the importer's bank will honor the draft, paying the exporter's bank or promising to pay after a period of time (60 days in the example in Exhibit 16.2). When the exporter's bank receives the funds, it passes them on to the exporter.

The importer's bank, in turn, collects from the importer in accordance with the terms agreed upon at the time the letter of credit was opened. The importer might pay at once in order to obtain the documents, including the order bill of lading that is needed to obtain physical possession of the merchandise. Alternatively, the bank may release the documents to the importer and the importer may promise to pay at some later date, usually under a trust receipt arrangement.

Essence of the Agreement

The essence of a letter of credit is the promise of the issuing bank to pay *against specified documents,* which must accompany any draft drawn against the credit. The letter of credit is not a guarantee of the underlying commercial transaction. Indeed, the letter of credit is a separate transaction from any sales or other contracts on which it might be based. To constitute a true letter of credit transaction, all of the following five elements must be present with respect to the issuing bank:

1. The issuing bank must receive a fee or other valid business consideration for issuing the letter of credit.

2. The bank's letter of credit must contain a specified expiration date or a definite maturity.

3. The bank's commitment must have a stated maximum amount of money.

4. The bank's obligation to pay must arise only on the presentation of specific documents, and the bank must not be called on to determine disputed questions of fact or law.

5. The bank's customer must have an unqualified obligation to reimburse the bank on the same condition as the bank has paid.

Variations in the Terms of a Letter of Credit

Most commercial letters of credit are *documentary,* meaning that certain documents must be included with any drafts drawn under their terms. Required documents usually include an order bill of lading, a commercial invoice, and any of the following: consular invoice, insurance certificate or policy, certificate of origin, weight list, certificate of analysis, packing list. Commercial letters of credit are also classified as follows.

Irrevocable Versus Revocable. An irrevocable letter of credit obligates the issuing bank to honor drafts drawn in compliance with the credit and can be neither canceled nor modified without the consent of all parties, including in particular the beneficiary (exporter). A revocable letter of credit can be canceled or amended at any time before payment; it is intended to serve as a means of arranging payment but not as a guarantee of payment.

Confirmed Versus Unconfirmed. A letter of credit issued by one bank can be confirmed by another, in which case both banks are obligated to honor drafts drawn in compliance with the credit. An unconfirmed letter of credit is the obligation only of the issuing bank. An exporter is likely to want a foreign bank's letter of credit confirmed by a domestic bank when the exporter has doubts about the foreign bank's ability to pay. Such doubts can arise when the exporter is unsure of the financial standing of the foreign bank, or if political or economical conditions in the foreign country are unstable.

Revolving Versus Nonrevolving. Most letters of credit are nonrevolving; they are valid for one transaction only. Under some circumstances, a revolving credit is issued. A $10,000 revolving weekly credit means the beneficiary is authorized to draw drafts up to $10,000 each week until the credit expires. The period of a revolving credit might be daily, weekly, or monthly. Because the maximum exposure under an irrevocable revolving credit is very great (the buyer cannot stop its obligation to pay for future shipments even if it is dissatisfied with the merchandise), most revolving credits are issued in revocable form. A revolving credit may be *noncumulative,* in which case any amount not used by the beneficiary during the specified period may not be drawn against in a later period; or it may be *cumulative,* in which case undrawn amounts carry over to future periods.

Issuers of Letters of Credit

From an exporter's point of view, a documentary letter of credit is one of the following types:

1. An irrevocable letter of credit issued by a domestic bank.

2. An irrevocable letter of credit issued by a foreign bank and confirmed irrevocably by a domestic bank, or on occasion confirmed by a third-country foreign bank.

3. An irrevocable letter of credit issued by a foreign bank without the confirmation of a domestic bank. In this situation the domestic bank simply transmits information (when the letter is opened) and forwards drafts for collection but does not guarantee payment.

4. A revocable letter of credit established to arrange for payment.

Exporters naturally prefer types 1 and 2, since they need look no further than a bank in their own country for compliance with the terms of the letter of credit. Although a letter of credit issued by a foreign bank alone (type 3) might well be of the highest esteem, many exporters, especially smaller firms, are not in a position to evaluate or deal with foreign banks directly if difficulties arise.

Every irrevocable letter of credit must indicate an expiration date beyond which documents for payment or acceptance will not be accepted. Documents, such as drafts or bills of lading, must be presented within a reasonable time after issue, for if there is undue delay, the bank may refuse to accept them.

Advantages and Disadvantages of Letters of Credit

The primary advantage of a letter of credit is that the exporter can sell against a bank's promise to pay rather than the promise of a commercial firm. The exporter is also in a more secure position as to the availability of foreign exchange to pay for the sale, since banks are more likely to be aware of foreign exchange conditions and rules than is the importing firm itself. If the importing country should change its foreign exchange rules during the course of a transaction, the government is likely to allow already outstanding bank letters of credit to be honored for fear of throwing its own domestic banks into international disrepute. Of course if the letter of credit is confirmed by a bank in the exporter's country, the exporter avoids any problem of blocked foreign exchange.

An exporter may find that an order backed by an irrevocable letter of credit will facilitate obtaining domestic pre-export financing. If the exporter's reputation for delivery is good, a local bank may lend funds to process and prepare the merchandise for shipment. Once the merchandise is shipped in compliance with the terms and conditions of the credit, payment for the business transaction is made and funds are generated to repay the pre-export loan.

The major advantage to the importer of a letter of credit is that the importer need not pay out funds until the documents have arrived at a local port or airfield and unless all conditions stated in the credit have been fulfilled. The main disadvantages are the fee charged by the importer's bank for issuing its letter of credit, and the possibility that the letter of credit reduces the importer's borrowing line of credit from its bank.

Liabilities of Banks Under Letters of Credit

When banks issue letters of credit they incur certain obligations that are specified in detail in *Uniform Customs and Practices for Documentary Credits,* published by the International Chamber of Commerce.[1]

The basic nature of a letter of credit is that the bank is obligated to pay against documents, not actual goods. Thus banks must carefully examine all documents to be sure they are in accordance with the original terms and conditions of the letter of credit. Banks are not liable for defects in the documents themselves, however, as long as any defect was not apparent on the face of the document. Thus, for example, the bank is not responsible for detecting false documents; for verifying that the quantities, quality, weights, or condition of the goods is other than what is stated on the documents; or for validating the good faith and performance of any of the parties to the underlying transaction. The bank is not responsible if messages are delayed or lost, or mistranslated; and it is not responsible for the consequences of such events as strikes, lockouts, riots, or war.

Draft

A *draft,* sometimes called a *bill of exchange (B/E)* or *first of exchange,* is the instrument normally used in international commerce to effect payment. A draft is simply an order written by an exporter (seller) instructing an importer (buyer) or its agent to pay a specified amount of money at a specified time. (A personal check is another type of draft; the drawer writes an order to a bank to pay a specified amount of money on demand to the order of a designated beneficiary.)

The person or business initiating the draft is known as the *maker, drawer,* or *originator.* Normally this is the exporter who sells and ships the merchandise. The party to whom the draft is addressed is the *drawee.* The drawee is asked to *honor* the draft, that is, to pay the amount requested according to the stated terms. In commercial transactions the drawee is either the buyer, in which case the draft is called a *trade draft,* or the buyer's bank, in which case the draft is called a *bank draft.* Bank drafts are usually drawn according to the terms of a letter of credit. A draft may be drawn as a bearer instrument, or it may designate a person to whom payment is to be made. This person,

---

[1]*Uniform Customs and Practice for Documentary Credits, 1993 Revision,* ICC Publication no. 500, issued in May 1993. The address of the International Chamber of Commerce is 38, Cours Albert 1er, 75008 Paris, France. Fax (1) 49.53.28.62. The U.S. office is at 156 Fifth Avenue, Suite 820, New York, NY 10010. Fax (212) 633–6025. The ICC has offices in most major cities around the world.

known as the payee, may be the drawer itself or it may be some other party such as the drawer's bank.

Negotiable Instruments

If properly drawn, drafts can become *negotiable instruments*. As such, they provide a convenient instrument for financing the international movement of the merchandise. To become a negotiable instrument, a draft or bill of exchange must conform to the following requirements:[2]

[handwritten note: person initiating draft]

- It must be in writing and signed by the maker or drawer.
- It must contain an unconditional promise or order to pay a definite sum of money.
- It must be payable on demand or at a fixed or determinable future date.
- It must be payable to order or to bearer.

If a draft is drawn in conformity with the requirements just listed, a person receiving it with proper endorsements becomes a "holder in due course." This is a privileged legal status that enables the holder to receive payment despite any personal disagreements between drawee and maker because of controversy over the underlying commercial transaction. If the drawee dishonors the draft, payment must be made to any holder in due course by any prior endorser or by the maker. This clear definition of the rights of parties who hold a negotiable instrument as a holder in due course has contributed significantly to the widespread acceptance of various forms of drafts, including personal checks.

Types of Drafts

Drafts are of two types: *sight drafts* and *time drafts*. A sight draft is payable on presentation to the drawee; the drawee must pay at once or dishonor the draft. A time draft, also called a *usance draft,* allows a delay in payment. It is presented to the drawee, who accepts it by writing or stamping a notice of acceptance on its face. Once accepted, the time draft becomes a promise to pay by the accepting party. When a time draft is drawn on and accepted by a bank, it becomes a *banker's acceptance*. When a time draft is drawn on and accepted by a business firm, it becomes a *trade acceptance*.

A time draft drawn by ABC Electronics Corporation of New Jersey for its export of bleached bag paper against the letter of credit shown earlier is illustrated in Exhibit 16.3. ABC Corporation is instructing Bank of America (Asia) to pay to Chemical Bank, New York, the sum of US$33,400.00 60 days after the draft is first presented to Bank of America (Asia). Chemical Bank would be ABC's U.S. banker. When the draft is presented to Bank of America (Asia), that bank will check to see all terms of the letter of credit have been complied with and will then stamp the face of the draft with the acceptance inscription shown with the draft in Exhibit 16.3. A bank officer will sign, and the draft becomes a bankers' acceptance maturing in 60 days. Because the draft in Exhibit 16.3 was accepted on December 15, 1993, it will mature on February 15, 1994.

---

[2]Uniform Commercial Code, Section 3104(1).

Exhibit 16.3   Time Draft and Stamp Indicating Acceptance by Bank

```
                                      No :  ___ABC-9330_____

Exchange for __USD33,400.00__ U.S.A. _December 10, 1993.___

____-60-_____ days after sight of this First of Exchange

(Second Unpaid) pay to the order of CHEMICAL BANK, NEW YORK

the sum of _Thirty-three thousand four hundred only._____

Value received DRAWN UNDER BANK OF AMERICA (ASIA) LTD.
LETTER OF CREDIT NO. YLC35666 DATED NOVEMBER 2, 1993.

To:   BANK OF AMERICA (ASIA) LTD.   ABC ELECTRONICS CORP.
      HONG KONG
                                    _____

                                         Managing Director
```

```
ACCEPTED ON DECEMBER 15, 1993
DUE ON FEBRUARY 15, 1994
PAYABLE AT BANK OF AMERICA (ASIA) LTD.        This chop, (stamp)
            HONG KONG                         on the face of the
                                              draft, represents
                                              the L/C issuing
_____                 bank's acceptance.
            Authorized Signature
```

The time period of a draft is referred to as its *tenor* or *usance*. To qualify as a negotiable instrument, and so be attractive to a holder in due course, a draft must be payable on a fixed or determinable future date. For example, 60 days after sight is a determinable date, such a maturity being established precisely at the time the draft is accepted. However, payment "on arrival of goods" is not determinable, since the date of arrival cannot be known in advance. Indeed, there is no assurance the goods will arrive at all. Third parties would have no interest in investing in it because they could not be certain they would ever be paid. Note, however, that a non-negotiable acceptance is still a legal device to obtain payment unless a defect exists in the underlying commercial transaction. That is, a non-negotiable draft creates a legal obligation between the original parties without giving third parties (holders in due course) any privileged claim.

Drafts are also classified as *clean* or *documentary*. A clean draft is an order to pay unaccompanied by any other documents. When it is used in trade, the seller has usually sent the shipping documents directly to the buyer, who thus obtains possession of the merchandise independent of its payment (on a clean sight draft) or acceptance (on a clean time draft). Clean drafts are often used by multinational firms shipping to their own affiliates because matters of trust and credit are not involved. Clean drafts are also used for nontrade remittances, for example, when collection of an outstanding debt is sought. Use of a clean draft puts pressure on a recalcitrant debtor by forcing it to convert an open-account obligation into documentary form. Failure to pay or accept such a draft when presented through a local bank can damage the drawee's reputation.

Most drafts in international trade are "documentary," which means various shipping documents are attached to the draft. Payment (for sight drafts) or acceptance (for time drafts) is required to obtain possession of those documents, which are in turn needed to obtain the goods involved in the transaction. If documents are to be delivered to the buyer on payment of the draft, it is known as a "D/P draft"; if the documents are delivered on acceptance, the draft is called a "D/A draft."

Bankers' Acceptances

When a draft is accepted by a bank, it becomes a *bankers' acceptance*. As such it is the unconditional promise of that bank to make payment on the draft when it matures. In quality the bankers' acceptance is practically identical to a marketable bank certificate of deposit (CD). The holder of a bankers' acceptance need not wait until maturity to liquidate the investment, but may sell the acceptance in the money market, where constant trading in such instruments occurs.

The first owner of the bankers' acceptance created from an international trade transaction will be the exporter, who receives the accepted draft back after the bank has stamped it "accepted." The exporter may hold the acceptance until maturity and then collect. On an acceptance of, say, $100,000 for six months, the exporter would receive the face amount less the bank's acceptance commission of 1.5% per annum:

Face amount of the acceptance	$100,000
Less 1.5% per annum commission for six months	−750
Amount received by exporter in six months	$ 99,250

Alternatively, the exporter may "discount"—that is, sell at a reduced price—the acceptance to its bank in order to receive funds at once. The exporter will then receive the face amount of the acceptance less both the acceptance fee and the going market rate of discount for bankers' acceptances. If the discount rate were 7% per annum, the exporter would receive the following:

Face amount of the acceptance	$100,000
Less 1.5% per annum commission for six months	−750
Less 7% per annum discount rate for six months	−3,500
Amount received by exporter at once	$ 95,750

The discounting bank may hold the acceptance in its own portfolio, earning for itself the 7% per annum discount rate, or the acceptance may be resold in the acceptance market to portfolio investors. Investors buying bankers' acceptances provide the funds that finance the underlying commercial transaction.

Bill of Lading

The third key document for financing international trade is the *bill of lading,* or B/L. The bill of lading is issued to the exporter by a common carrier transporting the merchandise. It serves three purposes: a receipt, a contract, and a document of title.

As a receipt, the bill of lading indicates the carrier has received the merchandise described on the face of the document. The carrier is not responsible for ascertaining that the containers hold what is alleged to be their contents, so descriptions of merchandise on bills of lading are usually short and simple. If shipping charges are paid in advance, the bill of lading will usually be stamped "freight paid" or "freight prepaid." If merchandise is shipped collect—a less common procedure internationally than domestically—the carrier maintains a lien on the goods until freight is paid.

As a contract, the bill of lading indicates the obligation of the carrier to provide certain transportation in return for certain charges. Common carriers cannot disclaim responsibility for their negligence through inserting special clauses in a bill of lading. The bill of lading may specify alternative ports in the event that delivery cannot be made to the designated port, or it may specify the goods will be returned to the exporter at the exporter's expense.

As a document of title, the bill of lading is used to obtain payment or a written promise of payment before the merchandise is released to the importer. The bill of lading can also function as collateral against which funds may be advanced to the exporter by its local bank prior to or during shipment and before final payment by the importer.

Characteristics of the Bill of Lading

Bills of lading are either *straight* or *to order.* A straight bill of lading stipulates that the carrier deliver the merchandise to the designated consignee. A straight bill of lading is not title to the goods and is not required for the consignee to obtain possession. Because a straight bill of lading is *not* title, it is not good collateral for loans. Therefore, a straight bill of lading is used when the merchandise has been paid for in advance, when the transaction is being financed by the exporter, or when the shipment is to an affiliate.

An order bill of lading directs the carrier to deliver the goods to the order of a designated party. An additional inscription may request the carrier to notify someone else of the arrival. The order bill of lading grants title to the merchandise only to the person to whom the document is addressed, and surrender of the order bill of lading is required to obtain the shipment.

The order bill of lading is typically made payable to the order of the exporter, who thus retains title to the goods after they have been handed to the carrier. Title to the merchandise remains with the exporter until payment is received, at which time the exporter endorses the order bill of lading (which is negotiable) in blank or to the party making the payment, usually a bank. The most common procedure would be for payment to be advanced against a documentary draft accompanied by the endorsed order bill of lading. After paying the draft, the exporter's bank forwards the documents through bank clearing channels to the bank of the importer. The importer's bank, in turn, releases the documents to the importer after payment (sight drafts), after acceptance (time drafts addressed to the importer and marked D/A), or after payment terms have been agreed (drafts drawn on the importer's bank under provisions of a letter of credit).

Variations in the Bill of Lading

A *clean* bill of lading indicates the goods were received by the carrier in apparently good condition. The carrier is not obligated to check the condition of the merchandise beyond external visual appearance. A *foul* bill of lading indicates the merchandise appeared to have suffered some damage before being received for shipment. A foul bill of lading lacks complete negotiability.

An *on-board* bill of lading indicates the merchandise has been placed on board the vessel whose name is designated on the document. This form is preferred to a *received-for-shipment* bill of lading, which allows for the possibility the goods are sitting on the dock and might remain there for some time. A received-for-shipment bill of lading is not an acceptable document unless it has been specifically authorized in the letter of credit. Similarly, unless authorized otherwise by the letter of credit, banks will refuse to accept *on-deck* bills of lading, indicating the goods have been stowed on deck. Received-for-shipment bills of lading may be issued when goods are first received on the carrier's premises; they can be converted to an on-board form by an appropriate stamp showing the name of the vessel, the date, and the signature of an official of the carrier.

Additional Documents

The draft, the bill of lading, and the letter of credit are the major documents required in most international transactions. However, additional documents may be needed as a condition of the letter of credit for honoring a draft. The more common additional documents include those described here.

A signed *commercial invoice* is issued by the seller and contains a precise description of the merchandise. Unit prices, financial terms of sale, and amount due from the buyer are indicated, as are shipping conditions related to charges, such as "FOB" (free on board), "FAS" (free alongside), "C & F" (cost and freight), or "CIF" (cost, insurance, freight).

Insurance documents must be as specified in the letter of credit and must be issued by insurance companies or their agents. The insurance may be issued to the exporter, who must then endorse the policy to the importer, or it may be issued in the name of the importer. The document must be expressed in the same currency as the credit and must not be dated later than the date of shipment carried on the face of the shipping documents. Insurance must be of types and for risks specified in the letter of credit.

Consular invoices are issued by the consulate of the importing country to provide customs information and statistics for that country and to help prevent false declarations of value. The consular invoice may be combined with a certificate of origin of the goods.

Certificates of analysis may be required to ascertain that certain specifications such as weight, purity, and sanitation have been met. These conditions may be required by health or other officials of the importing country—especially in the case of foods and drugs—or they may be insisted on by the importer as assurance that it is receiving what it ordered. The certificates may be issued by government or private organizations, as specified in the letter of credit.

Packing lists may be required so the contents of containers can be identified, either for customs purposes or for importer identification of the contents of separate containers.

An *export declaration* is a document prepared by the exporter to assist the government to prepare export statistics.

Summary: Documentation in a Typical Trade Transaction

A trade transaction could conceivably be handled in many ways. The transaction that would best illustrate the interactions of the various documents would be an export financed under a documentary commercial letter of credit, requiring an order bill of lading, with the exporter collecting via a time draft accepted by the importer's bank. Such a transaction is illustrated in Exhibit 16.4.

Exhibit 16.4   Typical Trade Transaction

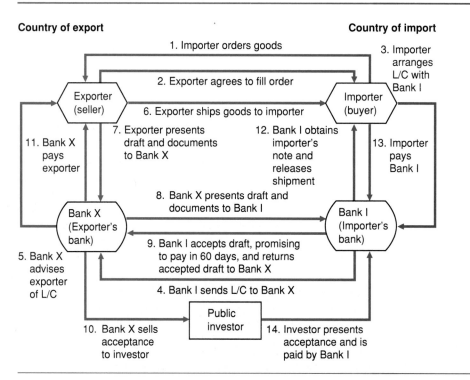

1. Importer places an order for the goods with Exporter, inquiring if Exporter would be willing to ship under a letter of credit.

2. Exporter agrees to ship under a letter of credit and specifies relevant information such as prices and terms.

3. Importer applies to its bank, Bank I, for a letter of credit to be issued in favor of Exporter for the merchandise Importer wishes to buy.

4. Bank I issues the letter of credit in favor of Exporter and sends it to Bank X, Exporter's bank, or to a correspondent bank in the country of export.

5. Bank X advises Exporter of the opening of a letter of credit in the Exporter's favor. Bank X may or may not confirm the letter of credit to add its own guarantee to the document.

6. Exporter ships the goods to Importer.

7. Exporter presents a time draft to Bank X, drawn on Bank I in accordance with Bank I's letter of credit and accompanied by such other documents as required, including the order bill of lading. Exporter endorses the order bill of lading in blank so that title to the goods goes with the holder of the documents—Bank X at this point in the transaction.

8. Bank X presents the draft and documents to Bank I. Bank I accepts the draft, taking possession of the documents and promising to pay the now-accepted draft at maturity (60 days).

9. Bank I returns the accepted draft to Bank X. Alternatively, Bank X could have asked Bank I to accept and discount the draft; then Bank I would have returned cash less a discount fee rather than the accepted draft to Bank X.

10. Bank X, having received back the accepted draft, now a bankers' acceptance, must choose between several alternatives. Bank X may sell the acceptance in the open market at a discount to a portfolio investor. The investor will typically be a corporation or financial institution with excess cash it wants to invest for a short period of time. Bank X may also hold the acceptance in its own portfolio.

11. If Bank X has discounted the acceptance with Bank I (mentioned in step 9) or has discounted it in the local money market, Bank X will transfer the proceeds less any fees and discount to Exporter. Another possibility would be for Exporter itself to take possession of the acceptance, hold it for 60 days, and present it for collection. Normally, however, exporters prefer to receive the discounted cash value of the acceptance at once rather than wait for the acceptance to mature and receive a slightly greater amount of cash.

12. Bank I notifies Importer of the arrival of the documents. Importer signs a note or makes some other agreed plan to pay the bank for the merchandise in 60 days, and Bank I releases the underlying documents so Importer can obtain physical possession of the shipment.

13. In 60 days Bank I receives from Importer funds to pay the maturing draft.

14. On the same day—the 60th day after acceptance—the holder of the matured

acceptance presents it for payment and receives its face value. The holder may present it directly to Bank I, as in the diagram, or return it to Bank X and have Bank X collect it through normal banking channels.

Government Programs to Help Finance Exports

Governments of most export-oriented industrialized countries have special financial institutions that provide some form of subsidized credit to their own national exporters. These export finance institutions offer terms that are better than those generally available from the competitive private sector. Thus domestic taxpayers are subsidizing lower financial costs for foreign buyers in order to create employment and maintain a technological edge. The most important institutions usually offer export credit insurance and a government-supported bank for export financing.

Export Credit Insurance

The exporter who insists on cash or letter of credit payment for foreign shipments is likely to lose orders to competitors from other countries that provide more favorable credit terms. Better credit terms are often made possible by means of export credit insurance, which provides assurance to the exporter or the exporter's bank that, should the foreign customer default on payment, the insurance company will pay for a major portion of the loss. Because of the availability of export credit insurance, commercial banks are willing to provide medium- to long-term financing (five to seven years) for exports.

Since credit has become an increasingly competitive component of the terms of export selling, governments of at least 35 countries have established entities that insure credit risks for exports. Details of these systems appear in the various editions of *the World's Principal Export Credit Insurance Systems* published by the International Export Credits Institute, New York.

Competition between nations to increase exports by lengthening the period for which credit transactions can be insured could lead to a credit war and to unsound credit decisions. To prevent such an unhealthy development, a number of leading trading nations joined together in 1934 to create the Berne Union (officially, the Union d'Assureurs des Crédits Internationaux) for the purpose of establishing a voluntary international understanding on export credit terms. The Berne Union recommends maximum credit terms for many items including, for example, heavy capital goods (five years), light capital goods (three years), and consumer durable goods (one year).

Export Credit Insurance in the United States

In the United States, export credit insurance is provided by the Foreign Credit Insurance Association (FCIA). This is an unincorporated association of private commercial insurance companies operating in cooperation with the Export-Import Bank, an independent agency of the U.S. government.

The FCIA provides policies protecting U.S. exporters against the risk of nonpayment by foreign debtors as a result of commercial and political risks. Losses due to commercial risk are those that result from the insolvency or protracted payment default of the buyer. Political losses arise from actions of governments beyond the control of buyer or seller. FCIA political coverage generally protects against the following events:

- A buyer's inability to legally obtain U.S. dollars or other approved currencies and to transfer those funds to the insured.

- Loss of transportation or insurance charges incurred after shipment because of the politically caused interruption of a voyage outside the United States, when it is not practical to recover the charges from the buyer.

- The occurrence after shipment of any of the following, when it is not the fault of the buyer, issuing bank, or the insured or its agents:
    1. Cancellation or nonrenewal of an export license, or the imposition of restrictions on the export of products that were not subject to license or restriction prior to shipment.
    2. Cancellation of authority to import the products of the buyer's country.
    3. Imposition of laws that prevent import of the products into the buyer's country, or that prevent exchange of local currency into U.S. dollars or some other approved currency.

- The occurrence of any of the following after shipment but on or before the date of default:
    1. War, hostilities, civil war, rebellion, revolution, insurrection, civil commotion, or similar disturbances.
    2. Governmentally authorized requisition, expropriation, confiscation of, or intervention in, the specific business of the buyer, issuing bank, or guarantors.

Foreign Credit Insurance Association (FCIA) Policies

The FCIA offers short-term policies, involving payment terms up to 180 days, and medium-term policies, with payment terms from 181 days to five years. Coverage up to seven years may be arranged on a case-by-case basis for aircraft, marine, and other sales if necessary to meet government-supported foreign competition. Coverage is for U.S. goods produced and shipped from the United States during the policy period, and applies to credit sales to a foreign buyer or to export letters of credit opened by a foreign issuing bank.

Generally, commercial coverage ranges from 90 to 95% and political coverage ranges from 95 to 100%, depending on the type of policy and options chosen by the exporter. Premiums depend on a number of variables, including the length of credit terms being offered, the exporter's previous experience with export sales, the risk associated with the countries to which goods are shipped or services are rendered, and the spread of risk covered by the policy. Details of the provisions of various types of policies can be obtained from the Foreign Credit Insurance Association at 40 Rector Street, 11th Floor, New York, NY 10006.

Export-Import Bank

The Export-Import Bank (also called Eximbank) is an independent agency of the U.S. government, established in 1934 to stimulate and facilitate the foreign trade of the United States. Interestingly, the Eximbank was originally created primarily to facilitate exports to the Soviet Union.

In 1945, the Eximbank was rechartered "to aid in financing and to facilitate exports and imports and the exchange of commodities between the United States and any foreign country or the agencies or nationals thereof." The bank has $1 billion of nonvoting stock paid in by the U.S. Treasury and has the option of borrowing an additional $6 billion from the Treasury if and when needed.

The Eximbank facilitates the financing of U.S. exports through various loan guarantee and insurance programs. The Eximbank guarantees repayment of medium-term (181 days to 5 years) and long-term (5 years to 10 years) export loans extended by U.S. banks to foreign borrowers.

The Eximbank's medium- and long-term direct-lending operation is based on participation with private sources of funds. Essentially the Eximbank lends dollars to borrowers outside the United States for the purchase of U.S. goods and services. Proceeds of such loans are paid to U.S. suppliers. The loans themselves are repaid with interest in dollars to the Eximbank. The Eximbank requires private participation in these direct loans in order to (1) ensure it complements rather than competes with private sources of export financing; (2) spread its resources more broadly; and (3) ensure that private financial institutions will continue to provide export credit.

The Eximbank also guarantees lease transactions, finances the costs involved in the preparation by U.S. firms of engineering, planning, and feasibility studies for non-U.S. clients on large capital projects, and supplies counseling for exporters, banks, or others needing help in finding financing for U.S. goods.

Countertrade   *is not really barter.*

The word *countertrade* refers to a variety of international trade arrangements "in which the sale of goods and services by a producer is linked to an import purchase of other goods and services."[3] In other words, an export sale is tied by contract to an import. The countertrade may take place at the same time as the original export, in which case credit is not an issue; or the countertrade may take place later, in which case financing becomes important.

Conventional wisdom is that countertrade is a variation of barter, used by developing countries because of their shortages of hard currency. However a recent study by Hennart and Anderson suggests a country's reliance on central planning, its political risk rating, and the level of barriers it puts on incoming foreign direct investment are the variables most important for countertrade.[4]

---

[3]Donald J. Lecraw, "The Management of Countertrade: Factors Influencing Success," *Journal of International Business Studies,* Spring 1989, p. 43.

[4]Jean-François Hennart and Erin Anderson, "Countertrade and the Minimization of Transaction Costs: An Empirical Examination," *Journal of Law, Economics, and Organization.*

Hennart, who classified countertrade practices according to the diagram in Exhibit 16.5, points out there are two broad categories of countertrade, each of which has three subcategories:[5] Category 1 transactions avoid the use of money: (1) simple barter; (2) clearing arrangements; and (3) switch trading. Category 2 transactions use money or credit but impose reciprocal commitments: (1) buyback; (2) counterpurchase; and (3) offset.

Exhibit 16.5 Classification of Forms of Countertrade

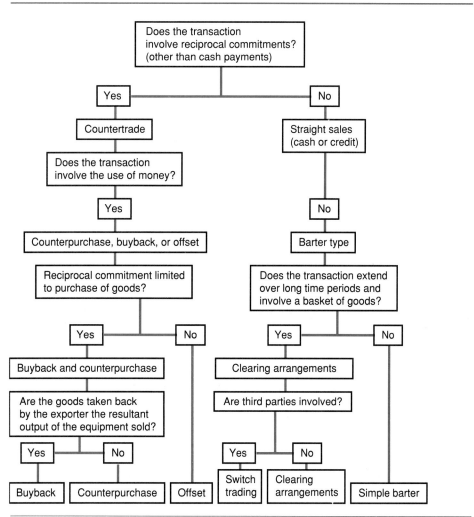

Source: Jean-François Hennart, "Some Empirical Dimensions of Countertrade," *Journal of International Business Studies,* Second Quarter 1990, p. 245. Reprinted with permission.

---

[5]Jean-François Hennart, "Some Empirical Dimensions of Countertrade," *Journal of International Business Studies,* Second Quarter 1990, pp. 243–270.

Simple Barter

Simple barter is a direct exchange of physical goods between two parties. It is a one-time transaction carried out under a single contract that specifies both the goods to be delivered and the goods to be received. The two parts of the transaction occur at the same time, and no money is exchanged. However money may be used as the numeraire by which the two values are established and the quantities of each good are determined.

A famous example of classical barter was an 18-year agreement whereby PepsiCo sent Pepsi syrup to 37 bottling plants in the former Soviet Union in return for Stolichnaya vodka, which Pepsi then marketed in the United States. An extension of that agreement involved PepsiCo's Pizza Hut subsidiary: Moscow agreed to compensate PepsiCo with 10 Soviet-made freighters to sell on the international market.[6]

A more complicated deal involved Philip Morris shipping cigarettes to the Russian Republic, for which it received urea for use in making fertilizer. Philip Morris shipped the urea to China, and China in turn shipped glassware to North America for retail sale by Philip Morris.[7]

Clearing Arrangements

In a clearing arrangement, each party agrees to purchase a specified (usually equal) value of goods and service from the other, with the cost of the transactions debited to a special account. At the end of the trading period any residual imbalances may be cleared by shipping additional goods or by a hard currency payment. In effect, the addition of a clearing agreement to a barter scheme allows for a time lag between barter components. Thus credit facilitates eventual matching of the transactions.

Switch Trading

Switch trade involves transferring use of bilateral clearing balances from one country to another. For example, an original export from Canada to Romania is paid for with a balance deposited in a clearing account in Romania. Although the clearing account may be measured in Canadian dollars (or in any other currency), the balance can be used only to purchase goods from Romania.

The original exporter from Canada might buy unrelated goods from Romania or it might sell the clearing balance at a substantial discount to a "switch trader," often located in Vienna, who in turn purchases goods from Romania for sale elsewhere. The Canadian exporter in effect exchanges the blocked clearing balance for hard currency at a substantial discount with a specialist firm equipped to export merchandise from Romania. The Romanian goods themselves are quite cheap, given the discount, so the switch trader can resell the merchandise at a low price in world markets. Those who oppose this practice note it is dumping below true cost, which hurts competing manufacturers in

---

[6]Robert W. Gibson, "Reform Makes It Harder to Do a Soviet Deal," *Los Angeles Times,* December 2, 1990, p. D10.

[7]Ibid.

other countries. However, because the "dumping" is not done by the original country of manufacture it escapes international agreements on dumping.

An example of a switch trade was a Polish/Greek clearing agreement that existed before Greece joined the EEC. Poland had sold Greece more goods than it had purchased, and so ended up with a dollar-denominated clearing balance in Greece. A switch trader bought the right to 250,000 clearing dollars from Poland for $225,000 and then resold them for $235,000 to a European sultana merchant, who in turn used them to purchase Greek sultanas through the Greek Foreign Trade Bank.[8] (A sultana is a small white seedless grape used for both raisins and wine making.)

Buyback, or Compensation Agreement

A compensation agreement, or buyback transaction, is an agreement by an exporter of plant or equipment to take compensation in the form of future output from that plant. A buyback contract is essentially two parallel money transactions, and the seller is fully compensated by receipts of output from the plant and equipment. Such an arrangement has attributes that make it, in effect, an alternative form of direct investment. The value of the buyback usually exceeds the value of the original sale, as would be appropriate to reflect the time value of money.

An example of a buyback was an agreement by several western European countries to provide steel pipe and compressors for a gas pipeline from the former Soviet Union to Europe, with compensation paid with gas delivered through that pipeline. Another example was an agreement between Occidental Petroleum and the Soviet Union under which Occidental supplied the former Soviet Union with 1 million tons of U.S. super-phosphoric acid per year for 20 years and in turn received 4 million tons of Soviet ammonia, urea, and potash. Occidental helped construct the extra ammonia production and pipeline capacity in the Soviet Union.

Production sharing is the term used for a similar arrangement involving natural resources or energy projects.

Counterpurchase

A counterpurchase transaction involves an initial export, but with the exporter receiving back merchandise that is unrelated to items the exporter manufactures. The importer provides a "shopping list" for the exporter. An early example of counterpurchase was an agreement between McDonnell Douglas and Yugoslavia in 1966 under which McDonnell Douglas sold DC-9's to Yugoslovenski Aerotransport for $199 million cash and $26 million in Yugoslav goods. The Yugoslav products, imported into the United States over subsequent decades, included Zagreb hams, wines, dehydrated vegetables, and even some power transmission towers that were resold to the Los Angeles Department of Water and Power.[9] McDonnell Douglas reportedly housed a

---

[8]Rupert Birley, "Can't Pay? Will Pay, But in Sultanas," *Euromoney,* May 1983, p. 187.

[9]Chris MacKenzie, "How Many Canned Hams Buy a Jet?" *The Travel Agent,* January 28, 1982, pp. 90–92.

Yugoslav trading firm at one of its aircraft plants to deal with the goods acquired in countertrade.

Other counterpurchase examples are the pre-German reunification purchase by West Germany's Volkswagenwerk of coal, oil, and machinery from then East Germany in return for selling 10,000 automobiles to East Germany; and Rolls Royce's sales of jet parts to Finland in return for Rolls Royce's marketing Finnish TV sets and other consumer durables in the United Kingdom.

Offset

Offset refers to the requirement of importing countries that their purchase price be offset in some way by the seller. Offset is common in the purchase of weapons and other large-ticket items. Reciprocal concessions may involve agreement to source some of the production locally, to increase imports from the buying country, or to transfer technology.

Reasons for the Growth of Countertrade

In theory, countertrade is a movement away from free multilateral trade. It is a slow, expensive, and convoluted way of conducting trade that often forces firms to set up operations to deal in products very remote from their expertise. The basic problem is that the agreement to take back goods in some form of barter suggests these goods cannot be sold in the open market for as high a price as is being locked into the countertrade agreement.

Nevertheless, several reasons are advanced in support of countertrade. First, from the perspective of a centrally planned economy, countertrade reduces the risk of fluctuations in export receipts by assuring that future exports will provide foreign exchange roughly equivalent to the cost of the original import.[10] Centrally planned economies have never been competent at marketing their products in foreign countries, perhaps because marketing was not necessary at home. Production plans in these countries are made by a central authority, and the production system does not respond well to sudden changes in export demand. Countertrade provides an assured market for a period of time, and can be negotiated by governmental officials who set economic production quotas, rather than by the managers of individual plants who do not control the availability of resources.

Second, countertrade exports avoid domestic price controls and base prices set by international cartels or commodity agreements. In the case of barter, goods change hands without the explicit use of prices. Consequently any domestic price controls are passed over. Goods can be "sold" abroad at "prices" that are substantially below those charged local customers. Nigeria, Iran, Libya, Indonesia, Iraq, Qatar, and Abu Dhabi are reported to have used barter deals to sell oil below the OPEC cartel agreed upon price.[11]

---

[10]Hennart, "Some Empirical Dimensions of Countertrade," p. 247.

[11]Ibid., p. 249, quoting *Petroleum Economist,* May 1984.

Third, because foreign exchange is not created, it need not be turned over to a central bank. Yet the entity that pays for its original imports with mandated countertrade exports in effect earns foreign exchange which it is able to keep to itself to pay for the import.

Fourth, countertrade enables a country to export merchandise of poor design or quality. The merchandise is often sold at a major discount in world markets. Whether or not this constitutes a discount on the original sale, or even dumping, depends on how that original sale was priced. To the extent that communist and former communist countries have a reputation for poor quality, the fact that the goods are marketed in foreign countries by reputable firms gives buyers some assurance of quality and after-sale service.

Donald Lecraw found that countertrade was most successful for large firms experienced in exporting large complex products; for firms vertically integrated or that could accommodate countertrade take backs; and for firms that traded with countries having inappropriate exchange rates, rationed foreign exchange, and import restrictions. Importers who were relatively inexperienced in assessing technology or in export marketing also enjoyed greater success.[12]

Summary

- Over many years, established procedures have arisen to finance international trade. The basic procedure rests on the interrelationship among three key documents: the letter of credit, the draft, and the bill of lading. Variations in each of these three key documents provide a variety of ways to accommodate any type of transaction.

- In the simplest transaction, in which all three documents are used and in which financing is desirable, an importer applies for and receives a letter of credit from its bank. In the letter of credit, the bank substitutes its credit for that of the importer and promises to pay if certain documents are submitted to the bank. The exporter may now rely on the promise of the bank rather than on the promise of the importer.

- The exporter typically ships on an order bill of lading, attaches the order bill of lading to a draft ordering payment from the importer's bank, and presents these documents, plus any of a number of additional documents, through its own bank to the importer's bank. If the documents are in order, the importer's bank either pays the draft (a sight draft) or accepts the draft (a time draft). In the latter case the bank promises to pay in the future. At this step the importer's bank acquires title to the merchandise through the bill of lading, and it then releases the merchandise to the importer against payment or promise of future payment.

- If a sight draft is used, the exporter is paid at once. If a time draft is used, the exporter receives the accepted draft, now a bankers' acceptance, back from the bank. The exporter may hold the bankers' acceptance until maturity or sell it at a discount in the money market.

[12]Lecraw, "The Management of Countertrade," p. 57.

- The process of international trade is facilitated by various national programs to provide export credit insurance and direct financial support.

- Countertrade provides an alternative to traditional importing and exporting. In countertrade, a seller provides a buyer with goods or services and promises in return to take back (barter) or purchase (other forms of countertrade) goods or services in partial or full payment.

Questions

1. Basic Needs
Explain the basic needs of import-export financing and the main instruments used to deal with those needs.

2. Baltimore Pump Company
Baltimore Pump Company has received an order for merchandise to be exported to Kuwait under the terms of a letter of credit issued by Swiss Bank Corporation on behalf of the Kuwaiti importer. The letter of credit specifies that the face value of the shipment, $8,000,000, will be paid nine months after Swiss Bank Corporation accepts a draft drawn by Baltimore Pump in accordance with the terms of the letter of credit.

The current discount rate on nine-month acceptances is 12% per annum, and Baltimore Pump judges its weighted average cost of capital to be 20%. The commission for selling in the discount market is 1.5% of the face amount.

Baltimore Pump wonders how much cash it can expect from the sale if it holds the acceptance until maturity. Alternatively, it wonders if it should sell the acceptance at once at a discount in the U.S. money market.

3. Naha Beach Club
Surfing has become very popular in Okinawa. In order to capitalize on this, Surfboards, Inc. of San Diego sold 1,000 surfboards to the Naha Beach Surf Shop. The terms of agreement were such that Surfboards, Inc. drew a six-month time draft against a letter of credit issued by Sanwa Bank (Tokyo) on behalf of the Naha Beach Surf Shop in the amount of ¥ 160,000,000. After the boards were shipped and all documentation completed, Surfboards, Inc., presented the draft to the San Diego branch of Sanwa Bank, which stamped it: *ACCEPTED. PAYABLE SIX MONTHS FROM TODAY,* dated it June 6 (today), and returned it to Surfboards, Inc.

Market rates today, the day of acceptance, are as follows:

Spot exchange rate:	¥ 140/$
Six-month forward exchange rate:	¥ 138/$
Discount rate on six-month yen-denominated bankers' acceptances:	8% p.a.
U.S. dollar T-bill rates:	7% p.a.

Euroyen deposit rates available to Surfboards, Inc. six-month
maturity, from a Tiajuana bank: 5% p.a.
Sanwa's rate for a yen loan to Surfboards, Inc.:   6% p.a.

Surfboards, Inc., has no immediate need for the cash within the business, but wants to
have funds available in six months to finance export sales to Australia. Furthermore,
Surfboards, Inc., does not want to expose itself to any exchange risk.

You are financial vice president of Surfboards, Inc. What would you do with the
accepted draft and why? (You may ignore transaction costs and taxes.)

4. Offset: The McDonnell Douglas-Finland Deal

In 1992, the government of Finland purchased $2 billion worth of F-18 Hornet aircraft
from McDonnell Douglas (US) over a number of major competitors such as the
Swedish-built JAS 39 Gripen and the French Mirage 2000-5. The "F-18" team, McDonnell Douglas and three of its major suppliers (Northrop, General Electric, and Hughes
Aircraft), agreed to "facilitate" or aid in the sale of an equivalent amount of business
over the coming 10-year period for Finnish industry.

Why do you think either of the two parties to this agreement would want to enter
into such a vague and complex purchase agreement?

5. Documenting an Export

Explain and diagram the steps involved in an export of canned peas from California to
Japan, using a confirmed letter of credit, payment to be made 90 days from sight.

6. Confirmed Letter of Credit

Explain why an exporter might want a confirmed letter of credit rather than an unconfirmed one. What are its advantages and disadvantages?

7. Bankers' Acceptances

Explain the advantages and disadvantages of using bankers' acceptances for financing
an export. Compare its cost to that of alternative methods of financing, using data from
current sources.

8. Countertrade

Using current sources of information, such as indexes to either the *Wall Street Journal*
or the *New York Times,* find an example of countertrade and explain how it is working.

Bibliography

Banks, Gary, "The Economics and Politics of Countertrade," *The World Economy,* June 1983, pp.
159–182.

Birley, Rupert, "Can't Pay? Will Pay, But in Sultanas," *Euromoney,* May 1983, pp. 187–189.

Blomstrom, Magnus, and Robert E. Lipsey, *Foreign Firms and Export Performance in Developing Countries: Lessons from the Debt
Crisis,* Cambridge, MA: National Bureau of
Economic Research, Inc., Working Paper no.
3412, 1990.

Cavusgil, S. Tamer, Shaoming Zou, and G.M.
Naidu, "Product and Promotion Adaption in
Export Ventures: An Empirical Investigation."
Journal of International Business Studies,
Third Quarter 1993, pp. 479–506.

Celi, Louis J., and I. James Czechowicz, *Export Financing, A Handbook of Sources and Techniques,* Morristown, N.J.: Financial Executives Research Foundation, 1985.

Cohen, Stephen S., and John Zysman, "Countertrade, Offsets, Barter and Buybacks," *California Management Review,* Winter 1986, pp. 41–56.

Dizard, John W., "The Explosion of International Barter," *Fortune,* February 7, 1983, pp. 88–95.

Dominguez, Luis V., and Carlos G. Sequeira, "Determinants of LDC Exporters' Performance: A Cross-National Study," *Journal of International Business Studies,* First Quarter, 1993, pp. 19–40.

Francis, Dick, *The Countertrade Handbook,* Westport, Conn.: Quorum Books, 1987.

The Guide to Export Finance 1988, London: Euromoney Publications, 1988.

Guild, Ian, and Rhodri Harris, *Forfaiting,* London: Euromoney Publications, 1985.

A Handbook on Financing U.S. Exports, 5th ed., Washington, D.C.: Machinery and Allied Products Institute (MAPI), 1988.

Hennart, Jean-François, "Some Empirical Dimensions of Countertrade," *Journal of International Business Studies,* Second Quarter 1990, pp. 243–270.

————, and Erin Anderson, "Countertrade and the Minimization of Transaction Costs: An Empirical Examination," *Journal of Law, Economics, and Organization.*

Huszagh, Sandra M., and Fredrick W. Huszagh, "International Barter and Countertrade," *International Marketing Review,* Summer 1986, pp. 7–19.

Korth, Christopher M., ed., *International Countertrade,* Westport, Conn.: Quorum Books, 1987.

Kryzanolwski, Lawrence, and Nancy D. Ursel, "Market Reaction to the Formation of Export Trading Companies by American Banks," *Journal of International Business Studies,* Second Quarter 1993, pp. 373–381.

Lecraw, Donald J., "The Management of Countertrade: Factors Influencing Success," *Journal of International Business Studies,* Spring 1989, pp. 41–59.

Mirus, Rolf, and Bernard Yeung, "Economic Incentives for Countertrade," *Journal of International Business Studies,* Fall 1986, pp. 27–40.

Uniform Customs and Practices for Documentary Credits, New York: United States Council of the International Chamber of Commerce, 1974.

Venedikian, Harry M., and Gerald A. Warfield, *Export-Import Financing,* 2nd ed., New York: Wiley, 1986.

Vernon-Wortzel, Heidi, Lawrence H. Wortzel, and Zhu Jingtian, *The People's Republic of China as an Exporter: A Far Road Travelled; A Far Road Yet to Go.* Boston: Boston University School of Management Working Paper no. 90–44, 1990.

Chapter 17
Corporate Strategy and Foreign Investment

Global View
Giants in China Build-Up

Leading multinational companies are moving aggressively in China to build up a dominant market share to pre-empt the entry of big rivals, according to a survey by management consulting firm McKinsey and Co. The survey covers multinationals which have a significant presence in China and are regarded by their peers as top performers in the China market.

"China is a large part of their future, and the future is now," say McKinsey principal Stephen Shaw and consultant Johannes Meier in their report. These typically successful companies are not in China just to take temporary advantage of its low labour costs before packing up and moving to another country when faster development inexorably drives costs up. They are there for the long haul, have already figured out how to make profits and sustain them over time, and are working hard to lock out slower competitors. The study found that many multinationals had gone through the learning process and were now moving aggressively into the second stage of involvement in China, focusing on managing local partners, keeping their business systems simple and laying the organisational foundations for a nationwide presence.

The multinationals are rapidly expanding both the number and size of their ventures in China. They are planning to raise their invested capital in the country from an average of US$50 million today to more than $200 million within three years. "The new objective is to build and hold a dominant share of the Chinese market, and to pre-empt, if possible, entry by other multinationals, and very importantly, to do so while making good money along the way," says the report.

Three Stages of MNC Business-Building in China

	STAGE 1 *Opportunistic experimenter*	STAGE 2 *Strategic investor*	STAGE 3 *Dominant local player*
Primary MNC objectives	• Establish small local presence • Learn about market • Learn how to operate and manage in China • Assess risks and rewards of making additional investments	• Build broader multiregional or national presence (through sales or facilities) • Pre-empt competitors by seizing first-mover advantages • Develop substantial local management capability	• Secure dominant share of market, within industry sector. • Shape industry structure and conduct to achieve sustained superior returns
Key characteristics of MNC operations in this phase	• One or two ventures achieving limited coverage; an extension of trading-base opportunities • Very simple operations with low asset commitment and exposure • Active experimentation with localisation, business system design, and partnerships • Footnote on corporate "radar screen"	• Multiple ventures in various geographic and or product areas with umbrella management • High exposure to China sales and assets • Substantially expanded business systems beyond basic manufacturing into sales, service, product design, etc. • High corporate attention and tracking of progress in China versus key competitors	• Highly localised management running significant operations (full business system) • Viewed as truly local player by consumers and market leader by customers and suppliers • Viewed by government as long-term partner in aiding China's economic progress • Key earnings engine for the corporation
Level of corporate commitment to China	Low	Very high	Extremely high

Source: Excerpted from "Giants in China Build-Up: Multinationals Move to Pre-Empt Entry by Rivals," Kent Chen, *South China Morning Post,* Hong Kong, 2/16/94, pp. 1, 20. Reprinted with permission.

The foreign investment decision results from a complex process that differs in many respects from that governing the domestic investment decision. Foreign investments are usually motivated by a wider and more complicated set of strategic, behavioral, and economic considerations. The investigation process is often longer, more costly, and yields less information on which to evaluate opportunities. Financial evaluations of foreign investments using traditional discounted cash flow techniques are not relied on as heavily as they are in domestic investments because of greater perceived business, political, and foreign exchange risks.

In this chapter we examine the three main managerial decisions that need to be considered before investment can be made. These decisions are (1) whether to invest abroad at all, (2) where to invest abroad, and (3) how to invest abroad. The main theories that bear on these decisions lie in the domain of the literature on strategy, international economics, industrial organization, and organization behavior, rather than in the literature of finance. Yet it is critical for financial executives to understand the strategic, behavioral, and economic motives that generate the basket of proposed foreign projects they are asked to evaluate and rank from a financial perspective. The details of foreign project analysis from a traditional financial capital budgeting perspective are covered in chapter 19.

An immense body of literature has emerged in the last 35 years to explain the rapid growth of direct foreign investment. Many theories have been proposed and tested. Each theory typically explains why direct foreign investment occurs in certain industries or in particular types of firms. No one theory has been able to explain direct foreign investment for all types of industries, firms, and countries. Nevertheless, significant attempts have been made to synthesize the various theories into one grand theory. Our approach in this chapter is to summarize these various theories and attempts at synthesis because in combination they constitute a good explanation of most direct foreign investment.

To place the theories in perspective, we note they have one theme in common. *They all attempt to explain why a firm resorts to 100%-owned direct foreign investment rather than relying on joint ventures, exporting, licensing, or management contracts.* The original classical theory of international trade was based only on exporting and importing as determined by comparative advantage and the law of factor proportions. Since direct foreign investment, joint ventures, licensing, and management contracts were not part of the classical theory, why have they become so important in recent years? More specifically, why does a firm establish direct foreign investments rather than alternative modes of foreign involvement? To answer these questions, we now examine the various strategic, behavioral, and economic theories that have been proposed and tested during the last 35 years.

Whether to Invest Abroad

Strategic motives drive the decision to invest abroad. They can be summarized as follows:

1. Market seekers.
2. Raw material seekers.
3. Production efficiency seekers.
4. Knowledge seekers.
5. Political safety seekers.[1]

---

[1]The first four classifications were suggested in W. Dickerson Hogue, "The Foreign Investment Decision Making Process," *Association for Education in International Business Proceedings,* December 29, 1967, pp. 1–2. They were also contained in Lee Nehrt and W. Dickerson Hogue, "The Foreign Investment Decision Process," *Quarterly Journal of AISEC International,* February/April 1968, pp. 43–48.

Market seekers produce in foreign markets either to satisfy local demand or to export to markets other than their home market. U.S. automobile firms manufacturing in Europe for local consumption are an example of market-seeking motivation.

Raw material seekers extract raw materials wherever they can be found, either for export or for further processing and sale in the host country. Firms in the oil, mining, plantation, and forest industries fall into this category.

Production efficiency seekers produce in countries where one or more of the factors of production are underpriced relative to their productivity. Labor-intensive production of electronic components in Taiwan, Malaysia, and Mexico is an example of this motivation.

Knowledge seekers operate in foreign countries to gain access to technology or managerial expertise. For example, German, Dutch, and Japanese firms have purchased U.S.-located electronics firms for their technology.

Political safety seekers acquire or establish new operations in countries that are considered unlikely to expropriate or interfere with private enterprise. For example, Hong Kong firms have invested heavily in manufacturing, services, and real estate in the United States, Canada, and Australia in anticipation of the consequences of China's takeover of the British colony in 1997.

The five types of strategic considerations just described are not mutually exclusive. For example, forest products firms seeking wood fiber in Brazil would also find a large Brazilian market for a portion of their output.

In industries characterized by worldwide oligopolistic competition, each of the strategic motives just described should be subclassified into *proactive* and *defensive* investments. Proactive investments are designed to enhance the growth and profitability of the firm itself. Defensive investments are designed to deny growth and profitability to the firm's competitors. Examples of the latter are investments that try to preempt a market before competitors can get established there, or attempts to capture raw material sources in order to deny them to competitors.

Does the Firm Have a Sustainable Competitive Advantage in the Home Market?

In deciding whether to invest abroad, management must first determine if the firm has some sustainable competitive advantage that enables it to compete effectively in the home market. The competitive advantage must be firm-specific, transferable, and powerful enough to compensate the firm for the potential disadvantages of operating abroad.

Based on observations of firms that have successfully invested abroad, some of the competitive advantages enjoyed by multinational firms are (1) economies of scale and scope arising from their large size, (2) managerial and marketing expertise, (3) superior technology owing to their heavy emphasis on research, (4) financial strength, (5) differentiated products, and (6) sometimes competitiveness of their home markets. We discuss each of these in turn.

Economies of Scale and Scope

Economies of scale and scope can be developed in production, marketing, finance, research and development, transportation, and purchasing. In each of these areas there are significant competitive advantages to being large, whether because of international or just domestic operations. Production economies can come from the use of large-scale automated plant and equipment or from an ability to rationalize production through worldwide specialization. For example, some automobile manufacturers, such as Ford, rationalize manufacturing by producing engines in one country, transmissions in another, bodies in another, and assembling still elsewhere, with the location often being dictated by comparative advantage. Marketing economies occur when firms are large enough to use the most efficient advertising media to create worldwide brand identification, as well as to establish worldwide distribution, warehousing, and servicing systems. Financial economies derive from access to the full range of financial instruments and sources of funds, such as the Eurocurrency, Euro-equity, and Eurobond markets. In-house research and development programs are typically restricted to large firms because of the minimum-size threshold for establishing a laboratory and scientific staff. Transportation economies accrue to firms that can ship in carload or shipload lots. Purchasing economies come from quantity discounts and market power.

Managerial and Marketing Expertise

Managerial expertise includes skill in managing large industrial organizations from both a human and technical viewpoint. It also encompasses knowledge of modern analytical techniques and their application in functional areas of business. Servan-Schreiber popularized the managerial expertise (and technology) thesis in *The American Challenge*.[2] For example, he cited the great depth of management in U.S. firms due to American educational opportunities to study business administration (management) at both the undergraduate and graduate levels. This situation contrasted with the elitist approach to management education in Europe at the time the book was written (1968).

Managerial expertise can be developed through prior experience in foreign markets. In most empirical studies multinational firms have been observed to export to a market before establishing a production facility there. Likewise, they have prior experience sourcing raw materials and human capital in other foreign countries either through imports, licensing, or direct foreign investments. In this manner the multinational firms can partially overcome the supposed superior local knowledge of host country firms.

Technology

Technology includes both scientific and engineering skills. It is not limited to multinationals, but firms in the most industrialized countries have had an advantage in terms of access to continuing new technology spin-offs from the military and space programs.

---

[2]J.J. Servan-Schreiber, *The American Challenge,* London: Hamish Hamilton, 1968.

Empirical studies have supported the importance of technology as a characteristic of multinational firms.[3]

Financial Strength

Financial strength includes not only economies of scale but the ability to reduce risk through diversification of operations and borrowing sources. Typically multinationals have had both lower cost and better availability of capital than foreign and domestic competitors, as we explained in Chapter 10.

Differentiated Products

Firms create their own firm-specific advantages by producing and marketing differentiated products.[4] Such products originate from research-based innovations or heavy marketing expenditures to gain brand identification. Furthermore, the research and marketing process continues to produce a steady stream of new differentiated products. It is difficult and costly for competitors to copy such products, and they always face a time lag if they try. Having developed differentiated products for the domestic home market, the firm may decide to market them worldwide, a decision consistent with the desire to maximize return on heavy research and marketing expenditures.

Competitiveness of the Home Market

A strongly competitive home market can sharpen a firm's competitive advantage relative to firms located in less competitive home markets. Michael Porter and his associates characterize this phenomenon as the "diamond of national advantage."[5] The diamond has four components:

1. Factor conditions.
2. Demand conditions.
3. Related and supporting industries.
4. Firm strategy, structure, and rivalry.

Success of a firm to compete in a particular industry depends partly on the availability of factors of production (land, labor, capital, and technology) appropriate for that

---

[3]W. Gruber, D. Mehta, and R. Vernon, "The R & D Factor in International Trade and International Investment of United States Industries," *Journal of Political Economy*, February 1967, pp. 20–37. Also see Se'ev Hirsch *Location of Industry and International Competitiveness*, Oxford: Oxford University Press, 1967; S. Hirsch, "Multinationals: How Different Are They?" in *The Growth of the Large Multinational Corporation*, G. Y. Bertin, ed., Paris: Centre Nationale de la Recherche Scientifique, 1973.

[4]Richard E. Caves, "International Corporations: The Industrial Economics of Foreign Investment," *Economica*, February 1971, pp. 1–27; and Raymond Vernon, "International Investment and International Trade in the Product Cycle," *Quarterly Journal of Economics*, May 1966, pp. 190–207.

[5]Michael Porter, *The Competitive Advantage of Nations*, London: Macmillan Press, 1990.

industry. Countries that are either naturally endowed with the appropriate factors or able to create them will probably spawn firms which are both competitive at home and potentially so abroad. For example, a well-educated work force in the home market creates a competitive advantage for firms in certain high-tech industries.

Firms facing sophisticated and demanding customers in the home market are able to hone their marketing, production, and quality control skills. Japan is such a market.

Firms in industries that are surrounded by a critical mass of related industries and suppliers will be more competitive because of this supporting cast. For example, electronic firms located in centers of excellence, such as in the San Francisco Bay area, are surrounded by efficient, creative suppliers, and enjoy access to educational institutions at the forefront of knowledge.

A competitive home market obliges firms to fine-tune their operational and control strategies. They are forced to customize these strategies for their specific industry and country environment. For example, Japanese firms learned how to organize to implement their famous "just-in-time" inventory control system. One key was to use numerous subcontractors and suppliers who were encouraged to locate near the final assembly plants.

Product and Factor Market Imperfections

Although a firm may develop a sustainable competitive advantage in its home market, its ability to transfer this advantage abroad depends on finding product or factor market imperfections abroad that open the door to direct foreign investment.[6]

Market Seekers and Raw Material Seekers

Market imperfections may occur naturally, but they are usually caused by policies of firms and governments. For example, market-seeking and raw material-seeking firms in oligopolistic industries seek to create unique competitive advantages through product differentiation and/or preemptive investments to capture foreign raw material sources. Governments create market imperfections through tariff and nontariff barriers to trade, preferential purchasing policies, tax incentives, capital market controls, and similar policies.

One of the most important market imperfections created by governments was the original formation of the EEC in 1957 and the European Free Trade Area (EFTA) in 1958. These trade blocs motivated a large influx of direct foreign investment from

---

[6]Steven Hymer's doctoral dissertation at MIT in 1960 was the first publication to identify product and factor market imperfections as necessary conditions for direct foreign investment. His study was later published as *The International Operations of National Firms: A Study of Direct Foreign Investment,* Cambridge, Mass.: MIT Press, 1976. Hymer's theory was later extended by Charles P. Kindleberger, *American Business Abroad: Six Lectures on Direct Foreign Investment,* New Haven, Conn.: Yale University Press, 1969; Richard E. Caves, "International Corporations," 1971; Rayond Vernon, "International Investment and International Trade in the Product Cycle," *Quarterly Journal of Economics,* May 1966, pp. 190–207.

nonmember countries during the latter 1950s, continuing throughout the 1960s. A second wave during the 1980s was motivated by the prospect of the final realization of the Single European Market after 1992.

Opportunities have also been created by governments in developing countries with large protected markets, such as Brazil, Indonesia, Nigeria, India, and China. At times they have offered multinational firms "pioneer" status, which could include tax breaks, tariff protection from later entrants to the market, and subsidized local infrastructure investments. Both market-seeking and raw material-seeking firms have received such inducements, but these benefits were more common during the colonial era when host governments were under foreign control. It should be noted, however, that government policies to create protected markets can attract direct foreign investment only if the market is sufficiently large, or protected, to overcome diseconomies of scale from production units of less than optimal size.

Although government policies, oligopolistic competition, or natural barriers may create potentially large protected markets, foreign firms operating manufacturing plants in these markets must enjoy some competitive advantages not possessed by local firms in order to be compensated for such inherent disadvantages as lack of knowledge about local customs, differing local tastes, and unfamiliar legal systems, as well as greater communication and control costs. Furthermore, the competitive advantages must allow the firm to earn a higher rate of return from direct foreign investment than would be earned by similar projects of comparable risk in the home market. If these conditions are not met, the firm will prefer to cover foreign markets through alternative modes of involvement.

Defensive Investments

Product and factor market imperfections also create openings for production efficiency seekers, knowledge seekers, and political safety seekers.

Product Cycle Theory. Differentiation with a time lag is the basis for the product cycle theory that was first proposed by Raymond Vernon and his colleagues at Harvard Business School.[7] It suggests that direct foreign investment is a natural stage in the life cycle of a new product from its inception to its maturity and eventual decline. The socioeconomic development, economies of scale, and oligopolistic competition that are found in the most advanced industrial countries lead firms in these countries to undertake intensive research and development efforts. New technologically advanced, or differentiable, products are discovered.

The new products are first introduced in the home market. Close coordination of production and sales is required while the product is improved and the production process standardized. After a short time lag the product is exported. As the new product reaches maturity, competition from nearly similar products narrows profit margins and threatens both export and the home markets.

At this stage foreign manufacturing locations are sought where market imperfections in the cost of factors of production create a chance for lower unit production costs.

---

[7]Raymond Vernon, "International Investment," 1966.

Thus the foreign investment is essentially a defensive investment designed to preserve profit margins in both export and home markets.

Examples of defensive investments can be found in many labor-intensive less developed countries. For example, the price of labor in Mexico, Puerto Rico, China, South Korea, Indonesia, Malaysia, Taiwan, and Thailand is low for its productivity.[8] This feature has attracted direct foreign investment in labor-intensive industries. If laborers in these countries earn the local currency equivalent of $2.50 per hour but are as productive as their U.S. counterparts, who earn $5 per hour, a firm can cut its per unit labor cost in half. Of course, other factors of production, such as shipping, tariffs, equipment, plant, and land, may cost much more in these countries, thereby offsetting the labor differential. Furthermore, over time labor costs may increase more rapidly in these countries than in the United States because of foreign demand for their services. In the meantime, however, a temporary market imperfection for labor exists and attracts direct foreign investment. Although the product cycle theory initiated the idea of defensive investments, many other theories of defensive investments followed.

Follow the Leader. Knickerbocker developed a follow-the-leader theory of defensive direct foreign investment.[9] He noted that in oligopolistic industries when one competitor undertakes a direct foreign investment, other competitors follow very quickly with defensive direct investments into that market. He hypothesized that the followers were motivated by a desire to deny any competitive advantages, such as the benefits of economies of scale, to the others. This is aptly illustrated by the strategy of direct foreign investors in China as described in the Global View at the beginning of this chapter.

Knickerbocker's theory does not explain why the leader initiates the original direct foreign investment, but presumably the reason springs from the opposite side of the same coin. For example, firms are observed entering potentially large markets prematurely with direct foreign investments in an attempt to gain economies of scale and preempt economies of scale from the other competitors. Some of the manufacturing investments in large, growing, less developed countries fall into this category. Even in countries where the size and growth potential of the market are permanently limited, multinationals will make direct investments or acquisitions of firms that are riskier and less profitable than themselves because of the favorable impact on their economies of scale and diversification of risk for the firms as a whole, and denial of these advantages to other oligopolistic competitors. Multinationals sometimes make direct investments of a defensive nature in the home markets of competitors even

---

[8]An empirical example of the product cycle theory, as it applies to defensive investments in offshore plants by U.S. firms, can be found in Richard W. Moxon, "The Motivation for Investment in Offshore Plants: The Case of the U.S. Electronics Industry," *Journal of International Business Studies,* Spring 1975, pp. 51–66. Also see Richard W. Moxon, "Offshore Production in the Less-Developed Countries: A Case Study of Multinationality in the Electronics Industry," *The Bulletin,* nos. 98 and 99, New York University, July 1974, pp. 1–90.

[9]A good synthesis of oligopoly theory and its relation to multinational firms can be found in Fred T. Knickerbocker, *Oligopolistic Reaction and the Multinational Enterprise,* Boston: Harvard Graduate School of Business Administration, 1973.

though such investments appear in accounting statements to be unprofitable. The purpose is to disrupt the easy market share of competitors in their home market in order to reduce their economies of scale and thereby their competitiveness in other markets. U.S., European, and Japanese automobile manufacturing firms have sometimes considered defensive investments in each other's markets in this light.

Defensive investments are even more apparent in the raw material-producing industries, such as in oil, tin, copper, bauxite, rubber, and forest products. Control over sources of raw material, and conversely denial of these sources to competitors, causes a number of preemptive, defensive-type investments, similar to those of market-seeking oligopolists.

Another characteristic that is an important motivation for direct investments in raw materials is the need to develop economies of scale through both horizontal and vertical integration. The raw materials are typically just one stage in a multistage production process reaching all the way from raw materials to final consumers. The independents who perform only one stage in the process are often in a poor bargaining position. The fully integrated producers have alternative sources of supply and control the final markets. Thus, although an investment in raw materials may not be profitable in itself, it creates the opportunity for downstream profits that are not available to the independents.

Credibility. Defensive investments also occur when credibility with an existing customer base becomes important. For example, this factor motivated Novo Industri, A/S to establish a plant to manufacture industrial enzymes in North Carolina in the United States.[10] Novo enjoyed a large export market for industrial enzymes in the United States. However, enzymes are intermediate products that are used in the production of such end products as detergents and fructose. Quality control and guaranteed availability are critical in the continuous production processes employed in such industries. Therefore, despite the loss of economies of scale in Denmark and suboptimal economies of scale in the United States, Novo felt obligated to establish a manufacturing presence in the United States to maintain its credibility in the marketplace.

Growth to Survive. Another version of defensive investments suggests that firms invest abroad because they have saturated the domestic market and any further expansion domestically would lead to destructive retaliation by the other oligopolists or antitrust action (in the United States).[11] Growth abroad, either through new investments

---

[10]This information came from a close working relationship between one of the authors and officials of the firm.

[11]For studies of the "growth" version of international oligopoly theory, see Bela Belassa, "American Direct Investment in the Common Market," *Banca Nazionale del Lavoro Quarterly Review,* June 1966, pp. 121–146. Also see Stephen Hymer and Robert Rowthorn, "Multinational Corporations and International Oligopoly: The Non-American Challenge," in *The International Corporation: A Symposium,* Charles P. Kindleberger, ed., Cambridge, Mass.: MIT Press, 1970, pp. 57–91.

or acquisitions, is the natural reaction of firms that have a "grow to survive" attitude. In these firms, however, there could also be an intuitive understanding that growth leads to improving economies of scale relative to competitors and therefore ultimately to superior financial performance.

Knowledge Seekers. Multinational firms that have been identified as knowledge seekers provide still another example of defensive investments. These are firms trying to maintain or acquire a better position in one or more of the key competitive variables. In particular, they are trying to improve managerial expertise, technology, or knowledge of product and factor markets. This goal is accomplished most efficiently by acquisition of foreign firms that already possess some of these attributes. There may also be an element of improving economies of scale and financial strength in these types of acquisitions. Philips (the Netherlands), Siemens (Germany), and NEC (Japan) have all made important acquisitions of U.S. firms in the integrated circuit and semiconductor business. Most acquisitions were located in the San Francisco Bay area. This area is one of several centers of excellence in the electronics field. In Chapter 12 we described how Hafslund Nycomed, the Norwegian pharmaceutical company, pursued an active strategy to acquire foreign firms that possessed technical expertise in its areas of specialization.

Follow the Customer. The growing presence abroad of service firms is a final example of defensive investments. Banking, advertising, legal, consulting, and accounting firms have typically followed their clients abroad. Their motivation is to counter efforts by other international and local service firms to steal their clients. They are forced to invest in facilities and staff in key foreign locations both for credibility and for convenience.

Internalization

The mere existence of competitive advantages and market imperfections is not sufficient to guarantee direct foreign investment. Instead, firms could exploit their advantages through traditional exports, licensed production, joint ventures, strategic alliances, or management contracts. For foreign direct investment to occur, competitive advantages must be firm specific, not easily copied, and in a form that allows them to be transferred to foreign subsidiaries. For example, economies of scale and financial strength are not necessarily firm specific because they can be and are achieved by many firms throughout the world. Certain kinds of technology can be purchased, licensed, or copied. Even differentiated products can lose their advantage to slightly altered versions given enough marketing effort and the right price.

According to the theory of internalization, the key ingredient for maintaining a firm-specific competitive advantage is possession of proprietary information and control of the human capital that can generate new information through expertise in research, management, marketing, and technology.[12] Needless to say, once again large research-intensive firms are most likely to fit this description.

Why does possession of information lead to direct foreign investment? In the words of Alan Rugman, one of the theory's proponents:

> Information is an intermediate product par excellence. It is the oil which lubricates the engine of the MNE [multinational enterprise]. There is no proper market for the sale of information created by the MNE and therefore no price for it. There are surrogate prices; for example, those found by evaluating the opportunity cost of factor inputs expended in the production and processing of a new research discovery or by an ex post evaluation of the extra profits generated by that discovery, assuming all other costs to remain the same. Yet there is no simple interaction of supply and demand to set a market price. Instead the MNE is driven to create an internal market of its own in order to overcome the failure of an external market to emerge for the sale of information. This internal market of the MNE is an efficient response to the given exogenous market imperfection in the determination of the price of information. Internalization allows the MNE to solve the appropriability problem by assigning property rights in knowledge to the MNE organization.
>
> The creation of an internal market by the MNE permits it to transform an intangible piece of research into a valuable property specific to the firm. The MNE will exploit its advantage in all available markets and will keep the use of information internal to the firm in order to recoup its initial expenditures on research and knowledge generation. Production by subsidiaries is preferable to licensing or joint ventures since the latter two arrangements cannot benefit from the internal market of an MNE. They would therefore dissipate the information monopoly of the MNE, unless foreign markets were segmented by effective international patent laws or other protective devices.[13]

Although the theory of internalization is appealing as a high-level synthesis of market imperfections theories, it lacks empirical verification. Testing such a theory is difficult where no observable market exists external to the firm. Furthermore, we do observe cases where multinational firms have been willing to license information in one market at the same time as they are exploiting it through export or direct foreign investment in other markets. Therefore, John Dunning has developed an eclectic theory of international production in which location-specific factors explain why a firm might serve a particular market by direct foreign investment or export or management contract or licensing.[14]

---

[12]The theory of internalization has its origins in transactions cost theory, which was first introduced by R.H. Coase, "The Nature of the Firm," *Economica* (New Series), 4; 1937, pp. 386–405. The theory was further developed by Oliver Williamson, *Markets and Hierarchies,* New York: Free Press, 1975, and *The Economic Institutions of Capitalism,* New York: Free Press, 1985. Its international dimension was first developed by Peter J. Buckley and Mark Casson, *The Future of the Multinational Enterprise,* London: Macmillan, 1976; and John H. Dunning, "Trade Location of Economic Activity and the MNE: A Search for an Eclectic Approach," in *The International Allocation of Economic Activity,* Bertil Ohlin, Per-Ove Hesselborn, and Per Magnus Wijkman, eds., New York: Holmes and Meier, 1977, pp. 395–418.

[13]Alan Rugman, "Internalization as a General Theory of Foreign Direct Investment: A Re-Appraisal of the Literature," *Weltwirtschaftliches Archiv,* vol. 116, no. 2, June 1980, pp. 368–369. Reprinted with permission.

[14]John Dunning, "The Eclectic Paradigm of International Production: A Restatement and Some Possible Extensions," *Journal of International Business Studies,* Spring 1988, pp. 1–32.

Where to Invest Abroad

The decision about where to invest abroad is influenced by economic and behavioral factors, as well as the stage of a firm's historical development. The decision about where to invest abroad for the first time is not the same as where to reinvest abroad. A firm learns from its first few investments abroad and this influences subsequent investments.

In theory, a firm should identify its competitive advantages. Then it should search worldwide for market imperfections and comparative advantage, until it finds a country where it expects to enjoy a competitive advantage large enough to generate a risk-adjusted return above the firm's hurdle rate.

In practice, firms have been observed to follow a sequential search pattern as described in the behavioral theory of the firm.[15] Human rationality is bounded by one's ability to gather and process all the information that would be needed to make a perfectly rational decision based on all the facts. This observation lies behind two related behavioral theories of direct foreign investment: the *internationalization process theory* and *international network theory*.

The Internationalization Process

The decision to invest abroad for the first time is often a stage in a firm's development process. The firm first develops a competitive advantage in its home market and then may find it can grow profitably by exporting to foreign markets. Eventually it experiences a stimulus from the external environment that leads it to consider production abroad.

In his classic study of the foreign investment decision process of 38 market-seeking U.S. firms that had considered investing in Israel, Yair Aharoni observed the following external stimuli:

1. An outside proposal, provided it comes from a source that cannot be easily ignored. The most frequent sources of such proposals are foreign governments, the distributors of the company's products, its clients, or a powerful member of the firm's board of directors.

2. Fear of losing a market.

3. The "bandwagon" effect: very successful activities abroad of a competing firm in the same line of business or a general belief that investment in some area is "a must."

4. Strong competition from abroad in the home market.[16]

The sequence and intensity of investigation, including the motivating force, was the major determinant of the foreign investment decision.

---

[15]Herbert Simon, *Administrative Behavior,* New York: Macmillan, 1947; and Richard Cyert and James March, *A Behavioral Theory of the Firm,* Englewood Cliffs, N.J.: Prentice-Hall, 1963.

[16]Yair Aharoni, *The Foreign Investment Decision Process,* Boston: Harvard Graduate School of Business Administration, Division of Research, 1966.

The behavioral approach to analyzing the foreign investment decision has been further developed by economists from Uppsala University in Sweden.[17] They have rather successfully explained not just the initial decision to invest abroad but also later decisions to reinvest elsewhere and to change the structure of a firm's international involvement over time. Based on the internationalization process of a large sample of Swedish multinational firms, they observed that these firms tended to invest first in countries which were not too far distant in "psychic" terms. Close psychic distance meant countries with a similar cultural, legal, and institutional environment to Sweden. Examples of such countries are Norway, Denmark, Finland, Germany, and the United Kingdom. The initial investments were modest in size to minimize the risk of an uncertain foreign environment. As the Swedish firms learned from their initial investments, they became willing to take greater risks both with respect to the psychic distance of the countries and the size of the investments.

Multinational Firms in a Network Perspective

As the Swedish multinational firms grew and matured, so did the nature of their international involvement. Today each multinational firm is perceived as being a member of an international network, with nodes based in each of the foreign subsidiaries, as well as in the parent firm itself.[18] Centralized (hierarchical) control has given way to decentralized (heterarchical) control.[19] Foreign subsidiaries compete with each other, and the parent, for expanded resource commitments, thus influencing the strategy and reinvestment decisions. Many of these multinational firms have become political coalitions with competing internal and external networks. Each subsidiary (and the parent) is embedded in its host country's network of suppliers and customers. It is also a member of a worldwide network based on its industry. Finally, it is a member of an organizational network under the nominal control of the parent firm. Complicating matters still further is the possibility that the parent itself may have evolved into a *transnational firm,* that is, one owned by a coalition of investors located in different countries.

Asea Brown Boveri (ABB) is an example of a firm that has passed through the international evolutionary process all the way to becoming a transnational firm. ABB was

---

[17]The internationalization process theory was first introduced by two Swedish scholars, John Johansen and F. Weidersheim-Paul, "The Internationalization of the Firm: Four Swedish Case Studies," *Journal of Management Studies,* vol. 12, no. 3, 1975. It was further developed by John Johansen and Jan Erik Vahlne, "The Internationalization of the Firm: A Model of Knowledge Development and Increasing Foreign Market Commitments," *Journal of International Business Studies,* vol. 8, no. 1, 1977.

[18]An excellent explanation of network theory as applied to multinational firms, written by one of its Swedish pioneers, can be found in Mats Forsgren, *Managing the Internationalization Process: The Swedish Case,* London: Routledge, 1989.

[19]Heterarchical control systems of multinational firms was first described by Gunnar Hedlund, "The Hypermodern MNC—A Heterarchy?" *Human Resource Management,* vol. 25, no. 1, pp. 9–35.

formed through a merger of Sweden-based ASEA and Switzerland-based Brown Boveri in 1991. Both firms were already dominant players internationally in the electrotechnical and engineering industries. ABB has literally hundreds of foreign subsidiaries, which are managed on a very decentralized basis. Percy Barnevik, a Swede, is chief executive officer. He manages the firm with a central staff of fewer than 70 persons from a base in Geneva, Switzerland. ABB's "flat" organization structure and transnational ownership encourage local initiative, quick response, and decentralized foreign investment decisions. Although overall strategic direction is the legal responsibility of the parent firm, foreign subsidiaries play a major role in all decision making. Their input in turn is strongly influenced by their own membership in their local and worldwide industry networks.

Global View
When Two Giants Meet

Since Daimler-Benz, Germany's biggest industrial company, and four members of Japan's giant Mitsubishi group announced a partnership over three years ago, they have found it easier to reject joint endeavours than to launch them. They passed up a project to develop together a four-wheel-drive vehicle, for example, and declined to work together on car engines. But on November 30th the two companies presented the first fruits of their partnership, and hinted at bigger ones to come.

To critics, all this proves is that two sluggish giants move even slower when they march together. It is up to the pair to prove them wrong. Tantalisingly, the most promising projects lie among the 30-odd ideas the two groups are still discussing. For example, they already shop together in Asia for supplies; if they did so globally, they would save much more. They may some day take symbolic shareholdings in each other—and perhaps even jointly develop a super-jumbo jet. Cynics will believe it when they see it.

Source: Adapted from "When Two Giants Meet," 12/4/93, p. 70. © 1970 *The Economist Newspaper Ltd.* Reprinted with permission.

How to Invest Abroad: Modes of Foreign Involvement

So far our analysis has concentrated on whether to and where to establish 100%-owned greenfield (new) subsidiaries abroad. However, there are several alternative modes of foreign involvement. The main choices are these:

1. A joint venture with one or more foreign partners.
2. A merger with or acquisition of an existing foreign firm

3. Licensing a foreign firm.

4. Undertaking a management contract for a foreign firm.

Joint Venture

A joint venture between a multinational firm and a host country partner is a viable strategy if, and only if, one finds the right local partner. Some of the obvious advantages of having a compatible local partner are as follows:

1. The local partner understands the customs, mores, and institutions of the local environment. This might take years for a multinational firm to acquire on its own with a 100%-owned greenfield subsidiary, especially if the psychic distance is large.

2. A key attribute is whether the local partner can provide competent management, not just at the top but also with respect to middle management.

3. Some host countries require, or certainly prefer, that foreign firms share ownership with local firms or investors. In such a case, 100% foreign ownership is not a realistic alternative to a joint venture.

4. Access to the host country's capital markets may be enhanced by the local partner's contacts and reputation.

5. In some cases a local partner may possess technology that is appropriate for the local environment, or maybe can be used worldwide. The difficulty of implementing this strategy is illustrated by the Daimler-Benz/Mitsubishi technology partnership described in the Global View on page 481.

6. If the purpose of the investment is to serve the local market, the public image of a firm that is partially locally owned may improve its sales possibilities.

Despite this impressive list of advantages, joint ventures are not as common as 100%-owned foreign subsidiaries because multinational firms fear interference by the local partner in certain critical decision areas. Indeed, what is optimal from the viewpoint of the local venture may be suboptimal for the multinational operation as a whole. The most important potential conflicts are these:

1. If the wrong partner is chosen, political risk is increased rather than reduced. Imagine the standing of joint ventures undertaken with the family or associates of General Noriega in Panama or Ferdinand Marcos in the Philippines just before their overthrow. The local partner must be credible and ethical or the venture is worse off for being a joint venture.

2. Local and foreign partners may have divergent views about the need for cash dividends or about the desirability of growth financed from retained earnings versus new financing.

3. Transfer pricing on products or components bought from or sold to related companies creates a potential for conflict of interest.

4. Control of financing is another problem area. A multinational firm must justify its use of cheap or available funds raised in one country to finance joint venture operations in another country.

5. Ability of a firm to rationalize production on a worldwide basis can be jeopardized.

6. In some cases financial disclosure of local results is made necessary by having locally traded shares, whereas if the firm is wholly owned from abroad such disclosure is not needed. Disclosure gives nondisclosing competitors an advantage in setting strategy.

7. The problem of valuation of equity shares is difficult. How much should the local partner pay for its share? What is the value of contributed technology, or of contributed land in a country like China where all land is state owned? It is highly unlikely that foreign and host country partners have similar opportunity costs of capital, expectations about the required rate of return, or similar perceptions of appropriate premiums for business risk. Insofar as the venture is a component of the portfolio of each investor, its contribution to portfolio return and variance may be quite different between them.

Mergers and Acquisitions

The 1980s was characterized by a spate of mergers and acquisitions both with domestic and with foreign partners. Cross-border mergers have played an important role in this activity. The 1992 completion of the European Union's Internal Market stimulated many of these investments as European, Japanese, and U.S. firms jockeyed for stronger market positions within the EU. However, the weak value of the U.S. dollar, a relatively undervalued U.S. stock market, good long-run U.S. growth prospects, and political safety in the United States motivated more takeovers of U.S. firms by foreign firms, particularly from the United Kingdom and Japan, than vice versa. This was a reversal of historical trends when U.S. firms were net buyers of foreign firms rather than net sellers to foreign firms.

Advantages and Disadvantages. As opposed to a greenfield investment, a cross-border merger has the following advantages:

1. It is a much quicker way to establish an operating presence in a host country, or a whole geographic market such as the EU.

2. It may be a cost-effective way to capture valuable technology rather than developing it internally.

3. It could have been a necessity to be "grandfathered" in with "insider" status in the EU before the 1992 Internal Market became a reality.

4. Economies of scale and scope can be gained with a larger base whether the merger is cross border or domestic.

5. Foreign exchange operating exposure can be reduced by servicing a market with local manufacturing rather than through imports. This is an implementation of the diversification strategy recommended in Chapter 8.

6. According to internalization theory, cross-border mergers are another way for a firm to exploit its proprietary knowledge and products internally when an efficient external market does not exist.

7. In the case of foreign takeovers in the United States, the price and timing may be right considering the weakness of the dollar.

As in the domestic merger case, cross-border mergers have some potential pitfalls:

1. Cultural differences may inhibit the melding of two organizations of different nationality, customs, and values.
2. The price paid by the acquirer may be too high and the method of financing too costly.
3. Unfavorable host country political reactions may occur when a takeover is by a foreign firm.
4. Labor troubles can arise because of unequal union contracts, seniority, favoritism, or a host of other potential grievances.
5. Contractual agreements, license fees, transfer prices, and other commercial relationships between the parties will be more closely scrutinized than when they were independent.

Unfriendly Takeovers

Whereas successful takeovers within the continental European countries and Japan have almost always been friendly, such has not been the case in the United Kingdom and the United States. This relates to some basic differences in corporate and investor philosophies between the Anglo-American equity markets and those in the rest of the world.

As suggested in Chapter 1, the Anglo-American equity markets are characterized by a philosophy that a corporation's objective should be to maximize shareholder wealth. Whether all firms behave in this manner is open to debate, but if management deviates too much from this objective they can be removed through the discipline of the marketplace, that is, a takeover by others. This discipline is made possible by the "one-share-one-vote" rule that dominates the Anglo-American markets.

In contrast, the continental European and Japanese equity markets are characterized by a philosophy that a corporation's objective should be to maximize corporate wealth.[20] This means a firm should treat shareholders on a par with other corporate interest groups, such as management, labor, the local community, suppliers, creditors, and even the government. The goal is to earn as much as possible in the long run but to retain enough to increase the corporate wealth for the benefit of all the interest groups.

One might wonder why shareholders do not enforce their own objectives when management does not act as their agent. The answer is that the non-Anglo-American countries are not characterized by the corporate "one-share-one-vote" rule. Furthermore, many other antitakeover defenses exist that make it virtually impossible to force an unfriendly merger.

---

[20]The best description of the corporate wealth maximization model from a financial perspective can be found in Gordon Donaldson, *Managing Corporate Wealth: The Operation of a Comprehensive Financial Goal System,* New York: Praeger, 1984.

Exhibit 17.1   A Survey of Takeover Defenses in Seven Non-Anglo-American Countries

Type of Takeover Defenses	Countries in the Survey in Which the Defense Is Used[a]
1. Dual classes of voting stock	Denmark, France, the Netherlands, Norway, West Germany, and Switzerland.
2. Restrictions on the number of shares that can be voted	West Germany and Switzerland
3. Restrictions on foreign ownerships of shares	France, Japan, Norway, and Switzerland
4. Provisions in the corporate charter that might require a super-majority vote on a takeover bid	Japan, Switzerland, and West Germany
5. Selling a special issue of voting shares or convertible preferred to "stable" or "friendly" investors	France, Japan, the Netherlands, Norway, Switzerland, and West Germany
6. Finding a "white knight"	France, the Netherlands, Norway, and Switzerland
7. Control by a foundation	Denmark, the Netherlands, and Switzerland
8. Forming a strategic alliance and/or having interlocking boards of directors	France, Japan, the Netherlands, Norway, and West Germany
9. Relying on a network of close personal relationships, that is, belonging to "the establishment"	Denmark, France, Japan, the Netherlands, Norway, Switzerland, and West Germany
10. Government regulations controlling competition and monopolies	France, the Netherlands, and West Germany

[a]The seven countries included in the survey were Denmark, France, Japan, the Netherlands, Norway, Switzerland, and Germany (West).

Source: Arthur Stonehill and Kåre Dullum, "Corporate Wealth Maximization, Takeovers, and the Market for Corporate Control," *Nationaløkonomisk Tidsskrift* (Denmark), no. 1, 1990, p. 87.

Exhibit 17.1 presents a survey of takeover defenses in seven non-Anglo-American countries. It shows that dual classes of voting stock are prevalent in six of the seven countries. The controlling class of stock is usually held by the founders, a foundation, or investors friendly to existing management. Nine other takeover defenses are listed along with the countries in which they are used. Note in particular the importance of strategic alliances (number 8) and close personal relationships (number 9). For example, it was the Belgian and European "establishment" that defeated Carlo de Benedetti's unsuccessful bid to take over Société Genérale de Belgique, Belgium's largest company, in 1988.

Strategic Alliances

Strategic alliances are currently in vogue in the world of international business. The definition of strategic alliance is unclear because it connotes different meanings to different observers. One form of cross-border strategic alliance is where two firms exchange a share of ownership with each other. As we pointed out in Exhibit 17.1, this can be a takeover defense if the prime purpose is for a firm to place some of its stock in stable and friendly hands. If that is all that occurs, it is just another form of portfolio investment, not direct foreign investment.

A more comprehensive strategic alliance is where, in addition to exchanging stock, the partners establish a separate joint venture to develop and manufacture a product or service. Numerous examples of such strategic alliances can be found in the automotive, electronics, telecommunications, and aircraft industries. Such alliances are particularly suited to high-tech products where the cost of research and development is high and timely introduction of improvements is important.

A third level of cooperation might involve joint marketing and servicing agreements where each partner represents the other in certain markets. Some observers believe such arrangements begin to resemble the cartels that were prevalent in the 1920s and 1930s. Because they reduce competition, cartels have been banned by international agreements and many national laws.

Strategic alliances involving joint ventures and marketing agreements are quasi direct foreign investment. They enjoy the same advantages and disadvantages as we identified previously for other types of joint ventures. The main difference here is that strategic alliances often also involve an exchange of stock between the parent firms.

It remains to be seen if the current wave of strategic alliances in the EU are stable and durable. It seems as if most firms feel they should be treating the Internal Market as if it were a "United States of Europe." Strategic alliances are a quick way to get EU-wide coverage before it is too late. This is particularly attractive to firms that have historically served the EU markets through exports, licensing, or minor direct investment in assembly and service facilities. Specifically, firms located in Austria, Sweden, Norway, Finland, and Switzerland are feeling the pressure to become "insiders." Strategic alliances with EU partners have also been popular with firms from the United States, Japan, Canada, and Australia. After the euphoria associated with 1992 wears off, it is possible many of these hurried strategic alliances will be dissolved and be replaced in a more deliberate manner by traditional types of direct foreign investment.

Licensing and Management Contracts as Alternatives to Direct Foreign Investment

In recent years a number of host countries have demanded that multinational firms sell their services in "unbundled form" rather than only through direct investment. For instance, they would like to purchase managerial expertise and knowledge of product and factor markets through management contracts, and technology through licensing agreements.

Licensing is a popular method for nonmultinational firms to profit from foreign markets without the need to commit sizable funds. Since the foreign producer is typically 100% locally owned, political risk is minimized.

The main disadvantage of licensing is that license fees are likely to be lower than direct investment profits, although the return on the marginal investment might be higher. Other disadvantages include possible loss of quality control, establishment of a potential competitor in third-country markets, possible improvement of the technology by the local licensee, which then enters the original firm's home market, and possible loss of opportunity to enter the licensee's market with a direct investment later on. Yet another disadvantage is the risk the technology will be stolen.

Multinational firms have not typically used licensing of independent firms. On the contrary, most licensing arrangements have been with their own foreign affiliates or joint ventures. License fees have been a way to spread the corporate research and development cost among all operating units and a means of repatriating profits in a form typically more acceptable to some host countries than dividends.

Management contracts are similar to licensing insofar as they provide for some cash flow from a foreign source without significant foreign investment or exposure. Management contracts probably lessen political risk because it is easy to repatriate the managers. International consulting and engineering firms have traditionally conducted their foreign business on the basis of a management contract.

Whether licensing and management contracts are cost effective compared to direct foreign investment depends on the price host countries are willing to pay for the unbundled services. If the price were high enough, many firms would prefer to take advantage of market imperfections in an unbundled way, particularly in view of the lower political, foreign exchange, and business risks. Since we observe multinationals continuing to prefer direct investments, we must assume the price for selling unbundled services is still too low.

Why is the price of unbundled services too low? The answer may lie in the synergy created when services are bundled as direct investments in the first place. Managerial expertise is often dependent on a delicate mix of organizational support factors that cannot be transferred abroad efficiently. Technology is a continuous process, but licensing usually captures only the technology at a particular time. Most important of all, however, economies of scale cannot be sold or transferred in small bundles. By definition they require large-scale operations. How can even a relatively large operation in a small market achieve the same economies of scale as a large operation in a large market?

Despite the handicaps, some multinationals have successfully sold unbundled services, for example, sales of managerial expertise and technology to the OPEC countries. In this case, however, the OPEC countries are both willing and able to pay a price high enough to approach the returns on direct foreign investment (bundled services) while only receiving the lesser benefits of the unbundled services.

Summary

- The direct foreign investment decision results from a complex process involving strategic, behavioral, and economic considerations.

- The decision on whether to invest abroad at all is driven by strategic motives that can be classified into five categories: market seekers, raw material seekers, production efficiency seekers, knowledge seekers, and political safety seekers.

- In order to invest abroad a firm must have a sustainable competitive advantage in the home market. This must be strong enough and transferable enough to overcome the disadvantages of operating abroad.

- Competitive advantages stem from economies of scale and scope arising from large size, managerial and marketing expertise, superior technology, financial strength, differentiated products, and competitiveness of the home market.

- Product and factor market imperfections abroad open the door to direct foreign investment.

- Oligopolistic competition also motivates firms to make defensive investments abroad to save both export and home markets from foreign competition.

- The product cycle theory suggests that new products are first developed in the most advanced countries by large firms which have the ability to undertake research and development. The new products are introduced into the home market and later exported. As the product matures and the production process becomes standardized, foreign competition reduces profit margins and threatens the home market. Part of the production process is then defensively relocated abroad to take advantage of lower unit costs of labor or other factors of production.

- Defensive direct foreign investments may also be motivated by "follow-the-leader" behavior, a desire to establish credibility with local customers, a "grow-to-survive" philosophy, a desire to gain knowledge by acquiring firms with valuable expertise, and a need to follow the customer in the case of service firms.

- The theory of internalization holds that firms having a competitive advantage because of their ability to generate valuable proprietary information can only capture the full benefits of innovation through direct foreign investment.

- The decision about where to invest abroad is influenced by the stage of a firm's historical development.

- Behavioral studies show that the foreign investment decision is often motivated by a strong stimulus from the external environment, or from within an organization on the basis of personal biases, needs, and commitments of individuals and groups. The investigation process itself, particularly the choice of projects to be investigated, is a major determinant of the foreign investment decision.

- Psychic distance plays a role in determining the sequence of foreign investment and later reinvestment. As firms learn from their early investments they venture further afield and are willing to risk larger commitments.

- The most internationalized firms can be viewed from a network perspective. The parent firm and each of the foreign subsidiaries are members of networks. The networks are composed of relationships within a worldwide industry, within the host countries with suppliers and customers, and within the multinational firm itself.

- Alternative (to 100%-owned foreign subsidiaries) modes of foreign involvement exist. They include joint venture, merger or acquisition, licensing, and management contracts.

- The success of a joint venture depends primarily on the right choice of a partner. For this reason and a number of issues related to possible conflicts in decision making between a joint venture and a multinational parent, the 100%-owned foreign subsidiary approach is more common.

- The surge in merger and acquisition activity in the 1980s focused attention on the distinction between the Anglo-American shareholder wealth maximization model and the continental European corporate wealth maximization model. The Anglo-American philosophy has led to much of the merger and acquisition activity in which a firm is taken over by others through the discipline of the marketplace. The continental European philosophy, however, treats shareholders on par with other corporate interest groups. Takeover defenses effectively stifle hostile takeovers.

- The completion of the European Internal Market at end-of-year 1992 induced a surge in cross-border entry through strategic alliances. Although some forms of strategic alliances share the same characteristics as joint ventures, they often also include an exchange of stock.

Decision Case
Silica Glass, Inc.[21]

The sparkle, color, and artistry were mesmerizing. Mike Harrelson was amazed as he held the crystalline Christmas tree ornament up to the firelight. It was May 15, 1991, and the ornament was the product of the world-renowned glass artistry of the Thüringen region of Germany, until recently East Germany. Mike Harrelson is president of Silica Glass, Inc., a firm which had just made an offer for one of the glass manufacturing firms of this Thüringen region. The Treuhandanstalt, the German government agency in charge of the privatization effort for enterprises formerly of East Germany, had not really rejected the offer, but made a counterproposal. The crystal ornament was elegantly simplistic; this acquisition was not. Mike wished to reevaluate his strategy.

Background

Silica Glass, Incorporated (U.S.), is a worldwide leader in the production of glass fiber. Silica fiber is a synthetic fiber of proprietary glass composition. The glass fiber is in turn used in many different industrial applications, some of which were in other divisions of the same company.

Silica's products had grown steadily in quality and sales for a number of years; however, the firm itself had undergone a number of significant ownership and strategy changes. The primary product lines had been developed under Silica Products in the early 1980s. The firm was taken over in 1984 by a takeover specialist who used it as a "cash cow," milking the enterprise for cash flows but reinvesting little. Two years later, operations were sold to Primavera, a southeastern U.S. holding company which had new plans for Silica.

Primavera saw more long-term growth potential for the series of products manufactured by Silica. Primavera's strategy was to expand sales and acquire additional

---

[21]Michael H. Moffett, Oregon State University, May 1991. Reprinted with permission.

operations which would increase the overall value of the total Silica operation, that is, grow the firm. Although several of the Silica divisions showed healthy profitability, the product lines were very narrow and market expansion limited. Rapid growth would likely be obtained through merger and acquisition, rather than direct sales growth. Moreover, sales, particularly in the domestic market, were being squeezed by new competitive products.

Silica's Markets

The glass fiber market is a highly specialized one. Silica's sales were currently split between intradivisional sales (50%) and external sales (50%). External sales were in turn divided between the United States (75%), Western Europe (20%), and the Pacific Rim (5%). Silica had grossed nearly $25 million in sales in 1989, and held approximately 25% market share worldwide in these specialized glass fiber products. World markets in general were expected to grow at a 10–15% per year rate in the coming decade.

The problem was intrafirm sales. While outside sales were expected to grow at nearly 30% per year for the next five years, the internal sales to other corporate divisions were expected to decline nearly 25% annually over the same period. Mike's division was looking at a substantial squeeze. The internal sales decline was fairly certain, as new nonglass synthetics were coming onto the market which would make the products of several other corporate divisions obsolete. Hence, Mike's division needed new sales outside the firm. The solution was fairly clear (or at least Mike had thought so initially): focus on external sales growth through increased market share.

Silica's major competitor, both in the United States and worldwide, is GlassPro, a major midwestern U.S. corporation. GlassPro is a firm of substantially larger size and product scope, but presently has only one glass fiber production facility, located in Ohio. GlassPro often experienced excess capacity in short periods of sluggish sales. GlassPro would therefore probably not be expanding into European production in the foreseeable future. A third but relatively minor competitor was Sonnenberg Glaswerks GmbH, located in Sonnenberg, East Germany. Although Sonnenberg produced glass fiber, sales were limited to the Eastern Bloc prior to German unification. With unification, however, Sonnenberg could constitute new competition for both U.S. firms throughout Western Europe.

European Production and 1992

Mike Harrelson had concluded that the rapid sales growth Silica was experiencing, both in the United States and Europe, required immediate manufacturing expansion. Initiating production in Europe was a strong possibility.

Silica believed it should locate new production capability in Europe for a number of reasons. First, the recent growth in the European market represented new opportunities which would be better served by producing within the region. Second, the possibility of a single-Europe, the 1992 program, also created increasing debate over a possible "Fortress Europe." Although the protectionism debate was not considered significant in many industries, Silica had reason to believe it was real. Silica was aware of tentative discussions between the European Commission (EC) in Brussels and a French

glass-fiber producer. The French producer is currently a world leader in glass-fiber production, but does not produce the technologically complex fibers of the two U.S.-based
firms. The EC's concern was clear: it was interested in fostering European production of
high quality (and high value-added) glass fiber. Mike had a suspicion that once European production of glass fiber began, new protectionist legislation might come forward
against foreign firms exporting into Europe.

With the support of Primavera Corporation, Mike Harrelson started exploring possibilities for European manufacturing in the spring of 1990. The question was where to
produce in Europe, and how to enter. Mike initially explored greenfield investment possibilities, searching first in the United Kingdom, France, western Germany, and Luxembourg, for affordable property for plant construction. What Mike found was costly, and
not encouraging. A second alternative was then explored: the acquisition of an existing
facility, one with a glass furnace in place which might allow a cheaper production
start-up.

Mike focused on Sonnenberg Glaswerks in the Thüringen region of former East
Germany. Sonnenberg, or what was left of it, was known to have had some of the most
advanced technology in the world in glass manufacturing for over four centuries. The
fame and product development had stopped with the inception of the communist government in East Germany in 1945. The following 45 years resulted in little advancement.
There had been no new capital investment. The facilities at Sonnenberg were a mix of
the technology of different eras. The two 15-ton furnaces in place were of a technology
over 50 years out of date.

By the spring of 1990 Sonnenberg was producing a mediocre glass fiber and was
badly in need of new capital, technology, and marketing skills if it was to survive the
transition to a capitalist market economy. The unification of Germany now provided
Mike Harrelson with the opportunity to salvage something of Sonnenberg's history and
productive capability while getting Silica's foot in the door of European production.

Privatization and the Treuhandanstalt

Whereas the opening of Eastern Europe produced massive drives for reindustrialization
and privatization for some countries (for example, Poland, Czechoslovakia, Hungary,
and Bulgaria), it was different for the former West and East Germanies. Because western
Germany was already one of the world's true industrial giants, its economy could provide a jump-start to the revitalization of the east. The east, however, could be absorbed
into the whole rather than independently reindustrialized like other Eastern European
economies. West Germany approached much of the redevelopment with triage analysis,
quietly separating the previous East German enterprises into: (1) those that would not be
competitive; (2) those that were well-positioned and prepared for competing with western businesses; (3) those that might survive if provided with infusions of capital, technology, and expertise. The major problem and motivation for selection and action was
maintenance of employment. Eastern Germany was rapidly falling into a depression.

To orchestrate the privatization process, a government-constructed holding company,
the Treuhandanstalt, was established. The Treuhandanstalt was charged with winding up
over 8,000 firms. The process required the formation of Western-style balance sheets and

Exhibit 17.2   East German Privatization: Glasring Thüringen AG

TREUHANDANSTALT
(German government organization for privatization,
and owner of regional holding companies including Glasring Thüringen)

Glasring Thüringen AG
(regional holding company for privatization of the following firms)

- Sühl[ER] Glaswerke GmbH
- Rudolstadt[ER] Thermometerwerk GmbH
- Sühl[ER] Glasmachinenbau GmbH
- Saalfeld[ER] Glaswerke GmbH
- Zella-Mehlisglas GmbH
- Deutsche Schaumglas GmbH
- Sonnenberg[ER] Christbaumschmuck GmbH
- Thüringer Glasschmuck GmbH
- Zella-Mehlis[ER] Metallchristbaumschmuck GmbH

- Staaken[ER] Quarzschmelze GmbH
- Schmalkalden Pharmaglas GmbH
- Haselbach[ER] Glaswerk GmbH
- Naumberg[ER] Glasfaser GmbH
- Sonnenberg[ER] Glaswerk GmbH
- Langewiesen[ER] Thermos GmbH
- Gotha[ER] Rhonglas GmbH
- Sühl[ER] Ilmkristall GmbH

GmbH is the German reference for corporation, the corporate entity with limited liability.

operating statements for every firm. It was also necessary to quickly assess which firms required immediate cash injections in order to stay afloat until they could be sold or closed.

Sonnenberg Glaswerk GmbH was held by a regional holding company known as Glasring Thüringen AG. Sonnenberg was one of 17 different enterprises for which Glasring Thüringen was responsible (see Exhibit 17.2). Thüringen's role was to follow the directives of the Treuhandanstalt and wind up the 18 firms while doing everything possible to ensure employment.

Proposed Acquisition

After initial exploratory meetings in the spring of 1990, a second visit in September resulted in a tentative arrangement. Silica proposed the acquisition of Sonnenberg Glaswerks, with 75% ownership by Silica, and the remaining 25% remaining with Sonnenberg (actually its present management). The 75% ownership level was necessary in order to obtain tax benefits under EU law. Although no one had actually owned Sonnenberg in the recent past (under a communist system), Glasring Thüringen AG would hold the 25% minority ownership under the proposal. Silica would be guaranteed first refusal on the sale of this 25% share (Silica had wanted 100% ownership, but this was unacceptable to Glasring Thüringen). Since Glasring Thüringen was really only a privatization agency, Mike suspected that its 25% ownership would be "given" to the present management of Sonnenberg. Sonnenberg management still saw itself as owners although they had no equity investment or legal standing. In fact, in the preliminary discussions with management, the chief operating officer of Sonnenberg had wished to discuss a joint venture with Silica in which he would be the other equity holder, albeit with no capital investment.

Silica's offer was to invest approximately DM1,500,000 ($1,000,000 at the present exchange rate of DM1.5000/$) in new capital and technology, and provide all marketing and sales expertise. One-fourth of this capital would be required for new plant and equipment, along with an additional 30% subsidy package provided by the German government for specific health, safety, environmental, and machinery needs. The remaining DM1,125,000 would provide working capital for expanded operations. Present contracts such as one with Naumburg Glasfaser would continue. These would provide some minimal cash flows during the transition.

Mike Harrelson returned to the United States to await the completion of balance sheet analysis, but feeling positive about the feasibility of the project. Mike waited for financial information throughout October, November, and into December. The process, which had moved so quickly and smoothly, had ground to a halt. Communication was difficult, and there seemed to be no response to queries for additional information.

Glasring Thüringen AG's Counterproposal

Mike Harrelson returned to Sonnenberg in mid-December to investigate the problems first-hand. The problems of the Treuhandanstalt and Glasring Thüringen had intensified as unemployment had continued to increase.[22] Glasring Thüringen now proposed an alternative arrangement: Silica would not only acquire Sonnenberg Glaswerks GmbH, but also acquire a second facility 50 kilometers away, Sfhl Glaswerke, GmbH. The two were to be sold together, and not singly. This was different. Silica would now be expected to split production between the two different facilities, thus adding to direct and indirect operating costs as well as overhead expenses. Mike explored the possibility of consolidating the two operations at one facility, Sfhl, but Glasring Thüringen's interests were firmly in the maintenance of regional employment without worker dislocation. In exchange for the acquisition of the second facility, Glasring Thüringen agreed to the same purchase price; two firms for one! This would increase operating costs substantially, but since there were still no balance sheets or operating statements available, the amount of the cost increase could not be identified.

By late January 1991 there was still no response on the requests for financial information on Sonnenberg. Without some estimates of production costs, material costs, and particularly energy costs, the competitiveness of the existing facilities could not be determined. There was also no word on the acquisition approval process.[23]

---

[22]The difficulties the Treuhandanstalt had been having in finding suitable joint venture partners were severe. For example, the offer by the West German firm BASF for Synthesewerk Schwarzheide, an East German polyurethane maker, had been low to say the least: BASF would pay nothing for Synthesewerk Schwarzheide; BASF would not be liable for any environmental liabilities resulting from Synthesewerk Schwarzheide's operations prior to purchase (1945–1990); BASF would be granted ownership by the end of September 1990. The offer was made in August 1990.

[23]The April 1 assassination of Detlev Rohwedder, the director of the Treuhandanstalt, did not aid in the process either. The murder of Rohwedder at his Dusseldorf villa by the German Red Army faction known as the Baader-Meinhof gang was a terrorist action intended to slow the restructuring of former East Germany. The Baader-Meinhof gang is thought to have had ties to the former East German secret police, the Stasi. Ironically, Rohwedder was born in the Thüringia region of East Germany.

Mike Harrelson decided to try and force the process. A fax to Glasring Thüringen explained that without positive movement on approval, financial documentation, and price negotiation by mid-March, the acquisition offer by Silica would be terminated. The fax went without response until early March when a hastily called meeting in Berlin once again brought Mike into negotiations, this time with an expanded cast: the director of Glasring Thüringen, the assistant chief administrator of the Treuhandanstalt, and the president of Deutsche Bank, Berlin. Mike was astounded to find out that the acquisition had only been brought to the attention of the directors of the Treuhandanstalt and Glasring Thüringen in the past two weeks. The offer and negotiation process had evidently been mired in the lower levels of the bureaucracy. In addition, the previous counterproposal was now expanded to include a third firm in the Glasring, Sonnenberg Christbaumschmuck GmbH, the actual producer of the famous crystal Christmas ornaments. Although small, the additional component would require some attention and capitalization by Silica. The meeting ended on a positive note with assurances of rapid progress, but no financial discussions or documents yet put forward.

The Netherlands Alternative

Upon Mike Harrelson's return to the United States back in December of 1990 he had decided to reopen consideration of greenfield investment within the EC. Mike had instructed Silica's representatives in the Netherlands to search out potential properties for use in a greenfield investment. The timing was fortunate.

Philips, one of the largest firms in Europe, had been forced to announce major plant closures and literally thousands of layoffs. The restructuring resulted from its own continuing problems and the recession in the United States and United Kingdom beginning in the third quarter of 1990. There was an abundance of available facilities and skilled employees, all in a region of extremely well-developed transportation and communication infrastructure. The city of Haarlem, according to Silica's representative, had two different properties which might be developed to the company's needs. Silica also had existing sales in the Netherlands, and an increasing number of clients in the bordering countries of Belgium, France, and Germany. It did constitute a relatively central location for servicing western Europe.

The Netherlands Foreign Investment Agency office in San Mateo, California, responded quickly with information regarding labor costs and benefit guidelines, estimates of electricity costs, and other needed material and facility cost information. Of particular note was that for major electrical power users like Silica, the Netherlands provided extremely cheap block-rate packages, which were even less than those in the Pacific Northwest of the United States. Mike now believed that the Netherlands, if they could provide investment subsidies that were competitive with those of Germany, could be a legitimate alternative to the Sonnenberg acquisition.

Entry Preference

Mike Harrelson now had serious doubts about the rapidly expanding acquisition in Germany. He had been negotiating with the German parties, and there seemed to be an ever-increasing number of interested parties for over a year, and still had little to show for it.

Much of what he was now reading indicated a worsening business environment in the former East Germany. On the other hand, the recession-induced events in the Netherlands as well as the rapid movement of the Dutch authorities had resulted in the Netherlands being a legitimate alternative. The two avenues to EC entrance were, however, inherently different.

As Mike Harrelson held the crystal Christmas tree ornament up to the light (a memento of the last meeting in Berlin when he was offered its maker, Sonnenberg Christbaumschmuck), he knew he must decide soon. December 31 of 1992 was no longer such a distant date.

Questions

1. Bergersen Shipping

In 1989, Bergersen Shipping (Norway) listed on both the Oslo and London stock exchanges, and sponsored ADRs in the United States. It needed additional tankers for its fleet quickly. Because rising expenses and increasing lead times made new construction impractical, Bergersen went shopping for tankers on the open market.

Sven Erik Amundsen, Bergersen's chief financial officer, approached Bulk Transport (Luxembourg) and offered to buy two of its four tankers. Bulk responded by stating that its tankers were not on the market, and would not be for sale at any price. So instead of buying the tankers, Bergersen simply bought Bulk Transport. After obtaining 69% of Bulk's publicly traded shares, Bergersen dissolved the unit and took three of the four tankers. (The remaining tanker was taken by the Saudi investment group holding the majority of the remaining outstanding shares.)

Bulk Transport's management considered the acquisition a "hostile" takeover. Amundsen responded he did not believe any of the shareholders who had sold their shares to Bergersen saw it that way. What do you think?

2. Rover Sells Out

Rover, the British automobile firm, announced in 1994 that it would sell controlling interest to BMW of Germany. Rover was 25% owned by Honda of Japan with which it had a strategic alliance and many cooperative agreements.

a. If you were Honda, how would you react to this new ownership structure?

b. Why do you think Rover sold out to BMW despite its partnership with Honda?

3. Japanese Direct Foreign Investment in the United States

Several Japanese firms have launched direct foreign investments in the United States, particularly in the automobile and electronics industries. What theories, if any, best explain the Japanese motives for these investments?

4. Japanese Direct Foreign Investment in Korea

Japanese firms have started new direct foreign investments in Korea. What do you think is the motivation behind these investments? What theories apply?

5. Pequot Indians and Foxwoods High Stakes Bingo and Casino

Firms often find it difficult to find capital for new and riskier investments. In 1992, the Pequot Indians of Ledyard, Connecticut (U.S.), wished to build and operate a casino on their reservation but could not find the capital necessary. After an extended search, a joint venture agreement was concluded with the Gentry Group, a Malaysian conglomerate with casino and gaming industry experience. The result was the formation of the Foxwoods High Stakes Bingo and Casino.

How would an international joint venture partner such as the Malaysian investment group in this case see the investment returns differently from a similar U.S.-based venture capital group?

6. Management Contracts Versus Direct Foreign Investment

What are the relative merits of management contracts compared to direct foreign investments? Answer this question both from the perspective of a host country as well as from the perspective of a firm that has the management contract.

7. Direct Foreign Investment in the Service Industries

Most of the service industries, such as accounting, law, advertising, and banking, have become multinational. What motivates these industries to establish offices abroad? What theories apply?

8. Joint Ventures

What are the advantages and disadvantages of joint ventures from the viewpoint of

    a.   the multinational firm?
    b.   the local joint venture partners?
    c.   the host country?

9. Licensing Versus Direct Foreign Investment

Compare licensing to direct foreign investment from the viewpoint of

    a.   the licensor (multinational firm)
    b.   the licensee (host country firm)
    c.   the host country

10. Networks of Multinational Corporations

Pick a multinational firm with which you are familiar. Identify and diagram its "network" in the home country, industry, and one host country of a foreign subsidiary.

11. Internationalization Process

Pick a multinational firm and trace its stages of internationalization from export to foreign subsidiary development. Identify the motives that explain the chronological order of countries into which it invested and expanded.

12. The Failed Merger of Volvo and Renault

One of the most ambitious, and in the end fruitless proposed mergers, was that in 1993 of Volvo of Sweden and Renault of France. Use your library to write a case history of this failed conglomeration.

    a.   What were the primary benefits that were thought to result from the merger?
    b.   Ultimately, what in the end do you believe caused the failure of the agreement? Could this failure have been foreseen?

Bibliography

Aharoni, Yair, *The Foreign Investment Decision Process,* Boston: Harvard Graduate School of Business Administration, Division of Research, 1966.

Akhter, Seyed H., and Robert F. Lusch, "Environmental Determinants of U.S. Foreign Direct Investment in Developed and Developing Countries: A Structural Analysis," *The International Trade Journal,* vol. 5, no. 3, Spring 1991, pp. 329–360.

Anderson, Erin, and Hubert Gatignon, "Modes of Foreign Entry: A Transaction Cost Analysis and Propositions," *Journal of International Business Studies,* Fall 1986, pp. 1–26.

Arpan, Jeffrey S., and David A. Ricks, "Foreign Direct Investment in the U.S., 1974–1984," *Journal of International Business Studies,* Fall 1986, pp. 149–154.

Beamish, Paul W., and John C. Banks, "Equity Joint Ventures and the Theory of the Multinational Enterprise," *Journal of International Business Studies,* Summer 1987, pp. 1–16.

BenDaniel, David J., and Arthur H. Rosenbloom, *The Handbook of International Mergers & Acquisitions,* Englewood Cliffs, N.J.: Prentice Hall, 1990.

Buckley, Peter J., "The Limits of Explanation: Testing the Internalization Theory of the Multinational Enterprise," *Journal of International Business Studies,* Summer 1988, pp. 181–193.

———, and Mark Casson, *The Future of the Multinational Enterprise,* London: Macmillan, 1976.

Casson, Mark, *The Firm and the Market: Studies on Multinational Enterprises and the Scope of the Firm,* Cambridge, Mass.: MIT Press, 1987.

Contractor, Farok J., "Ownership Patterns of U.S. Joint Ventures Abroad and the Liberalization of Foreign Government Regulations in the 1980s: Evidence from the Benchmark Surveys," *Journal of International Business Studies,* First Quarter 1990, pp. 55–73.

Doukas, John, and Nicholas G. Travlos, "The Effect of Corporate Multinationalism on Shareholders' Wealth: Evidence from International Acquisitions," *Journal of Finance,* December 1988, pp. 1161–1175.

Dunning, John H., *Explaining International Production,* Winchester, Mass.: Unwin Hyman, 1988.

———, "Trade Location of Economic Activity and the MNE: A Search for an Eclectic Approach," in *The International Allocation of Economic Activity,* Bertil Ohlin, Per-Ove Hesselborn, and Per Magnus Wijkman, eds., New York: Holmes and Meier, 1977, pp. 395–418.

———, "The Eclectic Paradigm of International Production: A Restatement and Some Possible Extensions," *Journal of International Business Studies,* Spring 1988, pp. 1–32.

———, ed., *Multinational Enterprises, Economic Structure, and International Competitiveness,* New York: Wiley, 1985.

———, and Alan M. Rugman, "The Influence of Hymer's Dissertation on the Theory of Foreign Direct Investment," *American Economic Review,* May 1985, pp. 228–232.

Ehrman, Chaim Meyer, and Morris Hamburg, "Information Search for Foreign Direct Investment Using Two-Stage Country Selection Procedures: A New Procedure," *Journal of International Business Studies,* Summer 1986, pp. 93–116.

Forsgren, Mats, *Managing the Internationalization Process: The Swedish Case,* London: Routledge, 1989.

Franko, Lawrence G., "Use of Minority and 50–50 Joint Ventures by United States Multinationals During the 1970s: The Interaction of Host Country Policies and Corporate Strategies," *Journal of International Business Studies,* Spring 1989, pp. 19–40.

Geringer, J. Michael, and Louis Hebert, "Control and Performance of International Joint Ventures," *Journal of International Business Studies,* Summer 1989, pp. 235–254.

Ghertman, Michel, "Foreign Subsidiary and Parents' Roles During Strategic Investment and Divestment Decisions," *Journal of International Business Studies,* Spring 1988, pp. 47–68.

Gomes-Casseres, Benjamin, "Firm Ownership Preferences and Host Government Restrictions: An Integrated Approach," *Journal of International Business Studies,* First Quarter 1990, pp. 1–22.

Gordon, Sara L., and Francis A. Lees, *Foreign Multinational Investment in the United States: Struggle for Industrial Supremacy,* Westport, Conn.: Quorum Books, 1986.

Grosse, Robert, "The Theory of Foreign Direct Investment," *Essays in International Business,* Columbia: University of South Carolina, Center for International Business Studies, December 1981.

Gruber, W., D. Mehta, and R. Vernon, "The R&D Factor in International Trade and Investment of United States Industries," *Journal of Political Economy,* February 1967, pp. 20–37.

Hedlund, Gunnar, "The Hypermodern MNC—A Heterarchy?," *Human Resource Management,* Volume 25, Number 1, pp. 9–35.

Hennart, Jean-François, "Internalization in Practice: Early Foreign Direct Investment in Malaysian Tin Mining," *Journal of International Business Studies,* Summer 1986, pp. 131–144.

————, "Can the New Forms of Investment Substitute for the Old Forms?' A Transaction Costs Perspective," *Journal of International Business Studies,* Summer 1989, pp. 211–234.

Hisey, Karen B., and Richard E. Caves, "Diversification Strategy and Choice of Country: Diversifying Acquisitions Abroad by U.S. Multinationals, 1978–1980," *Journal of International Business Studies,* Summer 1985, pp. 51–64.

Horaguchi, Haruo, and Brian Toyne, "Setting the Record Straight: Hymer, Internalization Theory and Transaction Cost Economics," *Journal of International Business Studies,* Third Quarter 1990, pp. 487–494.

Hymer, Stephen H., *The International Operations of National Firms: A Study of Direct Foreign Investment,* Cambridge, Mass.: MIT Press, 1976.

Kim, Wi Saeng, and Esmerelda O. Lyn, "FDI Theories and the Performance of Foreign Multinationals Operating in the U.S.," *Journal of International Business Studies,* First Quarter 1990, pp. 41–54.

Kimura, Yui, "Firm-Specific Strategic Advantages and Foreign Direct Investment Behavior of Firms: The Case of Japanese Semiconductor Firms," *Journal of International Business Studies,* Summer 1989, pp. 296–314.

Kogut, Bruce, and Harbir Singh, "The Effect of National Culture on the Choice of Entry Mode," *Journal of International Business Studies,* Fall 1988, pp. 411–432.

Kogut, Bruce, and Udo Zander, "Knowledge of the Firm and the Evolutionary Theory of the Multinational Corporation," *Journal of International Business Studies,* Fourth Quarter, 1993, pp. 625–645.

Mascarenhas, Briance, "International Strategies of Non-Dominant Firms," *Journal of International Business Studies,* Spring 1986, pp. 1–26.

Moxon, Richard W., "The Motivation for Investment in Offshore Plants: The Case of the U.S. Electronics Industry," *Journal of International Business Studies,* Spring 1975, pp. 51–66.

Murray, Alan I., and Carne Siehl, *Joint Ventures and Other Alliances: Creating a Successful Cooperative Linkage,* New York: Financial Executive Research Foundation, 1989.

Nigh, Douglas, "The Effect of Political Events on United States Direct Foreign Investment: A Pooled Time-Series Cross-Sectional Analysis," *Journal of International Business Studies,* Spring 1985, pp. 1–17.

Porter, Michael, *The Competitive Advantage of Nations,* London: Macmillan Press, 1990.

Ravichandran, R., and J. Michael Pinegar, "Risk Shifting in International Licensing Agreements: A Note," *Journal of International Financial Management and Accounting,* vol. 2, nos. 2 and 3, Summer and Autumn 1990, pp. 181–195.

Rugman, Alan, "Internalization Is Still a General Theory of Foreign Direct Investment," *Weltwirtschaftliches Archiv,* September 1985.

Sleuwaegen, Leo, "Monopolistic Advantages and the International Operations of Firms: Disaggregated Evidence from U.S. Based

Multinationals," *Journal of International Business Studies,* Fall 1985, pp. 125–134.

Swamidass, Paul M., "A Comparison of the Plant Location Strategies of Foreign and Domestic Manufacturers in the U.S.," *Journal of International Business Studies,* Second Quarter 1990, pp. 301–317.

Tallman, Stephen B., "Home Country Political Risk and Foreign Direct Investment in the United States," *Journal of International Business Studies,* Summer 1988, pp. 219–234.

Terpstra, Vern, and Chwo-Ming Yu, "Determinants of Foreign Investment of U.S. Advertising Agencies," *Journal of International Business Studies,* Spring 1988, pp. 33–46.

Vernon, Raymond, "International Investment and International Trade in the Product Cycle," *Quarterly Journal of Economics,* May 1966, pp. 190–207.

———, "The Product Cycle Hypothesis in a New Internationai Environment," *Oxford Bulletin of Economics and Statistics,* vol. 41, 1979, pp. 255–267.

Yang, Ho C., James W. Wansley, and William R. Lane, "A Direct Test of the Diversification Service Hypothesis of Foreign Direct Investment," *Advances in Financial Planning and Forecasting,* vol. 4, part A, 1990, pp. 215–238.

Yu, Chwo-Ming J., and Kiyohiko Ito, "Oligopolistic Reaction and Foreign Direct Investment: The Case of the U.S. Tire and Textiles Industries," *Journal of International Business Studies,* Fall 1988, pp. 449–460.

Chapter 18
Political Risk Management

Global View
Foreign Investment in China

A great deal of China's progress has been produced through joint ventures and foreign investment. But there's good foreign investment and bad foreign investment. A foreign investment is good if it comes in at roughly the same terms as domestic investment and generates good returns both for the investors and for the Chinese. But you know, very few foreign investors come to China to benefit China. They come in to make money. And one way they make money is by taking advantage of the special privileges the government has been conferring on foreign investors. Foreign investment that is attracted primarily by those privileges is good for the investor, but not for China. There really is no free lunch. Somebody has to pay for this.

If there's a lot of money to be made, people try to make it. And indeed, let me say a quick word in favor of corruption. In many cases much of what's called corruption is simply a black market that undoes the harm which is being done by the attempt by government to interfere with market practices. What's a black market? It's a market, a free market. And so what's called corruption is sometimes, not always, an introduction of market forces into a controlled economy.

Source: Milton Friedman, "China's Coming Revolution." An October 28, 1993 speech for the Hong Kong Centre for Economic Research, University of Hong Kong. Reprinted with permission.

Multinational firms are influenced by political events within host countries and by changes in political relationship between host countries, home countries, and even third countries. The possibility of such events occurring and having an influence on the economic well-being of the parent firm is called *political risk*. Although political events can have a positive or negative effect, managerial attention usually focuses on possible negative events.

Political risk management refers to steps taken by firms to assess the likelihood of unexpected political events, to anticipate how such events might influence corporate well-being, and to protect against loss (or to attempt to gain) from such events. This chapter classifies various types of political risk and identifies financially related techniques that reduce exposure to political risk.

For the first half of the twentieth century, political risk was more or less synonymous with expropriation of private assets, and often just foreign-owned private assets, by governments opposed to foreigners owning property or doing business within a country. Events in the latter half of the century have required a broadening of this definition. Stephen Kobrin has classified contemporary political risks along two dimensions. The first dimension distinguishes between *country-specific,* or macro, risks that affect all foreign firms in a country without regard to what they do, and *firm-specific,* or micro, risks that are specific to an industry, a firm, or a project.[1] Country-specific risk is of most concern to international bankers, who often set overall loan limits to specific countries based on their perception of country risk.[2] Firm-specific risk is of greater concern for multinational firms.

Kobrin's second dimension distinguishes between those political events that affect ownership of assets, such as requiring full or partial divestment, and those that affect the operations of a firm and thus its cash flows and returns.

Kobrin argues that most contemporary political risk for multinational firms involves firm-specific risks and operations rather than ownership. Consequently, political risk seldom leads to violence or a major discontinuity in the firm's operations. Most often politically inspired changes involve constraints, such as restrictions on the free setting of prices, limitations on the use of expatriate executives or workers, or local content regulations for manufactured goods.[3]

Taking into account changes in the world economic scene since the 1991 collapse of the Soviet Union, the current spectrum of political risks can be classified as shown in Exhibit 18.1.

---

[1]Stephen J. Kobrin, *Managing Political Risk Assessment: Strategic Response to Environmental Change,* Berkeley: University of California Press, 1982, p. 35.

[2]See, for example, Swiss Bank Corporation's detailed explanation of its own country risk assessment approach in its *Economic & Financial Prospects: Supplement,* February/March 1988.

[3]Kobrin, *Managing Political Risk Assessment,* 1982.

Exhibit 18.1   Micro-Macro Decomposition of Political Risk

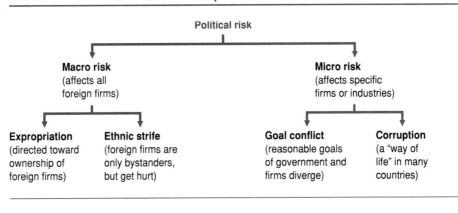

Macro Risks

Macro political risks include both expropriation and ethnic strife.

Expropriation Risk

To a reader briefed on world history in the years right after the Second World War, "political risk" brings to mind the abrupt expropriations of both domestic and foreign private businesses in eastern Europe and China as those territories came under communist control. Similar expropriations occurred in Cuba in 1960 after Fidel Castro imposed a communist government, and in Iran following the 1979 ouster of the shah by the Ayatollah Khomeini. Other examples also date from decades ago: Chile expropriated a number of U.S. companies, including several U.S. copper companies in 1971. Peru took over a subsidiary of Exxon in 1968. Libya expropriated Occidental Petroleum's oil fields in 1969. As one can see from the dates of these examples, expropriation has not been a major event for multinational firms in recent decades.

Expropriation is defined as official government seizure of private property. It is recognized by international law as the right of any sovereign state, provided the expropriated owners are given prompt compensation at fair market value in convertible currencies. Therein lies the rub, for promptness is usually delayed by extensive negotiations and appeals. Fair market value is in the eyes of the beholder, with firms usually arguing for a "going concern" value tied to the present value of lost future cash flows. Governments frequently argue for depreciated historical book value, which is typically lower. Prompt compensation in convertible currencies is usually difficult, for the kinds of governments given to expropriation do not usually have adequate foreign exchange reserves. Hence "payment" may be in par value of long-term bonds of dubious current market value.

Risk from Ethnic, Racial, Religious, Tribal, or Civil Strife

The decade of the 1990s has seen the sudden rise of a second type of macro political risk, caused by ethnic, racial, religious, tribal, or civil strife within a country. It has sprung forth at this time in history because of the sudden end of the overarching tension that had previously existed between the Soviet Union and the Euro-American alliance, which had as a by-product the suppression of "minor" conflicts. The most obvious examples at the present time are the slaughter in Bosnia and Herzegovina, and the general breakdown of any local authority in Somalia and Rwanda. The six-year-long war between Iran and Iraq, the Iraqi invasion of Kuwait in 1991, and the upsurge of Islamic fundamentalism in Algeria and Egypt, with attendant murders of foreigners, are other contemporary examples.

Civil strife arises when government authorities are unsure of their status or survival. This is the situation in Russia at the present time (1994), where the presumed democratic and privatization goals of President Boris Yeltsin are being contested by a democratically elected radical nationalist, Vladimir Zhirinovsky. A similar situation existed in post-Tiananmen China after 1989, but China's firm stance (no matter how brutal) against a disintegration of authority ameliorated business fears by the mid-1990s. The rise of neo-Nazism in Germany sits on the horizon as a potentially destabilizing force. The underlying principle is that when the basic nature of governance is changing rapidly, a firm cannot be sure which governmental representative speaks (or will be speaking next year) for the host country.

Strife between domestic forces, be they ethnic, tribal, religious, or political, may well become the major political risk for multinational firms in the remainder of this century. For the most part, multinational firms are bystanders, but threats to these firms, or to foreigners as individuals, create a significant macro risk to international business and investment.

Micro Risk: Goal Conflict

Micro risk is the second major form of contemporary political risk. Some micro risk arises from corruption, which we discuss later. The most important type of micro risk arises from a conflict between bona fide objectives of governments and private firms. Governments are normally responsive to a constituency consisting of their citizens. Firms are responsive to a constituency consisting of their owners and other stakeholders. The valid needs of these two separate sets of constituents need not be the same, but it is governments that set the rules. Consequently, governments impose constraints on the activities of private firms as part of their normal administrative and legislative functioning.

Goal Conflicts

Historically, conflicts between objectives of multinational firms and host governments have arisen over such issues as the firm's impact on economic development, perceived infringement on national sovereignty, foreign control of key industries, sharing of ownership and control with local interests, impact on a host country's balance of payments, influence on the foreign exchange value of its currency, control over export markets, use of domestic versus foreign executives and workers, and "exploitation" of natural resources. Attitudes about conflicts are often colored by views toward free enterprise versus state socialism, the degree of nationalism or internationalism present, or the place of religious views in determining appropriate economic and financial behavior.

From the viewpoint of the multinational firm, all national economic, political, social, cultural, and ideological goals, as well as the policy instruments to accomplish them, are parameters that circumscribe the firm's activities. It is unfortunate for the multinational firm that often government policies are unclear, or that two or more policies seem to be contradictory. Such ambiguity exists because ordering and implementing national priorities is not a science. Multinational firms must learn to live with such ambiguity. The important thing to remember is that they must be able to anticipate and adapt to changing national priorities and the resulting changes in the policy instruments.

Even when multinational firms succeed in adapting to host country priorities, host country governments may still feel ambivalent toward them. No consensus exists on what constitutes favorable or unfavorable performance by multinational firms with respect to national goals. Most empirical studies show a favorable impact of foreign-owned firms on such host country economic goals as growth, employment, price stability, and balance of payments. Such views are currently popular in ex-communist countries, as well as in China and Vietnam, which still claim to be communist. However, no methodology has been developed that quantifies the impact foreign-owned firms have on a host country's less tangible political, social, cultural, and ideological goals.

An attempt at understanding can be obtained by looking first at potential goal conflicts between the multinational firm and government economic policies and then at the multinational firm's impact on government noneconomic policies.

Goal Conflicts and Government Economic Policies

National economic priorities vary, but most countries seek a sustainable rate of growth in per capita gross national product and income, full employment, price stability, balance in their external accounts, and a fair distribution of income. Operations of multinational firms sometimes interfere with the smooth functioning of policy instruments chosen by the government to attain these ends. Major areas where conflict may arise include the following:

1. Monetary policy.
2. Fiscal policy.
3. Balance of payments and exchange rate policy.
4. Economic protectionism.
5. Economic development policies.

Monetary Policy. Governments want to control the cost and availability of domestic credit and long-term capital as a means of achieving the national economic priorities just listed. Affiliates of multinational firms in such a country are subject to these same monetary and credit constraints. However, they can often circumvent the spirit of such financial constraints, even when complying with the letter of the law. If local credit becomes too expensive or unavailable because of purposeful national monetary policy, the affiliate may turn to its parent or to sister affiliates for additional capital. Thus the affiliate is able to implement its spending plans while local, often smaller, competitors are restricted because of a lack of access to external capital.

National monetary policy is also frustrated when multinational firms suddenly convert large amounts of foreign exchange into local currency to buy out a local company or carry out a large new investment. Multinationals may also move excess working capital or speculative funds temporarily to other countries while riding out a foreign exchange crisis (so-called hot money flows). These activities create an instant change in the local money supply, which has to be offset by central bank open market or other operations. Hence multinational firm activities may be viewed as frustrating national monetary policy.

Fiscal Policy. Operations of multinational firms may influence government revenues and government expenses. On the revenue side, tax concessions used to lure the firm to that country mean the government fails to receive revenue it might later need. Recognizing such a concession is the fault of the government that granted it, a succeeding administration may denounce the actions of its predecessors and invalidate previous agreements. On the expenditure side, greenfield investments by multinational firms may create a need for governmental spending on new roads or railroads, public utilities, housing, schools, and health facilities. The government may lack the revenue to provide these. When a multinational firm provides them, a dependency relationship is established and the foreign firm may be accused of paternalism or economic imperialism.

Balance of Payments and Exchange Rate Policies. Balance of payments and exchange rate problems may lead governments to promulgate regulations that hamper the operations of foreign-owned firms. Latin American countries, in particular, have resorted to frequent devaluations, use of multiple exchange rates for different categories of imports and exports, licensing of imports, import deposit requirements, demands for extended credit terms to finance imports, and refinancing outstanding debt with loans from foreign lenders where possible. Exchange control, including inconvertibility of currency, can be particularly damaging to multinational firms because local inflation typically diminishes the value of blocked funds. Nevertheless, multinational firms must understand both the causes and likely policy responses to a host country's balance of payments deficit or strong pressure on its currency.

Economic Protectionism. National economic policy constraints are often motivated by protectionism, sometimes under the guise of balance of payments policies and sometimes under the guise of economic development. Negotiations under the General Agreement on Tariffs and Trade (GATT) have reduced the general level of tariffs during the past three decades, but nontariff barriers remain. Nontariff barriers, which restrict imports by something other than a financial cost, are often difficult to identify because they are promulgated as health, safety, or sanitation requirements. A list of the major types of nontariff barriers is shown in Exhibit 18.2. Removal of nontariff barriers was the main objective of the Uruguay Round of GATT negotiations that was concluded in 1994 after 8 years of tough negotiations.

Exhibit 18.2   Types of Nontariff Barriers

1. Specific limitations on trade, which either limit the amount of imports directly or establish import procedures that make importing more difficult.
   a. Quotas, which limit the quantity or value allowed for specific imported products for specific time periods.
   b. Licensing requirements that must be met before trading.
   c. Proportion restrictions of foreign to domestic goods or content.
   d. Minimum import price limits set equal to or above domestic prices.
   e. Embargoes prohibiting products originating in specific countries.
2. Customs and administrative entry procedures, which include inconsistent procedures for valuation, classification of documents, or assessing fees.
   a. Valuation of imports on an arbitrary basis at the discretion of customs officials.
   b. Antidumping countermeasures against imported goods sold below prices in the home market of the exporter.
   c. Tariff classifications that are inconsistent.
   d. Documentation requirements that are overburdensome.
   e. Fees charged to cover costs of entry procedures.
3. Unduly stringent or discriminating standards imposed in the name of protecting health, safety, and quality.
   a. Disparities between quality standards required by different countries.
   b. Differing intergovernmental acceptance standards or testing methods.
   c. Application of packaging and labeling standards in unduly stringent or discriminating ways.
4. Governmental participation in trade.
   a. Government procurement policies that favor domestic over imported products without regard to relative price or quality.
   b. Export subsidies, either directly or via taxes or export credit terms, provided by government.
   c. Countervailing duties charged by importing country to offset export subsidies granted by exporting country.
   d. Domestic assistance programs granted all domestic producers, both exporters and those producing for domestic consumption.
5. Charges on imports.
   a. Prior import deposit requirements, requiring a non-interest-bearing deposit equal to some percentage of import value (sometimes up to 100%) to be deposited prior to time of import and refunded at a later date. The "cost" is equal to the cost of capital on the funds so tied up.
   b. Border tax adjustments, in which border taxes are levied on imports to tax them in the same manner as domestic goods and are rebated on exports. Countries relying on indirect taxes (such as the value-added taxes used in Europe) are given an advantage over countries relying on direct taxes (such as corporate income taxes), since indirect taxes can be rebated but direct taxes cannot be rebated.
   c. Administrative fees levied.
   d. Special supplementary duties levied.
   e. Import credit discrimination.
   f. Variable levies.
6. Other nontariff barriers.
   a. Voluntary export restraints by exporting country, often at the request (with or without political pressure) of the importing country.
   b. Orderly marketing agreements, wherein countries agree formally to restrict trade.

Source: Adapted from material in A.D. Cao, "Non-Tariff Barriers to U.S. Manufactured Exports," *Columbia Journal of World Business,* Summer 1980, pp. 93–102.

Economic Development Policies. Protection of "infant industries" is sometimes advanced as a valid argument for protective tariffs or restrictions on foreign investment, even though many industries are protected long after they have matured. Historical examples include requirements in India, Mexico, Brazil, and Argentina that multinational firms manufacture an increasing proportion of components locally rather than assemble imported components with a minimum of local manufacture. Automobile firms are particularly vulnerable to such rules. Other restrictive rules require local majority ownership in joint ventures. Similar requirements specify mostly local rather than expatriate managers. While such requirements have some merit in the context of goal-driven governmental policies, they often inhibit a multinational firm from rationalizing production on a worldwide basis, and thus from lowering costs and sales prices to consumers.

Although direct foreign investment has often been heralded as contributing to economic development and is eagerly sought by many developing countries, the very fulfillment of its promise has often unintentionally created a "dual economy." Local citizens associated with the foreign firms, either as employees or suppliers, have prospered and advanced economically to become an elite class. Other citizens, untouched by the foreign firms or industry sector being developed, are left in their original state of poverty. Thus a two-class society is created, causing its own problems of internal dissension, jealousy, greed, and graft. The early plantation, oil, and mining investments were often the inadvertent victims of their own success, having been blamed for creating these dual economies.

Goal Conflicts and Noneconomic Policies

Even when all political groups within a host country agree that direct foreign investment is good economically for the country, some may oppose it on noneconomic grounds. Two common noneconomic arguments against multinational firms are (1) economic imperialism, and (2) national security and foreign policy.

Economic Imperialism. In many ex-colonial countries a widespread suspicion exists that multinational firms represent a new and invidious form of imperialism, albeit economic rather than political or military. These countries often fail to differentiate between profit-motivated private foreign enterprises and the home governments of such firms—a failure helped greatly when home governments seek a ban on foreign investments in politically unpopular countries. U.S. congressional pressure against granting Most Favored Nation (MFN) treatment to China because of its human rights abuses, although possibly justified on other grounds, gives credence to the idea that private firms are, after all, under the thumb of their home governments. It is not yet clear in the ideology of free enterprise at what point, short of war, a government should override the economic independence of its own multinational businesses.

It seems obvious to most U.S. citizens that the U.S. government and business do not cooperate closely on direct foreign investments. In fact, much U.S. political activity seems predicated on government and popular distrust of business and so suggests the opposite. Other governments, such as Japan, however actively support and encourage their own multinational firms, seeing such policies as necessary for a strong economy.

National Security and Foreign Policy. Host countries sometimes become alarmed that foreign control of key industry sectors will impair national security or an independent foreign policy. One need only read Servan-Schreiber's classic *The American Challenge* to perceive the French attitude of a quarter century ago toward U.S. dominance of the French computer, electronics, and other defense-related industries.[4] Canada screens and controls new direct foreign investments because of its concern that more than half of Canadian manufacturing and mining is U.S. owned, including most of the growth sectors and those related to national security. Japan severely restricts imports of foreign rice and certain other foodstuffs as part of a policy of remaining self-sufficient in food, albeit at an inordinately high cost to consumers. The United States blocked the Japanese purchase of Fairchild Industries in 1987 on grounds of national security. Fairchild was in the electronics business and had been the incubator for some of the most successful high-technology companies, including Intel, in the United States.

Micro Risk: Corruption

Although most contemporary political risk arises from goal conflict, political corruption and blackmail contribute to the risk of managing a foreign direct investment. Examples abound.

A 1989 political scandal in Venezuela arose after foreign corporations had legally transmitted funds out of the country through a government agency, Recadi, created to administer Venezuela's complex foreign exchange regulations. The agency was abolished early in 1989 by the new Venezuelan president, and an investigation started over alleged corruption. At the beginning of the investigation, arrest warrants were issued for some 47 foreign executives, and 60 others were ordered not to leave the country. About 100 top executives from major multinational firms were reported to have fled the country, not because they considered themselves guilty, but because under the Venezuelan judicial system they could be held in prison, without bail, for a very long time while claims against their firm were investigated.[5]

Firestone Tire and Rubber Company was reported to have sold all but 19% of its 70% interest in a Kenya factory after experiencing a prolonged period of delays in obtaining licenses to import critical raw materials, nonapproval of work permits for expatriate technicians, nonapproval of requests for price increases, and delays in approval of plans for plant expansion. After the sale to a holding company with ties to Kenya's president, the company's problems disappeared. Almost half of U.S.-owned

---

[4]J.J. Servan-Schreiber, *The American Challenge,* London: Hamish Hamilton, 1968.

[5]"A Crackdown in Caracas Sends Foreign Executives Fleeing," *Business Week,* July 31, 1989, p. 46; and "Many Executives Flee Venezuela in Scandal over Dollar Reserves—Even Multinational Officials Who Aren't Implicated Fear Jail and Slow Justice," *Wall Street Journal,* August 24, 1989, p. 1.

companies in Kenya are reported to have reduced their equities to as little as 14% by selling out to Kenyans with powerful political connections.[6]

Corruption is endemic in many developing countries. Chinese officials announced in early 1994 that some 300,000 officials, one-fifth of all cadres, in Anhui province, one of China's poorest, had been caught siphoning off or misusing public funds. Both Chinese and foreigners had complained that officials would deny services until they received "gifts" which ranged from a few packs of foreign cigarettes to cash, prostitutes, apartments, or offshore slush funds to pay the overseas tuition of their children.[7]

The *Asian Wall Street Journal* carried an article with a check list for doing business in Cambodia, a country returning to democracy after two decades of war and chaos.[8] Noting that potential gains in Cambodia far outweighed the difficulties posed by greedy and incompetent bureaucrats, the author nevertheless suggested a list of defensive activities, which shows the difficulty of operating in some parts of the world:

- Refuse bribery outright, or else demands will quickly multiply.

- Retain a knowledgeable local adviser, who among other tasks can diffuse demands by local officials for more taxes or operating fees than are required.

- Choose one's Cambodian partner with care, because under existing laws foreigners have little recourse if a local partner turns on them.

- Don't count on the justice system because it barely exists. Partners, suppliers, and officials can cheat with near impunity.

- Be prepared to spend lots of time at the airport and docks because imports will be held up in hope of a payoff or because paperwork is deemed incomplete.

- Spend lots of time training and overseeing local workers and be prepared to teach everything from personal hygiene to telephone usage. Educational levels are very low because most educated Cambodians did not live through the past 20 years of conflict.

- Plan for decayed and nonexistent infrastructure because most of the country's roads, bridges, and utilities have been all but destroyed. (Cellular phones are better than depending on a wired phone service.)

- Try to prevent theft, especially of vehicles, by hiring armed guards.

Host Government Regulations That Hinder Operations of Multinational Firms

In the pursuit of national goals, host governments often adopt laws and administrative rules that hinder operations of business firms in their jurisdictions. Either inadvertently

---

[6]"Kenya Corruption Overwhelms Investors," *Los Angeles Times,* Part I, June 25, 1989, p. 4.

[7]"Charges Against 300,000 Officials Reveal Deep Corruption in China," *Asian Wall Street Journal,* January 5, 1994; and "China: Corruption Suspects," *Far Eastern Economic Review,* January 20, 1994, p. 15.

[8]Sheila McNulty, "Welcome to Cambodia's Business Wilderness," *Asian Wall Street Journal,* January 13, 1994, p. 6.

or through intent such rules may be particularly burdensome to multinational firms. Regulations with the most potential for conflict can be classified as nondiscriminatory, discriminatory, and wealth depriving.

Nondiscriminatory Regulation

Nondiscriminatory regulations are usually mild and not particularly directed against foreign-controlled operations. Often they have an equal impact on foreign subsidiaries, joint ventures, local firms with management or licensing agreements with foreign firms, and purely domestic firms. Some examples of nondiscriminatory regulations are the following:

- Requiring that local nationals hold top management positions or seats on boards of directors.

- Establishing rules for transfer pricing that favor the host country's tax base.

- Requiring export industries to sell in the home market at a break-even price in order to subsidize local consumption of the particular product. (A common example is pharmaceutical firms.)

- Requiring construction of social overhead facilities (schools, workers' housing and health-care facilities, roads) by the investing firm.

- Requiring a given percentage of local content in manufactured goods.

- Allocating all foreign exchange to purchases deemed in the national interest, and consequently restricting the availability of foreign exchange for such "nonessential" purposes as dividends or royalty fee payments.

Discriminatory Regulation

Discriminatory regulations give local firms or national groups specific advantages over foreign firms. Often the intent is to protect weaker local firms from local-based foreign competition, much in the way that tariffs protect local firms from import competition. Some examples follow:

- Nationalizing an industry dominated by foreigners. In 1988, Brazil's Congress approved a constitutional provision that "exploration and mining of mineral resources and deposits may be carried out only by Brazilians or national companies" with government authorization.[9] The vote, 343 to 126, was reportedly followed by cheers of "Brazil, Brazil, Brazil," and singing of the national anthem by congressmen. Opposing congressmen pointed out that Brazilian businesses did not have the capital required for successful mining and the provision was "xenophobic" and detrimental to Brazil's development.[10]

- Allowing only joint ventures, with the foreign firms limited to less than 50% ownership. Local control may be required directly, or as a criteria for access to credit from local banks or the right to sell to the local government.

---

[9]"Brazil Plans to Bar Foreign Firms from Mining," *Los Angeles Times,* April 30, 1988.

[10]Ibid.

- Requiring special taxes or fees for a foreign firm to operate locally. Foreign firms, for example, may have to pay very high visa fees for expatriate managers, or very high income taxes on expatriates' salaries, which are based on salary levels back home.

- Requiring foreign firms to source labor through a host government agency, and to pay wages and social charges set by the government at a higher level than those required for local firms.

Wealth Deprivation by Host Governments

Wealth deprivation involves host government regulations that cause economic loss for foreign firms. That loss may be partial, as when the result is to weaken a foreign firm, or total, as in cases of expropriation. Wealth deprivation may take the form of nationalization of an entire industry or expropriation of a single firm.

Examples of wealth deprivation short of expropriation include the following:

- Enforcing price controls with threats. In 1988, a Brazilian court suspended price controls imposed on Autolatina, a holding company for Ford Motor Company and Volkswagen. The suspension was for the period the courts were to consider Autolatina's claim that such controls were illegal under Brazilian law. When Autolatina raised prices on the day after the price controls were suspended, the Brazilian Ministry of Finance ordered official bank credit cut off to the company, called in tax inspectors to examine Autolatina's books, and threatened to arrest Autolatina officials.[11] The Brazilian court subsequently ordered the government to stop punitive measures against Autolatina, but also rescinded its order suspending the price controls.

- Restricting distribution of products. In late 1986 and in 1987, the Singaporean government imposed severe circulation restrictions on the *Asian Wall Street Journal, Time, Asia Week,* and the *Far Eastern Economic Review.* The restrictions were punishment for unfavorable press coverage of the mid-1987 "detentions" (that is, imprisonments) without trial of 22 persons alleged to have organized a Marxist plot to overthrow the government. The government claimed it did not need to prove the allegations in a court of law.[12] Lee Hsien Loong, Singapore's minister for trade and industry, son of the then prime minister and a person widely regarded as the prime minister's eventual successor, stated, "In some cases, restricting the circulation of the journal is a sufficient countermeasure" because it "hurts its sales and advertising revenues, but does not deprive Singaporeans of access to information."[13] In 1990 the *Asian Wall Street Journal* stopped all circulation in Singapore because of the pressure.

---

[11]"Brazilian Court Sanctions Ford, VW Price Increase," *Wall Street Journal,* November 11, 1987.

[12] "Gov't Cuts Review's Sales to 500 Copies," *Straits Times* (overseas edition), January 2, 1988, p. 1.

[13]"When the Press Misinforms," address by Brig-Gen (Res) Lee Hsien Loong, minister for trade and industry and second minister for defense (services), Singapore, at the 40th World Congress of Newspaper Publishers on May 26, 1987, at Helsinki, Finland. Singapore Government Press Release, no. 40/May 15—1/87/05/26, p. 13.

- Imposing restrictions on dividends and mandating reinvestment. In 1985, Peruvian police armed with submachine guns seized U.S.-owned Belco Petroleum Company's Lima headquarters. This followed nationalization of the company, taking control of its assets, and freezing of its bank accounts. Peruvian president Alan Garcia claimed that Belco had refused to accept new conditions for required reinvestment of its profits in new exploration and production.[14]

Home Country Attempts at Wealth Deprivation

Not all attempts at wealth deprivation come from foreign governments. Home country political action groups, as well as home country governments, sometimes try to put their own companies in a bind. The U.S. Congress, in particular, often seeks domestic political gain by promulgating laws that hurt the international competitiveness of American firms. The decade-long prohibition on doing business in Vietnam is an example. The case in favor of ending the quarter-century old boycott has been stated: "The net effect of the American embargo is not to deny Vietnam access to western technology and financing, but rather to penalise U.S. companies to the benefit of our foreign competitors."[15] A side effect is that the boycott probably slows down rather than accelerates discovery of what happened to U.S. military personnel missing in action in the Vietnam war.

A similar claim can be made about U.S. policy on Cuba, which many assert to be dominated by political pressure from wealthy, conservative, anti-Castro Cuban exiles in Florida. A provision of the U.S. Cuban Democracy Act bars any vessel that enters Cuba from unloading freight in U.S. ports for 180 days after leaving Cuba. Britain has made it an offense for any person to comply with the extraterritorial provisions of the Act, and Canada has similarly objected. The United Nations General Assembly overwhelmingly sided with Cuba in condemning the embargo by a vote of 88 to 4 (Albania, Israel, Paraguay, and the United States) with 57 abstentions.[16]

The key issue is whether U.S. business should be allowed to deal with governments that the United States would like to censor, as compared to the view that a continued presence by U.S. business is likely to be advantageous in the long run. In line with the example just cited, in 1990 Vietnam Airlines was prevented from buying two European Airbus A310's to upgrade its international services. The purchase was blocked by the United States on the grounds the engines were manufactured in the United States. A political risk cost was imposed by the United States on its allies, France and the United Kingdom. Vietnam Airlines subsequently purchased six used Soviet-built Tupulov TU134's.[17]

---

[14] "Peru Seizes Assets of U.S. Oil Company," *Los Angeles Times,* December 29, 1985. Also see "Occidental Petroleum Avoids Seizure in Peru; Belco's Status Unclear," *Los Angeles Times,* December 28, 1985.

[15] Letter to U.S. President Clinton, initiated by Virginia Foote of the U.S.-Vietnam Trade Council and signed by 20 major U.S. companies. Susumu Awanohara, "Approaching Normal," *Far Eastern Economic Review,* January 20, 1994, pp. 12–13.

[16] "Change the Cuba Policy," editorial from the *New York Times* reprinted in the *International Herald Tribune,* November 9, 1993, p. 4.

[17] "Vietnam Opens Up to the West," *Far Eastern Economic Review,* November 29, 1990, p. 50.

In 1988, a U.S. grand jury indicted Manuel Noriega, then dictator of Panama, for drug dealings. The U.S. Internal Revenue Service then issued regulations instructing U.S. corporations in Panama that they would receive credit against their U.S. taxes for Panamanian taxes paid only if those taxes were paid to deposed Panamanian president Eric A. Delvalle. The goal was to deny cash to the Noriega regime, but one effect was to put U.S. corporations into the middle of a political squabble.

Global View
The U.S.'s Country-Risk Problem

The Von Roll company of Gerlafingen, Switzerland, is a global powerhouse in antipollution technology. Its recent triumphs include creating the world's most advanced hazardous waste incinerator. Built in Germany, this machine now merrily converts the toxic byproducts of German industry into benign compounds that don't poison the air and water. But Von Roll is in trouble with its gimlet-eyed Swiss banks. It seems the company was crazy enough to bring its technology to America and invest here.

"I don't want to compare the U.S. to Latin America, but when our banks are talking about 'country risk' in the U.S., it tells you something," says Rudolf Zaengerie, Von Roll's chief of environmental engineering.

Congress long ago divined the need for incineration and gave EPA [Environmental Protection Agency] the job of approving new projects. Yet after 13 years, $160 million and an unbroken string of 21 legal and regulatory victories, Von Roll's incinerator on the Ohio River sits idle. Whatever the law says, the plant makes an easy target for all kinds of political opportunists and legal harassers, from Greenpeace to Al Gore. So instead of vaporizing noxious gunk and making the world a cleaner place, Von Roll spends all its time in court and press conferences.

Foreign investors aren't the enemy. In today's world, what matters isn't where a company is headquartered, but where it chooses to build its factories and labs and offices. Von Roll's legalized water torture has been picked up by the European press and television. The message they're sending out doesn't bode well for winning America's share of the world's jobs and opportunities.

Assessing Political Risk

How can multinational firms anticipate government regulations which, from the firm's perspective, are discriminatory or wealth depriving? Normally a twofold approach is utilized.

At the macro level, firms attempt to assess a host country's political stability and attitude toward foreign investors. At the micro level, firms analyze whether their firm-specific activities are likely to conflict with host country goals as evidenced by existing regulations. The most difficult task, however, is to anticipate changes in host country goal priorities, new regulations to implement reordered priorities, and the likely impact of such changes on the firm's operations.

Predicting Political Stability

Macro political risk analysis is still an emerging field of study. Political scientists in academia, industry, and government study country risk for the benefit of multinational firms, government foreign policy decision makers, and defense planners.

Political risk studies usually include an analysis of the historical stability of the country in question, evidence of present turmoil or dissatisfaction, indications of economic stability, and trends in cultural and religious activities. Data is usually assembled by reading local newspapers, monitoring radio and television broadcasts, reading publications from diplomatic sources, tapping the knowledge of outstanding expert consultants, contacting other businesspeople who have had recent experience in the host country, and finally conducting on-site visits.

Despite this impressive list of activities, the prediction track record of business firms, the diplomatic service, and the military have been spotty at best. When one analyzes trends, whether in politics or economics, one tends to predict an extension of the same trends. It is rare a forecaster is able to predict a cataclysmic change in direction. For example, who predicted the overthrow of the shah of Iran and the ascent of a dogmatic theocratic government there? Who predicted the overthrow of Ferdinand Marcos in the Philippines and the emergence of Corazon Aquino to power in 1986? Who predicted the collapse of communism in eastern Europe and the turmoil in the Soviet Union in 1990, or the invasion of Kuwait by Iraq in 1990?

Predicting Firm-Specific Risk

From the viewpoint of a multinational firm, assessing the political stability of a host country is only the first step, since the real objective is to anticipate the effect of political changes on activities of a specific firm. Indeed, different foreign firms operating within the same country may have very different degrees of vulnerability to changes in host country policy or regulations. One does not expect a Kentucky Fried Chicken franchise to experience the same risk as a Ford manufacturing plant.

The need for firm-specific analyses of political risk has led to a demand for "tailor-made" studies undertaken in-house by professional political risk analysts. This demand is heightened by the observation that outside professional risk analysts rarely even agree on the degree of macro political risk which exists in any set of countries.

In-house political risk analysts relate the macro-risk attributes of specific countries to the particular characteristics and vulnerabilities of their client firms. Dan Haendel notes that the framework for such analysis depends on such attributes as the ratio of a firm's foreign to domestic investments, the political sensitivity of the particular industry, and the degree of diversification.[18] Mineral extractive firms, manufacturing firms, multinational banks, private insurance carriers, and worldwide hotel chains are all exposed in fundamentally different ways to politically inspired restrictions.

Even with the best possible firm-specific analysis, multinational firms cannot be assured the political or economic situation will not change. Thus it is necessary to plan protective steps in advance to minimize the risk of damage from such potential change. Possible protective steps can be divided into three categories, all of which have financial implications although they are not "pure" finance:

1. Negotiating the environment prior to foreign investment.

2. Establishing operating strategies after the investment is made.

3. Preparing a crisis plan in case the situation deteriorates.

Negotiating the Environment Prior to Investment

The best approach to political risk management is to anticipate problems and negotiate understandings beforehand. Different cultures apply different ethics to the question of honoring prior "contracts," especially when they were negotiated with a previous administration. Nevertheless, prenegotiation of all conceivable areas of conflict provides a better basis for a successful economic future for both parties than does overlooking the possibility that divergent objectives will evolve over time.

Negotiating Investment Agreements

An investment agreement spells out specific rights and responsibilities of both the foreign firm and the host government. The presence of multinational firms is as often sought by development-seeking host governments as is a particular foreign location sought by a multinational firm. All parties have alternatives, and so bargaining is appropriate.

An investment agreement should spell out policies on financial and managerial issues, including the following:

■ The basis on which fund flows, such as dividends, management fees, royalties, patent fees, and loan repayments, may be remitted.

■ The basis for setting transfer prices.

■ The right to export to third-country markets.

■ Obligations to build, or fund, social and economic overhead projects such as schools, hospitals, and retirement systems.

---

[18]Dan Haendel, *Foreign Investment and the Management of Risk,* Boulder, Colo.: Westview Press, 1979, p. 5.

- Methods of taxation, including the rate, the type of taxation, and how the rate base is determined.

- Access to host country capital markets, particularly for long-term borrowing.

- Permission for 100% foreign ownership versus required local ownership (joint venture) participation.

- Price controls, if any, applicable to sales in the host country markets.

- Requirements for local sourcing versus import of raw materials and components.

- Permission to use expatriate managerial and technical personnel, and to bring them and their personal possessions into the country free of exorbitant visa charges or import duties.

- Provision for arbitration of disputes.

- Provisions for planned divestment, should such be required, indicating how the going concern will be valued and to whom it will be sold.

Investment Insurance and Guarantees: OPIC

Multinational firms can sometimes transfer political risk to a home country public agency through an investment insurance and guarantee program. Many developed countries have such programs to protect investments by their nationals in developing countries.

The U.S. investment insurance and guarantee program is managed by the government-owned Overseas Private Investment Corporation (OPIC), organized in 1969 to replace earlier programs. OPIC's stated purpose is to mobilize and facilitate the participation of U.S. private capital and skills in the economic and social progress of less developed friendly countries and areas, thereby complementing the developmental assistance of the United States. OPIC offers insurance coverage for four separate types of political risk, which have their own specific definitions for insurance purposes:

- *Inconvertibility* is the risk that the investor will not be able to convert profits, royalties, fees, or other income, as well as the original capital invested, into dollars.

- *Expropriation* is the risk that the host government takes a specific step which for one year prevents the investor or the foreign affiliate from exercising effective control over use of the property.

- *War, revolution, insurrection, and civil strife* coverage applies primarily to the damage of physical property of the insured, although in some cases inability of a foreign affiliate to repay a loan because of a war may be covered.

- *Business income* coverage provides compensation for loss of business income resulting from events of political violence that directly cause damage to the assets of a foreign enterprise.

Operating Strategies After the Investment Decision

Although an investment agreement creates obligations on the part of both foreign investor and host government, conditions change and agreements are often revised in the light of such changes. The changed conditions may be economic, or they may be the result of political changes within the host government. The firm that sticks rigidly to the legal interpretation of its original agreement may well find the host government first applies pressure in areas not covered by the agreement and then possibly reinterprets the agreement to conform to the political reality of that country. Most multinational firms, in their own self-interest, follow a policy of adapting to changing host country priorities whenever possible.

The essence of such adaptation is *anticipating host country priorities and making the activities of the firm of continued value to the host country.* Such an approach assumes the host government acts rationally in seeking its country's self-interest and is based on the idea that the firm should initiate reductions in goal conflict. Future bargaining position can be enhanced by careful consideration of policies in production and logistics, marketing, finance, organization, and personnel.

Production and Logistic Strategies

Production and logistics policies to enhance bargaining position include local sourcing, location of facilities, control of transportation, and control of technology.

Local Sourcing. Host governments may require foreign firms to purchase raw material and components locally as a way to maximize value added and increase local employment. From the viewpoint of the foreign firm trying to adapt to host country goals, local sourcing reduces political risk, albeit at a trade-off with other factors. Local strikes or other turmoil may shut down the operation; and such issues as quality control, high local prices because of lack of economies of scale, and unreliable delivery schedules become important. Often the foreign firm acquires lower political risk only by increasing financial and commercial risk.

Facility Location. Production facilities may be located so as to minimize risk. The natural location of different stages of production may be resource oriented, footloose, or market oriented. Oil, for instance, is drilled in and around the Persian Gulf, Venezuela, and Indonesia. No choice exists for where this activity takes place. Refining is footloose. Whenever possible, oil companies have built refineries in politically safe countries, such as western Europe or small islands (such as Singapore or Curacao), even though costs might be reduced by refining nearer the oil fields. They have traded off reduced political risk and financial exposure for possibly higher transportation and refining costs.

Control of Transportation. Control of transportation has been an important means to reduce political risk. Control of oil pipelines that cross national frontiers, oil tankers, ore carriers, refrigerated ships, and railroads have all been used at times to influence the bargaining power of both nations and companies.

Control of Technology. Control of key patents and processes is a viable way to reduce political risk. If a host country cannot operate a plant because it does not have technicians capable of running the process, or of keeping up with changed technology, abrogation of an investment agreement with a foreign firm is unlikely. This works best when the foreign firm is steadily improving its technology.

Marketing Strategies

Marketing techniques to enhance a firm's bargaining position include control of markets, brand names, and trademarks.

Control of Markets. Control of markets is a common strategy to enhance a firm's bargaining position. As effective as the OPEC cartel was in raising the price received for crude oil by its member countries in the 1970s, marketing was still controlled by the international oil companies. OPEC's need of the oil companies limited the degree to which its members could dictate terms.

Control of export markets for manufactured goods is also a source of leverage in dealings between foreign-owned firms and host governments. The multinational firm would prefer to serve world markets from sources of its own choosing, basing the decision on considerations of production cost, transportation, tariff barriers, political risk exposure, and competition. The selling pattern that maximizes long-run profits from the overall viewpoint of the worldwide firm rarely maximizes exports, or value added, from the perspective of the host countries. Some will argue that if the same plants were owned by local nationals and were not part of a worldwide integrated system, more goods would be exported by the host country. The contrary argument is that self-standing local firms might never obtain foreign market share because they lack economies of scale on the production side and are unable to market in foreign countries.

Brand Name and Trademark Control. Control of a brand name or trademark can have an effect almost identical to that of controlling technology. It gives the multinational firm a monopoly on something that may or may not have substantive value but quite likely represents value in the eyes of consumers. Ability to produce for and market under a world brand name is valuable for local firms, and thus represents an important bargaining attribute for maintaining an investment position.

Financial Strategies

Financial strategies can be adopted to enhance the continued bargaining position of a multinational firm. Many of these are covered elsewhere in this book, so for the moment it is sufficient to list some of the more popular techniques.

Thin Equity Base. Foreign affiliates can be financed with a thin equity base and a large proportion of local debt. If the debt is borrowed from locally owned banks, host government actions that weaken the financial viability of the firm also endanger local creditors.

Multiple-Source Borrowing. If the firm must finance with foreign-source debt, it may borrow from banks in a number of countries rather than just from home country banks. If, for example, debt is owed to banks in Tokyo, Frankfurt, London, and New

York, nationals in a number of foreign countries have a vested interest in keeping the borrowing affiliate financially strong. If the multinational is U.S. owned, a fallout between the United States and the host government is less likely to cause the local government to move against the firm if it also owes funds to these other countries.

Shared Ownership. Local ownership, either directly via local shareholders or institutionally through a joint venture, means that local investors have a vested interest in the economic health of the firm.

Contractual Devices. Contractual devices such as hedging, swaps, linked financing, and export credit insurance reduce the risk to the firm.

Organizational Strategies

Organization ownership strategies designed to minimize political risk include the following:

- Finding the right local joint venture partner.
- Licensing a local firm to produce products or services.
- Managing a local business via a management contract.

One other organizational strategy worth discussing is the location of regional headquarters in safe places. Many U.S. and European firms have found it advantageous to locate their Latin American regional headquarters in Coral Gables, Florida, rather than in Latin America itself. Proximity to the Miami International Airport, cost savings such as avoiding cost-of-living allowances and school tuition for executives and families, lack of vulnerability to pressure for bribes and payoffs, and an efficient telecommunications system are some of the advantages cited.

It is equally important to avoid offending countries that would not have the regional headquarters. Because of jealousies between the various Latin American countries, individual political leaders have less objection to a regional headquarters in Florida than in a neighboring nation. The regional headquarters does not become a hostage to local politics and never has to be moved. If the political climate in any individual country deteriorates, the firm can simply hold back on local operations or pull out with a minimum of disturbance to other Latin American affiliates.

Crisis Planning[19]

Firms should plan in advance what they will do if or when the general uncertainty in a foreign environment turns to chaos. Anticipatory planning is essential because it forces management to think about its vulnerabilities. The major objective is to develop either companywide contingency plans or plans for parts of the firm that are vulnerable.

---

[19]The source of this section is Manolete V. Gonzalez and Edwin Villanueva, "Steering a Subsidiary Through a Political Crisis," *Risk Management,* October 1992, pp. 16–27.

Questions to ask include whether standard operating procedures cover perceived risks; what can be done to protect physical property; which executives or employees are likely to be in personal danger; and which records are so vital their protection should be attempted.

Three years before the February 1986 revolution in the Philippines, many firms doubted the Marcos administration could last up to the scheduled 1987 elections. To monitor developments, firms employed a wide array of channels of information. They used their respective embassies in Manila, trade associations, and the expatriate community. For example, Japanese businesspeople in Manila met regularly and exchanged information, as did businesspeople from the United States. Firms used different methods to assess the situation, including attending seminars held by local research centers, informal discussion with counterparts from other firms, and regular meetings of senior management. Some firms utilized the political risk analysis conducted by their head office, although the major responsibility for assessing the situation rested on the head of the local affiliate.

Suggestions derived from the Philippines experience included maintaining a low profile before any trouble starts. A foreign firm should keep itself neutral and employees should avoid activities that attract media attention.

A deteriorating political situation and a weak economy go hand in hand. This was particularly true in the Philippines in the last years of the Marcos administration. Firms sought to keep operations at a level that enabled them to retain the major portion of their trained staff. It was suggested that local nationals should be used to staff positions whenever possible, and their knowledge of the situation should be used as inputs in planning. Use of the greatly increased number of non-U.S. nationals who had received MBA or other equivalent training in the United States was recommended.

Specific planning in anticipation of disruption should be made if the situation calls for it. One firm dusted off its standard operating procedures manual, reviewed those parts that addressed the potential disruptions they anticipated, and made sure all concerned knew what was required of them. A firm with operations in a rebel-infested island in the Philippines instructed expatriate staff on procedures to take as a response to reports of kidnap threats, making sure to keep the procedures simple enough not to hamper the expatriates' day-to-day activities. Another firm instructed its expatriate staff to limit their evening activities to certain areas of the city to avoid exposure to random acts of kidnapping. As a rule, foreign employees should be sure they are registered with their local embassy so they can receive information on official evacuation plans. As a crisis actually unfolds, as it did during the February 1986 revolution and the August 1987 coup attempt in the Philippines, they should stay home to await instructions.

In the Philippines a few firms had even more elaborate plans. One firm was reported to have assigned radios to key executives and to have laid out a schedule of emergency meetings well in advance of anticipated trouble. Employees were briefed on what their firm would do to protect their lives and property, and emergency stores of food, water, and medical supplies were set aside. Some U.S. firms created "safe houses" in Manila from which employees could be evacuated to Clark Air Force Base (a U.S. facility) or U.S. naval ships.

These plans were not needed in the Philippines in February 1986 or August 1987 because the violence was confined to certain areas of Metro-Manila and was not directed at multinationals. However, political situations can deteriorate quickly and in directions difficult to anticipate. Having prepared plans and knowing what should be done is inexpensive insurance.

Summary

- Political risk is the possibility that a multinational firm may be adversely influenced by political events within a host country, or by a change of political relationships between that host country and another country.

- Most political risk arises because of a conflict in goals between host governments and firms when the normal functioning of governmental administrative and legislative processes leads to regulations that influence the well-being of the firm. Occasionally these political events constitute "expropriation," but far more frequently they are simply regulatory constraints imposed on the activities of private business firms.

- In recent years, ethnic, religious, racial, and civic strife has added another dimension to the political risks faced by multinational firms.

- Most political risk events are micro and project specific, affecting only certain firms in certain industries, rather than all foreign firms.

- To minimize vulnerability to political risk, multinational firms must constantly position themselves in a good bargaining position with their host governments. Before an investment is undertaken, an investment agreement is often negotiated in which all areas of possible future contention are discussed. Most multinational firms can also turn to a home country political risk insuring agency.

- Once an investment is undertaken, the parent firm should establish and maintain policies that will enhance the firm's continual value to the host country. A variety of risk-reducing policies can be undertaken in the areas of production and logistics, marketing, finance, organization, and personnel.

- Management should devise and rehearse a crisis plan to anticipate potential deteriorating conditions.

Questions

1. Goal Conflict: Nike Shoes in Turkey

Assume Nike is considering establishing a shoe manufacturing plant in Turkey. Prepare an analysis of all the potential areas of goal conflict between Nike and Turkey.

2. Political Risk Forecast: Turkey

Considering your answers to question 1, prepare a political risk forecast for a Nike shoe plant in Turkey. Consider both the potential for political unrest in Turkey and its neighbors, and whether a U.S.-owned shoe plant would be affected by such unrest. Use current periodicals and newspapers to gather your data.

3. Operating Strategies: Turkey

Assume Nike decides to build a shoe plant in Turkey. Recommend to Nike operating strategies that should reduce their political risk. Include strategies for marketing, production, finance, and organization.

4. Crisis Plan: Turkey

Prepare a crisis plan for Nike in Turkey in case political conditions should deteriorate.

5. Divestment: the Philippines

Assume Federated Department Stores owns a chain of retail clothing stores in the Philippines. Given the current situation in the Philippines, prepare a plan for Federated Department Stores that will enable them to divest their stores in the Philippines with maximum gain or minimum loss.

6. Iowa Foods, Inc.

Keith Smith, manager of Iowa Foods, Inc., is determining whether or not to purchase insurance through OPIC for a new capital investment in the Philippines. It is not clear if the government of President Fidel Ramos, who replaced Corazon Aquino in 1992, can reverse the decades of deterioration that began under Ferdinand Marcos.

Communists on the political left and former military officers on the political right are creating instability. The original analysis of the project assumed Ramos would be able to resolve interclass tensions that have left the Philippines controlled by an oligarchy.

After reading various political risk assessments, Smith concludes that if Ramos should fall, the odds are one in ten the communists will prevail. If that happens, the probability of expropriation is 70%. If expropriated, the best that can be hoped for is a 70% chance of 40% compensation for the equity two years after the situation has stabilized. The other possibility is a 30% probability of no compensation.

Should a military government take over, Smith judges the probability of expropriation at only 10%. In that case, there exists a probability of 30% for full compensation immediately, 60% for full compensation in one year, and 10% for no compensation.

Iowa Foods' equity in the Philippines is $1.5 million. Its weighted average cost of capital is 16%, and OPIC charges $0.80 per $100 of coverage. OPIC would pay immediately on any expropriation. Should Smith purchase OPIC insurance?

7. Political and Economic Barriers Facing the United States

Most Americans believe many political and economic barriers exist in other countries that inhibit exports to those markets from the United States. Explain some typical barriers and why they exclude U.S. goods and services.

8. U.S. Political and Economic Barriers Facing Other Countries

Citizens of other countries believe the United States has its own set of barriers that deny them equal access to the U.S. market. What are some of these barriers? Are the foreign complaints justified? Why?

9. Antibribery Law

The United States has passed a law prohibiting U.S. firms to bribe foreign officials and businesspersons even in countries where bribery is a common practice. Some U.S. firms claim this has placed the United States at a disadvantage compared to host country firms and other foreign firms that are not hampered by such a law. Discuss the ethics and practicality of the U.S. bribery law.

10. Colonial Legacy and Economic Imperialism

Some independent countries that were formerly colonies claim their economic development is still hampered by their colonial legacy and its aftermath, economic imperialism. Explain whether these arguments are justified or whether they are just excuses for poor performance because of other factors.

11. Contemporary Political Risk Examples

Have class members scan recent issues of *The Economist, Business Week, Far Eastern Economic Review,* or other current business magazines for recent examples of political risk. Acting as a class, classify these according to the scheme shown on page 502, or according to some other scheme if the text's classification seems inappropriate. What can you generalize about the present state of political risk?

Bibliography

Beaty, David, and Oren Harari, "Divestment and Disinvestment from South Africa: A Reappraisal," *California Management Review,* Summer 1987, pp. 31–50.

Brewer, Thomas L., *Political Risks in International Business,* New York: Praeger, 1985.

Chase, Carmen D., James L. Kuhle, and Carl H. Walther, "The Relevance of Political Risk in Direct Foreign Investment," *Management International Review,* vol. 28, no. 3, 1988, pp. 31–38.

Eiteman, David K., "A Model for Expropriation Settlement: The Peruvian-IPC Controversy," *Business Horizons,* April 1970, pp. 85–91.

Encarnation, Dennis J., and Sushil Vachani, "Foreign Ownership: When Hosts Change the Rules," *Harvard Business Review,* September/October 1985, pp. 152–160.

Fayerweather, John, ed., *Host National Attitudes Toward Multinational Corporations,* New York: Praeger, 1982.

Ghadar, Fariborz, Stephen J. Kobrin, and Theodore H. Moran, eds., *Managing International Political Risk: Strategies and Techniques,* Washington, D.C.: Ghadar and Associates, 1983.

Gonzalez, Manolete V., and Edwin Villanueva, "Steering a Subsidiary Through a Political Crisis," *Risk Management,* October 1992, pp. 16–27.

Green, Robert T., and Christopher M. Korth, "Political Instability and the Foreign Investor," *California Management Review,* Fall 1974, pp. 23–31.

Haendel, Dan, *Foreign Investment and the Management of Political Risk,* Boulder, Colo.: Westview Press, 1979.

Harvey, Michael G., "A Survey of Corporate Programs For Managing Terrorist Threats," *Journal of International Business Studies,* Third Quarter, 1993, pp. 465–478.

Kim, W. Chan, "Competition and the Management of Host Government Intervention," *Sloan Management Review,* Spring 1987, p. 33–39.

Kobrin, Stephen J., "The Environmental Determinants of Foreign Direct Manufacturing Investment: An Ex-Post Empirical Analysis," *Journal of International Business Studies,* Fall/Winter 1976, pp. 29-42.

———, "Political Risk: A Review and Reconsideration," *Journal of International Business Studies,* Spring/Summer 1979, pp. 67–80.

———, *Managing Political Risk Assessment: Strategic Response to Environmental Change,* Berkeley: University of California Press, 1982.

Lee, Suk Hun, "Relative Importance of Political Instability and Economic Variables on Perceived Country Creditworthiness," *Journal of International Business Studies,* Fourth Quarter, 1993, pp. 801–812.

Mandel, Robert, "The Overseas Private Investment Corporation and International Investment," *Columbia Journal of World Business,* Spring 1984, pp. 89-95.

Minor, Michael, "Changes in Developing Country Regimes for Foreign Direct Investment: The Raw Materials Sector, 1968–1985," *Essays in International Business,* no. 8, Columbia: University of South Carolina, September 1990.

Nigh, Douglas, "The Effect of Political Events on United States Direct Foreign Investment: A Pooled Time Series Cross-Sectional Analysis," *Journal of International Business Studies,* Spring 1985, pp. 1–17.

Rogers, Jerry, ed., *Global Risk Assessments: Issues, Concepts and Applications,* Riverside, Calif.: Global Risk Assessments, Inc., 1988.

Rummel, R. J., and David A. Heenan, "How Multinationals Analyze Political Risk," *Harvard Business Review,* January/February 1978, pp. 67–76.

Salehizadeh, Mehdi, "Regulation of Foreign Direct Investment by Host Country," *Essays in International Business,* no. 4, Columbia: University of South Carolina, 1983.

Sethi, S. Prakash, and K. A. N. Luther, "Political Risk Analysis and Direct Foreign Investment: Some Problems of Definition and Measurement," *California Management Review,* Winter 1986, pp. 57–68.

Tallman, Stephen B., "Home Country Political Risk and Foreign Direct Investment in the United States," *Journal of International Business Studies,* Summer 1988, pp. 219–234.

Vanden Bulcke, D., and J. J. Boddewyn, *Investment and Divestment Policies in Multinational Corporations in Europe,* London: Saxon/Teakfield; New York: Praeger, 1979.

Chapter 19
Multinational Capital Budgeting

Global View
Of Mice, Men and Money

Paris—It looks like being a winter of discontent for Euro Disney. On November 10th the company, which runs a big amusement park outside Paris modelled on American ones owned by its parent firm, Walt Disney, said that it had lost a whopping FFr5.3 billion ($960m) in the year to the end of September. Unless it can solve its problems soon, Euro Disney could end up on the scrap-heap.

Battered by currency changes, stingy visitors and soaring costs, the firm made a net loss before exceptional items of FFr1.7 billion, which was broadly what was expected. However, Euro Disney unexpectedly added a one-off charge of FFr3.6 billion, which mainly represents the start-up costs for the park. The firm had been planning to amortise these over periods of up to 20 years, but has changed its mind. Why?

The most plausible answer is that the new management team that took over Euro Disney in the summer wants to start with a clean sheet. By taking a big hit now, the new regime can blame this year's lousy results on its predecessors. There may be another reason for the red ink, too. Euro Disney is wrangling with its French bankers over a refinancing of its FFr21 billion debt. If the banks are convinced that the worst is behind them, they may be more generous.

Even if it can renegotiate its debts, Euro Disney will still need more cash to get back on its feet. Rebecca Winnington-Ingram, European media analyst at Morgan Stanley in London, puts the amount needed at FFr10 billion. For now, the firm is being kept alive thanks to help from Walt Disney, which says it has made $175m available to Euro Disney to tide it over until the spring.

What then? So far Walt Disney, which owns 49% of Euro Disney, has been steadfastly supportive of its troubled European offspring. Its approach is hardly altruistic.

Even when Euro Disney loses money, its parent can still cream off management fees and royalties. (Though it deferred the fees last year, Walt Disney still pocketed FFr262m in royalties.) But if it is asked to dip into its pocket again, some analysts believe it may refuse. If it does, the lights will go out on Euro Disney once and for all.

Source: "Of Mice, Men and Money," 11/13/93, p. 79. © 1993 The Economist Newspaper Ltd. Reprinted with permission.

Although the original decision to undertake an investment in a particular foreign country may be determined by a mix of strategic, behavioral, and economic decisions, the specific project, as well as all reinvestment decisions, should be justified by traditional financial analysis. For example, a production efficiency opportunity may exist for a U.S. firm to invest abroad, but the type of plant, mix of labor and capital, kinds of equipment, method of financing, and other project variables must be analyzed within the traditional financial framework of discounted cash flows. Consideration must also be given to the impact of the proposed foreign project on consolidated net earnings, cash flows from affiliates in other countries, and on the market value of the parent firm.

Foreign Complexities

Capital budgeting for a foreign project uses the same theoretical framework as domestic capital budgeting. Project cash flows are discounted at the firm's weighted average cost of capital, or the project's required rate of return, to determine net present value. Alternatively, the internal rate of return that equates project cash flows to the cost of the project is sought. However, capital budgeting analysis for a foreign project is considerably more complex than the domestic case for a number of reasons:

- Parent cash flows must be distinguished from project cash flows. Each of these two types of flows contributes to a different view of value.

- Parent cash flows often depend on the form of financing. Thus cash flows cannot be clearly separated from financing decisions, as is done in domestic capital budgeting.

- Additional cash flows generated by a new investment in one foreign affiliate may be in part or wholly taken away from another affiliate, with the net result that the project is favorable from a single affiliate point of view but contributes nothing to worldwide cash flows.

- Remittance of funds to the parent must be explicitly recognized because of differing tax systems, legal and political constraints on the movement of funds, local business norms, and differences in how financial markets and institutions function.

- Cash flows from affiliates to parent can be generated by an array of nonfinancial payments, including payment of license fees and payments for imports from the parent.

- Differing rates of national inflation must be anticipated because of their importance in causing changes in competitive position, and thus in cash flows over a period of time.

- The possibility of unanticipated foreign exchange rate changes must be remembered because of possible direct effects on the value to the parent of local cash flows, as well as an indirect effect on the competitive position of the foreign affiliate.

- Use of segmented national capital markets may create an opportunity for financial gains or may lead to additional financial costs.

- Use of host government subsidized loans complicates both capital structure and the ability to determine an appropriate weighted average cost of capital for discounting purposes.

- Political risk must be evaluated because political events can drastically reduce the value or availability of expected cash flows.

- Terminal value is more difficult to estimate because potential purchasers from the host, parent, or third countries, or from the private or public sector, may have widely divergent perspectives on the value to them of acquiring the project.

Since the same theoretical capital budgeting framework is used to choose among competing foreign and domestic projects, a common standard is critical. Thus all foreign complexities must be quantified as modifications to either expected cash flow or the rate of discount. Although in practice many firms make such modifications arbitrarily, readily available information, theoretical deduction, or just plain common sense can be used to make less arbitrary and more reasonable choices.

Project Versus Parent Valuation

A strong theoretical argument exists in favor of analyzing any foreign project from the viewpoint of the parent. Cash flows to the parent are ultimately the basis for dividends to stockholders, reinvestment elsewhere in the world, repayment of corporatewide debt, and other purposes that affect the firm's many interest groups. However, since most of a project's cash flows to its parent, or to sister affiliates, are financial cash flows rather than operating cash flows, the parent viewpoint usually violates a cardinal concept of capital budgeting, namely, that financial cash flows should not be mixed with operating cash flows. Often the difference is not important because the two are almost identical, but in some instances a sharp divergence in these cash flows exists. For example, funds that are permanently blocked from repatriation, or "forcibly reinvested," are not available for dividends to the stockholders or for repayment of parent corporate debt. Therefore shareholders will not perceive the blocked earnings as contributing to the value of the firm, and creditors will not count on them in calculating interest coverage ratios and other evidence of ability to service debt.

Exhibit 19.1 describes the four main avenues by which cash flows return to a parent firm. As also described, however, the manner in which the cash flows return to the parent has a significant impact on the tax liabilities of the foreign project itself.

Exhibit 19.1 Parent Valuation of Foreign Investment Projects: Cash Flows Derived from the Project

Cash Flows	Derivation of Cash Flow	Impact on Foreign Tax Liability
Dividends (financial cash flow)	Distributed profits arise only from a foreign project with positive net income in the period	No impact on foreign tax liability because dividends are distributed after tax, but there may be a dividend withholding tax.
Intrafirm Debt (financial cash flow)	Principal and interest payments flow back to the parent as scheduled in the loan agreement	Interest payments on debt (both intra- and extra-firm) are deductible expenses of the project and therefore lower foreign tax liability
Intrafirm Sales (operational cash flow)	Purchases of product or services from the parent firm arise from the operating needs of the project	Intrafirm purchases or transfers are an operating cost of the foreign project and therefore lower foreign tax liability
Royalties and License Fees (operational cash flow)	Royalties and other license fees are normally calculated as a percentage of project's sales revenue or volume	Royalties and license fees are expenses of the foreign project and therefore lower foreign tax liability

Evaluation of a project from the local viewpoint serves some useful purposes, but should be subordinated to evaluation from the parent's viewpoint. In evaluating a foreign project's performance relative to the potential of a competing project in the same host country, one must pay attention to the project's local return. Almost any project should at least be able to earn a cash return equal to the yield available on host government bonds with a maturity the same as the project's economic life, if a free market exists for such bonds. Host government bonds ordinarily reflect the local risk-free rate of return, including a premium equal to the expected rate of inflation. If a project cannot earn more than such a bond yield, the parent firm should buy host government bonds rather than invest in a riskier project—or, better yet, invest somewhere else!

If the theory of direct foreign investment is correct, multinational firms should invest only if they can earn on a project a risk-adjusted return greater than local-based competitors can earn on the same project. If they are unable to earn superior returns on foreign projects, their stockholders would be better off buying shares in local firms, where possible, and letting those companies carry out the local projects.

Apart from these theoretical arguments, surveys over the last 27 years show that in practice multinational firms continue to evaluate foreign investments from both the parent and project viewpoint. Responses of multinational firms to surveys by Stonehill and Nathanson (1968), Baker and Beardsley (1973), Oblak and Helm (1980), Bavishi (1981), Kelly and Philippatos (1982), and Stanley and Block (1983) reveal that firms calculate and evaluate rates of return by using cash flows to and from the parent alone, as well as to and from the foreign project alone.[1] In their study of 121 U.S. multinational firms, conducted in the early 1980s, Stanley and Block found that 48% of their 121 respondents evaluate foreign projects on the basis of the project's cash flows, 36% on the basis of parent cash flows, and 16% on both.[2]

The attention paid to project returns in the various survey results probably reflects emphasis on maximizing reported consolidated net earnings per share as a corporate financial goal. As long as foreign earnings are not blocked, they can be consolidated with the earnings of both the remaining affiliates and the parent.[3] Even in the case of temporarily blocked funds, some of the most mature multinational firms do not necessarily eliminate a project. They take a very long-run view of world business opportunities.

If reinvestment opportunities in the country where funds are blocked are at least equal to the parent firm's required rate of return (after adjusting for anticipated exchange rate changes), temporary blockage of transfer may have little practical effect on the capital budgeting outcome because future project cash flows will be increased by the returns on forced reinvestment. Since large multinationals hold a portfolio of domestic and foreign projects, corporate liquidity is not impaired if a few projects have blocked funds; alternate sources of funds are available to meet all planned uses of funds. Furthermore, a long-run historical perspective on blocked funds does indeed lend support to the belief that funds are almost never permanently blocked. However, waiting for the release of such funds can be frustrating, and sometimes the blocked funds lose value because of inflation or unexpected exchange rate deterioration while blocked, even though they have been reinvested in the host country to protect at least part of their value in real terms.

In conclusion, most firms appear to evaluate foreign projects from both parent and project viewpoints. The parent's viewpoint gives results closer to the traditional meaning of net present value in capital budgeting. Project valuation provides a closer

---

[1]Arthur Stonehill and Leonard Nathanson, "Capital Budgeting and the Multinational Corporation," *California Management Review,* Summer 1968, pp. 39–54. James C. Baker and Laurence J. Beardsley, "Multinational Companies' Use of Risk Evaluation and Profit Measurement for Capital Budgeting Decisions," *Journal of Business Finance,* Spring 1973, pp. 38–43. David J. Oblak and Roy J. Helm, Jr., "Survey and Analysis of Capital Budgeting Methods Used by Multinationals," *Financial Management,* Winter 1980, pp. 37–41. Vinod B. Bavishi, "Capital Budgeting Practices at Multinationals," *Management Accounting,* August 1981, pp. 32–35. Marie E. Wicks Kelly and George C. Philippatos, "Comparative Analysis of the Foreign Investment Evaluation Practices by U.S.-Based Manufacturing Multinational Corporations," *Journal of International Business Studies,* Winter 1982, pp. 19–42. Marjorie Stanley and Stanley Block, "An Empirical Study of Management and Financial Variables Influencing Capital Budgeting Decisions for Multinational Corporations in the 1980s," *Management International Review,* vol. 23, no. 3, 1983, pp. 61–71.

[2]Stanley and Block, "An Empirical Study of Management and Financial Variables Influencing Capital Budgeting Decisions for Multinational Corporations in the 1980s," pp. 66–67.

[3]U.S. firms must consolidate foreign affiliates that are over 50% owned. If an affiliate is between 20% and 50% owned, it is usually consolidated on a pro rata basis. Affiliates less than 20% owned are normally carried as unconsolidated investments.

approximation of the effect on consolidated earnings per share, which all surveys indicate is of major concern to practicing managers.

Adjusting for Risk: Parent Viewpoint

In analyzing a foreign project from the parent's point of view, the additional risk that stems from its "foreign" location can be handled in at least two ways. The first method is to treat all foreign risk as a single problem by increasing the discount rate applicable to foreign projects relative to the rate used for domestic projects to reflect the greater foreign exchange risk, political risk, and other uncertainties perceived in foreign operations.

In the second method, which we prefer, all foreign risks are incorporated in adjustments to forecasted cash flows of the project. The discount rate for the foreign project is risk adjusted only for overall business and financial risk, in the same manner as that for domestic projects.

Adjusting the Discount Rate. Adjusting the discount rate applied to a foreign project's cash flow to reflect political and foreign exchange uncertainties does not penalize net present value in proportion either to the actual amount at risk or to possible variations in the nature of that risk over time. Combining all risks into a single discount rate discards much information about the uncertainties of the future.

For example, political uncertainties are a threat to the entire investment, not just to annual cash flows. Potential loss depends partly on the terminal value of the unrecovered parent investment, which will vary depending on how the project was financed, whether political risk insurance was obtained, and what investment horizon is contemplated. Furthermore, if the political climate was expected to be unfavorable in the near future, any investment would probably be unacceptable. Political uncertainty usually relates to possible adverse events that might occur in the more distant future but cannot be foreseen at the present. Adjusting the discount rate for political risk thus penalizes early cash flows too heavily while not penalizing distant cash flows enough.

In the case of foreign exchange risk, changes in exchange rates have a potential effect on future cash flows because of operating exposure. The direction of the effect, however, can either decrease or increase net cash inflows, depending on where the products are sold and where inputs are sourced. We explained the variety of outcomes under operating exposure in the Instruments Napoleon example in Chapter 8. To increase the discount rate applicable to a foreign project, on the assumption the foreign currency might depreciate more than expected, ignores the possible favorable effect of a foreign currency's depreciation on the project's competitive position. Increased sales volume might more than offset a lower value of the local currency. Such an increase in the discount rate also ignores the possibility the foreign currency may appreciate. That is, foreign exchange risk is two sided.

Apart from anticipated political and foreign exchange risks, multinational firms sometimes worry that taking on foreign projects may increase the firm's overall cost of capital because of investors' perceptions of foreign risk. This worry seems reasonable if the firm has significant investments in Iran, Libya, Iraq, or Serbia in the 1990s, especially if the firm's operations are heavily centered in one such uncertain country and if that country is in the news frequently in a context of rising xenophobia. However, the argument loses persuasiveness when applied to diversified foreign investments with a heavy balance in the industrial countries of Canada, western Europe, Australia, and Asia, where in fact the bulk of direct foreign investment is located. These countries have a reputation for treating foreign investments by consistent standards, and empirical evidence confirms that a foreign presence in these countries may not increase the cost of capital. In fact, some studies indicate that required returns on foreign projects may even be lower than those for domestic projects.

Adjusting Cash Flows. In the rest of this chapter we use the method that adjusts cash flows rather than the discount rate in treating risk. Cash flows to the parent are discounted by the rate of return appropriate for the business and financial risks of comparable domestic projects. Any risk unique to the foreign location of the project is incorporated into project cash flows.

It should be noted that many multinational firms do adjust the discount rate for foreign projects despite the theoretical limits of this method. The aforementioned Baker and Beardsley survey found that 49% of the responding multinationals add a premium percentage for risk to their required rate of return on foreign investments.[4] The authors remark that these tended to be firms with a relatively small percentage of foreign sales. Firms with a larger foreign commitment did not typically change the discount rate, but instead presumably adjusted cash flows. The Oblak and Helm survey also reported that slightly more than half of the responding firms varied the discount rate for foreign projects, but the other half did not.[5] Of those that varied the discount rate, 40% subjectively varied their weighted average cost of capital; 44% used the local (that is, foreign) weighted average cost of capital.

In their 1983 study, Stanley and Block found that 62% of their respondents used some risk adjustment technique, but that risk-adjusted discount rates and risk-adjusted cash flows were used with similar frequency. They also found that the use of risk adjustment techniques is independent of the percentage of foreign sales to total sales.[6]

Adjusting for Risk: Project Viewpoint

From the project point of view, "foreign" risks also exist. A foreign affiliate has foreign exchange exposure on both its imports and exports. Since the prime purpose of finding a project rate of return is to compare it with alternative opportunities to invest funds locally, the appropriate discount rate should be the one required by local investors for projects of the same business and financial risk class. This approach forces the parent to

---

[4]Baker and Beardsley, "Risk Evaluation and Profit Measurement," p. 39.

[5]Oblak and Helm, "Capital Budgeting Methods," p. 39.

[6]Stanley and Block, "An Empirical Study of Management and Financial Variables Influencing Capital Budgeting Decisions for Multinational Corporations in the 1980s," pp. 66–67.

remember that local inflation and risk must be reflected in the required rate of return for local projects.

For comparisons within the host country, a project's actual financing or parent-influenced debt capacity should be overlooked, since these would probably be different for local investors than they are for a multinational owner. In addition, the risks of the project to local investors might differ from those perceived by a foreign multinational owner because of the opportunities a multinational firm has to take advantage of market imperfections. Moreover, the local project may be only one out of an internationally diversified portfolio of projects for the multinational owner, whereas it might have to stand alone, without international diversification, if undertaken by local investors. Since diversification reduces risk, the multinational firm can require a lower rate of return than is required by local investors.

Thus the discount rate used locally must be a hypothetical rate based on a judgment as to what independent local investors would probably demand were they to own the business. Consequently, application of the local discount rate to local cash flows provides only a rough measure of the value of the project as a stand-alone local venture, rather than an absolute valuation.

Kim Electronics (Kimtron)

To illustrate some of the foreign complexities of multinational capital budgeting, we analyze a hypothetical "market-seeking" investment by a U.S. manufacturing firm in Korea. A project analysis team has collected the following facts.

Product

Kim Electronics (Kimtron) is the wholly owned Korean affiliate of Fairtel, a U.S. electronic component manufacturer. Fairtel manufactures customized integrated circuits (ICs) for use in computers, automobiles, and robots. Kimtron has been Fairtel's distribution affiliate in Korea, but consideration is now being given to making Kimtron a manufacturing affiliate. Kimtron's products would be sold primarily in Korea, and all sales would be denominated in Korean won.

Sales

Sales in the first year are forecasted to be Won22,000 million. The physical volume of sales is expected to grow at 8% per annum for the foreseeable future.

Working Capital

Kimtron needs gross working capital (that is, cash, receivables, and inventory) equal to 20% of sales. Half of gross working capital can be financed by local accruals and accounts payable, but the other half must be financed by Kimtron or Fairtel.

Inflation

Prices are expected to increase as follows:

Korean general price level:	+6% per annum
Kimtron average sales price:	+6% per annum
Korean raw material costs:	+2% per annum
Korean labor costs:	+8% per annum
U.S. general price level:	+3% per annum

Parent-Supplied Components

Components sold to Kimtron by Fairtel have a direct cost to Fairtel equal to 96% of their sales price.

Depreciation

Plant and equipment will be depreciated on a straight-line basis for both accounting and tax purposes over an expected life of eight years. No salvage value is anticipated.

License Fees

Kimtron will pay a license fee of 2% of sales revenue to Fairtel. This fee is tax deductible in Korea but provides taxable income to Fairtel.

Taxes

The Korean corporate income tax rate is 30%, and the U.S. rate is 34%. Korea has no withholding tax on dividends, interest, or fees paid to foreign residents.

Cost of Capital

The weighted average cost of capital used in Korea by companies of comparable risk is 22%. Fairtel also uses 22% for its investments.

Exchange Rates

In the year in which the initial investment takes place, the exchange rate is Won800 to the dollar. Fairtel forecasts the won to depreciate relative to the dollar at 3% per annum. Consequently, year-end exchange rates are forecasted to be as follows:

Year	Calculation	Won/dollar
0	(given)	800.00
1	800.00 × 1.03 =	824.00
2	824.00 × 1.03 =	848.72
3	848.72 × 1.03 =	874.18
4	874.18 × 1.03 =	900.40
5	900.40 × 1.03 =	927.42

Dividend Policy

Kimtron will pay 65% of accounting net income to Fairtel as an annual cash dividend. Kimtron and Fairtel estimate that over a five-year period the other 35% of net income must be reinvested to finance working capital growth.

Financing

Kimtron will be financed by Fairtel with a $9,000,000 purchase of Won7,200,000,000 common stock, all to be owned by Fairtel. In order to prepare the normal cash flow projections, the project team has made the following assumptions:

1. Sales revenue in the first year of operations is expected to be Won22,000 million. Won sales revenue will increase annually at 8% because of physical growth and at an additional 6% because of price increases. Consequently, sales revenue will grow at (1.08) (1.06) = 1.1448, or 14.48% per annum.

2. Korean raw material costs in the first year are budgeted at Won3,000 million. Korean raw material costs are expected to increase at 8% per annum because of physical growth and at an additional 2% because of price increases. Consequently, raw material costs will grow at (1.08) (1.02) = 1.1016, or 10.16% per annum.

3. Parent-supplied component costs in the first year are budgeted at Won8,000 million. Parent-supplied component costs are expected to increase annually at 8% because of physical growth, plus an additional 3% because of U.S. inflation, plus another 3% in won terms because of the expected deterioration of the won relative to the dollar. Consequently the won cost of parent-supplied imports will increase at (1.08) (1.03) (1.03) = 1.1458, or 14.58% per annum.

4. Direct labor costs in the first year are budgeted at Won4,000 million. Korean direct labor costs are expected to increase at 8% per annum because of physical growth, and at an additional 8% because of increases in Korean wage rates. Consequently Korean direct labor will increase at (1.08) (1.08) = 1.1664, or 16.64% per annum.

5. General and administrative (G&A) expenses are budgeted at Won5,000 million in the first year. Although largely fixed, G&A expenses are nevertheless expected to rise 1% annually as Kimtron expands production and sales.

6. Liquidation value. At the end of five years, the project (including working capital) is expected to be sold on a going-concern basis to Korean investors for Won8,000 million, equal to $8,626,081 at the expected exchange rate of Won927.42/$. This sales price is free of all Korean and U.S. taxes, and will be used as a terminal value for capital budgeting purposes.

Given the facts and stated assumptions, the beginning balance sheet is presented in Exhibit 19.2; Exhibit 19.2 Won accounts are translated in year 0 at the current exchange rate of Won800 per dollar. Exhibit 19.3 shows revenue and cost projections for Kimtron over the expected five-year life of the project.

Exhibit 19.4 shows how the annual increase in working capital investment is calculated. According to the facts, half of gross working capital must be financed by Kimtron or Fairtel. Therefore half of any annual increase in working capital would represent an additional required capital investment.

Exhibit 19.2   Beginning Balance Sheet, Kimtron (year 0)

	Millions of won	Thousands of dollars
Assets		
(1) Cash balance	720	900
(2) Accounts receivable	0	0
(3) Inventory	1,280	1,600
(4) Net plant and equipment	6,000	7,500
(5) Total	8,000	10,000
Liabilities and Net Worth		
(6) Accounts payable	800	1,000
(7) Common stock equity	7,200	9,000
(8) Total	8,000	10,000

Exhibit 19.3   Revenue and Cost Data for Kimtron (millions of won)

Item (by year)	1	2	3	4	5
(1) Total sales revenue	22,000	25,186	28,832	33,007	37,787
(2) Korean raw material	3,000	3,305	3,641	4,010	4,418
(3) Components purchased from parent	8,000	9,166	10,502	12,033	13,787
(4) Korean labor	4,000	4,666	5,442	6,347	7,404
(5) Total variable costs [(2) + (3) + (4)]	15,000	17,137	19,585	22,391	25,609
(6) Gross profit	7,000	8,049	9,248	10,616	12,178
(7) License fee [2% of (1)]	440	504	577	660	756
(8) General and administrative expenses	5,000	5,050	5,101	5,152	5,203
(9) Depreciation	750	750	750	750	750
(10) EBIT [(6) − {(7) + (8) + (9)}]	810	1,745	2,820	4,055	5,469
(11) Korean income taxes (30%)	243	524	846	1,216	1,641
(12) Net income	567	1,222	1,974	2,838	3,828
(13) Cash dividend [65% of (12)]	369	794	1,283	1,845	2,488

Exhibit 19.5 forecasts project cash flows from the viewpoint of Kimtron. Thanks to a healthy liquidation value, the project has a positive net present value (NPV) and an internal rate of return (IRR) greater than the 22% local (Korean) cost of capital for projects of similar risk. Therefore Kimtron passes the first of the two tests of required rate of return.

Exhibit 19.4   Working Capital Calculation for Kimtron (millions of won)

Item (by year)	1	2	3	4	5
(1) Total revenue	22,000	25,186	28,832	33,007	37,787
(2) Net working capital needs at year end [20% of (1)]	4,400	5,037	5,766	6,601	7,557
(3) Less year-beginning working capital	2,000	4,400	5,037	5,766	6,601
(4) Required addition to working capital	2,400	637	729	835	956
(5) Less working capital financed in Korea by accruals and accounts payable	1,200	319	365	417	478
(6) Net new investment in working capital	1,200	319	365	418	478

Exhibit 19.5   Project Cash Flows for Kimtron, All-Equity Basis (millions of won)

Item (by year)	0	1	2	3	4	5
(1) EBIT [Exhibit 19.3 (10)]		810	1,745	2,820	4,055	5,469
(2) Korean income taxes (30%)		(243)	(524)	(846)	(1,216)	(1,641)
(3) Net income, all equity basis[a]		567	1,222	1,974	2,838	3,828
(4) Depreciation		750	750	750	750	750
(5) Liquidation value						8000
(6) Half of addition to working capital		(1,200)	(319)	(365)	(417)	(478)
(7) Cost of project	(7,200)					
(8) Net cash flow	(7,200)	117	1,653	2,360	3,171	12,100
(9) Present value (PV) factor (22%)	1.000	0.820	0.672	0.551	0.451	0.370
(10) PV each year	(7,200)	96	1,111	1,299	1,431	4,477
(11) Cumulative NPV	(7,200)	(7,104)	(5,993)	(4,694)	(3,263)	1,214
(12) IRR = 26.78%						

Conclusion: The project is viable from a project point of view, because net present value is a positive won1,214 million and IRR is 26.78%, which is greater than the 22% local (Korean) cost of capital for projects of similar risk.

[a]Because Kimtron has no long-term debt, and thus no interest expense, line (3) in this exhibit equals line (12) of Exhibit 19.3. If Kimtron had interest expense, line (12) of Exhibit 19.3 would have been calculated after deducting interest, whereas line (3) here would have been before interest expenses.

Does Kimtron also pass the second test? That is, does it show at least a 22% required rate of return from the viewpoint of Fairtel?

Exhibit 19.6 shows the calculation for expected after-tax dividends from Kimtron to be received by Fairtel. The manner in which dividends from abroad are taxed by the United States is explained in more detail in Chapter 21. For purposes of this example, note that Fairtel must pay regular U.S. corporate income taxes (34% rate) on dividends received from Kimtron. However, the U.S. tax law allows Fairtel

Exhibit 19.6   After-Tax Dividend Received by Fairtel from Kimtron

Item (by year)	0	1	2	3	4	5
In Millions of Won						
(1) Cash dividend paid [Exhibit 19.3, (13)]		369	794	1,283	1,845	2,488
(2) 65% of Korean income tax [Exhibit 19.3 (11)]		158	340	550	791	1,066
(3) Grossed-up dividend		527	1,134	1,833	2,635	3,555
(4) Exchange-rate (won/$)	800.00	824.00	848.72	874.18	900.40	927.42
In Thousands of Dollars						
(5) Grossed-up dividend [(3)/(4) × 1000]		639.0	1.336.7	2,097.2	2,926.9	3,833.1
(6) U.S. tax (34%)		217.2	454.5	713.0	995.2	1303.3
(7) Credit for Korean taxes [(2)/(4) × 1000]		191.7	401.0	629.1	878.1	1149.9
(8) Additional U.S. tax due [(6) − (7), if (6) is larger]		25.6	53.5	83.9	117.1	153.3
(9) Excess U.S. tax credit [(7) − (6), if (7) is larger]		-0-	-0-	-0-	-0-	-0-
(10) Dividend received by Fairtel, after all taxes[a] [(1)/(4) × 1000 − (8)]		421.7	882.2	1,384.1	1,931.8	2,529.9

[a]Values are taken from spreadsheet C19A.WK1, and therefore may not add due to internal values carried by the computer but not visible in tabular form shown here.

to claim a tax credit for income taxes paid to Korea on the Korean income that generated the dividend. The process of calculating the original income in Korea is called "grossing up" and is illustrated in Exhibit 19.6, lines (1), (2), and (3). This imputed Korean won income is converted from won to dollars in lines (4) and (5). Then the U.S. income tax is calculated at 34% in line (6). A tax credit is given for the Korean income taxes paid, as calculated in line (7). Line (8) then shows the net additional U.S. tax due, and line (10) shows the net dividend received by Fairtel after the additional U.S. tax is paid.

Finally, Exhibit 19.7 calculates the rate of return on cash flows from Kimtron from the viewpoint of Fairtel. Unfortunately, in this case Kimtron does not pass the test because it has a slightly negative net present value and an IRR of 21.26%, not quite enough for the 22% rate of return required by Fairtel.

Sensitivity Analysis

So far the project investigation team has used a set of "most likely" assumptions to forecast rates of return. It is now time to subject the most likely outcome to sensitivity analyses. The same probabilistic techniques are available to test the sensitivity of results to political and foreign exchange risks as are used to test sensitivity to business and financial risks. Popular techniques include the use of decision tree analysis, reducing cash flows to certainty equivalents, adjusting the discount rate to reflect the degree of

Exhibit 19.7   Net Present Value to Fairtel of Cash Flows from Kimtron

Item (by year)	0	1	2	3	4	5
In Millions of Won						
(1) License fee from Kimtron (2%) [Exhibit 19.3, (7)]		440	504	577	660	756
(2) Margin on exports to Kimtron [4% of (3) in Exhibit 19.3]		320	367	420	481	551
(3) Total receipts		760	870	997	1,141	1,307
(4) Exchange rate (won/$)	800.0	824.0	848.72	874.18	900.41	927.42
In Thousands of Dollars						
(5) Pretax receipts [(3)/(4) × 1000]		922.3	1,025.5	1,140.2	1,267.7	1,409.5
(6) U.S. taxes (34%)		(313.6)	(348.7)	(387.7)	(431.0)	(479.2)
(7) License fees and export profits, after tax		608.7	676.8	752.5	836.7	930.3
(8) After-tax dividend [Exhibit 19.6 (10)]		421.7	882.2	1,384.1	1,931.8	2,529.9
(9) Project cost	(9,000.0)					
(10) Liquidation value						8,626.1
(11) Net cash flow	(9,000.0)	1,030.4	1,559.0	2,136.7	2,768.5	12,086.2
(12) PV factor (22%)	1.000	0.820	0.672	0.551	0.451	0.370
(13) PV each year	(9,000.0)	844.6	1,047.5	1,176.7	1,249.7	4,471.9
(14) Cumulative NPV	(9,000.0)	(8,155.4)	(7,107.9)	(5,931.2)	(4,681.6)	(209.7)
(15) IRR = 21.26%						

Conclusion: The project as designed is not viable from a parent point of view because its net present value is negative $209,600, and its IRR is 21.26%, slightly less than the parent's 22% required rate of return.

riskiness of the project, and measuring the statistical dispersion of expected returns. Many decision makers feel more uncomfortable about the necessity to guess probabilities for unfamiliar political and foreign exchange events than they do about guessing their own more familiar business or financial risks. Therefore it is more common to test sensitivity to political and foreign exchange risk by simulating what would happen to net present value and earnings under a variety of "what if" scenarios.

Exhibit 19.8 illustrates the results of a possible sensitivity analysis on the rate of depreciation of the Korean won. The Net Present Value (NPV) Profile of the project from the parent's viewpoint is constructed from the net after-tax cash flows received by Fairtel, discounted over a range of discount rates. If the Korean won were to depreciate at a 6% annual rate as opposed to the 3% rate initially assumed, the project's value worsens (NPV profile shifts downward).

Political Risk

What if Korea should impose controls on the payment of dividends or license fees to Fairtel? The impact of blocked funds on the rate of return from Fairtel's perspective would depend on when the blockage occurs, what reinvestment opportunities exist for the blocked funds in Korea, and when the blocked funds would eventually be

Exhibit 19.8   Kimtron's Net Present Value Profile and Exchange Rate Sensitivity Analysis[a]

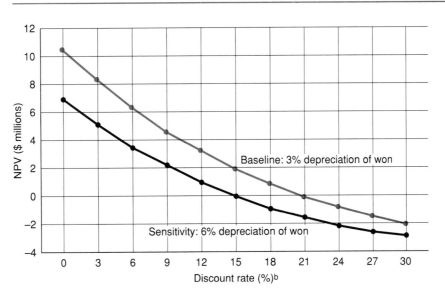

[a]Net present value profile shown is Kimtron's value from Fairtel's point of view. Net cash flows are from line 11 in Exhibit 19.7.

[b]The internal rate of return (IRR) is that discount rate which causes the project from the parent's point of view to have a net present value of zero. As seen above, it is just over 21% for the base line case and about 17% for the sensitivity case.

[c]Baseline NPV profile is the result of the assumptions discussed in the case. Sensitivity NPV profile is the result of assuming the Korean won to depreciate 6% per year rather than the baseline assumption of 3% per year.

released to Fairtel. One could simulate various scenarios for blocked funds and rerun the cash flow analysis in Exhibit 19.7 to estimate the effect on Fairtel's rate of return.

What if Korea should expropriate Kimtron? The effect of expropriation would depend on the following five factors:

1. When the expropriation occurs, in terms of the number of years after the business began operations.

2. How much compensation the Korean government will pay and how long after expropriation this will occur.

3. How much debt is still outstanding to Korean lenders and has the parent, Fairtel, guaranteed this debt.

4. The tax consequences of the expropriation.

5. The future cash flows forgone.

Many expropriations eventually result in some form of compensation to the former owners. This compensation can come from a negotiated settlement with the host government or from payment of political risk insurance by the parent government. Negotiating a settlement takes time, and the eventual compensation is sometimes paid in installments over a further period of time. Thus the present value of the compensation is often much lower than its nominal value. Furthermore, most settlements are based on book value of the firm at the time of expropriation rather than the firm's market value.

Repayment of local debt would usually receive first claim on any compensation funds paid. Thus the debt remaining to Korean lenders would be paid before Fairtel could receive the balance of settlement funds. If no compensation agreement can be negotiated, Kimtron, as an independently incorporated subsidiary of Fairtel, might default on its debt. Fairtel is not obligated for Kimtron's own debt, lacking a parent guarantee. As a practical matter, however, local debt might be supplied by a subsidiary of a U.S. bank in the host country. The parent bank would probably expect to be repaid by the parent firm from funds outside the expropriating country if necessary.

The tax consequences of expropriation would depend on the timing and amount of capital loss recognized by the U.S. government. This loss would usually be based on the uncompensated book value of the Korean investment. The problem is that there is often some doubt as to when a write-off is appropriate for tax purposes, particularly if negotiations for a settlement drag on. In some ways a nice clear expropriation without hope of compensation, such as occurred in Cuba in the early 1960s, is preferred to a slow "bleeding to death" in protracted negotiations. The former leads to an earlier use of the tax shield and a one-shot write-off against earnings, whereas the latter tends to depress earnings for years, as legal and other costs continue and no tax shelter is achieved.

The value of future cash inflows forgone is really the key to the effect of expropriation on project rate of return in capital budgeting. According to Exhibit 19.7, if expropriation comes after the fourth year, the project will have a $4,681,600 negative cumulative net present value. The project would have a break-even net present value of zero only if its terminal value is high enough to compensate for cash inflows forgone. In this case terminal value is composed of net compensation plus any tax shield. Therefore net compensation plus tax shield would need to have a net present value of $4,681,600 for Fairtel to realize the required 22% rate of return on Kimtron. The same type of analysis can be used to find a break-even year or terminal value if funds are permanently blocked. Blocked funds reduce net present value in the same manner as expropriation, but without the benefit of a tax shield or compensation.

Foreign Exchange Risk

The project team assumed the Korean won would depreciate versus the U.S. dollar at 3% per year (and the sensitivity analysis shown in Exhibit 19.8 showed another calculation for 6% per year). What if the rate of depreciation were 9% per year? Although this would make the assumed cash flows to Fairtel worth less in dollars, operating exposure analysis would be necessary to determine whether the cheaper won made Kimtron more competitive. Since all of Kimtron's sales are in Korea, and they import components priced in dollars from Fairtel, it would seem that Kimtron's profitability would be worse rather

Exhibit 19.9 Kimtron Project's Sensitivity to Exchange Rate Changes

Rate of Won Appreciation[a]	Year 5 Rate (Won/$)	Parent Viewpoint	
		NPV	*IRR*
+6%	587	6,400.1	40.07%
+3%	687	3,811.9	33.63%
0%	800	1,633.3	27.38%
−3%	927	(209.7)	21.26%
−6%	1071	(1,775.7)	15.22%

[a]Positive (+) percentage change is won appreciation, negative (−) percentage change is won depreciation versus the U.S. dollar.

than better. However, if Kimtron were exporting product, the lower value for the won should have a favorable impact on profits.

What if the won should *appreciate* by 6% per year against the dollar? The same kind of operating exposure analysis is needed. In this particular case we might guess that the effect would be positive on both local sales in Korea and the value in dollars of dividends and license fees paid to Fairtel by Kimtron. Exhibit 19.9 illustrates the impact on Fairtel's expected NPV and IRR if the won were to appreciate or depreciate over a relatively wide range of values.[7]

Other Sensitivity Variables

With reference to Exhibits 19.5 and 19.7, project rate of return to Fairtel would also be sensitive to a change in the assumed liquidation value, the margin percentage on exports to Kimtron, the size of the license fee paid by Kimtron, the size of the initial project cost, the amount of working capital financed locally, and the tax rates in Korea and the United States. Since some of these variables are within control of Fairtel, it is still possible the Kimtron project would qualify at the 22% required rate of return, particularly if the initial investment could be reduced, license fees raised, and the margin increased on exports to Kimtron from Fairtel.

Summary

- Capital budgeting for foreign projects involves many complexities that do not exist in domestic projects.

- A foreign project should be judged on its net present value from the viewpoint of funds that can be freely remitted to the parent.

---

[7]An appreciation or depreciation rate of 6% per year is a relatively high rate of change, particularly if it continues for a five-year period (compounding) as in the Kimtron case. Exchange rate sensitivities presented in Exhibit 19.9 were calculated using spreadsheet C19A.WK1.

- Comparison of a project's net present value to similar projects in the host country is useful for evaluating expected performance relative to potential.

- Risks that are peculiar to foreign operations, such as political risk and foreign exchange risk, can be best accommodated by adjusting project cash flows rather than adjusting the project's risk-adjusted discount rate.

- An illustrative example, Kimtron, was analyzed in some detail. Rates of return were calculated from both the project's viewpoint and the parent's viewpoint.

- Once the most likely outcome is determined, a sensitivity analysis is normally undertaken. Foreign project returns are particularly sensitive to changes in assumptions about exchange rate developments, political risk, and how the repatriation of funds is structured.

Questions

1. Kimtron Sensitivities (C19A.WK1)

Kimtron, the proposed Korean subsidiary of the U.S. parent corporation, Fairtel, was analyzed in the chapter on the basis of the baseline assumptions regarding sales, costs, interest rates, and exchange rates.

The chief financial officer at Fairtel asks you to conduct a number of sensitivity studies on the impact of other assumed values for these critical factors.

    a. What is the net present value of Kimtron from the parent's viewpoint if the Korean won were to appreciate at an annual rate of 5% against the dollar?

    b. What is the net present value of Kimtron from the project's and parent's viewpoint, if the sales price were to increase only 4% per year rather than 6% per year?

    c. What is the impact on both the project's and parent's potential returns from Kimtron if the proposed license fee paid by Kimtron to Fairtel was increased to 3.5% from the original 2%?

2. Knackwurst Corporation (C19B.WK1)

Knackwurst, Inc. is the wholly owned U.S. affiliate of a German parent, Bratwurst, A.G. Knackwurst, Inc. has been selling high-quality imported party sausages for $2 per can in the United States, but the United States has now banned all future imports of such sausages. Bratwurst, A.G. is now considering whether it should purchase an existing U.S. sausage factory and convert it to manufacturing German sausages.

If purchased, the new wholly owned subsidiary will have the following attributes:

1. The initial ($t = 1$) sales price in the United States will remain at $2 per can.

2. First-year production and sales will be 10 million cans per year, and physical sales will grow at 10% per annum over the next three years and then stabilize forever.

First-year production costs will be $1.50 per can. Administrative costs will be $1 million per year, and depreciation will be $1 million per year.

3. Prices and costs in future years will rise with U.S. inflation as follows:

   a. 4.00% p.a. for raw materials and labor.
   b. 3.50% p.a. for sausage sales prices.
   c. No change for administrative costs or depreciation.

4. The weighted average cost of capital in both countries is 15%.

5. Knackwurst, Inc.'s value to Bratwurst, A.G. at the end of the third year is assumed to be equal to an infinite stream of third-year dividends, discounted at 20% p.a. The higher discount rate is because of the perceived greater risk in the future.

6. Production is for sale; hence production volume equals sales volume. All sales are for cash.

7. Corporate tax rate for United States: 35%.
   Corporate tax rate for Germany: 50%.

8. Actual and expected exchange rates are: In $t = 0$, DM1.70/\$; $t = 1$, DM1.60/\$; $t = 2$, DM1.70/\$; $t = 3$, DM1.80/\$.

9. Knackwurst, Inc. is expected to pay 80% of its accounting profit to its German parent as an annual cash dividend. German taxes are calculated on grossed-up dividends from foreign countries, with a credit for local taxes already paid.

What is the maximum U.S. purchase price Bratwurst, A.G. can afford to pay (at $t = 0$) for the U.S. sausage factory acquisition?

3. Bols Canned Foods

Smith Company has been invited by the government of Lower Slobovia to open a manufacturing plant to can *bols,* a food delicacy favored by the local population. (Slobovia is named after the local population, Slobs, who got their name from a confused ancestor who spelled "bols" backward!)

The Lower Slobovian government has offered Smith Company favorable financing in the form of a $20,000,000 six-year loan at 4% per annum, to be repaid in six equal year-end payments of $3,815,238 each. Other information for Smith Company's proposed affiliate within Lower Slobovia is as follows:

Cost of equity: 24% p.a.
Market cost of debt: 10% p.a.
Optimal capital structure mix: D = 40%; E = 60%
T-bill rate in Lower Slobovia   8%
Corporate tax rate, both countries: 35%

   a. What discount rate should Smith Company use within Lower Slobovia to evaluate the proposed project?
   b. What is the value of the subsidized loan and how would such a loan affect Smith Company's capital budgeting analysis? Explain any controversial aspects.

4. Pasadena Electronics, Inc.

Pasadena Electronics, Inc. of California exports 24,000 sets of low-density light bulbs per year to Thailand under an import agreement that expires in five years. In Thailand the bulbs are sold for the baht equivalent of $60 per set. Direct manufacturing costs in the United States and shipping together amount to $40 per set, and there are no other costs. The market for this type of bulb in Thailand is stable, neither growing nor shrinking, and Pasadena holds the major portion of the market.

The Thai government has invited Pasadena to open an assembly plant so imported bulbs can be replaced by local production. If Pasadena makes the investment, it will operate the plant for five years and then sell the building and equipment to Thai investors at net book value at the time of sale plus the current amount of any working capital. Pasadena will be allowed to repatriate all net income and depreciation funds to the United States each year.

Pasadena's anticipated outlay in 1992 would be as follows:

Building and equipment	$1,000,000
Working capital	1,000,000
Total	$2,000,000

Depreciation and investment recovery. Building and equipment will be depreciated over five years on a straight-line basis. At the end of the fifth year, the $1,000,000 of working capital may also be repatriated to the United States, as may be the remaining net book value of the plant.

Sales price. Locally assembled sets of light bulbs will be sold for the Thai baht equivalent of $60 each.

Operating expenses per set of bulbs.

Materials purchased in Thailand (dollar amount of baht cost)	$20 per set
Raw materials imported from U.S. parent	10 per set
Variable costs per set	$30 per set

The $10 transfer price per set for raw materials sold by Pasadena to its Thai subsidiary consists of $5 of direct costs incurred in the United States and $5 of pretax profit to Pasadena. There are no other operating costs in either Thailand or the United States.

Taxes. Both Thailand and the United States have a corporate income tax rate of 40%.

Cost of capital. Pasadena uses a 15% discount rate to evaluate all domestic and foreign projects.

Assume the investment is made at the end of 1992, and all operating cash flows occur at the end of 1993 through 1997. The baht/dollar exchange rate is expected to remain constant over the next five years.

  a. Do you recommend that Pasadena make the investment?
  b. Pasadena learns that if it decides not to invest in Thailand, Matsushita Electronics will probably make an investment similar to that being considered by Pasadena. Matsushita would be protected by the Thai government against imports. How would this information affect your analysis and recommendations?

c. After the analysis in part b, you discover the following: The anticipated investment of $1,000,000 in building and equipment includes the book value of some surplus equipment now in the United States, which Pasadena intended to ship to Thailand and factor in at its book value of $400,000. However, that plant and equipment could have been sold in the United States for $800,000 after all taxes, that is, it is worth $800,000 rather than $400,000. How would this information affect your analysis and recommendations?

d. Assume the conditions of question b. Thailand reduces income tax charged to foreign firms from 40% to 20% in order to attract foreign investors. How would this information affect your analysis and recommendation?

e. How would your analysis and recommendation for d. differ if Pasadena expected to have a permanent presence in Thailand, and if it expected long-run growth opportunities in Thailand?

f. Assume the conditions of question b. Imports from the United States are paid for at once. However Thailand blocks all other cash remittances to the United States until the end of the fifth year, at which time all free cash may be repatriated. Funds invested in Thailand earn 3% per annum, compounded annually. How would this information affect your analysis and recommendation?

g. Assume the conditions of question f. Pasadena is able to enter into an arrangement to use operating cash (depreciation and earnings) to purchase canned tum yum soup for shipment to and eventual sale in the United States. The Thai cost of tum yum soup is charged against Thai earnings at full cost. The supply of tum yum is unlimited, but American tastes are such that it can be sold only at 80% of its Thai purchase price. How would this opportunity affect your analysis and recommendation?

Bibliography

Agmon, Tamir, "Capital Budgeting and Unanticipated Changes in the Exchange Rate," *Advances in Financial Planning and Forecasting,* vol. 4, part B, 1990, pp. 295–314.

Ang, James S., and Tsong-Yue Lai, "A Simple Rule for Multinational Capital Budgeting," *Global Finance Journal,* Fall 1989, pp. 71–75.

Baker, James C., and Laurence J. Beardsley, "Multinational Companies' Use of Risk Evaluation and Profit Measurement for Capital Budgeting Decisions," *Journal of Business Finance,* Spring 1973, pp. 38–43.

Bavishi, Vinod B., "Capital Budgeting Practices at Multinationals," *Management Accounting,* August 1981, pp. 32–35.

Booth, Laurence D., "Capital Budgeting Frameworks for the Multinational Corporation," *Journal of International Business Studies,* Fall 1982, pp. 113–123.

Dinwiddy, Caroline, and Francis Teal, "Project Appraisal Procedures and the Evaluation of Foreign Exchange," *Economics,* February 1986, pp. 97–107.

Dotan, Amihud, and Arie Ovadia, "A Capital-Budgeting Decision—The Case of a Multinational Corporation Operating in High-Inflation Countries," *Journal of Business Research,* October 1986, pp. 403–410.

Freitas, Lewis P., "Investment Decision Making in Japan," *Journal of Accounting, Auditing & Finance,* Summer 1981, pp. 378–382.

Gordon, Sara L., and Francis A. Lees, "Multinational Capital Budgeting: Foreign Investment Under Subsidy," *California Management Review,* Fall 1982, pp. 22–32.

Hodder, James E., "Evaluation of Manufacturing Investments: A Comparison of U.S. and Japanese Practices," *Financial Management,* Spring 1986, pp. 17–24.

Kelly, Marie E. Wicks, *Foreign Investment Evaluation Practices of U.S. Multinational Corporations,* Ann Arbor: UMI Research Press, 1983.

————, and George C. Philippatos, "Comparative Analysis of the Foreign Investment Evaluation Practices by U.S.-based Manufacturing Multinational Corporations," *Journal of International Business Studies,* Winter 1982, pp. 19–42.

Lessard, Donald R., "Evaluating International Projects: An Adjusted Present Value Approach," in *International Financial Management: Theory and Application,* Donald R. Lessard, ed., New York: Wiley, 1985, pp. 570–584.

Lin, James Wuh, and Jeff Madura, "Optimal Debt Financing for Multinational Projects," *Journal of Multinational Financial Management,* Volume 3, Numbers 1/2 1993, pp. 63–73.

Mehta, Dileep R., "Capital Budgeting Procedures for a Multinational," in *Management of Multinationals,* P. Sethi and R. Holton, eds., New York: Free Press, 1974, pp. 271–291.

Oblak, David J., and Roy J. Helm, Jr., "Survey and Analysis of Capital Budgeting Methods Used by Multinationals," *Financial Management,* Winter 1980, pp. 37–41.

Shao, Lawrence Peter, and Alan T. Shao, "Capital Budgeting Practices Employed by European Affiliates of U.S. Transnational Companies," *Journal of Multinational Financial Management,* Volume 3, Numbers 1/2, 1993, pp. 95–109.

Shapiro, Alan C., "Capital Budgeting for the Multinational Corporation," *Financial Management,* Spring 1978, pp. 7–16.

————, "International Capital Budgeting," *Midland Corporate Finance Journal,* Spring 1983, pp. 26–45.

Stanley, Marjorie, and Stanley Block, "An Empirical Study of Management and Financial Variables Influencing Capital Budgeting Decisions for Multinational Corporations in the 1980s," *Management International Review,* no. 3, 1983.

Stonehill, Arthur, and Leonard Nathanson, "Capital Budgeting and the Multinational Corporation," *California Management Review,* Summer 1968, pp. 39–54.

Chapter 20
International Portfolio Investments[1]

Global View
Currency Risk and Overseas Investments

How Florida Power & Light Is Using Inherent Currency Risk
as an Opportunity to Earn Incremental Returns in Overseas Investments

In the past four years, dealing with foreign currency risks associated with international securities held by U.S. pension funds has been theoretically simplified by hiring foreign exchange overlay managers. But as corporate plan sponsors nudge their holdings of foreign securities past 10% in search of higher returns, they are learning that simply hedging away foreign currency risk may not be the right thing to do.

Such a discovery has occurred for several reasons. Most studies show that the correlation between equities and the foreign exchange components of an international portfolio is very small. Add to that the fact that plenty of natural hedges exist in any international portfolio because the economies of some countries are tied closely to the dollar.

Then there is the degree of difficulties. Often, some currencies are so costly to hedge that proxy currencies have to be used. Indeed, hedging costs can ultimately hurt a portfolio's returns. Consider Florida Power & Light, which has 20%, or $340 million, of it's pension portfolio allocated to foreign equities. Hedging costs for such a portfolio could eat away at the very gains such diversity has produced. So FP&L turns to others. "We leave the decision to hedge back to the dollar to our international fund managers," says Fernando Donayre, a portfolio analyst who oversees equities in FP&L's $1.7 billion pension portfolio.

---

[1]This chapter was written by Cheol S. Eun.

One example is the use of State Street Global Advisors Currency Selection Fund, run by John Serhant, who has been a foreign exchange tactician for the past five years. But the weakness of the dollar so far this year hasn't helped Serhant add very much gain at all. "In the last six months, even with high volatility in currencies, foreign exchange opportunities have made very little change in FP&L's portfolio returns," he says.

Still, Donayre doesn't think of currencies as a separate asset class that produce returns like stocks or bonds. Why? Because FP&L doesn't use Serhant's currency fund as a basic investment. It is solely an incremental strategy based on the foreign exchange risk that is an inherent part of any international portfolio such as the High Value Country Fund. Says Donayre: "Since we already have currency risk, we are comfortable asking a manager to convert it to incremental returns."

Source: Adapted from "To Hedge or Not is Not the Question," Desmond MacRae, *Financial World's Corporate Finance*, November/December 1993, p. 48. Reprinted with permission.

In view of the recent trend toward liberalizing domestic capital markets, coupled with the widespread international multiple listings of shares, the hitherto parochial approach to portfolio investment has become outdated. In an integrated world capital market, the investor need not restrict portfolio choice to domestic securities, since it is possible to combine foreign with domestic securities in a portfolio. Indeed, increasing integration of international capital markets was identified earlier as one of the major trends in today's business world, with far-reaching implications not only for portfolio investment decisions but also for such important issues as capital asset pricing and corporate investment and financing decisions.

International portfolio diversification is not an entirely new idea. In Europe, where each domestic capital market was and still is relatively small, institutional investors have routinely invested internationally. In other developed countries, however, international diversification is still a relatively new concept that has caught on among institutional and individual investors. In what follows, we discuss various arguments for international portfolio diversification, risk/return characteristics of national stock markets, choice of optimal international portfolios, and a few related issues.

Global Risk Diversification: A Case for International Investment

An internationally diversified portfolio should be substantially less risky than a purely domestic portfolio. A risk-averse investor would hold a well-diversified portfolio, instead of a single or a few securities, in order to reduce risk. The extent to which risk is reduced by portfolio diversification, however, depends critically on how highly the individual securities included in the portfolio are correlated. The less highly correlated the individual securities are, the less risky the portfolio becomes.

Exhibit 20.1 Average Correlations of Stock Market Returns, 1973–1982 (all returns converted to U.S. dollars)

Stock Market	AUS	FRA	GER	JAP	NTH	SWZ	UNK	USA
Australia (AUS)	0.586							
France (FRA)	0.286	0.576						
Germany (GER)	0.183	0.312	0.653					
Japan (JAP)	0.152	0.238	0.300	0.416				
Netherlands (NTH)	0.241	0.344	0.509	0.282	0.624			
Switzerland (SWZ)	0.358	0.368	0.475	0.281	0.517	0.664		
United Kingdom (UNK)	0.315	0.378	0.299	0.209	0.393	0.431	0.698	
United States (USA)	0.304	0.225	0.170	0.137	0.271	0.272	0.279	0.439

Source: C. Eun and B. Resnick, "Estimating the Correlation Structure of International Share Prices," *Journal of Finance,* December 1984, p. 1314. Reprinted with permission.

To understand this point, consider a portfolio consisting of two stocks. If returns to these stocks are highly positively correlated so they move up and down together, the possibility of risk reduction by holding these stocks is minimal. On the other hand, if returns to the two stocks are not correlated with each other, risk reduction is very substantial, and, as a result, the portfolio will be much less risky than either of the two stocks.[2] The preceding analysis suggests that if security returns show lower positive correlation across countries than within a country, gains in terms of risk reduction will result from international diversification.

Exhibit 20.1 provides the average correlation of stock returns within each of eight major countries in the diagonal cells, and the average correlations of stock returns across countries in the off-diagonal cells during the period 1973 to 1982. It shows that stock returns display much lower positive correlation across countries than within a country. For example, the intracountry average correlation is 0.439 for the United States, 0.653 for Germany, and 0.416 for Japan, whereas the intercountry average correlation of the United States is only 0.170 with Germany and 0.137 with Japan. This correlation structure indicates that the potential for risk reduction via international diversification is indeed substantial. The observed low international correlations may reflect, among other things, independent monetary, fiscal, and exchange rate policies, different endowments of natural resources, divergent industrial bases, and nonsynchronous business cycles among countries.

As an investor increases the number of securities in a portfolio, the portfolio's risk declines rapidly at first and then asymptotically approaches the systematic risk of the market. Systematic risk measures the level of nondiversifiable risk in an economy.

---

[2]To be precise, as long as the two constituent stocks are less than perfectly positively correlated, it is possible to construct a portfolio that is less risky than either constituent stock. Risk reduction through portfolio diversification is one of the basic tenets of modern portfolio theory, which was pioneered by Harry Markowitz and James Tobin. For a detailed discussion of this topic, refer to any standard investment textbook.

Exhibit 20.2(a) illustrates this relationship for the United States. It shows that a fully diversified U.S. portfolio is only about 27% as risky as a typical individual stock. This relationship implies that about 73% of the risk associated with investing in a single stock is diversifiable in a fully diversified U.S. portfolio.[3]

Exhibit 20.2(b) shows the same relationship for international diversification as well as U.S. domestic diversification. The most striking fact revealed by Exhibit

Exhibit 20.2   Risk Reduction Through Diversification

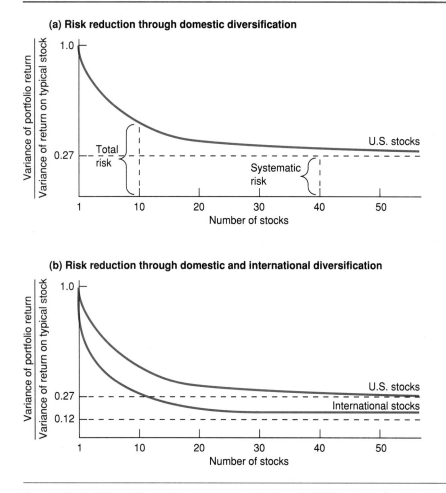

Source: B. Solnik, "Why Not Diversify Internationally Rather Than Domestically?" *Financial Analysts Journal,* July 1974, p. 17. Reprinted with permission.

---

[3]Although risk can be reduced substantially through portfolio diversification, it is not possible to totally eliminate risk. This is so because security returns are affected by a common set of factors.

20.2(b) is that a fully diversified international portfolio is less than half as risky as a fully diversified U.S. portfolio. Clearly, then, a significant portion of U.S. domestic systematic risk is diversifiable in the context of an international portfolio. Incidentally, a fully diversified international portfolio is found to be only about 12% as risky as a typical individual stock. In view of the well-established fact that security returns are much less highly correlated internationally than domestically, the case for international investment as a means of risk diversification seems to be rather convincing.

Risk and Return in the World Stock Markets

In the preceding section, we discussed the gains from international portfolio diversification in terms of risk reduction, without explicitly considering another important aspect of investment, that is, (expected) return. To the extent that investors prefer more wealth to less and are averse to risk, they try to minimize risk at a given return level, or maximize return at a given risk level. In other words, investors simultaneously consider both risk and return in making investment decisions. Therefore it is useful to examine risk/return characteristics of major stock markets of the world.

Exhibit 20.3 shows historical risk/return characteristics of each of 15 major stock market indices, which represent the 15 largest stock markets in the world in terms of capitalization value. For each stock market index, it shows the mean return (mean), the standard deviation (S.D.) of return as a measure of total risk, the beta (b), and the Sharpe performance measure (SHP). Betas were calculated using a world index, and they represent the systematic or nondiversifiable risk inherent in each national stock market index. The Sharpe performance measure, which is the mean excess return (above the risk-free rate) per standard deviation, was calculated using the (annualized) risk-free rate of 5%. Exhibit 20.3 provides these parameter values from a U.S. dollar investor's perspective, together with the correlation matrix. It was calculated for the 10-year period January 1973 to December 1982, a period characterized by flexible exchange rates.

As can be seen from Exhibit 20.3, the pairwise correlation varies widely—from 0.15 for Singapore/Spain and the United States/Spain to 0.78 for the Netherlands/Switzerland. Note that Spain and Italy generally have low correlations with other countries and that the correlations among three European countries, that is, Germany, the Netherlands, and Switzerland, are very high, 0.70 or higher. This result may partly reflect a high degree of economic integration as well as close coordination of economic policies among these countries. As would be expected, the United States and Canada have a high correlation, 0.68.

Exhibit 20.3 also shows that national stock markets display substantially different risk/return characteristics. Measured in U.S. dollars, for example, the mean monthly return ranges from −0.46% for Spain to 1.18% for Sweden. The standard deviation, on the other hand, ranges from 4.84% for the United States to 13.54% for Hong Kong; beta ranges from 0.45 for Spain to 1.54 for Singapore. Roughly speaking, the Hong Kong, Singapore, and U.K. stock markets are characterized by high risk and high return. In

Exhibit 20.3 Summary Statistics of the Monthly Returns for 15 Major Stock Markets, 1973–1982 (all returns converted to U.S. dollars)

Stock market	Correlation Coefficient														Mean (%)	S.D. (%)	β	SHP
	AU	BE	CA	FR	GE	HK	IT	JA	NE	SG	SP	SD	SW	UK				
Australia (AU)															0.63	7.97	1.25	0.027
Belgium (BE)	0.36														0.80	5.92	0.84	0.065
Canada (CA)	0.62	0.36													0.78	6.52	1.16	0.056
France (FR)	0.46	0.61	0.46												0.67	8.04	1.16	0.032
Germany (GE)	0.33	0.65	0.31	0.52											0.83	5.44	0.73	0.076
Hong Kong (HK)	0.34	0.36	0.27	0.30	0.33										1.10	14.54	1.52	0.047
Italy (IT)	0.29	0.36	0.28	0.39	0.28	0.21									0.27	8.47	0.74	0.017
Japan (JA)	0.34	0.43	0.29	0.40	0.49	0.45	0.37								0.85	5.77	0.78	0.075
Netherlands (NE)	0.43	0.69	0.53	0.59	0.70	0.45	0.30	0.44							1.01	5.80	1.06	0.102
Singapore (SG)	0.46	0.40	0.41	0.38	0.38	0.48	0.23	0.43	0.54						1.08	10.20	1.54	0.065
Spain (SP)	0.28	0.28	0.24	0.26	0.28	0.20	0.25	0.32	0.31	0.15					-0.46	6.12	0.45	-0.143
Sweden (SD)	0.30	0.44	0.28	0.29	0.42	0.24	0.16	0.35	0.46	0.34	0.23				1.18	5.89	0.66	0.130
Switzerland (SW)	0.48	0.72	0.46	0.60	0.75	0.38	0.38	0.46	0.78	0.53	0.25	0.52			0.77	6.01	1.00	0.059
United Kingdom (UK)	0.46	0.50	0.48	0.53	0.40	0.36	0.32	0.38	0.63	0.58	0.22	0.32	0.54		1.02	9.27	1.47	0.065
United States (US)	0.53	0.37	0.68	0.41	0.32	0.24	0.16	0.27	0.58	0.48	0.15	0.36	0.49	0.46	0.57	4.84	1.03	0.032

Source: C. Eun and B. Resnick. "International Diversification Under Estimation Risk: Actual vs. Potential Gains." Reprinted by permission of the publisher, from *Recent Developments in International Banking and Finance*, vol. 1, edited by Sarkis J. Khoury and Alo Ghosh, Lexington, Mass.: Lexington Books, D.C. Heath & Co. Copyright 1987, D.C. Heath.

contrast, the U.S. market is characterized by low risk and low return. Both the German and the Japanese markets yield medium returns at relatively low-risk levels. It is noteworthy that the Swedish market yields the highest return at a very low-risk level. Thus it is not surprising that Sweden turns out to be the best performing market with a Sharpe value of 0.130. Other high-performance countries include the Netherlands, Germany, and Japan, followed by Singapore, the United Kingdom, and Belgium. Countries like Spain, Australia, France, and the United States registered rather lackluster performances during the period examined.

Choice of an Optimal International Portfolio

In this section, we discuss choice of an optimal international portfolio, examine its composition, and finally compare the risk/return efficiency of an optimal international portfolio with that of a domestic portfolio. As is well known in portfolio analysis, utility-maximizing investors strive to identify an "optimal" portfolio—one that has, among all possible portfolios, the greatest ratio of excess return (above the risk-free interest rate) to risk. Once the optimal portfolio is identified, investors allocate their wealth between the optimal portfolio and the risk-free asset to achieve the desired combination of risk and return.

Exhibit 20.4 presents the composition of an optimal international portfolio, for the holding period 1973 to 1982, for each of the 15 national investors. Note that in solving for the optimal international portfolio, the following assumptions were made:

1. Investors can lend or borrow at the annual risk-free interest rate of 5%.

2. Investors use their respective domestic currencies to measure returns.

3. Investors are not allowed to sell stocks short; that is, investors cannot hold stocks in negative amounts.

4. Investors diversify internationally by investing in national stock market indices, rather than individual stocks.

As can be seen from Exhibit 20.4, a U.S. investor's optimal international portfolio consists of the Japan fund, with an investment weight of 11.68%; the Netherlands, with 27.82%; and Sweden, with 60.50%. For the British investor, on the other hand, the optimal international portfolio consists of Belgium (0.73%), Canada (2.63%), Germany (12.03%), Japan (18.44%), the Netherlands (20.62%), Sweden (38.89%), and the United Kingdom (6.65%). Clearly, composition of the optimal international portfolio varies substantially across investors' nationality. This, of course, reflects the fact that investors of different nationalities use different currencies to measure security returns.

It is noteworthy in Exhibit 20.4 that Sweden, the Netherlands, and Japan dominate all the other national markets in terms of the investment proportions, regardless of the investor's currency perspective. At a risk-free rate of 5%, the total investment in these three funds ranged from 65.20% (for the Italian investor) to 100% (for the U.S. investor). Moreover, both Sweden and the Netherlands were represented in every

Exhibit 20.4   Composition of the Optimal International Portfolio by Country (Holding Period: 1973–1982)

Stock market	From the Currency Perspective of Investors from														
	AU	BE	CA	FR	GE	HK	IT	JA	NE	SG	SP	SD	SW	UK	US
Belgium		0.1122		0.0209			0.0724				0.0347	0.0843		0.0073	
Canada	0.0916		0.1228				0.0466				0.0182			0.0263	
Germany		0.0891		0.1318			0.2133				0.0127	0.1553		0.1203	
Hong Kong	0.0130				0.0100	0.0106						0.0111	0.0300		
Italy							0.0157	0.0268	0.0045	0.0190					
Japan	0.2133	0.1803	0.1719	0.1714	0.0030	0.1728	0.1809	0.1491	0.0540	0.0037	0.2306	0.1780		0.1844	0.1168
Netherlands	0.2209	0.2169	0.2253	0.2312	0.3105	0.3054	0.1397	0.1740	0.3421	0.2747	0.2967	0.1400	0.1421	0.2062	0.2782
Singapore										0.0115			0.0053		
Sweden	0.4612	0.4015	0.4800	0.4447	0.6765	0.5112	0.3314	0.6501	0.5994	0.6912	0.4070	0.4313	0.8226	0.3889	0.6050
United Kingdom														0.0665	
Total	1.0000	1.0000	1.0000	1.0000	1.0000	1.0000	1.0000	1.0000	1.0000	1.0000	1.0000	1.0000	1.0000	1.0000	1.0000

Source: C. Eun and B. Resnick, "Currency Factor in International Portfolio Diversification," *Columbia Journal of World Business*, Summer 1985, p. 48. Reprinted with the permission of the *Columbia Journal of World Business*, copyright 1985.

Note: The risk-free interest rate is assumed to be 5% per annum. Country abbreviations are the same as in Exhibit 20.3.

national investor's optimal portfolio, and Japan was represented in every portfolio except that of the Swiss investor.

It is also noteworthy that five markets (Australia, France, Spain, Switzerland, and the United States) were not included in any national investor's optimal portfolio. The United States was excluded partly because of its lackluster performance and partly because of its high correlation with Canada, a market with a higher mean return. Switzerland was most probably excluded because of its high correlations with the Netherlands and Germany, both of which had higher mean returns. The United Kingdom and Italy were included in only one portfolio, that of the domestic investor. The reason the U.K. fund was not demanded by foreign investors was probably its high beta value. In the case of Italy, the mean return was just too low to be included in an optimal portfolio.[4]

Given the preceding analysis of optimal international portfolio selection, we can now compare the risk/return efficiency of the optimal international portfolio with that of the domestic portfolio and determine the efficiency gains from international diversification, from the viewpoint of each national investor. Let SHP(IP) denote the ratio of excess return to standard deviation of the optimal international portfolio and SHP(DP) the same ratio for the domestic portfolio. In other words,

$$SHP(IP) = \frac{(\bar{R}_{IP} - R_f)}{\sigma_{IP}}$$

and

$$SHP(DP) = \frac{(\bar{R}_{DP} - R_f)}{\sigma_{DP}}$$

where

R_{IP} = expected return on the international portfolio,

R_{DP} = expected return on the domestic portfolio,

R_f = the risk-free interest rate,

σ_{IP} = standard deviation of returns on the international portfolio,

σ_{DP} = standard deviation of returns on the domestic portfolio.

Then the efficiency gains from international diversification can be measured by the SHP differential:

$$\Delta SHP = SHP(IP) - SHP(DP)$$

As can be seen from Exhibit 20.5, the SHP differential measures the mean return differential, per unit of standard deviation, that accrues from holding the optimal international portfolio in lieu of the domestic portfolio.

---

[4]Casual observation of Exhibit 20.4 reveals that most optimal portfolios would be less than fully diversified. This result reflects, in part, the fact that no short sales were allowed in solving for optimal portfolios and, in part, the fact that ex-post rather than ex-ante parameter values were used. If short sales were allowed, investors would take either long or short positions in each country fund, resulting in fully diversified portfolios. Use of ex-ante parameters is also likely to result in more diversified portfolios even if short sales are not allowed.

Exhibit 20.5   Gains from International Portfolio Diversification

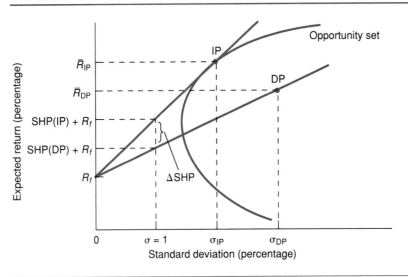

Exhibit 20.6 provides risk, return, and SHP measures of domestic and optimal international portfolios, as well as ΔSHP values, for each national investor. As can be seen from the exhibit, ΔSHP is positive for every national investor and substantial in magnitude for many national investors. This means every national investor can potentially benefit from international diversification. The gains from international diversification are found to be particularly large for the Australian, French, Italian, Spanish, and U.S. investors. For the Dutch and Swedish investors, on the other hand, the gains are relatively modest.

Considering that the U.S. stock market offers the most extensive diversification opportunity by virtue of its sheer size and well-diversified industry base, it is somewhat surprising that U.S. investors are among those who potentially stand to gain most from international diversification. Exhibit 20.6 shows that U.S. investors can nearly double their portfolio return (from 0.57% per month to 1.09%) at a comparable risk level by holding the optimal international portfolio, as opposed to the U.S. domestic portfolio.

Unlike U.S. investors, who benefit from international diversification mostly in terms of increased portfolio return, Hong Kong investors benefit mostly in terms of reduced portfolio risk. Note that with the standard deviation of 13.48%, Hong Kong is by far the most volatile market in the world. By holding the optimal international portfolio instead of the domestic portfolio, Hong Kong investors can drastically reduce risk from 13.48% to 4.47% at a comparable level of return. Other national investors, such as those in Australia, Canada, France, and Italy, substantially benefit in terms of both increased return and reduced risk. If the French investors hold their optimal international portfolio instead of the French domestic portfolio, for example, they can increase return from 0.64% per month to 1.08% and, at the same time, reduce risk from 6.62% to 3.93%.

Exhibit 20.6 Gains from International Diversification by Country (Monthly Returns: January 1973–December 1982)

Investor's currency	Domestic Portfolio $\bar{R}(\%)$	S.D.(%)	SHP	Optimal International Portfolio $\bar{R}(\%)$	S.D.(%)	SHP	ΔSHP
Australia	0.76	7.12	0.048	1.24	4.54	0.181	0.133
Belgium	0.82	4.40	0.092	1.08	3.83	0.172	0.080
Canada	0.93	5.94	0.086	1.21	4.40	0.181	0.095
France	0.64	6.62	0.034	1.08	3.93	0.170	0.136
Germany	0.61	3.87	0.024	0.85	4.50	0.096	0.072
Hong Kong	1.11	13.48	0.051	−1.17	4.47	0.168	0.117
Italy	0.92	7.84	0.064	1.68	4.34	0.290	0.226
Japan	0.55	4.10	0.032	0.87	4.64	0.097	0.065
Netherlands	0.76	4.83	0.071	0.88	4.29	0.108	0.037
Singapore	0.80	9.70	0.040	0.86	4.70	0.095	0.055
Spain	0.04	5.26	−0.072	1.61	4.91	0.244	0.316
Sweden	1.52	5.42	0.204	1.34	3.78	0.244	0.040
Switzerland	0.32	4.56	−0.021	0.77	5.07	0.069	0.090
United Kingdom	1.26	8.40	0.100	1.32	4.27	0.212	0.112
United States	0.57	4.84	0.032	1.09	4.87	0.139	0.107

Source: C. Eun and B. Resnick, "Currency Factor in International Portfolio Diversification," *Columbia Journal of World Business,* Summer 1985, p. 51. Reprinted with permission of the *Columbia Journal of World Business,* copyright 1985.

Effect of Fluctuating Exchange Rates

When a U.S. investor invests in a foreign stock market, the return on the foreign investment in terms of the U.S. dollar depends not only on the return on the foreign stock market in terms of local currency but also on the change in the exchange rate between the local currency and U.S. dollar. Since the exchange rates among major currencies have been volatile in recent years, exchange rate uncertainty has often been mentioned as one of the potential barriers to international investment.

In examining the effect of fluctuating exchange rates, we take the viewpoint of the U.S. investor investing in six major foreign stock markets, that is, Canada, France, Germany, Japan, Switzerland, and the United Kingdom. The dollar rate of return from investing in the ith foreign stock market, denoted by $R_{i\$}$, is given by

$$R_{i\$} = (1 + R_i)(1 + e_i) - 1,$$

where R_i is the local currency rate of return on the ith stock market and e_i is the rate of appreciation of the local currency against the U.S. dollar. Ignoring the cross-product term of secondary importance, we can well approximate the dollar rate of return by

$$R_{i\$} = R_i + e_i.$$

This equation simply states that the dollar rate of return on the ith foreign stock market is (approximately) equal to the local currency rate of return on the market plus the rate of appreciation of the local currency against the U.S. dollar.

From the preceding result, the variance of the dollar rate of return, $\text{Var}(R_i^\$)$, can be written as

$$\text{Var}(R_{i\$}) = \text{Var}(R_i) + \text{Var}(e_i) + 2\text{Cov}(R_i, e_i).$$

This equation shows that the exchange rate change contributes to the variance of dollar returns not only through its own variance, $\text{Var}(e_i)$, but also through its covariance with the local stock market returns, $\text{Cov}(R_i, e_i)$.

Exhibit 20.7 presents the breakdown of the volatility of dollar returns into different components. Contrary to the conventional belief that the exchange market should be substantially less volatile than the stock market, the dollar exchange rates of such major currencies as the German mark and the Japanese yen exhibit nearly as much volatility as their respective stock markets during the sample period of 1980 to 1985. In the case of Switzerland, the exchange market turns out to be even more volatile than the stock market. For other countries, that is, France, the United Kingdom, and especially Canada, the stock market remains more volatile than its exchange market counterpart. Also note that the covariance between the local stock market returns and the exchange rate changes is positive for each of the six foreign countries. This means that when a foreign currency appreciates against the U.S. dollar, the local stock market return also tends to go up. Exchange rate movements are thus found to reinforce, rather than offset, stock market movements. Exhibit 20.7 also shows that exchange rate changes, through their own variance as well as their covariance with the local stock market returns, account for a significant fraction of the volatility of dollar returns in each country, except Canada. For example, the fraction is 52.35% for Japan, 58.49% for Germany, 69.99% for Switzerland, and 48.77% for the United Kingdom. This figure is calculated by adding columns (7) and (8) in Exhibit 20.7.

As suspected, fluctuating exchange rates were indeed found to reduce potential gains from international investment by rendering foreign investment more risky. This result, however, does not mean it doesn't pay to diversify internationally. On the contrary, as we showed previously, every national investor can potentially benefit from international diversification in spite of the negative effect of fluctuating exchange rates. The proper conclusion to be drawn is that had the exchange rate uncertainty been absent or had it been controlled effectively, the potential gains from international diversification could have been greater.[5]

---

[5]In their study, "Exchange Rate Uncertainty, Forward Contract and International Portfolio Selection," *Journal of Finance,* March 1988, pp. 197–215, C. Eun and B. Resnick found that the exchange rate uncertainty is a largely nondiversifiable risk because of the high correlations among the exchange rate changes across currencies, and proposed that two methods of exchange risk reduction, that is, multicurrency diversification and the forward exchange contract on a currency-by-currency basis, should be employed simultaneously. They reported that the simultaneous use of these two methods led to nearly complete elimination of the negative effect of exchange rate uncertainty.

Exhibit 20.7 Decomposition of the Volatility of Stock Market Returns in U.S. Dollars[a] (Weekly Data: January 1980–December 1985)

Stock Market	(1) $Var(R_i)$	(2) $Var(e_i)$	(3) $Cov(R_i,e_i)$	(4) $Cor(R_i,e_i)$	(5) $Var(R_{i\$})$	(6) $\frac{(1)}{(5)} \times 100\%$	(7) $\frac{(2)}{(5)} \times 100\%$	(8) $\frac{2 \times (3)}{(5)} \times 100\%$
Canada	7.37	0.37	0.47	0.281	8.68	84.91	4.26	10.83
France	7.52	3.61	0.52	0.100	12.17	61.79	29.66	8.55
Germany	3.69	3.46	0.87	0.244	8.89	41.51	38.92	19.57
Japan	3.86	2.58	0.83	0.264	8.10	47.65	31.85	20.50
Switzerland	2.35	4.32	0.58	0.180	7.83	30.01	55.17	14.81
United Kingdom	5.21	3.28	0.84	0.205	10.17	51.23	32.25	16.52
United States	5.42	—	—	—	5.42	100.00	—	—

[a]The variances and covariances of columns (1), (2), (3), and (5) are stated in terms of squared percentages.

Source: C. Eun and B. Resnick, "Exchange Rate Uncertainty, Forward Contract and International Portfolio Selection," *Journal of Finance*, March 1988, p. 201. Reprinted with permission.

Performance of International Mutual Funds

Two different approaches exist for investors seeking international portfolio diversification. First, investors may evaluate risk/return characteristics of foreign securities themselves and invest directly in foreign securities on the basis of their evaluation. In this approach, investors are going to incur substantial information and transaction costs. In addition, they will have to perform security analysis themselves in order to construct optimal international portfolios. The alternative approach is to invest in existing international mutual funds. By investing in international mutual funds, investors can substantially reduce information and transaction costs and, at the same time, benefit from professional management. For the majority of investors, especially individual investors, international mutual funds are about the only practical means of diversifying into foreign securities.

Currently, at least 50 U.S.-based mutual funds invest a significant portion of their assets in foreign markets. By convention, these funds are classified into three categories: country funds, international funds, and global funds. A country fund is one that invests exclusively in the securities of a single country. A fund that invests at least 25% of its assets in foreign markets is classified as a global fund, whereas a fund investing at least 50% in foreign markets is considered an international fund. Some funds in each of these categories are as follows:

Country Funds

Japan Fund	Italy Fund
Australia Fund	Canada Fund
Mexico Fund	Korea Fund

Global Funds

Templeton World	Templeton Growth
New Perspective	Pru-Bache Global
Oppenheimer A.I.M.	Putnam International

International Funds

Fidelity Overseas	T. Rowe Price International
Scudder International	Merrill Lynch Pacific
Kemper International	Templeton Foreign

Note that most of the previous studies on the gains from international diversification have analyzed "hypothetical" portfolios, such as optimal international portfolios comprising national stock market indices. In reality, investors rarely invest in such a portfolio, but instead invest in international mutual funds. Therefore it is the performance of these funds that determines whether investors can actually reap gains from international diversification.

Proffitt and Seitz evaluated the performance of U.S.-based international mutual funds during the period 1974 to 1982 as shown in Exhibit 20.8. They used two alternative performance measures, namely, the Sharpe measure (SHP) and the Treynor measure (TRN). These measures are defined as follows:

$$\text{SHP} = \frac{\bar{R} - R_f}{\sigma_i}$$

Exhibit 20.8 Performance of International Mutual Funds (Monthly Returns: 1974–1982)

Fund	Performance Measure	
	Sharpe	*Treynor*
ASA Ltd.	0.0906	0.0107
New Perspective	−0.0479	−0.0024
Research Capital	0.1606	0.0119
International Investors	0.1485	0.0128
Keystone International	0.1047	0.0103
Putnam International	0.0111	0.0008
Scudder International	−0.0302	−0.0015
Sogen International	0.0544	0.0037
Templeton Growth	−0.0060	−0.0003
United Continental Growth	0.0415	0.0019
S&P 500 Index	−0.1000	−0.0033

Source: Dennis Proffitt and Neil Seitz, "The Performance of Internationally Diversified Mutual Funds," *Journal of the Midwest Finance Association*, December 1983, p. 45.

and

$$\text{TRN} = \frac{\bar{R}_i - r_f}{\beta_i}$$

where

R_i = mean return on the ith fund,

σ_i = standard deviation of returns to the ith fund,

β_i = systematic risk, or beta risk, of the ith fund,

R_f = risk-free interest rate.

Clearly, both Sharpe and Treynor criteria provide risk-adjusted performance measures. However, the kind of risk considered is different between the two performance criteria. The Sharpe criterion considers the total risk, measured by the standard deviation (s_i); the Treynor criterion considers the systematic risk, measured by the beta (β_i). Here, β_i measures the sensitivity of returns on the ith fund to return on the stock market index.[6] In a situation where an investor invests solely or mostly in an international fund, the investor

---

[6]Formally, the systematic risk of ith fund, β_i is defined as

$$\beta_i = \frac{\text{Cov}(R_i, R_M)}{\text{Var}(R_M)},$$

that is, the covariance between the rate of returns to the ith fund and the market portfolio, M, comprising all securities of the economy, divided by the variance of the market portfolio returns. Unlike the standard deviation, which measures the total risk, the systematic or beta risk measures the contribution of the fund to the risk of the (U.S.) market portfolio.

should be concerned with the total risk of the fund. Therefore the Sharpe measure would be relevant in this case. On the other hand, if an international mutual fund is held as a supplement to a well-diversified portfolio, the investor should be concerned with the systematic risk of the fund. Consequently the Treynor measure would be more appropriate.

Exhibit 20.8 presents numerical values for both Sharpe and Treynor performance measures for a selected sample of international mutual funds based in the United States. It shows that by either criterion, every international mutual fund in the sample outperformed the Standard & Poor's 500 Index, which is a broadly based U.S. stock market index. Four of the funds, namely, ASA, International Investors, Research Capital, and Keystone International, registered particularly strong performances. Note also that three international mutual funds and the Standard & Poor's 500 Index had negative performance measures. In other words, the mean returns on these three funds and the Index were less than the (average) risk-free interest rate during the sample period.[7] These empirical results from 1974 to 1982 offer convincing evidence that U.S. investors have historically been able to capture gains from international diversification via investing in existing international mutual funds.

Do Multinationals Provide International Diversification?

A multinational corporation (MNC) can be viewed as representing a portfolio of internationally diversified cash flows originated in a variety of countries and currencies. Since the cash flows of a MNC are likely to be strongly influenced by foreign factors, it has been suggested that investors may be able to achieve international diversification indirectly by investing in the shares of MNCs.

While this issue is far from complete resolution, Jacquillat and Solnik (1978) found that the share price behavior of MNCs is nearly indistinguishable from that of purely domestic firms. To illustrate this point, they selected MNCs of nine different nationalities and estimated the betas of the MNC shares with regard to both the domestic and the other eight foreign stock market indices. Exhibit 20.9 provides their estimated domestic and foreign beta measures of MNCs by country. The exhibit reveals that the share prices of MNCs act pretty much like those of purely domestic firms, showing far more sensitivity to the index of their home markets than to foreign market indices. It would seem, then, that investing in domestic MNCs is not an effective means of international diversification.[8]

---

[7]It is rather unusual that the mean returns on the risky portfolios fall short of the risk-free interest rate. This may be due to the fact that the inflation rate was unusually high during the sample period of 1974 to 1982. It is well known that the (nominal) interest rate varies directly with the inflation rate, and also that stock returns are negatively correlated with the inflation rate.

[8]In contrast to Jacquillat and Solnik (1978), Agmon and Lessard (1977) found in their study of the share price behavior of U.S. multinational firms that as the proportion of international sales increased, the share prices of multinationals exhibited an increasing (decreasing) sensitivity to the world (U.S.) factor. For a detailed discussion of their study, refer to T. Agmon and D. Lessard, "Investor Recognition of Corporate International Diversification," *Journal of Finance,* September 1977, pp. 1049–1055.

Exhibit 20.9 Domestic and Foreign Betas of Multinational Corporations

Nationalities of MNCs	National Stock Market Indices								
	United States	Netherlands	Belgium	West Germany	Italy	Sweden	France	Switzerland	United Kingdom
American	**0.94**	0.12	−0.05	−0.01	−0.04	0.04	0.02	−0.01	−0.07
Dutch	0.31	**0.76**	0.09	0.16	−0.02	−0.28	0.25	−0.21	−0.06
Belgian	−0.27	0.07	**1.04**	0.06	0.03	0.19	0.06	0.08	0.07
German	0.24	0.03	−0.21	**1.18**	−0.02	−0.01	0.10	−0.15	−0.11
Italian	−0.10	0.06	0.10	0.01	**0.83**	0.11	−0.19	−0.16	0.20
Swedish	0.06	−0.15	−0.02	0.08	−0.10	**0.96**	0.01	0.15	0.02
French	−0.10	0.14	0.33	0.18	0.02	−0.16	**0.95**	−0.22	0.03
Swiss	−0.12	−0.23	−0.04	−0.09	−0.02	0.16	−0.11	**1.74**	0.16
British	−0.10	−0.11	0.30	0.09	−0.04	−0.13	−0.09	0.07	**0.84**

Source: B. Jacquillat and B. Solnik, "Multinationals Are Poor Tools for International Diversification," *Journal of Portfolio Management*, Institutional Investor Systems, Inc., Winter 1978, p. 160. Reprinted with permission.

Note that investment in the shares of MNCs was initially proposed as a second-best alternative to direct international portfolio investment in the last decade, when the international capital market was much more segmented than it is now. Currently, investors can invest either in the dual-listed foreign shares or in the existing international mutual funds without incurring prohibitive costs; therefore the idea of investing in domestic MNCs as a substitute for international portfolio investment seems to be losing much of its appeal.

A Word of Caution

Despite the recent trend toward a greater integration of international capital markets, investors in the United States and other countries display a rather strong "home bias" in their portfolio holdings. This may imply there still exist significant barriers to international investment. These barriers may include the following:

1. excessive information and transaction costs associated with investing in foreign securities, especially those that are solely listed on the home markets,
2. foreign exchange regulations that make overseas investment costly and, sometimes, impossible,[9]
3. legal restrictions on the ownership of domestic securities by foreigners,[10]
4. double taxation of foreign investment income for certain investors, and, last but not least,
5. the persistence of parochial attitudes on the part of investors.

When investors have to make portfolio decisions subject to investment barriers, they should balance an increased portfolio efficiency accruing from international diversification against extra costs associated with incorporating foreign securities into their portfolios.

Paradoxical as it may sound, increasing integration of capital markets may also cause some of the benefits of international diversification to diminish. For example, since Denmark-based Novo Industri (Chapter 10) was listed on the New York Stock Exchange, its stock price appears to be significantly influenced by overall movements of the U.S. market, rather than those of its Danish home market. As returns on foreign

---

[9]In many developing countries, which are in need of importing capital, investors are not allowed to acquire foreign exchange for the purpose of foreign portfolio investment. Even in developed countries, overseas portfolio investment can be restricted to a fixed pool of foreign exchange. A historical example is provided by the "investment dollar premium" that existed in the United Kingdom until 1979. Under this system, British portfolio investors often had to purchase dollars at a substantial premium over the regular exchange rate.

[10]An example is the restrictions imposed by some governments on the fraction of equities of local firms that can be held by foreigners. Governments in developing as well as developed countries often impose this kind of restriction as a means of safeguarding the domestic control of local firms.

stocks become more closely correlated with returns on the investor's domestic market, the foreign stocks lose some of their diversification appeal.

One answer to this problem is to invest in internationally "nontraded" stocks. This strategy would typically result in higher transaction and information costs, but the pay-off in terms of risk reduction may be worth the effort.

Summary

- As international capital markets become more integrated, investors can more easily diversify their investment portfolios internationally, rather than just domestically, and benefit substantially from doing so. The most popular case for international investment is based on global risk diversification. Investors diversify their portfolio holdings in order to reduce risk. To the extent that security returns show lower positive correlation across countries than within a country, an internationally diversified portfolio will be less risky than a purely domestic portfolio. Empirical evidence shows that a fully diversified international portfolio could be only half as risky as a fully diversified U.S. portfolio.

- At a more general level, utility-maximizing investors would hold an "optimal" portfolio, one that has the greatest ratio of excess return to risk. The composition of an optimal international portfolio for each of 15 national investors can be examined, using different numeraire currencies. The risk/return efficiency of an optimal international portfolio can also be compared with that of a domestic portfolio. The comparison reveals that every national investor can potentially benefit from international diversification in terms of extra returns at the domestic-equivalent risk level.

- Investors can benefit from international investment despite the negative effect of fluctuating exchange rates. Examination of historical data shows that the exchange rate volatility often accounts for 50% or more of the volatility of dollar returns from major foreign stock markets. This result implies that controlling exchange rate uncertainty is the key to improving the efficiency of international portfolios.

- It has been suggested that investors may be able to benefit from international diversification by investing in the shares of multinational firms. While the jury is still out on this issue, the share price behavior of multinationals was observed to be very similar to that of domestic firms in their home market. This finding casts doubt on the argument that investing in multinational firms could be a good substitute for direct international portfolio investment.

- The examination of the performance of U.S.-based international mutual funds shows that they often outperformed the U.S. stock market in terms of risk/return efficiency. We may, then, infer that despite existing barriers to international investment, U.S. investors have successfully captured gains from international diversification via investing in international mutual funds. To conclude, the case for international, as opposed to purely domestic, diversification seems to be rather convincing.

Questions

1. Correlations of Security Returns
Exhibit 20.1 shows both the intercountry and intracountry correlations for major countries. Clearly, the intercountry correlations tend to be substantially lower than the intracountry correlations.

    a. Explain intuitively why this happens.

    b. What significance does this fact have for international investment?

2. Systematic Risk
Exhibit 20.2 shows that the international systematic risk is much less than the U.S. domestic systematic risk. Discuss what factor is responsible for this result.

3. Betting on the Nikkei
You are a U.S.-based investor who invests $1,000,000 on April 15 in a Japanese share listed on the Tokyo Stock Exchange. The spot rate on the day of purchase is ¥120/$, and the share price is ¥6,250/share.

    After one year you sell your shares at ¥7,000/share, and return the yen proceeds to the United States at a spot rate of ¥100/$.

    a. What is the total rate of return on your investment?

    b. What is the percentage return earned on the stock and on the currency independently?

    c. If when you sold the stock the share price was ¥7,250/share, and the spot exchange rate was ¥125/$, what would have been your total and decomposed rates of return?

4. Multinational Firms as International Diversification
What are the arguments for and against investing in the domestic multinational companies as a substitute for direct international portfolio investment?

5. Integrated Markets and Diversification Benefits (C20A.WK1)
An investor is evaluating an equally weighted two-asset portfolio of the following two securities:

	Return (mean)	Risk (std. dev.)
Boeing (U.S.)	18.6	22.8
Unilever (U.K.)	16.0	24.0

    a. What is the expected risk and return for the portfolio if the two securities have a correlation of +0.8?

    b. What is the expected risk and return for the portfolio if the two securities have a correlation of +0.2?

    c. Some have argued that increasing integration of international capital markets may cause some of the benefits of international portfolio diversification to diminish. Comment on this argument.

6. Sony Shares and Exchange Rate Changes

A U.S. investor just sold a share of Sony, a Japanese firm, for ¥100,000. The share was purchased a year ago for ¥120,000. The exchange rate is ¥140 per dollar now and was ¥190 per dollar a year ago. Compute the rate of return on this investment in dollars as well as in yen. Assume that no dividend payment was received during the holding period. If the U.S. investor had received ¥5,000 as a cash dividend immediately before the share was sold, how would this affect the return calculations?

7. Siemens Shares and Exchange Rate Changes

A U.S. investor is considering investing in the stock of Siemens, a German firm. The estimated standard deviation of the rate of return on Siemens in terms of marks is 20% and that of the rate of change in the dollar-mark exchange rate is 7%. Further, the correlation coefficient between the mark return on Siemens and the rate of change in the exchange rate is estimated at 0.25. Compute the standard deviation of the dollar rate of return on the investment in Siemens.

8. Domestic Portfolio Bias

Despite potential gains from international investment, investors tend to invest heavily in their domestic securities, displaying "home bias" in their portfolio holdings. What are some of the possible reasons for this phenomenon?

9. Adelaide, Ltd. and AB Lund

Adelaide, Ltd. and AB Lund are publicly held corporations in Australia and Sweden, respectively. Foreign exchange risk and political risk are the same in both countries. Each company would like to issue additional common stock. Assume the following:

	Adelaide, Ltd.	*AB Lund*
Beta	0.7	0.5
Risk-free rate	5.0%	9.0%
Market return	12.5%	14.5%

a. Compute the cost of equity capital for Adelaide, Ltd. and AB Lund.

b. Does the calculation here indicate whether the capital markets in Australia and Sweden are segmented or integrated? Explain.

Bibliography

Adler, Michael, and B. Dumas, "International Portfolio Choice and Corporation Finance: A Synthesis," *Journal of Finance*, June 1983, pp. 925–984.

Adler, Michael, and David Simon, "Exchange Risk Surprises in International Portfolios," *Journal of Portfolio Management*, Winter 1986, pp. 44–53.

Agmon, Tamir, and Donald Lessard, "Investor Recognition of Corporate International Diversification," *Journal of Finance*, September 1977, pp. 1049–1055.

———, "The Relations Among Equity Markets: A Study of Share Price Co-Movements in the U.S., U.K., Germany and Japan," *Journal of Finance*, September 1972. pp. 839–855.

Alexander, G., C. Eun, and S. Janakiramanan, "Asset Pricing and Dual Listing on Foreign Capital Markets: A Note," *Journal of Finance*, March 1987, pp. 151–158.

———, "International Listings and Stock Returns: Some Empirical Evidence," *Journal of Financial and Quantitative Analysis,* June 1988, pp. 135–151.

Black, Fischer, "Equilibrium Exchange Rate Hedging," *Journal of Finance,* July 1990, pp. 899–907.

———, "International Capital Market Equilibrium with Investment Barriers," *Journal of Financial Economics,* December 1974, pp. 337–352.

Bonser-Neal, Catherine, Greggory Brauer, Robert Neal, and Simon Wheatley, "International Investment Restrictions and Closed-End Country Fund Prices," *Journal of Finance,* June 1990, pp. 523–548.

Cho, D., C. Eun, and L. Senbet, "International Arbitrage Pricing Theory: An Empirical Investigation," *Journal of Finance,* June 1986, pp. 313–329.

Christofi, Andreas C., and George C. Philippatos, "An Empirical Investigation of the International Arbitrage Pricing Theory," *Management International Review,* no. 1, 1987, pp. 13–22.

Collins, J. Markham, "A Market Performance Comparison of U.S. Firms Active in Domestic, Developed and Developing Countries," *Journal of International Business Studies,* Second Quarter 1990, pp. 271–287.

Cumby, Robert E., and Jack D. Glen, "Evaluating the Performance of International Mutual Funds," *Journal of Finance,* June 1990, pp. 497–521.

Doukas, John, and Nickolaos G. Travlos, "The Effect of Corporate Multinationalism on Shareholders' Wealth: Evidence from International Acquisitions," *Journal of Finance,* December 1988, pp. 1161–1175.

Errunza, Vihang, and Etienne Losq, "Capital Flow Controls, International Asset Pricing, and Investors' Welfare: A Multi-Country Framework," *Journal of Finance,* September 1989, pp. 1025–1037.

———, "How Risky Are Emerging Markets?" *Journal of Portfolio Management,* vol. 14, no. 1, Fall 1987, pp. 62–67.

———, "International Asset Pricing Under Mild Segmentation: Theory and Test," *Journal of Finance,* March 1985, pp. 105–124.

———, and Barr Rosenberg, "Investment in Developed and Less Developed Countries," *Journal of Financial and Quantitative Analysis,* December 1982, pp. 741–762.

———, and L. W. Senbet, "The Effects of International Operations on the Market Value of the Firm: Theory and Evidence," *Journal of Finance,* May 1981, pp. 401–418.

Eun, Cheol S., and Bruce G. Resnick, "Currency Factor in International Portfolio Diversification," *Columbia Journal of World Business,* Summer 1985, pp. 45–53.

———, "Estimating the Correlation Structure of International Share Prices," *Journal of Finance,* December 1984, pp. 1311–1324.

———, "Exchange Rate Uncertainty, Forward Contract and International Portfolio Selection," *Journal of Finance,* March 1988, pp. 197–215.

———, "International Diversification Under Estimation Risk: Actual vs. Potential Gains," in *Recent Developments in International Banking and Finance,* S. Khoury and A. Gosh, eds., Lexington, Mass.: Heath, 1987, pp. 135–147.

Fatemi, Ali M., "Shareholder Benefits from Corporate International Diversification," *Journal of Finance,* December 1984, pp. 1325–1344.

Giovannini, Alberto, and Philippe Jorion, "The Time Variation of Risk and Return in the Foreign Exchange and Stock Markets," *Journal of Finance,* June 1989, pp. 307–326.

Grauer, Frederick A., Robert A. Litzenberger, and Richard E. Stehle, "Sharing Rules and Equilibrium in an International Capital Market Under Uncertainty," *Journal of Financial Economics,* June 1976, pp. 233–256.

Grauer, Robert R., and Nils H. Hakansson, "Gains from International Diversification: 1968–85 Returns on Portfolios of Stocks and Bonds," *Journal of Finance,* July 1987, pp. 721–741.

Grubel, Herbert G., "Internationally Diversified Portfolios: Welfare Gains and Capital Flows,"

American Economic Review, December 1968, pp. 1299–1314.

Hill, Joanne, Thomas Schneeweis, and Jot Yau, "International Multi-Asset Diversification: A Further Analysis," *Advances in Financial Planning and Forecasting,* vol. 4, part A, 1990, pp. 197–214.

Huang, Roger D., and Tsong-Yue Lai, "Financial Asset Substitutability and International Asset Pricing," *Advances in Financial Planning and Forecasting,* vol. 4, part A, 1990, pp. 171–196.

Jacquillat, Bertrand, and Bruno H. Solnik, "Multinationals Are Poor Tools for Diversification," *Journal of Portfolio Management,* Winter 1978, pp. 8–12.

Jorion, Philippe, "International Portfolio Diversification with Estimated Risk," *Journal of Business,* July 1985, pp. 259–278.

Lee, Adrian F., "International Asset and Currency Allocation," *Journal of Portfolio Management,* vol. 14, no. 1, Fall 1987, pp. 68–73.

Lee, W. Y., and K. S. Sachdeva, "The Role of the Multinational Firm in the Integration of Segmented Capital Markets," *Journal cf Finance,* May 1977, pp. 479–492.

Lessard, Donald R., "World, National, and Industry Factors in Equity Returns," *Journal of Finance,* May 1974, pp. 379–391.

Levy, Hiam, and Marshall Sarnat, "International Diversification of Investment Portfolios," *American Economic Review,* September 1970, pp. 668–675.

Lewellen, Wilbur G., and James S. Ang, "Inflation, Currency Exchange Rates, and the International Securities Markets," *Journal of Business Research,* March 1984, pp. 97–114.

Maldonado, Rita, and Anthony Saunders, "International Portfolio Diversification and the Inter-Temporal Stability of International Stock Market Relationships," *Financial Management,* Autumn 1981, pp. 54–63.

Philippatos, G. C., A. Christofi, and P. Christofi, "The Inter-Temporal Stability of International Stock Market Relationships: Another View," *Financial Management,* Winter 1983, pp. 63–69.

Rhee, S. Ghon, and Rosita P. Chang, eds., *Pacific Basin Capital Markets Research,* Amsterdam and New York: North-Holland, 1990.

Roll, Richard, and Bruno H. Solnik, "A Pure Foreign Exchange Asset Pricing Model," *Journal of International Economics,* no. 7, 1977, pp. 161–179.

Solnik, Bruno H., *International Investments,* 2nd ed., Reading, Mass.: Addison-Wesley, 1992.

———, "The International Pricing of Risk: An Empirical Investigation of the World Capital Market Structure," *Journal of Finance,* May 1974, pp. 365–378.

———, "Testing International Asset Pricing: Some Pessimistic Views," *Journal of Finance,* May 1977, pp. 503–512.

———, "Why Not Diversify Internationally Rather Than Domestically?" *Financial Analysts Journal,* July/August 1974, pp. 48–54.

Stehle, Richard F., "An Empirical Test of the Alternative Hypothesis of National and International Pricing of Risk Assets," *Journal of Finance,* May 1977, pp. 493–502.

Stulz, Rene M., "On the Effects of Barriers to International Investment," *Journal of Finance,* September 1981, pp. 923–933.

———, "Pricing Capital Assets in an International Setting: An Introduction," *Journal of International Business Studies,* Winter 1984, pp. 55–73.

Uppal, Raman, "The Economic Determinants of the Home Country Bias in Investors' Portfolios: A Survey," *Journal of International Financial Management and Accounting,* vol. 4, no. 3, Autumn 1992, pp. 171–189.

Chapter 21
Principles of Multinational Taxation

Global View
California's Unitary Tax and Barclays

The state of California (U.S.) and Barclays Bank (UK) have resolved, at least partially, a long-standing feud over taxation. California's "unitary-tax" system assesses multinational companies on a proportion of their worldwide profits, not simply those earned in California. The assessment is based on a formula that requires worldwide combined reporting (WWCR), which calculates taxes for multinational firms on the basis of local sales, payroll, and property as a proportion of the multinational's worldwide totals and income. Over 30 non-U.S.-based multinationals sued the state of California for over $4 billion in tax refunds.

The debate is not a new one. Barclays Bank has been leading the fight for over six years. After considerable pressure by the Reagan administration, California began offering multinational firms the ability to "opt-out" of a worldwide tax base and substitute for it a U.S.-based tax base back in 1988. Although not as expensive and burdensome as the unitary tax, the special documentation and filing still represented a burden on foreign firms that domestic firms did not bear.

The debate was settled in September 1993 when the state of California passed new legislation abolishing the fees and documentation requirements for opting out of unitary tax. The British government, however, is still pursuing the issue with the

Source: This global view draws from a number of sources including "Non-U.S. Firms Await Choice by Clinton in Tax Dispute," Rick Wartzman, *Wall Street Journal Europe*, August 20–21, 1993, p. 8; "Smart Move," *The Economist*, September 18, 1993, p. 86; "Tax Deficient," *The Economist*, May 22, 1993, p. 20; "United Kingdom Threatens Retaliation Against California Unitary Tax," M.F. Lynch, A.R. Biebl, et al., *Journal of Accountancy*, September 1993, pp. 34–36.; and "Locational Determinants of Japanese Manufacturing Startups in the United States," Douglas P. Woodward, *Southern Economic Journal*, January 1992, pp. 690–708.

U.S. Supreme Court. The British government and its fellow litigants hope to recoup some of the $4 billion paid under the previous unitary tax. In a related study, researchers found that unitary taxes were found to be a strong deterrent in the site selection process by Japanese-owned manufacturers in the United States.

Tax planning for multinational operations is an extremely complex but vitally important aspect of international business. To plan effectively, multinational firms must understand not only the intricacies of their own operations worldwide, but also the different structures and interpretations of tax liabilities across countries. The primary objective of multinational tax planning is to minimize the firm's worldwide tax burden. This objective, however, must not be pursued without full recognition that decision making within the firm must always be based on the economic fundamentals of the firm's line of business, and not on convoluted policies undertaken purely for the reduction of tax liability.

Executives with tax responsibility in a multinational firm should have a background in public finance so they can understand the principles of tax neutrality, equity, revenue, and morality. They should have experience in tax law in order to be able to follow the various tax rulings as they apply to international business practice, and they should also be able to read a number of foreign languages to keep abreast of foreign tax rulings. Naturally they should have accounting experience, since a large part of day-to-day tax administration involves decisions about whether specific transactions are tax deductible or whether a particular transfer price can be defended as an "arm's-length" transaction. Needless to say, the ideal international tax executive probably does not exist. Instead, tax planning is effected by group action, with each group member contributing expertise in one or more of the areas just described.

With tax planning so complex, this chapter cannot create tax experts. Rather it sets out to acquaint the reader with the overall international tax environment. At least a minimum of sophisticated knowledge of tax structures is needed by every international financial executive because many decisions require consideration of such factors. As evident from previous chapters, taxes have a major impact on corporate net income and cash flow through their influence on foreign investment decisions, financial structure, determination of the cost of capital, foreign exchange management, working capital management, and financial control.

The following sections explain the most important aspects of the international tax environments and specific features that affect multinational operations. Prior to explaining the specifics of multinational taxation in practice, however, we introduce two areas of fundamental importance: tax morality and tax neutrality.

Tax Morality

The multinational firm faces not only a morass of foreign taxes but also an ethical question. In many countries taxpayers, corporate or individual, do not voluntarily comply with the tax laws. Smaller domestic firms and individuals are the chief violators. The multinational firm must decide whether to follow a practice of full disclosure to tax authorities or adopt the philosophy of "when in Rome, do as the Romans do." Given the local prominence of most foreign affiliates and the political sensitivity of their position, most multinational firms follow the full disclosure practice. Some firms, however, believe their competitive position would be eroded if they did not avoid taxes to the same extent as their domestic competitors. Obviously there is no prescriptive answer to the problem, since business ethics are partly a function of cultural heritage and historical development.

There is also a potential morality problem on the part of the host country. Some countries have imposed what seem to be arbitrary punitive tax penalties on multinational firms for presumed violations of local tax laws. Property or wealth tax assessments are sometimes perceived by the foreign firm to be excessively large when compared with those levied on locally owned firms.

Tax Neutrality

When a government decides to levy a tax, it must consider not only the potential revenue from the tax, or how efficiently it can be collected, but also the effect the proposed tax can have on private economic behavior. For example, the U.S. government's policy on taxation of foreign-source income does not have as its sole objective the raising of revenue but has multiple objectives. These include the following:

- The desire to neutralize tax incentives that might favor (or disfavor) U.S. private investment in developed countries.
- Provision of an incentive for U.S. private investment in developing countries.
- Improvement of the U.S. balance of payments by removing the advantages of artificial tax havens and encouraging repatriation of funds.
- Raising of revenue.

The ideal tax should not only raise revenue efficiently but also have as few negative effects on economic behavior as possible. Some theorists argue that the ideal tax should be completely *neutral* in its effect on private decisions and completely *equitable* among taxpayers. However, other theorists claim that national policy objectives such as balance of payments or investment in developing countries should be encouraged through an active tax incentive policy rather than requiring taxes to be neutral and equitable. Most tax systems compromise between these two viewpoints.

One way to view neutrality is to require the burden of taxation on each dollar, mark, or yen of profit earned in domestic operations by a domestic multinational firm be equal to the burden of taxation on each currency-equivalent of profit earned by the same firm in its foreign operations. This is called *domestic neutrality*. A second way to view neutrality is to require the tax burden on each foreign affiliate of the firm be equal to the tax burden on its competitors in the same country. This is called *foreign neutrality*. The latter interpretation is often supported by multinational firms because it focuses more on the competitiveness of the individual firm in individual country markets.

The issue of *tax equity* is also difficult to define and measure. In theory, an equitable tax is one that imposes the same total tax burden on all taxpayers who are similarly situated and located in the same tax jurisdiction. In the case of foreign investment income, the U.S. Treasury argues that since the United States uses the nationality principle to claim tax jurisdiction, U.S.-owned foreign affiliates are in the same tax jurisdiction as U.S. domestic affiliates. Therefore a dollar earned in foreign operations should be taxed at the same rate and paid at the same time as a dollar earned in domestic operations.

National Tax Environments

Contrary to the fundamental objectives of national tax authorities, it is widely agreed that taxes do affect economic decisions made by multinational firms. Tax treaties between nations and differential tax structures, rates, and practices all result in a less than "level playing field" for the multinational firms competing on world markets.

Exhibit 21.1 provides an overview of corporate tax rates as applicable to the United States, Germany, and Japan. The categorizations of income (e.g., distributed versus undistributed profits), the differences in tax rates, and the discrimination in tax rates applicable to income earned in specific countries serves to introduce the critical dimensions of tax planning for the multinational firm.

National Tax Jurisdictions

Nations typically structure their tax systems along one of two basic approaches: the worldwide approach or the territorial approach. Both approaches are attempts to determine which firms, foreign or domestic by incorporation, or which incomes, foreign or domestic in origin, are subject to the taxation of host country tax authorities.

The *worldwide approach,* also referred to as the *residential* or *national approach,* levies taxes on the income earned by firms regardless of where the income was earned (domestically or abroad). A multinational firm earning income both at home and abroad would therefore find its worldwide income taxed by its home country tax authorities. For example, a country like the United States taxes the income earned by firms based in the United States regardless of whether the income earned by the firm is domestically sourced or foreign sourced.[1] The primary problem is that this does not address the income earned by foreign firms operating within the United States. Countries like the United States then apply the principle of *territorial taxation* to foreign firms within their legal jurisdiction, taxing all income earned by foreign firms in their borders as well.

The *territorial approach,* also termed the *source approach,* focuses on the income earned by firms within the legal jurisdiction of the host country, not on the country of firm incorporation. Countries like Germany, which follow the territorial approach, apply taxes equally to foreign or domestic firms on income earned within the country, but in principle not on income earned outside the country. The territorial approach, like the worldwide approach, results in a major gap in coverage if resident firms earn income outside the country, but are

---

[1]In the case of the United States, ordinary foreign-sourced income is taxed only as remitted to the parent firm. As with all questions of tax, however, there are numerous conditions and exceptions.

Exhibit 21.1   Comparison of Corporate Tax Rates: Japan, Germany, and the United States

Taxable Income Category	Japan[a]	Germany[b]	United States[c]
Corporate income tax rates:			
Profits distributed to stockholders	37.5%	36%	35%
Undistributed profits	37.5%	50%	35%
Branches of foreign corporations	37.5%	46%	35%
Withholding taxes on dividends (portfolio):			
with Japan	—	15%	15%
with Germany	15%	—	15%
with United States	15%	5%	—
Withholding taxes on dividends (substantial holdings):[d]			
with Japan	—	15%	10%
with Germany	10%	—	5%
with United States	10%	10%	—
Withholding taxes on interest:			
with Japan	—	10%	10%
with Germany	10%	—	0%
with United States	10%	0%	—
Withholding taxes on royalties:			
with Japan	—	10%	10%
with Germany	10%	—	0%
with United States	10%	0%	—

[a]Corporations operating in Japan, both foreign and domestic, whose accounting periods end between April 1, 1992, and March 31, 1994, are subject to a special corporate income tax surcharge of 2.5% for income above ¥4,000,000.

[b]German corporate income tax rates are scheduled to change by year:

	1992	1993	1994
Undistributed profits (%)	50.00	45.50	47.75
Branches of foreign corporations (%)	46.00	41.86	43.93

[c]The United States and Germany concluded a new bilateral tax agreement on August 21, 1991.

[d]"Substantial holdings" for the United States apply only to intercorporate dividends. In Germany and Japan, "substantial holdings" apply to corporate shareholders of greater than 25%.

Source: *Corporate Taxes: A Worldwide Summary,* Price Waterhouse, 1993. Rates are as in effect on January 1, 1993.

not taxed by the country in which the profits are earned. In this case, tax authorities extend tax coverage to income earned abroad if it is not currently covered by foreign tax jurisdictions. Once again, a mix of the two tax approaches is necessary for full coverage of income.[2]

If the worldwide approach to international taxation was followed to the letter, it would end the *tax-deferral* privilege for many multinational firms. Foreign affiliates of

---

[2]Government tax authorities are not inherently "mean spirited"; tax authorities generally attempt to treat all firms equitably so neutrality is approximately observed. A firm that escapes taxation internationally due to a gap or "loophole" in national tax jurisdictions would have an undue competitive advantage on world markets.

multinational firms pay host country corporate income taxes, but many parent countries defer claiming additional income taxes on that foreign-source income *until it is remitted to the parent firm.* For example, U.S. corporate income taxes on some types of foreign-source income of U.S.-owned affiliates incorporated abroad are deferred until the earnings are remitted to the U.S. parent. As we see in the case of the United States, the ability to defer corporate income taxes is highly restricted and has been the subject of many of the tax law changes in the past three decades.

Foreign Tax Credits

To prevent double taxation of the same income, most home countries grant a *foreign tax credit* for income taxes paid to a foreign host country. Countries differ on how they calculate the foreign tax credit and what kinds of limitations they place on the total amount claimed. We explain the U.S. method of calculating the foreign tax credit and limitations on its use later in this chapter. Normally foreign tax credits are also available for withholding taxes paid to other countries on dividends, royalties, interest, and other income remitted to the parent. The value-added tax and other sales taxes are not eligible for a foreign tax credit but are typically deductible from pretax income as an expense.

Tax Treaties

A network of bilateral tax treaties, many of which are modeled after one proposed by the Organization for Economic Cooperation and Development (OECD), provides another means of reducing double taxation. Tax treaties normally define how or if taxes are to be imposed on income earned in one country by the nationals of another. Tax treaties are bilateral, with the two signatories specifying what rates are applicable to which types of income. Exhibit 21.1's specification of withholding taxes on dividends, interest, and royalty payments between resident corporations of the United States, Germany, and Japan is a classic example of the structure of tax treaties. Note that Germany, for example, imposes a 10% withholding tax on royalty payments to Japanese investors; royalty payments to U.S. investors are withheld at a 0% rate.

   The individual bilateral tax jurisdictions as specified through tax treaties are particularly important for firms that are primarily exporting to another country rather than doing business there through a "permanent establishment." The latter would be the case for manufacturing operations. A firm that only exports would not want any of its other worldwide income taxed by the importing country. Tax treaties define what is a "permanent establishment" and what constitutes a limited presence for tax purposes.

   Tax treaties also typically result in reduced withholding tax rates between the two signatory countries, the negotiation of the treaty itself serving as a forum for opening and expanding business relationships between the two countries. This practice is important to both multinational firms operating through foreign affiliates, earning *active income,* and individual portfolio investors simply receiving *passive income* in the form of dividends, interest, or royalties.[3]

---

[3]Summaries of corporate taxes worldwide and the bilateral treaties in effect between countries are available from a number of sources. One of the most widely used is *Corporate Taxes: A Worldwide Summary,* Information Guide, Price Waterhouse, updated annually.

Exhibit 21.2   Corporate Tax Rates in Selected Countries (percentage of taxable income)

Country	Tax Rate	Country	Tax Rate	Country	Tax Rate
Antigua & Barbuda	40	Gibraltar	35	Papua New Guinea	25
Argentina	30	Greece	35	Paraguay	30
Australia	39	Guatemala	25	Peru	30
Austria	30	Guyana	35	Philippines	35
Bahamas	0	Honduras	35	Poland	40
Barbados	40	Hong Kong	17.5	Portugal	36
Belgium	39	Hungary	40	Puerto Rico	22
Belize	35	India	45	Qatar	50
Bermuda	0	Indonesia	35	Russian Federation	32
Bophutswana	40	Ireland	40	St. Lucia	33.33
Botswana	40	Isle of Man	20	Saudi Arabia	45
Brazil (monthly)	25	Italy	36	Senegal	35
British Virgin Islands	0/15	Ivory Coast	35	Singapore	30
Brunei	30	Jamaica	33.3	South Africa	48
Bulgaria	40	Japan	37.5	Spain	35
Cameroon	38.5	Kazakhstan	25	Swaziland	37.5
Canada	37.5	Kenya	35	Sweden	30
Cayman Islands	0	Korea	34	Switzerland	37.5
Channel Islands	20	Kuwait	55	Taiwan	25
Jersey	20	Liechtenstein	20	Tanzania	35
Chile	35	Luxembourg	33	Thailand	30
China	30	Macau	15 + 5	Trinidad & Tobago	45
Colombia	30	Malawi	35	Turkey	46
Congo	49	Malaysia	34	Uganda	35
Costa Rica	30	Malta	35	United Kingdom	33
Cyprus	25	Mauritius	35	United States	35
Czech Republic	45	Mexico	35	Uruguay	30
Denmark	34	Morocco	38	Vanuatu	0
Dominican Republic	27	Namibia	40	Venezuela	30
Ecuador	36	Netherlands	35	Western Samoa	48
Egypt	40	Netherlands Antilles	39	Zaire	50
El Salvador	25	New Caledonia	30	Zambia	40
Estonia	35	New Zealand	33	Zimbabwe	42.5
Fiji	35	Nicaragua	30		
Finland	25	Nigeria	35		
France	33.33	Norway	28		
Gabon	40	Oman	35		
Germany	36	Pakistan	55		
Ghana	35	Panama	0/45		

Corporate income tax rates for nonfinancial business. British Virgin Islands charge 0% corporate income tax for registered international business companies. Macau imposes base rate of 15% plus a 5% stamp duty. Panama imposes no income tax on foreign income of resident corporations. For actual tax liability calculations see original source.

Source: Price Waterhouse, *Corporate Taxes: A Worldwide Summary,* Information Guide, 1993 Edition.

Tax Types

Taxes are classified on the basis of whether they are applied directly to income, *direct taxes,* or on the basis of some other measurable performance characteristic of the firm, called *indirect taxes.* Exhibit 21.2 illustrates the wide range of corporate income taxes in the world today.

Income Tax. Many governments rely on income taxes, both personal and corporate, for their primary revenue source. Corporate income taxes are widely used among industrialized countries today. Many countries impose different corporate tax rates on distributed income versus undistributed income, as in the case of Germany in Exhibit 21.1. Corporate income tax rates vary over a relatively wide range, rising as high as 55% in Kuwait and Pakistan and as low as 17.5% in Hong Kong, 15% in the British Virgin Islands, and effectively 0% in a number of offshore tax havens discussed later in this chapter. Brazil, because of the hyperinflation suffered over the past decade, imposes a 25% income tax on *monthly income,* the firm's fiscal year being irrelevant!

Withholding Tax. Passive income (dividends, interest, royalties) earned by a resident of one country within the tax jurisdiction of a second country is normally subject to a withholding tax. The reason for the institution of withholding taxes is actually quite simple: Governments recognize that most international investors will not file a tax return in each country in which they invest, and the government therefore wishes to assure that a minimum tax payment is received. As the term *withholding* implies, the taxes are withheld by the corporation from the payment made to the investor, and the taxes withheld are then turned over to government authorities. Withholding taxes are a major subject of bilateral tax treaties, and generally range between 0 and 25%.

Value-Added Tax. One type of tax that has achieved great prominence is the value-added tax, a national sales tax collected at each stage of production or sale of consumption goods in proportion to the value added during that stage. In general, production goods such as plant and equipment have not been subject to the value-added tax. Certain basic necessities such as medicines and other health-related expenses, education and religious activities, and the postal service are usually exempt or taxed at lower rates. The value-added tax has been adopted as the main source of revenue from indirect taxation by all members of the European Union, most other countries in western Europe, a number of Latin American countries, and scattered other countries.[4] A numerical example of a value-added tax computation is shown in Exhibit 21.3.

Other National Taxes. There are a variety of other national taxes, which vary in importance from country to country. We mentioned the *turnover tax* (tax on the purchase or sale of securities in some country stock markets) and the *tax on undistributed profits* before. *Property* and *inheritance taxes,* also termed *transfer taxes,* are imposed in a

---

[4]An excellent summary of the experience of various countries with value-added taxes, as well as information on each country's system, can be found in Price Waterhouse, *Value-Added Tax,* November 1979.

Exhibit 21.3   Value-Added Taxes & Fence Posts

This is an example how a wooden fence post would be assessed for value-added taxes in the course of its production and subsequent sale. A value-added tax of 10% is assumed.

The original tree owner sells to the lumber mill, for $0.20, that part of a tree that ultimately becomes the fence post. The grower has added $0.20 in value up to this point by planting and raising the tree. While collecting $0.20 from the lumber mill, the grower must set aside $0.02 to pay the value-added tax to the government. The lumber mill processes the tree into fence posts and sells each post for $0.40 to the lumber wholesaler. The lumber mill has added $0.20 in value ($0.40 less $0.20) through its processing activities. Therefore the lumber mill owner must set aside $0.02 to pay the mill's value-added tax to the government.

In practice, the owner would probably calculate the mill's tax liability as 10% of $0.40, or $0.04, with a tax credit of $0.02 for the value-added tax already paid by the tree owner. The lumber wholesaler and retailer also add value to the fence post through their selling and distribution activities. They are assessed $0.01 and $0.03 respectively, making the cumulative value-added tax collected by the government $0.08, or 10% of the final sales price.

Stage of production	Sales price	Value added	Value-added tax at 10%	Cumulative Value-added tax
Tree owner	$0.20	$0.20	$0.02	$0.02
Lumber mill	$0.40	$0.20	$0.02	$0.04
Lumber wholesaler	$0.50	$0.10	$0.01	$0.05
Lumber retailer	$0.80	$0.30	$0.03	$0.08

variety of ways to achieve intended social redistribution of income and wealth as much as to raise revenue. There are a number of red-tape charges for public services that are in reality user taxes. Sometimes foreign exchange purchases or sales are in effect hidden taxes inasmuch as the government earns revenue rather than just regulates imports and exports for balance of payments reasons.

Tax Dimensions of Multinational Operations

Parent countries differ with respect to their treatment of foreign-source income earned by their own multinational firms. A partial list of the origins of these differences would appear as follows:

- Varying interpretations of how to achieve tax neutrality,
- The treatment of the tax deferral privilege,
- The method of granting credit for foreign income taxes already paid to host countries,
- Concessions gained in bilateral tax treaties, and
- The treatment of intercompany transactions.

The way a parent country taxes foreign-source income affects the way multinational firms organize their foreign operations. In particular, taxes have an important bearing on whether to operate overseas through foreign branches of the parent firm or locally incorporated foreign affiliates. Tax considerations also affect the perceived desirability of utilizing foreign affiliates located in tax-haven countries. A discussion of these issues follows.

Intercompany Transactions and Transfer Prices

The problem of intercompany transactions, particularly transfer pricing, is a substantial area of concern for the multinational firm. *Transfer pricing* refers to the prices charged, either domestically or internationally, for goods, services, and technology exchanged between related units. Although the problem is complex enough domestically, internationally it proves an area of continual management attention and government oversight. Because so much of the "business" of a multinational firm is with other affiliated units, and the nature of the product or service being transferred is so firm specific, firms can potentially alter tax liabilities per country through inappropriate or manipulated transfer prices. Transfer pricing is extremely technical, and involves a number of issues beyond that of simply tax. Chapter 22 considers transfer pricing in detail within the more general context of multinational working capital management.

Nevertheless, the transfer price implications of national tax codes, such as that of Section 482 of the United States, are worthy of a more detailed analysis from the tax viewpoint. This subject is highly technical and one that often changes because of tax court rulings. Therefore we cannot do it justice in this book but suggest that the reader refer to articles and other authorities cited in the bibliography.

Branch Versus Locally Incorporated Affiliate

A multinational firm normally has a choice of whether to organize a foreign affiliate as a branch of the parent or as a local corporation. Both tax and nontax consequences must be considered. Nontax factors include the locus of legal liability, public image in the host country, managerial incentive considerations, and local legal and political requirements. Although important, nontax considerations are really outside the scope of this chapter on tax planning.

One major tax consideration is whether the foreign affiliate is expected to run at a loss for several years after start-up. If so, it might be preferable to organize originally as a branch operation to permit these anticipated losses to be consolidated in the parent's income statement for tax purposes. For example, tax laws in the United States and many other countries do not permit a foreign corporation to be consolidated for tax purposes, even though it is consolidated for reporting purposes, but do permit consolidation of foreign branches for tax purposes.

A second tax consideration is the net tax burden after paying withholding taxes on dividends. A multinational firm must weigh the benefit of potential tax deferral of home country taxes on foreign-source income from an incorporated foreign unit versus the total tax burden of paying foreign corporate income taxes and withholding taxes once the income is distributed to the parent corporation. A foreign branch's income would typically be taxed by the host country but with full credit against home country taxes. Its income would be consolidated with the rest of home country income and taxed at the home country tax rate (less the foreign tax credit).

A third tax consideration is important for firms engaged in natural resource exploration and development. Some countries allow exploration costs, and possibly part of development costs, to be written off as a current expense rather than requiring them to be capitalized and amortized over succeeding years. Therefore many of the multinational oil and mining firms choose to operate these activities overseas as branches rather than subsidiaries. U.S. firms have an additional incentive to use the branch form of organization overseas because this practice permits their use of the special depletion allowances permitted under the U.S. tax laws.

Further complicating the choice of structure are the various special-purpose organization forms permitted or encouraged by some countries. These are normally motivated by a country's desire to increase its exports or to promote development of less developed countries. For example, a U.S. firm can reduce the effective tax on foreign income by establishing a so-called possessions corporation in a U.S. possession such as Puerto Rico, Guam, or American Samoa.

Tax-Haven Affiliates and International Offshore Financial Centers (IOFCs)

Many multinational firms have foreign affiliates that act as tax havens for corporate funds awaiting reinvestment or repatriation. Tax-haven affiliates are partially a result of tax deferral features on earned foreign income allowed by some of the parent countries to their multinational firms. Tax-haven affiliates, also known as International Offshore Financial Centers (IOFCs), are typically established in a country that can meet the following requirements:

- A low tax on foreign investment or sales income earned by resident corporations and a low dividend withholding tax on dividends paid to the parent firm.

- A stable currency to permit easy conversion of funds into and out of the local currency. This requirement can be met by permitting and facilitating the use of Eurocurrencies.

- The facilities to support financial services, for example, good communications, professional qualified office workers, and reputable banking services.

- A stable government that encourages the establishment of foreign-owned financial and service facilities within its borders.

Exhibit 21.4 provides a map of most of the world's major offshore IOFCs.

The typical tax-haven affiliate owns the common stock of its related operating foreign affiliates. (There might be several tax-haven affiliates spotted around the world.) The tax-haven affiliate's equity is typically 100% owned by the parent firm. All transfers of funds might go through the tax-haven affiliates, including dividends and equity financing. Thus the parent country's tax on foreign-source income, which might normally be paid when a dividend is declared by a foreign affiliate, could continue to be deferred until the tax-haven affiliate itself pays a dividend to the parent firm. This event can be postponed indefinitely if foreign operations continue to grow and require new internal financing from the tax-haven affiliate. Thus multinational firms are able to operate a corporate pool of funds for foreign operations without having to repatriate foreign earnings through the parent country's tax machine.

For U.S. multinational firms the tax deferral privilege operating through a foreign affiliate was not originally a tax loophole. On the contrary, it was granted by the U.S.

Exhibit 21.4 International Offshore Banking Centers

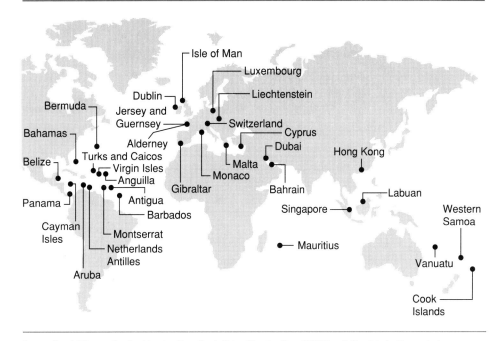

Isle of Man
Luxembourg
Liechtenstein
Dublin
Bermuda
Jersey and
Guernsey
Switzerland
Cyprus
Bahamas
Dubai
Alderney
Hong Kong
Belize
Turks and Caicos
Virgin Isles
Malta
Anguilla
Monaco
Panama
Gibraltar
Bahrain
Antigua
Labuan
Barbados
Singapore
Western
Samoa
Cayman
Isles
Montserrat
Mauritius
Netherlands
Antilles
Vanuatu
Aruba
Cook
Islands

Source: Special Report, *Sunday Morning Post, South China Morning Post,* 4/17/94, p. 7. Reprinted with permission.

government to allow U.S. firms to expand overseas and place them on a par with foreign competitors, which also enjoy similar types of tax deferral and export subsidies of one type or another.

Unfortunately, some U.S. firms distorted the original intent of tax deferral into tax avoidance. Transfer prices on goods and services bought from or sold to related affiliates were artificially rigged to leave all the income from the transaction in the tax-haven affiliate. This manipulation could be done by routing the legal title to the goods or services through the tax-haven affiliate, even though physically the goods or services never entered the tax-haven country. This maneuver left no residual tax base for either exporting or importing affiliates located outside the tax-haven country. Needless to say, tax authorities of both exporting and importing countries were dismayed by the lack of taxable income in such transactions.

One purpose of the U.S. Internal Revenue Act of 1962 was to eliminate the tax advantages of these "paper" foreign corporations without destroying the tax deferral privilege for those foreign manufacturing and sales affiliates that were established for business and economic motives rather than tax motives. Nevertheless, in some cases U.S. firms may have found loopholes in the law, permitting them to continue using their tax havens as originally intended. Others do not benefit from tax deferral but have found these affiliates useful as finance control centers for foreign operations.

U.S. Taxation of Foreign-Source Income

This section deals with U.S. government taxation of foreign-source income earned by U.S. multinational corporations, including certain key provisions of the U.S. tax code.

U.S. corporations are taxed within the United States on their worldwide income. The timing and amount of U.S. taxation, however, depends on the following key factors:

1. The type of income, *active* or *passive;*

2. The organizational structure of the U.S. multinational and its degree of ownership and control over the unit of income origination;

3. The relative corporate and withholding tax rates between the foreign country of income origin and the United States;

4. Whether the particular foreign-source income falls under one of a number of exceptions to the overall general principles.

Classification by Income Type and Country of Origin

Any home country could decide to tax separately income from each separate foreign country by each separate type of income. Alternatively, all types of income for each foreign country could be pooled, and a tax levied only on the sum of foreign income from each country. A third alternative would be to tax by type of income, with the parent allowed to pool income from many countries as long as it was of the same type. Similarly, all passive income from all countries would be pooled and taxed one time. Finally, of course, all foreign-source income from all countries and by all types could be put into one grand international pool and taxed once.

In general, the United States uses the third alternative (tax by type of income). Foreign-source income must be classified by type, or "basket," and separate taxes calculated and paid on the sum within that basket. However, within each basket, income from various countries may be pooled.

Combining by countries using pooling allows excess tax credits from countries with high effective tax rates on that basket to be used to neutralize taxes on income received from low-tax-rate countries. The effective combining of dividends from several countries to obtain the lowest effective overall rate is a major goal of tax planning.[5] However classifying income by baskets is a way for the United States tax code to limit the benefits of pooling.

---

[5]This offsetting of income from high-tax countries versus low-tax countries was important for U.S.-based multinationals as long as U.S. corporate income taxes were some of the lowest in the world. As was seen in Exhibit 21.2, however, this is no longer the case.

Classification by Earned Versus Distributed Income

Another classification is also possible. Within each cell, that is, for each type of income from each country, home country taxes could be levied on income (1) at the time earned abroad, or (2) only when that foreign-source income is returned to the home country as a dividend. With some important exceptions, the United States taxes foreign-source income of separately incorporated subsidiaries (in which the U.S. parent holds more than 10% voting equity) only at the time that income is returned to the United States as a dividend. However, earnings of unincorporated branches are taxed at the time earned.[6] The most important exception to this principle is *Subpart F income* (passive income) received from *controlled foreign corporations* (CFCs), a topic that we discuss separately later in this chapter.

The key principles of U.S. taxation of foreign-source income are summarized in Exhibit 21.5, which illustrates the two basic income classifications—active and passive—as they flow through the three primary international ownership structures: branches, subsidiaries, and affiliates.

Exhibit 21.5   Organizational Alternatives, Ownership Structure, and Income Classification of U.S. Foreign-Source Income

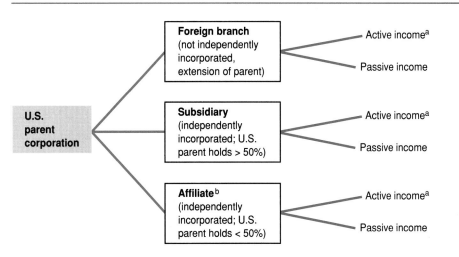

[a]*Active income* results from domestic production or provision of services by the firm itself. *Passive income* is any kind of remuneration derived from ownership of assets (dividends received from equity ownership in other enterprises or royalties for the use of technology or patents held) or the extension of credit (interest income from loans extended to affiliated or unaffiliated parties).

[b]10% is a widely accepted, yet arbitrary line, for distinguishing between *portfolio investment*, in which the holder does not intend to influence or control the operations of the entity, versus *foreign direct investment*, in which the investor intends to influence managerial or strategic decision making in the firm.

---

[6]In earlier chapters of this book we sometimes used the generic term *affiliate* to refer generally to all forms of foreign operation. In this section on taxation it is essential to differentiate between foreign-incorporated subsidiaries and other forms such as branches.

- Income (and losses) derived from a foreign branch of a U.S. corporation, regardless of whether the earnings are remitted to the U.S. parent during the current tax period, is consolidated with the domestic earnings of the parent firm for tax purposes.

- Active and passive income derived from an *uncontrolled foreign affiliate,* a foreign corporation in which a U.S. corporation holds more than 10% but less than 50% control, is taxed as remitted to the U.S. parent firm.

- Active income derived from a *controlled foreign corporation* (CFC), a foreign corporation in which a U.S. corporation holds more than 50% control, is taxed as remitted to its U.S. parent. Passive income, however, is taxed as earned (not as remitted) by the U.S. parent firm.

Foreign Tax Credits

U.S. corporations are taxed within the United States on their worldwide income (worldwide jurisdictional approach), under a system that allows U.S. tax credit for taxes *deemed paid* to foreign host governments. "Worldwide income" includes dividends and other distributions received from foreign-incorporated subsidiaries plus all profits (minus all losses) from branches. We first explain the basic concept and reason behind the allowance of foreign tax credits and then look at the particulars of how they are calculated under various circumstances.

Basic Concept of Foreign Tax Credits (FTCs)

A *tax credit* is a direct reduction of taxes that would otherwise be due and payable. It differs from a *deductible expense,* which is an expense used to reduce taxable income before the tax rate is applied. A $100 tax credit reduces taxes payable by the full $100, whereas a $100 deductible expense reduces taxable income by $100 and taxes payable by $100 × t, where t is the tax rate. Tax credits are more valuable on a dollar-for-dollar basis than are deductible expenses.

Without credits for foreign taxes paid, sequential taxation by the host government and then by the United States would result in a very high cumulative tax rate. To illustrate, assume the wholly owned foreign subsidiary of a U.S. parent earns $10,000 before local income taxes and pays a dividend equal to all of its after-tax income. The host country income tax rate is 30%, and the U.S. tax rate is 35%. For simplicity we assume no withholding taxes. Total taxation with and without allowances for tax credits is shown in Exhibit 21.6.

If tax credits are not allowed, sequential levying of both a 30% host country tax and then a 35% U.S. tax on the income that remains results in an effective 54.5% tax, a cumulative rate that would render many U.S. firms uncompetitive with single-country local firms. The effect of allowing tax credits is to limit total taxation on the *original* before-tax income to no more than the highest single rate among jurisdictions. In the case depicted in Exhibit 21.6, the effective overall tax rate of 35% with foreign tax credits is equivalent to the higher tax rate of the United States (and is the tax rate payable if the income had been earned at home).

Exhibit 21.6   Foreign Tax Credits as Calculated in the United States

	Without foreign tax credits	With foreign tax credits
Before-tax foreign income	$10,000	$10,000
Less foreign tax at 30%	−3,000	−3,000
Available to U.S. parent and paid as dividend	$ 7,000	$ 7,000
Less additional U.S. tax at 35%	−2,450	
Less incremental tax (after credits)		−500
Profit after all taxes	$ 4,550	$ 6,500
Total taxes, both jurisdictions	$ 5,450	$ 3,500
Effective overall tax rate (total taxes paid ÷ foreign income)	54.5%	35.0%

The $500 of additional U.S. tax under the tax credit system in Exhibit 21.6 is the amount needed to bring total taxation ($3,000 already paid plus the additional $500) up to but not beyond 35% of the original $10,000 of before-tax foreign income. We explain the calculation of this *foreign tax credit* next.

Calculating the Direct Foreign Tax Credit

Within each basket category, dividends received from U.S. corporate subsidiaries are fully taxable in the United States at U.S. tax rates but with tax credits allowed for direct taxes paid on income in a foreign country.[7] The amount of foreign tax allowed as a credit depends on five tax parameters (also illustrated as cases 1 to 5 in Exhibit 21.7):

1. Foreign corporate income tax rate;

2. U.S. corporate income tax rate;

3. Foreign corporate dividend withholding tax rate for nonresidents (per the applicable bilateral tax treaty between the specific country and the United States);

4. Proportion of ownership held by the U.S. corporation in the foreign firm;

5. Proportion of net income distributed, the dividend payout rate.

Other complicating factors are the basket classification and situations where the dividend exceeds that year's income. For the moment we ignore these complications.

The five cases depicted in Exhibit 21.7 are based on a foreign subsidiary of a U.S. corporation that earns $10,000 before local taxes. The U.S. corporate tax rate is 35%. The foreign tax rate is 30% in Cases 1 to 4 and 40% in Case 5.

Case 1: Foreign Subsidiary with 100% Payout (No Withholding Taxes).

Assuming the foreign subsidiary earns $10,000 before local taxes in its overall tax

---

[7]Exceptions to this general principle exist, especially for income that falls into specific baskets. Indirect taxes (valued-added taxes, sales taxes, excise taxes, and property taxes) are deductible as an expense, but do not serve as the base for tax credits.

Exhibit 21.7   U.S. Taxation of Foreign-Source Income

Baseline Values		Case 1	Case 2	Case 3	Case 4	Case 5
a	Foreign corporate income tax rate	30%	30%	30%	30%	40%
b	U.S. corporate income tax rate	35%	35%	35%	35%	35%
c	Foreign dividend withholding tax rate	0%	10%	10%	10%	10%
d	U.S. ownership in foreign firm	100%	100%	100%	40%	40%
e	Dividend payout rate of foreign firm	100%	100%	50%	50%	50%
Foreign Affiliate Tax Computation						
1.	Taxable income of foreign affiliate	$10,000	$10,000	$10,000	$10,000	$10,000
2.	Foreign corporate income taxes (rate a)	−3,000	−3,000	−3,000	−3,000	−4,000
3.	Net income available for profit distribution	$7,000	$7,000	$7,000	$7,000	$6,000
4.	Retained earnings ((1 − rate e) × line 3)	0	0	3,500	3,500	3,000
5.	Distributed earnings (rate e × line 3)	$7,000	$7,000	$3,500	$3,500	$3,000
6.	Distribution to U.S. corporation					
	(rate d × line 5)	$7,000	$7,000	$3,500	$1,400	$1,200
7.	Withholding taxes on dividends					
	(rate c × line 6)	0	700	350	140	120
8.	Net remittance to U.S. corporation	$7,000	$6,300	$3,150	$1,260	$1,080
U.S. Corporate Tax Computation on Foreign-Source Income						
9.	Dividend received (before withholding tax)	$7,000	$7,000	$3,500	$1,400	$1,200
10.	Add-back foreign deemed-paid tax					
	(line 6 ÷ line 3 × line 2)	3,000	3,000	1,500	600	800
11.	Grossed-up foreign dividend for U.S. taxation	$10,000	$10,000	$5,000	$2,000	$2,000
12.	Tentative U.S. tax liability (rate a × line 11)	3,500	3,500	1,750	700	700
13.	Less credit for foreign taxes:					
	a) Foreign income taxes paid	−3,000	−3,000	−1,500	−600	−800
	b) Foreign withholding taxes paid	−0	−700	−350	−140	−120
	c) Total	−3,000	−3,700	−1,850	−740	−920
14.	Additional U.S. taxes due (if line 12 > line 13c)	500	0	0	0	0
15.	Excess foreign tax credits (if line 12 < line 13c)	0	200	100	40	220
16.	After-tax income from foreign affiliate					
	(line 11 + line 13c − line 14)	$6,500	$6,300	$3,150	$1,260	$1,080
Tax Burden Measurement						
17.	Total taxes paid (foreign + domestic)	$3,500	$3,700	$1,850	$740	$920
18.	Effective tax rate on foreign income					
	(line 17 ÷ line 11)	35%	37%	37%	37%	46%

basket, it pays $3,000 in foreign taxes (30% foreign tax rate) and distributes all $7,000 in net income to its U.S. parent (100% payout rate). Because there are no withholding taxes, the U.S. parent receives a net remittance of the full $7,000.

The U.S. parent corporation takes the *full* before-tax foreign income of the foreign corporation—apportioned by its proportional ownership in the foreign corporation (in this case 100%)—into its taxable income. This is called *grossing up*.

The U.S. parent then calculates a tentative U.S. tax against the grossed-up foreign income. Assuming a 35% U.S. tax rate, the tentative U.S. tax on a grossed-up income of $10,000 is $3,500. The U.S. parent is then entitled under U.S. tax law to reduce this U.S. tax liability by a *deemed-paid foreign tax credit* for taxes already paid on the same income in the foreign country. The deemed-paid tax credit is calculated from *creditable taxes*. Creditable taxes are foreign income taxes paid on earnings by a foreign corporation that has paid a dividend to a qualifying U.S. corporation.[8] The deemed-paid credit in Case 1 is $3,000. The U.S. parent owes an additional $500 in U.S. taxes ($3,500 tentative U.S. tax less the deemed-paid credit of $3,000). The after-tax income earned by the U.S. parent corporation is $6,500, and the overall tax rate on the foreign income is 35% (total taxes of $3,500 on total income of $10,000). Note that although the foreign corporate tax rate was lower (30% to the U.S. 35% rate), the U.S. corporation ends up paying the higher effective rate.

Case 2: Foreign Subsidiary with 100% Payout (10% Withholding Tax). Assume the same foreign corporation earns the same income, but now all dividends paid to the U.S. parent corporation are subject to a 10% withholding tax. All other values remain the same as in Case 1. Although the actual net remittance to the U.S. parent is now lower, $6,300 instead of $7,000, the U.S. parent calculates the tentative U.S. tax on a grossed-up dividend of $7,000.

The tentative U.S. tax liability is again $3,500. The U.S. corporation can then deduct the amount of the deemed-paid credit ($3,000) and the full amount of withholding tax ($700) from its U.S. tax liability. Because the total foreign tax credits of $3,700 are greater than the tentative U.S. tax of $3,500, the U.S. parent owes no additional U.S. taxes. The U.S. parent has, in fact, an excess foreign tax credit of $200 ($3,700 − $3,500), which it can carry back two years or carry forward five years. The effective foreign tax rate is now 37% as a result of paying higher taxes abroad than it would have theoretically paid at home, including the withholding tax.

Case 3: Foreign Subsidiary with 50% Payout (10% Withholding Tax). In this case it is assumed all tax rates remain the same, but the foreign corporation chooses to pay out only 50% of net income rather than 100%. As a result, all dividends, withholding taxes, deemed-paid credits, tentative U.S. tax liabilities, foreign tax credits, after-tax income from the foreign subsidiary, and finally total taxes paid, are cut in half. The overall effective tax rate is again 37%, higher than what would have theoretically been paid if the income had been earned inside rather than outside the United States.

Case 4: Foreign Affiliate with 50% Payout (10% Withholding Tax). Case 4 illustrates to what degree these cash flows change when the U.S. parent corporation

---

[8]In order to qualify, a U.S. corporation must own at least 10% of the voting power of the distributing foreign corporation. Furthermore, if the 10% owned (first-tier) foreign corporation itself owns 10% or more of another (second-tier) foreign corporation, and the second-tier corporation owns 10% or more of a third-tier corporation, a portion of the second- and third-tier corporations' foreign income taxes will also be creditable to the U.S. taxpayer to the extent that earnings are distributed to the first- and second-tier corporations. However, there must be a minimum indirect ownership of 5% in the second- and third-tier corporations.

owns only 40% of the foreign corporation. As illustrated in Exhibit 21.7, the 40% ownership acts only as a "scale factor" in apportioning dividends paid, withholding tax withheld, and tax liabilities and credits resulting. Once again the U.S. parent corporation has excess foreign tax credits as a result of paying more taxes abroad than it is liable for at home. The overall effective tax rate on the reduced after-tax net income for the foreign affiliate of $1,260 is 37%.

Case 5: Foreign Affiliate with 50% Payout (40% Foreign Corporate Tax, 10% Withholding Tax). This fifth and final case illustrates the increasing tax burden on the U.S. parent corporation when the corporate income tax in the foreign country is higher than that in the United States. The combined impact of a 40% foreign income tax and a 10% withholding tax, even after calculation of deemed-paid foreign tax credits, results in a rising excess foreign tax credit and a substantially higher effective tax rate of 46%. Clearly, when the implications of Case 5 are combined with the number of countries with corporate tax rates higher than that of the United States (see Exhibit 21.2), the tax burden borne by U.S.-based multinational firms is a significant competitive concern.

Management Aspects of Using Foreign Tax Credits

As demonstrated in the previous cases, if income is received from a foreign country that imposes higher corporate income taxes than the United States (or combined income and withholding tax), total creditable taxes will exceed U.S. taxes on that foreign income. The result is excess foreign tax credits. The amount of credit a taxpayer can use in any year, however, is limited to the U.S. tax on that foreign income. Foreign tax credits *cannot* be used to reduce taxes levied on income that year from U.S. sources.

Nevertheless, excess foreign tax credits that cannot be used in a particular year can be carried back for two years and forward for five years and can be treated like foreign creditable taxes for those carry-over years. The total foreign tax creditable in any one year, however, is limited according to the following formula:

$$\text{Creditable tax limit} = \frac{\text{total foreign taxable income}}{\text{total taxable income}} \times \text{U.S. tax on total income.}$$

The preceding sample cases assumed that dividends were 100% or less of the net income of the foreign subsidiary. If dividends in any year *exceed* the earnings and profits of that year, the calculation is based on an accumulated pool of all post-December 31, 1986, undistributed earnings and foreign taxes.

Controlled Foreign Corporations and Subpart F Income

The rule that U.S. shareholders do not pay U.S. taxes on foreign-source income until that income is remitted to the United States is modified by an exception called *Subpart F* income. The exception is designed to prevent the use of arrangements between operating companies and base companies located in tax havens as a means of deferring U.S. taxes and to encourage greater repatriation of foreign incomes.

Several definitions are needed to understand Subpart F income:

- A *controlled foreign corporation* (CFC) is any foreign corporation in which U.S. shareholders, including corporate parents, own more than 50% of the combined voting power or total value.

- A U.S. *shareholder* is a U.S. person owning 10% or more of the voting power of a controlled foreign corporation. A U.S. *person* is a citizen or resident of the United States, a domestic partnership, a domestic corporation, or any nonforeign trust or estate. The required percentages are based on *constructive ownership,* under which an individual is deemed to own shares registered in the names of other family members, trusts, and so on.[9]

Under these definitions a more-than-50% owned "subsidiary" of a U.S. corporation would be a controlled foreign corporation, and the U.S. parent would be taxed on certain undistributed income (Subpart F income) of that controlled foreign corporation.

Subpart F income, subject to immediate U.S. taxation even when not remitted, is income of a type otherwise easily shifted offshore to avoid current taxation. It includes (1) passive income received by the foreign corporation such as dividends, interest, rents, royalties, net foreign currency gains, net commodities gains, and income from the sale of non-income-producing property, (2) income from the insurance of U.S. risks; (3) financial service income; (4) shipping income; (5) oil-related income; and (6) certain related-party sales and service income.

Subpart F, restated, provides that if a foreign corporation is considered to be a controlled foreign corporation, each U.S. shareholder owning 10% or more of that CFC must include the shareholder's prorated share of the CFC's Subpart F income in the shareholder's gross income. Thus Subpart F income is subject to current U.S. taxation at the shareholder level even though not remitted to the United States.

Foreign Sales Corporation (FSC)

Over the years the United States has introduced into U.S. tax laws special incentives dealing with international operations. To benefit from these incentives, a firm may have to form separate corporations for qualifying and nonqualifying activities. The most important U.S. special corporation is a foreign sales corporation (FSC).

FSCs were introduced in the Tax Reform Act of 1984 as a device to provide tax-exempt income for U.S. persons or corporations having export-oriented activities. FSCs replaced domestic international sales corporations (DISCs), which had been created by the Revenue Act of 1971 for somewhat similar purposes.

---

[9]Since 10% ownership is required by each U.S. shareholder, a foreign corporation in which six unrelated U.S. citizens and/or corporations each own 9% of the combined voting power or total value would not be a controlled foreign corporation, even though total U.S. ownership is 54%. Nor would a foreign corporation in which U.S. shareholders own exactly 50% be a controlled foreign corporation.

FSCs Versus DISCs

Briefly, a DISC was a U.S. corporation formed to export U.S.-produced goods to either foreign affiliates or unrelated foreign buyers. A portion of the earnings and profits of a DISC were not taxed to the DISC, but instead were taxed to the DISC's shareholders when distributed or deemed distributed to them.

Almost from their beginning, DISCs were the subject of dispute between the United States and other signatories of the General Agreement on Tariffs and Trade (GATT). Opponents contended that the DISC allowed an illegal export subsidy in violation of GATT regulations because it permitted indefinite deferral of direct taxes on income earned from U.S. exports. GATT permits indirect taxes such as value-added taxes to be rebated, but the provision on direct taxes such as income taxes is more complicated. Export income may be exempt from a member country's income taxes only if the economic processes by which that income arises occur outside the country. The United States did not concede that DISCs were in violation of GATT, but to avoid further disputes it replaced the DISC with the FSC.

A FSC differs from a DISC in that use of a FSC allows *permanent* exemption of certain income from U.S. taxes, whereas the DISC only allowed *deferral* of taxes. A FSC is a foreign corporation, whereas a DISC was a domestic U.S. corporation.

Tax Benefits of a FSC

"Exempt foreign trade income" of a FSC is not subject to U.S. income taxes. Exempt foreign trade income is income from foreign sources that is not effectively connected with the conduct of a trade or business within the United States. Exempt foreign trade income is a portion of total foreign trade income.

A FSC's total foreign trade income is derived from gross receipts from the sale of export property; lease or rental of export property; incidental services provided with the sale or lease of export property; and fees for engineering, architectural, or managerial services. The exempt portion of the FSC's total foreign trade income depends on the pricing rules used. "Export property" is manufactured, produced, grown, or extracted from the United States by an entity other than the FSC, and is sold, leased, or rented outside the United States.

If foreign trade income is based on arm's-length pricing between unrelated parties, or between related parties under the rules of Section 482 of the Internal Revenue Code, then exempt foreign trade income is defined as 34% of the income from the transaction. If prices are set under special administrative rules established for FSCs, exempt foreign trade income is the fraction 17/23 of income from the transaction. That portion of total foreign trade income not exempt is regarded as effectively derived from the conduct of trade or business by a permanent business establishment in the United States, and is therefore subject to U.S. income taxes.

Exempt income of a FSC may be distributed to its U.S. shareholders on a tax-free basis. Dividends paid from nonexempt income of a FSC are fully taxable to the U.S. parent. The legal requirements for the creation of a FSC are described in Exhibit 21.8.

Exhibit 21.8 Creation of a Foreign Sales Corporation

A corporation qualifies as a FSC if it maintains an adequate foreign presence, has foreign management, carries out some economic processes outside the United States that are related to its export income, and complies with appropriate transfer price legislation. These rules are to ensure the FSC is a bona fide foreign corporation that earns its exempt income from economic activities conducted outside the United States.

Adequate Foreign Presence

To establish an adequate foreign presence, a FSC must satisfy each of the following requirements:

1. The FSC must be a foreign corporation, incorporated under the laws of a foreign country or certain overseas possessions of the United States, such as Guam, American Samoa, the Commonwealth of the Northern Mariana Islands, and the Virgin Islands. Puerto Rico does not qualify because it is within the U.S. customs area. Most FSCs are owned by a single U.S. parent corporation. However, a FSC may have up to a maximum of 25 shareholders. This provision allows the benefits of FSCs to pass through directly to owners of closely held corporations.
2. A FSC may not issue preferred stock, although under some conditions separate classes of common stock are allowed. Congress was concerned that different classes of stock might be used to direct some dividends to shareholders having taxable income and other dividends to shareholders having net operating losses.
3. The FSC must maintain a permanent establishment outside the United States, including an office, books, and records. The office must be in a fixed location, be equipped for the performance of the firm's business, and be regularly used for business activity of the FSC.
4. At least one member of the FSC's board of directors must be a nonresident of the United States.
5. The FSC must elect to be treated as a FSC, and the FSC may not be a member of an affiliated group of corporations that also includes a DISC as a member.

Foreign Management

The FSC must be managed outside the United States, as indicated by the following requirements:

1. All board of directors meetings and all shareholders meetings must be held outside the United States.
2. The principal bank account of the corporation must be maintained outside the United States.
3. All dividends, legal and accounting fees, and salaries of members of the board of directors must be disbursed from bank accounts outside the United States.

Foreign Economic Process

Certain economic processes must take place outside the United States for each individual transaction for which tax exemption is sought.

1. The solicitation, negotiation, or making of the contract must take place outside the United States.
2. Foreign direct costs incurred by the FSC and attributable to each transaction must be paid by the FSC. Direct transaction costs are for processing customers' orders and arranging for delivery; billing customers and receiving payment; arranging and paying of transportation, advertising, and sales promotion; and assuming credit risk. The FSC must pay either 50% of each of the cost categories above, or 85% of the direct costs in any two categories.

Transfer Pricing Rules

Taxable income of the FSC must be determined from transfer prices that are either based on arm's-length pricing between unrelated parties or on use of Section 482 of the Internal Revenue Code for transactions between related parties. An alternative is for the FSC to price under certain "safe harbor" rules designated "administrative pricing rules."

Possessions Corporation

A business carried on to a substantial extent in a U.S. possession can be carried on by a separate U.S. corporation, which, if it meets the requirements for a possessions corporation, is not subject to U.S. tax on income earned outside the United States unless the income is *received* in the United States. Although technically a U.S. corporation, a possessions corporation is treated like a foreign corporation in nearly every respect. U.S. corporate shareholders of a possessions corporation may claim deemed-paid foreign tax credit if they own 10% of its stock. Its dividends do not qualify for the dividends-received deduction, and it may not be included in a consolidated U.S. return.

Requirements

To qualify as a possessions corporation, a corporation must satisfy the following requirements:

1. It is a domestic U.S. corporation.
2. At least 80% of its gross income is derived from within a U.S. possession.
3. At least 75% of its gross income is derived from the active conduct of a trade or business in a U.S. possession.

Requirements 2 and 3 must be met for the three years preceding the end of the tax year or from date of incorporation for a new corporation.

Possessions of the United States include the Commonwealth of Puerto Rico, the Panama Canal Zone, Guam, American Samoa, and Wake and Midway Islands.

The U.S. Virgin Islands, although a U.S. possession, are excluded from possessions corporation benefits because of their peculiar tax situation. A U.S. corporation operating in the U.S. Virgin Islands pays its taxes, as computed under the U.S. Internal Revenue Code, to the Islands Treasury. However, under the Islands' incentive legislation, a qualifying corporation would receive a subsidy from the Islands of up to 75% of the tax paid. Thus, in effect, qualifying corporations would pay tax of about 8.75% (25% of 35%) on Virgin Islands income. In order to qualify, the corporation must meet requirements similar to 2 and 3 as just listed and must also satisfy the incentive legislation requirements.

Exclusion from Gross Income

A corporation meeting the requirements just outlined excludes from U.S. gross income amounts earned outside the United States unless the income is received in the United States. Thus a possessions corporation should arrange to *receive* income initially outside the United States, although it may subsequently transfer it from a foreign bank account to a bank account in the United States.

Prior to 1976, a possessions corporation was exempt from U.S. tax until the income was paid as a dividend to the U.S. parent company. The exemption was granted in an indirect way by subjecting the income to U.S. tax and then allowing a credit equal to the U.S. tax. The 1986 tax revisions retain but tighten up certain 1982 changes in the possessions tax credit. The essence of these is that any portion of the income of a possessions corporation attributable to intangibles developed in the United States must be paid or allocated to a U.S.-related party in order for any of the income allocated to the intangible to be eligible for the possessions credit.

Thus the possessions corporation's income is subject to U.S. tax, but a tax-sparing credit is allowed for U.S. taxes on foreign-source income attributable to the conduct of a trade or business in a U.S. possession and qualified possessions-source investment income. The net result is that nonqualified income is subject to U.S. tax but possessions income is exempt from tax.

Global View
Puerto Rico's Shaky Tax Credit

Over the last 20 years Puerto Rico has emerged as a major manufacturing and financial center, thanks almost entirely to the benefits of the "possessions tax credit." The subsidy, outlined in Section 936 of the U.S. Internal Revenue Code, allows American companies a 100% tax credit on profits earned in Puerto Rico (as well as in other possessions, such as Guam and American Samoa, which have not taken advantage of it). All told, U.S. corporate assets in Puerto Rico amount to $18 to 20 billion, says Jose Ramon Gonzalez, president of First Boston Puerto Rico.

Some 520 companies, from chip manufacturer Intel to soft-drink maker Coca-Cola, operate on the island, a self-governing commonwealth that has been attached to the United States since the Spanish-American War in 1898. Nine U.S. securities firms—including Merrill Lynch, Kidder Peabody, and Shearson Lehman—have subsidiaries in Puerto Rico. But the greatest user of the tax credit is the pharmaceutical industry, with such U.S. companies as American Home Products, Johnson & Johnson, Squibb, Eli Lilly, and Upjohn all claiming a presence on the island. With a population of only 3.6 million, Puerto Rico manufactures 25% of the world's pharmaceutical products.

While Section 936 has been called the cornerstone of the Puerto Rican economy, the tax exemption costs the U.S. Treasury almost $3 billion each year in lost revenues. In addition, mainland labor unions charge that Section 936 encourages companies to relocate plants to the Caribbean. Many believe that 936 is being attacked because of abuse from drug companies—the United States' most profitable industry. A study by Congress's General Accounting Office notes that the pharmaceutical industry uses 50 to 55% of the islands tax credits but provides just 18% of the 115,000 jobs generated by 936.

Source: Adapted from "Puerto Rico's Shaky Tax Credit," by Paul Sweeney, *Global Finance,* 1993, p. 108. Reprinted with permission.

The income qualifying for this credit is as follows:

■ Income from foreign sources that is attributable to the conduct of a trade or business in a possession.

■ Qualified possessions-source investment income that is defined as investment income (1) from sources within the possession in which the business is carried on, and (2) which the taxpayer establishes is attributable to the funds derived from the business or investment in such possession.

Other investment is taxable in the United States on a current basis. No foreign tax credit is available to possessions corporations except to the extent a foreign tax is imposed on income subject to U.S. tax but not eligible for the tax-sparing credit. As regards the U.S. parent company of a possessions corporation, foreign taxes paid with respect to distributions from the possessions subsidiary are neither creditable nor deductible.

Dividends from possessions corporations are eligible for the 100% or 85% dividends-received deduction, regardless of when the income was earned. Thus accumulated earnings from prior years can be repatriated by the possessions corporation to the U.S. parent with little or no U.S. tax.

An *election* must be filed to obtain the tax benefit of possessions corporation status. The election is for a 10-year period and may be revoked during that period only with the consent of the commissioner. An electing corporation is not includable in a consolidated return. Income accumulated by a possessions corporation is not subject to the accumulated earnings tax.

Summary

■ Tax planning for multinational operations is a complex technical subject that requires the inputs of experienced tax and legal counsel in both parent and host countries. Nevertheless, the financial manager of a multinational firm should be acquainted with the national tax environments in the host countries where the firm operates. This environment includes the role of local income taxes, value-added taxes and other indirect taxes and the less tangible aspects of local tax morality.

■ The financial executive must also understand how the parent country taxes foreign-source income in order to organize efficiently for foreign operations. Important considerations include how the parent's country views tax neutrality as well as how it treats tax deferral, foreign tax credits, and intercompany transactions. Bilateral tax treaties may also influence the way foreign operations are structured.

■ Finally, the financial manager must choose the specific organization form that would be optimal for each foreign location as well as for the group as a whole. This activity typically involves choosing the branch or corporate form of organization. It also might require use of one or more special-purpose corporations or tax-haven affiliates.

Questions

☐ 1. U.S. Taxation of Foreign-Source Income (C21A.WK1)

Using the structure for calculating U.S. taxes for foreign-source income from Exhibit 21.7, assume a foreign subsidiary has $3,400,000 in gross earnings, U.S. and foreign corporate income taxes are 35% and 28%, respectively, and foreign withholding taxes are 15%.

    a. What is the total tax payment, foreign and domestic combined, for this income?

    b. What is the effective tax rate?

    c. What would be the total tax payment and effective tax rate if the income was earned by a branch of the U.S. corporation?

2. Macao Manufacturing

Jones Company (U.S.) has the following expectations for earnings from its wholly owned manufacturing subsidiary in Macao (in millions of *patacas,* the Macao currency unit).

	Year 1	*Year 2*	*Year 3*	*Year 4*
Earnings before interest and taxes (EBIT)	10,000	10,000	10,000	10,000
Interest	−2,000	−2,000	−2,000	−2,000
Pretax earnings	8,000	8,000	8,000	8,000
15% Macao tax	−1,200	−1,200	−1,200	−1,200
Net income	6,800	6,800	6,800	6,800

The Macao subsidiary plans to declare dividends equal to 40% of expected net income in years 1 and 2, and equal to 100% of expected net income in years 3 and 4. No carry back or carry forward of tax liability or credits is allowed. The effective Macao tax rate is 15% and the effective U.S. tax rate is 35%. The pataca/dollar (MOP/$) exchange rate is MOP8.00/US$ and is not expected to change.

What is the present value in dollars of the four dividends, after grossing up, to Jones Company if Jones's desired discount rate for an investment in Macao is 20% p.a.?

3. Schnapps & Schnitzel

Schnapps & Schnitzel (S&S) is the Austrian subsidiary of a U.S. fast-food chain. It is the U.S. firm's only foreign subsidiary. Austrian corporate taxes are 50% and U.S. corporate taxes are 35%. The current exchange rate is Schilling 11.00 = $1.00. S&S has no debt. S&S's earnings before interest and taxes (EBIT) are Sch1,100,000, which are currently being distributed as follows:

EBIT	Sch1,100,000
Less Austrian taxes (50%)	−550,000
Net Austrian income	550,000
Less cash dividend paid to United States	−440,000
Retained in Austria	110,000

Assume the cash dividend paid by S&S to its U.S. parent is reduced by half, and S&S pays a cash royalty to its U.S. parent equal to the amount by which the cash dividend is reduced (so that pretax total cash payments from S&S to the United States do not change). Fill out the following matrix to indicate the cash and earnings consequences. Show calculations separately.

	Before dividend reduction	After dividend reduction	Gain or loss
After-tax cash flow received in the United States:	US$	US$	US$
Austrian cash flow remaining after dividend:	Sch	Sch	Sch
Parent's worldwide consolidated net income:	US$	US$	US$

4. Reinvoicing Centers and Taxation

How could a reinvoicing center be used to shift profits from a high tax country market to a lower tax environment?

5. Schweinfurt Ball Bearings, GmbH (C21B.WK1)

Schweinfurt Ball Bearings, GmbH is the German subsidiary of a U.S. ball bearing company. German corporate tax rates are 50% and U.S. corporate tax rates are 34%. The current exchange rate is DM1.50/$. Schweinfurt Ball Bearing has no debt, and its earnings before taxes (EBT) are DM2,200,000, which it distributes as follows:

EBT	DM 2,200,000
Less German taxes (50%)	−1,100,000
Net income	DM 1,100,000
Less dividends (80% payout)	−880,000
Retained in Germany	DM 220,000

a. How would imposing a 5% royalty charge on Schweinfurt alter cash flows received in the United States, total worldwide taxes paid, and consolidated world income?

b. How would a combined 5% royalty charge and a reduced dividend payment rate, from 80% to 50%, alter U.S. cash flows, worldwide tax payments, and consolidated income?

Bibliography

Bannock, Graham, *VAT and Small Business: European Experience and Implications for North America,* Washington, D.C.: Canadian Federation of Independent Business Research and Education Foundation, 1986.

Brecher, Stephen M., Donald W. Moore, Michael M. Hoyle, and Peter G. B. Trasker, *The Economic Impact of the Introduction of VAT,* Morristown, N.J.: Financial Executives Research Foundation, 1982.

Chown, John F., "Tax Treatment of Foreign Exchange Fluctuations in the United States and United Kingdom," *Journal of International Law and Economics,* George Washington University, no. 2, 1982, pp. 201–237.

Christian, Ernest S., Jr., *State Taxation of Foreign Source Income,* New York: Financial Executives Research Foundation, 1981.

"DISC/FSC Legislation: The Case of the Phantom Profits," *Journal of Accountancy,* January 1985, pp. 83–97.

Dolan, D. Kevin, "Intercompany Transfer Pricing for the Layman," *Tax Notes,* October 8, 1990, pp. 211–228.

Frisch, Daniel J., "The Economics of International Tax Policy: Some Old and New Approaches," *Tax Notes,* April 30, 1990, pp. 581–591.

Gelinas, A. J. A., "Tax Considerations for U.S. Corporations Using Finance Subsidiaries to Borrow Funds Abroad," *Journal of Corporate Taxation,* Autumn 1980, pp. 230–263.

Goldberg, Honey L., "Conventions for the Elimination of International Double Taxation: Toward a Developing Country Model," *Law and Policy in International Business,* no. 3, 1983, pp. 833–909.

Hartman, David G., "Tax Policy and Foreign Direct Investment in the United States," *National Tax Journal,* December 1984, pp. 475–487.

Hemelt, James T., and Cynthia Spencer, "United States: Tax Effective Management of Foreign Exchange Risks," *European Taxation,* vol. 30, no. 3, 1990, pp. 67–71.

Kaplan, Wayne S., "Foreign Sales Corporations: Politics and Pragmatics," *Tax Executive,* April 1985, pp. 203–220.

OECD, *Taxation in Developed Countries,* Paris: Author, 1987.

Peat, Marwick, Mitchell & Co., *Foreign Sales Corporations,* New York: Author, 1984.

Price Waterhouse, *Corporate Taxes A Worldwide Summary,* New York: Price Waterhouse, 1993, updated annually.

Sharp, William M., Betty K. Steele, and Richard A. Jacobson, "Foreign Sales Corporations: Export Analysis and Planning," *Taxes, the Tax Magazine,* March 1985, pp. 163–200.

Sherman, H. Arnold, "Managing Taxes in the Multinational Corporation," *The Tax Executive,* Winter 1987, pp. 171–181.

Chapter 22
Working Capital Management

Management of working capital assets requires both a flow and a stock perspective. From a flow perspective, managing the location of liquid funds is most important. Location means both the currency in which liquid funds are held and the country where such holdings are placed. From a stock perspective, managing the appropriate levels and composition of cash balances, accounts receivable, inventories, and short-term debt is the main task.

The first part of this chapter discusses positioning: techniques to move liquid funds from one location to another, including dividend remittances, royalties and other fees, transfer pricing, and blocked funds. The second part deals with determining and maintaining appropriate international balances of cash, accounts receivable, and inventory.

Constraints on Positioning Funds

In domestic business, fund flows among units of a large company are generally unimpeded, and decisions about where to locate working cash balances or excess liquidity are usually based on marginal rates of return and gains from operating with minimal cash. With possibly minor exceptions all funds are denominated in the currency of the home country.

If a firm operates multinationally, political, tax, foreign exchange, and liquidity considerations impose significant restrictions on the idea that funds may easily and without cost be moved anywhere in the world. These constraints create the environment for special consideration of the problem of positioning funds multinationally.

Political constraints can block the transfer of funds either overtly or covertly. Overt blockage occurs when a currency becomes inconvertible or subject to other exchange controls that prevent its transfer at reasonable exchange rates. Covert blockage occurs when dividends or other forms of fund remittances are severely limited, heavily taxed, or prevented by other means.

Tax constraints arise because of the complex and possibly contradictory tax structures of various national governments through whose jurisdictions funds might pass.

Foreign exchange transaction costs are incurred when funds are moved from one currency to another. These costs, in the form of fees and the difference between bid and offer prices, are profit for the commercial banks and dealers that operate the foreign exchange market. Although usually a small percentage of the amount of money exchanged, such costs become quite significant for large sums or frequent transfers.

Liquidity constraints must be satisfied for each affiliate while maintaining good banking relationships locally and worldwide. This local interface is easily forgotten when trying to optimize worldwide corporate liquidity.

Unbundling International Fund Transfers

Multinational firms sometimes "unbundle" their transfer of funds into separate flows for each purpose. Host countries are then more likely to perceive that a part of what might otherwise be called "remittance of profits" constitutes an essential purchase of specific benefits that command worldwide values and benefit the host country. Unbundling allows a multinational firm to recover funds from its affiliates without piquing host country sensitivities with large "dividend drains." An item-by-item matching of remittance to input, in the form of royalties for patents, fees for services, and so on, is equitable to host country and foreign investor alike. If all investment inputs are unbundled, part of what might appear to be residual profits may turn out to be tax deductible expenses related to a specific purchased benefit. Unbundling also facilitates allocation of overhead from a parent's international division to each operating affiliate in accordance with a predetermined formula. Finally, unbundling facilitates the entry of local capital into joint venture projects, because total remuneration to different owners can be in proportion to the value of their different types of contribution rather than only in proportion to the ownership interest.

In the following sections we consider fund transfer techniques to pay for the bundle of contributions a parent might make to an affiliate and vice versa. Specifically we examine dividend policy, royalties, fees, contributions to overhead, transfer pricing, and reactions to blocked funds.

International Dividend Remittances

Payment of dividends is the most common way firms transfer funds from affiliate to parent. Determinants of dividend policy include tax considerations, political risk, foreign exchange risk, and several less important factors.

Taxes

Host country tax laws influence the dividend decision. Countries such as Germany tax retained earnings at one rate while taxing distributed earnings at a lower rate. Most countries levy withholding taxes on dividends paid to foreign parent firms. Parent country taxes also influence the decision. We discussed tax influences on decision making, including dividends, in detail in the previous chapter.

Political Risk

Political risk can motivate parent firms to require foreign affiliates to remit all locally generated funds in excess of stipulated working capital requirements and planned capital expansions. Such policies, however, are not universal. To enhance the financial self-reliance of affiliates, some parent firms do not demand remittances. In many cases neither of these extremes is followed. Instead, the normal managerial response to potential government restrictions is to maintain a constant dividend payout ratio so as to demonstrate an established policy is being consistently carried out. Host governments are more likely to accept the idea of regular dividend payments because they provide a framework based on precedent against which to judge whether a particular dividend is "normal," or is an attempt to flee from the currency to the detriment of host country foreign exchange reserves.

Foreign Exchange Risk

If a foreign exchange loss is anticipated, affiliates may speed up the transfer of funds to their parent through dividends. This "lead" is usually part of a larger strategy of moving from weak currencies to strong currencies, including speeding up intra-firm payments on accounts receivable or payable. However, decisions to accelerate dividend payments ahead of what might be normal must take into account interest rate differences and the negative impact on host country relations. Leads and lags were discussed in Chapter 8.

Other Factors

Among other factors that influence dividend policy are the age and size of the foreign affiliate. Older affiliates often provide a greater share of their earnings to their parent, presumably because as the affiliate matures it has fewer reinvestment opportunities. With regard to size, large firms tend to use rule-of-thumb guidelines to set policy, whereas small firms have few set policies and may improvise. Medium-sized firms often use dividend policy as one of several techniques for positioning funds throughout the system.[1]

Existence of joint venture partners or of local stockholders is also a factor influencing dividend policy. Optimal positioning of funds internationally cannot dominate the valid claims of partners or local stockholders for dividends. The latter do not necessarily benefit from the world perspective of the multinational parent. Robbins and Stobaugh found evidence that local stock ownership leads to more stable dividend payments regardless of earnings. Firms hesitate to reduce dividends when earnings falter; but they also hesitate to increase dividends following a spurt in earnings because it might be difficult to reduce dividends later, should earnings be lower.[2]

Royalties, Fees, and Home Office Overhead

Royalties represent remuneration paid to the owners of technology, patents, or trade names for the use of the technology or the right to manufacture or sell under the patents or trade names. A royalty rate may be expressed as a fixed monetary amount per unit or as a percentage of gross revenue.

A fee is compensation for professional services and expertise supplied to an affiliate by a parent or another affiliate. Fees are sometimes differentiated into management fees for general expertise and advice, and technical assistance fees for guidance in technical matters. Fees are usually paid for identifiable benefits received by the affiliate, in contrast to overhead charges, which are for more general benefits. Fees are usually a fixed charge, either in total for supplying the services for a stated period of time, or on a time-rate basis varying with the number of billable hours devoted to the affiliate. Fee provisions usually require an affiliate to pay travel and per diem expenses of the individuals involved.

A home office overhead allocation is a charge to compensate the parent for costs incurred in the general management of international operations and for other corporate overhead that must be recovered by the operating units. Overhead may be charged for

---

[1]Sidney M. Robbins and Robert B. Stobaugh, *Money in the Multinational Enterprise*, New York: Basic Books, 1973, p. 85.

[2]Ibid.

regional cash management, research and development, corporate public relations, legal and accounting costs for the entire enterprise, or a share of the salaries and other costs of top management. Home office overhead is often levied throughout an entire company as a predetermined percentage of sales. In other instances the charge may be based on a pro rata sharing of specific costs, which can be matched to the various units.

Financial Management Implications

Payment of royalties and fees is especially suitable when unbundling of remuneration is desired. In joint ventures the resources contributed by one of the partners may include technology and know-how; the other partner may be the primary supplier of monetary capital. The supplier of technology can readily accept royalty or fee compensation for that input and then accept a smaller proportion of net income as return on its investment of monetary capital.

Not all companies desire unbundling. Some parent firms do not want to impair the competitiveness of affiliates with charges for services that could be regarded as remote.

Sometimes royalty and fee payments are allowed by the host country, even when dividend payments are restricted. A company might organize the contractual part of its investment agreements so that if the free movement of funds via dividends is limited, options for repositioning funds via royalties and fees remain open.

Income Tax Aspects

Royalties and fees have certain tax advantages over dividends, especially when the host country income tax rate is above the parent rate. Royalties and fees are usually deductible locally. If the affiliate compensates the parent by dividends, local income taxes are paid before the dividend distribution and withholding taxes are paid on the dividend itself. The parent can take a tax credit for the local income and withholding taxes paid, but if the affiliate's combined tax rate is above that of the parent, part of the benefit may be lost. The entire benefit is gained when the payment is for royalties or fees.

The tax interaction is depicted in Exhibit 22.1. Assume the foreign affiliate of a U.S. parent earns $10,000 before paying cash to the parent and before host country income taxes. The parent wants to receive $4,000 before U.S. taxes. The host country tax rate is 50% and the U.S. rate is 34%. For simplicity we assume no dividend withholding taxes.

Case 1 is a "bundled" situation, where only dividends return cash to the parent. The $4,000 dividend (80% of the amount available for dividends) is "grossed-up" by adding back 80% of host country taxes. The U.S. tentative tax is 34% of the grossed-up $8,000, or $2,720; however, this amount is reduced by the foreign tax already paid. Since the foreign tax exceeds the U.S. tax, no additional tax is due. The U.S. parent receives $4,000 in cash, total worldwide taxes are $5,000 (all paid in the host country), and the foreign affiliate contributes $5,000 to consolidated worldwide income.

Case 2 is an "unbundled" situation. A royalty of $2,400 is combined with a dividend of $1,600 for a total $4,000 cash payment to the parent. The $1,600 dividend (about 42.1% of the amount available for dividends) is grossed-up by adding back 42.1% of host country taxes. The U.S. tentative tax is 34% of the grossed-up $3,200, or $1,088. Again, since payment is reduced by the foreign tax already paid, nothing more need be paid. The

Exhibit 22.1 Tax Effect, Bundled Versus Unbundled Compensation to Parent

	Case 1 Bundled: $4,000 dividend	Case 2 Unbundled: Royalty + $1,600 dividend	Case 3 Unbundled: Royalty + $2,416 dividend
Affiliate Statement			
Net income before taxes	$10,000	$10,000	$10,000
Less royalties and fees	—	2,400	2,400
Taxable income in host country	10,000	7,600	7,600
Less host country tax at 50%	5,000	3,800	3,800
Available for dividends	5,000	3,800	3,800
Cash dividend to parent	4,000	1,600	2,416
Reinvested locally	$ 1,000	$ 2,200	$ 1,384
Parent Statement			
Dividends received	$4,000	$1,600	$2,416
Add back foreign income tax	4,000	1,600	2,416
Grossed-up dividend in U.S.	8,000	3,200	4,832
Tentative U.S. tax at 34%	2,720	1,088	1,643
Less credit for foreign taxes	4,000	1,600	2,416
Additional U.S. tax on dividends	—	—	—
Royalty received	$ —	$2,400	$2,400
Less U.S. tax on royalty at 34%	—	816	816
Royalty received after U.S. tax	—	1,584	1,584
Net dividend after all taxes	$4,000	$1,600	$2,416
Net royalty after all taxes	—	1,584	1,584
Total cash received in the U.S.	$ 4,000	$ 3,184	$ 4,000
Total Taxes Paid			
Taxes paid to host government	$5,000	$3,800	$3,000
Taxes paid to U.S. government	—	816	816
Total taxes paid	$ 5,000	$ 4,616	$ 4,616
Contribution to Worldwide Income			
Original income before any taxes	$10,000	$10,000	$10,000
Less total worldwide taxes paid	5,000	4,616	4,616
Contribution to consolidated income	$ 5,000	$ 5,384	$ 5,384

[a]Dividends of $4,000 are 80% of available income of $5,000. Hence 80% of taxes of $5,000, or $4,000, is added back.

[b]Dividends of $1,600 are 42.1% of available income of $3,800. Hence 42.1% of taxes of $3,800, or $1,600, is added back.

[c]Dividends of $2,416 are 63.6% of available income of $3,800. Hence 63.6% of taxes of $3,800, or $2,416, is added back.

royalty, however, is fully taxed in the United States at 34%. After all taxes the U.S. parent retains only $3,184 in cash, total worldwide taxes are $4,616, and the foreign affiliate contributes $5,384 to consolidated worldwide income. In effect, worldwide income is up, worldwide cash retained is up, but cash positioned in the United States is down.

Case 3 is an alternate "unbundled" situation designed to leave exactly $4,000 cash after tax with the parent. The royalty of $2,400 is combined with a dividend of $2,416. The $2,416 dividend (about 63.6% of the amount available for dividends) is "grossed-up" by adding back 63.6% of host country taxes. The U.S. tentative tax is 34% of the grossed-up $4,832, or $1,643; however, nothing is to be paid because the host country tax is more than the tentative charge. As before, the royalty is fully taxed at 34%. After all taxes the U.S. parent retains $4,000, the same as in Case 1. Worldwide taxes are $4,616, the same as in Case 2, and the foreign affiliate contributes $5,384 to consolidated worldwide income. Worldwide consolidated income is above that in Case 1, and cash returned to the United States is more than in Case 2.

Transfer Pricing

A particularly sensitive problem for multinational firms is establishing a rational method for pricing the transfer of goods, services, and technology between related affiliates in different countries. Even purely domestic firms find it difficult to reach agreement on the best method for setting prices on transactions between affiliates. In the multinational case managers must balance conflicting considerations. These include fund positioning, income taxes, managerial incentives and evaluation, tariffs and quotas, and joint venture partners.

Fund Positioning Effect

Transfer price setting is a technique by which funds may be positioned within a multinational enterprise. A parent wishing to remove funds from a particular foreign country can charge higher prices on goods sold to its affiliate in that country. A foreign affiliate can be financed by the reverse technique, a lowering of transfer prices. Payment by the affiliate for imports from its parent transfers funds out of the affiliate. A higher transfer (sales) price permits funds to be accumulated within the selling country.

Transfer pricing may also be used to transfer funds between sister affiliates. Multiple sourcing of component parts on a worldwide basis allows changes in suppliers from within the corporate family to function as a device to transfer funds.

The flow of funds effect can be illustrated with the data in Exhibit 22.2. This exhibit shows two different results in which a manufacturing affiliate incurs costs of $1,000 for goods, which are then sold to a distribution affiliate. The distribution affiliate resells to an unrelated final customer for $2,000. The gross profit for the consolidated company is $1,000 under both combinations. If each affiliate has the same income tax rate and if other expenses are constant, net income on a consolidated basis is $400.

The low-markup policy, in which the manufacturing affiliate "charges" the distribution affiliate $1,400 for the goods, results in a cash transfer of $1,400 from the distribution country to the manufacturing country. The high-markup policy, where the goods are

Exhibit 22.2   Tax-Neutral Impact of Low Versus High Transfer Price on Flow
of Funds

Assumption: Both manufacturing affiliate and distribution affiliates pay income taxes of 50%.

	Manufacturing affiliate	Distribution affiliate	Consolidated company
Low-Markup Policy			
Sales	$1,400	$2,000	$2,000
Less cost of goods sold[a]	1,000	1,400	1,000
Gross profit	$ 400	$ 600	$1,000
Less operating expenses	100	100	200
Taxable income	$ 300	$ 500	$ 800
Less income taxes (50%)	150	250	400
Net income	$ 150	$ 250	$ 400
High-Markup Policy			
Sales	$1,700	$2,000	$2,000
Less cost of goods sold[a]	1,000	1,700	1,000
Gross profit	$ 700	$ 300	$1,000
Less operating expenses	100	100	200
Taxable income	$ 600	$ 200	$ 800
Less income taxes (50%)	300	100	400
Net income	$ 300	$ 100	$ 400

[a]Cost of goods sold for the distribution affiliate is the amount of sales of the manufacturing affiliate.

"sold" at $1,700, causes an additional $300 of cash to move from distribution to manufacturing country. If it were desirable to transfer funds out of the distribution country, the
high-markup policy would achieve this end.

Income Tax Effect

A major consideration in setting a transfer price is the income tax effect. Worldwide corporate profits may be influenced by setting transfer prices to minimize taxable income in
a country with a high income tax rate and maximize income in a country with a low
income tax rate.

The income tax effect is illustrated in Exhibit 22.3, which is identical to Exhibit
22.2 except the manufacturing affiliate pays income taxes of 25% while the distribution
affiliate pays income taxes of 50%. Under the low-markup policy the manufacturing
affiliate pays $75 of taxes and the distribution affiliate pays $250, for a total tax bill of
$325 and consolidated net income of $475.

If the firm adopts a high-markup policy, so the merchandise is transferred at an
intracompany sales price of $1,700, the same $800 of pretax consolidated income is
allocated more heavily to the manufacturing affiliate and less heavily to the distribution
affiliate. As a consequence, total taxes drop by $75 and consolidated net income
increases by $75.

Exhibit 22.3   Tax Effect of Low Versus High Transfer Price on Net Income

Assumption: Manufacturing affiliate pays income taxes at 25%. Distribution affiliate pays income taxes at 50%.

	Manufacturing affiliate	Distribution affiliate	Consolidated company
Low-Markup Policy			
Sales	$1,400	$2,000	$2,000
Less cost of goods sold[a]	1,000	1,400	1,000
Gross profit	$ 400	$ 600	$1,000
Less operating expenses	100	100	200
Taxable income	$ 300	$ 500	$ 800
Less income taxes (25%/50%)	75	250	325
Net income	$ 225	$ 250	$ 475
High-Markup Policy			
Sales	$1,700	$2,000	$2,000
Less cost of goods sold[a]	1,000	1,700	1,000
Gross profit	$ 700	$ 300	$1,000
Less operating expenses	100	100	200
Taxable income	$ 600	$ 200	$ 800
Less income taxes (25%/50%)	150	100	250
Net income	$ 450	$ 100	$ 550

[a]Cost of goods sold for the distribution affiliate is the amount of sales of the manufacturing affiliate.

In the absence of government interference, the firm would prefer the high-markup policy. Needless to say, government tax authorities are aware of the potential income distortion from transfer price manipulation. A variety of regulations and court cases exist on the reasonableness of transfer prices, including fees and royalties as well as prices set for merchandise. If a government taxing authority does not accept a transfer price, taxable income will be deemed larger than was calculated by the firm, and taxes will be increased. An even greater danger, from the corporate point of view, is that two or more governments will try to protect their respective tax bases by contradictory policies that subject the business to double taxation on the same income.

Typical of laws circumscribing freedom to set transfer prices is Section 482 of the U.S. Internal Revenue Code. Under this authority the Internal Revenue Service (IRS) can reallocate gross income, deductions, credits, or allowances between related corporations in order to prevent tax evasion or to reflect more clearly a proper allocation of income. Under the IRS guidelines and subsequent judicial interpretation, the burden of proof is on the taxpayer to show the IRS has been arbitrary or unreasonable in reallocating income. The "correct price" according to the guidelines is the one that reflects an *arm's-length price,* that is, a sale of the same goods or service to an unrelated customer.

IRS regulations provide three methods to establish arm's-length prices: comparable uncontrolled prices, resale prices, and cost-plus. A comparable uncontrolled price is regarded as the best evidence of arm's-length pricing. Such prices arise when transactions in the same goods or services occur between the multinational firm and unrelated customers, or between two unrelated firms. The second-best approach to arm's-length pricing starts with the final selling price to customers and subtracts an appropriate profit for the distribution affiliate to determine the allowable selling price for the manufacturing affiliate. The third method is to add an appropriate markup for profit to total costs of the manufacturing affiliate. The same three methods are recommended for use in member countries by the Organization for Economic Cooperation and Development (OECD) Committee on Fiscal Affairs.[3]

Although all governments have an interest in monitoring transfer pricing by multinational firms, not all governments use these powers to regulate transfer prices to the detriment of multinational firms. In particular, transfer pricing has some political advantages over other techniques of transferring funds. Although the recorded transfer price is known to the governments of both the exporting and importing countries, the underlying cost data are not available to the importing country. Thus the importing country finds it difficult to judge how reasonable the transfer price is, especially for nonstandard items such as manufactured components. Additionally, even if cost data could be obtained, some of the more sophisticated governments might continue to ignore the transfer pricing leak. They recognize that the foreign investors must be able to repatriate a reasonable profit by their own standards, even if this profit seems unreasonable locally. An unknown or unproven transfer price leak makes it more difficult for local critics to blame their government for allowing the country to be "exploited" by foreign investors. On the other hand, if the host government has soured on foreign investment, transfer price leaks are less likely to be overlooked. Thus within the potential and actual constraints established by governments, opportunities may exist for multinational firms to alter transfer prices away from an arm's-length market price.

Managerial Incentives and Evaluation

When a firm is organized with decentralized profit centers, transfer pricing between centers can disrupt evaluations of managerial performance. This problem is not unique to multinational firms but has been a controversial issue in the "centralization versus decentralization" debate in domestic circles. In the domestic case, however, a modicum of coordination at the corporate level can alleviate some of the distortion that occurs when any profit center suboptimizes its profit for the corporate good. This statement might also be true in the multinational case, but coordination is often hindered by longer and less efficient channels of communication and the need to consider the unique variables that influence international pricing. Even with the best of intent, a manager in one country finds it difficult to know what is best for the firm as a whole when buying at a negotiated price from an affiliate in another country. If corporate headquarters

---

[3]"Transfer Pricing and Multinational Enterprises," *Report of the Organization for Economic Cooperation and Development Committee on Fiscal Affairs,* Paris: OECD, 1979.

establishes transfer prices and sourcing alternatives, managerial disincentives arise if the prices seem arbitrary or unreasonable. Furthermore, if corporate headquarters makes more decisions, one of the main advantages of a decentralized profit center system disappears. Local management loses the incentive to act for its own benefit.

Tariff and Quota Effect

Transfer pricing may have an influence on the amount of import duties paid. If the importing affiliate pays ad valorem import duties, and if those duties are levied on the invoice (transfer) price, duties will rise under the high-markup policy.

The incidence of import duties is usually opposite to the incidence of income taxes in transfer pricing, but income taxes are usually a heavier burden than import duties. Therefore transfer prices are more often viewed from an income tax perspective. In some instances, however, import duties are actually levied against internationally posted prices, if such exist, rather than against the stated invoice price. If so, duties will not be influenced by the transfer price policy. Income taxes will still be affected by both the residual location of operating profit and the deductibility of the assessed import duties.

Related to the tariff effect is the ability to lower transfer prices to offset the volume effect of foreign exchange quotas. Should a host government allocate a limited amount of foreign exchange for importing a particular type of good, a lower transfer price on the import allows the firm to bring in a greater quantity. If, for example, the imported item is a component for a locally manufactured product, a lower transfer price may allow production volume to be sustained or expanded, albeit at the expense of profits in the supply affiliate.

Effect on Joint Venture Partners

Joint ventures pose a special problem in transfer pricing because serving the interest of local stockholders by maximizing local profit may be suboptimal from the overall viewpoint of the multinational firm. Often the conflicting interests are irreconcilable. When Ford Motor Company decided to rationalize production on a worldwide basis so each division could specialize in certain products or components, it was forced to abandon its policy of working with joint ventures partly because of the transfer pricing problem. It had to purchase the large British minority interest in Ford, Ltd. in 1961, despite the well-publicized and ill-timed drain on the U.S. balance of payments. For identical reasons, General Motors has seldom worked with joint ventures despite its recent arrangement with Toyota.

Transfer Pricing in Practice

Given the potential for conflicting objectives, what transfer pricing policies do multinational firms utilize in practice? A recent empirical study of 164 U.S. multinational firms by Al-Eryani, Alam, and Akhter sheds considerable light on this question.[4] Their findings are presented in Exhibit 22.4.

---

[4]Mohammad F. Al-Eryani, Pervaiz Alam, and Syed Akhter, "Transfer Pricing Determinants of U.S. Multinationals," *Journal of International Business Studies,* Third Quarter, 1990, pp. 409–425.

Exhibit 22.4 Frequency of Use of International Transfer Pricing Methods

	More Developed Countries		Less Developed Countries		TOTAL	
	#	%	#	%	#	%
Nonmarket-Based Methods						
Actual unit full cost	4	4	4	5	8	5
Actual unit full cost + fixed markup	15	15	11	15	26	15
Actual unit variable cost	0	0	0	0	0	0
Actual unit variable cost + fixed markup	3	3	2	3	5	3
Actual unit full cost + fixed markup	15	16	10	13	25	15
Standard unit full cost	5	5	0	0	5	3
Standard unit variable cost	1	1	0	0	1	0
Standard unit variable cost + fixed markup	5	5	4	5	9	5
Marginal cost	0	0	0	0	0	0
Opportunity cost	2	2	0	0	2	1
Negotiated price	13	13	12	16	25	15
Mathematical programming	1	1	3	4	4	2
Dual pricing	1	1	1	1	2	1
Total nonmarket based	65	66	47	62	112	65
Market-Based Methods						
Prevailing market price	17	18	12	16	29	17
Adjusted market price	15	16	16	22	31	18
Total market based	32	34	28	38	60	35
Total number of firms[a]	97	100	75	100	172	100

[a]Total number of responses exceeds 76 firms in the more developed country group because some firms identified the use of more than one transfer pricing method. On the other hand, the total number of responses for the less developed country group is less than 88 because some firms did not identify the transfer pricing method they used for multinational transfers.

Source: Mohammad F. Al-Eryani, Pervaiz Alam, and Syed Akhter, "Transfer Pricing Determinants of U.S. Multinationals," *Journal of International Business Studies,* Third Quarter, 1990, p. 420.

Although Section 482 of the U.S. Internal Revenue Code requires use of "arms-length" pricing, only 35% of the responding firms indicated they used "market-based" methods to set the "arms-length" transfer price (bottom of Exhibit 22.4). Almost all of the other firms used either some version of a "cost-plus" price or a "negotiated" price. This split presumably reflects the relative proportion of products which had a recognized external market price compared to products or components that had no external market price.

The authors of Exhibit 22.4 used the response data to test various hypotheses about the determinants motivating a firm's choice of a particular transfer pricing policy. They found that "legal" and "size" variables were statistically significant determinants of market-based transfer pricing. Legal considerations include compliance with tax rules (Section 482), customs regulations, antidumping laws, antitrust laws, and the accounting norms of host countries. Large-size firms with multiple products and locations were also likely to use market-based transfer pricing whenever possible. This was probably because they are highly visible and it would be difficult to customize transfer pricing given the complexities of their sales networks.

Another interesting finding of the study was that "economic restrictions (such as exchange controls, price controls, and restrictions on imports), political-social conditions, and the extent of economic development in host countries are either unimportant or are secondary determinants of a market-based transfer pricing strategy."[5] Furthermore, they found no statistical support for assuming these variables influenced nonmarket-based transfer pricing policies. These findings suggest that transfer pricing policies are not very sensitive to the positioning of funds considerations that we described earlier in this chapter.[6]

In a much earlier study of 60 non-U.S. multinational firms and their U.S. affiliates, Jeffrey S. Arpan found distinct national differences with respect to the weight accorded host country environmental variables and internal company parameters. Canadian, French, Italian, and U.S. parent firms judged that the tax effect of transfer pricing was the most important consideration.[7] British parent firms emphasized the strong financial appearance of their U.S. affiliates. Inflation was an important consideration by all parent firms except those in Scandinavia; these firms considered acceptability to the host government to be the most important determinant of their transfer pricing policies. German firms appeared to be least concerned about transfer pricing policies. Non-U.S. firms, in contrast to U.S. firms, did not consider the evaluation of managerial performance to be important because, contrary to the practice of many U.S. firms, they did not usually operate their foreign affiliates on a profit center basis.

Blocked Funds

When a government runs short of foreign exchange and cannot obtain additional funds through borrowing or attracting new foreign investment, it usually limits transfers of foreign exchange out of the country. In theory this does not discriminate against foreign-owned firms because it applies to everyone; in practice foreign firms have more at stake. Depending on the degree of shortage, the host government might simply require approval of all transfers of funds abroad, thus reserving the right to set a priority on the use of scarce foreign exchange in favor of necessities rather than luxuries. In very severe cases the government might make its currency nonconvertible into other currencies, thereby fully blocking transfers of funds abroad. In between these positions are policies that restrict the size and timing of dividends, debt amortization, royalties, and service fees.

---

[5]Ibid., p. 422.

[6]The study also found that internal considerations, such as performance evaluation of subsidiaries and their management, were not statistically significant determinants of transfer pricing policies. Presumably multinational firms prefer to maintain separate sets of books for that purpose.

[7]Jeffrey S. Arpan, "International Intracorporate Pricing: Non-American Systems and Views," *Journal of International Business Studies,* Spring 1972, p. 9.

Multinational firms can react to the potential for blocked funds at these three stages:

1. Prior to making an investment, they can analyze the effect of blocked funds on expected return on investment, the desired local financial structure, and optimal links with affiliates.

2. During operations they can attempt to move funds through a variety of positioning techniques.

3. Funds that cannot be moved must be reinvested in the local country in a manner that avoids deterioration in their real value because of inflation and/or exchange depreciation.

Preinvestment Strategy

Management can consider blocked funds in their capital budgeting analysis, (see example in Chapter 19). Temporary blockage of funds normally reduces the expected net present value and internal rate of return on a proposed investment. Whether the investment should nevertheless be undertaken depends on whether the expected rate of return, even with blocked funds, exceeds the required rate of return on investments of the same risk class. Preinvestment analysis also includes the potential to minimize the effect of blocked funds by means of heavy local borrowing, swap agreements, and other techniques to reduce local currency exposure and thus the need to repatriate funds. Sourcing and sales links with affiliates can be predetermined so as to maximize the potential for moving blocked funds.

Moving Blocked Funds

What can a multinational firm do to transfer funds out of countries having exchange or remittance restrictions? These three popular approaches have already been discussed:

1. Unbundling services, described earlier in this chapter.

2. Transfer pricing, also described earlier in this chapter.

3. Leading and lagging payments, described in Chapter 8.

Three additional approaches are the following:

1. Using fronting loans.

2. Creating unrelated exports.

3. Obtaining special dispensation.

Fronting Loans. A *fronting loan* is a parent-to-affiliate loan channeled through a financial intermediary, usually a large international bank. Fronting loans differ from "parallel" or "back-to-back" loans, discussed in Chapter 8, in that the latter involve offsetting loans between commercial businesses arranged outside the banking system. Fronting loans are sometimes referred to as *link financing*.

In a direct intracompany loan the parent or an affiliate loans directly to the borrowing affiliate, and at a later date the borrowing affiliate repays the principal and interest. In a fronting loan, by contrast, the "lending" U.S. parent deposits funds in, say, a London bank, and that bank loans the same amount to the borrowing affiliate in a third (host) country. From the bank's point of view the loan is risk free because the bank has 100% collateral in the form of the parent's deposit. In effect the bank "fronts" for the parent—hence the name. Interest paid by the borrowing affiliate to the bank is usually slightly higher than the rate paid by the bank to the parent, allowing the bank a margin for expenses and profit.

Use of fronting loans increases chances for repayment should political turmoil occur between the home and host countries. Government authorities are more likely to allow the local affiliate to repay a loan to a large international bank in a neutral country than to allow the same affiliate to repay a loan directly to its parent. To stop payment to the international bank would hurt the international credit image of the country, whereas to stop payment to the parent corporation would have minimal impact on that image and might even provide some domestic political advantage.

A fronting loan may have a tax advantage. Assume, as depicted in Exhibit 22.5, that a finance affiliate, wholly owned by the parent and located in a tax-haven country, deposits $1,000,000 in an intermediary commercial bank at 8% interest, and the bank in turn lends $1,000,000 to an operating affiliate at 9%. The operating affiliate is located in a country where the income tax rate is 50%. Interest payments net of income tax effect will be as follows:

1. The operating affiliate pays $90,000 interest to the intermediary bank. Deduction of interest from taxable income results in a net after-tax cost of $45,000.

2. The intermediary bank receives $90,000, retains $10,000 for its services, and pays $80,000 interest on the deposit of the finance affiliate.

3. The finance affiliate receives $80,000 interest on deposit, tax free.

The net result is that $80,000 of cash is moved from the operating affiliate to the finance affiliate. Since the after-tax cost to the borrowing affiliate is only $45,000, the

Exhibit 22.5   Tax Aspects of a Fronting Loan

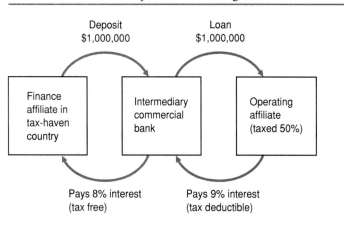

system has been able to move an additional $35,000 out of the country by virtue of the tax shield. If the finance affiliate had made a direct loan to the operating affiliate, the host government of the operating affiliate would be in a position to disallow the interest charge as a tax deductible expense by ruling it was a substantive dividend to the parent disguised as interest. Note that the fronting loan, as a device, provides no protection against changes in exchange rates.

Creating Unrelated Exports. One approach to blocked funds that benefits both affiliate and host country is the creation of unrelated exports. Because the main reason for stringent exchange controls is usually a country's persistent inability to earn hard currencies, anything a multinational firm can do to create new exports from the host country helps the situation and provides a potential means to transfer funds out.

Some new exports can often be created from present productive capacity with little or no additional investment, especially if they are in product lines related to existing operations. Other new exports may require reinvestment or new funds, although if the funds reinvested consist of those already blocked, little is lost in the way of opportunity costs. A multinational firm already in Brazil, for example, might locate research and development laboratories there and pay for them with blocked cruzeiros. Key research personnel could be transferred to Brazil to supplement local talent, their salaries and expenses being picked up on the local payroll. A Brazilian architectural and engineering firm might be hired to provide services for the worldwide enterprise, being paid in cruzeiros to design plants in France or Florida.

Export equivalents can also be created with little investment in certain service activities. The Brazilian affiliate, for example, could host conventions or other business meetings in Rio de Janeiro for its multinational parent. Employees of the firm might be sent on company-sponsored vacations to Brazil, and employees of the parent flying anywhere in the world might be asked to use Varig, the Brazilian national airline, wherever possible, flying on tickets purchased in Brazil by the Brazilian affiliate and paid for with cruzeiros.

All such activities benefit Brazil because they provide export-oriented jobs and earnings. They benefit the multinational firm because they provide a way to use effectively funds that would otherwise remain tied up in the Brazilian money market.

Another approach for a parent dealing with blocked currency is to arrange barter agreements. A country such as Brazil would probably not allow barter deals involving coffee or other commodities already sold on world markets for hard currencies, but it might permit a barter for exports of goods or services not normally exported. For example, Brazilian textiles might be bought from the Brazilian affiliate by the parent in exchange for imports into Brazil of the parent's products or equipment. The parent (not in the textile business) arranges for the sale of the textiles in the parent country. Countertrade, of which barter is one form, was discussed in Chapter 16.

Special Dispensation. If all else fails and the multinational firm is investing in an industry that is important to the economic development of the host country, the firm may bargain for special dispensation to repatriate some portion of the funds that otherwise would be blocked. Firms in "desirable" industries such as telecommunications, semiconductor manufacturing, instrumentation, pharmaceuticals, or other research and high-tech industries, may receive preference over firms in mature industries. The amount of preference received depends on bargaining among informed parties, the government and the business firm, either of which is free to back away from the proposed investment if unsatisfied with the terms.

Self-Fulfilling Prophecies. In seeking "escape routes" for blocked funds—or for that matter in trying to position funds through any of the techniques discussed in this chapter—the multinational firm may increase political risk and cause a change from partial blockage to full blockage. The possibility of such a self-fulfilling cycle exists any time a firm takes action that, no matter how legal, thwarts the underlying intent of politically authored controls. In the statehouses of the world, as in the editorial offices of the local press and TV, multinational firms and their affiliates are always a potential scapegoat.

Forced Reinvestment

If funds are indeed blocked from transfer into foreign exchange, they are by definition "reinvested." Under such a situation the firm must find local opportunities that will maximize rate of return for a given acceptable level of risk.

If blockage is expected to be temporary, the most obvious alternative is to invest in local money market instruments. Unfortunately, in many countries such instruments are not available in sufficient quantity or with adequate liquidity. In some cases government treasury bills, bank deposits, and other short-term instruments have yields that are kept artificially low relative to local rates of inflation or probable changes in exchange rates. Thus the firm often loses real value during the period of blockage.[8]

If short- or intermediate-term portfolio investments, such as bonds, bank time deposits, or direct loans to other companies, are not possible, direct investment in additional production facilities may be the only alternative. Often this investment is what the host country is seeking by its exchange controls, even if the fact of exchange controls is by itself counterproductive to the idea of additional foreign investment. Examples of forced direct reinvestment can be cited for Peru, where an airline invested in hotels and in maintenance facilities for other airlines; for Turkey, where a fish canning company constructed a plant to manufacture cans needed for packing the catch; and for Argentina, where an automobile company integrated vertically by acquiring an automobile transmission manufacturing plant previously owned by a supplier.

If investment opportunities in additional production facilities are not available, funds may simply be used to acquire other assets expected to increase in value with local inflation. Typical purchases might be land, office buildings, or commodities that are exported to global markets. Even inventory stockpiling might be a reasonable investment, given the low opportunity cost of the blocked funds.

---

[8]Forced reinvestment may take the form of direct loans. The back-to-back or parallel loan discussed in Chapter 8 is one type, as is the fronting loan discussed earlier in this chapter.

Managing International Cash Balances

Cash balances, including marketable securities, are held partly in anticipation of day-to-day cash disbursements and partly as protection against unanticipated variations from budgeted cash flows. These two motives are commonly called the transaction motive and the precautionary motive. Cash may also be held for speculative purposes; however, this aspect is beyond our consideration in this chapter because it does not involve normal day-to-day operations. Cash management in a multinational firm can benefit from both centralized depositories and multilateral netting.

Centralized Depositories

Operational benefits can be gained by centralizing cash management in any business with widely dispersed operating affiliates. Internationally the procedure calls for each affiliate to hold only a minimum cash balance for transaction purposes. No cash for precautionary purposes is held locally—unless management of the central pool issues specific instructions to override the general rule. All excess funds are remitted to a central cash depository, where a single authority has responsibility for placing the funds in such currencies and money market instruments as will best serve the firm as a whole.

The central depository has advantages of size and information. It is located where information can be collected and decisions made about the relative strengths and weaknesses of various currencies. Interest rate information on alternative investments for each currency is also available, as is experience with the mechanical functioning of the various money markets. Although in theory such information might be available to the treasurer of each affiliate, in practice that individual can seldom specialize in money market management alone.

Funds held in the central pool can quickly be returned to a local affiliate that is short of cash. This return is achieved either by wire transfer or by creating a worldwide bank credit line. The bank would instruct its branch office in the particular country to advance funds to the local affiliate.

Another reason for holding all precautionary balances in a central pool is that the total pool, if centralized, can be reduced in size without any loss in the level of protection. For example, assume a firm possesses three affiliate operations: Italy, Germany, and France. Each affiliate maintains a precautionary cash balance equal to the expected cash needs plus a safety margin of three standard deviations of the expected balance. Cash needs are assumed to be normally distributed in each country, and the needs are independent from one country to another. Three standard deviations means there exists a 99.87% chance that actual cash needs will be met.

The cash needs of the individual affiliates, and the total precautionary cash balances held, are shown in Exhibit 22.6. The total precautionary cash balances of the three affiliates is $46,000,000. This total includes $28,000,000 in expected cash needs and $18,000,000 in idle cash balances (the three standard deviations of the individual expected cash balances) held as the safety margin.

What would happen if the firm maintained all precautionary balances in a single account in one European financial center? Because variances are additive when

Exhibit 22.6   Decentralized Cash Budgeting Versus a Centralized Depository

DECENTRALIZED CASH BUDGETING

Country	Expected cash need (A)	One standard deviation (B)	Cash Balance budgeted for adequate protection[a] (A + 3B)
Italy	$10,000,000	$1,000,000	$13,000,000
Germany	6,000,000	2,000,000	12,000,000
France	12,000,000	3,000,000	21,000,000
Total	$28,000,000	$6,000,000	$46,000,000

CENTRALIZED DEPOSITORY

Country	Expected cash need (A)	One standard deviation (B)	Cash Balance budgeted for adequate protection[a] (A + 3B)
Italy	$10,000,000		
Germany	6,000,000		
France	12,000,000		
Total	$28,000,000	$3,741,657[b]	$39,224,972

[a]Adequate protection is defined as the expected cash balance plus three standard deviations, assuming the cash flows of all three individual affiliates are normally distributed.

[b]The standard deviation of the expected cash balance of the centralized depository is calculated as follows:

Std. Dev. of Centralized Depository $= \sqrt{(1,000,000)^2 + (2,000,000)^2 + (3,000,000)^2}$
$= \sqrt{14,000,000} = \$3,741,657.$

probability distributions are independent, the equivalent standard deviation for the single account would be as shown in footnote b of Exhibit 22.6. Therefore, a firm using a centralized depository would hold a centralized cash balance of the following:

$$\begin{array}{l} \text{Centralized} \quad \text{Sum of} \qquad \text{Three} \\ \text{cash} \quad = \text{expected} \quad + \text{ standard deviations} \\ \text{balance} \qquad \text{cash needs} \qquad \text{of expected sum} \end{array}$$

$$= \$28,000,000 + (3 \times \$3,741,657)$$
$$= \$39,224,972$$

A budgeted cash balance three standard deviations above the aggregate expected cash need would require only $11,224,972 in potentially idle cash, as opposed to the previous total idle cash balance of $18,000,000. Budgeted investment in cash balances is reduced by $6,775,028.

Central money pools are usually maintained in major money centers such as London, New York, Zurich, and Tokyo. Additional popular locations for money pools include Liechtenstein, Luxembourg, the Bahamas, and Bermuda. Although the latter countries do not have strong diversified economies, they offer most of the other prerequisites for a corporate financial center: freely convertible currency, political and economic stability, access to international communications, and clearly defined legal procedures. Their additional advantage as a so-called tax haven is also desirable.

A second advantage of centralized cash management is that one affiliate will not borrow at high rates while another holds surplus funds idle or invests them at low rates. Managers of the central pool can locate the least expensive sources of funds, worldwide, as well as the most advantageous returns to be earned on excess funds. If additional cash is desired, the central pool manager can determine the location of such borrowing. A local affiliate manager would never borrow at a rate above the minimum available to the pool manager. If the firm has a worldwide cash surplus, the central pool manager can evaluate comparative rates of return in various markets, transaction costs, exchange risks, and tax effects.

Use of a centralized depository system does not necessarily imply use of a single bank, for the essence of the centralized depository is centralized information and decisions. Actual funds may be placed in as many banks as desired.

Near-Term Cash Planning

Moving funds from country to country, as is required for the operation of a centralized depository, has a cash cost in terms of exchange rate spreads and a managerial cost in terms of loss of local affiliate control of its resources. These costs are particularly burdensome if such funds are mislocated, that is, denominated in the wrong currency from the viewpoint of near-term cash needs. Mislocated funds can be minimized by the use of a multinational cash forecasting system.

To illustrate, assume the European headquarters of a multinational firm operates a central cash pool in Belgium, and the firm has operating affiliates in the United Kingdom, Sweden, Germany, and France. At the close of daily banking hours in each country, the four affiliates report to Brussels by wire or fax their end-of-day cash balances in cleared funds. As is true for netting systems, the daily report will be in a designated reporting currency, with actual local currency cash balances translated at an exchange rate specified by the corporate treasurer. Assume the reporting currency is the U.S. dollar.

The daily cash report for each unit might appear as in Exhibit 22.7. According to the reports in Exhibit 22.7, the British affiliate has an end-of-day cash balance in pounds equivalent to $150,000. In other words, the British affiliate could have disbursed an additional $150,000 (in pounds) that day without creating a negative cash balance or exceeding intended overdraft privileges. Similarly, the Swedish affiliate has an end-of-day balance of $250,000, and the German and French affiliates have end-of-day balances equal to $600,000 and $500,000.

At the end of each day the central pool manager compiles a report in the form shown in Exhibit 22.8. This daily cash ledger shows the end-of-day cash balances at each affiliate and the previously agreed upon minimum operating balance to be maintained there for day-to-day operations. In the example, the British affiliate ended the day with a cash balance of $150,000, but it needed $200,000. At the end of the day it was $50,000 short of normal operating funds. Similarly the Swedish affiliate was short $375,000, while the

Exhibit 22.7   European Cash Management Pool: Daily Cash Reports (thousands of dollars)

DAILY CASH REPORT

Date_____March 7, 19XX_____

Location_____United Kingdom_____

End-of-day cash balance_____+150_____

	Five-day forecast:		
	receipt	*disburse*	*net*
+1	300	400	−100
+2	400	350	+50
+3	300	250	+50
+4	250	650	−400
+5	200	250	−50
Net for period			−450

DAILY CASH REPORT

Date_____March 7, 19XX_____

Location_____Sweden_____

End-of-day cash balance_____−250_____

	Five-day forecast:		
	receipt	*disburse*	*net*
+1	100	200	−100
+2	100	150	−50
+3	50	zero	+50
+4	200	75	+125
+5	200	200	zero
Net for period			+25

DAILY CASH REPORT

Date_____March 7, 19XX_____

Location_____Germany_____

End-of-day cash balance_____+600_____

	Five-day forecast:		
	receipt	*disburse*	*net*
+1	400	100	+300
+2	350	100	+250
+3	300	150	+150
+4	300	400	−100
+5	200	100	+100
Net for period			+700

DAILY CASH REPORT

Date_____March 7, 19XX_____

Location_____France_____

End-of-day cash balance_____+500_____

	Five-day forecast:		
	receipt	*disburse*	*net*
+1	100	400	−300
+2	300	100	+200
+3	500	200	+300
+4	100	100	zero
+5	150	225	−50
Net for period			+150

German and French affiliates had cash balances above their operating needs. For Europe as a whole, the company had a surplus cash of $225,000.

The essence of effective cash planning is to use the information in the daily cash ledger to cover any deficits, decide on any borrowing, and put any excess cash into the currency and/or money market instruments most appropriate in light of expectations about future cash needs, interest rates, and possible changes in exchange rates.

For example, if an imminent drop in value of the British pound was anticipated, the required minimum cash balance for the United Kingdom could be reduced from

Exhibit 22.8 European Cash Management Pool: Central Office Compilation

CASH LEDGER (March 7, 19XX)
(thousand-dollar equivalents of local currency)

Location	End-of-day cash balance	Required minimum	Excess local cash balance
United Kingdom	+150	200	−50
Sweden	−250	125	−375
Germany	+600	250	+350
France	+500	200	+300
Europe-wide cash gain (or loss)			+225

$200,000 to some lower level. If local overdrafts were possible, the required "minimum" might be a negative number.

As seen in Exhibit 22.7, one additional item of information is usually requested in each daily cash report. This is a forecast of expected cash receipts and disbursements for each of the following five days. Only local affiliate managers have the detailed knowledge for such near-term cash forecasting. This forecast, which moves forward day to day, serves at least three purposes: First, each affiliate is forced to revise its operating cash budget daily, and the actual cash result can be measured against the accuracy of the forecasts of each of the previous five days. Second, information that assists in the decision to transfer funds to or from the central pool is given. For example, although France currently has a cash surplus of $300,000 (Exhibit 22.8), the following day a deficit of $300,000 is expected. Depending on interest rates and the cost of exchange transactions, the central pool might instruct the French affiliate to invest its surplus funds overnight in France against the following day's deficit, rather than transmit the funds to Belgium and then have Belgium cover the next day's deficit with a remittance back to France.

Third, an estimate of future net cash flows for all of Europe is needed to determine the appropriate maturities for any investing or borrowing by the central pool. Should the Europe-wide net cash gain of $225,000 on March 7 (Exhibit 22.8) or any portion of it be put into longer maturities, or should it be put into the short-term money market because of cash needs the following day or week?

Information received and tabulated in the cash ledger, Exhibit 22.8, is used for decisions about where to direct cash movements. Given the needs (United Kingdom and Sweden) and excess cash balances (Germany and France), one possible set of routings that would clear balances for the day and leave the daily surplus of $225,000 in the central pool would be as shown in Exhibit 22.9. Many other combinations are possible, but both responsibility and supporting information are concentrated in one location—the European cash manager in Belgium.

Information from the individual affiliate five-day forecasts is also compiled into a Europe-wide forecast, as shown in Exhibit 22.10. The sum of columns for each day shows the Europe-wide cash gain or loss, and that figure is used for deciding whether or not daily excess funds should be sent to the pool or allowed to accumulate at the local

Exhibit 22.9   European Cash Management Pool: Possible Cash Routing
Instructions (thousands of dollars)

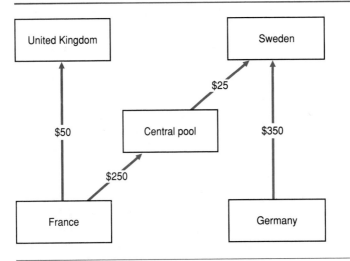

Exhibit 22.10   European Cash Management Pool: Five-Day Cash Forecast
(thousands of dollars)

Location	Days from the Present +1	+2	+3	+4	+5	Five-Day Total
United Kingdom	−100	+50	+50	−400	−50	−450
Sweden	−100	−50	+50	+125	zero	+25
Germany	+300	+250	+150	−100	+100	+700
France	−300	+200	+300	zero	−50	+150
European cash gain by day, forecast	−200	+450	+550	−375	zero	+425

level. It is also used to decide what investment maturities, if any, should be sought by the
central pool, for decisions to approach the company's banks to borrow more funds, for
deciding what currencies to borrow or invest, and for decisions to repay bank loans. In
this example, the company is going to gain $425,000 over the week, as shown in the
lower right corner, but will be short of cash on the first and fourth day that follow.

Multilateral Netting

Multilateral netting of payments is useful primarily when a large number of separate foreign exchange transactions occur between affiliates in the normal course of business.
Netting reduces the settlement cost of what would otherwise be a large number of crossing spot transactions.

Multilateral netting is an extension of bilateral netting. If a Belgian affiliate owes an Italian affiliate $5,000,000 while the Italian affiliate simultaneously owes the Belgian affiliate $3,000,000, a bilateral settlement calls for a single payment of $2,000,000 from Belgium to Italy and the cancellation, via offset, of the remainder of the debt.

A multilateral system is an expanded version of this simple bilateral concept. Assume payments are due between European affiliates of the same multinational firm at the end of a month of operations. Each obligation reflects the accumulated transactions of the prior month. These obligations are shown in the top third of Exhibit 22.11 on page 622.

Without netting, Belgium, for example, must make three separate payments and will receive three separate receipts. If Belgium paid each individual invoice, rather than accumulated balances at the end of the month, it would generate a multitude of costly small bank transactions every day. The daily totals would add up to the monthly accumulated balances shown in the diagram.

In order to reduce bank transaction costs, such as the spread between foreign exchange bid and ask quotations and transfer fees, many multinational firms have established their own multilateral netting centers. Others have contracted with banks to manage their netting activities. With netting, the affiliates transmit information about their obligations to a single center, which combines them in the form shown in Exhibit 22.11.

Note that total payments add up to $43,000,000. If the cost of foreign exchange transactions and transfer fees were 0.5%, the total cost of settlement would be $215,000. Using information from the netting matrix in the middle of Exhibit 22.11, the netting center can order three payments that settle the entire set of obligations. The United Kingdom can be instructed to remit $3,000,000 to Italy, and Belgium can be instructed to remit $1,000,000 each to France and Italy. Total foreign exchange transfers are reduced to $5,000,000, and transaction costs are reduced to $25,000.

Some countries limit or prohibit netting, and some permit netting on a "gross settlements" basis only. For a single settlement period all receipts may be combined into a single receipt and all payments into a single payment. However, these two may not be netted. Thus two large payments must pass through the local banking system. The reason for such a requirement is usually a desire to subsidize local banks by forcing firms to pay for transactions that are not necessary, although this real reason may be concealed behind a statement that certain types of data are needed.

Permission to net payments is granted by individual permit in some countries. Firms that manufacture locally are often given permission; those that only sell are often denied.

Managing Receivables

Multinational accounts receivable are created by two separate types of transactions: sales to related affiliates and sales to independent buyers having no ownership relationship with the selling firm. Within-family accounts receivable are usually managed by leads and lags and through reinvoicing centers, topics we discussed in Chapter 8.

Exhibit 22.11   Multilateral Netting Matrix (thousands of dollars)

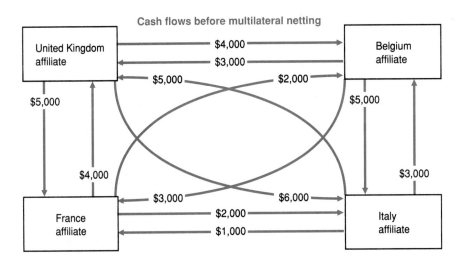

Cash flows before multilateral netting

Calculation of Net Obligation

	Paying Affiliate				Total receipts	Net receipts (payments)
Receiving affiliate	*U.K.*	*Belgium*	*France*	*Italy*		
United Kingdom	—	$3,000	$4,000	$5,000	$12,000	($3,000)
Belgium	4,000	—	2,000	3,000	9,000	($2,000)
France	5,000	3,000	—	1,000	9,000	$1,000
Italy	6,000	5,000	2,000	—	13,000	$4,000
Total payments	$15,000	$11,000	$ 8,000	$ 9,000	$43,000	—

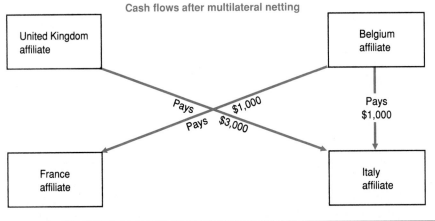

Cash flows after multilateral netting

Independent Customers

Management of accounts receivable from independent customers involves two types of decisions: In what currency should the transaction be denominated, and what should be the terms of payment? Domestic sales are almost always denominated in the local currency. At issue is whether export sales should be denominated in the currency of the exporter, the currency of the buyer, or a third-country currency. Competition or custom often dictates the answer, but if negotiating room exists, the seller should prefer to price and to invoice in the strongest currency. Since the buyer would prefer to pay in the weakest currency, and both parties are likely to be equally well informed about the risk involved, the usual result is a trade-off in which a price or a terms-of-payment concession is granted by the seller in order to obtain the sale in a hard currency. Alternatively, the buyer pays more or pays sooner if payment in a soft currency is desired.

Parties to the transaction are likely to deviate from this straightforward bargaining position only if they have different opinions about the relative strengths of the currencies involved or if their own financial situation is strong enough to absorb the weak currency position. For example, a seller is more willing to price and invoice in a weak currency if that seller already has debts in that currency, for the sales proceeds can be used to retire the debt without any obvious loss. From the point of view of opportunity cost, that seller nevertheless forgoes an exchange gain. The buyer may be willing to pay in a hard currency if the buyer intends to resell the merchandise in a hard currency.

Payment Terms

Another factor is terms of payment. Considered by themselves, receivables from sales in weak currencies should be collected as soon as possible to minimize loss of exchange value between sales date and collection date. Accounts receivable resulting from sales in hard currencies may be allowed to remain outstanding longer. In fact, if the seller is expecting an imminent devaluation of its home currency, it might want to encourage slow payment of its hard currency receivables, especially if the home government requires immediate exchange of foreign currency receipts into the home currency. An alternative, if legal, would be for the seller to accept the proceeds abroad and keep them on deposit abroad rather than return them to the home country.

In some economies accounts receivable are used as a basis for short-term financing in preference to inventory financing. This situation occurs most often in inflationary economies and in economies in which the banking system is institutionally oriented toward discounting paper rather than financing merchandise.

In inflationary economies the demand for credit usually exceeds the supply. Often, however, a large business (be it multinational or a large local concern) has better access to the limited, cheaper credit that is available locally than do smaller domestic businesses, such as local distributors, retail merchants, or smaller manufacturers. Assume, for example, that the cost of local credit to a large multinational manufacturer/seller is 30% per annum, while the cost of credit to a potential retailer/buyer in the same economy is 50% per annum. Both manufacturer and retailer will benefit by maximizing sales volume to the ultimate customer if the manufacturer finances the transactions as long as possible and adds the financing costs (at 30%) to the sales price. In other words, it is better for the seller to finance the buyer's inventory at 30% per annum in the form of long-term receivables than for the buyer to finance the inventory directly for 50% per annum.

Self-Liquidating Bills

Some banking systems, often for reasons of tradition, have a predilection toward self-liquidating, discountable bills. In many European countries it is easier to borrow from a bank on the security of bills (receivables in negotiable form) generated from sales than on the security of physical inventory. Napoleon is alleged to have had a philosophy that no good French merchant should be required to wait for funds if good merchandise has been sold to good people, provided a document exists showing sales of the items. The document must have the signature of the buyer and the endorsement of the seller and the rediscounting bank. Thus in France it is often possible to reduce net investment in receivables to zero by selling entirely on trade acceptances that can be discounted at the bank.[9]

Other Terms

In many countries government bodies facilitate inventory financing in the guise of receivable financing by extending export credit or by guaranteeing export credit from banks at advantageous interest rates. When the term of the special export financing can be extended to match the payment of the foreign purchaser, the foreign purchaser is in effect able to finance its inventory through the courtesy of the exporter's government.

In some environments credit terms extended by manufacturers to retailers are of such long maturities as to constitute "purchase" of the retailer, such "purchase" being necessary to build an operational distribution system between manufacturer and ultimate customer. In Japan, for example, customer payment terms of 120 days are fairly common, and a manufacturer's sales effort is not competitive unless sufficient financial aid is provided to retailers to make it possible or beneficial for them to buy the manufacturer's product. Financial aid is reported to take the form of outright purchase of the retailer's capital stock, working capital loans, equipment purchase, subsidy or loan, and consideration of payment terms. Yet this is a normal way of doing business in the Japanese environment.

In summary, a multinational firm often manufactures or sells a product in a credit-short or inflationary economy, in a country where the banking system is oriented toward self-liquidating bills, or in locations where competition causes suppliers to finance their commercial customers. Longer collection periods have implications not only for the amount of financing that must be budgeted for a venture but also for the criteria by which the performance of local managers is evaluated.

---

[9]The European predilection for discountable bills has a very real rationale behind it. According to European commercial law, which is based on the "Code Napoleon," the claim certified by the signature of the buyer on the bill is separated from the claim based on the underlying transaction. For example, a bill is easily negotiable because objections about the quality of the merchandise by the buyer do not affect the claim of the bill holder. In addition, defaulted bills can be collected through a particularly speedy judicial process that is much faster than the collection of normal receivables. Thus there is nothing mystical about the preference of European countries for commercial bills, and retail buyers often finance their entire inventory with receivable financing from the manufacturer/seller.

In-House Banks

Some multinational firms have found their financial resources and needs are becoming either too large or too sophisticated for the financial services that are available in many of their local subsidiary markets. One solution to this has been the establishment of an *in-house* or *internal bank* within the firm. Such an in-house bank is not a separate corporation; rather, it is a set of functions performed by the existing treasury department. Acting as an independent entity, the central treasury of the firm transacts with the various business units of the firm on an arms-length basis. The purpose of the in-house bank is to provide banking-like services to the various units of the firm. The in-house bank may be able to provide services not available in many country markets, and do so at lower cost when they are available. In addition to traditional banking activities, the in-house bank may be able to offer services to units of the firm that aid in the management of ongoing transaction exposures. Lastly, because it is "in-house" credit, analysis is not a part of decision making.

Exhibit 22.12 illustrates how the in-house bank of a French multinational firm may work with the firm's Irish manufacturing unit and its Spanish distributor. There are two common benefits to the Irish business unit. First, since the Irish unit sells all foreign currency receivables to the in-house bank as they arise, the working capital needs of the unit are reduced. Secondly, the remaining working capital needs of the Irish unit are supplied by the in-house bank at lower cost. Because the two units are part of the same company, the interest rates charged by the in-house bank may often be significantly lower than what the Irish unit could obtain on its own. The source of funds for the in-house bank may arise from the deposits of excess cash balances from the Spanish affiliate. If the in-house bank can pay the Spanish affiliate a higher deposit rate than it could obtain on its own in Spain, and if the in-house bank can lend funds to the Irish unit at an interest rate

Exhibit 22.12   In-House Bank of a French Multinational Firm

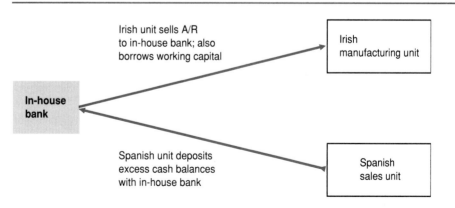

The French firm's in-house bank purchases the foreign currency receivables of the Irish manufacturing unit, reducing the working capital financing needs of the Irish unit. The remaining working capital needs of the Irish unit are provided by the in-house bank at interest rates cheaper than available in local markets. The in-house bank obtains its funds from deposits of excess cash balances by other units such as the Spanish sales unit, which earns higher deposit rates that it alone would have access to.

lower than it could obtain on its own in Ireland, then both operating units benefit. Assuming the loan rate is greater than the deposit rate, the in-house bank profits by the margin between the two.

How can the in-house bank be more efficient than a large outside bank? First, its costs are lower. In-house banks do not have to conform to the stringent capital requirements imposed on commercial banks worldwide. Secondly, in-house banks do not have the large overhead costs of supporting large dealing rooms, branch networks, and other services required for commercial bank competitiveness. Thirdly, they need not assess the creditworthiness of the corporate units they deal with, since the units are all in the same family. Nor need they provide for credit losses.

In addition to providing financing benefits, in-house banks allow for more effective currency risk management. In the case of the Irish affiliate shown in Exhibit 22.12, the sale of the foreign currency receivable to the in-house bank shifts the transaction exposure to the bank. The in-house bank is better equipped to deal with currency exposures and has a greater volume of international cash flows, allowing the firm to gain from more effective use of netting and matching. This frees the units of the firm from struggling to finance working capital and manage transaction exposures and allows them to focus on their primary business activities.

A variety of different structures are used for in-house banks. Many firms allow their units to use outside banks if the same services are available at lower cost. This forces the in-house bank to be operationally competitive. In this case, the in-house bank cannot rely on captive customers for its business, but must compete with commercial banks openly. Many firms, however, require their units to use the in-house bank in order to assure the bank of having an adequate level of activity to take advantage of economies of scale.

Inventory Management

Operations in inflationary, devaluation-prone economies sometimes force management to modify its normal approach to inventory management. In some cases management may choose to maintain inventory and reorder levels far in excess of what would be called for in an economic order quantity model.

Under conditions where local currency devaluation is likely, management must decide whether to build up inventory of imported items in anticipation of the expected devaluation. After the devaluation imported inventory will cost more in local currency terms. One trade-off is a higher holding cost because of the bloated level of inventory and high local interest rates, which normally reflect the expected devaluation. A less obvious trade-off is the possibility that local government will enforce a price freeze following devaluation. This freeze would prevent the imported inventory from being sold for an appropriate markup above its now higher replacement value. Still worse, the devaluation may not occur as anticipated, leaving management holding an excessive level of inventory until it can be worked down. Disposing of excessive inventory will be particularly painful if competitors have followed the same strategy of speculating on imported inventory.

Anticipating Price Freezes

To circumvent an anticipated price freeze, management can establish the local currency price of an imported item at a high level, with actual sales being made at a discount from this posted price. In the event of a devaluation, sales continue at the posted prices but discounts are withdrawn. This technique circumvents the price freeze only if that freeze is expressed in terms of posted rather than effective price. In any event it provides no protection against competitive price squeezes. An alternative is to sell at the posted price but increase selling, promotion, or other marketing mix activities, which can later be reduced.

If imported inventory is a commodity, another strategy is to purchase the commodity in the forward market. Then if local prices are frozen, the forward contract can be sold abroad for the same currency in which it is denominated. On the other hand, if local price controls are based on a fixed markup over cost, the forward contract can be exercised and the commodity imported at the now higher local currency cost, which becomes the basis for the markup. If options on the commodity are available, the same benefit can be achieved. The certain cost of the option should be compared with the uncertain trading gain or loss on the forward contract.

Free-Trade Zones

A free-trade zone is a combination of the old idea of duty-free ports and new legislation that gives breaks on customs duties to manufacturers that structure their operations to benefit from the technique. The old duty-free ports were typically in the dock area of major seaports. Modern free-trade zones, by comparison, are often located away from a port area. For example, the Italian firm of Olivetti uses such a zone in Harrisburg, Pennsylvania.

Free-trade zones increasingly are locations for assembly or manufacturing activity. Retailers use the zones to sort, label, or store imported clothing and appliances until the date of final sale. Manufacturers often complete work on partially assembled imports within the zone. When work is performed in a free-trade zone, import duties are usually assessed only on the lower import cost and not on the higher value created by work performed within the zone. Additionally, the time of payment of duties is usually delayed. An item imported into the United States in January for, say, three months of additional finishing and storage before an April sale will be charged duty in January. The same item left in a free-trade zone until April will be assessed the same amount of duty, but payment will not be made until April. Free financing of the duty charges for three months is obtained!

A free-trade zone can also be used to circumvent a price freeze because merchandise in the zone has not yet been formally imported. Often a price freeze will not apply to items not yet imported into the country. Alternatively, the importer retains an option to sell the merchandise elsewhere at world market prices without the loss of import duties and transactions costs that would have already been paid if the merchandise had been formally imported.

Summary

- Financial managers of multinational firms must control international liquid assets in order to maintain adequate liquidity in a variety of currencies while also minimizing political and foreign exchange risk.

- The first half of this chapter looked at ways that funds can be positioned in a multinational firm. The concept of unbundling remittances was described. We explained determinants of dividend policy and discussed the use of royalties, fees, and home office overhead.

- Transfer pricing was considered in terms of possible conflicting goals of fund positioning, tax and tariff minimization, and fair treatment of managers and joint venture partners.

- Techniques for moving blocked funds, such as fronting loans, creating unrelated exports, and obtaining special dispensation were discussed, and the deployment of funds under forcible reinvestment was examined.

- The second half of the chapter looked at uniquely international aspects of managing cash, accounts receivable, and inventories. Cash balances are held to provide planned disbursements and to protect the firm against unanticipated variations from budgeted cash flows in an array of currencies. Techniques of cash management include the use of centralized depositories and multilateral netting.

- Accounts receivable management was discussed in terms of receivables from independent customers. Inventory management was viewed in terms of ways to protect inventory values in the face of adverse exchange rate changes and anticipated price freezes.

Decision Case
Tektronix B[10]

In late December 1983 Barbara Block, Assistant Treasurer-International, Tektronix, Inc., was reviewing one more time various alternative approaches to managing Tektronix's foreign exchange exposure and working capital management practices. During the period 1981–1983 the increasing strength of the U.S. dollar had led to mounting foreign exchange transaction losses totaling nearly $9 million. These were primarily incurred by the foreign manufacturing and sales affiliates. In addition, Tektronix was suffering from adverse economic exposure due to producing equipment in Oregon, U.S.A., for export to

---

[10]Doug Schafer and Barbara Block of Tektronix, and Arthur Stonehill, Oregon State University, 1988. Reprinted with permission.

the foreign affiliates. These exports were invoiced in U.S. dollars to the affiliates but sold to customers who were billed in local currency by the affiliates. The increasing strength of the U.S. dollar made it difficult for the affiliates to maintain their operating margins when pricing larger custom orders which would not be delivered and billed for several months. It also complicated routine updating of catalogs and price lists for more standardized products.

Background

Tektronix is a U.S. corporation, headquartered in Beaverton, Oregon, that develops, manufactures, sells, and services electronic measurement, display and control instruments and systems throughout the industrialized world and in certain developing countries. The financial results of these activities are measured in U.S. dollars.

Almost since the company's beginning in 1946, Tektronix has had product sales outside of the United States. In 1948 Tektronix established its first foreign distribution agreement in Sweden. During the early 1950s Tektronix established other distribution networks in Belgium, Germany, Austria, and Canada. In 1958 Tektronix commenced manufacturing operations on the Isle of Guernsey, followed by other manufacturing affiliates located in the Netherlands and the United Kingdom. A major manufacturing joint venture in Japan was also established with Sony. By late 1983 Tektronix had 21 foreign operating subsidiaries and joint ventures.

During the late 1970s and early 1980s Tektronix established subsidiaries in Austria, Finland, Germany, Italy, Norway, and Spain. Since Tektronix follows a policy of establishing subsidiaries with a minimum of equity capital, the majority of each subsidiary's capital came from intercompany U.S. dollar loans, lagged intercompany payables, and local bank credit. The capital mix decision for each subsidiary is made by the corporate finance department in Beaverton, Oregon.

In the case of Finland, Italy, Norway, and Spain there were credit restrictions in each country that resulted in inadequate availability of local credit facilities. The decision was made to finance the start-up of these subsidiaries with mostly intercompany U.S. dollar loans and lagged intercompany payables to supplement the local credit facilities.

For several years, as these subsidiaries became established in their local market, they experienced operational difficulties and losses requiring additional working capital funds. Again these requirements were funded by further lagging the subsidiaries' intercompany payables. Some additional share capital increases were also made. Since all of the intercompany loans and payables were denominated in U.S. dollars the company experienced large exposures to changes in the value of the dollar.

Exchange Rates

In late 1980, the U.S. dollar began strengthening and this trend continued, with vigor, for several more years. Many competitors sourced from European factories and pricing competition became very fierce. Tektronix's marketing affiliates tried to minimize price increases as the dollar soared in order to hold market share. In 1981 the DM traded from 1.80 to a low of 2.55 against the dollar, and the French franc declined from 4.45 to 6.00. Tektronix's prices to most European customers had increased as much as 30%. During the three-year period 1981–1983 the dollar continued to strengthen with the DM hitting a low of almost 2.80 and the French franc weakening to almost 8.50.

Pricing Procedures

Tektronix's products are not stocked at the local sales affiliates, so orders take an average of three months between order and shipment. Terms range from 30 days to 180 days after shipment with the majority being under 90 days. The sales affiliates bill their customers in their local currency and pay the factories for the products in dollars. They price the products by applying a profit margin to the dollar cost and then use an estimated future exchange rate to convert the quote to local currency. However, in actual practice the competition does not allow very much discretion in anticipatory pricing.

The affiliates' cost of sales varied as the exchange rates changed and they had to buy U.S. dollars to pay the factories. Their sales prices in local currency, however, were generally fixed. In some countries the affiliates had the ability to use currency clauses which allowed them to share the currency fluctuations, from the time of the quote until the goods were received, with the customer. This practice was used to varying degrees from 90–100% in Scandinavia to almost 0% in Germany. The affiliates could only use this practice where competition allowed.

Foreign Exchange Exposure Management

The affiliates were in a losing battle for the past three years. They were taking fewer and fewer orders at higher and higher prices. Many times their markup in local currency was not enough to cover the cost of their intercompany purchases due to the local currency weakening beyond their anticipated price list rate. Tektronix's policies forbid the use of forward currency contracts for backlog hedges. Forward currency contracts were used by the parent company in Beaverton for transaction exposures (intercompany payables that were already on the affiliates books). This was a policy that had been in place since the inception of the overseas affiliates.

Many of the sales affiliates had limited or no ability to do forward currency contracts, at the time, due to foreign exchange controls. A change in company policy that would allow Tektronix's subsidiaries to hedge backlog would therefore be of little or no benefit to them. The Operations Managers of the subsidiaries were crying for help. Their margins were shrinking, or disappearing altogether, and they were losing market share due to the frequent price list changes and requests for currency clauses (see Exhibit 22.13).

Tektronix's main concern about letting the affiliates use forward contracts was one of control. The company's treasury functions are very centralized and therefore the affiliates' finance departments are staffed with accounting and administrative personnel. They did not have the necessary knowledge and experience to manage a backlog exposure management program.

At the same time backlog exposures originally became a major issue, Tektronix undertook a study to evaluate all of its various types of exposures and the hedging

Exhibit 22.13 Selected Financial Data for Tektronix's Foreign Affiliates and Joint Ventures (thousands of dollars)

FOREIGN AFFILIATES

Tektronix has 18 foreign operating subsidiaries located in Australia, Belgium, Brazil, Canada, Denmark, Finland, France, Germany, Guernsey, Italy, the Netherlands, Norway, Spain, Sweden, Switzerland, and the United Kingdom with a branch in Ireland. The assets, liabilities, sales, and income of foreign subsidiaries are included in the consolidated financial statements in these amounts:

	1983	1982	1981	1980	1979	1978
Current Assets	$233,030	$218,375	$208,864	$169,051	$141,446	$106,098
Current Liabilities	69,334	68,528	68,207	55,483	39,090	32,105
Facilities	29,727	34,787	28,938	22,185	18,585	15,337
Other Assets	95	603	410	907	1,118	889
Other Liabilities	7,598	9,449	8,228	7,857	6,732	2,222
Net Sales	$367,215	$377,167	$364,785	$321,741	$252,597	$185,472
Gross Profit	106,268	109,479	105,403	97,367	77,878	57,352
Operating Income	34,760	30,808	34,285	37,446	29,941	22,281
Income Before Taxes	34,916	34,326	33,301	39,781	31,809	23,632
Earnings	21,787	23,426	19,401	29,882	22,583	16,714

JOINT VENTURES

Tektronix also has investments in three joint venture companies located in Austria, Japan, and Mexico. The company's share of the assets, liabilities, sales, and income of these unconsolidated affiliates consisted of the following:

	1983	1982	1981	1980	1979	1978
Current Assets	$31,166	$33,429	$32,173	$24,873	$21,713	$12,991
Current Liabilities	15,149	16,166	16,892	12,903	10,936	7,359
Facilities	13,023	9,114	8,686	5,477	3,939	3,577
Other Assets	4,213	3,895	4,236	3,063	3,202	3,662
Other Liabilities	1,560	1,237	1,417	1,558	1,145	1,772
Net Sales	$57,368	$61,520	$59,660	$46,064	$40,551	$25,457
Gross Profit	18,668	21,613	23,728	16,107	16,740	10,118
Operating Income	7,761	11,161	14,181	8,859	10,385	6,017
Income Before Taxes	7,966	10,419	15,575	8,041	10,618	7,235
Earnings	3,636	4,023	7,597	2,930	5,222	4,249

alternatives (strategic and tactical) available to best manage those exposures. The study covered reinvoicing, netting, finance companies, and traditional hedging tools such as leads, lags, and forward currency contracts.

When the study was completed and presented to management in late 1982, the company was experiencing a slowdown in growth (see Exhibits 22.14 and 22.15) and expense-cutting procedures were being evaluated. Another factor impacting the choice

Exhibit 22.14   Tektronix Consolidated Financial Statement (thousands of dollars)

	1983	1982	1981	1980	1979	1978
Current Assets	$639,680	$621,981	$573,791	$540,917	$428,787	$357,704
Cash	96,867	73,331	47,862	57,145	41,788	66,208
Accounts Receivable	210,843	230,573	204,952	198,069	153,568	115,100
Inventories	292,885	290,268	293,705	263,563	214,533	163,523
Prepaid Expenses	39,085	27,809	27,272	22,140	18,898	12,873
Current Liabilities	$197,428	$233,267	$214,527	$193,831	$153,135	$107,556
Short-Term Debt	33,675	66,334	50,175	45,809	28,997	10,351
Accounts Payable	78,569	63,856	60,405	49,034	42,033	33,108
Income Taxes Payable	15,280	23,118	28,778	27,404	20,444	18,458
Accrued Compensation	69,904	79,959	75,159	71,584	61,661	45,639
Working Capital	$442,252	$388,714	$359,264	$347,086	$257,652	$250,148
Facilities	397,290	379,122	304,912	276,771	194,454	119,533
Other Assets	50,444	41,184	30,050	24,005	19,666	13,893
Long-Term Debt	152,342	132,060	146,143	136,196	62,094	37,086
Deferred Tax Liability	43,691	441,124	30,765	23,974	19,150	16,029
Other Liabilities	32,258	5,387	4,774	4,354	5,728	3,763
Shareowners' Equity	$661,695	$630,449	$557,544	$483,338	$402,800	$326,696
Share Capital	78,097	64,277	52,515	41,884	31,950	24,332
Reinvested Earnings	595,957	566,172	505,029	441,494	370,850	302,364
Currency Adjustment	(12,359)					
Common Shares (thousands)	19,059	18,807	18,574	18,372	18,143	17,913

of alternative currency management techniques was that approximately 30% of all international orders from affiliates were naturally hedged with currency clauses with varying percentages in each country.

As of December 1983 recommendations made by the study had not yet been accepted. However, Barbara Block continued to be concerned about the potential for further exchange losses. The most recent foreign exchange exposure report had just been compiled and is shown in Exhibit 22.16.

Cash Management

Another related concern facing Barbara Block was in the area of cash management. As the number of Tektronix's international affiliates increased in the 1970s and early 1980s the problems and complexities of managing cash within the intercompany payment network increased to the point that the system was almost unmanageable (see Exhibit 22.17).

Each sales affiliate sourced products from up to four different factories. Therefore, each factory received payments from as many as eighteen different affiliates. The payment procedure had each affiliate paying on a fixed day each month, theoretically, but

Exhibit 22.15   Consolidated Income and Reinvested Earnings (thousands of dollars)

	1983	1982	1981	1980	1979	1978
Net Sales	$1,191,380	$1,195,748	$1,061,834	$971,306	$786,936	$598,886
Cost of Sales	615,941	595,340	513,145	485,464	359,740	266,474
Gross Income	$575,439	$600,408	$548,689	$512,842	$427,196	$332,412
Engineering Expense	125,393	109,086	91,147	77,797	60,561	49,832
Selling Expense	185,355	180,631	157,105	135,405	113,461	86,850
Administrative Expense	120,920	108,977	100,715	88,343	68,044	53,063
Profit Sharing	29,316	55,267	61,686	63,448	63,682	48,528
Operating Income	$114,455	$146,447	$138,036	$147,849	$121,448	$94,139
Interest Expense	25,832	29,537	25,274	15,956	6,428	4,246
Nonoperating Income	(25,509)	9,493	19,360	5,029	11,631	6,068
Income Before Taxes	$63,114	$126,403	$132,392	$136,922	$126,651	$95,961
Income Taxes	14,400	46,950	52,225	51,850	49,500	39,115
Earnings	$48,714	$79,453	$80,167	$85,072	$44,152	$56,846
Nonoperating Income (Expense) From Currency Gains (Losses)	($3,035)	($2,679)	($3,039)	$1,729	$435	($15)

this system did not always work, since an affiliate could decide at the last moment not to pay.

When making intercompany payments the procedure stated that the sending affiliate was to telex the receiving affiliate details of the payment (i.e., amount of transfer, date of transfer, sending bank, and receiving bank) before the transfer was sent, so that the receiving affiliate could manage its cash in a more efficient manner. This procedure encountered problems such as the sending affiliate forgetting to send a notification telex and also lost telexes. These problems made it very difficult for the person responsible for managing the cash in each factory.

Another problem with the current intercompany payment procedure was the loss of value on float that occurred between the paying affiliate and the receiving affiliate. It was not uncommon for the paying affiliate's bank to charge its account one or two days before the receiving affiliate's bank credited its account. With over $300 million flowing between the sales affiliates and the factories on an annual basis, this situation was very expensive.

Buying the necessary U.S. dollars to pay their intercompany purchases also caused problems for the sales affiliates. Some of them had relatively small intercompany payables each month. Commissions as a percent of the dollars purchased are substantially higher for smaller foreign exchange transactions. Therefore, they were paying relatively large commissions to purchase their U.S. dollars.

The final major concern regarding the current intercompany payment procedure was the large transfer costs that some of the international banks charged. With the large

Exhibit 22.16   Exposures, December 1983 (thousands of dollars)[a]

	Equity	Earnings	Backlog
EMS Exposures			
Belgian franc	426	394	1,835
Danish krone	128	1,387	2,471
Deutschemark	105	5,365	10,538
Dutch guilder	5,275	25,391[b]	12,393
Irish punt	429	1,491	
Italian lira	3,710	1,847	3,634
Total EMS	$9,644	$34,813	$32,362
Other European Exposures			
Austrian schilling	122	1,115	2,237
British pound	20,375	(9,846)[c]	23,783
Finnish markka	199	590	1,254
Norwegian krone	235	1,350	3,125
Spanish peseta	175	2,340	4,528
Swedish krona	2,035	5,248	1,349
Swiss franc	32,890	398	1,532
Total Other	$56,031	$1,195	$37,808
AM/PAC Exposures			
Australian dollar	5,378	458	2,548
Brazilian cruzado	0	400	2,103
Canadian dollar	10,745	2,583	6,381
Japanese yen	45,958	3,169	7,436
Mexican peso	0	142	283
Total Am/Pac	$62,081	$6,752	$18,751
Exposure Summary			
EMS	9,644	34,813	32,362
Other European	56,031	1,195	37,808
Am/Pac	62,081	6,752	18,751
Total Exposures	$127,756	$42,760	$88,921

[a]Not actual numbers

[b]Includes $25,990 translation, ($525) transaction.

[c]Includes ($5,428) translation, ($4,418) transaction.

amount of money being transferred and the large number of transfers, bank transfer charges were becoming substantial for the consolidated company.

Recommendation

The desire to minimize the effect of currency fluctuations at the subsidiary level, the limited flexibility to hedge backlog exposures in certain countries, the lack of timely transaction exposure information, and the numerous problems with effectively

Exhibit 22.17   Tektronix's Current Settlement System

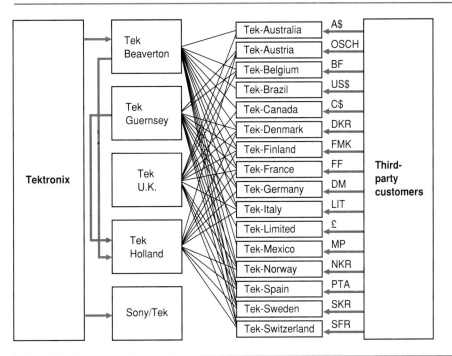

Note: All cash payments occur from right to left. All intracompany payables are denominated in U.S. dollars.

managing cash with the current system contributed to Tektronix's desire to review alternative approaches to currency management. Barbara Block knew that she needed to develop a comprehensive set of tools to address these concerns and she wondered what she should recommend in light of the current internal and external financial environments.

Case Questions

1. Which problems now confronting Tektronix are most immediately critical? Which of these can be managed in the short term, and which will require longer term solutions?

2. How can the multitude of cash flows and transactions between units of Tektronix be reduced?

3. If Tektronix was to stop the lagging of payables by its foreign affiliates, how are the affiliates going to cover their working capital needs?

4. Which of Tektronix's problems seem to be arising from the macro-environment, and which from internal policies and organizational issues?

5. If you were Barbara Block, what would you recommend to management?

Questions

1. Namur Refrigerator Company

Namur Refrigerator Company of Belgium manufactures electric refrigerators for sale to retail outlets in Belgium and, through a wholly owned distribution affiliate, to the Netherlands. Annual capacity of the Belgian factory is 4,000 refrigerators, but present production is only 3,000, of which 2,000 are sold in Belgium and 1,000 are exported to the Netherlands. Income tax rates in both Belgium and the Netherlands are 50%.

Within Belgium, refrigerators are sold by Namur to retail outlets at a manufacturer's price of BF12,000 each. After-tax profit is BF1,200 per refrigerator, calculated as follows:

Manufacturer's unit sales price	BF12,000
Direct labor	2,400
Direct material	3,600
Manufacturing overhead	2,000
Total manufacturing costs	8,000
Factory margin	BF4,000
Selling and administrative costs	1,600
Realized pretax profit per unit	BF2,400
Belgian income tax at 50%	1,200
After-tax profit per unit	BF1,200

Direct labor consists of hourly payroll costs for Belgian workers, and direct material is for components purchased in Belgium. Manufacturing overhead is a fixed cost that includes production line supervision and depreciation. Selling and administrative costs are fixed, and are for office salaries and rent.

Namur Refrigerator Company sells to its Netherlands affiliate at BF8,800 per refrigerator, this being its manufacturing cost of BF8,000 plus a profit markup of BF800. Transportation and distribution costs add an additional BF800, and the refrigerators are resold to Dutch retailers at the guilder equivalent of BF12,000. This pricing decision was based on the following analysis of elasticity of demand in the Netherlands. (All prices are expressed in Belgian francs.)

Unit sales price	BF12,800	BF12,000	BF11,200	BF10,400	BF9,600
Import cost	8,800	8,800	8,800	8,800	8,800
Transportation	800	800	800	800	800
Unit profit before tax	3,200	2,400	1,600	800	0
Less 50% Dutch tax	−1,600	−1,200	−800	−400	0
Unit profit after tax	1,600	1,200	800	400	0
Times sales volume	× 700	× 1,000	× 1,400	× 2,000	× 2,500
Total profit (000)	1,120	1,200	1,120	800	0

(Note: Unit demand is a function only of the final unit price in the Netherlands.)

It was self-evident to Namur's management that the unit price of BF12,000 in the Netherlands maximized Dutch contribution to profits at a total figure of BF1,200,000.

    a. Is Namur's present pricing strategy for the Netherlands correct?

    b. Assume Namur wants to divide profits on export sales evenly between Belgium and the Netherlands so as to avoid difficulties with either tax authority. What final unit price in the Netherlands and transfer price should the firm adopt for its sales to the Netherlands?

    c. If the Netherlands income tax rate remains at 50%, but Belgium lowers its tax rate to 30%, should a new transfer price be adopted? What policy issues are involved?

2. Torino Lock, S.A. (C22A.WK1)

Miller Lock Company has manufactured standardized door locks in Connecticut for many years. Each lock has per unit direct labor costs of $10, direct material costs of $5, and overhead of $2. A portion of production is sold (transferred) to Torino Lock, S.A., Miller's wholly owned distribution affiliate in Italy, for $22 per unit. Torino Lock incurs an additional $3 per lock of direct costs and resells to European builders for $30 per lock. No other costs are involved, except for income taxes, which until 1986 were 46% in both countries.

Comprehensive tax reform legislation passed by the U.S. Congress in 1986 lowered U.S. corporate income taxes to 34%, effective in 1987, but at that time Miller made no change in its transfer price to Torino. In 1991, Sarah Lodge, Miller's new director of international operations, was reviewing current transfer price policy. She judged that Miller could raise or lower its export sales price to Torino by up to 10% without causing a tax challenge from either Italian or U.S. tax authorities. She wondered if Miller should change the transfer price applied to exports to Italy.

    a. In 1991, what was Miller's consolidated after-tax profit per unit sold to Italy?

    b. What do you recommend for a transfer price in 1992?

    c. If your recommendation were adopted, what will be Miller's consolidated after-tax profit per unit sold to Torino?

    d. Miller becomes concerned that the Italian lire might devalue. How would this information influence your recommendation in question b?

3. Cuzco, S.A.

Cuzco, S.A. of Peru is 100% owned by Berkeley Manufacturing Company of the United States. Net escudo sales of Cuzco this past year were equal to $80,000,000, when measured in U.S. dollars, and net income before taxes and before any royalty payments was $10,000,000. The corporate income tax rate in Peru is 50% and the corporate income tax rate in the United States is 35%.

Cuzco is allowed to distribute 80% of its after-tax Peruvian income to Berkeley Manufacturing Company as a dividend. Alternatively Cuzco may remit royalties of 2% of net sales revenue. Royalty fees would be paid out of Peruvian pretax income, and if paid the Peruvian affiliate could still pay dividends up to 70% of after-tax income.

Royalties and dividends received in the United States are subject to the U.S. tax rate of 35%, grossed-up in the case of dividends for the proportion of income taxes paid in Peru and with a U.S. tax credit for Peruvian taxes.

    a. What distribution policy should Berkeley apply to Cuzco to maximize parent cash flow?

    b. If Berkeley wanted to maximize consolidated net income, and did not care about dividends, should it adopt a different policy?

4. Eurowide Corporation (C22B.WK1)

Eurowide Corporation has subsidiaries in Italy, France, Germany, and Denmark. It does its accounting in Deutschemarks. Historically Eurowide has maintained separate precautionary cash balances for each of these countries at a level equal to three standard deviations above the expected cash need in each country.

    a. What could Eurowide save by maintaining all precautionary balances in a single concentrated account in one European financial center? (Assume cash needs in each country are normally distributed and are independent of each other.)

Country	Expected Cash Need	One Standard Deviation
Italy	DM50,000,000	DM10,000,000
France	45,000,000	5,000,000
Germany	30,000,000	3,000,000
Denmark	40,000,000	7,000,000

    b. What other advantages might accrue to Eurowide from centralizing its European cash holdings? Are these advantages realistic?

5. Hietaniemi Brewery

Hietaniemi's VII-A Lager beer has a world reputation. It is brewed and sold in Hong Kong and the United States as well as in the home country of Finland. At the end of September 1992, unsettled intracompany debts in U.S. dollars are as follows:

Hong Kong unit:	owes $7,000,000 to U.S. affiliate.
	owes $9,000,000 to Finnish parent.
U.S. unit:	owes $3,000,000 to Finnish parent.
	owes $4,000,000 to Hong Kong affiliate.
Finnish parent:	owes $3,000,000 to U.S. affiliate.
	owes $5,000,000 to Hong Kong affiliate.

Foreign exchange transaction spreads average 0.5% of funds transferred.

    a. How should Hietaniemi Brewery settle these intracompany obligations? What would be the savings in transaction expenses over the no-netting alternative?

    b. Before settling the above accounts, Hietaniemi Brewery decides to invest US$6,000,000 in Australia to build a new brewery in Adelaide. Can this type of decision be incorporated into the settlement process? How, and what would be the total bank charges? Explain.

Bibliography

Al-Eryani, Mohammad F., Pervaiz Alam, and Syed H. Akhter, "Transfer Pricing Determinants of U.S. Multinationals," *Journal of International Business Studies,* Third Quarter 1990, pp. 409–425.

Anvari, M., "Efficient Scheduling of Cross-Border Cash Transfers," *Financial Management,* Summer 1986, pp. 40–49.

Arpan, Jeffrey S., "International Intracorporate Pricing: Non-American Systems and Views," *Journal of International Business Studies,* Spring 1972, pp. 1–18.

Barrett, M. Edgar, "Case of the Tangled Transfer Price," *Harvard Business Review,* May/June 1977, pp. 20–36, 176–178.

Benvignati, A. M., "An Empirical Investigation of International Transfer Pricing by U.S. Manufacturing Firms," in *Multinationals and Transfer Pricing,* A. M. Rugman and L. Eden, eds., New York: St. Martin's Press, 1985.

Bergendahl, Göran, "Multi-Currency Netting in a Multi-National Firm," *International Financial Management,* in Göran Bergendahl, ed., Stockholm: Norstedts, 1982, pp. 149–173.

Burns, Jane O., "Transfer Pricing Decisions in U.S. Multinational Corporations," *Journal of International Business Studies,* Fall 1980, pp. 23–39.

Business International, *Automating Global Financial Management,* Morristown, N.J.: Financial Executives Research Foundation, 1988.

Crum, Roy L., and Lee A. Tavis, "Allocating Multinational Resources When Objectives Conflict: A Problem of Overlapping Systems," *Advances in Financial Planning and Forecasting,* vol. 4, part B, 1990, pp. 271–294.

Fowler, D. J., "Transfer Prices and Profit Maximization in Multinational Enterprise Operations," *Journal of International Business Studies,* Winter 1978, pp. 9–26.

Gentry, James A., Dileep R. Mehta, S. K. Bhattacharya, Robert Cobbaut, and Jean-Louis Scaringella, "An International Study of Management Perceptions of the Working Capital Process," *Journal of International Business Studies,* Spring-Summer 1979, pp. 28–38.

Granick, David, "National Differences in the Use of Internal Transfer Prices," *California Management Review,* Summer 1975, pp. 28–40.

Greenhill, C.R., and E. O. Herbolzheimer, "Control of Transfer Prices in International Transactions: The Restrictive Business Practices Approach," in *Multinationals Beyond the Market,* R. Murray, ed., New York: Wiley, 1981, pp. 185–194.

Kim, Seung, H., and Stephen W. Miller, "Constituents of the International Transfer Pricing Decision," *Columbia Journal of World Business,* Spring 1979, pp. 69–77.

Kopits, George F., "Intra-Firm Royalties Crossing Frontiers and Transfer-Pricing Behaviour," *Economic Journal,* December 1976, pp. 791–805.

Lecraw, D. J., "Some Evidence on Transfer Pricing by Multinational Corporations," in *Multinationals and Transfer Pricing,* A. M. Rugman and L. Eden, eds., New York: St. Martin's Press, 1985.

Masson, Dubos J., "Planning and Forecasting of Cash Flows for the Multinational Firm: International Cash Management," *Advances in Financial Planning and Forecasting,* vol. 4, part B, 1990, pp. 195–228.

Mirus, Rolf, and Bernard Yeung, "The Relevance of the Invoicing Currency in Intra-Firm Trade Transactions," *Journal of International Money and Finance,* vol. 6, No. 4, December 1987, pp. 449–464.

Ness, Walter L., Jr., "U.S. Corporate Income Taxation and the Dividend Remittance Policy of Multinational Corporations," *Journal of International Business Studies,* Spring 1975, pp. 67–77.

Plasschaert, S. R. F., "Transfer Pricing Problems in Developing Countries," in *Multinationals and Transfer Pricing,* A. M. Rugman and L. Eden, eds., New York: St. Martin's Press, 1985, pp. 247–266.

Pugel, Thomas, and Judith L. Ugelow, "Transfer Pricing and Profit Maximization in Multinational Enterprise Operations," *Journal of International Business Studies,* Spring/Summer 1982, pp. 115–119.

Rutenberg, David P., "Maneuvering Liquid Assets in a Multinational Company: Formulation and Deterministic Solution Procedures," *Management Science,* June 1970, pp. B-671–B-684.

Shapiro, Alan C., "Optimal Inventory and Credit-Granting Strategies Under Inflation and Devaluation," *Journal of Financial and Quantitative Analysis,* January 1973, pp. 37–46.

Soenen, L. A., "International Cash Management: A Study of Practices of U.K.-Based Companies," *Journal of Business Research,* August 1986, pp. 345–354.

Soenen, L. A., and Raj Aggarwal, "Corporate Foreign Exchange and Cash Management Practices," *Journal of Cash Management,* March-April 1987, pp. 62–64.

Srinivasan, VenKat, and Yong H. Kim, "Payments Netting in International Cash Management: A Network Optimization Approach," *Journal of*

International Business Studies, Summer 1986, pp. 1–20.

———, Susan E. Moeller and Yong H. Kim, "International Cash Management: State-of-the-Art and Research Directions," *Advances in Financial Planning and Forecasting,* vol. 4, part B, 1990, pp. 161–194.

Tansuhaj, Patriya S., and James W. Gentry, "Foreign Trade Zones in Global Marketing and Logistics," *Journal of International Business Studies,* Spring 1987, pp. 19–34.

Transfer Pricing and Multinational Enterprises, *Report of the OECD Committee on Fiscal Affairs,* Paris: Organization for Economic Cooperation and Development, 1979.

UNCTAD (United Nations Commission on Trade and Development), *Dominant Positions of Market Power of Transnational Corporations: Use of the Transfer Pricing Mechanisms,* Geneva: UNCTAD/ST/MD/6, 1977.

Yunker, Penelope J., "A Survey of Subsidiary Autonomy, Performance Evaluation and Transfer Pricing in Multinational Corporations," *Columbia Journal of World Business,* Fall 1983, pp. 51–64.

———, *Transfer Pricing and Performance Evaluation in Multinational Corporations: A Survey Study,* New York: Praeger, 1982.

Chapter 23
Advanced Topics in Currency Risk Management

Global View
Lost in a Maze of Hedges

Volatile exchange rates in recent weeks have sent many a nervous boss scurrying to his or her finance department to check up on its currency-hedging strategy. Few of them will emerge much the wiser, for the typical multinational's strategy can seem impenetrable.

Hedging is simple enough in theory. Just doing business exposes many firms to foreign-exchange risk: if an exchange rate moves the wrong way, profit or the balance sheet suffers. Suppose a British exporter sells goods that will be paid for in dollars three months later. If the dollar weakens against the pound, the exporter will get less in sterling than it expected. Hedging lets firms reduce or eliminate this risk by using a financial instrument that moves in the opposite way when exchange rates change. For the British exporter, that means one which is worth more pounds as the dollar falls.

The best way to hedge is to do it "naturally." Firms can design their trading, borrowing, and investment strategies to match their sales and assets in a particular currency with their purchases and liabilities in it. If, say, a British firm owns an asset valued in dollars, it can hedge by borrowing in dollars. No matter what happens to the pound-dollar exchange rate there will be no net effect on the firm's balance sheet.

Few firms can hedge all, or even most, of their risk naturally. So many hedge actively in the financial markets, mainly using forward contracts and options. Forward contracts—agreements to buy or sell a given amount of a currency at an agreed exchange rate on a particular date—get rid of all exchange-rate risk, and are often thought of as the perfect hedge. Options—which give firms the right, but not the obligation, to use a particular forward contract—are more flexible. Imagine that the

British exporter buys an option to sell dollars in three months at the forward rate. If the exchange rate moves against the firm, it can use its option and limit the damage; if the rate goes in its favor, it can let the option lapse and enjoy the windfall.

Firms seem to use forward contracts at least twice as much as options. One reason is cost. Forward contracts are no dearer than an ordinary trade in the spot market. Options, by contrast, are expensive and must be paid for whether or not they are used. Option prices can jump about wildly, depending on which currencies are involved and how volatile the market is. Prices have gone through the roof recently; on September 29 Swiss Bank Corporation priced a three-month option to sell dollars at 2.7% of the contract—a hefty $27,000 for a British exporter wanting to hedge $1 million.

Source: Abstracted from "Lost in a Maze of Hedges," 10/3/92, p. 84. © 1992 *The Economist Newspaper Ltd.* Reprinted with permission.

This chapter provides a more rigorous presentation of a number of topics introduced in previous chapters, including the determination of the optimal currency hedge ratio, cross-currency "proxy" hedging, delta-neutral hedging strategies, and the construction and use of a number of increasingly accepted second-generation option products such as range forwards and participating forwards.

This chapter is optional. Only those interested in more detailed theoretical foundations and additional knowledge in the use of complex options for risk management need read further.

The Currency Hedge Ratio

Chapter 7's discussion of transaction exposure management assumed—without discussion—a *hedge ratio* of 1.0. The hedge ratio, frequently termed *beta* (β), is the percentage of an individual exposure's nominal amount covered by a financial instrument such as a forward contract or currency option. Beta is then defined as follows:

$$\beta = \frac{\text{Value of currency hedge}}{\text{Value of currency exposure}}.$$

This section describes the theoretical methodology for determining the optimal hedge ratio, the optimal beta.

The Optimal Hedge

The value of an individual currency position can be expressed as a portfolio of two assets: a spot asset (the exposure) and a hedge asset (a forward, future, or option). The hedge is constructed so that whatever spot value is lost as a result of adverse exchange rate movements (ΔS) is replaced by an equal but opposite change in the value of the hedge asset, the futures position (ΔF):

$$\Delta\text{Position Value} = \Delta\text{Spot} - \Delta\text{Futures} \approx 0.$$

The goal is to formulate the effective hedge that will indeed result in $\Delta V = 0$.

The *optimal currency hedge* can be found by minimizing the terminal (end-of-period) variance of the two-asset portfolio.[1] The hedge asset amount as a percentage of the exposure is altered to minimize the terminal portfolio variance.

For example, a multinational firm is expecting a foreign currency-denominated payment, an account receivable at a future date, time t_1, which is termed here the spot or *cash position*. The amount of the hedge, however, must be determined now, at time t_0. We can then specify the *expected value* of this receivable at the future date as

$$E(X_1^\$) = X_1 \times E(S_1)$$

where $E(X_1^\$)$ is the expected dollar value of the foreign currency receivable at time 1;
   X_1 is the amount of the foreign currency to be received (in foreign currency);
   $E(S_1)$ is the expected spot rate to occur at time 1 (dollars per unit of foreign currency).

Note that the *present* spot rate is not a part of the expected value at the end of the period.

Because it does not know what the exchange rate will actually be on the future date, the firm would like to hedge its foreign currency exposure. It can sign a forward contract that would guarantee it a specific exchange rate for U.S. dollars per unit of foreign currency at time t_1, for whatever amount of foreign currency it wishes. The firm then forms a portfolio of this cash position above and a forward contract as a hedge asset. The expected value of the portfolio, $E(P_1)$, at the end of the period, is

$$E(P_1^\$) = X_1\, E(S_1) + X_f[E(F_1) - F_0],$$

where X_f is the amount of foreign currency sold forward at time 0;
   F_0 is the current price of the futures contract;
   $E(F_1)$ is the expected futures price at time 1.

This is the expectation now of the portfolio's total value when the receivable is paid in 90 days.

The expected spot rate in 90 days is the only true unknown. The *decision variable* is the amount of the foreign currency it chooses to sell forward. The question is, what is the specific (mathematical) goal the firm is pursuing when it chooses the amount of the hedge? Answer: to minimize the variance of the expected return. This would translate mathematically into selecting the X_f value, which results in the minimum variance of the portfolio's final value.

The variance of the expected portfolio value is

$$\text{var}[E(P_1^\$)] = X^2\, \text{var}(S_1) + X_f^2 \text{var}(F_1) + 2XX_f\, \text{cov}(S_1, F_1).$$

---

[1]This section is based on Joe Kerkvliet and Michael H. Moffett, "The Hedging of an Uncertain Future Foreign Currency Payment," *Journal of Financial and Quantitative Analysis,* vol. 26, no. 4, December 1991, pp. 565–578.

Thus the quantitative problem at hand is the *minimization of this variance* with respect to the decision variable, X_f:

$$\underset{X_f}{\text{MIN}} \ \text{var}[E(P_1^\$)] = X^2 \ \text{var}(S_1) + X_f^2 \text{var}(F_1) + 2XX_f \text{cov}(S_1,F_1).$$

Differentiating the total variance with respect to X_f and setting the results equal to zero yields the following:[2]

$$2X_f \text{var}(F_1) = -2X \text{cov}(S_1,F_1)$$

If this equation is then solved for the amount of foreign currency to be sold forward (X_f) to minimize the portfolio's terminal variance:

$$X_f = \frac{-2X \text{cov}(S_1,F_1)}{2 \ \text{var}(F_1)} = \frac{-X \text{cov}(S_1,F_1)}{\text{var}(F_1)}.$$

Finally, if this equation is rearranged to determine the relative size of the optimal hedge amount to the amount of the original exposure, the *optimal hedge ratio* or *Beta*, is found.

$$\frac{X_f}{X} = \beta = \frac{-\text{cov}(S_1,F_1)}{\text{var}(F_1)}.$$

Optimal Hedge Calculation Example

What are the implications in practice for this theoretical model of the optimal hedge? Assume a U.S.-based firm expects the receipt of DM1,000,000 in 90 days. With this model, the only values necessary for the determination of the optimal hedge percentage, beta, are the variance of the 90-day forward, .005573, and the covariance between the spot rate ($\$$/DM) and the forward rate ($\$$/DM) of .0054998.[3] The optimal hedge ratio is

$$\beta = \frac{X_f}{X} = \frac{-0.0054998}{0.005573} = -.986865 \approx 98.69\%.$$

This optimal hedge ratio indicates that if the firm wishes to minimize the expected value of the two-asset portfolio (spot position and forward position) at the end of the 90 days it should sell 98.68% of the DM exposure forward, or .986865 × DM1,000,000 = DM986,865.

A beta of 1.0 would imply the entire amount of the exposure (100%) should be sold forward, yet the theoretical model implies a value slightly less than 1. Why is that? The reason is the spot rate and the futures rate are not perfectly correlated. This less than

---

[2]Differentiation of the entire equation with respect to X_f results in the left-hand side equaling zero, and the first term on the right-hand side also equaling zero. The remaining terms would appear as:
$$0 = 0 + 2X_f \text{var}(F_1) + 2XX_f \text{cov}(S_1,F_1)$$

[3]Variance and covariance are for the monthly U.S. dollar/Deutschemark spot rate for the 1981 to 1987 period (see Kerkvliet and Moffett, 1991).

perfect correlation is called *basis risk*. Given that the spot and forward rates for most major currencies typically indicate similar high hedge ratios (.97 and up), hedgers generally do not bother to evaluate and hedge less than the beta of 1.0 when selling currency forward to eliminate exchange rate risk.

Cross-Hedging

Sometimes there are no available futures or forward markets for currencies. In these cases, the risk manager may wish to use a substitute, or *proxy,* for the underlying currency that is available. The methodology used for determining the optimal hedge ratio in the previous section is also helpful in the analysis of *proxy-hedging* or *cross-hedging*.

The cross hedger would likely go through a simple two-step process to determine the optimal cross-hedge: first, find the currency futures that is most highly correlated with the actual currency of exposure; second, find the optimal hedge ratio using the covariance between the proxy futures and the actual currency as in the preceding model. This would then tell the risk manager the amount of the proxy future that should be purchased to hedge the currency exposure.

The Deutschemark (DM) has long been used as a proxy for the hedging of all European Monetary System (EMS) currencies. A U.S.-resident firm with long currency positions in many EMS currencies could effectively hedge all positions at once using the DM as a proxy futures. The validity of the proxy hedge, however, depends on the covariance and variance of the recent past applying to the future (as in the case of volatility in options). And in periods in which the fundamental relations between EMS currencies change, as in September 1992 or July 1993, the proxy hedge may prove suboptimal.

Many of the newly industrializing countries of Latin American and the Asia-Pacific are just now beginning to allow the formation of derivative markets (forwards, futures, and options) in their currencies. Exhibit 23.1 describes the currency regime and status of currency derivatives in many of these so-called *exotic currencies*. It is clear, however, that for many multinational firms exposed to these currencies, cross-hedging will continue to be utilized to manage the currency risks arising as these derivative markets slowly develop.

Delta-Hedging

A slightly more sophisticated currency hedging strategy than the traditional one demonstrated in Chapter 7 is called *delta-hedging*. The objective of *delta-hedging* is to construct a position—the combined exposure and hedging instrument—whose *market values* (not terminal values) will change in opposite directions with changes in the spot exchange rate; it is the value of the position at all times that is being managed, not the value of the position only at termination.

Returning to the basic position valuation principle introduced at the beginning of this chapter, if the hedge is constructed so the changes in the spot position and hedge position are equal and opposite in currency value at all times in the life span of the

Exhibit 23.1   Exotic Currencies and Derivative Markets

Currency	Rate Regime	Spot Market	Derivatives Market
Mexican peso	Managed devaluation versus the U.S. dollar	US$10 million; spread of 10 b.p.	Coberturas (1 year maximum)
Argentinean peso	Pegged to the U.S. dollar	US$5 million; spread 5 b.p.	Forwards (to 3 months)
Chilean peso	Pegged to a U.S. dollar-denominated basket	Less than US$5 million; spread 10 b.p.	Forwards (to 18 months)
Brazilian cruzeiro real	Floating	Less than US$5 million; spread 10 b.p.	Options (to 1 month)
Singapore dollar	Loosely pegged to the U.S. dollar	US$5 million; spread 5 b.p.	Forwards (maximum S$5 million per contract)
Malaysian ringgit	Linked to currency basket	US$5 million; spread 5 b.p.	Forwards (to 6 months; maximum M$4 million per day)
Thai baht	Linked to trade-weighted basket	US$10 million; spread 0.01 baht	Forwards (to 1 year)
Hong Kong dollar	Pegged to U.S. dollar	US$10 million; US$70 billion daily turnover; spread 5 b.p.	Forwards (to 6 months; US$20 million common); limited swaps and options
Indonesian rupiah	Linked to trade-weighted basket	US$ 5 million; US$1 billion daily turnover; spread 1 rupiah	Forwards (to 1 year); swaps and options starting
New Taiwan dollar	Not freely convertible; government licensing	US$100 million daily turnover	Government approval needed for forwards; 6 months maximum
South Korean won	Not freely convertible; rate vs US$ fixed daily; 1% fluctuation allowed	US$2 billion daily turnover	Forwards for nonbanks allowed only for trade transactions
Chinese renminbi	Not freely convertible	Swap centres US$200 million daily turnover	None
Indian rupee	Floating since March 1, 1993	Outside India of US$300,000; spread 100b.p.	Government approval needed for swaps; options planned
Greek drachma	Managed depreciation versus DM and ECU	US$10 million; spread 0.5 drachma	Options starting; derivatives of less than 3 months must be trade related
Turkish lira	Managed depreciation versus DM and US$	US$30 million daily turnover	Forwards (to 3 months)

Source: Adapted from "Special FX," by Graham Cooper, *Risk*, October 1993, p. 47. Reprinted with permission.

exposure, it is termed *delta neutral*.

$$\Delta \text{ Position Value} = \Delta \text{ Spot} - \Delta \text{ Futures} \approx 0.$$

What is lost (gained) on the spot position as a result of exchange rate changes is exactly offset by the gain (loss) in the market value of the hedge instrument.

A numerical example helps to differentiate this strategy from the generic hedging we have described up to now. Assume a U.S.-based firm has an account payable in 90 days in the amount of £1,000,000. The current exchange rate and interest rate values are the same as those used in Chapter 6 in the explanation of currency option valuation and its corresponding "Greeks."

Spot rate	= $1.7000/£
90-day forward	= $1.7000/£
Strike rate	= $1.7000/£
U.S. dollar interest rate	= 8.00 % (per annum)
British pound interest rate	= 8.00 % (per annum)
Time (days)	= 90
Standard deviation (volatility)	= 10.00 %

This call option on British pounds, with strike price of $1.70/£ (forward at-the-money), has a premium of 3.3 cents/£. The delta of this option is 0.5. This means the value of the option, the option premium, will change by $(0.5) \times$ (change in spot rate). For example, if the spot rate moves from $1.70/£ to $1.71/£, the option premium changes by:

$$\Delta \text{ Option Premium} = 0.5 \times (\$1.71/£ - \$1.70/£) = \$0.005/£.$$

It is this delta that is the focal point of a delta-hedging strategy.

Exhibit 23.2 illustrates how a delta-neutral hedge would be constructed for this exposure. The firm that is *short* foreign currency fears a foreign currency appreciation versus the domestic currency. If the spot rate were to rise to $1.71/£, while all other values remained the same, the expected cost in U.S. dollars of making the payment would rise from $1,700,000 to $1,710,000, an increase of $10,000.

Exhibit 23.2   Construction and Valuation of a Delta-Neutral Hedging Strategy

(1) Spot Rate	(2) Value of Exposure	(3) US$ Value of Exposure[a]	(4) Call Option Premium[b]	(5) Option Contract[c]	(6) Market Value of Option[d]
$1.70/£	£1,000,000	$1,700,000	$0.033/£	£2,000,000	$66,000
$1.71/£	£1,000,000	$1,710,000	$0.038/£	£2,000,000	$76,000
Change in value:		$10,000	$0.005/£		+$10,000

[a]column (3) = column (1) × column (2)

[b]Call option strike price of $1.70/£, 90-day maturity, volatility of 10% per annum, delta = 0.5.

[c]Option contract size for delta-neutral hedge = exposure/delta = £1,000,000/0.5 = £2,000,000. The delta of the same call option (strike price $1.70/£) rises to .546 after spot rate moves to $1.71/£.

[d]column (6) = column (4) × column (5)

At the same time, the value of the call option on British pounds—the market price of the option—would rise from 3.3 cents/£ to 3.8 cents/£; a half cent per pound purchased. Since the cost of the foreign currency payable has increased one cent per pound, and the option's value changes by only one-half cent per pound, if the value of the option position is to offset the change in the exposure, the option contract would need to be for twice the amount of the exposure, or £2,000,000. An option for £2,000,000 would increase in value from the purchase price of $66,000 to $76,000 in market value after the spot rate changes. The impact of the exchange rate change has been "neutralized" by the combined position.

Delta-hedging strategies utilize the *total value* of the option (the market value that includes both intrinsic value and time value) as the hedge instrument's value, not simply the *intrinsic value* that we have utilized throughout previous chapters. Although this is more theoretically correct, delta-hedging has two major drawbacks:

1. Delta-neutral positions such as the example shown here require the purchase of option or other financial derivative contracts that are often substantially larger in currency amount than the exposure itself. In this case the option contract is for £2,000,000 in order to hedge an exposure of £1,000,000. Many firms believe this is inherently speculative and overly expensive in capital outlays.

2. Delta-neutral positions must be constantly monitored and frequently rebalanced. For example, after the spot rate in the previous example has moved to $1.71/£, the delta of the option has now risen to approximately 0.55 from 0.50. In order to maintain a delta-neutral position, the firm needs currency coverage of only £1,818,182 (£1,000,000 ÷ .55). It would sell part of the existing option position down to the new delta-neutral position. This requires active management and more frequent transactions, which many firms do not wish to undertake.

Financial Engineering and Risk Management

Financial engineering has come to mean very different things to different people. Probably one of the best definitions is that provided by John Finnerty, himself one of the innovators in this field:

> Financial engineering involves the design, the development, and the implementation of innovative financial instruments and processes, and the formulation of creative solutions to problems in finance.[4]

We use it here to describe the use of the basic financial building blocks (spot positions, forwards, options) to construct positions that provide the user with desired risk and return characteristics. The number of combinations and deviations is indeed infinite.[5]

---

[4]John D. Finnerty, "Financial Engineering in Corporate Finance: An Overview," *Financial Management,* Winter 1988, p. 14.

[5]For a more detailed description of the developing area of financial engineering see Clifford W. Smith, Jr., and Charles W. Smithson, "Financial Engineering: An Overview," in *The Handbook of Financial Engineering,* Clifford W. Smith, Jr., and Charles W. Smithson, eds., New York: Harper & Row, 1990, pp. 3–29.

The following techniques are, however, simply tools. They are a means to an end, foreign currency risk management, and not an end themselves. This section demonstrates the mechanics of their construction and highlights for which types of currency exposures they may be appropriate. Many of these products have been developed for a specific risk management problem, a problem that may or may not be applicable to all firms. With a few notable exceptions, the following products can be acquired either as risk management products from financial institutions or constructed by the firm itself.

Chapter Problem: U.S.-Resident Firm with £1,000,000 90-Day Account Receivable

Exhibit 23.3 illustrates the problem used throughout the remainder of this chapter. A U.S.-based firm possesses a long £1,000,000 exposure—an account receivable—to be settled in 90 days. The firm believes the exchange rate will move in its favor over the 90-day period (the British pound will appreciate versus the U.S. dollar). This is a movement to the right along the horizontal axis of Exhibit 23.3. Although having this *directional view* or *currency expectation,* the firm wishes downside protection in the event the pound were to depreciate instead. Exhibit 23.3 also lists the assumptions and option values used throughout the remainder of the chapter.[6]

The exposure management zones that are of most interest to the firm are the two opposing *triangles* formed by the uncovered and forward rate profiles. The firm would like to retain all potential area in the upper right triangle, but minimize its own potential exposure to the bottom left triangle. The put option's "kinked profile" is consistent with what the firm wishes if it believes the pound will appreciate (dollar will depreciate).

The firm could consider any number of different put option strike prices, depending on what minimum assured value—degree of self-insurance—the firm is willing to accept. Exhibit 23.3 illustrates two different put option alternatives, a forward at-the-money (ATM) put of strike price $1.4700/£, and a forward out-of-the-money (OTM) put with strike price $1.4400/£.[7] The forward OTM put provides protection at lower cost, but also at a lower level of protection.

The Synthetic Forward

At a forward rate of $1.4700/£, the proceeds of the forward contract in 90 days will yield $1,470,000. A second alternative for the firm would be to construct a *synthetic forward* using options. The synthetic forward requires the firm to combine three different elements:

1. long position in £ (A/R of £1,000,000);

2. buy a put option on £ at a strike price of $1.4700/£, paying a premium of $0.0318/£;

3. sell a call option on £ at a strike price of $1.4700/£, earning a premium of $0.0318/£.

---

[6]Values are roughly those in existence on December 31, 1993. Note that the Euro-pound interest rate has been set so the forward rate is exactly $1.4700/£ (interest rate parity holds).

[7]Because foreign currency options are actually priced about the forward rate (see Chapter 6), not the spot rate, the correct specification of whether an option, put or call, is ITM, ATM, or OTM, is in reference to the same maturity forward rate.

Exhibit 23.3 Chapter Problem Assumptions and Option Values

Spot rate:	$1.4790/£	90-Day forward rate:	$1.4700/£
A/R due:	90 days	90-Day Euro-dollar interest rate:	3.250%
$/£ volatility:	11.0%	90-Day Euro-pound interest rate:	5.720%

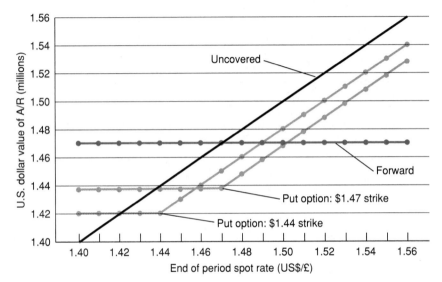

Value of £1,000,000 90-day A/R by hedging alternative

Strike Price	Put Premium		Call Premium		
($/£)	($/£)	(%)	($/£)	(%)	
$1.4000	$0.0079	0.6	$0.0774	5.5	
1.4200	0.0125	0.9	0.0621	4.4	
1.4400	0.0188	1.3	0.0486	3.4	
1.4500	0.0226	1.6	0.0425	2.9	
1.4600	0.0269	1.8	0.0369	2.5	
1.4700	0.0318	2.2	0.0318	2.2	"Forward-ATM"
1.4800	0.0371	2.5	0.0272	1.8	
1.4900	0.0429	2.9	0.0231	1.6	
1.5000	0.0491	3.3	0.0194	1.3	
1.5200	0.0630	4.1	0.0134	0.9	
1.5400	0.0784	5.1	0.0089	0.6	

All premiums are for European-style options, and calculated using the currency option pricing spreadsheet "OPTION.WK1" introduced in Chapter 6. All premiums are rounded to the nearest hundredth of a cent. Premiums are shown stated both in absolute terms of $/£ and as a percentage of the strike price (industry practice).

Exhibit 23.4 Construction of a Synthetic Forward for a Long FX Position

Instruments	Strike Rates	Premium	Amount (£)
Buy a put	$1.4700/£ (OTM)	$0.0318/£	£1,000,000
Sell a call	$1.4700/£ (OTM)	$0.0318/£	£1,000,000

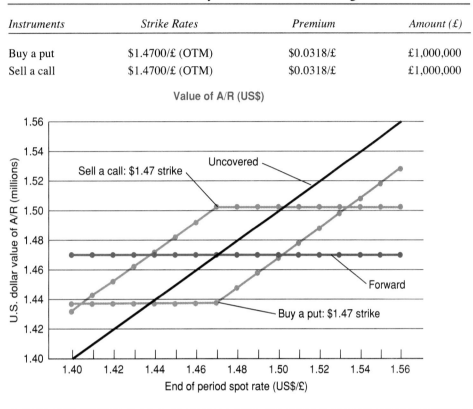

The purchase of the put option requires a premium payment whereas the sale of the call option earns the firm the premium payment. If both options are struck at the forward rate (forward ATM), the premiums should be identical and the net premium payment a value of zero.

Exhibit 23.4 illustrates the uncovered position, the basic forward rate hedge, and the individual profiles of the put and call options for the chapter problem. The outcome of the combined position is easily confirmed by simply tracing what would happen at all exchange rates to the left of $1.4700/£, and what would happen to the right of $1.4700/£.

At all exchange rates to the left of $1.4700/£:

1. the firm would receive £1,000,000 in 90 days;

2. the call option on £ sold by the firm would expire out-of-the-money;

3. the firm would exercise the put option on £ to sell the £ received at $1.4700/£.

At all exchange rates below $1.4700/£ the U.S.-based firm would earn $1,470,000 from the receivable. At all exchange rates to the right of $1.4700/£:

1. the firm would receive £1,000,000 in 90 days;

2. the put option on £ purchased by the firm would expire out-of-the-money;

3. the firm would turn over the £1,000,000 received to the buyer of the call who now exercises the call option against the firm. The firm receives $1.4700/£ from the call option buyer.

Thus at all exchange rates above or below $1.4700/£, the U.S.-based firm nets $1,470,000 in domestic currency. The combined spot-option position has behaved identically to that of a forward contract. A firm with the exact opposite position, a £1,000,000 payable 90 days in the future, could similarly construct a synthetic forward using options.[8]

But why would a firm undertake this relatively complex position in order to simply create a forward contract? The answer is found by looking at the option premiums earned and paid. We have assumed the option strike prices used were precisely forward ATM rates, and the resulting option premiums paid and earned were exactly equal. But this need not be the case. If the option strike prices (remember they must be identical for both options, bought and sold) are not precisely on the forward ATM, the two premiums may differ by a slight amount. The net premium position may then end up as a net premium earning or a net premium payment. If positive, this amount would be added to the proceeds from the receivable to result in a higher total dollar value received.[9]

Second-Generation Currency Risk Management Products

Second-generation risk management products are constructed from the two basic derivatives used throughout this book: the forward and the option. We subdivide them into two groups: (1) the *zero-premium option products* that focus on pricing in and around the forward rate; and (2) the *exotic option products* (for want of a better name) that focus on alternative pricing targets. Although all of the following derivatives are sold as financial products by risk management firms, we present each as simply the construction of the position from common building blocks, or LEGO®s as they have been termed, used in

---

[8]A U.S.-resident firm possessing a future foreign currency-denominated payment of £1,000,000 could construct a synthetic forward in the following way:
    1. the firm would pay £1,000,000 in 90 days;
    2. buy a call option on pounds at a strike price of $1.4700/£;
    3. sell a put option on pounds at a strike price of $1.4700/£.

[9]An additional possibility is that the firm finds, for the moment at which the position is taken, that the call option premium earned may actually slightly exceed the put option premium paid. This means the options market is temporarily out of equilibrium (parity). This is quite possible given the judgment required in the pricing of options (different banks pricing options do not necessarily use the identical volatilities at all times) and the inherent decentralized structure of the currency and currency option markets.

Global View

Hedging With the Mexican Cobertura

Mexico's novel hedging tool—the cobertura—was introduced in 1987 to help local companies protect themselves against fluctuations in the peso/dollar exchange rate. It was not until September of 1993, however, after various changes to the instrument, that this OTC market was opened to foreigners. The market has since flourished against the background of the NAFTA (North American Free Trade Agreement) talks, which many see as a make-or-break issue for the Mexican economy.

A cobertura has characteristics of an option and a forward, says Stephen Leach, a vice-president for corporate foreign exchange at Citibank, New York. A buyer pays a premium in pesos for each dollar covered by the contract, giving him the right to receive the peso amount of any depreciation of the peso/dollar exchange rate that occurs during the contract. But it also imposes the obligation to pay the seller the peso amount of any appreciation in the rate over the same period. For a seller of coberturas, the rights and obligations in the event of peso depreciation and appreciation are, of course, reversed.

The premium paid thus represents the income an investor is willing to forego to lock in the current spot exchange rate for the duration of the contract. Most cobertura contracts are for one, two, three or six months, but any maturity between three days and one year is possible in principle. "Liquidity dries up a bit after 180 days," says Carlos Kretschmer, a trader at Mexican broker Serfin Securities in New York. The contracts are denominated in dollars but redeemed in pesos at the free official spot exchange rate. This rate is the average of 48-hour forward rates from a number of Mexican banks, weighted by size of transactions.

The reference rate for the cobertura is therefore the free official spot rate that prevails two days before the contract begins. As the exchange rate at maturity is determined in the same way, the dollar hedge actually expires two business days before the contract is settled. To protect the position against possible peso weakness during these two days, the investor would have to buy dollars in the spot market (48 hours forward) at the free-market rate, two business days before the expiry of the cobertura. However, this will not be a perfect hedge as this market rate may differ from the official rate set at the close of the cobertura contract, which is an average of several spot market rates.

This difference between the two rates also leaves the investor with conversion risk when the cobertura is bought and redeemed. For example, if the free official spot rate at the start of the contract is weaker than the free-market rate used to convert dollars into pesos with which to buy the cobertura, then the investor will lose the peso difference between the two rates for each dollar of coverage.

Coberturas are generally held to maturity and no secondary market exists. Foreigners can only access the market via Mexican banks or brokerages and these participants are regulated by the Bank of Mexico to minimize counterparty risk.

Source: "Break for the Banker," by Graham Cooper. *Risk,* Volume 65, No. 10, October 1993, p. 48.
Reprinted with permission.

traditional currency risk management, forwards, and options.[10] As a group, they are collectively referred to as *complex options*.

Zero-Premium Option Products

The primary "problem" with the use of options for risk management in the eyes of the firms is the up-front premium payment. Although the premium payment is only a portion of the total payoff profile of the hedge, many firms view the expenditure of substantial funds for the *purchase* of a financial derivative as prohibitively expensive. In comparison, the forward contract that eliminates currency risk requires no out-of-pocket expenditure by the firm (and requires no real specification of expectations regarding exchange rate movements).

Zero-premium option products (or financially engineered derivative combinations) are designed to require no out-of-pocket premium payment at the initiation of the hedge. This set of products includes what are most frequently labeled the *range forward* and the *participating forward*.[11] Both of these products (1) are priced on the basis of the forward rate; (2) are constructed to provide a zero-premium payment up front; and (3) allow the hedger to take advantage of expectations of the direction of exchange rate movements.

For the case problem at hand in which the U.S.-resident firm possesses a long position in British pounds, this means all of the following products are applicable to an expectation that the U.S. dollar will depreciate versus the pound. If the hedgers have no such *view*, they should turn back now (and buy a forward, or nothing at all)!

Ratio Spreads

Before describing the most widely accepted second-generation option products, it is helpful to demonstrate one of the older methods of obtaining a zero-premium option combination: an alternative that leaves the hedger with a large uncovered exposure.

The U.S.-based firm in our chapter problem decides it wishes to establish a floor level of protection by purchasing a \$1.4700/£ put option (forward ATM) at a cost of \$0.0318/£ (total cost of \$31,800). This is a substantial outlay of capital up front for the option premium, and the firm's risk management division has no budget funding this magnitude of expenditures. The firm, feeling strongly the dollar will depreciate against the pound, decides to "finance" the purchase of the put with the sale of an OTM call option. The firm reviews market conditions and considers a number of call

---

[10]One of the original works in this field is entitled "A LEGO® Approach to Financial Engineering: An Introduction to Forwards, Futures, Swaps, and Options," Charles W. Smithson, *Midland Corporate Finance Journal,* vol. 4, no. 4, 1987, pp. 16–28.

[11]This zero-premium section draws on Sam Srinivasulu, "Second-Generation Forwards: A Comparative Analysis," *Business International Money Report,* September 21, 1987, pp. 297–299, 303. There are, in fact, a number of other products such as the *break forward* and the *deferred premium option,* which are used to a much lesser extent.

option strike prices that are significantly OTM; strike prices of $1.5200/£, $1.5400/£, or further out.

It is decided the $1.5400/£ call option, with a premium of $0.0089/£, is to be written and sold to earn the premium and finance the put purchase. However, because the premium on the OTM call is so much smaller than the forward ATM put premium, the size of the call option written must be larger. The firm determines the amount of the call by solving the simple problem of premium equivalency:

$$\text{Cost of put premium} = \text{Earnings call premium},$$

Substituting in the put and call option premiums yields

$$\$0.0318/£ \times £1,000,000 = \$0.0089/£ \times £ \text{ call},$$

and then solving for the size of the call option to be written:

$$\frac{\$31,800}{\$0.0089/£} = £3,573,034.$$

The reason this strategy is called a *ratio spread* is that the final position, call option size to put option size, is a ratio greater than 1 (£3,573,034 ÷ £1,000,000 or a ratio of about 3.57).[12]

As a number of firms using this strategy have learned the hard way, however, if the expectations of the hedger prove incorrect, and the spot rate moves past the strike price of the call option written, the firm is faced with delivering a foreign currency it does not have. In this example, if the spot rate moved above $1.5400/£, the firm would have to cover a net position of £2,573,034.

The Range Forward

The basic *range forward* has been marketed under a variety of other names, including the *collar, flexible forward, cylinder option, option fence* or simply *fence, mini-max,* or *zero-cost tunnel*. The range forward is constructed by:

1. buying a put option with a strike rate *below* the forward rate, for the full amount of the long currency exposure (100% coverage);

2. selling a call option with a strike rate *above* the forward rate, for the full amount of the long currency exposure (100% coverage).

The hedger chooses one side of the "range" or spread, normally the down side (put strike rate), which then dictates the strike rate at which the call option will be sold. The call option must be chosen at an equal distance from the forward rate as the put option strike price from the forward rate. If the hedger believes there is a significant possibility

---

[12]An alternative form of the ratio spread is the *calendar spread*. The calendar spread would combine the 90-day put option with the sale of an OTM call option with a maturity that is longer, for example 120 or 180 days. The longer maturity of the call option written earns the firm larger premium earnings requiring a smaller "ratio."

Exhibit 23.5   The Range Forward

Instruments	Strike Rates	Premium	Amount (£)
Buy a put	$1.4500/£ (OTM)	$0.0226/£	£1,000,000
Sell a call	$1.4900/£ (OTM)	$0.0231/£	£1,000,000

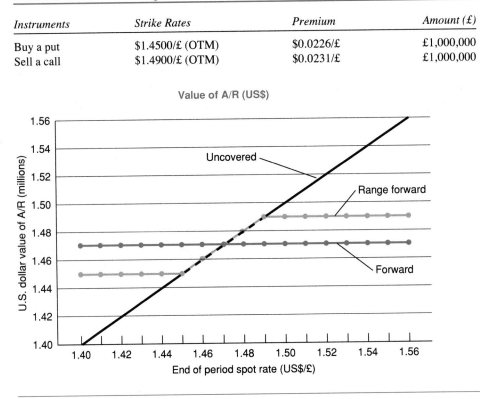

the currency will move in the firm's favor, and by a sizable degree, the put floor rate may be set relatively low in order for the ceiling to be higher or further out from the forward rate and still enjoy a zero net premium.[13]

Exhibit 23.5 illustrates the final outcome of a range forward constructed by buying a put with strike price $1.4500/£, paying a premium of $0.0226/£, with selling a call option with strike price $1.4900/£, earning a premium of $0.0231/£. The hedger has bounded the range over which the firm's A/R value moves as an uncovered position, with a put option floor and a sold call option ceiling.

There are a number of variations on the basic range forward. If both strike prices are the same, it is a *synthetic forward* as described in the previous section. If both strike prices chosen are equal to the actual forward rate, the synthetic equals the actual forward contract. This synthetic forward should theoretically have a near zero-net pre-

---

[13]How far down the downside protection is set is a difficult issue for the firm to determine. Often the firm's treasurer will determine at what bottom exchange rate the firm would be able to recover the minimum necessary margin on the business underlying the cash flow exposure, the *budget rate* (see Chapter 7).

mium.[14] If the strike rates of the options are selected independently of the desire for an exact zero-net premium up front (it must still bracket the forward rate), it is termed an *option collar* or *cylinder option.*

The Participating Forward

The *participating forward,* also called a *zero-cost ratio option* and *forward participation agreement,* is an option combination that allows the hedger to take a position which will share in potential upside movements in the exchange rate, while providing option-based downside protection, all at a net-zero premium. The participating forward is constructed by:

1. buying a put option with a strike price below the forward rate, for the full amount of the long currency exposure (100% coverage);

2. selling a call option with a strike price *which is the same as the put option,* for a *portion* of the total currency exposure (<100% coverage).

Similar to the range forward, the buyer of a participating forward will normally choose the put option strike rate first. Because the call option strike rate is the same as the put, all that remains is to determine the participation rate, the proportion of the exposure sold as a call option.

Exhibit 23.6 illustrates the construction of a participating forward for the chapter problem. The firm first chooses the put option protection level, in this case $1.4500/£, with a premium of $0.0226/£. A call option sold with the same strike rate of $1.4500/£ would earn the firm $0.0425/£. The call premium is substantially higher than the put premium because the call option is already in-the-money (ITM).

The percentage cover for the call option is then determined so that call premium earnings exactly offset put premiums paid:

$$\text{Put premium} = \text{Percent cover} \times \text{Call premium.}$$

Using the chapter problem premiums, the percent cover is found:

$$\text{Percent cover} = \frac{\$0.0226\pounds}{\$0.0425\pounds} = .5318 \approx 53.2\%.$$

The firm must sell a call option of .532 × £1,000,000, or £532,000, in order to achieve a net-zero premium.

The *participation rate* is the residual percentage of the exposure that is not covered by the sale of the call option. For example, if the percent cover is 53.2%, the participation rate would be 1 − the percent cover, or 46.8%. This means that for all favorable exchange rate movements, those above $1.4500/£, the hedger would "participate" or

---

[14]Although the put and call option premiums are in this case not identical, they are close enough to result in a near-zero net premium:

$$\text{Net premium} = (\$0.0226/\pounds - \$0.0231/\pounds) \times \pounds1,000,000 = -\$500.$$

The benefits of the combined position are readily observable given that the put option premium alone amounts to $22,600.

Exhibit 23.6   The Participating Forward

Instruments	Strike Rates	Premium	Amount (£)
Buy a put	$1.4500/£ (OTM)	$0.0262/£	£1,000,000
Sell a call	$1.4500/£ (ITM)	$0.0425/£	£532,000

Value of A/R (US$)

enjoy 46.8% of the differential. However, like all option-based hedges, downside exposure is bounded by the put option strike rate.

The expectations of the buyer are similar to the range forward, only the degree of foreign currency bullishness is greater. For the participating forward to be superior in outcome to the range forward it is necessary for the exchange rate to move further in the favorable direction than for the range forward.

Exotic Options

This second set of instruments offers alternative pricing, timing, or exercise provisions of the product. All of these in some way have altered the valuation principles of the basic option-pricing model, hence the term *exotic*.[15] These products are therefore products

---

[15]The term *exotic* is not to be confused with its occasional usage as the collective term for currencies of the Asian-Pacific countries.

only, and not easily reproducible (though generally possible) by the corporate risk manager independently. Their pricing is generally complex and they are generally produced and sold by risk management departments of major multinational banks.

Most exotic options are European-style options whose values change with the direction and the *path* the spot rate follows over their life span (they are in fact often referred to as path-dependent in value). We briefly discuss a few of these exotics: the *knock-out option,* the *average rate option, compound option,* and the *chooser option.* This is only a sampling of some of these increasingly complex—even bizarre—option-based instruments. We continue discussing each of these currency derivative products in the context of a U.S.-based firm with a long British pound exposure. But, as they warn spectators during daredevil exhibitions, "don't try this at home."

The Knock-Out Option

The knock-out option, also often referred to as the *down and out option (DAOO), barrier option, extinguishable option,* or *activate/deactivate option,* differs markedly from previous products covered. The knock-out option is designed to behave like any option, offering downside protection, but to offer only a limited upside range before crossing a previously specified barrier or knock-out level, at which it automatically expires. Because the knock-out level is in the upside direction, the automatic expiration of the option would occur only after the exchange rate has moved in the expected direction of the hedger (a favorable movement). In return for giving up the full maturity period coverage, the premium of the option—being a shorter term option—is smaller.[16]

Exhibit 23.7 depicts the knock-out option for the chapter problem, and compares its basic profile with that of the standard put option (strike price $1.4700/£ at premium $0.0318/£). The knock-out strike price is also $1.4700/£ (forward ATM), with a barrier of $1.4900/£. The premium of the barrier option is significantly lower, only $0.0103/£.[17] As illustrated, the knock-out appears to be the obviously better choice with the same strike price at a lower premium. The problem, however, is that the diagram is not able to illustrate the possibility the spot rate could rise in the early days of the exposure to $1.4900/£ or higher, crossing the barrier and therefore canceling the option protection. The exposure would still have many days left until maturity, during which the spot rate could easily rise or fall in essentially unlimited magnitudes. The standard put option, although higher in premium, will not expire prior to the maturity of the exposure. In the end, the cheaper cost of the knock-out option may prove to be an added cost for a final protection level of zero.

---

[16]For a more detailed evaluation of the pro and con arguments on the use of knock-out options see Martyn Turner, "Break-even Analysis of Knock-Out Options," *Corporate Finance,* September 1993, pp. 43–45.

[17]The premium of the barrier option is quite sensitive to the specification of the barrier level. The further the barrier is from the forward rate, the less likely the barrier will be crossed and therefore the more likely the option will not automatically expire. In that case, the premium must rise to compensate the writer of the knock-out option for the probability of providing coverage for a longer period of time.

Exhibit 23.7   The Knock-Out Option

Instruments	Strike Rates	Premium	Amount (£)
Buy a put	$1.4700/£ (ATM) Barrier: $1.4900/£	$0.0103/£	£1,000,000

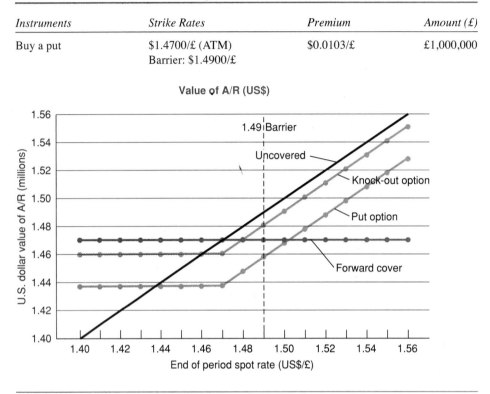

The Average Rate Option

These options are the most recent second-generation (possibly third-generation) currency derivatives. They are normally classified as "path-dependent" currency options because their values depend on averages of spot rates over some prespecified period of time. Here we describe two examples of path-dependent options, the average rate option and the average strike option:

1. *Average rate option (ARO),* also known as an *Asian option,* sets the option strike rate up front, and is exercised at maturity if the average spot rate over the period (as observed by scheduled sampling) is less than the preset option strike rate.

2. *Average strike option (ASO)* establishes the option strike rate as the average of the spot rate experienced over the option's life, and is exercised if the strike rate is greater than the end-of-period spot rate.

   Like the knock-out option, the average rate option is difficult to depict because its value depends not on the ending spot rate, but rather the path the spot rate takes over its specified life span. For example, an average rate option with strike price $1.4700/£

would have a premium of only \$0.0186/£. The "average rate" would be calculated by weekly observations (12 full weeks, the first observation occurring 13 days from purchase) of the spot rate. The number of different averages or paths of spot rate movement are obviously innumerable. A few different scenarios aid in understanding how the ARO differs in valuation:

1. The spot rate moves very little over the first 70 to 80 days of the period, with a sudden movement in the spot rate below \$1.4700/£ in the days prior to expiration. Although the final spot rate is below \$1.4700/£, the average for the period is above \$1.4700, so the option cannot be exercised. The receivable is exchanged at the spot rate (below \$1.4700/£) and the cost of the option premium is still incurred.

2. The dollar slowly and steadily depreciates versus the pound, the rate rising from \$1.4790/£ to \$1.48, \$1.49, and on up. At the end of the 90-day period the option expires out-of-the-money, the receivable is exchanged at the favorable spot rate, and the firm has enjoyed average rate option protection at substantially lower premium expense.

A variety of different types of average rate currency option products are sold by banking institutions, each having a distinct payoff structure. Because of the intricacy of the path-dependent option's value, care must be taken in the use of these instruments. As in all markets, buyer beware.[18]

The Compound Option

The *compound option* is an option to either buy or sell an option on a specific future date. Also referred to as *options on options*, a call compound option gives the buyer the right to buy a specific option on a future date, whereas a put compound option gives the buyer the right to sell a specific option on a future date. The underlying option—the option the first option is written on—is fully defined in terms of premium, strike price, amount, and maturity. Because the first option is an option on an option, the up-front premium is substantially smaller.

It is ironic that these "third-generation" currency risk management products are focused on contingent currency exposures, the same exposure that only a few years ago the simple put and call options were thought appropriate for.[19] For example, a firm making a bid on a contract that will result in a substantial exposure in terms of foreign

---

[18]A variation on the average rate and average strike option is the *lookback option, with strike* and *without strike*. A *lookback option with strike* is a European-style option with a preset strike rate, which on maturity is valued versus the highest or lowest spot rate reached over the option life. A *lookback option without strike* is typically a European-style option that sets the strike rate at maturity as the lowest exchange rate achieved over the period if a call option, or the highest exchange rate experienced over the period for a put option, and is exercised on the basis of this strike rate versus the ending spot rate.

[19]For a more detailed illustration of the use of compound options, including a description of an additional variety known as the *installment option,* see Stephanie Mon, "Hedging Bids Made in Foreign Currencies," *Treasury,* Fall 1991, pp. 46–47.

currency cash flows, positive or negative, may be able to cover the bid exposure with a smaller initial premium payment than a standard option would require. But it must be remembered that the first premium is to maintain the right to pay (receive) the second premium if the right is exercised. The hedger must be careful and clear as to what cash flows and premiums will be required at what points in time if the compound option is purchased.

The compound option has two different points in time of maturity. The first, the *near-date* or *first-date*, is the date on which the buyer of the compound option must decide whether the right is to be exercised to buy or sell the underlying option. The second point in time is the *last-date* or *second-date*, on which the actual underlying option expires. Because of this sequencing of time periods, the compound option may in the future be one method firms use for distant currency exposures that are highly contingent without committing substantial quantities of corporate capital to the payment of option premia.

The Chooser Option

A final alternative is—at least for the moment—the extreme of option flexibility. The *chooser option* allows the buyer to lock in a specific option strike price, amount, and maturity now, and choose at a later date ("chooser date") whether the option is to be a call option or put option. The primary use of such a hedge instrument is in cases in which the exposure's final net long or net short position is unknown until further into the life of the exposure.

Summary

- The determination of the optimal hedge ratio for an individual exposure can be derived by constructing a two-asset portfolio and minimizing its expected terminal value.

- Alternative hedging methodologies such as delta-hedging and proxy-hedging are often useful and necessary when dealing with exotic currencies or exposures.

- The rapidly developing field of financial engineering allows the corporate treasurer to construct financial positions with financial derivatives that possess desired risk/return profiles to match and manage complex exposures and detailed market expectations.

- Second-generation option products like range forwards and participating forwards allow hedgers to acquire option protection with a zero net up-front premium payment.

- Exotic option products, sometimes called third-generation products, are options constructed to provide values and protection that are functions of the path the spot rate takes over the life span of the option, and not simply on the value at expiration (ending spot rate). The primary benefit is the reduction of the option premium paid by the buyer.

Decision Case
ZAPA Chemical and BuBa[20]

Stephanie Mayo, currency analyst for ZAPA Chemical of Cleveland, stared at her Reuters screen, her option pricing screen, and then out the window. It was Monday, September 21, 1992, and the markets seemed much calmer this morning. The French had voted "oui" by 50.95% to "non" of 49.05% to approve the Maastricht treaty the previous day. Stephanie was now debating what to do about her put option on Deutschemarks she had been holding for the last month.

The Original Exposure and Rate View

Stephanie had originally been given the exposure for management in mid-August. ZAPA Chemical had sold a specialty chemical distributorship in Stuttgart, Germany. The proceeds of the sale, approximately DM7.6 million, would be brought back to the United States sometime in November. Because of special tax and sales document filings in Germany, it could not yet be determined when exactly the funds would be available for repatriation.

The U.S. dollar had been falling like a rock since late March. The central bank of Germany, the Bundesbank or as it is affectionately known "BuBa," had added momentum to the drop when it had increased the German base lending rate by 75 basis points (3/4 of a percent) to 9.75% on July 16. By August 17, when Steph was given the exposure, the DM/$ rate looked as if it had settled down to a historically weak dollar rate of DM1.4649/$ (see Exhibit 23.8). At that time Steph had debated whether the dollar was as low as it was going to go, or just hesitating before sliding further. Steph felt there were a number of forces that could still drive the dollar lower.

- **The Bundesbank.** The Bundesbank had become very high profile in the last month as German interest rates continued to rise. The Bundesbank was slowing monetary growth to a crawl and driving interest rates up, all in an effort to stop the inflationary forces resulting from reunification. Of the many rumors emanating from the central bank, the ones about further interest rate hikes were the loudest.

- **Dollar-DM Interest Differentials.** The anemic growth of the U.S. economy continued. The U.S. Federal Reserve was attempting to provide needed stimulus through lower interest rates. The United States was now enjoying the lowest interest rates in 20 years. The high interest rates in Germany and the low interest rates in the U.S., an unusual scenario by any account, was resulting in a massive capital flow from dollar-denominated assets into Deutschemarks. Three-month Eurodollar deposits

---

[20]Michael H. Moffett, University of Michigan, December 1992. Reprinted with permission. This case is intended for class discussion only, and does not represent effective or ineffective financial management practices. This case concerns a Fortune 500 company. All names and values have been changed to preserve confidentiality.

Exhibit 23.8   The Falling Value of the U.S. Dollar Versus the Deutschemark
(Friday closing, January-August 1992)

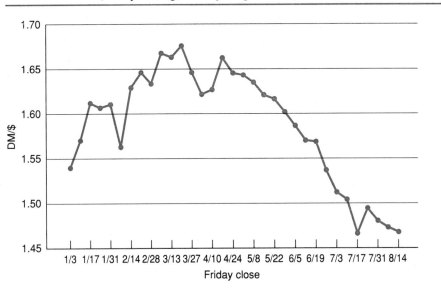

were paying 3.3125%; similar Euro-Deutschemark deposits were paying 9.750%. And there were no signs of either rate moving toward the other.

- **The French Vote on the Maastricht Treaty.** The European Community had now painted itself into a corner with the escalating debate on the willingness of individual countries to actually pursue true European economic integration. The Maastricht Treaty had been signed by the Council of Ministers in December 1991, but had to be ratified by each country. The Treaty had formalized the steps and timetable for the adoption of a single European banking system and currency by the end of the decade. But the Danes had voted no in June 1992, and yesterday (September 20th) the French had narrowly approved the Treaty.

- **Stress in the EMS.** Not only were the high German interest rates causing a strengthening of the DM versus the dollar, but for the same reasons, they were putting pressure on all EMS currencies as they tried to maintain their parities with the Deutschemark. The Italian lira and the British pound were both trading at the bottom of their allowable ranges (according to the agreed ranges within the ERM of the EMS) versus the Deutschemark.

To top it all off this was an election year in the United States. In mid-August President George Bush was 18 to 20 percentage points behind Democratic presidential candidate Bill Clinton in the polls. The markets had historically favored and rewarded Republican economic policies as opposed to the policies of the Democrats.

The Risk Tolerance of ZAPA

ZAPA was a rather unusual firm in its approach to currency risk management. Although the parent corporation, ZAPA Oil, did not use foreign currency options for risk management, ZAPA Chemical used them exclusively. Because of losses caused by forward contracts in the previous year, Treasury now used foreign exchange options whenever possible. If needed, synthetic forwards were created by simply buying calls and selling puts for the same strike prices and maturities (or vice versa).

ZAPA Chemical considered Treasury a cost center. Treasury therefore saw its primary responsibility as conservative management of exposures. Profit through currency speculation was not its purpose. In addition to an in-house aversion to forwards, the group could not write uncovered options (with their corresponding unlimited loss potential). The fiasco in 1991 at Allied-Lyons, the British food conglomerate, had sparked an internal review of all activities of International Treasury at ZAPA Chemical. Allied-Lyons had suffered losses of $150 million as a result of unwise and uncontrolled currency speculation. Although ZAPA did not in any way mirror Allied-Lyons, the review had resulted in the exclusion of writing uncovered call options, as well as the requirement that the use of new instruments was allowed only after approval of the operating committee. But, all things considered, management was appreciative when the expenses of running the cost center were lower.

Hedge Decision: August 17

On August 17 the Deutschemark had traded around the DM1.4649/$ point all day. After discussion with her risk manager, Steph had decided a safety net was called for. Her logic was relatively simple. First, she believed the dollar would fall further. Most currency forecasters felt the dollar was already at bottom, but then again, they had said the same thing at the magic DM1.50/$ level. She believed the DM would move in her favor. Secondly, although she held the directional view of dollar down, she also felt there were too many unknowns to feel secure. Currency volatility would by all guesses increase in the coming four to six weeks, with uncertainty over Bundesbank policies rising and the French vote on Maastricht forthcoming.

Before making her decision, Steph had reviewed an alternative that was not considered by ZAPA to be a true alternative: the forward. The coming volatility of the markets—and Stephanie felt sure things would be heating up—posed many uncertainties. Selling the entire DM exposure forward would at least allow her to sleep nights. But there were two distinct negative characteristics of the forward at this time. First, the huge interest differentials between dollar and Deutschemark assets resulted in forward rates that were extremely unattractive. The 120-day forward on August 17 was DM1.4957/$. Given the spot rate of DM1.4649/$, this was an annual discount of nearly 6.2%—expensive protection. By selling the Deutschemarks forward she would be locking in a rate she sincerely felt was in the wrong direction from that which the spot rate would move. The forward was quite unattractive.

Exhibit 23.9   Hedge Alternatives for ZAPA Chemical's DM Exposure
(millions of US$)

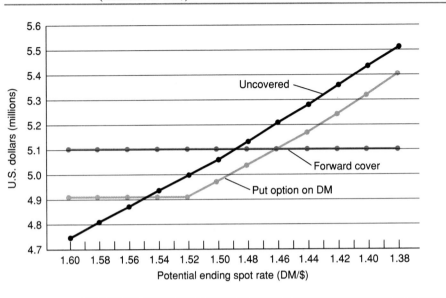

The safety net Steph had chosen was an out-of-the-money (OTM) put option (bank option) on Deutschemarks. Gotham Bank (NY) was willing to sell ZAPA a December put on the DM 7.6 million for a premium of 1.40 cents per DM ($0.0140/DM) for a strike of 66 ($0.66/DM or DM1.5152/$). This was a total outlay of $106,400 for the DM December put option. Although seemingly a lot of money, the option price was a paltry 2.1% premium ($0.0140 ÷ $0.6600/DM) for a substantial amount of protection against a dollar rebound.

Steph, as she did with all her major stand-alone exposures, took a look at her option position versus the totally unhedged and total forward cover alternatives. Exhibit 23.9 reproduces her exposure valuation analysis. The put option's value would parallel the uncovered position, but with the added benefit of a safety net if the spot rate were to actually move in the opposite direction.

Daily Position Monitoring

Given the size of the position and the tension in the markets, Steph had watched the markets and the DM put option position daily. The next two weeks yielded good news and bad news. The good news was that Steph's intuition had been right on target. The dollar had declined rapidly in the days following her put option purchase, so the prospective dollar value of the DM7.6 million was rising by the minute. The bad news, however, was the December put option was also falling, falling in value. As the put option moved further and further out-of-the-money, the market value of the option (the premium) had fallen.

By September 1 the U.S. dollar was at an all-time low of DM1.39/$, and the option's premium was approximately 50 cents per DM. The potential loss on the option was $68,400.

$$(\$.0050/DM - \$.0140/DM) \times DM7,600,000 = (\$68,400).$$

Although a bit unsettling when expressed in this manner, Steph recognized that this is what the corporate hedger wanted to happen when purchasing an OTM put option for protection. The U.S. dollar declined to approximately DM1.40/$ and stayed there for the first two work weeks of September. Stephanie watched and waited.

September Turbulence

The week of September 14 had been a literal nightmare. The dollar had fallen, risen, and fallen again. The British pound had been withdrawn from the ERM. The Italian lira had been first devalued by over 7%, then finally withdrawn from the ERM as it came under further pressure. The Spanish peseta had been devalued 5% in the ERM. Other currencies had come under speculative attacks on Friday. The high interest rates in Germany had continued to bleed capital out of the other major European capital markets. Exhibit 23.10 reviews the roller coaster of events in these turbulent times.

In Great Britain the events of the previous weeks continued to have substantial news value. With the pound still floating freely against the Deutschemark, the long-standing critics of Britain's participation in the EMS were once more making a lot of noise. The lead critic, former British prime minister Lady Margaret Thatcher (often known as the "iron maiden" for her tough political stands), commented in a speech on September 20 that ". . . there is a tendency in Europe to treat the exchange rate as a type of virility symbol. I myself, have never felt the need for such a symbol."

The cynics still seemed to have carried the day. Many EC analysts now saw the Maastricht Treaty and the idea of economic integration as something of a dead issue. The fundamental economic pressures that had led to the currency events of the previous weeks were still present: extremely high interest differentials between Germany and the United States; extreme devaluation pressures on most of the currencies of the EMS versus the Deutschemark.

Steph now wished to reevaluate her put option hedge position on the DM exposure. She now knew that the DM 7.6 million would be repatriated to the American parent on December 15. This would match the maturity of the DM put option's expiration. But the massive volatility in the markets the previous week had sent option values straight up. Steph was wondering whether it would be better to sell her put option and either cover the position with a forward or wait a few days until the markets calmed to replace the put position.

Exhibit 23.10   EMS in Crisis: The Events of September 1992

Sept. 1	The U.S. dollar falls below DM1.39/$.
Sept. 4	The Italian lira trades below the ERM floor. Italian central bank raises discount rate from 13.25% to 15% to protect the lira.
Sept. 6	EC finance ministers and central bank governors reaffirm their unwillingness to realign the EMS and promise massive intervention to protect the status quo.
Sept. 8	Finland announces that it will no longer fix the markka to the ECU following a week of increasing speculation against the markka. The markka immediately falls against the DM and the dollar. The Swedish krona is hit by speculation as capital flows out of the Nordic countries to DM-denominated assets accelerate; Swedish monetary authorities begin raising interest rates to protect the krona.
Sept. 9	Swedish central bank raises interest rates from 24% to 75% and plans to raise up to ECU 31 billion to protect the krona. Bundesbank is quoted as believing the Italian lira, Spanish peseta, and British pound should be devalued.
Sept. 13	The Bundesbank cuts the Lombard borrowing rate, the base bank borrowing rate, by 25 basis points, from 9.75% to 9.50%. It is the first interest rate cut by the Bundesbank in five years. Italy/EMS announce that the Italian lira will be devalued by 7.6%. The Netherlands, Belgium, Austria, and Switzerland announce their interest rates will be allowed to fall. Sweden announces it will lower its marginal lending rate, the rate of interest that governs overnight interest rates between banks, to 20%.
Sept. 14	The currency markets react favorably, the dollar rising from Friday's close of DM1.44/$ to DM1.49/$, a 2.4% appreciation. The markets wait for more interest rate cuts from the Bundesbank.
Sept. 15	Bundesbank president Helmut Schlesinger makes it clear in an interview that the German monetary authority has not changed course toward expansionary policy. The Italian lira finds itself once more under attack as no interest rate cuts follow Sunday's devaluation. Rumors abound that Giuliano Amato, the Italian prime minister, is about to resign. The British pound comes under increasing speculative pressure as it falls below the allowed floor value against the Deutschemark.
Sept. 16	The Bank of England raises its base lending rate to defend the falling British pound. By afternoon the Bank considers a further rate increase, but instead withdraws from the Exchange Rate Mechanism (ERM) of the EMS. Sweden raises the base lending rate from 75% to 500% to stop speculators from shorting the krona. Currency volatilities and option premiums skyrocket as crisis continues.
Sept. 17	The Bundesbank refuses all pressure to cut German interest rates. The Spanish peseta is devalued 5% in the European Monetary System grid. The Italian lira withdraws from the exchange rate mechanism of the EMS. Official trading in the lira is suspended until the following Tuesday. The U.S. dollar falls from the previous day's high against the Deutschemark in response to rumors that the Bundesbank may be waiting to cut interest rates until after Sunday's French vote on Maastricht.
Sept. 18	Sweden announces that it will cut the bank borrowing rate from 500% to 50%. The markets remain tense as all is put on hold awaiting the results of the French referendum on Sunday September 20.
Sept. 20	The French vote on the Maastricht treaty and its proposed monetary unification of the EC.

Exhibit 23.11   Daily Changes in the DM/$ Spot Rate and the DM Put
                    Option Premium

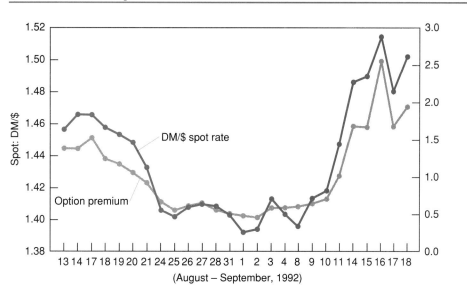

(August – September, 1992)

Steph quickly downloaded data on the daily spot rate and the December put option
premium value. The graphic results of the comparison are shown in Exhibit 23.11. The
put option premium had closed at 1.95 cents per DM on Friday (September 18) while the
spot and 90-day forward rates were DM1.5015/$ and DM1.5255/$, respectively. The 90-
day Eurocurrency interest rates had not changed since August. Steph thought she would
have to move fast if—and it was a big if—she wished to sell her option while values
(and volatilities) were still high.

Case Questions

1. Should Stephanie Mayo sell the put option protection already in place? Use the cur-
    rent market rates and prices to defend your logic.

2. How have the events of September altered Stephanie's directional view of the DM/$
    exchange rate?

3. How has the volatility of the put option changed between August and September?
    Use the option pricing spreadsheet OPTION.WK1 to estimate the volatilities.

4. If you were the vice president for Treasury at ZAPA, what *benchmarks* would you
    use to measure Stephanie's hedging effectiveness? How would this alter Stephanie's
    hedging?

Questions

1. Optimal Hedges

You are confronted by a simple, but seemingly difficult question: Why is the optimal amount of cover for a SF100,000 account receivable not necessarily SF100,000?

2. Delta-Neutral Hedging

Which is more appropriate for the multinational firm's accounting purposes, the typical end-of-period currency hedging strategy or the continuing market value hedging strategy used in delta-neutral hedging?

3. Financial Derivatives and Emerging Markets

Although many countries are increasingly "freeing up" their currency and financial derivative markets, many of the largest traders of the Asian-Pacific and Latin America (the so-called emerging markets) still do not have widely quoted and traded financial hedges available. Why do you think many countries are slow to allow the use of financial derivatives in their country on their domestic currency?

4. Synthetic Forwards

Assume the same identical values hold as in the chapter problem, except the £1,000,000 exposure is a 90-day account payable, not receivable. All other rates and values are the same.

    a.   Explain precisely how a synthetic forward position would be constructed.

    b.   Diagram the construction of the synthetic forward position.

5. Ikea's Yen Exposure and Range Forward (C24A.WK1 and OPTION.WK1)

Ikea, the Swedish household furnishings firm that has so successfully penetrated the American market, is now betting on a major change in U.S. consumer taste. Ikea believes that many of the simple Japanese furnishing designs will be in demand in the 1995–1996 period, and is willing to spend nearly $25,000,000 quarterly in new materials and inventory in anticipation of this market shift. It is expecting its first shipment of merchandise from a Japanese wholesaler in 90 days, with a payment on receipt of ¥2.7 billion.

Ikea has long been considered a leader in not only its understanding of consumer tastes, but in its ability to manage and anticipate currency exposures and their impacts on competitiveness. Ikea (US) had originally sourced all merchandise from Europe until the early 1990s when the U.S. dollar weakened considerably against major European currencies. Since that time it had shifted to domestic sourcing to the point that over 80% of all merchandise was now derived domestically.

Ikea wishes to consider the use of currency options, but due to the limited budget of finance and treasury, it will need to finance these option purchases by writing offsetting positions. Current market conditions are as follows:

Spot exchange rate:	¥108.20/$
90-day forward rate:	¥107.88/$
90-day Eurodollar deposit rate:	3.3750%

90-day Euroyen deposit rate: 2.1875%
90-day ¥/$ volatility quote: 11.8%

a. Construct and diagram a range forward that is ± 2% around the forward rate. What precisely would Ikea like the spot rate to do in the coming 90 days to maximize the use of this range forward?

b. Construct and diagram a range forward that is ± 5% around the forward rate. What precisely would Ikea like the spot rate to do in the coming 90 days to maximize the use of this range forward?

6. Participating Forward (C24B.WK1 and OPTION.WK1)

Using the same assumptions as used in the chapter problem to construct a participating forward with a 65% participation rate,

a. What is the size of the call option that must now be sold to yield a net-zero up-front premium?

b. Why is the size different?

c. What would be the forward break-even spot rate, the rate at which the participating forward would yield the same results as the forward contract, for this participating forward?

7. Nokia Oy's Acquisition Bid

Nokia Oy is one of the largest and fastest growing technology-based firms in Finland, and in effect, all of Europe. As the leading manufacturer of cellular telephones in the European market (both in and out of the European Union), the firm has been increasingly aggressive in its expansion into new markets.

Nokia has decided that if it is to compete in the United States against the market leader, Motorola, it needs an assembly and service center located there. After months of working with industry consultants and investment bankers, it has now made a bid on an electronics assembly facility presently owned and operated by Philips (Netherlands) in Winnetka, Illinois. Although Philips is still operating the facility, albeit at a low capacity rate, Philips has decided to withdraw from the American markets due to its continuing financial woes, both in the United States and its home markets in Europe. Nokia wishes to take ownership of the facility prior to shutdown and "mothballing" by Philips because of the added costs associated with reopening a closed facility and rehiring some of the trained labor already in place, and the time involved. So the actual bid is important.

The analysts have concluded that the plant, equipment, and facilities, are roughly worth $17,000,000. Because Philips is planning to get out, the investment bankers think it could be had for less, somewhere between $12 and $14 million. But Nokia's corporate strategy group has argued it is critical that the first bid be acceptable to Philips, otherwise negotiations may drag on and time is money for Nokia's competitiveness in North America. (Rumors have already surfaced on Motorola's plans to use the North American Free Trade Agreement's provisions on open access to attack both the Canadian and Mexican markets.)

Timo Hakkonen is head of risk management within the treasury group at Nokia's central office. He has been asked in to offer additional advice on the purchase price given the sizable currency exposure of making a bid of $12 to $17 million. Nokia has some U.S. dollar cash flows, but they are nothing in magnitude compared to the bid price. And the Finnish markka-U.S. dollar exchange rate has been anything but stable over the past few years. Timo's preliminary analysis for the coming 90-day period looks like the following:

Spot exchange rate:	FIM5.6136/$
90-day forward rate:	FIM5.6487/$
90-day Eurodollar deposit rate:	3.3750%
90-day Euro-Finmark deposit rate:	5.9000%
90-day FIM/$ volatility:	14.8%

Most importantly, because of stabilizing economic conditions in Finland (finally), and the overheating of the U.S. economy, Timo expects the Finmark to strengthen versus the dollar.

a. What would be the premium expense of buying a forward ATM option to cover the exposure if Timo assumes a purchase price of $14,000,000?

b. What spot rate is needed to make the option cover superior to simple forward cover with the current exchange rate and interest rate conditions?

Timo explains to management that the purchase of this option cover is beyond the current budgetary allotment for Treasury, and in order to finance this cover he should consider a "complex option" position which would essentially pay for the option but limit the potential benefits. He suggests they use either a range forward or a participating forward for the position.

c. Price and construct a range forward that sets the strike prices ± 3% of the forward rate.

d. Price and construct a participating forward in which Nokia could participate in 60% of all favorable exchange rate movements.

e. Contrast and compare the alternatives. What would clearly distinguish the choice between the range forward and participating forward?

As a final note. Timo feels strongly the markka is about to appreciate versus the U.S. dollar by anywhere from 5 to 10%. He suggests they consider using a ratio spread, in which they would purchase forward ATM option protection by selling a far OTM option to yield a net-zero premium. If Timo's expectations are correct,

f. How could he construct the ratio spread to cover the exposure?

g. How could the potential "savings" from these expectations be put to use in the actual amount bid for the Winnetka, Illinois, facility?

Bibliography

Ahm, Mark J., and William D. Falloon, *Strategic Risk Management,* Chicago: Probus, 1991.

Andersen, Torben Juul, *Currency and Interest Rate Hedging,* 2nd ed., New York: New York Institute of Finance, 1993.

Anderson, R.W., and J.P. Danthine, "Cross-Hedging," *Journal of Political Economy,* December 1981, pp. 1182–1196.

Bessembinder, Hendrik, "Forward Contracts and Firm Value: Investment Incentive and Contracting

Effects," *Journal of Financial and Quantitative Analysis,* vol. 26, no. 4, December 1991, pp. 519–532.

Euromoney, "Dictionary of Derivatives," *Euromoney Supplement,* June 1992, London.

Franke, G., "Uncertain Perception of Economic Exchange Risk and Financial Hedging," *Managerial Finance,* vol. 18, no. 3/4, 1991, pp. 53–70.

Grabbe, J. Orlin, *International Financial Markets,* 2nd ed., New York: Elsevier, 1991.

Howcroft, Barry, and Christopher Storey, *Management and Control of Currency and Interest Rate Risk,* Chicago: Probus, 1989.

Kerkvliet, Joe, and Michael H. Moffett, "The Hedging of an Uncertain Future Foreign Currency Payment," *Journal of Financial and Quantitative Analysis,* vol. 26, no.4, December 1991, pp. 565–578.

Levi, Maurice D., and Piet Sercu, "Erroneous and Valid Reasons for Hedging Foreign Exchange Rate Exposure," *Journal of Multinational Financial Management,* vol. 1, no. 2, 1991, pp. 25–37.

Marshall, John F., and Vipul K. Bansal, *Financial Engineering: A Complete Guide to Financial Innovation,* New York: New York Institute of Finance, 1992.

Modigliani, Franco, and Merton Miller, "The Cost of Capital, Corporation Finance, and the Theory of Investment," *American Economic Review,* vol. 48, June 1958, pp. 261–297.

Quinn, Lawrence R., "How Corporate America Views Financial Risk Management," *Futures,* vol. 18, no. 1, January 1989, pp. 40–41.

Rawls, S. Waite, III, and Charles W. Smithson, "Strategic Risk Management," *Continental Bank Journal of Applied Corporate Finance,* Winter 1990, pp. 6–18.

Shapiro, Alan, and S. Titman, "An Integrated Approach to Corporate Risk Management," *Midland Corporate Finance Journal,* vol. 3, Fall 1985, pp. 41–55.

Smith, Clifford W., and Rene M. Stulz, "The Determinants of Firms' Hedging Policies," *Journal of Financial and Quantitative Analysis,* vol. 20, no. 4, December 1985, pp. 390–405.

Smith, Clifford W., Jr., and Charles W. Smithson, "Financial Engineering: An Overview," in *The Handbook of Financial Engineering,* Clifford W. Smith, Jr., and Charles W. Smithson, eds., New York: Harper & Row, 1990, pp. 3–29.

Smith, Clifford W., Jr., Charles W. Smithson, and D. Sykes Wilford, *Managing Financial Risk,* Institutional Investor Series in Finance, New York: Harper & Row, 1990.

———, "Why Hedge?" *Intermarket,* July 1989, pp. 12–16.

Stulz, Rene M., "Optimal Hedging Policies," *Journal of Financial and Quantitative Analysis,* vol. 19, no. 2, June 1984, pp. 127–140.

Sutton, William H., *Trading in Currency Options,* New York Institute of Finance, New York: Simon & Schuster, 1988.

Walmsley, Julian, *The Foreign Exchange and Money Markets Guide,* New York: Wiley, 1992.

Wunnicke, Diane B., David R. Wilson, and Brooke Wunnicke, *Corporate Financial Risk Management,* New York: Wiley, 1992.

Glossary

A.B. *Aktiebolag.* Swedish word for incorporated or stock company.

A.G. *Aktiengesellschaft.* German word for incorporated or stock company.

Accounting exposure. The potential for an accounting-derived change in owners' equity resulting from exchange rate changes and the need to restate financial statements of foreign affiliates in the single currency of the parent corporation. Also called "translation exposure."

ACU. *See* Asian currency unit.

ADB. Asian Development Bank.

Adjusted present value. A type of present value analysis in capital budgeting in which operating cash flows are discounted separately from (1) the various tax shields provided by the deductibility of interest and other financial charges, and (2) the benefits of project-specific concessional financing. Each component cash flow is discounted at a rate appropriate for the risk involved.

ADR. *See* American Depositary Receipt.

Ad valorem duty. A customs duty levied as a percentage of the assessed value of goods entering a country.

AfDB. African Development Bank.

Affiliate. A foreign operation, formed as either a branch or a foreign-incorporated subsidiary.

Agency for International Development (AID). A unit of the U.S. government dealing with foreign aid.

AID. *See* Agency for International Development.

All-equity discount rate. A discount rate in capital budgeting that would be appropriate for discounting operating cash flows if the project were financed entirely with owners' equity.

American Depositary Receipt (ADR). A certificate of ownership, issued by a U.S. bank, representing a claim on underlying foreign securities. ADRs may be traded in lieu of trading in the actual underlying shares.

American option. An option that can be exercised at any time up to and including the expiration date.

American selling price (ASP). For customs purposes, the use of the domestic price of competing merchandise in the United States as a tax base for determining import duties. The ASP is generally higher than the actual foreign price, so its use is a protectionist technique.

American terms. Foreign exchange quotations for the U.S. dollar, expressed as the number of U.S. dollars per unit of non-U.S. currency.

A/P. In international trade documentation, abbreviation for "authority to purchase" or "authority to pay." In accounting, abbreviation for "accounts payable."

Appreciation. In the context of exchange rate changes, a rise in the foreign exchange value of a currency that is pegged to other currencies or to gold. Also called "revaluation."

Arbitrage. A trading strategy based on the purchase of a commodity, including foreign exchange, in one market at one price while simultaneously selling it in another market at a more advantageous price, in order to obtain a risk-free profit on the price differential.

Arbitrageur. An individual or company which practices arbitrage.

Arm's-length price. The price at which a willing buyer and a willing unrelated seller freely agree to carry out a transaction. In effect, a free market price. Applied by tax authorities in judging the appropriateness of transfer prices between related affiliates.

Asian currency unit. A trading department within a Singaporean bank that deals in foreign (non-Singaporean) currency deposits and loans.

Ask price. The price at which a dealer is willing to sell foreign exchange, securities or commodities. Also called "offer price."

ASP. *See* American selling price.

Back-to-back loan. A loan in which two companies in separate countries borrow each other's currency for a specific period of time, and repay the other's currency at an agreed maturity.

Sometimes the two loans are channelled through an intermediate bank. Back-to-back financing is also called "link financing."

Balance of payments. A financial statement summarizing the flow of goods, services, and investment funds between residents of a given country and residents of the rest of the world.

Balance of trade. An entry in the balance of payments measuring the difference between the monetary value of merchandise exports and merchandise imports.

Balance on current account. *See* Current account.

Bank for International Settlements. (BIS) A bank in Basle, Switzerland, that functions as a bank for European central banks.

Bank rate. The interest rate at which central banks for various countries lend to their own monetary institutions.

Bankers' acceptance. An unconditional promise of a bank to make payment on a draft when it matures. The acceptance is in the form of the bank's endorsement ("acceptance") of a draft drawn against that bank in accordance with the terms of a letter of credit issued by the bank.

Barter. International trade conducted by the direct exchange of physical goods, rather than by separate purchases and sales at prices and exchange rates set by a free market.

Basic Balance. In a country's balance of payments, the net of exports and imports of goods and services, unilateral transfers, and long-term capital flows.

Basis point. One one-hundredth of one percentage point, often used in quotations of spreads between

interest rates or to describe changes in yields in securities.

B/E. *See* Bill of exchange.

Bearer bond. Corporate or governmental debt in bond form that is not registered to any owner. Possession of the bond implies ownership, and interest is obtained by clipping a coupon attached to the bond. The advantage of the bearer form is easy transfer at the time of a sale, easy use as collateral for a debt, and what some cynics call "taxpayer anonymity," meaning that governments find it hard to trace interest payments in order to collect income taxes. Bearer bonds are common in Europe, but are seldom issued any more in the United States. The alternate form to a bearer bond is a registered bond.

Beta. Second letter of Greek alphabet, used as a statistical measure of risk in the Capital Asset Pricing Model. Beta is the covariance between returns on a given asset and returns on the market portfolio, divided by the variance of returns on the market portfolio.

Bid. The price which a dealer is willing to pay for (i.e., buy) foreign exchange or a security.

BID. *Banco Interamericano de Desarrollo.* Spanish name for the Inter-American Development Bank.

Bid-ask spread. The difference between a bid and an ask quotation.

Big Bang. The October 1986 liberalization of the London capital markets.

Bill of exchange (B/E). A written order requesting one party (such as an importer) to pay a specified amount of money at a specified time to the order of the writer of the bill of exchange. Also called a "draft." *See* Sight draft.

Bill of lading (B/L). A contract between a common carrier and a shipper to transport goods to a named destination. The bill of lading is also a receipt for the goods. Bills of lading are usually negotiable, meaning they are made to the order of a particular party and can be endorsed to transfer title to another party.

BIS. *See* Bank for International Settlements.

B/L. *See* Bill of lading.

Black market. An illegal foreign exchange market.

Blocked funds. Funds in one country's currency that may not be exchanged freely for foreign currencies because of exchange controls.

Border tax adjustments. The fiscal practice, under the General Agreement on Tariffs and Trade, by which imported goods are subject to some or all of the tax charged in the importing country and reexported goods are exempt from some or all of the tax charged in the exporting country.

Branch. A foreign operation not incorporated in the host country, in contradistinction to a "subsidiary."

Bretton Woods Conference. An international conference in 1944 that established the international monetary system in effect from 1945 to 1971. The conference was held in Bretton Woods, New Hampshire, USA.

Bridge financing. Short-term financing from a bank, used while a borrower obtains medium- or long-term fixed-rate financing from capital markets.

Bulldogs. British pound-denominated bonds issued within the United Kingdom by a foreign borrower.

Cable. The U.S. dollar per British pound crossrate.

CAD. "Cash against documents." International trade term.

Call option. The right, but not the obligation, to buy foreign exchange or some other financial contract at a specified price within a specified time. *See* Option.

Capital account. That portion of the balance of payments that measures public and private international lending and investment.

Capital Asset Pricing Model (CAPM). A theoretical model that relates the return on an asset to its risk, where risk is the contribution of the asset to the volatility of a portfolio. Risk and return are presumed determined in competitive and efficient financial markets.

Capital budgeting. The analytical approach used to determine whether investment in long-lived assets or projects is viable.

Capital flight. Movement of funds out of a country because of political risk.

Capital markets. The financial markets in various countries in which various types of long-term debt and/or ownership securities, or claims on those securities, are purchased and sold.

Capital mobility. The degree to which private capital moves freely from country to country seeking the most promising investment opportunities.

CAPM. *See* Capital Asset Pricing Model.

Certificate of Deposit (CD). A negotiable receipt issued by a bank for funds deposited for a certain period of time. CD's can be purchased or sold prior to their maturity in a secondary market,

making them an interest-earning marketable security.

CFC. *See* Controlled foreign corporation.

C&F. *See* Cost and freight.

Cia. *Companía.* Spanish word for company.

CHIPS. *See* Clearinghouse Interbank Payments System.

CIF. *See* Cost, insurance, and freight.

Closing rate method. Another name for the current rate method of creating consolidated financial statements. *See* Current rate method.

CKD. "Completely knocked down." International trade term for components shipped into a country for assembly there. Often used in the automobile industry.

Clearing house. An institution through which financial obligations are cleared by the process of netting obligations of various members.

Clearinghouse Interbank Payments System (CHIPS). A New York-based computerized clearing system used by banks to settle interbank foreign exchange obligations (mostly U.S. dollars) between members.

Collar option. The simultaneous purchase of a put option and sale of a call option, or vice versa. Thus a form of hybrid option.

COMECON. Acronym for Council for Mutual Economic Assistance. An association of the former Soviet Union and Eastern European governments formed to facilitate international trade among European Communist countries. COMECON ceased to exist after the breakup of the Soviet Union.

Commercial risk. In banking, the likelihood that a foreign debtor will be unable to repay its debts because

of business (as distinct from political) events.

Common market. An association through treaty of two or more countries that agree to remove all trade barriers between themselves. The best known is the European Common Market, now called the European Union.

Comparative advantage. A theory that everyone gains if each nation specializes in the production of those goods that it produces relatively most efficiently and imports those goods that other countries produce relatively most efficiently. The theory supports free trade arguments.

Concession agreement. An understanding or contract between a foreign corporation and a host government defining the rules under which the corporation may operate in that country.

Consolidated financial statement. A corporate financial statement in which accounts of subsidiaries and the parent are added together to produce a statement which reports the status of the worldwide enterprise as if it were a single corporation. Inter-affiliate obligations are eliminated in consolidated statements.

Consolidation. In the context of accounting for multinational corporations, the process of preparing a single "reporting currency" financial statement that combines financial statements of affiliates that are in fact measured in different currencies.

Consortium bank. A banking joint venture, owned by two or more individual banks often of different nationalities. Consortium banks are formed in order to offer loans that are larger than the capacity of any one single bank, as well as to engage in other aspects of international banking.

Controlled foreign corporation (CFC). A foreign corporation in which U.S. shareholders own more than 50% of the combined voting power or total value. Under U.S. tax law, U.S. shareholders may be liable for taxes on undistributed earnings of the controlled foreign corporation.

Convertible bond. A bond or other fixed-income security which may be exchanged for a number of shares of common stock.

Convertible currency. A currency that can be exchanged freely for any other currency without government restrictions.

Correspondent bank. A bank that holds deposits for and provides services to another bank, located in another geographic area, on a reciprocal basis.

Cost and freight (C&F). Price, quoted by an exporter, that includes the cost of transportation to the named port of destination.

Cost, insurance, and freight (CIF). Exporter's quoted price including the cost of packaging, freight or carriage, insurance premium, and other charges paid in respect of the goods from the time of loading in the country of export to their arrival at the named port of destination or place of transshipment.

Cost of capital. *See* Weighted average cost of capital.

Countertrade. A type of international trade in which parties exchange goods directly rather than for money. Hence a type of barter.

Countervailing duty. An import duty charged to offset an export subsidy by another country.

Country risk. In banking, the likelihood that unexpected events within a host country will influence a client's or a government's ability to repay a loan. Country risk is often divided into sovereign (political) risk and foreign exchange (currency) risk.

Covered interest arbitrage. The process whereby an investor earns a risk-free profit by (1) borrowing funds in one currency, (2) exchanging those funds in the spot market for a foreign currency, (3) investing the foreign currency at interest rates in a foreign country, (4) selling forward, at the time of original investment, the investment proceeds to be received at maturity, (5) using the proceeds of the forward sale to repay the original loan, and (6) having a remaining profit balance.

Covering. A transaction in the forward foreign exchange market or money market which protects the value of future cash flows. Covering is another term for hedging. *See* Hedge.

Crawling peg. A foreign exchange rate system in which the exchange rate is adjusted very frequently to reflect prevailing rate of inflation.

Cross rate. An exchange rate between two currencies derived by dividing each currency's exchange rate with a third currency. For example, if ¥/$ is 140 and DM/$ is 1.5000, the cross rate between ¥ and DM is ¥140/$ ÷ DM1.5000 = ¥93.3333/DM.

CTA account. *See* Cumulative translation adjustment account.

Cumulative translation adjustment (CTA) account. An entry in a translated balance sheet in which gains and/or losses from translation have been accumulated over a period of years.

Currency basket. The value of a portfolio of specific amounts of individual currencies, used as the basis for setting the market value of another currency. Also called currency cocktail.

Currency cocktail. *See* Currency basket.

Currency swap. A transaction in which two counterparties exchange specific amounts of two different currencies at the outset and then repay over time according to an agreed upon contract which reflects interest payments and possibly amortization of principal. In a currency swap, the cash flows are similar to those in a spot and forward foreign exchange transaction. *Also see* Swaps.

Current account. In the balance of payments, the net flow of goods, services, and unilateral transfers (such as gifts) between a country and all foreign countries.

Current rate method. A method of translating the financial statements of foreign affiliates into the parent's reporting currency. All assets and liabilities are translated at the current exchange rate.

Current/noncurrent method. A method of translating the financial statements of foreign affiliates into the parent's reporting currency. All current assets and current liabilities are translated at the current rate, and all noncurrent accounts at their historical rates.

D/A. "Documents against acceptance." International trade term.

Deemed-tax paid. That portion of taxes paid to a foreign government that is allowed as a credit (reduction) in taxes due to a home government.

Delta. The change in an Option's price divided by the change in the price of the underlying instrument. Hedging strategies are based on delta ratios.

Demand deposit. A bank deposit that can be withdrawn or transferred at any time without notice, in contradistinction to a time deposit where (theoretically) the bank may require a waiting period before the deposit can be withdrawn. Demand deposits may or may not earn interest. A "time deposit" is the opposite of a demand deposit.

Depreciate. In the context of foreign exchange rates, a drop in the spot foreign exchange value of a floating currency; i.e., a currency the value of which is determined by open market transactions. *See* Devaluation. In the context of accounting, a periodic charge (expense) that represents the allocation of the cost of a fixed asset to various time periods.

Devaluation. A drop in the spot foreign exchange value of a currency that is pegged to other currencies or to gold. *See* Depreciate.

Direct quote. The price of a unit of foreign exchange expressed in the home country's currency. The term has meaning only when the "home country" is specified.

"Dirty" float. A system of floating (i.e., market-determined) exchange rates in which the government intervenes from time to time to influence the foreign exchange value of its currency.

Discount (in foreign exchange market). The amount by which a currency is cheaper for future delivery than for spot (immediate) delivery. The opposite of "discount" is "premium."

DISC. *See* Domestic International Sales Corporation.

Domestic International Sales Corporation (DISC). Under the U.S. tax code, a type of subsidiary formed to export U.S.-produced goods. A portion of the earnings and profits of DISCs is not taxed to the DISC but is instead taxed directly to its shareholders.

D/P. "Documents against payment." International trade term.

Draft. An unconditional written order requesting one party (such as an importer) to pay a specified amount of money at a specified time to the order of the writer of the draft. Also called a "bill of exchange." Personal checks are one type of draft.

D/S. "Days after sight." International trade term.

Dragon bond. A U.S. dollar denominated bond sold in the so-called "Dragon" economies of Asia, such as Hong Kong, Taiwan, and Singapore.

Dumping. The practice of offering goods for sale in a foreign market at a price that is lower than that of the same product in the home market or a third country. As used in GATT, a special case of "differential pricing."

Economic exposure. Another name for operating exposure. *See* Operating exposure.

ECU. *See* European Currency Unit.

Edge Act and Agreement Corporation. Subsidiary of a U.S. bank incorporated under federal law to engage in various international banking and financing operations, including equity participations which are not allowed to regular domestic banks. The Edge Act subsidiary may be located in a state other than that of the parent bank.

EEC. *See* European Economic Community.

Effective exchange rate. An index measuring the change in value of a foreign currency determined by calculating a weighted average of bilateral exchange rates. The weighting reflects the importance of each foreign country's trade with the home country.

Efficient market. A market in which all relevant information is already reflected in market prices. The term is most frequently applied to foreign exchange markets and securities markets.

EFTA. *See* European Free Trade Association.

EMS. *See* European Monetary System.

EOM. "End of month." International trade term.

Eurobank. A bank, or bank department, which bids for time deposits and makes loans in currencies other than that of the country where the bank is located.

Eurobond. A bond originally offered outside the country in whose currency it is denominated. For example, a dollar-denominated bond originally offered for sale to investors outside of the United States.

Euro-Commercial Paper. Short-term notes (30, 60, 90, 120, 180, 270, and 360 days) sold in international money markets.

Eurocurrency. A currency deposited in a bank located in a country other than the country issuing the currency.

Eurodollar. A U.S. dollar deposited in a bank outside the United States. A Eurodollar is one type of Eurocurrency.

Euronote. Short- to medium-term debt instruments sold in the Eurocurrency market.

European Currency Unit (ECU). Composite currency created by the European Monetary System to function as a reserve currency numeraire. The ECU is used as the numeraire for denominating a number of financial instruments and obligations.

European Economic Community (EEC). The European common

market composed of Belgium, Denmark, France, Germany, Greece, Ireland, Italy, Luxembourg, the Netherlands, Portugal, Spain, and the United Kingdom. Officially renamed the European Union (EU) January 1, 1994.

European Free Trade Association (EFTA). European countries not part of the EEC (EU) but having no internal tariffs. EFTA consists of Austria, Iceland, Finland, Sweden, and Switzerland.

European Monetary System (EMS). A monetary alliance of twelve European countries (same members as the European Union), formed to maintain member exchange rates within specified margins about fixed central rates. As of July 1994, the United Kingdom and Italy are not active members.

European option. An option that can be exercised only on the day on which it expires.

European terms. Foreign exchange quotations for the U.S. dollar, expressed as the number of non-U.S. currency units per U.S. dollar.

European Union (EU). The official name of the former European Economic Community (EEC) as of January 1, 1994.

Exchange rate. The price of a unit of one country's currency expressed in terms of the currency of some other country.

Exchange Rate Mechanism (ERM). The means by which members of the EMS maintain their currency exchange rates within an agreed upon range with respect to the other member currencies.

Exchange risk. *See* Foreign exchange risk.

Ex dock, followed by the name of a port of import. International trade term in which seller agrees to pay for the costs (shipping, insurance, customs duties, etc.) of placing the goods on the dock at the named port.

Exim Bank. *See* Export-Import Bank.

Export-Import Bank (Eximbank). A U.S. government agency created to finance and otherwise facilitate imports and exports.

Expropriation. Official government seizure of private property, recognized by international law as the right of any sovereign state provided expropriated owners are given prompt compensation and fair market value in convertible currencies.

FAF. "Fly away free." International trade term.

FAQ. "Free at quay." International trade term.

FAS. *See* Free alongside.

FASB 8. A regulation of the Financial Accounting Standards Board requiring U.S. companies to translate foreign affiliate financial statements by the temporal method. FASB was in effect from 1976 to 1981.

FASB 52. A regulation of the Financial Accounting Standards Board requiring U.S. companies to translate foreign affiliate financial statements by the current rate (closing rate) method. FASB 52 became effective in 1981.

FCIA. *See* Foreign Credit Insurance Association.

FDI. *See* Foreign direct investment.

FI. "Free in." International trade term meaning that all expenses for loading into the hold of a vessel are for the account of the consignee.

FIFO. "First in, first out." An inventory valuation approach in which the cost of the earliest inventory purchases is charged against current sales. The opposite is LIFO, or "last in, first out."

Fisher Effect. A theory that nominal interest rates in two or more countries should be equal to the required real rate of return to investors plus compensation for the expected amount of inflation in each country.

Fixed exchange rates. Foreign exchange rates tied to the currency of a major country (such as the United States), to gold, or to a basket of currencies such as Special Drawing Rights.

Floating exchange rates. Foreign exchange rates determined by demand and supply in an open market that is presumably free of government interference.

Floating rate note (FRN). Medium-term securities with interest rates pegged to LIBOR and adjusted quarterly or semiannually.

FOB. "Free on board." International trade term in which exporter's quoted price includes the cost of loading goods into transport vessels at a named point.

Foreign bond. A bond issued by a foreign corporation or government for sale in the domestic capital market of another country, and denominated in the currency of that country.

Foreign Corrupt Practices Act of 1977. A U.S. law that punishes companies and their executives if they pay bribes or make other improper payments to foreigners.

Foreign Credit Insurance Association (FCIA). Private U.S. insurance association that insures exporters in conjunction with Exim Bank.

Foreign currency translation. The process of restating foreign currency accounts of subsidiaries into the reporting currency of the parent company in order to prepare a consolidated financial statement.

Foreign direct investment (FDI). Purchase of physical assets, such as plant and equipment, in a foreign country, to be managed by the parent corporation. FDI is in contradistinction to foreign portfolio investment.

Foreign exchange broker. An individual or firm which arranges foreign exchange transactions between two parties, but is not itself a principal in the trade. Foreign exchange brokers earn a commission for their efforts.

Foreign exchange option. *See* Option.

Foreign exchange risk. The likelihood that an unexpected change in exchange rates will alter the home currency value of foreign currency cash payments expected from a foreign source. Also, the likelihood that an unexpected change in exchange rates will alter the amount of home currency needed to repay a debt denominated in a foreign currency.

Foreign exchange dealer (or trader). An individual or firm that buys foreign exchange from one party (at a "bid" price), and then sells it (at an "ask" price) to another party. The dealer is a principal in two transactions and makes a profit on the spread between its buying and selling prices.

Foreign sales corporation (FSC). Under U.S. tax code, a type of foreign corporation that provides tax-exempt or tax-deferred income for U.S. persons or corporations having export-oriented activities.

Foreign tax credit. The amount by which a domestic firm may reduce (credit) domestic income taxes for income tax payments to a foreign government.

Forfaiting. A technique for arranging nonrecourse medium-term export financing, used most frequently to finance imports into Eastern Europe. A third party, usually a specialized financial institution, guarantees the financing.

Forward contract. An agreement to exchange currencies of different countries at a specified future date and at a specified forward rate.

Forward differential. The difference between spot and forward rates, expressed as an annual percentage.

Forward discount or premium. The same as "forward differential."

Forward rate. An exchange rate quoted today for settlement at some future date. The rate used in a forward transaction.

Forward transaction. A foreign exchange transaction agreed upon today but to be settled at some specified future date, often one, two, or three months after the transaction date.

Free alongside (FAS). An international trade term in which the seller's quoted price for goods includes all costs of delivery of the goods alongside a vessel at the port of embarkation.

Freely floating exchange rates. Exchange rates determined in a free market without government interference, in contradistinction to "dirty" float.

Free trade zone. An area within a country into which foreign goods may be brought duty free, often for purposes of additional manufacture, inventory storage, or packaging. Such goods are subject to duty only when they leave the duty-free zone to enter other parts of the country.

FRN. *See* Floating rate note.

Fronting loan. A parent-to-affiliate loan channelled through a financial intermediary such as a large international bank in order to reduce political risk. Presumably government authorities are less likely to prevent a foreign affiliate repaying an established bank than repaying the affiliate's corporate parent.

FSC. *See* Foreign sales corporation.

Functional currency. In the context of translating financial statements, the currency of the primary economic environment in which a foreign affiliate operates and in which it generates cash flows.

Futures, or futures contracts. Exchange-traded agreements calling for future delivery of a standard amount of any good, e.g., foreign exchange, at a fixed time, place, and price.

Gamma. A measure of the sensitivity of an option's delta ratio to small unit changes in the price of the underlying security.

GATT. *See* General Agreement on Tariffs and Trade.

General Agreement on Tariffs and Trade (GATT). A framework of rules for nations to manage their trade policies, negotiate lower international tariff barriers, and settle trade disputes.

Glasnost. Russian language word for the political reform policies of President Mikhail S. Gorbachev in the Soviet Union.

G.m.b.H. *Gesellschaft mit beschraenkter Haftung.* German term for limited liability company.

Gold standard. A monetary system in which currencies are defined in terms of their gold content, and payment imbalances between countries are settled in gold.

Gross up. *See* Deemed paid credit.

Group of Five. France, Japan, United Kingdom, United States, and Germany. Central bankers and finance ministers of these countries met in the mid-1980's to discuss coordinating economic policies.

Group of Seven. Canada, France, Germany, Italy, Japan, United Kingdom, and the United States. Political leaders of these countries met in 1990 and 1991 to discuss, among other topics, economic aid to the Soviet Union and whether to intervene in the foreign exchange markets to try to stop the rise in the international value of the U.S. dollar.

Group of Ten. Germany, France, Belgium, the Netherlands, Italy, the United Kingdom, Sweden, Canada, Japan, and the United States. These countries pledged in 1962 to stand ready to lend their currencies to the International Monetary Fund. They have been active in the design and operation of the world's international monetary system.

Hard currency. A freely convertible currency that is not expected to depreciate in value in the foreseeable future.

Hedge. The purchase of a contract (including forward foreign exchange) or tangible good that will rise in value and offset a drop in value of another contract or tangible good. Hedges are undertaken to reduce risk by protecting an owner from loss.

Hijo(s). Spanish word for son(s).

Historical exchange rate. In accounting, the exchange rate in effect when an asset or liability was acquired.

Hnos. Hermanos. Spanish word for brothers.

Hot money. Money which moves internationally from one currency and/or country to another in response to interest rate differences, and moves away immediately when the interest advantage disappears.

Hybrid foreign currency options. Purchase of a put option and the simultaneous sale of a call (or vice versa) so that the overall cost is less than the cost of a straight option.

Hyperinflation countries. Countries with a very high rate of inflation. Under United States FASB 52, these are defined as countries where the cumulative three-year inflation amounts to 100% or more.

IBF. *See* International Banking Facility.

IBRD. *See* International Bank for Reconstruction and Development.

IMF. *See* International Monetary Fund.

IMM. International Monetary Market. A division of the Chicago Mercantile Exchange.

Inc. "Incorporated." American English word for a business formed as a corporation. *Also see* Limited.

Indirect quote. The price of a unit of a home country's currency expressed in terms of a foreign country's currency.

Interest equalization tax. A 1963 U.S. tax imposed on U.S. residents who purchased foreign securities. The law was repealed in 1973. The purpose of the tax was to penalize U.S. residents who invested outside of the United States, and so help the U.S. balance of payments.

Interest rate parity. A theory that the differences in national interest rates for securities of similar risk and maturity should be equal to but opposite in sign to the forward exchange rate discount or premium for the foreign currency.

Interest rate swap. A transaction in which two counterparties exchange interest payment streams of different character (such as floating vs. fixed), based on an underlying notional principal amount.

International Bank for Reconstruction and Development (IBRD, or World Bank). International development bank owned by member nations that makes development loans to member countries.

International Banking Facility (IBF). A department within a U.S. bank that may accept foreign deposits and make loans to foreign borrowers as if it were a foreign subsidiary. IBF's are free of U.S. reserve requirements, deposit insurance, and interest rate regulations.

Internal rate of return (IRR). A capital budgeting approach in which the discount rate is found that matches the present value of expected future cash inflows with the present value of outflows.

International Fisher Effect. A theory that the spot exchange rate should change by an amount equal to the difference in interest rates between two countries.

International Monetary Fund (IMF). An international organization created in 1944 to promote exchange rate stability and provided temporary financing for countries experiencing balance of payments difficulties.

International Monetary Market (IMM). A branch of the Chicago Mercantile Exchange which specializes in trading currency and financial futures contracts.

IRR. *See* Internal rate of return.

Joint venture. A business venture that is owned by two or more other business ventures. Often the several business owners are from different countries.

Jumbo loans. Loans of $1 billion or more.

Kangaroo bonds. Australian dollar-denominated bonds issued within Australia by a foreign borrower.

KK. *Kabushiki-Kaishi.* Japanese term for stock company.

Lag. In the context of leads and lags, payment of a financial obligation later than is expected or required.

L/C. *See* Letter of credit.

Lead. In the context of leads and lags, payment of a financial obligation earlier than is expected or required.

Letter of credit (L/C). An instrument issued by a bank, in which the bank promises to pay a beneficiary upon presentation of documents specified in the letter of credit.

LIBOR. *See* London Interbank Offered Rate.

LIFO. "Last in, first out." An inventory valuation approach in which the cost of the latest inventory purchases is charged against current sales. The opposite is FIFO, or "first in, first out."

Limited (Ltd). British English word for a business formed as a corporation.

Link financing. *See* Back-to-back loan.

Lombard rate. The interest rate on a "Lombard loan," which is an advance against the collateral of specified European securities.

London Interbank Offered Rate (LIBOR). The deposit rate applicable to interbank loans in London. LIBOR is used as the reference rate for many international interest rate transactions.

Long position. A position in which foreign currency assets exceed foreign currency liabilities to deliver. The opposite of a long position is a short position.

Ltd. *See* Limited.

Managed float. *See* "Dirty" float.

Margin. A deposit made as security for a financial transaction otherwise financed on credit.

Merchant bank. A bank that specializes in helping corporations and governments finance by any of a variety of market and/or traditional techniques. In Europe, merchant banks combine in one institution what in the United States are separated into commercial banks or investment banks. European merchant banks are sometimes differentiated from clearing banks, which tend to focus on bank deposits and clearing balances for the majority of the population.

MFN. *See* Most-favored-nation treatment.

Monetary/nonmonetary method. A method of translating the financial statements of foreign affiliates into the parent's reporting currency. All monetary accounts are translated at the current rate, and all nonmonetary accounts are translated at their historical rates. Sometimes called "temporal method" in the United States.

Money market hedge. Use of foreign currency borrowing to reduce transaction or accounting foreign exchange exposure.

Money Markets. The financial markets in various countries in which various types of short-term debt instruments, including bank loans, are purchased and sold.

Monetary assets or liabilities. Assets in the form of cash or claims to cash (such as accounts receivable), or liabilities payable in cash. Monetary assets minus mone-tary liabilities are called "net monetary assets."

m.n. *Moneda nacional.* Spanish language term for "national money," the local currency.

Most-favored-nation (MFN) treatment. Application by a country of import duties on the same, or "most favored," basis to all countries accorded such treatment. Any tariff reduction granted in a bilateral negotiation will be extended to all other nations that have been granted most-favored-nation status. Hence in fact most-favored nation status means normal treatment rather than being discriminated against.

Negotiable instrument. A draft or promissory note that is in writing, signed by the maker or drawer, contains an unconditional promise or order to pay a definite sum of money on demand or at a determinable future date, and is payable to order or to bearer. A "holder in due course" of a negotiable instrument is entitled to payment despite any personal disagreements between drawee and maker.

Net present value. A capital budgeting approach in which the present value of expected future case inflows is subtracted from the present value of outflows to determine the "net" present value.

Nominal exchange rate. The actual foreign exchange quotation, in contradistinction to "real exchange rate," which is adjusted for changes in purchasing power.

Nontariff barrier. Trade restrictive practices other than custom tariffs. Examples are import quotas, "voluntary" restrictions, variable levies, and special health regulations.

Note issuance facility (NIF). An agreement by which a syndicate of banks indicate a willingness to accept short-term notes from borrowers and resell those notes in the Eurocurrency markets. The discount rate is often tied to LIBOR.

NPV. *See* Net present value.

n.s.f. "Not sufficient funds." Term used by a bank when a draft or check is drawn on an account not having sufficient credit balance.

N.V. *Naamloze vennootschap.* Dutch term for stock company or corporation.

O/A. "Open account." Arrangement in which the importer (or other buyer) pays for the goods only after the goods are received and inspected. The importer is billed directly after shipment, and payment is not tied to any promissory notes or similar documents.

Offer. The price at which a trader is willing to sell foreign exchange, securities, or commodities. Also called "ask."

Offshore finance subsidiary. A foreign financial subsidiary owned by a corporation in another country. Offshore finance subsidiaries are usually located in tax-free or low-tax jurisdictions to enable the parent multinational firm to finance international operations without being subject to home country taxes or regulations.

Operating exposure. The potential for a change in expected cash flows, and thus in value, of a foreign affiliate as a result of an unexpected change in exchange rates. Also called "economic exposure."

Option. In foreign exchange, a contract giving the purchaser the right, but not the obligation, to buy or sell a given amount of foreign exchange at a fixed price per unit

for a specified time period. Options to buy are "calls" and options to sell are "puts."

Order bill of lading. A shipping document through which possession and title to the shipment reside with the owner of the order bill of lading.

Outright quotation. The full price, in one currency, of a unit of another currency. *See* Points quotation.

Parallel loan. Another name for a back-to-back loan, in which two companies in separate countries borrow each other's currency for a specific period of time, and repay the other's currency at an agreed maturity.

Parallel market. An unofficial foreign exchange market tolerated by a government but not officially sanctioned. The exact boundary between a parallel market and a black market is not very clear, but official tolerance of what would otherwise be a black market leads to use of the term parallel market.

Perestroika. Russian language word for the economic reform policies of President Mikhail S. Gorbachev of the Soviet Union.

P/N. "Promissory note."

Points. A "point" is the smallest unit of price change quoted, given a conventional number of digits in which a quotation is stated. Deutschemarks per dollar are usually quoted to four decimal points, DM1.5624/$. In this quote, a change from 1.5624 to 1.5625 would be an increase of one point. A 12 point increase would bring the quote to 1.5636.

Points quotation. A forward quotation expressed only as the number of decimal points (usually four decimal points) by which it differs from the spot quotation.

Political risk. The possibility that political events in a particular country will have an influence on the economic well-being of firms in that country. *Also see* Sovereign risk.

Portfolio investment. Purchase of foreign stocks and bonds, in contradistinction to "foreign direct investment."

Possessions corporation. Under U.S. tax code, a type of corporation organized to conduct business in U.S. possessions. Certain tax benefits exist for income of possessions corporations.

Premium (in foreign exchange market). The amount by which a currency is more expensive for future delivery than for spot (immediate) delivery. The opposite of "premium" is "discount."

Protectionism. A political attitude or policy intended to inhibit or prohibit the import of foreign goods and services. The opposite of "free trade" policies.

Pty. Ltd. "Proprietary Limited." Term used in Australia, Singapore, and other countries for a privately owned corporation.

Purchasing power parity. A theory that the price of internationally traded commodities should be the same in every country, and hence the exchange rate between the two currencies should be the ratio of prices in the two countries.

Put. An option to sell foreign exchange or financial contracts. *See* Option.

Quota. A limit, mandatory or "voluntary," set on the import of a product.

Quotation. In foreign exchange trading, the pair of prices (bid and ask) at which a dealer is willing to buy or sell foreign exchange.

Real exchange rate. An index of foreign exchange adjusted for relative price level changes since a base period. Sometimes referred to as "real effective exchange rate," it is used to measure purchasing-power-adjusted changes in exchange rates.

Registered bond. Corporate or governmental debt in a bond form in which the owner's name appears on the bond and in the issuer's records, and interest payments are mailed to the owner. Transfer, as at the time of sale or if the bond is being possessed as collateral for a loan in default, requires power of attorney and the return of the physical bond to a transfer agent. The transfer agent replaces the old bond with a new one registered to the new owner.

Reinvoicing center. A central financial subsidiary used by a multinational firm to reduce transaction exposure by having all home country exports billed in the home currency and then reinvoiced to each operating affiliate in that affiliate's local currency.

Rembrandt bonds. Dutch guilder-denominated bonds issued within the Netherlands by a foreign borrower.

Reporting currency. In the context of translating financial statements, the currency in which a parent firm prepares its own financial statements. Usually this is the parent's home currency.

Revaluation. A rise in the foreign exchange value of a currency that is pegged to other currencies or to gold. Also called "appreciation."

SA. *Sociedad Anónima* (Spanish), or *Societe Anonyme* (French). Term meaning corporation.

SACI or SAIC. *Sociedad Anónima de Capital e Industria.* Spanish term for company of capital and industry.

Samurai bonds. Yen-denominated bonds issued within Japan by a foreign borrower.

SARL. *Società a Responsabilità Limitada* (Italian), or *Société a Responsabilité Limitée* (French). Term for company with limited liability.

S/D. "Sight draft." International trade term.

S/D-B/L. "Sight draft and bill of lading attached." International trade term.

SDR. *See* Special drawing right.

S. de R.L. *Sociedad de Responsabilidad Limitada.* Spanish term for limited partnership.

Section 482. The set of U.S. Treasury regulations governing transfer prices.

S. en C. *Sociedad en Comandita.* Spanish term for silent partnership.

Shogun bonds. Foreign currency-denominated bonds issued within Japan by Japanese corporations.

Short position. *See* Long position.

SIBOR. Singapore interbank offered rate.

Sight draft. A bill of exchange (B/E) that is due on demand; i.e., when presented to the bank. *Also see* Bill of exchange.

SIMEX. Singapore International Monetary Exchange.

Soft currency. A currency expected to drop in value relative to other currencies. Free trading in a currency deemed soft is often restricted by the monetary authorities of the issuing country.

Snake. Informal name for European Narrow Margins (or Joint Float) Agreement, in which European governments agreed to keep their currencies within a plus or minus 2.25% trading band around an agreed central value. Superceded by the EMS agreement.

Society for Worldwide Interbank Financial Telecommunications (SWIFT). A dedicated computer network providing funds transfer messages between member banks around the world.

Sovereign risk. The risk that a host government may unilaterally repudiate its foreign obligations or may prevent local firms from honoring their foreign obligations. Sovereign risk is often regarded as a subset of political risk.

SPA. *Societa per Azioni.* Italian term for corporation.

Special Drawing Right (SDR). An international reserve asset, defined by the International Monetary Fund as the value of a weighted basket of five currencies.

Speculation. An attempt to make a profit by trading on expectations about future prices.

Spot rate. The price at which foreign exchange can be purchased (its bid) or sold (its ask) in a spot transaction. *See* Spot transaction.

Spot transaction. A foreign exchange transaction to be settled (paid for) on the second following business day.

Spread. The difference between the bid (buying) quote and the ask (selling) quote.

SPRL. *Societe de Personnes a Responsabilite Limitee.* Belgian term for company of persons with limited liability.

Stripped bonds. Bonds issued by investment bankers against coupons or the maturity (corpus) portion of original bearer bonds, where the original bonds are held in trust by the investment banker. Whereas the original bonds will have coupons promising interest at each interest date (say June and December for each of the next twenty years), a given stripped bond will represent a claim against all interest payments from the entire original issue due on a particular interest date. A stripped bond is in effect a zero coupon bond manufactured by the investment banker.

Subpart F. A type of foreign income, as defined in the U.S. tax code, which under certain conditions is taxed in the United States even though it has not been repatriated to the United States.

Subsidiary. A foreign operation incorporated in the host country and owned 50% or more by a parent corporation. Foreign operations that are not incorporated are called "branches."

Sushi bonds. Eurodollar, or other non-yen denominated, bonds issued by a Japanese corporation for sale to Japanese investors.

Swap. This term is used in many contexts. In general it is the simultaneous purchase and sale of foreign exchange or securities, with the purchase being effected at once and the sale back to the same party to be carried out at a price agreed upon today but to be completed at a specified future date. Swaps include interest rate swaps, currency swaps, and credit swaps. A "swap rate" is a forward foreign exchange quotation expressed in terms of the number of points by which the forward rate differs from the spot rate.

SWIFT. *See* Society for Worldwide Interbank Financial Telecommunications.

Syndicated loan. A large loan made by a group of banks to a large multinational firm or government. Syndicated loans allow the participating banks to maintain diversification by not lending too much to a single borrower.

Systematic risk. In a portfolio, the amount of risk that cannot be diversified away.

T/A. "Trade acceptance." International trade term.

Tariff. A duty or tax on imports that can be levied as a percentage of cost or as a specific amount per unit of import.

Tax haven. A country with either no or very low tax rates that uses its tax structure to attract foreign investment or international financial dealings.

Temporal method. In the United States, term for a codification of a translation method essentially similar to the "monetary/nonmonetary method."

Terms of trade. The weighted average exchange ratio between a nation's export prices and its import prices, used to measure gains from trade. Gains from trade refers to increases in total consumption resulting from production specialization and international trade.

Trade acceptance. A draft accepted by a commercial enterprise, instead of by a bank.

Transaction exposure. The potential for a change in the value of outstanding financial obligations entered into prior to a change in exchange rates but not due to be settled until after the exchange rates change.

Transfer pricing. The setting of prices to be charged by one unit (such as a foreign affiliate) of a multiunit corporation to another unit (such as the parent corporation) for goods or services sold between such related units.

Translation exposure. *See* Accounting exposure.

Unbiased predictor. A theory that spot prices at some future date will be equal to today's forward rates.

Unbundling. Dividing cash flows from an affiliate to a parent into their many separate components, such as royalties, lease payments, dividends, etc., so as to increase the likelihood that some fund flows will be allowed during economically difficult times.

Unsystematic risk. In a portfolio, the amount of risk that can be eliminated by diversification.

Value-added tax. A type of national sales tax collected at each stage of production or sale of consumption goods, and levied in proportion to the value added during that stage.

Value date. The date when value is given (i.e., funds are deposited) for foreign exchange transactions between banks.

Value today. A spot foreign exchange transaction in which delivery and payment are made on the same day as the contract. Normal delivery is two business days after the contract.

Value tomorrow. A spot foreign exchange transaction in which delivery and payment are made on the next business day after the contract. Normal delivery is two business days after the contract.

VAT. *See* Value-added tax.

WACC. *See* Weighted average cost of capital.

Weighted average cost of capital (WACC). The sum of the proportionally weighted costs of different sources of capital, used as the minimum acceptable target return on new investments.

World Bank. *See* International Bank for Reconstruction and Development.

Yankee bonds. Dollar-denominated bonds issued within the United States by a foreign borrower.

Yield to maturity. The rate of interest (discount) which equates future cash flows of a bond, both interest and principal, with the present market price. Yield to maturity is thus the time-adjusted rate of return earned by a bond investor.

Y.K. *Yugen-Kaisha.* Japanese term for limited liability company.

Zero coupon bond. A bond which pays no periodic interest, but simply returns a given amount of principal at a stated maturity date.

Zero coupon bonds are sold at a discount from the maturity amount to provide the holder a compound rate of return for the holding period.

Zoonen. Dutch word for sons.

Author Index

Page numbers followed by n indicate footnotes.

Aggarwal, Raj, 199n, 310n
Agmon, Tamir, 562n
Aharoni, Yair, 479
Akhter, Syad, 608
Alam, Pervaiz, 608
Al-Eryani, Mohammad, F., 608
Alexander, Gordon J., 324
Alford, Alan, 295n
Altman, Edward, 113n
Anderson, Erin, 458
Arpan, Jeffrey S., 610
Awanohara, Susumu, 512n

Baker, Hikent, 323n
Baker, James C., 528, 531
Bates, Thomas, 312n
Batten, Jonathan, 199n
Bavishi, Vinod B., 528
Beardsley, Laurence J., 528, 531
Beekhuisen, Theo, 312n
Belassa, Bela, 476n
Belk, P.A., 199n
Biddle, Gary C., 326n
Biger, Nahum, 148n
Bilson, John F.O., 127n
Birley, Rupert, 461n
Black, Fischer, 148, 176
Block, Stanley, 528, 529, 531, 628n
Bodurtha, James N. Jr., 176
Breeden, Richard, 398
Buckley, Peter, 478n

Cahn, Rosanne M., 1
Cao, A.D., 506n
Casson, Mark, 478n
Caves, Richard, 472n, 473n
Chan, K. Hung, 199n
Chan, Su Han, 339n
Chatterjee, Sangit, 310n
Chen, Kent, 468n
Choi, Frederick D.S., 258n, 326
Clarke, Stephen V.O., 432n
Coase, R.H., 478n
Collins, J. Markham, 310–311
Cooper, Graham, 646n, 653n
Courtadon, Georges R., 176
Cox, J.C., 176
Cumby, Robert E., 118n
Cyert, Richard, 479n

Dale, Richard S., 428n
Darby, Michael R., 113n

Davis, Steven I., 428n
Dawson, Steven, 349
Dominguez, Kathryn, 25
Donaldson, Gordon, 12n
Drew, Daniel, 190n
Drucker, Peter, 10
Dufey, Gunter, 47n, 124n, 126, 201n, 413n, 415n
Dullum, Kåre B., 222n, 288n, 293n
Dunning, John, 478

Edelshain, David, 199n, 200
Egan, Douglas, 312n
Engel, Charles, 132n
Errunza, Vihang, 310n
Eun, Cheol, 324, 547n, 549n, 552n, 554n, 557n, 558n, 559n

Falloon, William, 369n
Fama, Eugene, 126, 127n
Finnerty, John, 648
Fisher, Irving, 118
Folks, William R., Jr., 295n
Forsgren, Mats, 480n
Frankel, Jeffrey, 25
Frenkel, Jacob A., 113n, 124n
Friedman, Irving S., 428n
Friedman, Milton, 500n
Froot, Kenneth A., 185n

Garman, Mark, 148n, 176
Gernon, Helen, 254n
Gibson, Robert W., 460n
Giddy, Ian H., 47n, 48n, 124n, 126, 413n, 415n, 417n
Glaum, M., 199n
Gonzalez, Manolete, 519n
Goodman, Stephen, 127n
Goodwin, Barry K., 113n
Grabbe, J. Orlin, 148n
Grennes, Thomas, 113n
Gruber, W., 472n
Gultekin, Mustafa N., 295n
Gultekin, N. Bulent, 295n

Hachey, George A., 118n
Haendel, Dan, 515
Hamilton, David P., 181n
Hamilton, James D., 132n
Hedlund, Gunnar, 480n
Helm, Roy J., 528, 531
Hennart, Jean-François, 458, 459, 462n

Hirsch, Se'ev, 472n
Hodder, James E., 310n
Hogue, W. Dickerson, 469n
Houpt, James V., 421n, 422n
Howe, John, 324
Huang, Roger D., 327n
Hull, John, 148n
Husted, Steven, 113n
Hymer, Stephen, 473n, 476n

Jaaskelainen, Veikko, 48n
Jacque, Laurent L., 126n, 562n
Jacquillat, Bertrand, 563n
Janakiramanan, S., 324
Johansen, John, 480n
Johnson, Harry G., 113n, 124n
Jones, R.A., 414n

Kaen, Fred R., 118n
Kearney, A., John, 242n
Kelly, Marie E. Wicks, 528
Kelm, Kathrun, 324
Kensinger, John W., 339n
Keown, Arthur J., 339n
Kerkvliet, Joe, 463n
Kester, Carl, 304n, 310n, 312
Khoury, Sarkis, 199n, 428n
Kindleberger, Charles, 473n
Knickerbocker, Frederick, 475
Kobrin, Stephen, 501
Kohlhagen, Steven, 126, 148n, 176
Kwok, C.K. Chuck, 309, 310n

Lau, Sie Ting, 323n
Laughlin, Terrence, 400n
Lecraw, David, 458n, 463
Lee, Hsien Loong, 511
Lee, Kwang Chul, 309, 310n
Lessard, Don, 562n
Levi, Maurice D., 184n
Levich, Richard M., 124n, 127n
Lewent, Judy C., 242n
Logue, Dennis E., 124n
Lothian, James R., 113n
Lorsch, Jay, 12n
Lynch, M.F., 570

MacKenzie, Chris, 461n
Magee, Stephen P., 113n, 116n
Mann, Catherine L., 116n
Manzur, Meher, 113n
March, James, 479n

Markowitz, Harry, 549n
Mascarenhas, Briance, 433n
Mattione, Richard P., 428n
McCartney, Robert J., 147n
Meek, Gary, 254n
Mehta, D., 472n
Mellor, Robert, 199n
Michel, Allen, 309n
Miller, Merton, 312
Mishkin, Frederick, 118n
Modigliani, Franco, 312
Moffett, Michael H., 48n, 74n, 116n, 204n, 400n, 423n, 489n, 643n, 663n
Mon, Stephanie, 661n
Moxon, Richard, 475n
Mueller, Gerhard, 254n, 258n

Nathanson, Leonard, 528
Nehrt, Lee, 469n
Ness, Walter L., 303n

Oblak, David J., 528, 531
Obstfeld, Maurice, 118n
Officer, Lawrence H., 113n
Ohmae, Kenichi, 59n

Papp, Bela, 439n
Parés, Antonio, 312n
Penati, Alessandro, 295n
Philippatos, George C., 528
Porter, Michael, 472
Proffitt, Dennis, 560, 561n

Raghavan, Anita, 282n
Ravn, Niels, 222n
Ree, Howard C., 413n
Reed, Barbara M., 269n
Reed, Howard C., 413n
Remmers, Lee, 310n, 312n
Ricardo, David, 2–3

Robbins, Sidney M., 601
Rogalski, Richard J., 113n
Ross, S.A., 174
Rowthorn, Robert, 476n
Rubenstein, M., 174
Rugman, Alan R., 478
Rush, Mark, 113n
Rutterford, Janette, 312

Sand, Ole C., 433n
Sarathy, Ravi, 310n
Saudagaran, Shahrokh M., 323n, 324, 326n
Schaefer, Doug, 628n
Scharfstein, David S., 185n
Scherreik, Susan, 322n
Scholes, Myron, 148, 176
Seitz,, Neil, 560, 561n
Sekely, William, 310–311
Senbet, Lemma W., 310n
Sercu, Piet, 184n
Servan-Schreiber, J.J., 471, 508
Sesit, Michael R., 282n, 345n
Shaked, Israel, 309n
Shapiro, Alan C., 310n, 312n
Sharpe, William F., 561, 562
Siconolfi, Michael, 84n
Siltz, J. David, 323n
Simon, Herbert, 479n
Simos, Evangelos O., 118n
Smith, Adam, 2–3
Smith, Clifford W., Jr., 184n, 648n
Smithson, Charles W., 184n, 648n
Soen, Luc A., 199n
Solnick, Bruno H., 130–131, 550n, 562n, 563n
Srinivasulu, Sam, 654n
Stanley, Marjorie, 310n, 528, 529, 531
Stapleton, Richard C., 286n
Steely, Robert, 439n
Stein, Jeremy C., 185n

Stitzel, Tom, 310n
Stobaugh, Robert B., 601
Stoll, Hans, R., 327n
Stonehill, Arthur I., 222n, 288n, 294n, 310n, 312n, 423n, 528, 628n
Stultz, Rene M., 184n, 185n
Subrahmanyam, Màrti, 286n
Sutton, William, 204n
Suzuki, Sadahiko, 310n
Sweeney, Paul, 593n
Sweeney, Richard J., 124n

Taussig, Russell, 257
Tobin, James, 549n
Tomkins, Robert, 395n
Toy, Norman, 310n, 312n
Treynor, Jack, 561, 562
Trimble, John L., 295n
Turner, Martyn, 659n

Vahlne, Jan Erik, 480n
Varma, Raj, 295n
Vernon, Raymond, 472n, 473n, 474
Villanueva, Edwin, 519n
Vinso, Joseph D., 113n

Wakeman, Lee MacDonald, 388n
Walter, Ingo, 71, 113n, 418
Wartzman, Rick, 570n
Wan, Victor, 199n
Wehataley, S., 295n
Weidersheim-Paul, F., 480n
White, Bouck, 190
Wihlborg, Clas, 127n
Wilford, D. Sykes, 184n
Willett, Thomas D., 124n
Williamson, Oliver, 478n
Wohlgenant, Michael K., 113n
Woodward, Douglas P., 570n
Wright, Richard, 310n, 312n

Subject Index

Page numbers followed by n indicate footnotes.

Absolute purchasing power parity, 112
Acceptances, 449–451
Accounting exposure
  balance sheet hedge, 265–267
  comparison with operating exposure, 261–262
  current rate method, 252–253, 256–260, 266–267
  consolidated accounts, 262–265
  cumulative translation adjustment (CTA) account, 253, 256, 258–259
  described, 251–254
  exposure reports, 262–265
  exposed assets, 258–260, 265
  functional currency, 251–252, 254–257
  hyperinflation countries, 257
  income statement translation, 258
  management of, 261, 265–268, 347
  minimizing exposure, transaction or accounting, 267–268
  monetary balance, 265
  monetary/non-monetary method, 252–254, 257–261, 265–267
  reporting currency, 254–256
  technical aspects of, 254–257
  temporal method, 252, 254, 256
  time of recognizing gains and losses, 256–257
  translation example, 257–264
Accounts receivable
  payment terms, 623–624
  sales to independent customers, 623
  self-liquidating bills, 624
Acquisition investments, 70–71, 325
ADR. See American Depository Receipt.
Ad valorem duty, 608
Affiliates, in banking, 422
Agency theory, 11–12
Agreement Corporation. See Edge Act and Agreement Corporation.
Allied-Lyons, 4–5
Algebraic parity, 142–145
American Depository Receipt (ADR), 292, 321–324, 337–338
American terms (in foreign exchange market), 92–93
Apple Computer, 369
APV. See Adjusted present value.

Arbitrage, 84, 99, 334–336
ARO. See Average Rate Option.
ARCO, 4–5
Argentina, 14, 36, 80
Arm's length banking, 416
Arm's length price, 606, 609
Asian option, 660–661
Ask quotation, 94
Average rate option (ARO), 660–661

Back-to-back
  loans, 238–240, 611
  swaps, 385–387
Balance of payments
  "above the line," 61
  analytical arrangement, 61–66
  basic balance, 64–66
  "below the line," 61
  capital flow impact, 70–71
  current account, 63–64, 66
  debits and credits, 61–63
  deficit and/or surplus, 60
  defined, 60
  economic development, 68–69
  exceptional financing, 65
  forecasting exchange rate changes, 10, 108–109, 129–133
  foreign authorities' reserves, 65–66
  Germany's balance of payments, 73
  imbalances, 67–69
  interpretation of, 59, 66–67, 70–71
  Japan's balance of payments, 72–73
  liabilities constituting foreign authorities' reserves, 65–66
  managed float, 68
  measurement of, 60–67
  monetary reserves, 66
  official settlements balance, 65–66
  overall balance, 65–66
  trade balance, 62, 66
  United States' balance of payments, 62–63, 72–73
Balance of trade, 62, 66
Balance sheet hedge, 265–267
Bang & Olufsen, 336, 339
Bank for International Settlements (BIS), 86–92
Banking, international
  affiliates, 422
  branch banks, 420–421
  capital adequacy standards, 418

  centralized cash depositories, 615–617
  commercial risk, 427
  correspondent banks, 419
  country risk, 412, 427–434
  currency risk, 431
  Edge Act and Agreement Corporation, 419, 422–425
  Giro transfer systems, 425–426
  in-house banks, 625–626
  interest charge calculation, 426
  International Banking Facility (IBF), 416–417, 419, 422–423
  international financial centers, 412–416, 580–582
  letters of credit, 440–448, 454–455
  loans, 350–352
  representative offices, 419–420
  risks, 427–433
  services, of banks, 425–427
  sovereign risk, 71, 430
  strategies, 416–419
  subsidiaries, 421–422
  syndicated loans, 352–354, 429
  types of offices, 419–425
Banque Commercial pour L'Europe du Nord, 47
Barclays Bank PLC, 4–5, 570–571
Barter, 438, 460
Basic balance, balance of payments, 64–66
Basis risk, 370–371
B/E (bill of exchange). See Draft.
Below the line, balance of payments, 61
Bid and offer (ask) foreign exchange quotations, 94–95
"Big bang," 17, 284
"Big Mac" standard, 110–112
Bill of exchange. See Draft.
Bill of lading, 440–441, 452–453
BIS. See Bank for International Settlements.
B/L. See Bill of lading.
Blocked funds, 610–614
Bond market, 350, 357–363
Bond ratings, 361–363
Branch banks, 420–421
Branch form of organization for taxes, 421
Bretton Woods Agreement, 30–31
Brokers, foreign exchange, 85–86

Bulldogs, 357
Buyback agreement, 461

California unitary tax, 570–571
Call options, 147, 153–156
Capital adequacy, banks, 418
Capital budgeting
  defined, 6, 9
  cash flows, 526–528, 531, 536–540
  discount rate, 526, 530
  foreign complexities, 526–527
  foreign exchange risk, 540–541
  illustrative case (Kimtron), 532–541
  political risk, 538–540
  project vs. parent valuation, 527–532
  risk adjustment, parent viewpoint, 530
  risk adjustment, project viewpoint, 531–532
  sensitivity analysis, 537–539, 541
  working capital, 532
Capital flight, 71
Capital flows, 41, 70–71, 308–309
Capital markets, 282–288, 294–295
Capital structure. See Financial structure.
Caps, interest rate, 387–393, 395
Cash-balances
  blocked funds, 610–611
  centralized depositories, 615–617
  dividend remittances, 600–601
  management of, 615–621
  multinational netting, 620–621
  planning, 617–620
  royalties and fees, 601–604
  transfer pricing, 604–610
Cash flows, 10, 221, 526–528, 531, 536–540
Cayman Islands, 9, 414
Centralized cash depositories, 615–617
Certificate of analysis, 453–454
CFO. See Chief financial officer.
Cheung Kong Holdings, 9
Chicago Board Options Exchange, 146, 148
Chicago Mercantile Exchange.
  See also International Money Market.
Chief financial officer, 10
China, People's Republic of, 80, 467, 512
CHIPS. See Clearing House Interbank Payments System.
CIA. See Covered interest arbitrage.
Clearing arrangements in countertrade, 460
Clearing House Interbank Payments System (CHIPS), 91
Clinton, Bill, 16
Coberturas, 646, 652–653

Code Napoléon, 624n
Collars, option, 393–394
Commercial letter of credit. See Credit, letter of.
Comparative advantage, 2, 22–24
Compensation agreements, 461
Competitive advantage, 470
Competitive exposure. See Operating exposure.
Complex options, 654
Consolidated financial statements, 262–265
Consular invoices, 453
Contractual hedges, 188–203
Controlled foreign corporations, 588–590
Convergence criteria, for European Monetary Union, 45
Corporate wealth maximization model (CWM), 12
Correspondent banks, 419
Corruption and risk, 508–509
Cost of capital
  adjustment for risk, 530–531
  debt, 302–303, 305–306, 347–349
  equity, 301–302, 305–306.
  market imperfections,
  market liquidity, 282–284
  market segmentation, 281–282, 284–288, 294–295
  optimal structure, 283
  taxation, 289–290, 302–303
  weighted average, 282, 301–303, 305–308
Cost of debt, 302–303, 305–306, 347–349
Cost of equity, 301–302, 305–306
Counterparty risk, 240n, 397–399
Counterpurchase, 461–462
Countertrade, 438, 458–463
Country risk, 412, 427–434
Covered interest arbitrage (CIA), 121–124, 143
Covering against exchange risk. See Hedging against transaction exposure.
Credit, in balance of payments, 61–63
Credit, letter of (L/C), 440–448, 454–455
Credit swaps, 238–240
Crisis of 1971, 32
Crisis planning and risk, 519–521
Cross border financial markets, 345
Cross hedging, 645
Cross listing, 322–331
Cross rates, 98–99
CTA Account. See Cumulative translation adjustment account.
Cuba, 80, 502, 512–513
Cumulative translation adjustment

account (CTA), 253, 256, 258–259
Currency arrangements, 37–41
Currency clauses, and risk sharing, 234–235
Currency futures. See Futures in foreign exchange.
Currency hedge ratio, 642–648
Currency matching, 347
Currency options. See Options.
Currency risk, management of, 641–663. See also Exposure.
Currency swaps, 240–241, 384–387
Currency switching, 238
Current account, in balance of payments, 63–64, 66
Current assets, 346–347
Current rate translation method, 252–253, 256–260, 266–267
CWM. See Corporate wealth maximization model.

Daimler-Benz, 16, 281–282, 295, 326
Dealers, foreign exchange, 83–84
Debt capital, sourcing
  bond markets, 357–363
  debt management and funding goals, 345–350
  Eurocredits, 351–352
  Euronotes, 353–357
  foreign exchange risk, 347–349
  instrument choices, 350–357
  cost of debt, 302–303, 305–306, 347–349
  currency matching, 347
  maturity matching, 345–347
  syndicated credits, 352–354, 429
Debit, in balance of payments, 61–63
Debt crisis, 36
Debt for equity swaps, 433–434
Deemed paid credit, 584, 587
Deficit, in balance of payments, 60
Delta hedge, 645–648
Depository receipts, 323–324. See also American Depository receipts.
Depreciation, of exchange rates, 27
Derivatives, 396–397, 646
Deterioration, of exchange rates, 27
Devaluation, of exchange rates, 27
DFI. See Direct foreign investment.
Direct foreign exchange quotations, 93, 97, 100
Direct foreign investment (DFI), 3, 9, 70
DISC. See Domestic international sales corporation.
Disclosure requirements, 281–282, 325–327, 360–361
Discriminatory regulation, 510–511

Disney. *See* Euro-Disney.
Diversification, 230–233
Dividend remittances, 600–601
Dollar sign, history, 93
Domestic International Sales
    Corporation (DISC), 589–590
Draft, 440–441, 448–451

Eastman Kodak, 219–220, 242–243
Economic development, 68–69, 507
Economic exposure. *See* Operating
    exposure.
Economic motives, for direct foreign
    investment, 9
Economies of scale, 471
ECP. *See* Euro-Commercial paper.
ECU. *See* European Currency Unit.
Edge Act and Agreement Corporation,
    419, 422–425
EEC. *See* European Economic Commu-
    nity.
Efficient capital markets, 11, 284–285
EFTA. *See* European Free Trade Associ-
    ation.
EMS. *See* European Monetary System.
EMTN. *See* Euro-medium-term notes.
EMU. *See* European Monetary Union.
Equilibrium in foreign exchange
    markets, 122–124, 127–128.
Equity capital, sourcing, 331–334
Equity-related bonds, 358–360
ERM. *See* European Rate Mechanism.
Eurobanks, 47
Eurobonds
    market, 349, 357–358
    Novo Industri issue, 291
    rating systems, 361–363
    unique characteristics, 360–361
Euro-commercial paper (ECP), 353,
    355–356
Eurocredits, 351–352
Eurocurrencies, 46–48, 422, 429. *See
    also* Eurodollars.
Euro-Disney, 3, 525–526
Eurodollars
    characteristics, 46–47
    creation, 56–58
    credits, 351–352
    defined, 351
    history, 47–48
    line of credit, 352
    loans, 417
    revolving commitment, 352
    syndicated credit, 352–353
Euro-equities, 331, 333–334
Euromarkets, 283, 296
Euromarks, 46
Euro medium term notes (EMTN), 353,
    356–357

Euronote market, 353–357
Eurosterling, 46
Euroyen, 46
European Currency Unit (ECU), 41–46
European Economic Community (EEC),
    473
European Free Trade Association
    (EFTA), 473
European Monetary System (EMS),
    33–34, 36, 38, 41–46, 85
European Monetary Union (EMU),
    45–46.
European rate mechanism (ERM),
    25–26, 43–45
European terms, in foreign exchange
    market, 92–93
European Union, 38, 417–418
Exchange rate mechanism, 43–45
Exchange rate regimes, 27, 37–41
Exchange rates. *See also* Foreign
    exchange.
    American terms, 92–93
    appreciation, 27
    balance of payments, 67–68
    defined, 26–27
    depreciation, 27
    deterioration, 27
    devaluation, 27
    dirty float, 40
    exotic currencies, 645–646
    fixed, 27–28, 31–32, 41, 67–68
    flexible, 27–29, 127–128
    floating, 27, 32, 38–40, 68
    forecasting (predicting), 10, 108–109,
        129–133
    foreign exchange market, 80–100
    forward, 91–92, 124
    gold standard, 28–30
    hard, 27
    managed, 27, 39–40, 68
    parity conditions, 6, 108–133,
        142–145
    par value, 27–28
    pass-through, 116–117
    pegged, 37–38, 40
    portfolio implications, 557–559
    quotations, 92–100
    real effective rates, 114–115
    revaluation, 27
    risk, 10
    soft, 27
    spot, 91
    strengthening, 27
    upvaluation, 27
    weakening, 27
Exchange risk and exposure. *See*
    Exposure.
Ex-Im Bank. *See* Export-Import Bank.
Exotic currencies, 645–646

Exotic options, 653, 658–662
Export credit insurance, 456–458
Export-Import Bank (of U.S.), 458
Exports. *See* Imports and Exports.
Exposed assets, 258–260, 265
Exposure
    accounting, 8, 182
    advanced approaches, 641–662
    operating, 8, 182, 219–244
    transaction, 8, 181–204
Expropriation, 502. *See also* Political
    risk.

Factor market imperfections, 473–477
FAS No. 8. *See* Statement of Financial
    Accounting Standards No. 8.
FAS No. 52. *See* Statement of Financial
    Accounting Standards No. 52.
FASB No. 8. *See* Statement of Financial
    Accounting Standards No. 8.
FASB No. 52. *See* Statement of
    Financial Accounting Standards
    No. 52.
FCIA. *See* Foreign Credit Insurance
    Association.
Fifth directive of European Union, 19
Finance theory. *See* Theory of finance.
Financial Accounting Standards Board.
    See Statement of Financial
    Accounting Standards.
Financial strategies and risk, 518–519
Financial structure
    capital availability, 306–308
    debt norms, 310–313
    foreign affiliates, 309–315
    operating exposure, 232
    optimal, 283, 305–309
    risk reduction, 308–309
    sources of funds, 315–317
Finland, 48–53
Fisher Effect, 118–119, 144–145, 232
Fixed exchange rates, 27–28, 31–32, 41,
    67–68
Flexible exchange rates, 27–29,
    127–128
Floating exchange rates, 15, 109
Floating rate notes (FRN), 358
Follow the customer theory, 477
Follow the leader theory, 475–476
Ford Motor Company, 256
Forecasting exchange rate changes, 10,
    108–109, 129–133
Foreign bonds, 357
Foreign Credit Insurance Association
    (FCIA), 456–457
Foreign currency futures. *See* Futures in
    foreign exchange.
Foreign exchange. *See also* Exchange
    rates.

arbitragers, 84
brokers, 85–86
cross rates, 98–99
dealers, 83–84
defined, 81
forecasting, 108–109, 129–133
functions of market, 10, 82–83
futures, 105–107
market, 80–100
market participants, 83–86
market size, 86–91
options. *See* Options.
quotations, 92–100
regimes, 27, 37–41
reserves, 62, 65–66
risk, 15, 83, 286, 600
speculation, 84
transactions, 81, 91–92
Foreign interest rates, 374–375
Foreign investment decision, 468
Foreign sales corporation (FSC),
    589–591
Foreign tax credit (FTC), 584–588
Forward market hedge, 189–190,
    193–196
Forward exchange rates
    contracts, 6
    spot rates, 374–375
    synthetic forward, 649–652
    transactions, 91–92
    unbiased predictors, 124–127, 143
Forward rate agreement (FRA),
    375–376, 378–379, 395
Forward swaps, 377–378
FRA. *See* Forward rate agreement.
Free trade zones, 627
FRN. *See* Floating rate notes.
Fronting loans, 611–613
FSC. *See* Foreign sales corporation.
FTC. *See* Foreign Tax Credit.
Functional currency, 251–252,
    254–256, 257
Futures in foreign exchange
    compared to forward markets, 107
    contract specifications, 105–106
    quotations, 106–107

GAB. *See* General Agreement to
    Borrow.
Gap risk, 370
General Agreement on Tariffs and Trade
    (GATT), 590
General Agreement to Borrow (GAB),
    31
Giro transfer system, 425–426
Glaxo Holdings, plc., 359
Goal conflict, 15, 503–504, 507–508
Goals of management, 11
Gold exchange standard, 30–31

Gold standard, classical, 28–30
Gold tranche, 30
Gorbachev, Mikhail S., 9
Greenfield investments, 70–71
Grossed up, in dividend taxation, 537,
    586
Group of Five, 34, 36, 108
Group of Ten, 36
Growth to survive attitude, 476–477

"Hamburger Standard," 110–112
Hard currency, defined, 27
Havens, in taxation, 580–582
Hedge ratio, 642–648
Hedging, against transaction exposure,
    188–199
Hidden reserves, 281–282
Holder in due course, 449
Hyperinflation countries, 257

IBF. *See* International Banking Facility.
IMF. *See* International Monetary Fund.
IMM. *See* International Money Market
    of Chicago.
Imperfections in markets, 13
Imperialism, 507–508
Imports and Exports
    additional documents, 453–454
    benefits of system, 440–442
    blocked funds, 610–614
    countertrade, 438, 458–463
    credit systems, 456–458
    bill of lading, 440–441, 452–453
    dilemma, 439–440
    documentation example, 454–456
    draft, 440–441, 448–451
    letter of credit (L/C), 440, 441–448
    negotiable instruments, 449
    world trade profile, 69
Indexes of stock markets, 296
Indirect foreign exchange quotation,
    92–93, 96–97, 99–100
Infant industry protection, 507
Information barriers, 285
Interbank quotations, 92–94
Interest charge calculation, banks,
    426–427
Interest rate cap and floor, 387–393,
    395
Interest rate collars, 393–395
Interest rate parity, 119–124, 143–144
Interest rate risk
    counterparty risk, 240n, 397–399
    defined, 369–373
    management of, 370, 373–376
    option-based instruments and
        techniques, 387–397
    outright instruments and techniques,
        377–387

Interest rate swaps, 379–384
Internalization theory, 477–478
International Bank for Reconstruction
    and Development. *See* World
    Bank.
International Banking Facility (IBF),
    416–417, 419, 422–423
International financial centers,
    412–416, 580–582
International firms, defined, 3
International Fisher effect, 118–119
International Monetary Fund (IMF),
    30–31, 114
International monetary system. *See*
    Monetary system.
International Money Market of Chicago
    (IMM), 105–107
International Offshore Financial
    Centers (IOFC), 580–582
Inventory management, 626–627
IOFC. *See* International Offshore Finan-
    cial Centers.
Irrevocable letter of credit, 446

Jamaica Agreement of 1976, 33–34, 36
Japan, 16, 59, 231, 304, 334–336
Joint float, 38
Joint ventures, 482–483

Kiwi, 94
Knowledge seekers, 469–470, 477

Lags. *See* Leads and lags.
Latin American debt crisis, 36
Law of one price, 110–115, 142
L/C. *See* Credit, letter of.
Leads and lags, 233–234
Letter of credit. *See* Credit, letter of.
LIBOR. *See* London Interbank Offered
    Rate.
Licensing, 486–487
Link financing, 611–613
Liquidity, 282–284, 328
Loan syndication, 352–354, 429
London Stock Exchange, 330–331
London Interbank Offered Rate
    (LIBOR), 352–353, 369,
    372–373, 380–382,384,
    388–390, 392–394
Louvre Accord, 34, 36

Maastrich, 45–46
Managed exchange rates, 15, 39–40
Management contracts, 486–487
Managerial expertise, 471
Maquiladora plants, 256
Market seekers, 469–470, 473–474
Marketing expertise, 471
Marketing strategies and risk, 518

Maturity matching of debt, 345–347, 376–377, 395
Merck, 242–243, 247
Merger mode of entry, 483
Mexico, 36, 81, 256, 411, 652–653
Moody's Investors Services, 361
Monetary/nonmonetary translation method, 252–254, 257–261, 265–267
Monetary balance, 265
Monetary policy, 41, 504–505
Monetary system
  international system, 25–48
  Bretton Woods Agreement, 30–31
  contemporary currency arrangements, 37–46
  crisis, 32
  currencies adjusted according to indicators, 38
  defined, 26
  European Currency Unit (ECU), 41–43
  European Monetary System (EMS), 41–46
  Exchange Rate Mechanism (ERM), 43–45
  Eurocurrencies, 46–48, 56–58
  fixed exchange rate period, 31–32
  flexible currencies, 37
  floating exchange rates, 15, 109
  foreign exchange markets, 80–110
  gold standard, 28–31
  history of, 28–37
  independently floating currencies, 40
  inter-war years (1914–1944), 29–30
  Jamaica Agreement of 1976, 33
  joint float currencies, 38
  managed float currencies, 39–40
  Maastricht, 45–46
  pegged currencies, 37
  terminology, 26–27
  world currency events table, 36
Money market hedge, 190–192, 195–196
Morgan Grenfell Group PLC, 290–292
Morgan Guaranty Trust Company, 33, 291
Moscow Narodny Bank, 47
Motives for direct foreign investment, 9
Multinational firms, defined, 3
Mutual fund performance, 560–562

NAFTA. See North American Free Trade Agreement.
Natural hedges, 237–238
Negotiable instruments, 449
Netting, multilateral cash, 620–621
New York Stock Exchange, 281, 295, 328–331

Newspaper quotations, 97–98, 106–107
Nixon, Richard M., 36
Noncompletion risk. See counterparty risk.
Nondiscriminatory regulation, 510
Nominal effective exchange rates, 114–115
Nontariff barriers, 505–506
North American Free Trade Agreement (NAFTA), 2, 411, 653
Novo-Nordisk A/S, 288n
Novo Industri, A/S, 288–294, 325, 332, 476, 564

OECD. See Organization for Economic Cooperation and Development.
Official settlements balance, balance of payments, 65–66
Oklahoma letter, 417
One-share-one-vote rule, 12
OPEC. See Organization of Petroleum Exporting Countries.
Operating cash flow, 221
Operating exposure
  compared with accounting exposure, 261–262
  compared with transaction exposure, 220–221
  contractual hedging, 242–243
  defined and contrasted, 182
  example of (Eastman Kodak), 220–221
  illustration of, 223–230
  impact of, 222–223
  management of, 230–243, 347
  survey of practices, 241–242
  vocabulary of, 147–148
OPIC. See Overseas Private Investment Corporation.
Options
  activate/deactivate options, 659–660
  average rate options (ARO), 660–661
  average strike options (ASO), 660–661
  barrier options, 659–660
  calendar spread options, 655n
  chooser options, 662
  collar options, 655
  complex options, 654
  compound options, 661–662
  cylinder options, 655
  definitions, 147–148
  delta (spot rate sensitivity), 161–162, 170, 645–648
  down and out options (DAO), 659–660
  exotic options, 653, 658–662
  extinguishable options, 659–660
  fence options, 655

flexible forward options, 655
forward participation agreement, 657
knock-out options, 659–660
markets, 148–151
mini-max options, 655
options on options, 661–662
optimal hedge ratio, 642–645
participating forward options, 654, 657–658
path-dependent options, 660
quotations and prices, 150–151
phi (foreign interest rate sensitivity), 167–168, 170
pricing and valuation, 158–170, 176–178
range forward options, 654–657
ratio spreads, 654–655
rho (domestic interest rate sensitivity), 167–168, 170
speculation with, 151–158
synthetic forward options, 656
theta (time to maturity changes), 162–164, 170
used as a hedge, 146, 192–196
vega (volatility sensitivity), 164, 170
zero cost ratio options, 657
zero-cost tunnel options, 655
zero premium options, 653–654
Organization for Economic Cooperation and Development (OECD), 231
Organization of Petroleum Exporting Countries (OPEC), 36
Outright foreign exchange quotation, 94–95
Outright forward transaction, 91–92
Overall balance, balance of payments, 65–66
Overdraft, 426
Overseas Private Investment Corporation (OPIC), 516
Overvalued currency, 115
Ownership structure. See Financial structure.

Parallel loans, 238–240, 611
Parent guarantees, 316
Parity in exchange rates, 6, 108–133, 142–145
Pass-through, 116–117
Percentage quotations, 96–97
Philadelphia Stock Exchange, 148–149
Philippines, 520–521
Plain vanilla swap, 379
Plaza Accord, 34, 36, 108
Points in forward exchange market, 94–96
Political risk
  assessing, 513–515
  capital budgeting, 538–540

corruption, 508–509
cost of capital, 285–286
crisis planning, 519–521
defined, 501
dividend policy, 600
ethnic, racial, religious, tribal, and civil strife, 503
expropriation risk, 502
goal conflict, 503–504, 507–508
host government regulations, 509–513
micro risks, 503–509
techniques for dealing with, 515–521
Political safety seekers, 469–470
Portfolio approach to country risk, 431–433
Portfolio investors, 290
Portfolio optimization, 553–557
Portfolio theory, 9, 431–433, 547–565
Positioning of funds, 599
Possessions corporation, 592–593
PPP. See purchasing power parity.
Price freezes, 627
Prices and exchange rates, 110
Product cycle theory, 474–475
Product market imperfections, 473–477
Production-efficiency seekers, 469–470
Production strategies and risk, 517–518
Protectionism, 505–506
Purchasing power parity, 110–117, 127–128, 142–143
Puts, in options, 147, 156–158

Quotations of exchange rates, 92–100

Random walks, 284
Range forward options, 654–657
Raw material seekers, 469–470, 473–474
Real effective exchange rates, 114–115
Receivables. See Accounts receivable.
Regulatory barriers, 285
Reinvoicing centers, 235–237
Reporting currency, 254–256
Reporting, financial. See Accounting, in multinational business.
Representative offices in banking, 419–420
Revaluation of exchange rates, 27
Revolving commitment, Eurodollars, 352
Revolving underwriting facility (RUF), 353
Risk
advanced approaches to managing, 641–662
banking, 427–433

capital budgeting considerations, 530–532
commercial, 427
cost of capital influenced by, 286, 290–291
counterparty, 398–399
country, 427–433
currency, 428, 431
financial, 370
interest rate, 370–376
measurement, 9
political, 428
portfolio diversification, 548–560
refunding of debt, 347
risk/return trade-off, 13, 551–560
sovereign, 428–430
systematic and unsystematic, 11
Royalties, 601–604
RUF. See Revolving underwriting facilities.

Samurai bonds, 357
SDR. See Special drawing right.
Section 482, Internal Revenue Code, 609
Securities and Exchange Commission (U.S.), 325, 327, 332–333
Segmented capital markets, 281–282, 284–288, 294–295
Self-fulfilling prophecies, 614
SFAS. See Statement of Financial Accounting Standards No. 8 and No. 52.
Shareholder wealth maximization model (SWM), 11
SIMEX. See Singapore International Monetary Exchange.
Singapore, 14, 94, 511
Singapore International Monetary Exchange, 105
Single European Act of 1985, 417.
Single European Market (1992), 417, 474
Small country bias, 285–286
Smithsonian Agreement of 1971, 32, 36
SNIF. See Standby note issuance facility
Soft currency, defined, 27
Sourcing debt. See Debt capital, sourcing.
Sourcing equity. See Equity capital, sourcing.
Sovereign risk, 71, 430
Soviet Union, 30
Special drawing right (SDR), 31
Speculation in foreign exchange markets, 84
Spot exchange rates and transactions, 91, 94–98
Standard and Poor's, 361–363

Standby note issuance facility (SNIF), 353
Statement of Financial Accounting Standards No. 8 (FAS No. 8, SFAS No. 8, or FASB No. 8), 254
Statement of Financial Accounting Standards No. 52 (FAS No. 52, SFAS No. 52, or FASB No. 52), 253, 257
Sterling, 94
Stock exchanges, 328–331
Stock market indices, 296
Straight fixed-rate bonds, 358
Strategic alliances, 485–486
Strategic motives for direct foreign investment, 9
Subpart F, 583, 588–590
Subsidiaries of banks, 421–422
Swaps
back-to-back loans, 238–240
credit, 238–240
currency, 240–241, 379, 384–387
debt for equity, 433–434
derivatives, 396–397
forward, 377–378
interest rate, 379–384
parallel loans, 238–240
plain vanilla, 379
rate, 95–96
shares of stock, 325
swaption, 395
transaction, 92
Switch trade, 460–461
SWM. See Shareholder wealth maximization model.
Syndicated loans, 352–354, 429
Synthetic forward, 649–652
Systematic risk, 11

Takeover defenses, 285–286, 484–485
Tariffs, 608
Taxes
ad valorem duties, 608
anonymity, 361
branch taxation, 579–580
controlled foreign corporations, 588–590
cost of capital, 289–290, 302–303
credit, foreign, 575, 584–588
deemed paid credit, 584, 587. See also Grossed up.
deferral, 580–582
dividend remittances, 600
Domestic International Sales Corporation (DISC), 589–590
environment, in nations, 573–578
foreign sales corporation (FSC), 589–591

foreign source income, 582–584
fronting loans, 612
grossed up, 537, 586
havens, 580–582
income, 577
intercompany transactions, 579
International Offshore Financial Centers (IOFC), 580–582
jurisdictions, 573–575
morality, 571–572
neutrality, 572–573
passive income, 583–584
planning, 571
possessions corporation, 592–593
royalties and fees, 602–604
Subpart F, 583, 588–590
subsidiary (incorporated), 579–580
transaction losses, 348n
transfer pricing, 579, 605–607
treaties, 575
types of, 577–578
value-added, 577
withholding, 577
Technical analysis of exchange rates, 129, 132
Technology, 471–472
Technology transfer, 15
Temporal translation method, 252, 254, 256
Tokyo Stock Exchange, 17, 329, 331, 334–336
Trade balance, balance of payments, 62, 66

Trade financing, 9, 438–463
Tranche, 30, 333
Transaction costs, in capital market segmentation, 285
Transaction exposure
  contractual hedges, 188–203
  defined, 182
  management of, 347
  measurement of, 186–188, 348
  operating hedges, 188
  strategy choice, 196–197
  types, 182–186
Transfer pricing
  fund positioning, 604–607
  joint ventures, 608
  managerial incentives, 607–608
  practices of corporations, 608–610
  tariff and quota effects, 608
  taxation effect, 579, 605–607
Translation exposure. See Accounting exposure.
Transnational corporations, 3, 14

Unbiased predictor, 124–128
Unbundling fund transfers, 486
Undervalued currencies, 115
Uniform Customs and Practices for Documentary Credits, 448
Unsystematic risk, 11

Value-added tax, 577–578
Vanilla (plain) swap, 379
Vietnam, 80, 512

WACC. See Weighted average cost of capital.
Weakening, of exchange rates, 27
Wealth deprivation, 511–513
Weighted average cost of capital (WACC), 282, 301–303, 526
Working capital management
  blocked funds, 610–614
  capital budgeting considerations, 532, 536
  cash balances, management of, 615–621
  dividend remittances, 600–601
  flows and stocks of funds, 598–599
  fronting loans, 611–613
  in-house banks, 625–626
  inventories, management of, 626–627
  overhead in home office, 601–604
  positioning funds, 599
  receivables, management of, 621–625
  royalties and fees, 601–604
  transfer pricing, 604–608
  unbundling fund transfers, 599
World Bank, 30
Writer of option contract, 147

Yankee bonds, 344, 357
Yeltsin, Boris, 503
YPF Sociedad Anonima, 337–338

Zero cost ratio option, 657
Zero cost tunnel options, 655
Zero-premium options, 653–654
Zhirinovsky, Vladimir, 503

Index of Named Cases and Problems

Adelaide, Ltd., and AB Lund (portfolio theory), 567
Allied-Lyons: Option Hedging Run Amok (options), 173–174
Austrian Exchange Rate and Tyrolean Rents (parity conditions), 135

Baltimore Pump Company (imports & exports), 464
Bank of Credit and Commerce International (BCCI) (banking), 435
Bayonne, S.A. (accounting exposure), 277
Bergersen Shipping (strategy), 495
Betting on the Nikkei (portfolio theory), 566
BOC Group, plc. (sourcing debt), 364
Bols Canned Foods (capital budgeting), 543
Borrowing Mexican Pesos (parity conditions), 137
British Columbia Hydro (interest rate risk), 400–406

Cache la Poudre Products of Colorado (sourcing debt), 365
CIA in Montreal (parity conditions), 137
Compaq's Hedging Policies (transaction exposure), 214
Computer International, Inc. (accounting exposure), 269–276
Computer Trading Screen: Spot Currency Quotations (foreign exchange market), 102
Covered Interest Arbitrage in Japan (parity conditions), 137
Cross Rates and Percentage Change (foreign exchange market), 101
Currency Cross Rates (foreign exchange market), 103
Currency Option Premiums and Alternative Strike Prices (options), 171
Cuzco, S.A. (working capital management), 637–638

Danish Segmentation: J. Lauritzen Holding & Carlsberg (sourcing equity), 341

Dayton Manufacturing (transaction exposure), 210. See also text, pp. 188–199.
Deutschebank's Strategy (banking), 435
Dole Pineapple: Hedging a Note Payable (transaction exposure), 215

Eastman Kodak: Hedging the Unhedgeable (operating exposure), 245–246
Ecuadorian Debt for Development (balance of payments), 74–77, 136
Eurocurrency Interest Rates and Forward Rates (foreign exchange market), 102–103
Euro-Currency Yield Curves (interest rate risk), 406
Eurowide Corporation (working capital management), 638

Failed Merger of Volvo and Renault (strategy), 496
Federal Republic of Brazil (sourcing debt), 364
Finnish Markka (monetary system), 48–53
Ford in Hungary (transaction exposure), 212
Ford Motor Company (sourcing debt), 365–366
Foreign Currency Pricing at K2 (parity conditions), 136
Forward Rates on the Australian Dollar (foreign exchange market), 102

Gekko & Fox Investment Banking (sourcing debt), 366
Gulliver Radio, Inc. (transaction exposure), 214–215

Hammersmith & Fulham Debacle (interest rate risk), 409. Also see text, p. 399
Hedging Hogs: Risk Sharing at Harley Davidson (operating exposure), 246–247
Hietaniemi Brewery (working capital management), 638

Ikea's Yen Exposure and Range Forward (advanced currency risk management), 670–671

Indian Rupiah (parity conditions), 138
Instruments Napoleon (operating exposure), 245; (accounting exposure), 276. Also see text, pp. 223–230, 257–267.
Integrated Markets and Diversification Benefits (portfolio theory), 566
Interest Rate Floors at SafeTeNet (interest rate risk), 408–409
Iowa Foods, Inc. (political risk), 522

Japan and Germany (parity conditions), 135

Kimtron Sensitivities (capital budgeting), 542. Also see text, pp. 532–541.
Knackwurst Corporation (capital budgeting), 542–543

L.A. Lever, Inc. (transaction exposure), 214
Lufthansa (transaction exposure), 204–209
Luxembourg Franc (foreign exchange market), 101

Macao Manufacturing (taxation), 595
McDonald's Hamburger Standard and the Law of One Price (parity conditions), 135. Also see text, pp. 110–112.
Mismatched Freddie Laker (operating exposure), 248

Naha Beach Club (imports and exports), 464–465
Namur Refrigeration Company (working capital management), 636–437
Nations of Alpine & Bayshore (parity conditions), 138
Nokia Oy's Acquisition Bid (advanced currency risk management), 671–672
Norwegian Transport (sourcing debt), 365
Novo Industri A/S (cost of capital), 288–294

Offset: The McDonnell Douglas-Finland Deal (imports & exports), 465

Operating Exposure at Compaq Computer (accounting exposure), 277

Operating Exposure: Merck (operating exposure), 247

Option Volatilities and Trader Expectations (options), 173

Pasadena Electronics (capital budgeting), 544–545

Pequot Indians and Foxwoods High Stakes Bingo Casino (strategy), 496

Platz-Ho, Inc. (sourcing debt), 366

Pricing Your Own Options: Calls on British Pounds (options), 171

Pricing Your Own Options: Puts on Deutschemarks (options), 171

Rover Sells Out (strategy), 495

Schnapps & Schnitzel (taxation), 595

Schweinfurt Ball Bearings, GmbH (taxation), 596

Shell Showa and Forward Contracts (transaction exposure), 213

Siemens Shares and Exchange Rate Changes (portfolio theory), 567

Silaca Glass, Inc. (strategy), 489–495

Sourcing from Thailand (operating exposure), 246

Smith and Jones (interest rate risk), 407

Sony Shares and Exchange Rate Changes (portfolio theory), 567

Speculation on the Movement of the Dutch Guilder (options), 173

Spich Corporation (sourcing debt), 365

Spot and Forward Market Sizes (foreign exchange market), 101

Statoil of Norway (operating exposure), 244–245, 246

Suislaw Corporation (cost of capital), 297–298

Teknekron Euro-Medium-Term Notes (sourcing debt), 366–367

Tektronix B (working capital management), 628–635

Tektronix: Hedging an Account Receivable (transaction exposure), 215–216

Torino Lock, S.A. (working capital management), 637

Unilever: Motives for Crosslisting (sourcing equity), 340

Utah International and Tokyo Power & Electric (transaction exposure), 212–213

Valdivia Vineyards (cost of capital), 299

Vivaldi Spice BHD (accounting exposure), 278

Willem Koopmans and Call Options Speculation (options), 171

Willem Koopmans and Put Options Speculation (options), 171

William Wong: CIA Back in Hong Kong (parity conditions), 137–138

Winnemucca's Interest Rate Cap (interest rate risk), 408

Wheat Trading (parity conditions), 135

Yankee Corporation and Kiso Kaido, K.K. (interest rate risk), 407

Yorkshire Industries and Huron River Salt Company (interest rate risk), 407–408

Yount Aircraft Parts of Phoenix (transaction exposure), 210

ZAPA Chemical and Buba (advanced currency risk management), 663–669

CURRENCY TRADING FROM THE WALL STREET JOURNAL

EXCHANGE RATES
Thursday, August 4, 1994

The New York foreign exchange selling rates below apply to trading among banks in amounts of $1 million and more, as quoted at 3 p.m. Eastern time by Bankers Trust Co., Dow Jones Telerate Inc. and other sources. Retail transactions provide fewer units of foreign currency per dollar.

Country	U.S. $ equiv. Thurs.	Wed.	Currency per U.S. $ Thurs.	Wed.
Argentina (Peso)	1.01	1.01	.99	.99
Australia (Dollar)	.7373	.7313	1.3563	1.3674
Austria (Schilling)	.08954	.09021	11.17	11.09
Bahrain (Dinar)	2.6522	2.6522	.3771	.3771
Belgium (Franc)	.03060	.03083	32.68	32.43
Brazil (Real)	1.1025358	1.1037528	.91	.91
Britain (Pound)	1.5350	1.5420	.6515	.6485
30-Day Forward	1.5338	1.5408	.6520	.6490
90-Day Forward	1.5317	1.5387	.6529	.6499
180-Day Forward	1.5290	1.5360	.6540	.6510
Canada (Dollar)	.7210	.7207	1.3870	1.3875
30-Day Forward	.7203	.7200	1.3883	1.3888
90-Day Forward	.7190	.7188	1.3908	1.3913
180-Day Forward	.7160	.7158	1.3966	1.3971
Czech. Rep. (Koruna)				
Commercial rate	.0351593	.0351593	28.4420	28.4420
Chile (Peso)	.002417	.002417	413.72	413.72
China (Renminbi)	.115221	.115221	8.6790	8.6790
Colombia (Peso)	.001226	.001226	815.62	815.62
Denmark (Krone)	.1601	.1615	6.2455	6.1929
Ecuador (Sucre)				
Floating rate	.000456	.000456	2192.02	2192.02
Finland (Markka)	.19135	.19303	5.2260	5.1804
France (Franc)	.18408	.18561	5.4325	5.3875
30-Day Forward	.18391	.18545	5.4373	5.3923
90-Day Forward	.18373	.18526	5.4428	5.3978
180-Day Forward	.18360	.18513	5.4465	5.4015
Germany (Mark)	.6299	.6346	1.5875	1.5758
30-Day Forward	.6296	.6343	1.5883	1.5766
90-Day Forward	.6296	.6343	1.5883	1.5766
180-Day Forward	.6305	.6352	1.5861	1.5744
Greece (Drachma)	.004169	.004206	239.85	237.75
Hong Kong (Dollar)	.12944	.12945	7.7255	7.7250
Hungary (Forint)	.0098971	.0098522	101.0400	101.5000
India (Rupee)	.03212	.03212	31.13	31.13
Indonesia (Rupiah)	.0004619	.0004619	2165.02	2165.02
Ireland (Punt)	1.5153	1.5246	.6599	.6559
Israel (Shekel)	.3298	.3298	3.0320	3.0320
Italy (Lira)	.0006312	.0006371	1584.33	1569.51
Japan (Yen)	.009968	.009965	100.32	100.35
30-Day Forward	.009990	.009987	100.10	100.13
90-Day Forward	.010033	.010030	99.67	99.70
180-Day Forward	.010113	.010110	98.88	98.91
Jordan (Dinar)	1.4725	1.4725	.6791	.6791
Kuwait (Dinar)	3.3565	3.3565	.2979	.2979
Lebanon (Pound)	.000596	.000596	1676.50	1676.50
Malaysia (Ringgit)	.3896	.3883	2.5665	2.5750
Malta (Lira)	2.7027	2.7027	.3700	.3700
Mexico (Peso)				
Floating rate	.2963402	.2966039	3.3745	3.3715
Netherland (Guilder)	.5610	.5652	1.7826	1.7692
New Zealand (Dollar)	.6032	.6003	1.6578	1.6658
Norway (Krone)	.1441	.1453	6.9382	6.8807
Pakistan (Rupee)	.0328	.0328	30.53	30.53
Peru (New Sol)	.4696	.4696	2.13	2.13
Philippines (Peso)	.03812	.03812	26.23	26.23
Poland (Zloty)	.00004366	.00004380	22906.00	22833.01
Portugal (Escudo)	.006187	.006222	161.62	160.73
Saudi Arabia (Riyal)	.26664	.26664	3.7504	3.7504
Singapore (Dollar)	.6631	.6636	1.5080	1.5070
Slovak Rep. (Koruna)	.0315557	.0315557	31.6900	31.6900
South Africa (Rand)				
Commercial rate	.2760	.2747	3.6233	3.6400
Financial rate	.2198	.2198	4.5500	4.5500
South Korea (Won)	.0012460	.0012460	802.60	802.60
Spain (Peseta)	.007657	.007704	130.60	129.80
Sweden (Krona)	.1289	.1297	7.7557	7.7112
Switzerland (Franc)	.7460	.7508	1.3405	1.3320
30-Day Forward	.7461	.7509	1.3403	1.3318
90-Day Forward	.7468	.7515	1.3391	1.3306
180-Day Forward	.7486	.7534	1.3358	1.3273
Taiwan (Dollar)	.037682	.037682	26.54	26.54
Thailand (Baht)	.04005	.04005	24.97	24.97
Turkey (Lira)	.0000320	.0000319	31207.76	31361.61
United Arab (Dirham)	.2723	.2723	3.6725	3.6725
Uruguay (New Peso)				
Financial	.199860	.199860	5.00	5.00
Venezuela (Bolivar)	.00590	.00590	169.57	169.57
SDR	1.45168	1.44546	.68886	.69182
ECU	1.20320	1.21440	...	...

Special Drawing Rights (SDR) are based on exchange rates for the U.S., German, British, French and Japanese currencies. Source: International Monetary Fund.

European Currency Unit (ECU) is based on a basket of community currencies.

OPTIONS
PHILADELPHIA EXCHANGE

	Calls Vol.	Last	Puts Vol.	Last
Australian Dollar				73.66
50,000 Australian Dollars-European Style.				
73 Sep	...	...	10	0.80
50,000 Australian Dollars-cents per unit.				
72 Sep	...	...	21	0.38
73 Sep	3	0.89	30	0.80
74 Sep	1	0.57	...	...
British Pound				153.39
31,250 British Pounds-cents per unit.				
152½ Dec	...	...	320	2.92
155 Sep	200	1.32	...	...
155 Dec	320	2.98	...	...
British Pound-GMark				243.36
31,250 British Pound-German mark EOM.				
240 Sep	...	...	100	1.50
244 Sep	100	1.90	...	...
250 Sep	100	0.50	...	...
Canadian Dollar				72.08